FULLNESS RECEIVED AND RETURNED

FULLNESS RECEIVED AND RETURNED

TRINITY AND PARTICIPATION IN JONATHAN EDWARDS

SENG-KONG TAN

Fortress Press
Minneapolis

FULLNESS RECEIVED AND RETURNED

Trinity and Participation in Jonathan Edwards

Cover design: Alisha Lofgren

Library of Congress Cataloging-in-Publication Data is available

Print ISBN: 978-1-4514-6932-5

eBook ISBN: 978-1-4514-7242-4

The paper used in this publication meets the minimum requirements of American National Standard for Information Sciences — Permanence of Paper for Printed Library Materials, ANSI Z329.48-1984.

Manufactured in the U.S.A.

This book was produced using PressBooks.com, and PDF rendering was done by PrinceXML.

CONTENTS

Abbreviations

CD *Church Dogmatics.* 14 vols. Edited by G. W. Bromiley and T. F. Torrance. Edinburgh: T&T Clark, 1956–75.

NPNF *A Select Library of the Nicene and Post-Nicene Fathers of the Christian Church: Series 2.* 14 vols. Edited by Philip Schaff and Henry Wace. Peabody, MA: Hendrickson, 1994.

PG *Patrologiae cursus completus. Series graeca.* 161 vols. Paris, 1857–66.

PL *Patrologiae cursus completus. Series latina.* 221 vols. Paris, 1844–49.

STh *St. Thomas Aquinas: Summa Theologica.* 5 vols. Translated by Fathers of the English Dominican Province. New York: Benzinger Bros., 1948. Reprint, Allen, TX: Christian Classics, 1981.

PRRD *Post Reformation Reformed Dogmatics: The Rise and Development of Reformed Orthodoxy, ca. 1520 to ca. 1725.* 4 vols. Grand Rapids, MI: Baker Academic, 2003.

PTJE *The Philosophical Theology of Jonathan Edwards.* Expanded ed. Princeton, NJ: Princeton University Press, 2000.

TG *Treatise on Grace and Other Posthumously Published Writings.* Edited by Paul Helm. Cambridge: James Clarke, 1971.

WJE *Works of Jonathan Edwards.* Vols. 1–26. New Haven: Yale University Press, 1957–2008.
Works of Jonathan Edwards Online. Vols. 27–73. New Haven: Jonathan Edwards Center at Yale University, 2008–.

WTG *The Works of Thomas Goodwin. D.D., Sometime President of Magdelene College, Oxford.* 12 vols. With general preface by John C. Miller and memoir by Robert Halley. Nichol's Series of Standard Divines: Puritan Period. Edinburgh: James Nichol, 1863.

Introduction

The emanation or communication of the divine fulness, consisting in the knowledge of God, love to him, and joy in him, has relation indeed both to God and the creature: but it has relation to God as its fountain, as the thing communicated is something of its internal fulness. . . . In the creature's knowing, esteeming, loving, rejoicing in, and praising God, the glory of God is both exhibited and acknowledged; his fulness is received and returned. Here is both an emanation and remanation. . . . So that the whole is of God, and in God, and to God; and he is the beginning, the middle, and the end.

–JONATHAN EDWARDS, CONCERNING
THE END FOR WHICH GOD CREATED THE
WORLD

Echoing the Apostle Peter, Jonathan Edwards claims that "being partakers of the divine nature" is not only a soteriological benefit that is "peculiar to the saints," but also "one of the highest privileges of the saints."[1] Human participation in the divine life is, therefore, a central theme in Edwards's soteriology and a defining motif in his overall theological thinking.[2] This project seeks to present an internally coherent picture of Edwards's doctrine of participation in God as a uniquely Reformed-Puritan construct, at once traditional yet creative.[3]

SECONDARY LITERATURE ON EDWARDS'S SOTERIOLOGY

In his monograph, Anri Morimoto compares Edwards's soteriology of participation in God with the various doctrines of grace in medieval Catholicism.[4] Michael McClymond outlines, in an essay, similarities between the soteriologies of Gregory Palamas and Edwards.[5] He attends to Edwards's construal of participation in God as a form of Christianized Neoplatonism

1

mediated through the Cambridge Platonists. While Morimoto helpfully situates Edwards's theology of grace within the context of the larger pre-Reformation Latin tradition, and McClymond has briefly outlined the parallels between Palamas and Edwards, no systematic and broad account of Edwards's doctrine of participation in the divine life has been attempted thus far. This project is an initial attempt to fill the lacuna and, in doing so, to locate the key secondary interpretations of Edwards's thought—that is, his Trinitarianism and aesthetics—in relation to his soteriology of participation in God.[6]

METHOD AND THEOLOGICAL PERSPECTIVE

My approach, while not denying Edwards's philosophical originality, concentrates on his creative retrieval and synthesis of theological motifs both from his own Puritan-Reformed-Augustinian tradition and the larger Western theological tradition.[7] The method is not, however, oriented toward the genetic-historical, but rather focuses on the synthetic-comparative.

The primary thrust of the project aims to systematically draw together Edwards's various ideas related to participation in God. Because human participation in God is inextricably linked to Trinitarian self-communication, I argue that Edwards's motif of *exitus et reditus*, or, in his nomenclature, emanation and remanation, is the key to explicating this dialectic (table 1.2).[8]

A BRIEF OUTLINE OF CHAPTERS

The chapters following this introduction are arranged around three interrelated loci: the doctrines of the Trinity, Christ, and salvation. As I shall show, the ground of possibility for Edwards's doctrine of participation in God is his doctrine of self-communication within God. In chapter 1, I discuss Edwards's understanding of the self-communication of essence and persons within the ontological Trinity. The focus is on the procession of the Spirit as an eternal movement of procession and return *ad intra*.

Chapter 2 works out this emanation and remanation theme in creation and redemption as grounded in the Trinitarian internal processions and divine counsels. The Holy Spirit, as the bond of love between Father and Son, is the basis for the willed egress of creatures from God in creation and their return to God in redemption.

Chapter 3 bridges Edwards's doctrines of the Trinity and Christology. We investigate his Trinitarian construal of the *pactum salutis* by which the Son compacted with the Father in the Spirit to become incarnate. As this self-communication of the Son in human form was the work of the Trinity *ad extra*, we look at how the Father and Spirit inseparably and distinctly participate in incarnating the Son.

In the next two chapters, the focus shifts to Christology proper. Chapter 4 centers on the relation between the divine Word and his assumed human nature. The central question is this: How does Jesus as man participate in the being and operations of the divine Son? In chapter 5, the study looks at the mutual interaction and participation between the two natures in Christ. Here, we look at two lines of inquiry: Is the human nature deified? Does the divine nature suffer?

Subsequently, the center of gravity moves to Edwards's soteriology. In chapter 6, I present the theme of union with Christ as fundamental to Edwards's understanding of the manner in which the saints participate in Christ and his benefits. While the investigation covers various aspects of salvation—regeneration, faith, adoption, justification, and sanctification—the prime focus of this chapter is on Edwards's doctrine of justification. In the penultimate chapter, the dissertation analyzes his doctrine of grace, looking in detail into the nature of the Spirit's self-communication in sanctification and the saint's participation in "the divine nature." The concluding chapter looks briefly at Edwards's doctrine of glorification as the continuation and culmination of sanctification.

Notes

1. Edwards, "Treatise on Grace," in *WJE* 21:156. See also Jaroslav Pelikan, *The Christian Tradition Christian*, vol. 5, *Doctrine and Modern Culture* (Chicago: University of Chicago Press, 1989), 161.

2. See also Roland André Delattre, *Beauty and Sensibility in the Thought of Jonathan Edwards: An Essay in Aesthetics and Theological Ethics* (New Haven: Yale University Press, 1968); Robert W. Jenson, *America's Theologian: A Recommendation of Jonathan Edwards* (New York: Oxford University Press, 1988). Delattre even argues that the idea of participation in God is the central interpretive key to Jonathan Edwards's ethics; see his "The Theological Ethics of Jonathan Edwards: A Homage to Paul Ramsey," *Journal of Religious Ethics* 19, no. 2 (Fall 1991): 74.

3. Conrad Cherry argues for Edwards's Calvinism and against his mysticism in *The Theology of Jonathan Edwards: A Reappraisal* (Bloomington: Indiana University Press, 1990). James M. Gustafson points to the Reformed Augustinianism of Edwards; see *Ethics from a Theocentric Perspective: Theology and Ethics* (Chicago: University of Chicago Press, 1981), 171–76.

4. Anri Morimoto, *Jonathan Edwards and the Catholic Vision of Salvation* (University Park: Pennsylvania State University Press, 1995).

5. Michael McClymond, "Salvation as Divinization: Jonathan Edwards, Gregory Palamas and the Theological Uses of Neoplatonism," in *Jonathan Edwards: Philosophical Theologian*, ed. Paul Helm and Oliver D. Crisp (Aldershot, England: Ashgate, 2003), 139–60. McClymond highlights the parallels between Palamite soteriology and Edwards's theology, which include divine

illumination, direct "mystical" experience, the divine essence-energies distinction, everlasting spiritual progress, and an embodied, holistic anthropology.

6. On Edwards's doctrine of the Trinity, see Amy Plantinga Pauw's seminal monograph, *The Supreme Harmony of All: The Trinitarian Theology of Jonathan Edwards* (Grand Rapids, MI: Eerdmans, 2002), which is the revision of her similarly titled dissertation: "'The Supreme Harmony of All': Jonathan Edwards and the Trinity" (Ph.D. diss., Yale University, 1990). On this aesthetics, see Delattre, *Beauty and Sensibility*, passim.

7. Beginning with Perry Miller's landmark work, many other seminal studies have demonstrated Edwards's creativity in the "modern" sense; see Perry Miller, *Jonathan Edwards* (Cleveland, OH: World, 1959). He not only restated the Reformed tradition by appropriating many philosophical ideas of his time but also advanced a thorough reconstruction of the substance ontology of the Western theological tradition. Thus, Sang Hyun Lee argues that the traditional metaphysics of substance and form was reconceived by Edwards as an ontology of dispositions and habits. See his *The Philosophical Theology of Jonathan Edwards* (Princeton, NJ: Princeton University Press, 1988); see also idem, *The Philosophical Theology of Jonathan Edwards*, expanded ed. (Princeton, NJ: Princeton University Press, 2000). All citations hereafter shall refer to the expanded edition. See also Avihu Zakai, *Jonathan Edwards's Philosophy of History: The Reenchantment of the World in the Age of Enlightenment* (Princeton, NJ: Princeton University Press, 2003); Edwards appropriated the Enlightenment idea of progress, without its human-centered emphasis, into his theocentric notion of an ever-advancing redemptive history.

8. See particularly Lee, *PTJE*, ch. 7ff.

1

Communication of Being *Ad Intra*

The Trinity as Origin, Medium, and End of the Divine Emanation and Remanation

Human participation in God through divine self-communication *ad extra* is grounded in Edwards's doctrine of self-communication *within* the Deity. How does he conceive of this divine self-communication *ad intra*, both among the divine persons and between the divine essence and persons? We shall begin by examining the latter part of the question.

DO THE DIVINE PROCESSIONS INVOLVE A COMMUNICATION OF ESSENCE?

With the mainstream tradition, Edwards affirms a perfect being theology and the consubstantiality of the divine persons.[1] He is thus explicit in his rejection of tritheism and, with that, any form of ontological subordinationism.[2] In siding with the Catholic tradition, Edwards holds that the origination of a divine person is coterminous with a communication of the divine essence.[3]

COMMUNICATIO ESSENTIA: EDWARDS'S DISTINCTION BETWEEN ABSOLUTE BEING AND RELATIVE BEING

Echoing the Augustinianism of John Calvin, Edwards conceives of the divine persons as internal essential relations, as the "union of several divine persons *in* one Essence."[4] Yet, in a late, untitled fragment on the Trinity, Edwards comes across as undeniably Nicene: "The Son derives the divine essence from the Father, and the Holy Spirit derives the divine essence from the Father and the Son."[5] Flatly contradicting Calvin, he insists that the Son is "begotten by him [the Father] from eternity and continually through eternity."[6]

However, in a sermon written just a few years earlier, Edwards appears to deny the *communicatio essentiae*.[7] In the divine generation, the Son "in some sense is derived from the Father yet he is not a dependent being though his subsistence be from the Father yet his essence is from none and chief."[8] That a divine person is "God of himself" or *autotheos* seems to be at odds with the notion of *communicatio essentiae*, which assumes that a divine person has being from another.[9] In what way, then, can the Son's divine essence be understood as both derived and underived?[10]

Edwards frames his response in terms of a twofold distinction of the divine essence: being or relative being, derived or underived, independent or dependent. Here, he follows the Reformed scholastics, such as Turretin, who modified Calvin's strict interpretation of the *autotheos*.[11] With this distinction, Edwards subtly shifts the terms of the debate. No longer are the divine persons directly referred to as *autotheos*, for the term is now predicated of the divine essence. Or, as Edwards himself presents the issue, how can *communicatio essentiae* meet the objection that "the divine essence" should be "undivided and independent," and not "in any dependence or by derivation"?[12]

The divine essence is thought of as absolute or underived because its *esse* and *essentia* are self-posited.[13] The divine essence has "relative being" or is derived when it is contemplated in the distinction of persons, or as "belonging to such persons."[14] Hence, the Son is said to be derived insofar as he eternally receives this same divine essence from the Father.[15] But when, *in abstracto*, "the divine essence [is] in itself considered," it is *autotheos*.[16] In fine, the Son is God from himself (*autotheos*) because of being or having the divine essence, yet the Son is not Son from himself since the divine essence is received not from himself, but from the Father. Clearly, derived personhood, for Edwards, is not opposed to consubstantiality precisely because the perpetual communication of the divine essence is coincident with the divine processions.[17]

To discount any ontological subordinationism, Edwards evacuates the *communicatio essentiae* of any idea of volitional derivation. The Son and Spirit receive the divine essence by "a necessary, essential, and so an independent communication."[18] Edwards echoes the orthodox divines in refusing to speak of the divine processions as willed by another divine person, in order to maintain the distinction between created and uncreated.[19] The *communicatio essentiae* is necessary yet unforced just as God must will good with utmost freedom.[20]

In other words, the divine processions come under the freedom of nature and not of the divine will.[21] God's natural will means that the Trinity, of absolute necessity, exists as Will-to-Love, which cannot not be.[22] God's free will, on the other hand, wills things God can choose not to will, but once actualized, a created entity may be considered relatively necessary.[23]

In summary, Edwards's version of the *autotheos* incorporates the idea of the communicability of the divine essence within the Trinity. For a divine person to have a derived essence is to possess relative being by natural or absolute necessity. How is the divine essence instantiated by the divine persons in the *actus personales*?

GOD AS MIND, IDEA, AND LOVE: THE PSYCHOLOGICAL TRINITY

Edwards uses a range of Trinitarian models for the ontological Trinity, ranging from the unipersonal to the tripersonal.[24] However, he focuses on a psychological description of the divine processions and, in particular, the Augustinian bipersonal model of the Trinity.[25] In the following, I will argue that Edwards's various Trinitarian models may be fruitfully integrated through a conceptual *exitus-reditus* framework.[26]

Seen in context, Edwards's first entry on the Trinity in his private notebook is hardly original: traditional Western filioquism is restated with an eighteenth-century confidence in rationality.[27] In his fuller Trinitarian account, Edwards describes the two divine processions as self-ideation/self-image and self-love/self-operation within God.[28]

> When we speak of God's happiness, the account that we are wont to give of it is that God is infinitely happy in the enjoyment of himself, in perfectly beholding and infinitely loving, and rejoicing in, his own essence and perfections. And accordingly it must be supposed that God perpetually and eternally has a most perfect idea of himself, as it were an exact image and representation of himself ever before him and in actual view. And from hence arises a most pure and perfect energy in the Godhead, which is the divine love, complacence and joy.[29]

Clearly, this sort of psychological account of the Trinity was not absent in Edwards's earlier writings.[30] Yet, Edwards's development of this Trinitarian model is, in some sense, novel.

EDWARDS'S HISTORICAL SOURCES AND INFLUENCES: AUGUSTINIAN, THOMISTIC, AND REFORMED TRADITIONS

Edwards stands against the mainstream of Reformed scholasticism in his speculative amplification of the distinctive personal properties of the Son and the Spirit, and within the tradition of appropriating Augustinian psychological metaphors for the Trinity.[31] In fact, Edwards comes closer to Aquinas's trinitarianism based on a metaphysical examination of the immanent acts of the mind than Augustine's psychological analogy based on the human soul.[32]

Here, he could be accused of moving away from the apophatic reserve exercised by patristic and mainstream Reformed theologians, who refused to positively define the difference between the eternal *generatio* and *spiratio* as analogous to the immanent operations of the human intellect (*per modum intellectus*) and volition (*per modum voluntatis*).[33] With the medieval Schoolmen and the marginal Reformed scholastic thinkers, Edwards obviously does not regard such a posteriori demonstration of the divine processions as *alogon*—that is to say, scripturally and rationally unfounded.[34] Edwards regards the biblical expressions "God is Spirit"/"God is Love" and "God is Light" as having pneumatological and christological import, respectively.[35] For him, as with Aquinas, the names Idea and Love are not merely appropriations applied to the Son and Spirit, but proper personal names.[36] Such medieval influences found their way into Edwards's psychological Trinity through Chevalier de Ramsay, a convert to Catholicism.[37] The divine essence, according to Ramsay, is analogous with "an infinitely active mind that conceives; or as an infinite idea that is the object of this conception; or as an infinite love that proceeds from this idea."[38] This infinitely active mind is God the Father.

FIRST DIVINE PERSON AS THE UNSOURCED SOURCE OF THE DIVINE IDEA AND THE DIVINE LOVE

Edwards notes that since the biblical use of *Theos* is primarily in reference to God the Father, Christian tradition rightly names God the Father "the fountain of the Godhead," wherein "all is from him, all is in him originally."[39] "The Father," as Edwards describes in another place, "is the deity subsisting in the prime, unoriginated and most absolute manner, or the deity in its direct existence."[40] Though he distances himself from Augustine on this point, Edwards's identification of the Father as *arche* must not be understood to make his theology more Greek than Latin.[41] This personalism does nothing to undermine the Latin influences on his theology.[42] Both traditions, as Richard Cross has argued persuasively, affirm the monarchy of the Father and subordinate the essence to the person.[43]

Even though Edwards does not emphasize (as did Aquinas) the personal distinctions in terms of Father-Son language, the Father is not self-posited apart from the Son. The Father's unoriginatedness or inascibility is the negative counterpart of that which is derived.[44] Furthermore, unengenderedness has a positive content because it implies fecundity.[45] As such, it is a relational term since the person who "neither is begotten or proceeds" is only so in relation to the Son and Spirit.[46] As the "Deity without distinction," the Father is the *plenitudo fontalis* from whence the other two divine persons are produced.[47]

However, Edwards is careful to qualify that the processions of the Son and Spirit are not "natural" or "voluntary," whereby their "being or well-being" is dependent on the Father's will.[48] Though the Father has a "priority of subsistence" and "though one proceeds from another, and so may be said to be in some respects dependent on another," this does not imply any superiority of nature and essential glory, as the Son and the Spirit are perfect self-repetitions of the Father's entire being and excellence.[49] Therefore, as much as the Son and the Spirit are dependent on the Father in their eternal relations of origin, they are constitutive of the Father's personhood as self-knowledge and self-love.[50]

The Father, in two distinct reflexive exercises of the divine essence, repeats the divine actuality in the "forms" of divine self-consciousness and self-love, thus generating the Son and spirating the Holy Spirit.[51] Edwards explains: "God is glorified within himself these two ways: (1) by appearing or being manifested to himself in his own perfect idea, or, in his Son, who is the brightness of his glory; (2) by enjoying and delighting in himself, by flowing forth in infinite love and delight towards himself, or, in his Holy Spirit."[52] This would seem to imply a Photian monopatrism, which would contradict Edwards's explicit defense of the Western filioquist position: that the Spirit "derives the divine essence from the Father and the Son."[53] The primacy that Edwards gives to the first divine person explains, in part, why Edwards seems to favor conceptions of the Trinitarian *hypostaseis* as analogous to the distinction of mind, knowledge, and love and like the sun, its light, and its heat.[54]

However, he also asserts that God's "love" and "knowledge of everything possible" must be thought of as rationally prior and so identical to the Father, or "the essence of the Godhead in its first subsistence."[55] Edwards's contrast between a mind's "mere direct consciousness" and its "reflex or contemplative idea" is analogous to the Father-Son distinction.[56] He regards the divine knowledge of all possibilities, as part of God's natural knowledge, to be prevolitional.[57] Is Edwards implying that the Son should be God's knowledge of everything actual? This seems to be the case, since all knowledge in God must be rationally thought of as *a fieri* unless the Son is "actualized" in the divine generation.[58] The Father is the "author or generator" of "divine wisdom."[59] In that one simple act of divine generation, God beholds God's own wisdom and omniscience with greatest clarity.[60]

The Father cannot exist without the Son, and so the Father must have actual knowledge in perpetual generation yet immanent in the Father. Edwards explains, "[I]t cannot be that Christ is called the wisdom of God only in a figurative sense . . . but that he is the real proper wisdom of God."[61] And God's wisdom and omniscience—the Son—must include God's knowledge of other necessary truths (apart from all possibles) and free knowledge of all contingents.[62]

WHERE IS THE FATHER-SON RELATION?

Edwards certainly regards paternity and filiation as *propria* of the Father and the Son respectively.[63] Though he rarely uses the term "paternity," he conceptualizes the Father under the notions of innascibility and generation. Like Aquinas, these two ideas are encapsulated under the term "principle" or "fountain."[64] The divine generation from the principle cannot exclude a communication of essence, for the Father must beget a Son of the same nature.[65] Because persons act, the Father begets because of being Father; the Father's identity as Father is not a result of begetting.[66] Edwards affirms the patristic notion of the *monogenes*—the "natural," only-begotten Son of the Father.[67] Hence, "the Father's begetting of the Son is a complete communication of all his happiness, and so an eternal, adequate and infinite exercise of perfect goodness, that is completely equal to such an inclination in perfection."[68] Although Edwards does not apply the property of "paternity" to the first subsistence, he regards begetting to be properly descriptive of the Father. "The Holy Spirit . . . cannot be confounded in God, either with God begetting or [with] his idea and image, or Son."[69] Because Edwards sees "generation" as an act of love, the Father-Son relation must therefore include the presence of the Spirit.[70]

FIRST, DIVINE SELF-COMMUNICATION: THE SON AS GOD'S REFLEXIVE IDEA AND SELF-IMAGE

For Edwards, self-intellection involves a duality, since to have in view a perfect idea of a thing is identical to seeing the thing itself.[71] God's perpetual self-ideation or self-image *is* the Father's eternal generation of the Son.[72] In this pure reflex act of knowing, the Father begets "the eternal, necessary, perfect, substantial and personal idea" of God's own self—the Son of God.[73] In that loaded phrase, Edwards recapitulates key Trinitarian assertions along traditional lines.

On the eternity and perfection of the Son, Edwards asserts that neither time nor space is implied in the generation of the Son by the Father.[74] The Son is said to be God's substantial and necessary idea because, unlike human intellection, the Word of God is not a contingent accident of a mind's cogitation.[75] Yet, the production of the Logos is analogous to the active conception of a human idea; in this sense, the Son may be seen as "an absolutely infinite effect, and object of the absolutely infinite mind."[76] God, in reflecting upon and beholding God's own self, must generate a perfect self-repetition—the exact image of God.[77] As Edwards writes, "And joining this with what was observed before, I think we may be bold to say that that which is the form, face, and express and perfect image of God, in beholding which God has eternal delight, and is also the wisdom, knowledge, logos and truth of God, is God's idea of himself."[78]

Using the Platonic notion of *mimesis*, Edwards states that since the "very being" and definition of an idea "consists in similitude or representation," the Son is "not only *in* the image of the Father, but he *is* the image itself in the most proper sense."[79] Or, as Bonaventure phrased it, the Son comes forth from the Father *per modum exemplaritatis*.[80] The Son is the Father's eternal self-reflection, "his aspect, form or appearance, whereby God eternally appears to himself."[81] This points to the Son's eternal simultaneity with the Father.[82] As the Son is begotten of the Father, as idea from mind, so God generates God's own perfect image.[83]

TRITHEISM AND THE PROBLEM OF INFINITE REGRESSION

Edwards's idealism, especially in relation to his trinitarianism, can be traced directly to Locke's influence.[84]

> And though there be a priority of subsistence, and so a kind of dependence of the Son, in his subsistence, on the Father—because with respect to his subsistence he is wholly from the Father and begotten by him—yet this is more properly called priority than superiority, as we ordinarily use such terms. There is dependence without inferiority of Deity, because in the Son the Deity, the whole Deity and glory of the Father, is as it [were] repeated or duplicated: everything in the Father is repeated or expressed again, and that fully, so that there is properly no inferiority.[85]

Edwards is clearly aware that if a similar logic of self-repetition were to be applied to the Son's (as well as the Spirit's) understanding of the Father, one could conclude that "there would not only be three persons but an indefinite number." Nonetheless, he thinks that such an "objection is but a color without substance" and advances a twofold appeal to the doctrine of divine simplicity to overturn the issue of infinite regression.

In the first place, since the three divine persons are "the same understanding divine essence," one would commit the tritheistic error of attributing "to each of them . . . a distinct understanding of their own."[86] These two distinct, immanent modes of action (of understanding and love) in God have as their content the numerically identical divine essence.[87] "We never suppose," Edwards contends, "the Father generated the Son by understanding the Son, but that God generated the Son by understanding his own essence." [88] As such, the Father and Son are two modes of the same divine essence: "It is the divine essence [that] understands, and it is the divine essence [that] is understood."[89] This line of reasoning is clearly similar to Aquinas's notion of the divine persons as subsistent relations.[90]

Secondly, the Father's generation and understanding are not two successive and distinct acts. Analogous to a perfect human concept, the comprehension and production of the idea within God is simple and identical, for "the Father understands the idea he has merely in his having that idea, without any other act."[91] Since the divine understanding is not discursive but consists in a single, undivided act of the one divine essence, there cannot be multiple acts of understanding within God, and therefore there can only be that one perfect generation of the Idea of God.[92]

Edwards's alleged philosophical idealism—that is, his application of Lockean ontology to explain the divine processions—also opens him to the charge of tritheism.[93] What, then, does Edwards mean by the word "same" in reference to the divine coequality and consubstantiality in the *actus personales*?[94] His answer is that commonality (*quidditas* or whatness) and self-identity (*haecceitas* or thisness) coexist in the divine repetition *ad intra*: A perfect idea of a concept is no different from the concept.[95] Divine repetition is the deity of the Father being "expressed again, and that fully": it is the divine essence perfectly articulated in another mode.[96] For Edwards, this notion of divine self-repetition *ad intra* is not philosophically grounded, but is first and foremost a biblical notion.[97] His use of Locke is an instance of metaphysically explicating the *Trisagion* with the tools of his time.

How does Edwards resolve the question of the Son's ideation of the Father? The Son's perception of the Father, he answers, is no different from the Son's own existence.[98] In other words, the Son does not generate another Son. That being the case, it is nothing else but the Son. On this same argumentation, wouldn't the Spirit's ideation of the Father imply an *ex Patre spirituque*?[99] For Edwards, there can be no procession of the Son from the Spirit, since the will is, by *ordo naturae*, posterior to reason.[100] As the eternal exemplar, the procession of the Son cannot be mediated, for its existence depends directly on the prototype.[101] Employing a kind of wordplay, Edwards insists that whether it is the Son or the Spirit having a self-ideation, "'tis still the idea of the Father."[102] If the Holy Spirit possesses the divine Idea who derives from the Father, how does Edwards distinguish the Spirit from the other two divine persons?

SECOND DIVINE SELF-COMMUNICATION: THE PROCESSION OF THE SPIRIT IN THREE MOVEMENTS

The Father, Son, and Spirit must be distinguished in a way analogous to the distinction between a human mind, its immanent idea, and the act of love: "The Holy Spirit . . . is certainly distinct from the other two; the delight and energy that is begotten in us by an idea is distinct from the idea. So it cannot be confounded in God, either with God begetting or [with] his idea and image, or Son. It is distinct from each of the other two, and yet it is God; for the pure and perfect act of God is God, because God is a pure act."[103] Accordingly, "the Holy Spirit is this act of the Deity, even love and delight, because from eternity there was no other act in God but thus acting with respect to himself."[104] Just as the Father directly exists in "the most absolute manner" and is thus the origin of Deity, the Holy Spirit "is the . . . most perfect . . . act of the divine nature, wherein the Godhead acts to an infinite degree and in the most perfect manner possible."[105] Since the Holy Spirit is "that personal energy" of God in infinite and complete exercise, this "perfect act of God must be a substantial act."[106] With this, Edwards recaps Thomas's understanding of the Holy Spirit as the "subsistent operation" (*operatio subsistens*) distinct from the Son, who is a "subsistent term" of an immanent procession in God.[107] The Spirit is also simultaneously the disposition of God.[108]

Here, the charge of philosophical idealism recedes as Edwards does not portray the procession of the Spirit as God's self-reflexive love. With most of the Augustinian-Latin tradition, he relies on the Holy Spirit to act as a unifying principle within the Trinity by appropriating to the Spirit the title of Love.[109] However, Edwards's trinitarianism comes under fire for depersonalizing the Holy Spirit—the well-worn critique of the Augustinian, psychological analogy.[110] In his defense, such use of nonpersonal analogies is in accord with Scripture, and Edwards does not hesitate in referring to the Holy Spirit as a divine person.[111]

First Movement of Love: The Spirit qui procedit ex Patre toward the Beloved Object

This psychological analogy is consonant with the first "movement" of the bipersonal analogy in that the eternal Happiness of God emanates from the Father to the Son.[112] He states this explicitly elsewhere: "God's love to himself, that is, to his Son, I suppose to be the Holy Spirit."[113]

The procession of the Spirit, thus, begins from the source of divinity—the Father, who eternally gives to the Son God's own Spirit. Edwards does not restrict the names Messiah and Christ to the realm of the divine economy. "Christ is the Messiah, or Christ, or the anointed in his divine nature only, without any consideration of his human nature, or his office of mediator." He is such insofar "as he is the object of the infinite love and delight of the Father, and as the Father doth eternally pour forth the Spirit of love . . . infinitely upon him."[114] Like the patristic writers, Edwards seems to think of the Spirit of the Father not only as resting upon but also abiding in the Son.[115]

The Son has a sort of priority over the Father inasmuch as "the Father depends on him as his object."[116] The Son is not only the subsistent term or eternal Object whom the Father sees, but also the eternal Object of Love. It is in the Beloved that the Father finds the divine love, joy, and happiness. "And therefore the Father's infinite happiness is in [the Son], and the way that the Father enjoys the glory of the Deity is in enjoying him."[117] The Holy Spirit, as the divine Happiness, actualizes the eternal, beatific vision of God. The generation of the Son is God's eternal *visio*, but it is only *beatifica* as the Spirit abides in the Son. The Son is perceived as the beautiful object because of an intrinsic divine beauty received from the Father.[118] This apparent monopatrism clearly has not accounted for how Edwards integrates the *filioque* into his trinitarianism.

The Second Movement of Mediation: The Spirit qui procedit ex Patre per Filium

At the Ecumenical Council of Florence, the procession of Spirit *ex patre filioque* was interpreted as *ex patre per filium*.[119] The Reformed scholastics were well aware of this ontological *per filium* and Edwards continues its usage.[120] "And even *ad intra*, though the Holy Ghost proceeds both from the Father and the Son, yet he proceeds from the Father mediately by the Son."[121]

Though Edwards reiterates Aquinas in saying that the Spirit proceeds "from the Father originally and primarily," they differ in emphasis.[122] Aquinas regarded the *per filium* from the point of origination, so "the Holy Ghost proceeds from the Father immediately."[123] In contrast, since Edwards's perspective is from the *terminus*, the "Spirit is from the Son immediately by himself."[124]

The procession of the Holy Spirit, as the second *communicatio essentiae* from the Father, is indirect and distinguished from the first, which is direct; that is why the Son's generation can be termed a procession also, albeit an unmediated one.[125]

Though Edwards does not say it overtly, he certainly does not think of the double procession as implying two sources. Although the Spirit proceeds from Father and Son, making them both "infinitely holy and . . . infinitely happy," they are to be regarded as a single "fountain of holiness" or "fountain of happiness."[126] This notion of a double procession of the Spirit from a single principle prevents the Son from being construed as an instrumental cause.[127]

Aquinas understood that because the Son is wholly receptive toward the Father, the Spirit proceeds from the Son, thus signifying the *per filium*.[128] Similarly, for Edwards, in the first logical movement, "the Son receives the infinite good, the Holy Spirit, from the Father," and is thus dependent on the Father. Yet, there is a kind of reciprocal dependency for the Father "enjoys the infinite good through the Son."[129] Here, Edwards follows the Puritans in regarding the Son as "the middle person of the Trinity," the one who is the mediator or "intermediate between the Spirit and the Father, or between the third person and the first."[130] According to Edwards, then, the Spirit is from the Father "originally and primarily," and "from the Son," or God's reflexive idea, "as it were secondarily."[131] How, then, is the Spirit "secondarily" from the Son?

As we have seen, by describing of the Son as preexistent within the Father, that is, as the "outward" revelation of God's interiority, Edwards echoes Marius Victorinus's analysis of self-ideation.[132] The Father in seeing himself begets the Son, while the Son in seeing the Father exists. On the one hand, it is in the Father's self-perception of an Other that the Spirit proceeds from the Father through the Son.[133] On the other hand, since the Son perceives the Father in the Son's own self, the Spirit proceeds from the Son directly.[134] In other words, it is from the Son and the Father mutually beholding each other that the Spirit proceeds. This completes the third movement of the *spiratio*.

THIRD MOVEMENT OF REMANATION: THE "END OF ALL PROCESSION" AS THE SON'S ETERNAL RESPONSE TO THE FATHER

Edwards assigns a preeminent place to the Holy Spirit as the aesthetic principle in God, the culmination of the Trinity.[135] The Spirit is "the beauty of the Godhead, and the divinity of Divinity (if I may so speak), the good of the infinite Fountain of Good."[136] As God's disposition is identical to God's act, divine Love is in perfect fruition in God.[137] The Holy Spirit is thus "the end of the other two [divine persons], the good that they enjoy, the end of all procession."[138]

> And the Son of God is not only the infinite object of love, but he is also an infinite subject of it. He is not only the infinite object of the Father's love, but he also infinitely loves the Father. The infinite essential love of God is, as it were, an infinite and eternal mutual holy energy between the Father and the Son, a pure, holy act whereby the Deity becomes nothing but an infinite and unchangeable act of love, which proceeds from both the Father and the Son.[139]

The virtue and beatitude of the Trinity is the Holy Spirit as "[b]oth the holiness and happiness of the Godhead consists in this love."[140] The procession of the Spirit makes the Trinity in facto esse.

Edwards's use of the unipersonal analogy leaves him with the difficulty of portraying the divine persons as three truly relational agencies in the Trinity.[141] However, he also appropriates Augustine's bipersonal analogy of the Trinity and imbues it with a sense of aesthetic relationality, or consent between persons.[142] Nonetheless, while this love is internally dual or reciprocal, it is never social in the full sense.[143] Unlike Richard of Victor, Edwards does not describe the Spirit as *condilectio* in God; there is mutual, but not shared, love in the Deity.[144] Since the *propria* of the Son and Spirit are Beloved and Love, respectively, the Holy Spirit may only be improperly said to be loved with the love of complacence.[145]

For Edwards, God must be social because God is fundamentally self-communicative as well as beautiful. Firstly, there must be an Other to which the Father can communicate the entire divine goodness.[146] Secondly, the Son must exist in perfect concord with the Father if there is to be infinite consent within God.[147] And this infinite and eternal consent is

> the act of God between the Father and the Son infinitely loving and delighting in each other. . . . It is distinct from each of the other two, and yet it is God; for the pure and perfect act of God is God, because God is pure act . . . so that the Scripture has implicitly told us, that that love which is between the Father and the Son is God.[148]

Edwards's modification of the unipersonal-psychological analogy permits him to affirm both intersubjectivity within God and Augustine's *filioque* clause—the latter placing him squarely in the Western tradition.[149] However, this configuration ironically grants a special significance to the third person—as the common Spirit of the Father and the Son—thus according to the Spirit the status of unifying principle in this analogy.[150]

Drawing from the Augustinian well within the Reformed tradition, Edwards sees the Spirit as "that infinite delight there is between the Father and the Son."[151] In this way, the Spirit is the *vinculum caritatis* or *amoris* "between the Father and the Son: for their love is mutual."[152] God as Spirit is not only the bond of love (*vinculum caritatis*) but also the "vehicle of eternity (*vehiculum aeternitatis*)."[153] The eternal movement of love within God does not culminate in the Father's gift of the Spirit to the Son, for the Spirit is mutually returned to the Father by the Son, in order that the Spirit might be "the end of the other two . . . the end of all procession."[154] This, then, may be interpreted as the eternal "emanation" and "remanation" within the divine life—the perfect reciprocity of love between the Father and the Son. The psychological Trinity modeled after an individual is transcended, for love creates communion.[155] Because mutual love is greater than mere loving, God the Father "must have an object on which it exerts itself . . . into which it flows, and that flows back to it again."[156] For Edwards, self-love and mutual love are not antithetical, as he unifies all his Trinitarian models under the rubric of divine love.[157] He explains, "From hence also it is evident that the divine virtue, or the virtue of the divine mind, must consist primarily in love to himself, or in the mutual love and friendship which subsists eternally and necessarily between the several persons in the Godhead, or that infinitely strong propensity there is in these divine persons one to another."[158]

Though Edwards could speak of the "social" Trinity and a "society of persons," his predominant imagery is that of a bipersonality of Father and Son.[159] Hence, the Father, Son, and Spirit are the eternal Subject, Object, and Act within the divine Being.[160] In this final "movement" of the Spirit's *processio*, the Son is both the object as well as the secondary subject of the Father's love. The Son is receptive in relation to the Father but is both receptive and active in relation to the Spirit (of the Father and Son). However, the Father is solely active in relation to the Son's being.[161]

TWO HANDS OF GOD: THE COINCIDENT PROCESSIONS OF IDEA AND LOVE

The two processions, as the two "hands" of God, are the simultaneous exercise of the fundamental twofold powers or faculties in God.[162] Does Edwards conflate the eternal generation of the Son with the emanation of the Spirit when he asserts that "the Father's begetting of the Son is a complete communication of all his happiness"?[163] What he is implying here is that since God is *actus purus*, there is only one immanent act (in two modes) whereby God is differentiated as three persons.[164] In other words, the generation of the Son is not without the procession of the Spirit. But where is the Son in the Spirit's procession?

In a remarkable statement, Edwards exclaims, "Understanding is in the Holy Ghost because the Son is in Him, not as proceeding from Him but as flowing out in Him."[165] Just as the Son exists as an object through the Father's ideation while remaining immanent in the Father, the Son is present in and with the Spirit's procession. In short, the Son flows out in the Spirit's procession. Although divine Love is posterior to, and so proceeds, from the divine Idea, the Spirit remains in the Son in procession.[166] The Son is not only the eternal object *of*, but also *in*, the Father's love.[167] In the procession or flowing out of the Spirit from the Father, the Son's generation is not excluded. In God, then, there is no "blind love" but rather a "seeing and understanding will," or, as Aquinas phrased it, "a sweet knowledge."[168] In other words, there is a double self-communication of the Father, which, though distinct, is never separable, whether ontologically or rationally.

Is this similar to Gregory of Cyprus's idea of an eternal "shining" forth of the Spirit *per filium*, appropriated by modern theologians to distinguish communication of essence and energy *ad intra*?[169] The case is quite the opposite. For Edwards, as we have seen, there is no procession of the Spirit that involves a *communicatio essentiae* from the Father alone; his is a Western ontological construal of the *ex Patre per filium* within the ambit of an *ex Patre filioque*. Rather, it is the Son who is the (ontological) epiphany of the Father. In being begotten, the Son not only mediates but accompanies the Spirit in procession.

Is the Divine Essence or God the Father Self-Communicative?

We now return to Edwards's understanding of the divine essence. Clearly, he does not have a generic conception of the divine essence; that is to say, it is not a genus or species.[170] The divine essence is indivisible "for God is not made up of parts for he is a simple pure act."[171] Edwards's conception is clearly Western: the divine essence is a particular singularity wholly resident in each and all three persons simultaneously.[172] "The Son," he explains, "has the same, not only specifically the same or the same in kind, but numerically the same individual glory so that [Father and Son] have but one glory that is common to both."[173] There is no difference in essential glory as their understanding is identical.[174]

Nonetheless, Edwards gives the impression, at times, that he propounds a bare derivation model of the Trinity, whereby the divine essence is simply identified with the Father.[175] On occasion, his sloppy attribution of processional terms to the Godhead seems to confirm the case.[176] Classical theology has held that the divine essence is communicated by the person, not begotten nor spirated.[177] Is Edwards here guilty of positing a self-generative essence, some sort of emanationism?[178] Can the distinction of absolute and relative being be applied to the Father? Edwards himself seems to waver on this account—a tension clearly reflected in secondary studies.[179] Interpreting Edwards's trinitarianism from the perspectives of *in fieri* and *in facto esse* accounts for his apparent fudging of the absolute/relative distinction of the divine essence as well as the monopatrism and egalitarianism of this theology.[180]

Like Aquinas, Edwards believes that the Father is the one *archē* within God; there is shared *triadikē archē* of the Trinity only *ad extra*.[181] Although he, like the Cappadocians, conceptualizes the divine processions as a movement from one to three, he sides with the Western tradition by denying that the Father is *causa* of the other two persons.[182] The Son and Spirit are not dependent on the will of another divine person for their being. They possess the divine essence independently because the *communicatio essentiae* is necessary and independent.

While the Father is the originator of the divine persons, the "first person" of the Trinity is not ontologically prior to the other two.[183] Edwards, in contrast to Augustine, thinks that the Father is not wise without the Son. Though the Son is causally dependent on the Father for existence, there is a relation of counterfactual dependence of the Father upon the Son.[184] An ontological Trinity *in fieri* can only exist in thought, for the Trinitarian processions are ontologically foundational. And this leads to another issue—Edwards's apparent conflation of the personal and essential attributes in the Trinity.

Proprietas Personales et Essentiales: Did Edwards Properly Distinguish between the Two?

In the history of theology, an undue emphasis on the simplicity of the divine essence has had the effect of undermining the divine attributes.[185] A pure nominalism of the divine attributes would leave only a simple, unknown, bare divine essence.[186] Reformed theology, by and large, upheld a virtual/modal distinction between the essence and attributes of God.[187] Yet, how the multiplicity of the attributes relates to the simple divine essence is not often delineated but instead is simply affirmed, at best, as antinomical.[188] More rarely still have the divine attributes been thought to derive from the doctrine of the Trinity.[189]

Edwards stands out as an exception to the rule, although his is not a completely consistent account.[190] There are instances where he veers toward nominalism.[191] Frequently, he recaps the simplicity tradition: all the essential attributes belong indistinctly to the three divine persons.[192] Nonetheless, he does not accept without qualification the simplicity axiom: "everything that is in God is God."[193] For Edwards, excepting the two "real attributes" of idea and love, all other divine perfections are but "mere modes or relations of existence" of the *essentia*.[194]

Applied notionally, God's Idea and Love are, respectively, the Son's and Spirit's *propria*.[195] But when used essentially, love is specially appropriated to the Spirit.[196] Comprehended under the divine idea, then, are the divine understanding, wisdom, and omniscience as its various modes. Similarly, God's holiness, justice, goodness, mercy, and grace are modalities of the divine love. Clearly, on this take, Edwards stands with the minority view within the West.[197]

In his earlier writings, however, Edwards listed three basic attributes in God—omnipotence, knowledge, and love—which he seems to appropriate to the divine persons.[198] In his later "Discourse on the Trinity," however, he asserts that there are "three distinct real things in God" but lists only two real attributes—"his understanding and love . . . for Deity subsists in them distinctly."[199] Why is the first divine person not classed a *proprietas* but only an *aliud*?

Apparently, since Edwards identifies the first divine person with the *essentia*, or "God (absolutely considered)," the Godhead cannot be reduced to omnipotence.[200] That is why he goes on to define God's omnipotence as the joint exercise of the divine understanding and will in relation to creatures *ad extra*.[201] The essence of God, as Trinity, is the perfect exercise of the power of God *ad intra*.[202] If that is the case, is the Father or "God (absolutely considered)" distinguished from the two real divine attributes only negatively?[203]

Attributively, the Father is to be understood (but not really) as the divine power *in fieri*, or the essence of God in latency.[204] It is as God eternally exercises God's essential attributes of understanding and love that God's Self-Ideation and Self-Love unfold, so to speak, into subsistences distinct from the Father.[205] Edwards, like the medieval theologians, considers God's essential powers of memory and will not only as logically prior to but also the ground (if not the cause) of the divine processions.[206] God the "Father," as the divine essence *in fieri,* is distinct from yet comprehends (or possesses) God's primal attributes of knowledge and love.[207] Hence, the Father knows and loves only by the Son and Spirit.[208] Only in exerting this primal understanding in a "reflex act of knowledge and . . . so knowing his own knowledge" does the Son come into subsistence.[209] And in God's operation of perpetually loving God's reflex idea, the Spirit thus subsists as the act and bond between Father and Son. As noted earlier, by differentiating the Son and Spirit as subsistent relations, Edwards modulates the grammar of essential attributes or powers (of understanding/idea and will/love) into that of notional properties.[210]

We now return to Edwards's distinction between "being" and "relative being" in one of his later fragments on the Trinity.[211] Here, he attempts an argument for Trinitarian coequality based not primarily on essential identity, but upon a parity of personal otherness.[212] Based on the distinction of the divine persons, Edwards claims that they each must possess unique *propria,* which he variously terms "personal glory," "peculiar glory," or "personal dignity."[213] But this does not commit one to tritheism because the referencing of distinctive properties to the divine persons is not like attributing separate "perfections" or essences to the divine persons.[214]

How can Father, Son, and Spirit be distinct and yet not be three Gods? "Their personal glory," Edwards avers, "is only a relative glory, or a glory of relation, and therefore may be entirely distinct."[215] Beyond the traditional appeals to identity of *ousia* and *perichoresis,* Edwards points to personal distinction as a basis for their equivalence. What is surprising here is that he seeks to justify their coequality using reciprocal relations of hierarchy. He contends that there are other proper relations of "priority" and "dependence" among the persons to be perceived beyond the traditional Trinitarian *taxis* of origination or "priority of subsistence": Father, Son, and Spirit.[216]

Being the "fountain of Deity" and *principium sine principium,* the Father is "the first person from whom the others proceed, and herein has a peculiar personal honor." The Son exercises a "superiority" over the Father as "the great and first object of divine love," or the Beloved.[217] From Edwards's perspective, receptivity is more than just a positive perfection, for without it, the *principium sine principium* would remain inactive or purely negative.[218] The Father is unoriginate *in se* but is only fecund because of the Son; the Father is *sine principium* in the Father's own self but *principium* because of the Son (and Spirit). The Son is not only the object of the Father's love, but also a second subject who returns the Father's love. More precisely, the Son is the mediating subject, by whom the Father enjoys the Spirit.[219] Here, the eternal *exitus-reditus* is not denied, but is viewed as a single movement of *processio*.[220]

The Holy Spirit, as "the end of the other two in their acting *ad intra*," has dominance as the governing will of the Father and Son. "In another respect the Holy Ghost, that is, divine love, has the superiority, as that is the principle that as it were reigns over the Godhead and governs his heart, and wholly influences both the Father and the Son in all they do."[221] In other words, the Holy Spirit as personal Love, directs and regulates that eternal *perichoretic* relation between Father and Son, Lover and Beloved.[222]

Edwards imports this idea of reciprocal relations of dependence into the Trinity *ad intra* from the "social" trinitarianism that was common currency in the Puritan-Reformed tradition.[223] Despite Edwards's dependence on the psychological analogy, the Boethian influence within medieval theology acts as a strong corrective against the modalistic tendency of this Trinitarian model.[224] This is evident in Ramsay's account of the Trinity, which influenced Edwards's own psychological model of the Trinity.[225]

ANTINOMY OF ONE AND THREE: *PERICHORESIS*

Edwards uses the psychological analogy to characterize the Father and Son as persons, with understanding and will.[226] However, he admits that describing the Spirit as Love would seem to deprive the Spirit of understanding.[227] He solves this difficulty by appealing to the doctrine of *perichoresis*. The divine persons are not individuals possessing three separate minds but in-exist one in another.

This clearly mitigates the monopatrism and binitarianism implicit in the psychological and mutual-love analogies (the Trinity *in fieri*). The Trinitarian *perichoresis* is concurrent with but logically posterior to the divine processions.[228] On the one hand, the *actus personales* and the *communicatio essentiae* both underlie the divine dynamism by which the divine persons are united and distinguished; here is a *circumincessio* of the divine persons.[229] We thus observe a kind of divine circumambulation or eternal movement of one toward another. On the other hand, the *perichoresis* secures the immanence of these processions as a kind of *stasis*, viz., a *circuminsessio*, or the mutual inhabitation and resting of the persons one in the other.

In the most primal logical configuration, the Son and Spirit are latent and distinguished as the Father's "faculties" of understanding and will.[230] Edwards describes the acts of God *ad intra* before the creation of the world as "a fire enfolding itself."[231] The two divine processions of the Son and Spirit are analogous to the eternal self-reception of light and heat within the eternal fire of God.[232] The Father as *arche* is the principle of both personal otherness and consubstantiality.[233] If, however, divine understanding and will are considered as identical to the divine essence, the divine persons are ineffably one.[234] It is not that the divine essence is logically prerelational, but that the real relations (persons) are comprehended in the divine essence.[235] Hence, the entire Trinity *is* the divine essence, for the Father, Son, and Spirit in-exist as three real relations (*aliud*) and not three substances (*alius*). "There are," as Edwards himself phrases it, "but these three distinct real things in God."[236] This makes sense of Edwards's derivative Trinity for here the plurality of the divine essence is internal—that is, three-in-one.[237] He thus maintains "that this is the true Trinity" because there are "these distinctions in the Deity, viz. God (absolutely considered), and the idea of God, and love and delight."[238]

In the first divine self-communication *in facto esse*, the Father sees himself in the Son while the Son sees the Father in himself. And in this reciprocity, the Son exists.[239] Simultaneously, the Son receives the Spirit from the Father as the second divine self-communication. This makes sense of that psychological model in which both the Son and Spirit seem to proceed from the Father alone. For from this perspective, the second divine self-communication is *in fieri*. The Father and Son exist one in another, and the Spirit exists in the Son. Here, the Spirit is to be considered as abiding in the Son before proceeding from/through the Son.[240]

In the second movement of the second divine self-communication *in facto esse*, the Spirit proceeds through the Son while remaining in the Son.[241] The Son "flows out" in the Spirit, who proceeds as the Son's love toward the Father.[242] In the final movement of eternal remanation, where the Spirit is returned to the Father, the Son is not excluded in this response of Love.

As Trinity *in facto esse*, the divine essence—as relative being—is to be considered as residing within each of the divine persons in their distinct expressions: one-in-three.[243] Here, the relations are properly subsistent as relations toward one another (an opposition of relations).[244] This triune culmination is not to be seen as a regression of the divine persons into an undifferentiated unity.[245] That logically primal moment—of God and God's two real "faculties"—must be viewed as sublated into an interexistence of the divine persons: one-in-three and three-in-one.

In summary, the *communicatio essentiae* allows Edwards to affirm the identity of essence in each of the divine persons in such manner "that the whole divine essence is supposed truly and properly to subsist in each of these three—viz. God, and his understanding, and love."[246] He is also able to spell out how, as coincident with the *actus personales*, the divine persons process while remaining in each other, with the exception of how the Father in-exists in the Spirit. It is only in the Trinitarian *perichoresis* that he is finally able to account for the total reciprocity of divine persons. As Edwards so vividly describes in his "Discourse on the Trinity," in this *circumincessio* and *circuminsessio* of the divine persons,

> there is such a wonderful union between them that they are, after an ineffable and inconceivable manner, one in another, so that one hath another and they have communion in one another and are as it were predicable one of another . . . so it may be said concerning all the persons in the Trinity, the Father is in the Son and the Son in the Father, the Holy Ghost is in the Father, and the Father in the Holy Ghost, the Holy Ghost is in the Son and the Son in the Holy Ghost.[247]

CONCLUSION

As we have seen, Edwards interprets the double procession of the Spirit (*filioque*) as both a *communicatio essentiae* from the Father through the Son (*per filium*) and the Son returning this eternal hypostatic Love to the Father in an eternal act of reciprocity. Thus, he employs the Augustinian bipersonal model of the Trinity, where the *nexus amoris*, or mutual love—the Holy Spirit of the Father and Son—is the primordial locus of the divine *exitus et reditus ad intra*.

In the following chapter, we shall explore how remanation or human participation in God is, for Edwards, founded on God's temporal self-communication, the Trinitarian emanation in the history and economy of God.[248] Edwards thus seeks to establish a correspondence between the Trinity in the immanent and economic "forms." In this way, Christ is described as the Mediator by whom the Holy Spirit, as "the end of the other two [divine persons and] . . . the end of all procession" accomplishes the "end for which God created the world" in time.[249]

Notes

1. Edwards defines the divine being, signified by the "proper name" *Jehovah* in the Old Testament, as "self-existent, eternal, all sufficient, perfect and immutable Essence." See Edwards, "Miscellanies," no. 1102, in *WJE* 20:487. Since the plural *Elohim* is always attached to *Jehovah*, he sees this to be an intimation of the divine Trinity. Echoing the Reformed orthodox theologians, like Voetius, God is to be regarded as singularly independent, noncontingent, and "absolutely *in se,*

per se, per existentiam." See Gisbertus Voetius, *Selectarum Disputationum theologicarum* Pars. 1–V (Utrecht, 1688), as quoted in Heinrich Heppe, *Reformed Dogmatics Set Out and Illustrated from the Sources*, rev. and ed. by Ernst Bizer, trans. G. T. Thomson, foreword by Karl Barth (London: George Allen & Unwin, 1950), 50. "Each of the persons of the Trinity, as they are the same God, they have the same divine essence." See Edwards, 321. Sermon on Heb. 1:3, in *WJE* 49. Since "they are all the same substance . . . whatsoever perfection, dignity or excellency" of "the divine essence, belongs to every one of them." See Jonathan Edwards, "The Threefold Work of the Holy Ghost," in *WJE* 14:379.

2. It is wrong to conceive of the "Father, Son and Holy Ghost as three distinct gods." See Jonathan Edwards, "Miscellanies," no. 539, in *WJE* 18:84. This is so because they are not "a plurality of essences or beings." See "Miscellanies," no. 1105, in *WJE* 20:488. That being the case, "there is no such thing as a natural superiority, because all have the same divine essence." See Jonathan Edwards, "Of God the Father," in *WJE* 25:147. This echoes Gregory's use of the indivisibility of the divine substance as a rebuttal of Eunomian subordinationism (Richard Cross, "Divine Monarchy in Gregory of Nazianzus." *Journal of Early Christian Studies* 14, no. 1 [Spring 2006]: 109–13). No denial of the causal priority of the Father is necessary (*pace* Thomas F. Torrance, *Trinitarian Faith: The Evangelical Theology of the Ancient Catholic Faith.* [Edinburgh: T&T Clark, 2006], 319–22).

3. Edwards is also *catholic* (hence, Nicene) since an equivalent concept is found in the East, in which the *homoousion* and the monarchy of the Father are acknowledged without the double procession of the Spirit. He is *Catholic* insofar as the Latin *communication essentiae* assumes the *filioque.*

4. Edwards, "Miscellanies," no. 1102, in *WJE* 20:487 (emphasis mine). According to Calvin, "in God's essence reside three persons in whom one God is known." See John Calvin, *Calvin: Institutes of Christian Religion*, 2 vols, ed. John T. McNeill, trans. Ford Lewis Battles, Library of Christian Classics 20 (Philadelphia: Westminster, 1960), I.13.16.

5. Jonathan Edwards, "On the Equality of the Persons of the Trinity," in *WJE* 21:147. Similar in handwriting to "Discourse on the Trinity," Lee surmises that it "was probably written in the very early 1740s, and no later than 1742" (Lee, "On the Equality," in *WJE* 21:145). Evidently, for Edwards, derivation of being within God need not entail subordinationism.

6. Edwards, "Miscellanies," no. 143 (*133*), in *WJE* 13:298. This applies also to "the Holy Spirit . . . [who] eternally and continually proceeds from both" (ibid.).

7. Edwards, 498b. Sermon on 1 John 4:12 (1738), in *WJE* 53. Edwards's corpus of sermons ranges over a period of thirty-eight years (from 1720 to the year of his death, 1758). This particular sermon may be considered mid-career, roughly eighteen years into his preaching ministry.

8. Ibid.

9. This was highlighted in the ecumenical Council of Florence. The two alternate views posit a radical person/essence distinction. The first is Calvin's, where the persons, but not the substance, are thought to be derived. The other is the εκπορευσις/*processio* distinction, in which the Greek term denotes the *communicatio essentiae* without implying the production of persons. This latter view is promulgated in "The Greek and Latin Traditions Regarding the Procession of the Holy Spirit," *L'Osservatore Romano*, 20 September 1995, as cited by David Coffey, "The Roman 'Clarification' of the Doctrine of the Filioque," *International Journal of Systematic Theology* 5, no. 1 (March 2003): 7–10.

10. My choice of these two chronologically proximate texts is intentional and, hopefully, obvious. Hence, I do not assume that Edwards changed his mind and so must face the more difficult task of accounting for the apparent contradiction.

11. For a historical account, see appendix 2, "The Doctrine of *Autotheos* in Calvin and the Reformed Tradition" below.

12. Edwards, "On the Equality," in *WJE* 21:147–48.

13. "With respect to its being . . . or, to speak more plainly, that the divine essence should be, and should be what it is, is not in any respect in any dependence or by derivation" (ibid.).

14. Differently stated, "that [the divine essence] should be here or there" does not threaten the simplicity of the essence (ibid.).

15. "That though the Son has life in himself because he is possessed of the divine essence, that has life in itself and in an independence, yet the Father has given him to have life in himself" (ibid., 148).

16. Ibid.,147–48. It may be thought of as the divine essence being identical to the Trinity. Thus, "the Scriptures speak of God absolutely, and *secundùm essentiam*, whereby we are to understand the whole Godhead, from which none of the Persons is excluded, [or *as it comprehends all three Persons*]" (Benedictus Aretius, *A Short History of Valentinus Gentilis the Tritheist. . . .* [London: E. Whitlock, 1696], ch. 10, 74–75).

17. "Hence we see how generation by the Father and yet coeternity with the Father . . . are consistent" (Edwards, "Miscellanies," no. 143 [*133*], in *WJE* 13:298).

18. Edwards, "On the Equality," in *WJE* 21:147–48. Divine consubstantiality excludes any "natural superiourity . . . because all have the same divine essence." See Edwards, 813. Sermon on 1 Cor. 11:3 [Mar 1746], in *WJE* 64:64.

19. "There is such an union between the Persons of the Trinity that it is impossible there should be any such thing as one compelling another; it is impossible but that they should all act in the most perfect agreement." See Edwards, 234. Sermon on Matt. 16:21–23 [1731], in *WJE* 47. This reiterates the classical distinction between the essential, necessary (without compulsion) willing of God's own internal being and the contingent willing of realities outside of God's own being, viz., John of Damascus's *ergon physeos* and *ergon theleseos*. As Barth put it, the "older dogmaticians . . . distinguish[ed] between a natural will, which wills what it is not able not to will (himself), and a free will, which wills what it is able not to will (creation)." See Karl Barth, *The Göttingen Dogmatics: Instruction in the Christian Religion*, vol. 1, ed. Hannelotte Reiffen, trans. Geoffrey W. Bromiley (Grand Rapids, MI: Eerdmans, 1991), §17, 416.

20. "For most certainly, God's will is free . . . yet there is the greatest and most absolute necessity imaginable, that God should always will good and never evil" (Edwards, "Miscellanies," no. 31, in *WJE* 13:271). "Compulsion is a thing that is not compatible to the Deity." See Jonathan Edwards, "The Free and Voluntary Suffering and Death of Christ," in *WJE* 19:497. As Cheynell put it, though the procession of the Spirit is "natural" and "necessary," this does not mean that it is "involuntary," as if there was "any *coaction or compulsion*" in God. See Francis Cheynell, *The divine triunity of the Father, Son, and Holy Spirit. . . .* (London: Samuel Gellibrand, 1650), 220–21.

21. "True it is, that the will of God is the nature of God, but . . . according to our manner of apprehension . . . it is more proper to say that the Father and the Son did breath forth the Spirit *by the perfection of their nature*, then to say they breathed him forth *of their own will, or by some arbitrary decree*," since the latter would mean "that the holy Spirit doth exist and subsist *Contingently*" (Cheynell, *The divine triunity*, 221–22).

22. Aquinas's two conceptions of necessity, the one "absolutely" and the other relatively or "by supposition," extend Damascus's distinction between *ergon physeon* and *ergon theleseon*. Just as something is absolutely necessary as a predicate is defined by its subject (for example, a human being is an animal), so it is that God necessarily and absolutely wills God's own goodness. Apart from such constancy, God would be less than good if the divine essence were changeable and perfectible. However, something is only relatively necessary insofar as it is willed contingently, for example, in one's act of sitting. As Aquinas illustrates, Socrates "must necessarily sit, as long as he is sitting." See Aquinas, *STh* I, q. 19, a. 3, 104–5.

23. In the same way, God willing things *ad extra* is only necessary insofar as God wills them to be, since the divine goodness does not stand in need of them. However, once God wills something to be, "then He is unable not to will it, as His will cannot change": it becomes necessary by supposition (Aquinas, *STh* I, q. 19, a. 3, 105).

24. See Amy Plantinga Pauw, *The Supreme Harmony of All: The Trinitarian Theology of Jonathan Edwards* (Grand Rapids, MI: Eerdmans, 2002), passim. Sang Hyun Lee acknowledges that Edwards uses many Trinitarian models and rightly highlights the psychological model as basic, with the social-relational element circumscribed within an ontology of divine self-repetition (Lee, "Editor's Introduction," in *WJE* 21:20–27).

25. Pauw's thesis has been challenged by Steven M. Studebaker. See his article, "Jonathan Edwards' Social Augustinian Trinitarianism: An Alternative to a Recent Trend," *Scottish Journal of Theology* 56 (2003): 268–85. He expands on Edwards's central use of the Augustinian bipersonal analogy in his book, *Jonathan Edwards' Social Augustinian Trinitarianism in Historical and Contemporary Perspectives* (Piscataway, NJ: Gorgias, 2008). Studebaker's interpretation is confirmed by Robert W. Caldwell III, who argues for the primacy of the mutual-love model, in his "The Holy Spirit as the Bond of Union in the Theology of Jonathan Edwards" (Ph.D. diss., Trinity Evangelical Divinity School, 2003). This was revised and published as *Communion in the Spirit: The Holy Spirit as the Bond of Union in the Theology of Jonathan Edwards*, Studies in Evangelical History and Thought (Milton Keynes, UK: Paternoster, 2006).

26. Here, our interpretation is similar to that proposed by David M. Coffey, "The Holy Spirit as the Mutual Love of the Father and the Son," *Theological Studies* 51, no. 2 (June 1990): 193–229. This proposal is further developed in his *Deus Trinitas: The Doctrine of the Triune God* (New York: Oxford University Press, 1999). While Edwards nowhere (to my knowledge) overtly links the *exitus-reditus* image with the divine procession of the Holy Spirit, my proposal is not inconsistent with his trinitarianism, as it provides a synthetic account of his various models, which further elucidates the emanation-remanation theme in his cosmology/soteriology.

27. "I think that it is within the reach of naked reason to perceive certainly that there are three distinct in God, each of which is the same [God], three that must be distinct; and that there are not nor can be any more distinct, really and truly distinct, but three, either distinct persons or properties or anything else; and that of these three, one is (more properly than anything else) begotten of the other, and that the third proceeds alike from both, and that the first is neither begotten nor proceed" (Edwards, "Miscellanies," no. 94, in *WJE* 13:257). Evidently, Edwards stands in the history of theology as one of the few thinkers (along with Hugh and Richard of St. Victor, and Richard Swinburne) who endeavored to supply a rational justification of the Trinity.

28. See Jonathan Edwards, "An Essay on the Trinity," in *Treatise on Grace and Other Posthumously Published Writing*, ed. Paul Helm (Cambridge: James Clarke, 1971), 99. Edwards, as we shall see, conceptualizes God within both social and psychological analogies based on human experience, but without introducing any notion of conflict (Randall B. Bush, "Trinitarian Conflict: A Re-assessment of Trinitarian Analogies in the Light of Modern Psychological and Sociological Conflict Theories," *Perspectives in Religious Studies* 19, no. 1 [Spring 1992]: 9–12).

29. Edwards, "Discourse on the Trinity," in *WJE* 21:113.

30. Even in his early twenties, Edwards denies that God is an unknowable *res extensa*. "We ought to conceive of God as being omnipotence, perfect knowledge and perfect love" (Edwards, "Miscellanies," no. 194, in *WJE* 13:335). Schafer dates this entry between July and August 1725. "'Tis evident that there are no more than these three really distinct in God: God, and his idea, and his love or delight" (Edwards, "Miscellanies," no. 259, in *WJE* 13:367).

31. For Augustine, the psychological analogies were secondary to his elucidation of the ontological Trinity, for they were located after his reflections on the divine processions and missions. And the triad of the human mind, knowledge, and love is a "lesser" analogy as compared to the triad of memory, knowledge, and love oriented toward God. While Edwards follows the Western tradition in using the psychological analogy, this was not absent in the East, e.g., Athenagoras of Athens. See Laurent A. Cleenewerk, *His Broken Body: Understanding and Healing the Schism between the Roman Catholic and Eastern Orthodox Churches* (Washington, DC: Euclid University Consortium Press, 2007), 330.

32. Bernard J. Lonergan chronicles Aquinas's modification of the Augustinian psychological analogy into a more metaphysical account based on Aristotelian categories in his *Collected Works of*

Bernard Lonergan, vol. 2, *Verbum: Word and Idea in Aquinas*, ed. Frederick E. Crowe and Robert M. Doran (Toronto: University of Toronto Press, 1997). As with Thomas, Augustine's most famous (and favorite) triad of *memoria, intelligentia*, and *voluntas* is noticeably missing in Edwards's own account of the Trinity (William B. Stevenson, "The Problem of Trinitarian Processions in Thomas's Romans Commentary," Thomist 64 [October 2000]: 620).

33. On this theological reticence, Richard Muller lists Turretin, Heidegger, Pictet, Rijssen, Voetius, and Ridgley. See Muller, *PRRD* 4:162, 376. Of course, Edwards would agree with William Ames that the divine processions are beyond definition—a point that Gregory of Nazianzen had pointed out. "The difference between (these two) to be begotten, which agrees to the Son, and to proceed, which is proper to the holy Ghost, cannot be explained by us in proper words." See William Ames, *The Marrow of Sacred Divinity Drawne Out of the Holy Scriptures, and the Interpreters thereof, and Brought into Method* (London: Henry Overton, 1642), ch. 5, 18.

34. Muller, *PRRD* 4:162. Keckermann, Ainsworth, and Burman stood within this Reformed minority. Appealing to the idea of progressive revelation, Edwards admits that in spite of the logical difficulties and "objections" that might be raised, he believes that his speculations do not threaten "the mysteriousness and incomprehensibleness" of the Trinity. See Edwards, "Discourse on the Trinity," in *WJE* 21:139: "I think the Word of God teaches us more things concerning it to be believed by us than have been generally taken [notice of]."

35. Edwards, "Miscellanies," no. 331, in *WJE* 13:409. "He is seen by his image, the Son, and is felt by the Holy Spirit, as fire is perceived only by its light and heat, seen by one and felt by the other. Fire, by its light, represents the Son of God, and by its heat, the Holy Spirit. God is light, and he is love. This light, in the manner of the subsisting of the Father and the Son, shines on itself; it receives its own brightness into its own bosom." See Edwards, "Notes on Scripture," no. 393, in *WJE* 15:387.

36. Aquinas was even more insistent: "If the procession of the Word and of Love is not sufficient for suggesting personal distinction, then there can be no personal distinction." See Thomas Aquinas, *De Potentia* 9, 9, ad 7, as cited in Gilles Emery, "The Doctrine of the Trinity in St Thomas Aquinas," in *Aquinas on Doctrine: A Critical Introduction*, ed. Thomas G. Weinandy, Daniel A. Keating, and John P. Yocum (London: T&T Clark, 2004), 59.

37. To form Miscellany 1253, Edwards excerpted Ramsay's posthumous work *Philosophical Principles of Natural and Revealed Religion* (1748–49) (Edwards, "Miscellanies," no. 1253, in *WJE* 23:184–88). A brief biography of Sir Andrew Michael Ramsay can be found in Sweeney, "Editor's Introduction," in *WJE* 23:13.

38. Edwards, "Miscellanies," no. 1253, in *WJE* 23:187.

39. "Hereby we see how the Father is the fountain of the Godhead, and why when he is spoken of in Scripture he is so often, without any addition or distinction, called God, which has led some to think that he only was truly and properly God." While this may be the case, Edwards also uses God in reference to the Godhead and to the particular persons where he deems fit (Edwards, "Essay," in *TG*, 122). See also, Edwards, "Observations," in *TG*, 79. The predominant reference to the Father as *theos*, though biblical and creedal, should not be exclusive. See John D. Zizioulas, *Communion and Otherness: Further Studies in Personhood and the Church*, ed. Paul McPartlan (London: T&T Clark, 2006), 136–37.

40. Edwards, "An Essay," in *TG*, 118; "Discourse on the Trinity," in *WJE* 21:131.

41. Augustine asserted that God, when defined absolutely, is the Trinity. See Leonardo Boff, *Trinity and Society*, trans. Paul Burns, Theology and Liberation Series (Maryknoll, NY: Orbis Books, 1988), 55. While Gibson highlights remarkable similarities between Edwards's and Maximus's trinitarianism, he does so by suppressing the robust account of the *filioque* as ontological *per filium* in Edwards. Furthermore, these similarities (the Father as *arche*; the Son as the Father's *ikon, logos*, and glory; the *per filium* as economical) are not more Greek in tone; if anything, they point to the ecumenical significance of both Edwards and Maximus. See Michael D. Gibson, "The Beauty of the Redemption of the World: The Theological Aesthetics of Maximus

the Confessor and Jonathan Edwards," *Harvard Theological Review* 101, no. 1 (2008): 54–58. Elsewhere, it has been argued that Edwards departs from the long history of Western philosophical theology in his concept of Being—one that is founded on plurality-in-relations and not on pure unity and simplicity of being. See Wallace E. Anderson, "Editor's Introduction," in *WJE* 6:84.

42. Much of twentieth-century Trinitarian theological research rests on Theodore de Regnon's stereotyping of the Greek-Byzantine and Latin-Scholastic traditions as respectively personalist and essentialist. While he regarded both Trinitarian approaches as equally legitimate, a number of scholars (e.g., Colin Gunton, Robert Jenson) appropriated his thesis with a theological bias toward so-called Eastern personalism. Karl Rahner has also alleged that God's unity not only funded the Latin dogmatic treatises but that, as a result of such a starting point, Christian theology and spirituality had become practically unitarian. See Karl Rahner, *The Trinity*, trans. Joseph Donceel (London: Herder & Herder, 1970), 10–15. Augustine as well as Aquinas was blamed for this Western ill, and such finger-pointing deservedly triggered strong critical responses. See Michel R. Barnes, "Augustine in Contemporary Trinitarian Theology," *Theological Studies* 56 (June 1995): 237–51; Michel R. Barnes, "De Regnon Reconsidered," *Augustinian Studies* 26 (1995): 51–79. On Aquinas's personalism, Gilles Emery has written extensively and convincingly on it; see his *Trinity in Aquinas* (Ann Arbor, MI: Sapientia, 2006).

43. Cross compares the "generic" conception of the *homoousion* of Gregory of Nyssa (as representative of the Greek tradition) with the more "unitary" conception of Augustine. The divine essence, in both views, is numerically one and "is the metaphysical 'place' where these persons overlap, and as such posterior to the persons themselves." See Richard Cross, "On Generic and Derivation Views of God's Trinitarian Substance," *Scottish Journal of Theology* 56, no. 4 (2003): 464.

44. "There is this difference between God the Father and the Son: that the Father in his person is unoriginated, underived and from none other; the person of the Son is originated, derived and proceeding from the Father" (Edwards, 321. Sermon on Heb. 1:3, in *WJE* 49).

45. Gilles Emery, *The Trinitarian Theology of Thomas Aquinas*, trans. Francesca A. Murphy (New York: Oxford University Press, 2007), 171. Aquinas would have challenged Bonaventure's contention that the hypostasis of the first person might be conceived without paternity as its property; that is to say, it is prerelational.

46. Edwards, "Miscellanies," no. 94, in *WJE* 13:257.

47. "That as the Father with respect to the subsistences [of the Son and the Spirit] is the fountain of the deity, wholly and entirely so" (Edwards, "Observations," in *TG*, 79). See also "Miscellanies," no. 143 (*133*), in *WJE* 13:298. The idea of originary plenitude is Bonaventure's (Emery, *Trinitarian Theology of Thomas Aquinas*, 171).

48. "'Tis not because one person of the Trinity is by nature above another: there is no such thing as a natural superiority" (Edwards, "Of God the Father," in *WJE* 25:147).

49. Edwards, "Observations," in *TG*, 77. With regard to the Son: "There is dependence without inferiority of deity; because in the Son the deity, the whole deity and glory of the Father, is as it were repeated and duplicated."

50. "All three are persons for they all have understanding and will. There is understanding and will in the Father, as the Son and the Holy Ghost are in Him and proceed from Him" (Edwards, "Essay," in *TG*, 120–21). This is to be read in light of Edwards's subjective definition of "a person [as] that which hath understanding and will" (Edwards, "Discourse on the Trinity," in *WJE* 21:133).

51. Lee, *PTJE*, 189. According to Lee, the divine persons are three distinct actualities as the primordial actuality of knowing and loving, the two perfect divine self-repetitions in reflexive knowledge and love. The dispositional essence of the Father is "expressed" in the persons of the Son and the Spirit as a "manifestation" of self-consciousness and a "flowing out" of self-enjoyment, respectively.

52. Edwards, "Miscellanies," no. 448, in *WJE* 13:495.

53. Edwards, "On the Equality," in *WJE* 21:147.

54. Edwards, "Discourse on the Trinity," in *WJE* 21:138. Lee accurately highlights this emphasis within Edwards's theological schema in his analysis of Edwards's dispositional reconception of the divine being. Pauw, who seems to lean toward a more social Trinitarian position, faults Lee on this point; see her *Supreme Harmony of All*, 15n52.

55. Edwards, "Discourse on the Trinity," in *WJE* 21:141.

56. Ibid. Edwards defined a mind's "reflex or contemplative idea" as someone "having a view of himself so as to delight in his own beauty or excellency" (ibid.).

57. "If there had never been any such thing as sin committed, there would have been infinite numbers of possible beings, which would have failed of existence, by God's appointment. God has appointed not to bring into existence numberless possible worlds, each replenished with innumerable possible inhabitants" (Edwards, *WJE* 3:249).

58. Though applied to creation, we can take it as axiomatic that Edwards considers actuality as greater than virtuality/disposition. "Understanding and will are the highest kind of created existence. And if they be valuable, it must be in their exercise. But the highest and most excellent kind of their exercise is in some actual knowledge and exercise of will." See Jonathan Edwards, "Concerning the End for which God Created the World," in *WJE* 8:454. Of course, faculty, habit, and act are all one in God.

59. Edwards, "Discourse on the Trinity," in *WJE* 21:135.

60. "But God's wisdom and omnisciency shines clearest of all in his perfect knowledge of himself, who is the infinite object of his own knowledge." God comprehends the divine self in "one simple view." See Jonathan Edwards, "God is Infinitely Exalted in Gloriousness and Excellency Above All Created Beings," in *WJE* 10:423.

61. Edwards, "On the Equality," in *WJE* 21:147.

62. Edwards seems to identify divine omniscience with God's free knowledge when he asserts that God "must necessarily be omniscient and know every least thing that must happen throughout eternity" (Edwards, "Things to be Considered and Written Fully About," in *WJE* 6:231). In another place, he alludes to God's knowledge of necessary truths: "But God, being omniscient, must necessarily perfectly perceive all excellency, and fully know what is contrary to it; and therefore, that all excellency is perfectly agreeable to his will, and all evil perfectly disagreeable; and therefore, that he cannot will to do anything but what is excellent" (Edwards, "Miscellanies," no. 89, in *WJE* 13:253).

63. "His proceeding from the Father in his eternal generation, or filiation, argues no proper dependence on the will of the Father; for that proceeding was natural and necessary and not arbitrary" (Edwards, "The Excellency of Christ," in *WJE* 19:572).

64. "The paternity of a family, tribe or nation, in the language of the Old Testament, is called a 'fountain.'" See Edwards, "Types of the Messiah," in *WJE* 11:196. See also, Emery, *Trinity in Aquinas*, 145–48.

65. The Son "has the nature of the infinite Jehovah in him. He is the Son of God. When a father begets a son he begets one of the same nature" (Edwards, 79. Sermon on Song of Sol. 1:3 (a), in *WJE* 43).

66. "Begetting is the proper act of a father." See Jonathan Edwards, "Blank Bible," note on 1 Pet. 1:3, in *WJE* 24:1177. In this context, he was referring to spiritual regeneration: "'Hath begotten us.' 'Tis probable that the Apostle uses this expression the rather because he was speaking of the work of God the Father as agreeing with his paternity." This is restated in his note on James 1:18, in *WJE* 24:1168, which reiterates Aquinas's famous axiom: *Quia Pater est, generat* (Emery, *Trinity in Aquinas*, 192), grounded on the more general principle that "an action presupposes a person acting" (Aquinas, *STh* I, q. 40, a. 4, 207).

67. "And [Christ] is not only his own natural Son, of the same nature with him, but is his only begotten Son." See Jonathan Edwards, "The Threefold Work of the Holy Ghost," in *WJE* 14:430. Again, "In this family or household, God [is] the Father, Jesus Christ is his own natural and eternally begotten Son" (Edwards, "Miscellanies," no. 571, *WJE* 18:110). On "the verb γεννάω, 'to beget'" in relation to human nature, "two ways of being begotten [are] spoken of in the New

Testament, one natural, and the other spiritual; one being the first generation, the other regeneration" (Edwards, *WJE* 3:300).

68. Edwards, "Miscellanies," no. 104, in *WJE* 13:272.

69. Edwards, "Miscellanies," no. 94, in *WJE* 13:260.

70. Edwards, "Miscellanies," no. 294, in *WJE* 13:385. For Hastings, Edwards overemphasizes his pneumatology to the extent of ascribing the Father's *proprium* of generation to the Spirit. See W. Ross Hastings, "'Honouring the Spirit': Analysis and Evaluation of Jonathan Edwards' Pneumatological Doctrine of the Incarnation," *International Journal of Systematic Theology* 7, no. 3 (July 2005): 293. This will be clear in Edwards when we look at the role of the Spirit in the incarnation, whereby the Spirit serves as the bond of the Father-Son relation in the human Jesus: "God hath respect to this man and loveth him as his own Son; this man hath communion with the Logos, in the love which the Father hath to him as his only begotten Son. Now the love of God is the Holy Ghost" (Edwards, Miscellanies," no. 487, in *WJE* 13:529).

71. Edwards, "Miscellanies," no. 260, in *WJE* 13:368. If a person could have a perfect reflex idea of every thought within the span of an hour, this person would "really be two during that time" (Edwards, "Essay," in *TG*, 102).

72. "The Son is the deity generated by God's understanding, or having an idea of Himself and subsisting in that idea" (Edwards, "Essay," in *TG*, 118). The *hypostasis* of the Son is "[t]he Godhead being thus begotten by God's loving an idea of Himself and shewing forth in a distinct subsistence or person in that idea" (Edwards, "Essay," in *TG*, 108). See also Edwards, "Miscellanies," no. 405, in *WJE* 13:468.

73. Edwards, "Essay," in *TG*, 103. See also Edwards, "Miscellanies," no. 94, in *WJE* 13:258–60.

74. "In this generation we must note: 1. That the begetter and begotten are together in time. 2. He that begets communicates to him that is begotten, not a part of his Essence but the whole Essence; that which is begotten is within, not without the begetter." See Edward Leigh, *A treatise of divinity consisting of three bookes . . .* (London: William Lee, 1646), 137. For the Damascene, the Word of God is unlike a human concept insofar as it is an immanent procession and subsists and exists in God even while proceeding from the Father. However, just as a human idea reveals the mind yet proceeds from it, the Son is one with the Father in nature (as manifested by the attributes) but distinguished as to derivation of subsistence. See John of Damascus, *Exposition of the Orthodox Faith*, trans. S. D. F. Salmond, bk. 1, ch. 6, 4–5 (*NPNF* 9).

75. Aquinas, *STh* I, q. 34, a. 2, ad. 1. Citing John of Damascus as an authority, Aquinas extends this position based on the distinction of being and intellection in human beings as opposed to the divine simplicity. The Father cannot be *causa* of the Son.

76. Ramsay, *Principles* 1:74–85, as quoted by Edwards, "Miscellanies," no. 1253, in *WJE* 23:185.

77. "And accordingly it must be supposed that God perpetually and eternally has a most perfect idea of himself, as it were an exact image and representation of himself ever before him and in actual view" (Edwards, "Essay," in *TG*, 100–101; "Discourse on the Trinity," in *WJE* 21:113).

78. Edwards, "Discourse on the Trinity," in *WJE* 21:120.

79. Ibid., 117; italics original. "Insofar as the image is defined by similarity, the production of the same, not of the other." See Gunter Gebauer and Christoph Wulf, *Mimesis: Culture, Art, Society*, trans. Don Reneau (Berkeley: University of California Press, 1992), 41. Of course, for Plato, this is a representation of the real by the unreal.

80. Bonaventure, *Sent.* I, d. 6, q. 3, c. On von Balthasar's appropriation of this idea, see Robert A. Pesarchick, *The Trinitarian Foundation of Human Sexuality as Revealed by Christ according to Hans Urs von Balthasar: The Revelatory Significance of the Male Christ and the Male Ministerial Priesthood*, Tesi Gregoriana, Serie Teologia 63 (Rome: Gregorian University Press, 2000), 148.

81. Edwards, "Discourse on the Trinity," in *WJE* 21:118.

82. God "has at every moment a view of his own essence," for God's perfect image "is what is eminently in God's presence" (ibid., 118–19).

83. He is "the Son of God, . . . the express image of the Father, and . . . from the Father as begotten of him" ("Notes on Scripture," note on 2 Pet. 3:16–18, in *WJE* 15:216).

84. Edwards's ontological presupposition that God encompasses all being within God's own self correlates with his epistemological idealism, which asserts that all truth correlates with reality, which in turn exists in God's mind (George Rupp, "The 'Idealism' of Jonathan Edwards," *Harvard Theological Review* 62 [1969]: 209–26). The logical conclusion of Edwards's ontological, epistemological, and theological idealism is that all being and knowledge must be in the Son. See Norman Fiering, "The Rationalist Foundations of Edwards' Metaphysics," in *Jonathan Edwards and the American Experience*, ed. Nathan Hatch and Harry Stout (New York: Oxford University Press, 1988), 83.

85. Edwards, "Miscellanies," no. 1062, in *WJE* 20:430. The idea that God constitutes another (*alius*) immanently through self-cogitation, analogous to the human thought process, appears already in the third century, for example, in Tertullian's *Adv. Prax.* 5. See J. N. D. Kelly, *Early Christian Doctrines* (New York: Harper & Brothers, 1958), 111.

86. Edwards, "Miscellanies," no. 308, in *WJE* 13:392.

87. Ibid.

88. Ibid.

89. Similarly, with regard to the procession of the Holy Spirit "'tis the divine being that loves, and it is the divine being that is loved" (ibid.).

90. As McCabe summarizes Aquinas's thinking, "the Holy Spirit is not *what* is loved, any more than the concept or word or Son is *what* is known; what is known and loved is the divine nature itself, it is a question of *self*-knowledge and *self*-love; the Word is what is formed in this self-knowledge and the Holy Spirit is what is formed in this self-love." See Herbert McCabe, "Aquinas on the Trinity," in *Silence and the Word: Negative Theology and Incarnation,* ed. Oliver Davies and Denys Turner (Cambridge: Cambridge University Press, 2002), 90. For Edwards, it would seem that what God is—namely, the divine essence as love and understanding—is just the Father. In the Father's eternal act of self-understanding and self-love, the Son and Spirit exist. The Puritan writers, like Aquinas, denied that there is any real distinction between the divine essence and persons. St. Thomas affirmed that "in God essence is not really distinct from person; and yet that the persons are really distinguished from each other." So "essence and person in God differ in our way of thinking" (Aquinas, *S.Th* I, q. 39, a. 1). Yet, the Puritans nuanced Thomas's rational distinction into a modal–virtual distinction. "The Persons differ," as Leigh put it, "from the Essence, not really as things and things, but modally, as manners from the things whereof they are manners, as degrees of heat from heat, and light from light" (Leigh, *A Treatise of Divinity,* 136). "Thus the person may be said to differ from the essence not really (*realiter*), i.e., essentially (*essentialiter*) as thing and thing, but modally (*modaliter*)—as a mode from the thing (*modus a re*)" (Francis Turretin, *Institutes of Elenctic Theology,* trans. George Musgrave Giger, ed. James T. Dennison [Phillipsburg, NJ: P&R, 1992–94], 1:278). Clearly, Aquinas is Augustinian in this regard. Arguably, whether Augustine failed to grasp the Cappadocian distinction between *hypostasis* and *ousia*, he certainly rejected the idea that the divine essence could be conceived apart from the persons as if the essence were the material cause of the persons. Of the Trinity, "we do talk of three persons of the same being, or three persons one being; but we do not talk about three persons out of the same thing, as though what being is were one thing and what person is another, as we can talk about three statues out of the same gold." See St. Augustine, *The Works of Saint Augustine, Part I, Vol. 5: The Trinity,* publications of the Augustinian Heritage Institute, ed. John E. Rotelle, introduction, translation, and notes by Edmund Hill (Brooklyn, NY: New City, 1991), bk. 7, ch. 3, 230. Neither should we think, he argued, that the identity of person and essence should confuse the distinction of persons. "There must be neither confusion or mixing up of the persons, nor such distinction of them as may imply any disparity" (Augustine, *Trinity,* bk. 7, ch. 4, 232). Recently, in response to Gunton's critique, Cross has argued that Augustine's diffidence on

the term "person" (*hypostasis*) is philosophical rather than theological. "What Augustine does not understand. . . . is what species the divine persons have in common, since 'person/ὑπόστασις' is (on Augustine's analysis) a genus word." See Richard Cross, "*Quid tres?* On What Precisely Augustine Professes Not to Understand in *De Trinitate* 5 and 7," *Harvard Theological Review* 100, no. 2 (June 2007): 215–32.

91. Edwards, "Miscellanies," no. 308, in *WJE* 13:393.

92. "So the Son understands the Father in that the essence of the Son understands the essence of the Father, as in himself being the understanding of that essence; and so of the Holy Ghost" (ibid.). Edwards is not implying that the Father and Son are two (distinct) essences understanding each other, but two modes of the same (numerical) essence in relation to each other. As Aquinas put it, since "God understands all things by one simple act . . . there cannot exist in Him a procession of Word from Word" (Aquinas, *STh* I, q. 27, a. 5, ad 3). In the same vein, as God "by one act also He wills all things . . . there cannot exist in Him a procession . . . of Love from Love." Therefore, there is in God, "only one perfect Word, and one perfect Love" (ibid.).

93. "It may be objected, that at this rate one may prove an infinite number of persons in the Godhead, for each person has an idea of the other persons" (Edwards, "Miscellanies," no. 94, in *WJE* 13:261; see also, Edwards, "Miscellanies," no. 308, in *WJE* 13:392). As Pauw notes, the issue of infinite regress is problematic because of Edwards's ambivalence toward the tradition of divine simplicity; he did not consistently identify each of the persons with the one divine essence (Amy Plantinga Pauw, "'The Supreme Harmony of All': Jonathan Edwards and the Trinity" [Ph.D. diss., Yale University, 1990], 70). For example, Edwards says that the Godhead is "repeated or duplicated." According to Helm, "if a perfect idea of x entails that x exists then Edwards has proved too much—not the second person of a trinity of persons but a second *theos*." Helm's contention that Edwards's idealism is "implicitly tritheistic" is not accurate because this logical strategy need not imply two Gods since the Spirit is not another ideation of God (*TG*, 21). It may well be that this was Edwards's deliberate strategy of countering the tacit modalism of the psychological analogy.

94. For example: "So that by God's thinking of the Deity, [the Deity] must certainly be generated. Hereby there is another person begotten; there is another infinite, eternal, almighty, and most holy and the *same* God, the very *same* divine nature" (Edwards, "Discourse on the Trinity," in *WJE* 21:116; italics mine). "The Father hath no glory peculiar to himself distinguishing of him from the son . . . no superiority above him in excellency of nature" (Edwards, 321. Sermon on Heb. 1:3, in *WJE* 49).

95. "Thus, when I have a perfect idea of my idea of an equilateral triangle, it is an idea of the same equilateral triangle, to all intents and purposes" (Edwards, "Miscellanies," no. 94, in *WJE* 13:261–62).

96. Edwards, "Miscellanies," no. 1062, in *WJE* 20:430.

97. "Revelation 4:8. 'Holy, holy, holy.'] I believe that this threefold repetition, and that in Isaiah 6:3, is because of the three persons in the Trinity, and not only as an expression of God's superlative holiness, as the threefold repetition of the word 'woe' [Rev. 8:13] signifies not so much exceeding great woe, but three distinct woes, and the threefold repeating of the word 'overturn' [Ezek. 21:27] signifies three distinct overturnings of the crown or supreme authority in Israel, first to the Persian monarchs, secondly to the Grecian, and thirdly to the Roman" (Edwards, "Blank Bible," note on Rev. 4:8, in *WJE* 24:1213).

98. The Son's "beholding the Father is nothing but his existence. . . . The idea's beholding is the idea's existing" (Edwards, "Discourse on the Trinity," in *WJE* 21:143).

99. "And if you say, the Holy Spirit has an idea of the Father; I answer, the Holy Ghost is himself the delight and joyfulness of the Father in that idea, and of the idea in the Father: 'tis still the idea of the Father" (Edwards, "Miscellanies," no. 94, in *WJE* 13:262).

100. "The Son is in the Holy Spirit, though it don't proceed from him, by reason that the understanding must be considered as prior in the order of nature to the will or love or act, both in creature and in the Creator" (Edwards, "Discourse on the Trinity," in *WJE* 21:134).

101. "If it don't actually represent to the beholder, it ceases to be. And the being of it is immediately dependent on its pattern. Its reference to that ceasing, it ceases to be its idea" (Edwards, "Discourse on the Trinity," in *WJE* 21:117). He also expresses this idea through the analogy of light emanating from a lamp. Unlike external ideas of the human mind, "the understanding of the divine mind originally proceeds from this mind itself and is derived from no other" (ibid.,119).

102. "So that," Edwards continues, "if we turn it all the ways in the world, we shall never be able to make more than these three: God, the idea of God, and delight in God" (Edwards, "Miscellanies," no. 94, in *WJE* 13:262).

103. Ibid., 260.

104. Ibid., 261.

105. Edwards, "Discourse on the Trinity," in *WJE* 21:131, 121.

106. Edwards, "Miscellanies," no. 143 (*133*), in *WJE* 13:298. Edwards, "Miscellanies," no. 94, in *WJE* 13:260. "The Holy Spirit [as] . . . the pure and perfect act of God is God, because God is a pure act" (ibid., 259).

107. In contrast, "the object of the divine mind is God's Son and idea" (ibid., 261). The terms "subsistent operation" and "subsistent term" are David Coffey's. See his "The 'Incarnation' of the Holy Spirit in Christ," *Theological Studies* 45 (1984): 471. "Si autem ab intellectu hujus verbi diligit separetur actus originis per quem efficitur notionale; et remaneret tantum id quod personale est, scilicet ipse amor: sic spiritui sancto conveniret: quia ipse procedit ut operatio subsistens." See St. Thomas Aquinas, *Scriptum super Sententiis*, lib. 1, d. 32, q. 1, a. 2, ad 4, trans. Roberto Busa S.J. (Parma, 1856), in *Corpus Thomisticum*, http://www.corpusthomisticum.org/snp1026.html.

108. As the Holy Spirit is "the divine nature [that] subsists in pure act and perfect energy," and since for Edwards there is "no distinction to be made between habit and act, between temper, disposition and exercise," he is, therefore, the spirit or "the disposition, temper or affection of the divine mind" (Edwards, "Discourse on the Trinity," in *WJE* 21:122).

109. "Though all the divine perfections are to be attributed to each person of the Trinity, yet the Holy Ghost is in a peculiar manner called by the name of love" (Edwards, "Treatise on Grace," in *WJE* 21:181).

110. Pauw blames this on his reliance on the psychological analogy and his use of Neoplatonic terminology (Pauw, "Supreme Harmony," 279). His trinitarianism has been seen as too literal and Sabellian (Jan Ridderbos, *De Theologie van Jonathan Edwards*, 274, as quoted in Pauw, "Supreme Harmony," 70). Edwards himself was well aware that his descriptions of the Trinity were "exceedingly analogous to the gospel scheme and agreeable to the tenour of the whole New Testament and abundantly illustrative of gospel doctrines" (Edwards, "An Essay," in *TG*, 122).

111. Edwards uses biblical metaphors such as breath ("Miscellanies," no. 157, in *WJE* 13:307), grace ("Miscellanies," no. 223, in *WJE* 13:346), oil or ointment ("Miscellanies," no. 209, in *WJE* 13:342; "Miscellanies," no. 226, *WJE* 13:347), lamps ("Miscellanies," no. 227, in *WJE* 13:347), and love ("Miscellanies," no. 305, in *WJE* 13:390). "He is often spoken of [in Scripture] as a person, revealed under personal characters and personal acts, and it speaks of His being acted on as a person" even though "the word person be rarely used in the Scriptures" (Edwards, "Treatise on Grace," in *TG*, 57).

112. David Coffey thinks that this *in fieri* love of the Father toward the Son can only be identical with the Father's own person. The answering love of the Son should be identical with the person of the Son but is "sublated into mutual love" as the Spirit is hypostatized *in facto esse* (Coffey, "Roman 'Clarification' of the Doctrine of the Filioque," 18–19).

113. Edwards, "Miscellanies," no. 151 (*141*), in *WJE* 13:302.

114. Edwards, "Blank Bible," note on Dan. 9: 25, in *WJE* 24:767. Elsewhere, he reiterates that these designations are not true of "Christ only as man, or as Mediator," but "God the Son from all eternity was Christ, or anointed with the Holy Spirit without measure, strictly speaking, or

with the infinite love of the Father toward him" (Edwards, "Miscellanies," no. 225, in *WJE* 13:346).

115. Thus, "God has His infinite happiness but one way . . . that the infinite joy He has in His own idea and that which He has in his Son are but one and the same" (Edwards, "Essay," in *TG*, 105). Similarly, "God is also Holy Spirit . . . proceeding from the Father without separation, and resting in the Son" (John of Damascus, *Orthodox Faith*, bk. 1, ch. 13, 16 [*NPNF* 9]). "It is manifest that the Paraclete Spirit proceedeth from the Father and abideth in the Son" (Gregory the Great, *Dial.* ii.38, as cited in Edward B. Pusey, *On the Clause "and the Son" in regard to the Eastern Church and the Bonn Conference: A Letter to the Rev. H. P. Liddon, D.D.* [Oxford: James Parker; New York: Potts, Young, 1876], 101). It is "the Holy Ghost, Who proceedeth from the Father, but dwells essentially and reposes in the Son" (Andrew of Crete, *In. Transfig.*, 52–53, in Pusey, *On the Clause*, 101).

116. Edwards, "On the Equality," in *WJE* 21:146.

117. Edwards, "Miscellanies," no. 1062, in *WJE* 20:430.

118. Thus, "the Holy Ghost . . . is the beauty and happiness of both the other persons" (Edwards, "Discourse on the Trinity," in *WJE* 21:135). According to Delattre, divine beauty is original, apparent, and inherent in the Father, Son, and Spirit, respectively. The Spirit and the Son are the substance and form of God's beauty (Roland André Delattre, *Beauty and Sensibility in the Thought of Jonathan Edwards: An Essay in Aesthetics and Theological Ethics* [New Haven: Yale University Press, 1968], 151).

119. The Council declared "that the holy Spirit is eternally from the Father and the Son, and has his essence and his subsistent being from the Father together with the Son, and proceeds from both eternally as from one principle and a single spiration. We declare that when holy doctors and fathers say that the holy Spirit proceeds from the Father through the Son, this bears the sense that thereby also the Son should be signified, according to the Greeks indeed as cause, and according to the Latins as principle of the subsistence of the holy Spirit, just like the Father." See Ecumenical Council of Florence (1438–1445), Session 6 (6 July 1439), in Norman P. Tanner, ed., *Decrees of the Ecumenical Councils*, vol. 1, *Nicaea 1 to Lateran V* (Washington, DC: Georgetown University Press, 1990). The use of the *per filium* is implicit in Athanasius and explicit in the Cappadocians. See Edmund J. Fortman, *The Triune God: A Historical Study of the Doctrine of the Trinity* (Philadelphia: Westminster, 1972), 75.

120. The Father "is the mind, the depth of reason, begetter of the Word, and through the Word the Producer of the revealing Spirit. . . . And we speak of the Spirit of the Son, not as though proceeding from Him, but as proceeding through Him from the Father" (John of Damascus, *Orthodox Faith*, bk. 1, ch. 13, 15 [*NPNF* 9]). "Tandem in Concilio Florentino onno 1439, temperamentum aliquod quaesitum est ad concordiam ineundam, ut statueretur Spiritus Sanctus à Patre per Filium procedere." See François Turrettini, *Institutio theologiae elencticae* (New York: [s.n.], 1847), 340. Van Mastricht (Edwards's favorite "divine") concludes that the Florentine Council proved that the Greek and Latin trinitarian positions were merely verbal. See Peter van Mastricht, *Theoretico-practica theologia, qua, per singula capita theologica, pars exegetica, dogmatica, elenchtica & practica, perpetuâ successione coniugantur* (Traiecti ad Rhenum: Ex officinâ Thomae Appels, 1699), 267.

121. Edwards, "Discourse on the Trinity," in *WJE* 21:143. By the color of the ink and handwriting, Lee dates the insertion to be sometime in the late 1730s. "But if we consider the persons themselves spirating, then, as the Holy Ghost proceeds both from the Father and from the Son, the Holy Ghost proceeds from the Father immediately, as from Him, and mediately, as from the Son; and thus He is said to proceed from the Father through the Son" (Aquinas, *STh* I-I, q. 36, art. 3, 186).

122. Edwards, "Discourse on the Trinity," in *WJE* 21:143. For Aquinas, the Spirit is said to "proceed principally or properly from the Father" (Aquinas, *STh* I-I, q. 36, a. 3, 186). This, of course, is thoroughly Augustinian inasmuch as the Father, as the *principium sine principium*, is the

unoriginate source of the other divine persons. Or, differently stated in the Latin tradition, the "the Father is the *principium non principiatum*, the Son the *principium principiatum*, and the Holy Spirit the *principiatum tantum*." See David M. Coffey, "*Quaestio Disputata*: Respond to Neil Ormerod, and Beyond," *Theological Studies* 68 (December 2007): 902.

123. Aquinas, *STh* I-I, q. 36, a. 3, 186.

124. Edwards, "Discourse on the Trinity," in *WJE* 21:143.

125. "The Son derives the divine essence from the Father, and the Holy Spirit derives the divine essence from the Father and the Son." (Edwards, "On the Equality," in WJE 21:147). "But the understanding of the divine mind originally proceeds from this mind itself and is derived from no other" (Edwards, "Discourse on the Trinity," in *WJE* 21:119)

126. Ibid., 135.

127. "So if we consider in the Father and the Son the power whereby they spirate the Holy Ghost, there is no mean, for this is one and the same power" (Aquinas, *STh* I-I, q. 36, a. 3, 186). Hence, the Father and Son are to be thought of as *unum principium*, since the Spirit proceeds from the two distinct Persons as one "spirating power," and so "as the unitive love of both" (Aquinas, *STh* I-I, q. 36, a. 4, 188).

128. Aquinas, *STh* I-I, q. 36, a. 3, 186. The Father actively generates and the Son is passively generated, but the Spirit is actively spirated by the Father and Son as a single principle.

129. Edwards, "On the Equality," in *WJE* 21:146.

130. Edwards, "Miscellanies," no. 733, in *WJE* 18:359. Elsewhere, he reiterates this understanding of the Son as being the "mediator between the Father and the Spirit" and "the middle person between them." (Edwards, "Miscellanies," no. 614, in *WJE* 18:146).

131. Edwards, "Discourse on the Trinity," in *WJE* 21:143.

132. Victorinus' source is Plotinus: "The same movement [of the Father], when it looks to the exterior . . . is precisely to will to see oneself, to think of and to know oneself; but the one who sees himself exists and is understood as double, both as seeing and as that which is seen . . . this turning toward the exterior is, therefore, coming to be or existing toward the exterior (*foris genitus vel exsistens*) in order to know what one is—therefore, if this movement is toward the exterior, it is begotten, and if begotten, this is the Son." See Marius Victorinus, *Adv. Arium* III.2.44–51, as cited in David Bradshaw, *Aristotle East and West: Metaphysics and the Division of Christendom* (Cambridge, UK: Cambridge University Press, 2004), 112.

133. The Spirit proceeds from Father in the Father's "beholding himself in the Son," and is thus mediated (Edwards, "Discourse on the Trinity," in *WJE* 21:143).

134. The Spirit proceeds "from the Son by his beholding the Father." But this seeing is the Son's beholding "the Father in himself," and the Son "beholds him no otherwise than in the idea of the Father, which is himself." Hence, the Spirit proceeds immediately from the Son since the Father is in the Son (ibid.).

135. "The honor of the Father and the Son is, they are infinitely happy and are the original and fountain of happiness; and the honor of the Holy Ghost is equal, for he is infinite happiness and joy itself" (ibid., 135). Edwards identifies God's natural perfection of knowledge with the Son, and the moral perfections of holiness and joy with the Holy Spirit (Delattre, *Beauty and Sensibility*, 150). And if "[m]oral excellency is the excellency of natural excellencies," holiness is not only a perfection of God but is *the* primary perfection that is fundamental to all others. (ibid.)

136. Edwards, *WJE* 2:274. Without the the divine beauty, "God himself (if that were possible to be) would be an infinite evil: without which, we ourselves had better never have been; and without which there had better have been no being" (ibid.).

137. "There is no distinction between act and habit in him . . . so that the eternal being of Love and the eternal exercise of Love are the same. For, indeed, God's own being and essence is a sure act" (Edwards, 528. Sermon on Rom. 8:29–30 [Dec 1739], in *WJE* 54). "Love is certainly the perfection as well as happiness of a spirit. God, doubtless, as he is infinitely perfect and happy, has infinite love" (Edwards, "Miscellanies," no. 117, in *WJE* 13:283).

138. Edwards, "On the Equality," in *WJE* 21:146.

139. Edwards, "Sermon Fifteen: Heaven is a World of Love," in *WJE* 8:373.

140. Edwards, "Treatise on Grace," in TG, 63.

141. That Edwards's sudden demise left us without a fully developed classical trinitarianism that would have included his own interpretation of "ontologically foundational relations" is a point well noted in Robert W. Jenson, *America's Theologian: A Recommendation of Jonathan Edwards* (New York: Oxford University Press, 1988), 97.

142. Robert Caldwell has brought out this dimension of Edwards's theology in his *Communion in the Spirit*. Augustine's role in identifying the Holy Spirit as a kind of social bond between the Father and the Son is well known (Augustine, *The Trinity*, bk. 5, ch. 3, 197). Pauw contends that Augustine's theology, on the other hand, was too governed by the notion of divine simplicity to permit this. This, in part, is due to her idiosyncratic reading of Augustine's trinitarianism as insufficiently relational, departing from the standard scholarly consensus (Pauw, "Supreme Harmony," 48).

143. Even the church's communion is with the Father and Son but not the Spirit, for "[w]e read of the communion of the Holy Ghost; but not of communion with Him, which are two very different things" (Edwards, "Treatise on Grace," in TG, 65).

144. "God is never said to love the Holy Ghost . . . Yea such epithets seem to be ascribed to the Son as tho' there were no person whatsoever to share the love of the Father with the Son." (Edwards, "An Essay," in TG, 129).

145. "The third person may be said to be beloved of God, but not so properly, because he is the infinite love of God itself" (Edwards, "Miscellanies," no. 737, in *WJE* 18: 363–64). To say that the Spirit is loved as divine Love is both *alogon* and poses the problem of infinite regression. Edwards observes that, in the Bible, "we have never any account of the Holy Ghost's loving either the Father or the Son, or of the Son's or the Father's loving the Holy Ghost, or of the Holy Ghost's loving the saints, tho' these things are so often predicated of both the other persons" (Edwards, "An Essay," in TG, 117–18). "A person may be said to love the delight he has in a person that he loves, but not so properly as he loves that person, because this would make love to that love, and delight in that delight, and again delight in the delight that he has in that delight, and so on in infinitum" (Edwards, "Miscellanies," no. 737, in *WJE* 18:364).

146. "No reasonable creature can be happy, we find, without society and communion, not only because he finds something in others that is not in himself, but because he delights to communicate himself to another." God also is inclined to communicate goodness in proportion to God's perfection. Thus, God must have an object equal to capacity to communicate goodness (Edwards, "Miscellanies," no. 96, in *WJE* 13:264).

147. He defines love as that which arises from consent to being-in-general, or consent to a particular sentient being, which cannot include any improper "self-love" or selfishness. Infinite consent, therefore, must consist in either infinite consent to being-in-general or to God, which is the same because God, in Edwards's metaphysics, is "the general and proper entity of all things." It follows then that there must be an object that God infinitely loves and that this object which is in perfect agreement with God, must be of the same essence as Godself. Therefore, God the Father, who is the perfect Lover, must be in illimitable accord with an infinite, particular Beloved—the Son—in order to be the infinitely consenting God. There must be plurality in God because "one alone cannot be excellent," for "there can be no consent" in a monopersonal God (Edwards, "Miscellanies," no. 117, in *WJE* 13: 283–84).

148. Edwards, "Miscellanies," no. 94, in *WJE* 13:261–62.

149. It should be noted that Augustine affirmed the procession of the Spirit from the Father and Son as from a single origin (Augustine, *Trinity*, 5.15, 199).

150. "Love is an uniting principle; the lover is united by his love to the beloved" (Edwards, 202. Sermon on Exod 33:18-19 [n.d.], in *WJE* 46). While Edwards sides with Augustine in identifying the *hypostasis* of the Spirit with Love, it would be logically consistent to appropriate this title to the person of the Father within the schema of the Greek triadology (John D. Zizioulas,

Being and Communion: Studies in Personhood and the Church [Crestwood, NY: St. Vladimir's Seminary Press, 1997], 46–47). In this, Edwards is not original, for the characterization of the Spirit as the *vinculum* within the *trinitas, theanthropos* and the *totus Christus* was affirmed by Puritan writers like Goodwin. "There is an higher correspondency yet: The Holy Ghost is *Vinculum Trinitatis,* the Union of the Father and the Son, as proceeding from both by way of Love, and who so meet to be the Union of God and Man in Christ, of Christ and Men in us, as he that was the Bond of Union among themselves?" (Goodwin, *WTG* 5:43).

    151. See esp. "Miscellanies," no. 1047, in WJE 20:389, where Edwards cites passages from John Owen's *Pneumatologia: Or, a discourse concerning the Holy Spirit. . . .* (London: Nathaniel Ponder, 1674).

    152. Edwards, "Discourse on the Trinity," in *WJE* 21:121. This clearly reiterates Augustine's idea of the Holy Spirit, who is "a kind of inexpressible communion or fellowship of Father and Son" (Augustine, *Trinity*, bk. 5, ch. 3, 197).

    153. The descriptor is taken from Eberhard Jüngel, *God as the Mystery of the World: On the Foundation of the Theology of the Crucified One in the Dispute between Theism and Atheism* (Grand Rapids, MI: Eerdmans, 1983), 388. Although Edwards would not say that the Spirit is the future of God, this phrase corresponds to his characterization of the Spirit's role as the "means of conveyance" between the natures in Christ (Edwards, "Miscellanies," no. 766, in *WJE* 18: 412). And, though he sees no succession in God, "God's love" may be said to be "extended from eternity to eternity" (Edwards, 528. Sermon on Rom. 8:29-30 [Dec 1739], in *WJE* 54).

    154. Edwards, "On the Equality," in *WJE* 21:146.

    155. "The Spirit," in the words of David Hart, "is not only the bond of love, but also the one who always breaks the bonds of self-love." See David Bentley Hart, *The Beauty of the Infinite: The Aesthetics of Christian Truth* (Grand Rapids, MI: Eerdmans, 2003), 176. Thus, in contrast to created being, only God is the true self-sufficient individual: "'Tis God only is happy in loving and rejoicing in himself." Yet, he qualifies himself in mid-sentence "and even the joy that God has in himself may be conceived of as the joy of union and society, the infinite joy and happiness in the eternal union and fellowship of the persons of the Trinity." See Jonathan Edwards, 131. Sermon on 1 Pet. 1:8 (a) (Jul 1757), in *WJE* 44. Elsewhere, he states: "Love is the uniting bond of all societies." See Jonathan Edwards, 297. Sermon on Ps. 139:23-24 (Sep 1733), in *WJE* 48.

    156. Ramsay, *Principles*, 1:74–85, as quoted in Edwards, "Miscellanies," no. 1253, in *WJE* 23:187.

    157. Thus, the more unipersonal (mind, knowledge and love; sun, light and heat), Augustinian-bipersonal (lover, beloved and love), and the social model of covenant theology are integrated within the rubric of divine love.

    158. Edwards, "True Virtue," in *WJE* 8:557.

    159. "Indeed, the eternal, infinite happiness of the divine being seems to be social, consisting in the infinitely blessed union and society of the persons of the Trinity, so that they are happy in one another: so God the Father and God the Son are represented as rejoicing from eternity, one in another" (Edwards, "Christ's Sacrifice An Inducement To His Ministers," in *WJE* 25:662).

    160. "And it also appears that *the Holy Spirit is this act of the Deity*, even love and delight, because from eternity there was no other act of God but thus acting with respect to himself . . . or that infinite delight there is between the Father and the Son; for the object of God's perfect act must necessarily be himself, because there is no other. But we have shown that the object of the divine mind is God's Son or idea" (Edwards, "Miscellanies," no. 94, in *WJE* 13:261). The bipersonal-aesthetical analogy enables Edwards to portray the Father and Son loving each other in their Spirit. "And the Son of God is not only the infinite object of love, but he is also an infinite subject of it." See Jonathan Edwards, "Heaven Is a World of Love," in *Charity and Its Fruits: Christian Love as Manifested in the Heart and Life,* ed. Tryon Edwards (London: Banner of Truth Trust, 1969), 333.

161. This is because "the Father is not a communication of the Son, and therefore not the object of the Son's goodness" (Edwards, "Miscellanies," no. 115, in *WJE* 13:282).

162. In Edwards's research on "intimations of the Trinity" in Jewish scriptures, he notes that Philo had seen the Wisdom in God as related to God's "own consubstantial powers, which are not simple attributes, but eternal uncreated infinite principles of action." They are the two real attributes in God that sum up all the others, which are modes or relations. Furthermore, Philo (as Ireneaus later on) regarded the Son and the Spirit as "the two hands of God" (Edwards, "Miscellanies," no. 1256, in *WJE* 23:192). Edwards cites Chevalier Ramsay's *Principles* (2:116) as referred to by Dr. Alix).

163. Edwards, "Miscellanies," no. 104, in *WJE* 13:272.

164. "God is in himself but one simple and pure act, but as we are forced to conceive and speak of him, his acts are innumerable" (Edwards, 107. Sermon on Num. 23:19 [1729], in *WJE* 44).

165. Edwards, "Essay," in *TG*, 121.

166. "The Son is in the Holy Spirit, though it don't proceed from him, by reason that the understanding must be considered as prior in the order of nature to the will or love or act." (Edwards, "Discourse on the Trinity," in *WJE* 21:134). Again, Aquinas says much the same: "Now love must proceed from a word. For we do not love anything unless we apprehend it by a mental conception" (Aquinas, *STh* I, q. 36, a. 2). Like Edwards, Aquinas posits an ordering of knowledge and will in God: "For the procession of love occurs in due order as regards the procession of the Word; since nothing can be loved by the will unless it is conceived in the intellect. So . . . although in God the will and the intellect are the same, still . . . there is a distinction of order between the procession of love and the procession of the Word in God" (Aquinas, *STh* I, q. 27, a. 3, ad 3).

167. "So the Holy Ghost, or the divine essence subsisting in divine love, understands because the Son, the divine idea, is in him" (Edwards, "Discourse on the Trinity," in *WJE* 21:134). "However, if God beholds himself so as thence to have delight and joy in himself, he must become his own object: there must be a duplicity" (ibid., 141).

168. Edwards, "Essay," in *TG*, 121. Because "the Son is the Word, not any sort of word, but one Who breathes forth Love," so the soul is accorded an "experimental knowledge; and this is properly called wisdom [*sapientia*], as it were a sweet knowledge [*sapida scientia*]" (Aquinas, *STh* I, q. 43, a. 5, ad 2).

169. For example, Vladimir Lossky's dogmatic distinction between the "hypostatic" and "energetic" processions within God, which he attributes to Gregory of Palamas. See esp. chapter 2, in Vladimir Lossky, *In the Image and Likeness of God*, ed. J. H. Erickson and T. E. Bird (Crestwood, NY: St. Vladimir's Seminary Press, 1974), 71–96; and chapters 3 and 4 in *The Mystical Theology of the Eastern Church* (Crestwood, NY: St. Vladimir's Seminary Press, 1997), 44–90. This "energetic" domain is where the Son and Spirit stand in a non-causal relationship, mutually "manifesting" one another, by which they "shine through one another, flow through one another, eternally" (Duncan Reid, *Energies of the Spirit: Trinitarian Models in Eastern Orthodox and Western Theology*, American Academy of Religion Academy Series [Atlanta: Scholars, 1997], 100). A Protestant representative is Moltmann. While Joost van Rossum argues that an explicit identification of Gregory of Palamas's notion of the divine energies with Gregory of Cyprus's idea of the eternal manifestation of the Spirit *per filium* may be an anachronistic "*hineininterpretieren*" by modern scholars, he concedes that the two conceptions are not incompatible. See Joost van Rossum, "Gregory of Cyprus and Palamism," in *Papers Presented at the Thirteenth International Conference on Patristic Studies held in Oxford 1999*, ed. M. F. Wiles and E. J. Yarnold, Studia Patristica 37 (Leuven, Belgium: Peeters, 2001), 626–30. Van Rossum is correct on two counts: (1) No textual evidence exists pointing to Palamas's appropriation of Gregory of Cyprus, and (2) their intents were different insofar as Palamas was more concerned with the existential implications of the divine energies in relation to the hesychastic controversy, while the other Gregory was more interested in clarifying the *per filium* usage within the Greek-Byzantine tradition. However, it is

not the case that Gregory of Cyprus was interested in the proper distinction of *theologia* from *oikonomia*, and that "Palamas's main concern was the divine *economy* only." The central concern of Palamas may not have been "the eternal relations of the Divine Persons in themselves," but Palamas's emphasis on the *uncreated* character of the divine energies surely points to *theologia* (ibid., 626–27).

170. The generic view portrays the divine persons as possessing their own distinctive properties, while sharing a universal essence (Gregory of Nyssa). This view, Cross argues, is not opposed to the Western conception of the Trinity (Augustine and Aquinas), as both affirm a shared Godhead and the monarchy of the Father. The idea of a *nuda essentia* is rejected since the divine substance is dependent on the persons (Cross, "On Generic and Derivation Views of God's Trinitarian Substance," 464–77). Yet, Gregory's generic model does not presume "a collective theory of universals," as if the divine persons were three individuals of a species, which presumes a divisible essence. The persons are "exemplifications of an immanent universal" essence (Richard Cross, "Gregory of Nyssa on Universals," *Vigiliae Christianae* 56 [2002]: 406). In short, Gregory (*pace* Harnack) is not guilty of *homoiousion*.

171. Edwards, 44. Sermon on Ps. 139:7-10, in *WJE* 42.

172. Since the divine essence is indivisible, the Son and Spirit do not receive a partial communication of a specific substance (as do human beings), but "have the same numerical essence communicated" to them. See Francis Turretin, *Institutes of Elenctic Theology*, 2 vols. trans. George Musgrave Giger, ed. James T. Dennison (Phillipsburg, NJ: P&R, 1992–1994), 1:256. This is the position of Calvin as well (*Institutes*, I.xiii.2). See B. B. Warfield, "Calvin's Doctrine of the Trinity," *Princeton Theological Review* 7, no. 4 (1909): 609. For a summary description of Latin trinitarianism, see Brian Leftow, "Modes without Modalism," in *Persons: Human and Divine*, ed. Peter van Inwagen and Dean Zimmerman (New York: Oxford University Press, 2007), esp. 357–60. See also Leftow's now-classic defense of Latin trinitarianism or, rather, his strident critique of social trinitarianism (Brian Leftow, "Anti Social Trinitarianism," in *The Trinity: An Interdisciplinary Symposium on the Trinity*, ed. Stephen T. Davis, Daniel Kendall, and Gerald O'Collins [New York: Oxford University Press, 2002], 203–50).

173. Edwards, 321. Sermon on Heb. 1:3 (Apr 1734), in *WJE* 49. Leftow proposes an interesting analogy for the Latin model, in which a time-traveler exists in three different modes in simultaneity (Brian Leftow, "A Latin Trinity," *Faith and Philosophy* 21, no. 3 [2004]: 304–33).

174. In clarifying that the Son's generation is the Father's understanding the singular divine essence, Edwards flatly denies tritheism: "In the first place, we don't suppose that the Father, the Son, and the Holy Ghost are three distinct beings that have three distinct understandings." The divine persons understand "because every one is the same understanding divine essence" (Edwards, "Miscellanies," no. 308, in *WJE* 13:392).

175. "And it confirms me in it, that . . . there must be these distinctions in the Deity, viz. of God (absolutely considered), and the idea of God, and love and delight" (Edwards, "Discourse on the Trinity," in *WJE* 21:131). Cross argues that Athanasius's identification of the Father with the divine essence tout court (implying that the Father is without any *proprietas personales*) is contradictory, since the Father would not have the property of generating the Son. This undermines the very point he wishes to defend, viz., the monarchy of the Father (Cross, "On Generic and Derivation Views," 469). See John R. Meyer's critique (which is heavily dependent of Thomas Torrance's interpretation) of Cross's view of Athanasius ("God's Trinitarian Substance in Athanasian Theology," *Scottish Journal of Theology* 59, no. 1 [2006]: 81–97).

176. "The Godhead being thus begotten by God's having an idea of himself" (Edwards, "Discourse on the Trinity," in *WJE* 21:114). Thus, Aquinas reminds us of the distinction between substantive and adjectival denominations of God. A "substantive personal term," like "the essence is the thing begotten" or "God begotten" is interchangeable with the person of Son. Yet, one cannot say that "essence is a thing begotten." If that distinction is observed, then (in reference to the Father), "there exists no contradiction in saying that 'essence is a thing begetting,' and 'a thing not

begetting'; because in the first case 'thing' stands for person, and in the second it stands for the essence" (Aquinas, *STh* I-I, q. 39, a. 5).

177. Goodwin rejects the idea that divine fatherhood means that God the Father "did beget the Godhead of Christ"; rather, "the Object of his Father-hood in that sense is only of the Person of Christ" (Goodwin, *WTG* 1:328). The scholastic axiom that the divine essence neither begets nor is begotten merely affirms the Nicene confession that God may be said to generate God in the concrete, but not in the abstract. "Quia vero substantia vel essentia significat in abstractione, ideo nec generat nec generatur." See St. Bonaventure of Bagnoregio, *Commentaria in Librum Primum Sententiarum*, bk. 1, a. 2, q. 1, English translation by the Franciscan Archive, accompanied by the Latin text of the Quaracchi Edition, http://www.franciscan-archive.org/bonaventura/1-Sent.html. Conversely, the *propria* of the Father, Son and Spirit are incommunicable: "*Essentia communicatio facit omnia communia*; The Godhead being communicated by the Father, all things of the Godhead, or that can be attributed thereunto, are communicated to all Three, only the distinction of Persons excepted" (Goodwin, *WTG* 9:136).

178. "The divine essence" in "its relative being may be dependent on a necessary, essential, and so an independent communication" (Edwards, "On the Equality," in *WJE* 21:148).

179. In the same treatise, Edwards refers to the Father as both "God (absolutely considered)" and "the deity subsisting in the . . . most absolute manner," the latter implying less absolute modes (Edwards, "Discourse on the Trinity," in *WJE* 21:131). Pauw's observation of this vacillation between an essentialism and personalism of the Father, in great part, justifies her conclusion that Edwards held to a "cobbled trinitarianism" of the psychological and social analogies (*Supreme Harmony*, ch. 6). Similarly, Lee's initial emphasis on the Father as actuality and disposition (in the first edition of his *Philosophical Theology*, 1988) was amended to include all three divine persons as exemplifications of the divine essence that are actual and dispositional (*Philosophical Theology*, exp. ed., 2000, 186–96).

180. This is implicitly stated by Edwards: "'tis by God's idea that his glory shines forth and appears to himself. God may be conceived of as glorious, antecedent to his idea of himself; but then his glory is latent. But 'tis the idea by which it shines forth and appears to God's view, so that he can delight in it" (Edwards, "Discourse on the Trinity," in *WJE* 21:119). One notes that the notion of subsistent relations and his frequent references to the "Father" are evident in Edwards's later Trinitarian treatise, "Equality" (c. 1740s) as compared to the "Discourse" (begun c. 1730). Yet, he continues to add entries to the "Discourse" into the 1740s without repudiating his earlier ideas. Thus, no polarity between an earlier and later Edwards should be posited to iron out the apparent contradiction.

181. Catherine M. LaCugna, *God for Us: The Trinity and Christian Life* (New York: HarperCollins, 1991), 388–90. Richard Cross has made a strong case, textually and philosophically, that Gregory of Nazianzus primarily uses the divine *monarchia* to refer to the action of the entire Trinity *ad extra*. However, "when used of the relation between the essence and persons, it is used as a way of asserting the indivisibility of this essence." These uses neither preclude nor contradict his affirmation of the divine causal relations (Cross, "Divine Monarchy in Gregory of Nazianzus," 114).

182. See esp. ch. 3 in Zizioulas, *Communion and Otherness*, 113–54.

183. The standard textbook criticism is that any conceptual priority to the Father as the sole fontal principle posits a hierarchical, rather than a relational, unity within the immanent Trinity. See William J. Hill, *The Three-Personed God: The Trinity as a Mystery of Salvation* (Washington, DC: Catholic University of America Press, 1982), 77–78. There is a sense of ontological priority in Damascus: "All then that the Son and the Spirit have is from the Father, even their very being: and unless the Father is, neither the Son nor the Spirit is. And unless the Father possesses a certain attribute, neither the Son nor the Spirit possesses it: and through the Father, that is, because of the Father's existence . . . the Son and the Spirit have all their qualities, those of birth and of procession being excepted" (John of Damascus, *Orthodox Faith*, bk. 1, ch. 8 [*NPNF* 9]).

184. As Cross points out, causal derivation need not imply subordinationism, though more philosophical work would need to be done to justify this. For, even in our conventional way of looking at things, "causal derivation . . . is perfectly consistent with the thought that something could counterfactually depend on its effect (if the sun were not producing heat, it would not exist: it counterfactually, though not causally, depends on the heat it produces" (Cross, "Divine Monarchy in Gregory of Nazianzus," 111n31).

185. This nominalism takes two forms. In its strong variety, an absolutely simple essence (like Eunomius's *nuda essentia*) means that the divine attributes are pure human concepts. In its mild form, a partial nominalism considers the *proprietas* of God real and nonaccidental to God's being but logically posterior to the divine simplicity insofar as they appear as multiple in God's relation to the world. That the divine attributes are affirmed to be objectively true in God (*proprie*) and their multiplicity merely subjectively true to us (*improprie*) leads once again to an unknown, abstract divine essence (Barth, *CD* II.1, 327–30). If the divine attributes were merely "the divine essence itself in its relation to the world," and if they were undifferentiated from the divine essence, then God would have no attributes apart from the world (Heppe, *Reformed Dogmatics*, 57).

186. Absolute nominalism was characteristic of medieval theologians like William of Occam and Gabriel Biel and modern ones like Schleiermacher. See Karl Barth, *CD* 2.1, 327. The positive delineation of the *proprietates Dei* over against an unknown *essentia* was not limited to the West. For John of Damascus, the various divine names and attributes, whether positive or negative, point to the essence but do not "explain his actual essence." Even God's "most proper" name (*ho on*) only "conveys the notion of His existence and of the nature of His existence." Just as one knows only the attributes of the essence of the human body or soul without apprehending their essence, "we do not apprehend the [divine] essence itself but only the attributes of the essence" (John of Damascus, *Orthodox Faith*, bk. 1, ch. 10, 12 [*NPNF* 9]).

187. Our formal ideas of the various divine attributes are not merely speculative (*ratio ratiocinans*), but correspond in content to objective concepts in God, which are revealed to us (*ratio ratiocinata*) (Heppe, *Reformed Dogmatics*, 59–60). Polanus, for example, says: "As God's essential attributes are not distinguished *realiter*, so too they are not distinguished by the nature of the thing but by the *ratio* or rather mode; i.e., by our conception and comprehension, or by our mode of understanding them" (Amandus Polanus a Polansdorf, *Syntagma Theologiae Christianae* [Hanover, 1624], II: 7, in Heppe, *Reformed Dogmatics*, 58). Barth considers Thomistic and Reformed scholasticism (Polanus, Quenstedt, and van Mastricht) as seminominalistic, and its rejection by nineteenth-century German theologians (like Thomasius and Dorner) to be correct (Barth, *CD* II.1, 329–30). This position was restated by later Reformed dogmaticians, like Charles Hodge, who argued against both the *distinctio ratio* of the medieval nominalists and the *distinctio realiter* of the medieval realists. See Charles Hodge, *Systematic Theology*, 3 vols. (Grand Rapids: Eerdmans, 1993; originally published, 1872), vol. 1, pt. 1, ch. 5, § 2, 369–74.

188. An example would be the Eastern idea of the single *energeia* expressed in a multiplicity of *energeias*. According to Palamas, we designate God by many names because of the multiplicity of the energies, since they are the manifestations of the divine superessence, but by doing so, the simplicity of God is not denied. That is why he affirms that the superessential Essence transcends the energies as Cause, not that the latter are created, but that "God subsist[s] entirely in each [energy] without any division at all." See Gregory Palamas, *The Triads*, ed. John Meyendorff, trans. Nicholas Gendell, with a preface by Jaroslav Pelikan, Classics of Western Spirituality (Mahwah, NJ: Paulist, 1983), 96. Scotus's formal distinction, while asserting that the various attributes are commensurate with their different "lexical definitions," nonetheless, does not state how they are so. See Richard Cross, *Duns Scotus*, Great Medieval Thinkers (New York: Oxford University Press, 1999), 43.

189. Even the personal names of Father, Son, and Spirit and their corresponding personal properties "do not explain the essence, but the mutual relationship and manner of existence." (John of Damascus, *Orthodox Faith*, bk. 1, ch. 10, 12 [*NPNF* 9]).

190. Oliver D. Crisp highlights, in particular, the problematic nature of Edwards's partitioning of the divine attributes into the real and relative. See his "Jonathan Edwards on Divine Simplicity," *Religious Studies* 39 (2003): 23–41.

191. "As we are forced to distinguish understanding and will in God in one way of conceiving of him (although they are indeed one in a manner that we cannot conceive of him), so . . . his will is always influenced and governed by his understanding and judgment" (Edwards, 107. Sermon on Num. 23:19 [1729], in *WJE* 44).

192. "Whatsoever power or wisdom or holiness, etc. belongs to the divine nature, still belongs to the same divine nature in whatsoever person it subsists, whether it subsists in the {Father, Son or Holy Ghost}." Edwards, "Threefold Work of the Holy Ghost,"in *WJE* 14:379.

193. "If a man should tell me that the immutability of God is God, or that the omnipresence of God and authority of God [is God], I should not be able to think of any rational meaning of what he said" (Edwards, "Discourse on the Trinity," in *WJE* 21:132). In scholastic theology, no real distinction exists between the *essentia*, *esse* and *proprietates Dei*. In affirming that the divine attributes are neither parts nor accidents of the divine essence, the basic Thomistic axiom that "in God's nature there is nothing which is not God himself" is affirmed (Heppe, *Reformed Dogmatics*, 57). The Thomistic thesis of the identity of the divine *essentia* and *esse* was certainly not foreign to Puritan writers like Nicolas Estwick. "For God is a most pure act: not of *Esse* and Essence, for the *Esse* of God is his Essence, and that Essence of God is his *Esse*; God's greatness is God's Essence; God's goodness is God's Essence; God's justice is God's Essence; and it's true of the rest." See Nicolas Estwick, *Pneumatología: Or, a treatise of the holy ghost. In which, the God-head of the third person of the Trinitie is strongly asserted by Scripture-arguments. And defended against the sophisticall subtleties of John Bidle* (London: Ralph Smith, 1648), 88. This treatise was written to refute the antitrinitarian writings of a founding father of English Socinianism, John Biddle (1615–1652).

194. Edwards, "Discourse on the Trinity," in *WJE* 21:131. Clearly, real distinction does not mean an essential difference (*essentialiter* or *distinctionem realem majorem*), for this would amount to tritheism. If it is a real minor distinction (*distinctionem realem minorem*), then it is no different from a modal distinction (*modaliter*), which is consistent with *tropoi hyparxeōs*. But if this is the case, then what of the other attributes that are modes of the real attributes? If these are not merely nominal or conceptual, then it must be the Scotistic virtual/formal distinction (*ex parte rei*), viz., a reasoned distinction with a foundation in the thing itself. The difference is probably similar to the essence/person and person/person distinctions, the latter being the greater (Turretin, *Institutes of Elenctic Theology*, trans. George Musgrave Giger, ed. James T. Dennison [Phillipsburg, NJ: P&R, 1992–94], 1: 279). In Thomas, they have respectively been characterized as conceptual and real distinctions in God. (Aquinas, *STh* III, q. 2, a. 2, 2028). Unlike God, there is a real distinction between *essentia* and *supposita* in created things. Individual entities or *supposita* composed of matter and form (including human beings) are made up of the defining properties of its nature together with accidental and individuating principles.

195. According to Holmes, this represents "a radical extension of the doctrine of appropriation." See Stephen R. Holmes, *God of Grace and God of Glory: An Account of the Theology of Jonathan Edwards* (Edinburgh: T&T Clark, 2000), 71.

196. "Though all the divine perfections are to be attributed to each person of the Trinity, yet the Holy Ghost is in a peculiar manner called by the name love" (Edwards, "Treatise on Grace," in *WJE* 21:181).

197. Wolfhart Pannenberg, *Systematic Theology*, 3 vols, trans. Geoffrey W. Bromiley (Grand Rapids, MI: Eerdmans, 1998), 1:362. Augustine's important contribution to subsequent Trinitarian discourse is to have cast the difference of Father, Son, and Holy Spirit in their relationships to each other; he insisted that the divine persons cannot be distinguished absolutely, either functionally or attributively (Hill, "Introduction," in *The Trinity*, 50–51). Muller notes that Heidegger rejected the attribution of intellection and volition to the Son and Spirit respectively since he regarded them as

belonging indistinctly to the divine essence (Heidegger, *Corpus theol.*, IV.4, as cited in Muller, *PRRD* 4:377).

198. "We ought to conceive of God as being omnipotence, perfect knowledge and perfect love; and not extended any otherwise than as power, knowledge and love extended; and not as if it was a sort of unknown thing that we call substance, that is extended" (Edwards, "Miscellanies," no. 194, in *WJE* 13:335). Schafer dates this entry between July and August 1725.

199. Edwards, "Discourse on the Trinity," in *WJE* 21:132.

200. Ibid., 131. There is the biblical basis as well: "I don't remember that any other attributes are said to be God, and God to be them, but λόγος and 'αγάπη, or reason and love; I conclude, because no other are in that (a personal) sense." See Edwards, "Miscellanies," no. 146 (*136*), in *WJE* 13: 299–300, where he refers to 1 John 4.

201. "There is God's power or ability to bring things to pass. But this is not really distinct from his understanding and will; it is the same, but only with the relation they have to those effects that are or are to be produced" (Edwards, "Discourse on the Trinity," in *WJE* 21:131).

202. Thus God's perfect exercise of power and operation *ad intra* is distinct from God's omnipotence or "the power of God" considered as "a relation of adequateness and sufficiency of the essence to everything. But if we distinguish it from relation, 'tis nothing else but the essence of God" (Edwards, "Miscellanies," no. 94, in *WJE* 13:262).

203. Since he classifies some of the negative attributes as modally distinguished from the divine essence, they are thus not really distinct from the first divine subsistence: "There are his attributes of infinity, eternity and immutability: they are mere modes of existence" (Edwards, "Discourse on the Trinity," in *WJE* 21:131).

204. "And if we take it [the divine power] for that by which God exerts himself, 'tis no other than the Father" (Edwards, "Miscellanies," no. 94, in *WJE* 13:262). In one sense, the Father is the most primal instance of the divine dispositional essence—the necessary disposition to self-communicate (Lee, *PTJE*, 186–87). The divine essence as disposition to self-communication *ad extra* is contingent.

205. "The Father is . . . the Deity in its direct existence. The Son is the Deity generated by God's understanding . . . and subsisting in that idea. The Holy Ghost is the Deity subsisting in act" (Edwards, "Discourse on the Trinity," in *WJE* 21:131).

206. Duns Scotus agreed that the essential acts are the ground of the notional, but rejected the Henrician claim of "essential knowledge as the causal principle of generated knowledge." See Richard Cross, *Duns Scotus on God*, Ashgate Studies in the History of Philosophical Theology (Burlington, VT: Ashgate, 2005), 225.

207. Edwards considers the Holy Spirit as both divine person (which is identical to the essence) and as a real distinction within the essence, as the Spirit is "not only infinitely holy as the Father and the Son are, but He is the holiness of God itself in the abstract" (Edwards, "Treatise on Grace," in *TG*, 64). Since "the Father" is "the fountain of the Godhead . . . All is from him, all is in him originally" (Edwards, "Discourse on the Trinity, in *WJE* 21:143).

208. Thus, "the Father understands because the Son, who is the divine understanding, is in him" (Edwards, "Discourse on the Trinity," in *WJE* 21:133). This was rejected by Scotus, who thought that Henry's description of the relation between God and the Word was too anthropomorphic since, according to Cross, the "generated Word is a divine person, and as such is not related to another person as attribute to subject" (Cross, *Duns Scotus on God*, 226).

209. "That knowledge or understanding in God which we must conceive of as first is His knowledge of everything possible. That love which must be this knowledge is what we must conceive of as belonging to the essence of the Godhead in its first subsistence" (Edwards, "Discourse on the Trinity," in *WJE* 21:141). This is akin to Ames's description of the divine processions: "The Son is produced as it were by an act of understanding or speaking, from the understanding, or fruitful memory of the Father: the holy Spirit is produced by an act of loving or breathing from the fruitful will of the Father and the Son." As reflected in the human being, the Father, Son, and Holy Spirit may be described respectively "as . . . *Deus intelligens*, God

understanding . . . *Deus intellectus*, God understood," and "*Deus dilectus*, God beloved" (Ames, *Marrow of Sacred Divinity*, ch. 5, 18).

210. "And I believe the whole divine essence does truly and distinctly subsist both in the divine idea and divine love, and that therefore each of them are properly distinct persons" (Edwards, "Discourse on the Trinity, in *WJE* 21:143). Aquinas's distinction between essential and notional attributes is echoed in Ames's distinction between "inherent qualities" of the common divine essence and the "relative affections" distinguishing the divine persons. "Now these properties are not inherent qualities, but relative affections, unto which agrees all that perfection, which is found in the like affections of the creature, but no imperfection agrees to them" (Ames, *Marrow of Sacred Divinity*, ch. 5, 17). While the divine persons are similar to the two distinct human affections *via eminentiae*, yet, *via negativa*, these do not subsist in human beings.

211. Edwards, "On the Equality," in *WJE* 21: 146–48. The fragment was probably written sometime between the beginning of 1740 and 1742, according to Lee, and has handwriting similar to later entries at the end of Edwards's "Discourse on the Trinity" (Lee, introduction to "On the Equality," in *WJE* 21:145).

212. "To show how the personal glory of each of the persons in the Trinity is equal, though each one, as they have a distinct personality, have a distinct glory, and so one has a peculiar glory that another has not" (Edwards, "On the Equality," in *WJE* 21:146).

213. Ibid. While other Puritan writers, like Patrick Gillespie, distinguished between the essential and personal glory of the divine persons, they applied it to the *oikonomia* alone. Patrick Gillespie (1617–1675), the younger brother of George Gillespie (who represented Scotland at the Westminster Assembly), was a contemporary of John Owen. Referring to the divine persons in the covenant of redemption, Gillespie asserted that "(beside the glory that was common to all the three Persons) there did accrue a peculiar glory to the distinct Persons of the Godhead, in regard of their distinct offices and working in this business of Redemption; a peculiar glory to the Father, who gave Christ . . . A peculiar honour to the Son . . . that wrought the Redemption . . . A peculiar glory unto the *eternal Spirit* . . . to whom the effectual application of the purchased Redemption by peculiar office belongs" See Patrick Gillespie, *The ark of the covenant opened. . . . Grounds of comfort from the covenant of suretyship.* (London: Tho. Parkhurst, 1677), 41–42.

214. While Edwards is aware that the theological tradition has distinguished the persons in attributive terms (e.g., unbegottenness, begottenness, procession), he recognizes the polyvalence of the term "attribute." Hence, "to apply a distinct glory to the Father, Son and Spirit in that sense, don't at all infer an application of proper distinct perfections or attributes, and so a distinct essence . . . for personal relations are not the divine essence" (Edwards, "On the Equality," in *WJE* 21:146).

215. Ibid. It is interesting that Edwards, anticipating John MacMurray, calls the glory common to the persons an "individual glory," in contradistinction to personal or relative glory (Edwards, 321. Sermon on Heb. 1:3 [Apr 1734], in *WJE* 49). Owen succinctly defines it: "For glory adds a supposition of relation unto being." However, he thinks of God's essential glory not as an *ad intra* relation; rather, it "is the being of God, with that respect which all creatures have unto it." See John Owen, *Christologia: Or, a Declaration of The Glorious Mystery of the Person of Christ, God and Man, to which are Subjoined, Meditations and Discourses on the Glory of Christ*, vol. 1 of *The Works of John Owen, D.D.*, ed. William H. Goold (New York: Robert Carter & Brothers, 1851), ch. 20, 262.

216. Edwards could even use the term "superiority" ("Discourse on the Trinity," in *WJE* 21:147) but elsewhere clarifies that its usage is not so appropriate as it may imply "inferiority." Hence, this ontological *taxis* is better described as a "priority of subsistence" ("Miscellanies," no. 1062, in *WJE* 21:430).

217. "The beloved has as it were the superiority over the lover, and reigns over him" (Edwards, "On the Equality," in *WJE* 21:147).

218. W. Norris Clarke, "To Be is to Be Substance-in-Relation," in *Metaphysics as Foundation: Essays in Honor of Ivor Leclerc*, ed. Paul A. Bogaard and Gordon Treash (Albany: State University of New York Press, 1993), 164–83.

219. "The Father has good, and though the Son receives the infinite good, the Holy Spirit, from the Father, the Father enjoys the infinite good through the Son" (Edwards, "On the Equality," in *WJE* 21:147).

220. Clearly, Edwards thinks that a temporal *processio* could either be seen from the perspective of ascending or descending (Edwards, "Miscellanies," no. 1263, in *WJE* 23:205–6).

221. Edwards, "On the Equality," in *WJE* 21:147.

222. With the help of a little "Hegeling," Coffey clarifies that the successive moments and order of the Trinity *in fieri* (Father loving the Son and vice versa) "have not been lost, but they have been sublated (preserved but transcended) as the reciprocal love itself has been sublated into mutual love" in the Trinity *in facto esse.* (Coffey, "Roman 'Clarification,'" 18).

223. "Hereby we may more clearly understand the equality of the persons among themselves, and that they are every way equal in the society or family of the three. They are equal in honor besides the honor which is common to 'em all, viz. that they are all God; each has his peculiar honor in the society or family. They are equal not only in essence" (Edwards, "Discourse on the Trinity," in *WJE* 21:135).

224. Here, one notes that the modalist tendency of the "psychological" analogy stands in stark contrast to a tritheist undertone in Ramsay's discourse, where he held to a Boethian definition of person as three self-aware *res*. Yet, he goes on to deny the major Trinitarian heresies in favor of Nicaea: "These three distinctions in the Deity are neither three distinct independent minds, as the tritheists alleged; nor three attributes of the same substance represented as persons, as the Sabellians affirmed: nor one supreme, and two subordinate intellectual agents, as some refined Arians maintained: but three co-eternal, consubstantial, coordinate persons co-equal in all things, self-origination only excepted" (Ramsay, *Philosophical Principles of Natural and Revealed Religion*, as cited in Edwards, "Miscellanies," no. 1253, in *WJE* 23:188). Boethius's understanding is clearly carried on into the Puritan tradition. Edward Leigh, for example, understood a person to be substantial, intelligent, hypostatic, incommunicable, non-*enypostatos*, and nonpartitive (Leigh, *Treatise of Divinity*, 130–31). Pauw has observed a similar sort of tension in Edwards (Pauw, *Supreme Harmony*, passim).

225. This "infinite life, light, and love" are not simply properties but are "self-conscious agents . . . three distinct beings, realities, somethings, or persons" (Ramsay, *Philosophical Principles of Natural and Revealed Religion*, as cited in Edwards, "Miscellanies," no. 1253, in *WJE* 23:187).

226. According to Edwards, "a person is that which hath understanding and will" (Edwards, "Discourse on the Trinity," in *WJE* 21:133). From the Father proceeds idea and love; the Son is idea and processes love with the Father.

227. "If the three in the Godhead are persons, they doubtless each of 'em have understanding: but this makes the understanding one distinct person, and love another. How therefore can this love be said to have understanding?" (ibid.).

228. Torrance appeals to Calvin's notion of *in solidum* to justify the idea of *autotheos* as grounded in a *perichoresis* that is logically prior to the divine processions. Calvin borrowed this term from Cyprian, who originally used it to describe the collegiality of the episcopacy. See Thomas F. Torrance, *The Christian Doctrine of God: One Being, Three Persons* (Edinburgh: T&T Clark, 1996), 201. In reference to the divine essence, Calvin says that "it is wholly and altogether (*tota est in solidum*) common to the Father and Son" (*Institutes*, I.xii.28). The Puritans were not unaware of this: "And thus have we discovered the blessed agents and undertakers in this work their several actions and orderly concurrence unto the whole; which, though they may be thus distinguished, yet they are not so divided but that every one must be ascribed to the whole nature, whereof each person is 'in solidum' partaker." See John Owen, "Death of Death in the Death of

Christ," in *Theomachia Auteousiastike: A Display of Arminianism*, vol. 10 of *The Works of John Owen, D.D.*, ed. William H. Goold (New York: Robert Carter & Brothers, 1852), 179.

229. The *communicatio essentiae* makes the divine persons, for Edwards, more like verbs (or verbal nouns). The "divine essence . . . represents the action of the deity towards itself, in the action of the persons of the TRINITY towards each other" (Edwards, "Notes on Scripture," no. 383, in *WJE* 15:387). This God is "infinitely, eternally and essentially active and productive," contrary to any "state of inaction and indolence." The divine processions as the "eternal commerce of the co-eternal three is the secret fund of the Deity" (Chevalier Ramsay, *Philosophical Principles of Religion*, 1:74–85, as cited in Edwards, "Miscellanies," no. 1253, in *WJE* 23:184, 188). This is very much like Thomas' construal of the divine persons as substantial activity or "action-based subsisting relations" (Fergus Kerr, *After Aquinas: Versions of Thomism* [Malden, MA: Blackwell, 2002], 200).

230. "And the Father understands because the Son, who is the divine understanding, is in him. The Father loves because the Holy Ghost is in him. . . . There is understanding and will in the Father, as the Son and the Holy Spirit are in him and proceed from [him]" (Edwards, "Discourse on the Trinity," in *WJE* 21:133–34).

231. Edwards, "Notes on Scripture," no. 393, in *WJE* 15: 388. Exegeting Ezek. 1:4, Edwards concludes: "And therefore this 'fire enfolding itself' does especially represent the deity before the creation of the world, or before the beginning of the being of this chariot with its wheels, when all God's acts were only towards himself, for then there was no other being but he."

232. Ibid., 387. The Father is the "substance" or "internal constitution" of the sun, the Son is its manifested "glory" or "form," the Spirit is its "intestine heat," which emanates from it and is communicated outwardly (Edwards, "Discourse on the Trinity," in *WJE* 21:138). Here, the Father or "Godhead" is not known apart from the Son and the Spirit: "He is seen by his image, the Son, and is felt by the Holy Spirit, as fire is perceived only by its light and heat, seen by one and felt by the other" (Edwards, "Notes on Scriptures," no. 393, in *WJE* 15:387). Edwards uses the term "divine essence" to include all three persons of the Trinity, or more accurately "the action of the deity toward itself" or "the action of the persons of the TRINITY towards each other." The Godhead is the hidden Father, spoken of in John 1:18, revealed by the Son and Spirit.

233. Zizioulas's opposition to any idea of the *actus personales* as involving natural necessity forces him to construe the Father as the principle of otherness *ad intra*. He thus rejects the idea of the Father being the fount of the *communicatio essentiae*, positing a sharp distinction between the divine essence (the "what") and the divine person (the "how"). The divine essence, being the common possession of the divine persons, is thus posterior to the divine processions (Zizioulas, *Communion and Otherness*, 126–30). That being the case, the Father would then be the *arche* of personhood-in-general but not *divine* personhood. The Father freely wills the Son and Spirit into existence, but is only divine as a result. But if persons are the divinity, and if the Father is their *aition*, then how is the Father not ultimately the cause of divinity? On this account, the Father is not only a vacuous person but becomes the willer of the Father's own essence. Here, Aquinas reminds us of the inseparability of essence and person for "common terms . . . are included in the understanding of proper terms." Hence, "in the concept of the person of the Father, God is understood" (*STh* I, q. 33, a. 3, ad 1). See also Emery, *Trinity in Aquinas*, 133–34.

234. "As we are forced to distinguish understanding and will in God in our way of conceiving of him (although they are indeed one in a manner that we cannot conceive of him), so, to speak of him according to our way of conceiving, his will is always influenced and governed by his understanding or judgment" (Edwards, 107. Sermon on Num. 23:19, in *WJE* 44).

235. The relations are comprehended within the essence because they are identical to it. See Matthew Levering, *Scripture and Metaphysics: Aquinas and the Renewal of Trinitarian Theology*, Challenges in Contemporary Theology (Oxford: Blackwell, 2004), 225.

236. Edwards does not describe the Son and Spirit as two real attributes of the Father, but explains that there are "three distinct real things in God," the first as the divine essence "absolutely

considered" and the other two as relative to the first (Edwards, "Discourse on the Trinity," in *WJE* 21:131).

237. At this primal "moment," the "Godhead or the divine nature and essence" neither stands forth as "substantial and personal idea" nor does it yet "subsist in love" (Edwards, "Discourse on the Trinity," in *WJE* 21:117, 121).

238. "These three—God, and the idea of God, and the inclination, affection or love of God—must be conceived as really distinct" (Edwards, "Discourse on the Trinity," in *WJE* 21:131–32).

239. The term *in facto esse* here should not be understood as an act of becoming actual. The divine processions are in perpetual operation and so are "said to be terminated by a termination of perfection, not by a termination of duration" (Turretin, *Institutes*, 1:294).

240. "So the Son loves because the Holy Spirit is in him and proceeds from him. . . . There is understanding and will in the Son, as he is understanding and as the Holy Ghost is in him and proceeds from him" (Edwards, "Discourse on the Trinity," in *WJE* 21:133–34).

241. "So the Holy Ghost, or the divine essence subsisting in divine love, understands because the Son, the divine idea, is in him. . . . There is understanding and will in the Holy Ghost, as he is the divine will and the Son is in him" (ibid.).

242. "Understanding may be predicated of this love, because it is the love of the understanding both objectively and subjectively. God loves the understanding and the understanding also flows out in love, so that the divine understanding is in the Deity subsisting in love" (ibid., 133).

243. This kind of thinking is not too far off from Gregory of Nazianzen: "For this reason, the One (μονάς) having moved from the beginning (from all eternity) to a Dyad, stopped (or rested) in Triad. And this is for us the Father and the Son and the Holy Spirit. The one as the Begetter and the Emitter (γεννήτωρ και προβολεύς), without passion of course and without reference to time, and not in a corporeal manner, of whom the others are one of them the begotten and the other the emission" (Gregory Naz., *Theol. Or.* 3.2, in Zizioulas, *Communion and Otherness*, 133). Zizioulas argues that "the One" refers to the Father alone and, as such, excludes the one *ousia*. But we may also interpret "the One" as meaning the *ousia* identified as the "Father." In fact, this makes more sense of the above passage as the One cannot be called Father except in the Dyad (viz., apart from the Son) and, therefore, the Father, Son and Holy Spirit are named only in the Triad. Thus, the Father begets and emits the Son and Spirit.

244. "The idea of relation, however, necessarily means regard of one to another, according as one is relatively opposed to another" (Aquinas, *STh* I, q. 28, a. 3). See also, *STh* I, q. 40, a. 1. Emery cautions us that the term "relation of opposition" used in much contemporary theology in reference to Aquinas is inaccurate. The terms used by St. Thomas include "relative opposition," "opposition of relations," "opposed relations," "mutually opposed relations," or "relations which have a mutual opposition." (Emery, *Trinitarian Theology of Thomas Aquinas*, 99).

245. Ratzinger parses the mutual love model using Gregory's idiom: "The dyad returns into unity in the Trinity without breaking up the dialogue. Dialogue is actually confirmed in just this way. A mediation back into unity which was not another Person would break up the dialogue as dialogue" (Joseph Ratzinger, "The Holy Spirit as Communio: Concerning the Relationship of Pneumatology and Spirituality in Augustine," *Communio: International Catholic Review* 25 [Summer 1998]: 326). This is comparable to Victorinus's conception of the Trinity as an eternal movement of *status, progressio,* and *regressus,* where the Spirit joins the Father and Son as the *reditus* within the divinity. He regarded the Son as the revelation of the unknowable Godhead, and the return of the Spirit as the eternal self-understanding of God (Kelly, *Early Christian Doctrines*, 271).

246. Edwards, "Discourse on the Trinity," in *WJE* 21:133. Ratzinger would prefer to interpret the Augustinian Trinitarian tradition in only personalist, and not substantialist, terms when he proposes that the *unitas* in *trinitas* as founded not on "a universal, ontic, *consubstantialitas,* but as *communio.*" See Ratzinger, "Holy Spirit as Communio," 326.

247. Edwards, "Discourse on the Trinity," in *WJE* 21:133.

248. The Father, in two distinct reflexive exercises of the dispositional essence, repeats his own actuality in the "forms" of divine self-consciousness and self-love, thus generating the Son and spirating the Holy Spirit. See esp. ch. 7 in Lee, *PTJE*, 170–210.

249. As we have seen, Edwards does not restrict the names "Messiah" and "Christ" to the realm of the divine economy. Accordingly, these designations are not true of "Christ only as man, or as Mediator," but "God the Son from all eternity was Christ" (Edwards, "Miscellanies," no. 225, in *WJE* 13:346). Edwards, "On the Equality," in *Works* 21:146. As "the Holy Spirit is the sum of all good" or "the fullness of God," the end for which God *created* the world is "to communicate . . . his own infinite fullness of good," so that the "diffusion" of the Holy Spirit *ad extra* was what God sought "as his last end" of creation (Edwards, "Concerning the End," in *WJE* 8:433).

2

Communication of Being *Ad Extra*
Trinitarian Creation

Previously, we examined Edwards's postulation of an eternal movement of emanation and remanation in the eternal procession of the Spirit *ad intra*. This mode of self-communication of essence within God is the basis of the telos of created reality. In this chapter, we will look at how Edwards uses the doctrines of *creatio ex nihilo* and *imago Dei* to posit a similarity and dissimilarity between God and created reality. Beginning from the creation's natural participation of likeness in the divine, we shall move on to analyze Edwards's portrayal of the end for which God created the world—the church's participation in the divine life. As he explains, "God is a communicative being. This communication is really only to intelligent beings: the communication of himself to their understandings is his glory, and the communication of himself with respect to their wills, the enjoying faculty, is their happiness. God created the world for the shining forth of his excellency and for the flowing forth of his happiness."[1] Here, we will see how the circle of emanation/creation and remanation/redemption is but a temporal reflection of the dynamism within God. But first, we shall briefly study how Edwards links the action of the Trinity *ad extra* and *ad intra* through the divine counsels.

OPERA INTERNUM AD EXTRA: THE BRIDGE BETWEEN THE IMMANENT TRINITY AND ECONOMIC TRINITY

For Edwards, God's immutable, divine nature secures the permanence of the divine decrees as well as their regulative function for both the divine and human.[2] The triune God has freely willed to be bound to God's own decrees.[3] While Edwards admits that God's decrees are eternal, they are to be distinguished from the divine attributes.[4] Here, he reiterates the Reformed stance that the divine decrees are modally distinguished from the divine will as possessing a relation *ad extra*.[5] For Edwards, the modal divine attributes, in turn, are founded upon the real attributes of God—the Son and the Spirit.[6] That is why the Son and Spirit are the *fundamenta*, *causa*, and *ratio* of the divine decrees.[7] Nonetheless, due to God's simplicity and the unity of essence, the ordering of the divine decrees is a rational distinction.[8] The decrees themselves arise from these deliberative counsels within God—a Reformed construct that Edwards inherits.

ŒCONOMY OF THE TRINITY: COMMUNION OF WILL FOR COMMUNICATION OF FULLNESS *AD EXTRA*

The notion of the divine counsels enables Edwards to ground the temporal *opera ad extra* of the Trinity in their eternal *opera ad intra*.[9] He posits two levels of divine intratrinitarian counsels where the Father, Son, and the Spirit agree to order themselves in their general economical action in the world and particularly in the work of redemption.[10] In the following section, we examine the first of these—the œconomical Trinity—and will study the covenant of redemption (*pactum salutis*) in the next chapter.[11]

"SOCIETY OF THE PERSONS OF THE TRINITY": EDWARDS'S "SOCIAL" TRINITARIANISM

Nowhere in Edwards's writings is the foundational divine parity more evident than in his metaphorical description of the three divine persons as a "family" or "society" united in loving consent.[12] In a manner consistent with the Puritan tradition, Edwards applies the analogy of the divine society or family to the œconomical Trinity. "The persons of the Trinity thus acting as a society in an established order is what divines call the 'economy of the persons of the Trinity,' comparing it to the order of a family."[13] It is at this level of the œconomy that Edwards brings the Father-Son relation to the fore.[14]

According to Edwards, this "œconomical" *taxis* comes about through neither an arbitrary nor teleologically expedient decision of the divine persons.[15] It is grounded in the immanent Trinity in *facto esse*, particularly in Edwards's Augustinian mutual-love analogy. "Indeed the eternal infinite happiness of the divine being seems to be social consisting in the infinitely blessed union and society of the persons of the Trinity so that they are happy in one another so God the Father and God the Son are represented as rejoicing from eternity one in another."[16] But Edwards's notion of the divine society, though comprehending the *familia*, is not identical to it. The perichoretic mutuality of the persons is included.

In light of the mutual in-existence of Father, Son, and Spirit, the divine persons mutually appropriate distinct roles to each other in the "economy [œconomy] of the persons of the Trinity."[17] This mutual concurrence is expressed in the *oikonomia* in which the divine persons function "as joint actors and co-workers in an affair of common concern," yet each has "his distinct part" or "office."[18] Implicit to this schema of the œconomical Trinity is the presupposition of three deliberating and consenting subjects, which stands in tension with Edwards's psychological model of the Trinity.[19] Well aware of their tritheistic implications, Edwards qualifies the figural character of these intratrinitarian counsels. The three divine persons "have *as it were* formed themselves into a society" for their economic works and also "*as it were* confederated in the design and a covenant of redemption."[20] Edwards's "social" trinitarianism is to be regarded as a second-order analogy since his language of joint action signifies three actors with one identical action in three modes of expression. Here, the singularity of being and action is not compromised because "the persons of the Trinity of their own *will* have as it were formed themselves into a society."[21] His partitive grammar, being analogical, must not be read as introducing division into the divine essence. The one action of God is not only modal but also ordered.

A HIERARCHICAL TRINITY: GENERAL ORDERING TO OPERATIONS AD EXTRA

What is the *ratio* of the œconomy of the Trinity? It is an ordering of the divine persons to their entire works *ad extra*, which involves a functional subordinationism.[22] Edwards, of course, recognizes that the "subordination of the persons of the Trinity, in their acting with respect to the creature" seems to contradict their ontological egalitarianism since it is "very manifest that the persons of the Trinity are not inferior one to another in glory and excellency of nature."[23] But such a contradiction is only apparent, as the order of their œconomy mirrors their order of subsistence: Father—Son—Spirit.[24]

As the Source of the being of the Son and their Spirit, the Father is aptly the originator of their modes of operation.[25] Since the Son and the Spirit process from the Father from all eternity, their entire activity *ad extra* should "originate from him, act from him and [be] in dependence on him."[26] It is in this œconomy that God the Father is "in the first place vested with the authority, right, and ruling power of the Godhead."[27] This hierarchical ordering of the œconomy is reflective of the Father's "necessary" position as the *fons divinitatis* within the immanent Trinity and is the result of all three persons consenting to an œconomical order that beautifully reflects their ontological relations.[28]

It is "the will of the persons of the Trinity to act" *per conveniens*—that is to say, "in that order that is in itself fit and decent" to "what the order of their subsisting requires."[29] Though the œconomy of the Trinity is not oriented toward any particular work, this generality does not obviate its ultimate purpose. In this "subordination of the persons of the Trinity in their actings . . . the persons of the Trinity of their own will have as it were formed themselves into a society for carrying on the great design of glorifying the Deity and communicating its fullness."[30] It is this telos of the œconomy to which we will now turn our attention.

PURPOSE OF THE ŒCONOMY: DIVINE SELF-COMMUNICATION AD EXTRA

As observed in the previous chapter, Edwards conceives of God's internal self-communication as the Father's epiphany in the Son and God's rapture in the Spirit.[31] And based on Edwards's theological aesthetics, there must be a fittingness between the Trinitarian *theologia* and *oikonomia*: "It is condecent that correspondent to these proceedings of the divinity *ad intra*, God should also flow forth *ad extra*."[32] On the divine self-communication *ad extra*, Edwards adds:

> God glorifies himself toward the creatures also two ways: (1) by appearing to them, being manifested to their understandings; (2) in communicating himself to their hearts, and in their rejoicing and delighting in, and enjoying the manifestations which he makes of himself. They both of them may be called his glory in the more extensive sense of the word, viz. his shining forth, or the going forth of his excellency, beauty and essential glory *ad extra*. By one way it goes forth towards their understandings; by the other it goes forth towards their wills or hearts.[33]

Where lies this tendency to Trinitarian self-communication *ad extra*? Edwards maintains that God's glory in creation does not arise out of a lack in God but out of the "natural propensity in the divine nature" to be happy in loving another.[34] Accordingly, God would be a lesser Being if God lacked the disposition to self-communicate.[35] Although the emanation of God's glory *ad extra* follows creation *ex nihilo* in time and is thus its end, this emanation is to be countenanced as ontologically and logically prior as the motive force or disposition that moved God to create the world. Three points should be noted here.

The first deals with the question of means and ends. The final purpose of creaturely participation in God (or the divine self-communication *ad extra*) is that which was intended first by God. Though the creation of the universe was the first to be executed in time, it is nonetheless secondary in the divine intention. Here, Edwards affirms (and qualifies) the Aristotelian axiom, which was adopted by the medieval and Reformed scholastics: "that that is the first in execution, is last in intention with regard to the ultimate end."[36]

The second point is that God's disposition to self-emanate is identical to God's act of emanation. "Therefore, to speak strictly according to truth, we may suppose *that a disposition in God, as an original property of his nature, to an emanation of his own infinite fullness, was what excited him to create the world; and so that the emanation itself was aimed by him as a last end of the creation.*"[37] This disposition in God—the Holy Spirit—is both the moving and final cause of the creation.

The final point, and related to the previous, is Edwards's crucial distinction between creation *simpliciter* and perfected creation, or the end of creation. For God's achievement of this ultimate end of creation, there must first be a creation in which God could be glorified.

DIVINE SELF-ENLARGEMENT AS THE END OF CREATION?

Creation, as derived being, does not and cannot add to God, as God is the "all-comprehending being."[38] The divine disposition is not geared toward reception but toward communication since there is no lack in God. Rather, God is not only self-sufficient but "has more than enough" and having "infinite fullness . . . which doth as it were overflow to the creature."[39] The saints are, in one sense, "containers" of divinity: the crystal is distinct from the light of the sun.[40] Although God's essential glory *ad intra* is infinite and cannot increase, Edwards frequently affirms that God's "declarative" glory could be enlarged.[41] From the divine perspective, an increase can be spoken of "so that God's declarative glory, as it is in God's view, is truly an infinitely great thing." But what does this mean for God's eternal omniscience, which comprehensively grasps everything, *ad intra*? Edwards concedes that this could only be said of God improperly: "For creatures' happiness does not properly add anything to God's happiness, any more than God's being glorified in the view of the creature and by the creature adds something to God's happiness."[42]

Is there a problem with Edwards's idea that there would be unexercised perfections in God—divine power, wisdom, goodness, and justice—had there been no creation?[43] If so, wouldn't they cease to be primary divine properties insofar as they are latent *in se* and not actualized apart from the world? Not so, for God eternally and perfectly cognized them, as they were "virtually contained" in the Holy Spirit *ad intra*. By the Son and Spirit, these latent attributes are expressed *ad extra* through they are "not the same kind of exercise" *opera ad intra*.[44] This "act of God within himself and toward himself," while "virtually [containing]" the above attributes, were not "the same kind of exercise."[45] God's self-enlargement in time is the exercise of God's "good disposition in his nature to communicate of his own fullness in general."[46] This is the crowning or fulfillment of creation whereby God exists *ad extra* in the redeemed creation. It is from this primordial disposition to self-communicate that God gave "creatures existence in order to it."[47]

How does one reconcile Edwards's idea of *creatio ex nihilo* with his notion of God as a *pleroma* of life?[48] Only if the creation, which resides "in" God, is differentiated from the end of creation, which is God coming to reside in creaturely reality. It is only in the latter that humankind comes to participate in the glory and life of God. In one sense, the moral world represents a historical outflow of God's eternal glory and happiness.[49] Just as God's Parousia is God's coming to indwell the world by the Word and Spirit, the original creation of the universe is similarly an operation of the triune God.

PACTUM CREATIONIS: CREATION OF THE WORLD
AS A TRINITARIAN ACT

With the entire theological tradition, Edwards affirms the indivisibility of the outward operation of the Trinity, who possesses a singular essence and will.[50] The unity of the cosmos "shows a common disposer, and that the whole is regulated by a common wisdom and a common will and a common power that governs everywhere."[51] Similar to the covenant of redemption, the work of creation involved the united yet distinct operation of the Trinity.[52]

Since "the Son is the adequate communication of the Father's goodness," Edwards asks, "Why, then, did God incline further to communicate himself, seeing he had done [so] infinitely and completely?"[53] His reply is that the universe is not the Father's self-communication or image, but the Son's.[54] As such, he argues that the Son "has also an inclination to communicate himself."[55] Christ's inclination of self-giving is not to be understood "metaphorically" but realistically "for it is his essence to incline to communicate himself."[56] In the

Father and the Son, the disposition to self-communication is exercised *ad intra* and *ad extra*, respectively. In Edwards's ontology of divine self-communication, the "Son is the fullness of God, and the church is the fullness of the Son of God."[57]

Creation is more immediately the Son's work since it is the Father who has "wrought all through Christ." All creation is *per filium* as "God created the world by his Son," with the exception of Christ's human nature, which was more a work of the Father.[58] By this distinction, Edwards could say that all creation is "more immediately" a manifestation of "the glory of the Son of God," while Christ's humanity is "from the glory of the Father."[59] "Christ . . . as God-man" is truly the Creator in actuality or in anticipation prior to the incarnation.[60] Since the end of creation is union with Christ, the Son is the divine person who both appropriately maintains and perfects the creation and originally brought it into being.[61] "Seeing that Christ created the world only to communicate his excellency and happiness, hence . . . all the excellency, virtue and happiness of the godly is wrought in them by Jesus Christ."[62] The sentient and conative creation that Christ created—humankind—will culminate in the church, which is "the completeness of Christ."[63] In the Parousia, then, Christ will be revealed as the mediating *principium* of created things.[64] And as the eternal Logos—God's self-ideation—Christ is appropriately given the office as the great prophet and "the revealer of God to creatures."[65] The work of giving spiritual insight or "imparting the knowledge of God is here appropriated to the Son of God, as his sole prerogative."[66]

Although all creation is brought about "universally" by the Spirit, Edwards specially assigns the work of creation, with the exception of Jesus' *conceptio*, to "the Spirit of the Son."[67] As we have noted, although the work of creation was an *opus Trinitatis*, "wherein the three persons were conjunct," the making of the human will was the Holy Spirit's "proper work." It is the Spirit's special work "to infuse this principle" because this "part of the natural image of God" mirrors the divine volition, "which will is the same with the Holy Ghost."[68] In the creation of humankind, Edwards correlates the Trinitarian modes of action on the *imago Dei* with his psychological model of the Trinity:

> Here is a consultation of the persons of the Trinity about the creation of man, for every person had his particular and distinct concern in it, as well as in the redemption of man. The Father employed the Son and the Holy Ghost in this work. The Son endued man with understanding and reason. The Holy Ghost endued him with a holy will and inclination, with original righteousness.[69]

And this he links to the divine counsels, indicating that creation was a free act by God. We turn now to Edwards's cosmology, wherein God willed the emanation of creatures in time.

Emanation of Creatures from the Uncreated God: *Creatio Ex Nihilo*

The emanationistic notion of *bonum diffusivum sui* is clearly observed in Edwards's theology. In the tradition of St. Bonaventure, he asserts not only that creation derives its "being and excellency" from God, but that true humanity imitates God in its possession of divine knowledge and love.[70] Edwards evidently drew from Goodwin, who described the character of perfect goodness as a disposition not only to self-communicate (*bonum est sui communicativum*) but also to self-reveal (*manifestativum sui*).[71] The divine happiness *ad intra* points to God's essence as having a "tendency or propensity to communicate of himself and of his own happiness." Human participation in the divine fullness is the possession of a particular Godlikeness—a measure of God's own integral knowledge, love, and happiness of God's own self.[72]

Active human participation in imaging the divine is, in some respect, real and necessary in the economic sphere of God's self-repetition of divine glory in time.[73] As such, Edwards could paradoxically affirm the perfect and unchanging yet increasingly affective life of this sovereign God:

> Though it be true, that God's glory and happiness are in and of himself, are infinite and cannot be added to, and unchangeable, for the whole and every part of which he is perfectly independent of the creature. . . . And yet, in some sense, it can be truly said, that God has the more delight and pleasure for the holiness and happiness of his creatures.[74]

Was the World Freely Created *Ex Nihilo* without Remainder?

Is Edwards guilty of a philosophical monism or theological pantheism, as many authors have alleged?[75] While Edwards acknowledges that God's "general" disposition to self-enlargement is primary, if not preeminent, to the divine constitution, this does not mean that this universe is either necessary for or identical to the divine. In other words, that God is necessarily self-communicative does not mean that the creation, as we have it, is necessary to God's being or well-being.[76]

Indeed, many scholars suggest that Edwards establishes a clear distinction between created and uncreated through the doctrine of creation out of nothing.[77] There are many instances in his writings where Edwards affirms that the world was created ex nihilo by God.[78] For example, Edwards insists that "the notion of creation . . . implies a being's receiving its existence, and all that belongs to its being, out of nothing."[79]

By affirming this classical idea of creation from nothing, Edwards effectively rejects the notion that human beings are necessary emanations from the divine.[80] God may be necessarily self-communicative, but God is not necessarily creative. The failure to account for this distinction between God's self-communication *ad extra* (the end of creation) and the creation ex nihilo has made Edwards out to be a natural panentheist by necessity.[81]

While the persons of the Son and the Spirit derive their divine essence and personhood from the Father by necessity, human beings are given being solely by an act of divine fiat.[82] The doctrine of *creatio ex nihilo* posits a mode of origination that is volitional or, in Edwards's term, "arbitrary" as compared to the divine processions *ad intra*, which are necessary. The outward operation of God in divine *oikonomia* (creation and redemption) and God's outward self-communication of God's perfections are contingent: they are *ergon theleseon*.[83] Notwithstanding the distinction between necessity and contingency, how does Edwards interpret the ex nihilo?

Aquinas rejected the interpretation of *nihil* as preexisting matter.[84] For Edwards, absolute nothingness is contradictory and inconceivable, for God just is.[85] However, a relative nothingness as can be posited as the counterfactual of created being.[86] In fact, on the premise of divine simplicity, Edwards equates God with uncreated, nonmaterial space that is prior to and beyond created space.[87] He would later describe this space as that uncreated, metaphorical heaven where God dwells; this is God's infinite space that both transcends yet contains created space.

> The only heaven that is unalterable is the state of God's own infinite and unchangeable glory, the heaven which God dwelt in from all eternity . . . which may metaphorically be represented as heaven that was the eternal abode of the blessed Trinity, and of the happiness and glory they have one in another; and is an heaven that is uncreated, . . . which [we] conceive of as the infinite and unchangeable expanse of space that is above and beyond the whole universe, and encompasses the whole.[88]

If this is the case, could not God have created the world *ex Dei* as a kind of *nihil per excellentiam?*[89] All created being, weighed on the scale of being, may be compared to a kind of "nothingness by privation" (*nihil per privationem*). Accordingly, "all other beings are as nothing to him, and all other excellency be as nothing and less than nothing, and vanity in comparison of his."[90]

From the perspective of Edwards's objective idealism, the universe is created and preserved within God's "incomprehensible void," or "infinite emptiness" of God's own being.[91] Creation is thus created in contrast to relative nothingness but is sustained "within" (though distinct from) the divine infinity. Pictured spatially, God is *ad extra* or "outside" of the universe from the point of view of created reality.

PRESERVATION AS *CREATIO CONTINUA* AND EDWARDS'S OBJECTIVE IDEALISM

The idea of preservation of *creatio continua* was not unknown to the Puritans, who had read Aquinas, and Edwards subscribes to this idea consistently throughout his writings.[92] He points to the doctrine of *creatio ex nihilo* as justification of God's conservative action, but he also sees preservation to be a kind of a continual *creatio ex nihilo*.[93] Preservation only differs from creation "circumstantially"—namely, as a divine sequencing of new effects of the same kind according to "an established order" and "method."[94] For Edwards, then, since preservation is identical to "a continued creation, . . . consequently, creating of the world is but the beginning of upholding of it, if I may so say, the beginning to give the world a supported and dependent existence."[95] He thinks that this is clearly biblical: "It [is] most agreeable to the Scripture, to suppose creation to be performed new every moment. The Scripture speaks of it not only as past but as a present, remaining, continual act."[96]

Edwards's belief in a *creatio continua* does not need to entail a strong occasionalism.[97] He is willing to allow for a conservationism as long as it is admitted that God created the world with its natural laws.[98] If Edwards's occasionalism is interpreted as an "ontology of temporal parts," as Paul Helm interprets it, it would provide no basis for immanent connections between the discrete world stages because they would be solely recreated and identically reconstituted by immediate, divine power.[99] Are created things to be understood as merely numerically distinct and successive instances (of the like or same kind) that God regards as continuously identical through time, such that "no created being can be preserved in existence beyond a moment, not even by God"?[100] There are a few points worth noting here regarding Helm's robust occasionalist interpretation of Edwards.

Firstly, such an argument reifies the *nihil* such that it becomes (at least) as ontologically basic as God. On this account, preservation seems to be God's perpetual contention against the threat of creation being constantly overcome by non-Being. As we have noted above, the only primordial *nihil* possible in Edwards's ontology is a *nihil per excellentiam*, which is not an other but God's own self. Secondly, although Edwards concedes that animals are annihilated at death, this is no default condition but is caused by "the constant law of God, according to harmony, that that principle in beasts should cease with their bodies."[101] De jure, this state of bestial nonexistence is divinely constituted and only as such does it become de facto at an animal's death. Even for an animal, there is no non-Being to speak of that annihilates it at death. Thirdly, the law that governs the existence of humankind is not a telos of annihilation but of eternal life. In fact, human immortality is necessary for God's end for creation, and, just so, annihilationism has no place in Edwards's anthropology.[102] Lastly, if Helm's construal is to be taken seriously, then the state of humankind's "natural" existence would be similar to that of hell, minus the suffering. As Edwards puts it, "eternal death is a continual thing. They are always a-dying . . . 'tis a dying all the while forever."[103] And even such a state is positively ordained by God.

EDWARDS'S OBJECTIVE IDEALISM

Edwards rejects the idea of *res extensa* upholding the being of created entities.[104] Since created, physical entities have no underlying substance, solidity is none other than the divine, creative causality acting in created space.[105] God, by Word and Will, causes and communicates ongoing existence to all physical beings according the rules God has set. Hence, "that which truly is the substance of all bodies is the infinitely exact and precise and perfectly stable idea in God's mind, together with his stable will that the same shall gradually be communicated to us, and to other minds, according to certain fixed and exact established methods and laws."[106]

Edwards, according to some scholars, not only affirms early Berkeleyian idealism, where reality is identical to that which is perceived (*esse est percipi*), but also Berkeley's later conception that created existence is grounded in God's *concipi*, or the divine ideas.[107] If, however, happiness is to be the end of creation, being cannot consist in merely being perceived "because the creation has as good not to be, as not rejoice in its being."[108] Although the basis of the unity and communication between body and soul inheres in neither but is grounded in the divine causality and constitution, God has nevertheless given dispositional powers to human beings.[109] Though the universe "does not exist anywhere perfectly but in the divine mind," created being is not identical to the divine ideas. This means that God knows all things by the Son but does not will through the Spirit all that God knows.[110]

Personal identity is not merely mental or forensic on God's side but is founded on a real, ontological union of successive parts (see table 1.1). We may take as axiomatic in Edwards's ontology that "what is real . . . is the foundation of what is legal" or mental.[111] Although Edwards conceives of spiritual unions, whether Trinitarian, incarnational, or mystical, to be caused by the immanent Spirit of God, cosmological identity may be analogously considered.[112]

That Edwards regards created, personal identity as upheld solely by God is incontestable, yet it is not simply by God's mental perception or regard that genidentical parts should be one.[113] The distinction between the divine supposition, unition, and treatment of ongoing creation needs to be accounted for. Firstly, the Spirit so wills and realizes the contexts, relations, and characteristics between created effects *ad extra* so that created identity is recognized consequentially by both the divine being and created, sentient beings. In light of the continual coming-into-being of all created realities, God "so unites these successive new effects, that he treats them as one, by communicating to them like properties, relations, and circumstances; and so, leads us to regard and treat them as one."[114] The divine communication of existence to created beings underlies God's perpetual communication of "properties, relations and circumstances" in creating their personal identities.[115] God does not merely think (and will) creation into existence but also perceives and so acknowledges the contiguity of an objective universe God establishes through an ongoing communication of being.

That "God supposes its [the world's] existence" is Edwards's philosophical cognate for the biblical "Let there be."[116] But God's (eternally) thinking physical things into being is God's willing divine ideas into existence *ad extra* and so distinct from (but at the same time comprehended by) God's mind and other created minds: this is Edwards's objective idealism.[117] Material entities do not exist in the confines of a created brain, but their being is as objectively ideal (and so real) as their location.[118] Thus Edwards regards the older realist and substantive way of conceiving the creation as an equally viable manner of expression.[119] God not only causes entities to persevere through time but grants them bodily and personal identity.

In Edwards's schema, the "arbitrary constitution" of the universe is not by any means unstable, since God ensures the permanent identity and unity of all such occasions (table 1.1). They have ontic identity and so God recognizes them as such and causes other minds to regard them similarly. This is God's subjective approbation or recognition of the perduring and objectively ideal world that he continually creates and unifies. This is Edwards's way of parsing God's recognition of creaturely integrity ("God saw that it was good") in the face of its objective reality ("And it was so").[120] This perpetual communication of created being through natural laws is nothing but God's outworking of God's plans, by Word and Spirit.[121] The notion of divine communication of existence, therefore, is indispensably linked to the idea of creaturely and human participation in the divine workings.[122]

HUMAN PARTICIPATION IN GOD: EDWARDS'S UNDERSTANDING OF THE *IMAGO DEI*

Edwards interprets the *imago Dei* within both christological and Trinitarian grids.[123] The human's soul, in its natural constitution, is triadic as it reflects God, the idea of God, and the love of God. However, the saint is to imitate Christ as "the perfect example of true religion and virtue"; the Son is "not only in the image of the Father, but He is the image itself in the most proper sense."[124] Elsewhere, Edwards also understands the *imago Dei* christologically:

> [B]y which four things are typified (1) Christ, the antitype of Adam, his being the brightness of God's glory, and the express image of his person. (2) The man Christ Jesus being made in union with the divine nature, so as to be in the divine person. He was made in that person that was the essential image of God; and so had in a sense the Godhead communicated to him. (3) Christ's having the image of God as God-man: as such, representing the person of God the Father as his vicegerent in governing and judging the world. (4) The transcendent advancement of men in their union with God, whereby they partake of the beauty, life, honor and joy of the eternal Son of God; and so are made as gods by communion of his Spirit, whereby they are made partakers of the divine nature.[125]

Edwards also posits a relational notion of the image, in which the Christian loves others "either because they are in some respect like God, in the possession of his nature and spiritual image, or because of the relation they stand in to him as his children or creatures."[126] Accordingly, humans are ontologically relational beings as "we are made to subsist by society and union, one with another, and God has made us with such a nature that we can't subsist without the help of one another."[127]

In his essay, "True Virtue," Edwards defines true virtue—the relational beauty of a moral being—as the love to being-in-general.[128] The object of true virtue is, primarily, being simply considered and, secondarily, loving being. As such, true spiritual beauty consists in love to God, for God is being with the highest existence and greatest love. In human beings, this relationality is fundamentally theocentric, as it is primarily love to God (as the greatest Being) and secondarily love to a lovely God (as the most virtuous Being).[129] It is from this foundational love to God that true love can have others and self as its object. "The saints" in heaven "love God for his own sake, and each other for God's sake, and for the sake of the relation which they bear to God, and the image of God which is upon them."[130] What does Edwards think about the *imago Dei* protologically?

Natural Image of God: Human Persons as Created Analogues of the Trinity

Having sentient and conative capacities, human beings are created analogues of the divine mind. Human beings, therefore, not only image God but are the highest creatures: "they are next to the First Cause."[131] As the "principal parts of the visible creation," their creative ability mirrors their Maker.[132] They are also purposive like the First Cause who "does things for final causes."[133]

Whereas the eternal Son is the perfect and whole repetition of the Father's essence and goodness *ad intra*—"he is not only in the image of the Father, but he is the image itself in the most proper sense," the creation of the world "is an image of his [Christ's] person" in order for Christ's happiness to be ultimately communicated.[134] And such an image of this idealistic self resides in the human conscience.[135] Imaging the generation of the Word in God, human beings are in a sort of perpetual self-communication internally.[136] In view of this similarity between the Logos and human rationality, Edwards points out that "God gave man the faculty of understanding, chiefly, that he might understand divine things."[137] That is why true theology is mediated through Christ.[138]

What about the role of the Spirit in Edwards's construal of the natural *imago Dei*? The creation mirrors the nature of God, particularly in God's holiness and beauty.[139] Hence, it is the function of the Holy Spirit to convict the natural conscience of moral transgressions.[140] And, since Word and Act are inseparable, a universe without motion is merely conceptual.[141] The interposition of the Spirit, as the Will and Act of God, is needed to actualize the static, divine ideas. Through the Word and Spirit, created existence is given being and motion.[142] Clearly, Edwards's psychological depiction of the Trinity informs his understanding of the *imago Dei*. We now examine this in closer detail.

IMAGO DEI AND ANALOGIA DEI: SIMILARITY AND DISSIMILARITY

God is the divine happiness that exists in an eternal, infinite, and dynamic movement of self-loving and self-understanding.[143] Echoing Augustine, Edwards's vision of God, who exists as the perfectly integrated triunity of mind, understanding, and will, finds in the human soul, with its two faculties of perception and inclination, a finite and imperfect image.[144] "There is yet more of an image of the Trinity in the soul of man: there is the mind, and its understanding or idea, and the will or the affection or love—the heart, comprising inclination, affection, etc.—answering to God, the idea of God, and the love of God."[145]

Clearly, Edwards's anthropology has a sort of dialectical convertibility with his psychological model of the Trinity.[146] Just as God the Father is the ground of both the Son and the Spirit, the human mind is "the proper seat" of human willing and understanding.[147] True faith or spiritual knowledge is the mind's ability both to sense and to judge true spiritual beauty, which requires the cooperative acting of the will and understanding.[148] Edwards's vision of the mind as the unitive center of human psychology correlates with his model of the Trinity as a unified psychological entity—the perfect spiritual Being.[149] What is the role of analogical thinking in Edwards's ruminations on this psychological *imago trinitatis*?

ANALOGICAL PREDICATION AND PARTICIPATION OF LIKENESS

The Thomistic understanding of analogical predication and the doctrine of participation of likeness was not unknown to Puritans, such as the similarly named John Edwards, an English Calvinist divine from the late seventeenth century.[150] When Jonathan Edwards asserts that human "reason and conscience seem to be a participation of the divine essence," he is speaking, as John Preston did, of a participation of likeness found in the natural image.[151] Edwards thinks that the term "divine" may be applied nontechnically and analogously to created things, and not only to grace possessed by a human being.[152] He suggests that we only know "anything about intelligent moral agents" through substitution, that is, by "transferring the ideas we obtain of such things in our own minds by consciousness, into their place."[153] Just as we have knowledge of another human person in this manner, so "this is the only way that we come to be capable of having ideas of any perception or act even of the Godhead."[154] Having these human notions, "we can add degrees, and deny limits, and remove changeableness and other imperfections, and ascribe them to God."[155] With the tradition, Edwards affirms the validity of the *viae eminentiae, negationis,* and *causalitatis* in speech about God.[156]

The divine omniscience and *aseitas* ensures the divine immutability, since "either ignorance, or error or change of nature" could change God's mind.[157] God loves in a passionless manner since divine love transcends the manner of human love. By virtue of the *ratio nomina*, we apply love to both God and human, yet the *modus significandi* is radically different.[158] By *via negationis*, one denies the imperfection of human love, but at the same time, by *via eminentiae,* the perfection of human love is affirmed transcendently of God.[159] Nonetheless, Edwards was more inclined to affirm the *via eminentiae,* or similarity "between the nature of the Deity and created spirits," than the *via negationis*.[160] In fact, in his less careful moments he admits a sort of univocity that even Scotus was careful to avoid.[161]

But, in general, Edwards affirms that one cannot explicate what divine goodness is (the *res significata*) because of the transcendence of the Cause. Even in his early philosophical writings where he applies the term "being" to God and creation, he states that "there is no proportion between finite being, however great, and universal being."[162] While there is a correspondence between the divine nature and human nature in their psychological makeup, God's nature is "vastly different" from ours in "perfection of degree and manner."[163] God is not only infinitely wise and loving, but there is also perfect integrity within God as there is no difference between power, faculty, habit, and act.[164] In God, the power of perception or idea, the habit of reasoning, and the act of judgment are one, as are the faculty of will, the habit of inclination, and the act of love.[165] Being *actus purus*, "the acting of love and the being of love are the same in God," which is quite unlike human beings, where "the habit or principle differs from the act."[166] In this, Edwards echoes Aquinas's real distinction between being and act in creatures.[167]

That self-love is a divine virtue within God (because in the infinite being it is not a private affection) and not in human beings secures, for Edwards, a fundamental distinction between the divine and the human. While the notion of communion and society allow for coordination between divine and human personhood, God's identity includes an independence and aseity, which does not characterize the creature. God's being is both grounded in the self (Being itself) and others (Being-in-communion), while the true identity of human beings is fundamentally social.[168]

Due to finitude and imperfection, humans are in need of others for their happiness.[169] This is because the primary constituents of human happiness—love and friendship—demand union with another.[170] In contrast, the divine persons are identical to the divine essence, which is uncreated and self-positing. Arguing from God's unity—God's self-sufficiency, omniscience, infinity, and perfection—Edwards concludes that, "'Tis peculiar to the divine being to have happiness and satisfaction in himself alone."[171] Evidently, all these caveats about dissimilarity do not negate speech about human beings as the *imago Dei*—in both its protological and its eschatological dimensions.[172]

CREATION AND "THE END FOR WHICH GOD CREATED THE WORLD" AS REFLECTED IN THE TWOFOLD *IMAGO DEI*

Original humanity has not only a structural-natural similarity to God (as knowing and willing beings) but also a moral-spiritual participation in God (as united to the Holy Spirit). Edwards's "psychological" analogy of the Trinity is, therefore, key to his anthropological account of both human constitution and vocation.[173] Edwards's natural and spiritual *imago Dei* approximates the patristic distinction between "image" and "likeness"; the one is structural and psychological, the other dynamic and eschatological.[174] Similar notions of the double *imago Dei* can be found in earlier Puritan writings, such as John Preston's.[175]

What is the correlation between the *exitus* and *reditus* of creatures and the natural and moral image? According to Edwards, the natural image is oriented toward the spiritual, wherein the created powers of intellection and volition participate, by grace, in God's own knowledge, love, and joy. True knowledge and virtue in humanity are temporal self-communications or "emanations" from God, a fitting reflection of the eternal self-glorification within the Trinity.[176] As such, the union of God and humankind by the Spirit, who is the divine Good, is the end of creation: "'Tis certain that what God aimed at in the creation of the world was the good that would be the consequence of the creation, in the whole continuance of the thing created."[177] Notably, divine glory communicated *ad extra* is distinct from *creatio ex nihilo*. Nonetheless, the goodness of human nature is both protological and eschatological, whether God is recognized as its source or seen as its chief and final cause.[178]

What, then, is the relation between *exitus* as creation and *reditus* as redemption? Human existence, as that which is natural to human beings, is subordinate to grace and goodness. The latter is a real participation in the divine nature, which the saints shall obtain in redemption: "And therefore God is pleased to make goodness the end of greatness: for he would make that in the creature, which is properly belonging to the nature of the creature, subordinate to that which is of God, or a communication of the divine nature in the creature."[179]

In correlation with the "first movement" of the Spirit's procession *ad intra*, the Father creates the world for the Son *ad extra*. In terms of the Father creating the world *per filium*, Edwards states: "This seems to have been one reason why God made the world by Jesus Christ, viz. that the creation of the world was a work that was subordinate to the work of redemption."[180]

Though the moral image of humanity is attributed to the presence of the Holy Spirit in both prelapsarian and regenerate humans, Edwards posits a difference between the principle, or disposition, and its circumstances.[181] Since the possibility of a higher degree of holiness exists now than it did for Adam, the possibility of greater love to God exceeds that at Adam's innocence.[182] "So, gospel holiness differs greatly from the holiness of man in innocency: man had the Holy Ghost then, as the Spirit of God; but now he must have it as the Spirit of the Son of God, the Spirit of a Redeemer."[183] As such, the saint not only possesses the Spirit immediately of God, he is also more dependent on God for holiness than Adam was.[184] The consequent "good" that the redeemed creature participates in is God's existential self-communication or the emanation of God's glory, in which she is enabled to know, love, and praise God in an act of remanation. We shall now look at this emanation-remanation motif in greater detail.

Spirit as Bond: The One Emanation and Remanation of Creation and Redemption

This *exitus-reditus* schema appears in the writings of the Cambridge Platonists, which were familiar to Edwards.[185] This is the great theme of Christian theology: in Christ, the *deitas* is the *principium et finis* of salvation, the *humanitas*, the *via*.[186] Edwards, in continuity with Calvin, embraced this and integrated it into his theology.[187] God's temporal self-glorification is achieved through the *exitus* of God's divine fullness to redeemed humanity and the *reditus* back to God in humanity's ontological transformation into the *imago Dei*.[188] In Edwards's words:

The emanation or communication of the divine fullness, consisting in the knowledge of God, love to God, and joy in God, has relation indeed both to God and the creature: but it has relation to God as its fountain, as it is an emanation from God; and as the communication itself, or thing communicated, is something divine, something of God, something of his internal fullness; as the water in the stream is something of the fountain; and as the beams are of the sun. And again, they have relation to God as they have respect to him as their object: for the knowledge communicated is the knowledge of God; and so God is the object of the knowledge: and the love communicated, is the love of God; so God is the object of that love: and the happiness communicated, is joy in God; and so he is the object of the joy communicated. In the creature's knowing, esteeming, loving, rejoicing in, and praising God, the glory of God is both exhibited and acknowledged; his fullness is received and returned. Here is both an emanation and remanation. The refulgence shines upon and into the creature, and is reflected back to the luminary. The beams of glory come from God, and are something of God, and are refunded back again to their original.[189]

This dynamism of God's providential action in history is analogous to rivers issuing from and returning to the ocean.[190] In accordance to the emanation and remanation theme, God is both the "first efficient cause and fountain" or principle of origination of all and their term or "the last final cause."[191] "That glory of God that is . . . the end of God's works," Edwards writes elsewhere, "is the egress and reception of God's fullness, the egress of it from God and the reception of it by the creature."[192] Even *creatio continua* may be regarded as a kind of *exitus-reditus*: "All dependent existence whatsoever is in a constant flux, ever passing and returning; renewed every moment . . . and all is constantly proceeding from God, as light from the sun. 'In him we live, and move, and have our being.'"[193]

As the Spirit is the *vehiculum* and "end of all procession" in God, the Spirit terminates the efficient causation of humans' "being and motion" as well as the final causation of their "tendency and aim."[194] Though Edwards speaks of the Spirit as the "end of all procession," he does not by this exclude the idea of a *reditus* or remanation. The remanation, when regarded as divine action, is the creation being returned to God by God. Hence, Edwards regards creation and redemption as a single parabolic movement of *processio*, which includes *descendus* and *ascensus*, a coming from and returning to God.[195] The ascending movement, insofar as it involves active, intelligent beings, is a remanation on their part. Just as creation is subordinate to providence, redemption is the content and goal of creation and providence.[196]

Seen in the light of these Miscellany entries, the self-communication of God's glory in the "End of Creation," which includes divine knowledge, love, and joy to the creature, could be interpreted as the existential giving of the Son and the Spirit to the saints.[197] The saints' divine vision and enjoyment is by the operation of God's self-revelation and self-love in them.[198] The end is one, since God, in seeking the "creature's good" or happiness, is not different from God giving God's own goodness to the creature, "viz. God's internal glory or fullness extant externally, or existing in its emanation."[199]

As Ramsey reminds us, for Edwards redemption was the predetermined, "original and independent end for which God created the world," since there cannot be two ultimate ends in Edwards's argument.[200] This single ultimate end may be regarded in relation to both God as communicator and the creaturely recipient.

Edwards wishes to underline that God is the source and term (the *of* and *to*) of this goodness: "it is an emanation from himself, and a communication of himself, and as the thing communicated, in its nature returned to himself, as its final term."[201] The goodness and glory proceeds from God "as its fountain," returns to God as "reflected back to the luminary," and is divinity itself, "something divine, something of God."[202] God is also the content (the *in*) of this self-communication, which resides in the creature: "And he had regard to it also as the emanation was to the creature, and as a thing communicated was in the creature, as its subject."[203]

Edwards application of the prepositions *of*, *in*, and *to* in reference to the divine self-communication in another text is worth analyzing. "The beams of glory come from God, and are something of God, and are refunded back again to their original. So that the whole is *of* God, and *in* God, and *to* God; and God is the beginning, middle, and end in this affair."[204] We suggest that this could be read as procession, remaining, and return: the glory of God proceeds to the creature and, remaining within that subject, returns to God with the creature in the end.[205] Procession distinguishes the *gloria Dei ad intra* as cause from its expression or effect *ad extra*. Remaining maintains the identity of content of that which is communicated as the *res* in itself and in its relation to the creature. This *res* communicated to the church may be regarded as the Spirit of Christ.

SPIRIT AS BOND BETWEEN CHRIST AND THE CHURCH

Edwards conceives of the triad of Christ, church, and Spirit as "an image of the eternal Trinity; wherein the Christ is the everlasting father, and believers are his seed, and the Holy Spirit . . . is the third person in Christ, being his delight and love flowing out toward the church."[206] And as there is an eternal procession and return of the Spirit between the Father and the Son *ad intra*, so in time there is an emanation and remanation of the Spirit between Christ and the church.[207] Christ, as *Logos asarkos* and *ensarkos*, not only is eternally anointed by the Father but also is anointed by the church in time.[208] Christ procures the Holy Spirit for the saints so that they might return this Spirit back. A being that is capable of knowing and willing finds happiness only in mutually enjoying another mind. A sentient being cannot exercise its will appropriately—that is, love another—without "answerable returns, which is mutual love."[209] Such reciprocity is grounded in the Father-Son relation *ad intra*.

SPIRIT AS BOND BETWEEN FATHER AND SON

God, the ultimate knowing and loving Being, is eternally diffusive and unitive.[210] Love, as the consent of spirits, or "that disposition and affection whereby one is dear to another," is essentially unitive and relational; the three persons in the Godhead are so united in affective love that they are, at the same time, one in nature.[211] As such, Edwards admits to a similarity and incomprehensibility of all "spiritual unions—of the persons of the Trinity, of the two natures of Christ, of Christ and the mind of saints," all of which are effected by the Spirit.[212] In other words, "there is no other way of different spirits' being thus united, but by love."[213] Just as the Spirit acts as the bond of love between the Father and the Son within God's own life, the saints' union with God and human communion are also pneumatological realities.[214]

By casting the Spirit as the fundamental, dynamic Love between the Father and Son that moves *ad extra* toward redeemed humanity, Edwards construes the Spirit as the active essence, expression, and goal of the work of redemption.[215] The love and concern of the Spirit in the work of salvation is equal to the Father's love that sacrificed the Son and the Son's self-sacrificial love because the Spirit is that *essential* Love.[216] The Gospel accounts of Christ's suffering in obedience to the Father's will and the Father's glorification of the Son are but *expressions* of the unitive "love eternally existing between the Father and the Son."[217] The christological *exinanitio* and *exaltatio* mirror the eternal *exitus* and *reditus* within God—the Son's reception and return of divine Love to the Father. The saints' having the spirit of love, the unitive principle between the

Father and the Son, is the *goal* of the work of redemption.[218] This Spirit, who brings about the hypostatic union between the divine and human natures in the incarnation, also enables our intimate union of affection with the Father and the Son.[219] This participation in the Spirit of Father and Son is not a private event, but is fundamentally social.[220] That is because divine and human felicity can only exist within a relational matrix.[221] For Edwards, beatified creatures participate in the Spirit and are thus united to the Father and the Son in a spiritual and not perichoretic union.[222] This human participation in the Father-Son relation may also be viewed as a sharing in the Father's Word and Spirit *ad extra*.

God's Twofold Communication of Creatures *Ad Extra*: The Inseparability of Divine Knowledge and Love

Following Aquinas, Edwards regards the divine processions or emanations as encompassing both eternal and temporal dimensions.[223] Edwards regards the "invisible" missions of the Son and Spirit as corresponding to the *actus personales*. "This twofold way of the Deity's flowing forth *ad extra* answers to the twofold way of the Deity's proceeding *ad intra*, in the proceeding and generation of the Son and the proceeding and breathing forth of the Holy Spirit; and indeed is only a kind of second proceeding of the same persons, their going forth *ad extra*, as before they proceeded *ad intra*."[224]

From the divine perspective, God's communication *ad extra* is expressed by the "two ways of the divine good" flowing forth, by the gifting of the Son and Spirit to the world. This, as we have noted, corresponds to "the two ways of the divine essence . . . proceeding from eternity within the Godhead, in the person of the Son and Holy Spirit."[225] Because humans mirror God as knowing and willing beings, their highest end is participation in God through knowing and loving God. This is the anthropological corollary to divine self-communication.

The integrated psychology of the human soul is an imperfect image of God's "seeing and understanding will" as "the Son is in the Holy Spirit."[226] Edwards at times distinguishes the communication of the Spirit and manifestation of the Word from the understanding and will of the elect. Though distinct, they are inseparably given to the church variously as "God flowing forth," God's self-glorification and self-communication *ad extra*.[227] "The glory of God implies these two things: manifestation and communication, the latter called grace, the former, truth."[228] Edwards makes a distinction between the manifestation of the Son (divine excellency) and the communication of the Spirit (divine happiness), which corresponds to the two human faculties of perception and volition.[229] As Edwards makes clear, this twofold communication of God is "Christ's being in the creature in the name, idea or knowledge of God being in them, and the Holy Spirit's being in them in the love of God's being in them."[230] In God *ad intra*, the Son is God's self-manifestation while the Spirit is God's self-enjoyment. Correlative to the *actus personales* are the invisible missions, where the Word is manifested to believers for their knowledge of God and the Spirit is communicated to them for their enjoyment of God.[231]

As God's eternal act, beauty, holiness, and happiness, the Spirit acts in time "to quicken, enliven and beautify all things; to sanctify intelligent [creatures]; and to comfort and delight them."[232] This is the believer's knowledge and worship by which God is "manifested and respected."[233] Since happiness is both "the perception and possession of excellency," true virtue of the saints cannot be mere disengaged perception of God's glory but necessarily includes a participation in God's very own glory.[234] God's glory may be appropriated to the Son or Spirit.[235]

Rational beings, as the "consciousness of creation," realize the summit of their existence insofar as they are "moved with joy at the sight" of God's perfection and inasmuch as they "raise joy in [themselves] and others at what is declared."[236] "Divine knowledge and divine love go together."[237] As the very beauty of God, the Spirit is the divine person who confers order and harmony in the triune act of creation.[238] In relation to the Father and the Son, the Holy Spirit is "the end of the other two in their acting *ad intra*, and also in his acting *ad extra*, in all they do in redemption and their distinct economical concern."[239] As "the Holy Spirit is the sum of all good" or "the fullness of God," the "last end" for which God created the world is to communicate the Spirit or "infinite good" *ad extra*.[240]

"LIGHT AND LOVE": GRACE AS THE INVISIBLE MISSION OF GOD

In the *oikonomia*, Edwards affirms a reciprocity in the missions of the Son and the Spirit, since *ad intra*, the Spirit proceeds *ex Patre per filium*, and the Son is in the Spirit "not as proceeding from him but flowing out in him."[241] Union with God is participation in the inseparable Light and Love of God.[242] Here, Edwards is drawing on the scholastic tradition of the invisible mission of grace, which involves the saint's reception of the Son and Spirit.[243] Faith and spiritual illumination are effects of the invisible mission of the Word and Spirit.[244] That is why regeneration is an invisible reality.[245] The Word and Spirit of God come invisibly to Christians in special seasons of grace.[246] Like Aquinas, Edwards distinguishes between an imperfect fruition of grace for believers *in via* and the perfect fruition of grace in the beatific.[247]

Just as Word is prior to Love *ad intra*, so God gives the Spirit to the church *per filium:* "God communicates his love to enjoyment by manifestation. None can enjoy [but] only as God manifests."[248] The consubstantiality and *perichoresis* of Word and Spirit *ad intra* is reflected in their corresponding operation *ad extra*. As Edwards puts it, "the enjoyment," as such, "will be proportionable to the manifestation."[249] This echoes Thomas's notion of the highest human act of enjoying God (*frui, fruitio*), by which the saints achieve their end, possess happiness, and are united to God.[250]

Only the triune God can bring about our participation in God's own knowledge and love. The Father does this by the two divine hands: "As 'tis God alone that can enlighten us so 'tis he alone that can love himself in us. As no man can know the Father but by the Son so no man can love the Father but by the holy Ghost."[251] The twofold emanation is one in purpose, for God's self-exertion *ad extra* and the creature's happiness are not two ultimate ends. God's end in creating the world is one: "'Tis himself exerted and himself communicated."[252] God is revealed through his Son and God self-communicates in the Spirit.[253] The saints see and enjoy God in the divine glory, and God is glorified in self-revealing and in communicating happiness to them.

CONCLUSION

The gap between a natural creation and a soteriological panentheism means that distinction and continuity need to be established between the divine and human *exitus* and *reditus*. In the former, creation is contained in God's uncreated spatiality yet distinguished (by *creatio continua ex nihilo*) as *ad extra* in relation to God's essence. In the latter, God comes to be contained or indwell the church by the Son and Spirit. Absent the influence of God's Spirit—the "superior principle" of love to God—humankind lost its "original righteousness," resulting in the reign of inordinate self-love.[254] The sinful nature, in "the absence of the image and love of God," has lost the divine beauty and glory.[255] Without a participation in the spiritual Image and Love of God, "the mind of man shrank from its primitive greatness and expandedness, to an exceeding smallness and contractedness."[256] Fallen humanity, therefore, retains the natural but not the spiritual *imago Dei*.[257] For Edwards, there is no such thing as a natural beatific end for humankind, for divine truth and love can only come from God.[258] How this spiritual image and beatific end is restored to humankind is the subject of our next chapter, where, through the covenant of redemption, God elects to send the Son to be incarnated by the Spirit. Through the incarnation, the end for which God created the world is once again made possible.

Notes

1. Edwards, "Miscellanies," no. 332, in *WJE* 13:410.
2. The covenant of works (as well as the covenant of grace) is "what God has made a rule to himself, as well as a rule to men" (Edwards, 107. Sermon on Num. 23:19 [1729], in *WJE* 44).
3. "God is pleased to act by rules which he fixes" (Edwards, Edwards, 107. Sermon on Num. 23:19, in *WJE* 44).
4. While Edwards acknowledges that the language of "cause and effect, antecedent and consequent, fundamental and dependent, determining and determined" are improperly applied to God due to the divine simplicity, "we are obliged" to distinguish between the real divine attributes and the divine decrees (Edwards, *WJE* 1:376–77).
5. As Quenstedt notes, not all the *opera interna* are *opera ad intra*, nor are all the *opera ad intra actus personales*—God's covenants, will, and processions must be distinguished (Quenstedt, *Conf*, 1.X.1, as cited in Heppe, *Reformed Dogmatics Set Out and Illustrated from the Sources*, rev. and ed. Ernst Bizer, trans. G. T. Thomson [London: George Allen & Unwin, 1950], 137). Reformed orthodoxy denied any *distinctio realiter* between the divine essence, will, and decrees (Heppe, *Reformed Dogmatics*, 137). In great part, this was to combat the Socinian distinction between eternal and temporal decrees, through which accidents, mutability, and composition were introduced into the divine being (Heppe, *Reformed Dogmatics*, 139). For example, Braun says, "Hence also it follows that the decrees do not inhere in God in the manner of an accident and inherently, changing hourly, as the *Socinians*, *Vorstius* and the *Arminians* madly suggest, but more perfectly, by attribution and denomination, like God's attributes, which do not differ in reality from His essence" (Johannes Braunius I, ii, 9, 4, as cited in Heppe, *Reformed Dogmatics*, 139). While no real distinction exists between the divine essence and decrees, the latter are not identical to the divine will per se, but are modally distinguished as "acts of the will with a tendency to externalization (*cum schect ad extra*)" (Joh. Henricus Hottingerus, 74, as cited in Heppe, *Reformed Dogmatics*, 139). Johannes Marckius described the divine decrees more precisely as "acts of the divine will, as it tends towards the future existence in time of things known from their ideas, and towards their just limits, or towards the actual will tending in this direction." Consistent with the doctrine of divine simplicity, the divine decrees are not to be thought of as the Platonic divine forms or ideas, that is, "things existing from eternity outwith the divine essence" (Johannes Marckius VI, 5, as cited in Heppe, *Reformed Dogmatics*, 139).
6. Inasmuch as "we must conceive of the knowledge and holiness of God as prior in the order of nature to his happiness," divine idea and will are to be thought of as metaphysically prior to the divine wisdom (Edwards, *WJE* 1:376). Edwards denies that God's omniscience, as comprehended in the divine self-knowledge, is virtually distinct from the divine essence. "'Tis also said that God's knowledge of himself includes the knowledge of all things; and that he knows, and from eternity knew, all things by the looking on himself and by the idea of himself, because he is virtually all things; so that all God's knowledge is the idea of himself. But yet it would suppose imperfection in God, to suppose that God's idea of himself is anything different from himself" (Edwards, "Miscellanies," no. 94, in *WJE* 13:257). Understood in this manner, the Son is the divine essence.
7. Thus, "the perfection of his understanding" must be thought of "as the foundation of his wise purposes and decrees," just as "the holiness of his nature, as the cause and reason of his holy determinations" (Edwards, *WJE* 1:376).

8. Edwards clearly rejects any kind of preexisting eternal time before creation as well as infinite succession in God, but equates divine duration with the Boethian *aeternitas:* "The eternal duration which was before the world, being only the eternity of God's existence; which is nothing else but his immediate, perfect and invariable possession of the whole of his unlimited life, together and at once; *vita interminabilis, tota, simul et perfecta possessio*" (Edwards, *WJE* 1:385–86).

9. "Some things were done before the world was created, yea from all eternity" (Edwards, *WJE* 9:118).

10. Edwards, "Observations," in *TG*, 93. Edwards enlarges the notion of social consensus beyond the limits of the "economic" trinitarianism extant in the Reformed tradition (Amy Plantinga Pauw, "'The Supreme Harmony of All': Jonathan Edwards and the Trinity" [Ph.D. diss., Yale University, 1990], 91). According to Pauw, the Puritans' unwillingness to amplify the role of covenant theology into the immanent Trinity resulted in a basic disconnection between God's eternal being and God's exterior activity (ibid., 100).

11. To designate this Trinitarian counsel, we shall follow Edwards's original manuscript spelling, "œconomy of the Trinity" or "œconomical Trinity," in contradistinction to the economical Trinity, whereby the designs and ordering of the former are actualized *ad extra*.

12. "The word 'economy' signifies family order" (Edwards, "Of God the Father," in *WJE* 25:146).

13. Edwards, "Of God the Father," in *WJE* 25:146. Elsewhere, Edwards terms this "the social order of acting" among the divine persons (Edwards, 813. Sermon on 1 Cor. 11:3 [Mar 1746], in *WJE* 64). See Edwards's reference to Peter Mastricht's *Theoretico-practica theologia,* II.24, § 11, in "Miscellanies," no. 482, in *WJE* 13: 524). Although Mastricht speaks of the Son as being begotten and the Father as "Pater-familias," Schafer notes that "of particular interest to JE was Mastricht's representation of God as having taken up the church into the 'communion' and 'society' of this family" (Schafer, in *WJE* 13:534n1).

14. Though Edwards refers to the first and second person as Father and Son at the causal level, the logic of derivation revolves around the psychological images of Mind and Idea. Evidently, language of God's Fatherhood is sort of "second order": still describing the immanent Trinity but relegated to the œconomical. This is evident in Edwards's sermon entitled "Of God the Father," in *WJE* 25:144–54.

15. Edwards, "Observations," in *TG*, 78. There is "free and voluntary agreement" in this social ordering, which harmonizes with their order of subsistence (Edwards, "Of God the Father," in *WJE* 25:147).

16. Edwards, 1114. Sermon on Acts 20:28(b) (Mar 1754), in *WJE* 72. He cites Prov. 8:30 here. By analogy, since it may be said that "the persons of the Trinity gave one another happiness as derived happiness one from another," this demonstrates that God is absolutely independent from creation (ibid.).

17. "Among the three persons of the Trinity each one has as it were his distinct office assigned him by agreement among themselves" (Edwards, 547. Sermon on Heb. 12:22-24(d), in *WJE* 55). The *opera internum ad intra* arises from "natural," causal relations while the *opera internum ad extra* comes out of "the mutual agreement of the persons . . . [and] not from the necessity of God's nature, not from any natural subordination" (Edwards, "Of God the Father," in *WJE* 25:147).

18. Edwards, "Of God the Father," in *WJE* 25:145–46. Yet, only the distinct roles of the Son and Spirit may properly be styled "offices," since the term signifies an assignment or charge "by a superiour."

19. With reference to the psychological analogy and Edwards's definition of a person as "that which hath understanding and will," he says: "Here I would observe that divines have not been wont to suppose that these three had three distinct understandings, but all one and the same understanding" (Edwards, "Essay," in *TG*, 120; "Discourse on the Trinity," in *WJE* 21:133).

20. Emphases mine. Edwards, "Observations," in *TG*, 78; "Sermon One," in *WJE* 9:118.

21. Emphases mine. Edwards, "Miscellanies," no. 1062, in *WJE* 20:431.

22. "The establishment of the economy is a determination that, in whatever work is done, the persons shall act in such a subordination; but the determining what works shall be done is not implied in that establishment" (Edwards, "Miscellanies," no. 1062, in *WJE* 20:438).

23. Edwards, "Miscellanies," no. 1062, in *WJE* 20:430; "Observations," in *TG*, 77. "Hereby we may more clearly understand the equality of the persons among themselves, and that they are every way equal in the society or family of the three" (Edwards, "An Essay," in *TG*, 122).

24. The œconomical Trinity has "an established order in it and a subordination of members, one being chief and head of the society and others in their order subject and dependent. There is one of 'em that is first in the affair and head of all. Another acts as second in the affair and as an intermediate person between the first and the last. The other acts as last and as subject to and dependent on the other two" (Edwards, 813. Sermon on 1 Cor. 11:13 [Mar 1746], in *WJE* 64).

25. Thus, "as the Father, with respect to the subsistences, is the fountain of the Deity, wholly and entirely so, so he should be the fountain in all the acts of the Deity" (Edwards, "Miscellanies," no. 1062, in *WJE* 20:431).

26. Edwards, "Observations," in *TG*, 78–79. The Father, in his œconomical office, preserves the interest and integrity of the Trinity because the Father is, in essence, the "fountain of the Godhead" (Edwards, "Essay," in *TG*, 122).

27. Edwards, "God the Father," in *WJE* 25:151.

28. "'Tis fit that the order of the acting of the persons of the Trinity should be agreeable to the order of their subsisting: that as the Father is first in the order of subsisting, so he should be first in the order of acting; that as the other two persons are from the Father in their subsistence, and as to their subsistence naturally originated from him and dependent on him, so that, in all that they act, they should originate from him, act from him and in a dependence on him; that as the Father, with respect to the subsistences, is the fountain of the Deity, wholly and entirely so, so he should be the fountain in all the acts of the Deity" (Edwards, "Miscellanies," no. 1062, in *WJE* 20:431). All Three consent to this *taxis* "as they all naturally delight in what is in itself fit, suitable and beautiful" (ibid.).

29. Ibid., 432.

30. Ibid., 431. That God is not static substance, in Edwards's thinking, but dynamic dispositional essence is a thesis that has received wide scholarly consensus. See esp. ch. 7 in Lee, *PTJE*, exp. ed., 170–210. A group of British interlocutors, like Paul Helm and Oliver Crisp, interpreting Edwards within a strict occasionalist framework, have challenged this reading. Stephen Holmes admits the coherence of Lee's dispositional account of reality but finds it anachronistic. See Stephen R. Holmes, "Does Edwards Use a Dispositional Ontology?" in *Jonathan Edwards: Philosophical Theologian*, ed. Paul Helm and Oliver D. Crisp (Aldershot, England: Ashgate, 2003), 104. Here, Holmes's characterization of Edwards's system as a "combination of philosophical radicalism and theological conservatism" echoes Riley's thesis of a duality between Edwards's metaphysics and theology. Unlike Riley, he does not conclude that there exists material incompatibility between the two, but instead that Edwards restated "inherited doctrine in a new philosophical idiom" (Holmes, "Does Edwards Use," 102).

31. Expressed differently, the first divine procession is "an expression of [God's] glory, in the idea or knowledge of it"; the second, "the flowing out of the essence in love or joy" (Edwards, "Miscellanies," no. 1151, in *WJE* 20:525).

32. Ibid.

33. Edwards, "Miscellanies," no. 448, in *WJE* 13:495. This is fully developed in Edwards's treatise, "Concerning the End," in *WJE* 8:403–526. "These two ways of the divine good beaming forth are agreeable to the two ways of the divine essence flowing out, or proceeding from eternity within the Godhead, in the person of the Son and Holy Spirit: the one, in an expression of his glory, in the idea or knowledge of it; the other, the flowing out of the essence in love or joy" (Edwards, "Miscellanies," no. 1151, *WJE* 20:525).

34. Edwards, "Miscellanies," no. 271, in *WJE* 13:374.

35. "Because God would be less happy, if he were less good: or if he had not that perfection of nature which consists in a propensity of nature to diffuse his own fulness. And he would be less happy, if it were possible for him to be hindered in the exercise of his goodness, as his other perfections, in their proper effects. And this surely is not, because he is dependent; but because he is independent on any other that should hinder him" (Edwards, "Concerning the End," in *WJE* 8:447).

36. The caveat is that "that which is last in execution is first in intention" is applicable only "to the end and all the proper means, but not with . . . every prerequisite condition." For, creation cannot be a proper means to conversion since it would be absurd to assert that "man was created . . . that he might repent!" (Edwards, "Miscellanies," no. 292, in *WJE* 13:383). See Aquinas, *STh* Q. 123, A. 7.

37. Edwards, "Concerning the End," in *WJE* 8:435.

38. "Communications of being ben't additions of being" (Edwards, "Miscellanies," no. 697, in *WJE* 18:281).

39. Edwards, 52. Sermon on Luke 2:14(b) (1743), in *WJE* 42.

40. "And as God delights in his own beauty, he must necessarily delight in the creature's holiness; which is a conformity to, and participation of it, as truly as the brightness of a jewel, held in the sun's beams, is a participation, or derivation of the sun's brightness, though immensely less in degree" (Edwards, "Concerning the End," in *WJE* 8:442).

41. He even describes this in quantitative terms: "For the sum total of the glory that God is to receive is infinite" (Edwards, "Miscellanies," no. 1099, in *WJE* 20:485).

42. Edwards, "Miscellanies," no. 1151, in *WJE* 20:525.

43. "There are many of the divine attributes that, if God had not created the world, never would have had any exercise: the power of God, the wisdom and prudence and contrivance of God, and the goodness and mercy and grace of God, and the justice of God" (Edwards, "Miscellanies," no. 553, in *WJE* 18:97).

44. "Indeed God knew as perfectly, that there were these attributes fundamentally in himself before they were in exercise, as since . . . [t]hat eternal act or energy of the divine nature within him, whereby he infinitely loves and delights in himself, I suppose does imply fundamentally goodness and grace towards creatures, if there be that occasion which infinite wisdom sees fit" (Edwards, "Miscellanies," no. 553, in *WJE* 18:97).

45. Edwards, "Miscellanies," no. 553, in *WJE* 18:97.

46. Edwards, "Concerning the End," in *WJE* 8:438.

47. Ibid., 439.

48. Douglas Sweeney suggests that Edwards understood *creatio ex nihilo* as creation "out of nothing . . . but God's own Trinitarian life" (Douglas A. Sweeney, "Editor's Introduction," in *WJE* 23:32).

49. "God is a communicative being. This communication is really only to intelligent beings: the communication of himself to their understandings is his glory, and the communication of himself with respect to their wills, the enjoying faculty, is their happiness. God created the world for the shining forth of his excellency and for the flowing forth of his happiness" (Edwards, "Miscellanies," no. 332, *WJE* 13:410).

50. The Western theological tradition, following Augustine, affirms that *opera trinitatis ad extra sunt indivisa* due to the consubstantiality of the divine persons. Commenting on the conception of Christ, St. Thomas affirms the indivisibility of all divine works, appealing to "Augustine [who] says (De Trin. i), 'The works of the Trinity are indivisible, just as the Essence of the Trinity is indivisible'" (Aquinas, *STh* 3, q. 32, a. 1). The Greeks would concur since they similarly confess a singular triune will and operation. Thus, "the operation of the Father, the Son, and the Holy Spirit is one, differing or varying in nothing, the oneness of their nature must needs be inferred from the identity of their operation." See Gregory of Nyssa, "On the Holy Trinity, and of the Godhead of the Holy Spirit to Eustathius," trans. William More and Henry Austin Wilson, 328 (*NPNF* 5).

51. Edwards, "Miscellanies," no. 976, in *WJE* 20:283. The interrelatedness, beauty, and "mutual action and reaction" of the different parts of the universe, as well as the harmony of the natural laws, point to the unity of God. Polytheism would demand multiple, independent universes or distinct galaxies within a whole. But since "parts of these different systems are not only communicated to and diffused through one another" such that they "become one great system," only "one cause" is to be concluded (Edwards, "Miscellanies," no. 976, in *WJE* 20:286). He shows an awareness that the practice of appropriations was used by polytheistic writers in making sense of the unity of the cosmos to a single *Theos*. "'The greater popularity,' as Tertullian speaks, 'of mankind, even when idolatry obscured the sense of divine providence, did however appropriate the name of God especially to one; in their usual expressions; being wont to say, if God grant, and what pleases God, and I commend it to God.'" (Edwards, "Miscellanies," no. 975, in *WJE* 20:278)

52. "The word is Elohim from the radix אָלָה, 'adjurare,' signifying the three persons of the Trinity confederated together as to the grand scheme and design of the creation, as they are in the eternal covenant of redemption" (Edwards, "Blank Bible," note on Gen. 1:1, in *WJE* 24:123). Though Aquinas clearly regarded the principal cause of the creation as the divine essence, he suggests that the Son and Spirit are the *ratio* for the willed processions of creatures from God. "Hence, as the Father speaks Himself and every creature by His begotten Word, inasmuch as the Word *begotten* adequately represents the Father and every creature; so He loves Himself and every creature by the Holy Ghost, inasmuch as the Holy Ghost proceeds as the love of the primal goodness whereby the Father loves Himself and every creature" (Aquinas, *STh* 1, q. 37, a. 2, ad 3). Norris interprets the "*a Patre, and per Filium*" to mean that both the Father and Son are the one Creator, originating all things in two modes: the first, as the efficient cause; the second, exemplary. "For indeed 'tis but Reason that the Father who is *Principium Essendi ad intra* should be also so *ad extra*, that the Things without should derive from him as well as the Persons within, and that he should be the Fountain of the *Creature*, as well as of the Deity." See John Norris, *Philosophical and Theological Writings*, 8 vols., ed. and intro. Richard Acworth (Bristol: Thoemmes, 2001), 6:277.

53. Edwards, "Miscellanies," no. 104, in *WJE* 13:272.

54. "But yet the Son has also an inclination to communicate himself, in an image of his person that may partake of his happiness: and this was the end of the creation, even the communication of the happiness of the Son of God . . . and man, the consciousness of perception of the creation, is the immediate subject of this" (Edwards, "Miscellanies," no. 104, in *WJE* 13:272).

55. Edwards, "Miscellanies," no. 104, in *WJE* 13:272. Edwards defines perfect goodness as the inclination to communicate one's happiness in equal measure to one's enjoyment of this happiness. Edwards argues that for the infinite God to exercise perfect goodness, it is impossible for God to communicate happiness fully to a finite or created being. As such, God the Father "must have the fellowship of a person equal to himself," and this person is the Son (Edwards, "Miscellanies," no. 96, *WJE* 13:263–64).

56. Edwards, "Miscellanies," no. 107(b), in *WJE* 13:277–78.

57. Edwards, "Miscellanies," no. 104, in *WJE* 13:273.

58. Edwards, "Miscellanies," no. 958, in *WJE* 20:234. "That which more especially was God's end in his eternal purpose of creating the world, and of the sum of his purposes with respect to creatures, was to procure a spouse, or a mystical body, for his Son" (Edwards, "Miscellanies," no. 1245, in *WJE* 23:178).

59. Edwards, "Miscellanies," no. 958, in *WJE* 20:239.

60. Ibid., 238.

61. "And all was decreed to be brought to pass by his Son. He being the end of all God's works *ad extra*, therefore the accomplishment of all was committed to him" (Edwards, "Miscellanies," no. 1245, in *WJE* 23:178). "Therefore the Son created and doth govern the world; seeing that the world was a communication of him, and seeing the communicating of his happiness is the end of the world" (Edwards, "Miscellanies," no. 104, corol. 3, in *WJE* 13:273).

Elsewhere, "the Son of God created the world for his very end, to communicate himself in an image of his own excellency." Although Christ "communicates himself properly only to spirits," yet "he communicates a sort of a shadow or glimpse of his excellencies to bodies" (Edwards, "Miscellanies," no. 108, in *WJE* 13:279).

62. Edwards, "Miscellanies," no. 107(b), in *WJE* 13:277.

63. Creation and the church "are a gift of the Father to the Son" (Edwards, "Miscellanies," no. 148 [138], in *WJE* 13:301). Only spirits, as they are real beings, can be said to be proper images of the Son; the rest of creation is but a shadow of Christ's excellency (Edwards, "Miscellanies," no. 108, in *WJE* 13:279).

64. "In heaven, Christ appears and acts most visibly and sensibly as the creator and life and soul and fountain of all being and perfection, and he of whom and through whom [all things] are, and by whom all immediately consists" (Edwards, "Miscellanies," no. 952, in *WJE* 20:216).

65. Edwards, "Miscellanies," no. 331, *WJE* 13:409.

66. Edwards says this in the context of Matt. 11:25-27 (Edwards, "A Divine and Supernatural Light," in *WJE* 17:417).

67. Edwards, "Miscellanies," no. 958, in *WJE* 20:234.

68. Edwards, "Miscellanies," no. 732, in *WJE* 18:359. Without the supernatural principle, unregenerate persons are not only incapable of a rational conviction and judgment of evil, but also a "sense of the heart of this evil." By common grace, the Spirit of God assists these natural capacities by mitigating "the prejudicing blinding tendency of sin" (ibid., 358).

69. Here, Edwards is commenting on the phrase "Let us make man" (Edwards, "Blank Bible," note on Gen. 1:26, in *WJE* 24:126).

70. Edwards, "True Virtue," in *WJE* 21:323. While this emphasis on the continuity between the immanent and economic Trinity using the framework of the psychological analogy was frequently employed by Western theologians, Edwards's use of it finds its clearest resemblance in Bonaventure (Pauw, "Supreme Harmony," 121–22). Bonaventure's concept of the divine fecundity within the Trinity, a synthesis of Pseudo-Dionysius's notion that the Good is self-diffusive and Anselm's logic of perfection, states that the diffusion of infinite goodness can only be actualized perfectly in the Trinitarian processions. As such, while creation is unnecessary to God's eternal self-communication, nevertheless it represents an overflow and a spatiotemporal manifestation of this fecundity. See Ewert Cousins, "Introduction," *The Soul's Journey into God. The Tree of Life. The Life of St. Francis*, trans. and intro. Ewert Cousins, The Classics of Western Spirituality (Mahwah, NJ: Paulist, 1978), 25.

71. Goodwin, "The Glory of the Gospel," *Works* 1, pt. 3, 63, as quoted in Edwards, "Miscellanies," no. 1275, in *WJE* 23:223.

72. Paul Ramsey highlights that Edwards's description of "communication of the divine fullness, consisting in the knowledge of God, love to God, and joy in God" to human beings demands more than just an ordinary reading. For "[t]he knowledge of God is God's own knowledge of himself. The love communicated is not love to God approximating its object; it is God's own love indwelling the will. The happiness communicated is a participation in God's own felicity." In other words, it is, in some sense, a communication of the persons of the Son and the Spirit, God's own personal knowledge and love or joy (Ramsey, in *WJE* 8:531n7).

73. Emanation includes a remanation, or the human responsibility of glorifying God through worship (Rachel Stahle, "The Trinitarian Spirit of Jonathan Edwards' Theology" [Ph.D diss., Boston University, 1999], 60). "[Y]et it does not hence follow, nor is it true, that God has no real or proper delight, pleasure, or happiness, in any of his acts or communications relative to the creature, or effects he produces in them; or in any thing he sees in the creature's qualifications, dispositions, actions and state" (Edwards, "Concerning the End," in *WJE* 8:531).

74. Edwards, "Concerning the End," in *WJE* 8:447. Edwards argues against those who "strongly insist that God cannot make his own glory his ultimate end, for that reason, because he can't make his own happiness his end, being already infinitely happy, and does not need any

manifestation of his glory to make him more happy" (Edwards, "Miscellanies," no. 1182, in *WJE* 23:104).

75. Scholars have compared Edwards's notion of divine self-communication to more modern approaches, like process theology, or to classical Neoplatonic emanationism, and conclusions are varied as to his position. See Douglas J. Elwood, *The Philosophical Theology of Jonathan Edwards* (New York: Columbia University Press, 1960); and R. C. de Prospo, *Theism in the Discourse of Jonathan Edwards* (Newark: University of Delaware Press, 1985). Recently, Michael Gibson has argued that the way in which Platonism was absorbed into Edwards's theology through the Cambridge Platonists finds its parallel in the manner by which neo-Platonism had influenced Eastern Christianity of the late antiquity via Plotinus and Proclus ("The Beauty of the Redemption of the World: The Theological Aesthetics of Maximus the Confessor and Jonathan Edwards," *Harvard Theological Review* 101, no. 1 [2008]: passim). It has been charged that Edwards's identification of the divine love and glory *ad extra* with human love of God in the saints' glorification is nothing less than pantheism and a logical outworking of his Calvinism. See Leslie Stephen, "Jonathan Edwards," in *Critical Essays on Jonathan Edwards*, ed. William J. Scheick (Boston: G. K. Hall, 1980), 73. Even the staunchest defenders of Edwards's theological orthodoxy have concluded that he was "pantheistic by implication and panentheistic by intention" (John H. Gerstner, *Rational Biblical Theology of Jonathan Edwards* [Powhatan, VA: Berea Publications; Orlando, FL: Ligonier Ministries, (1992)], 2:13).

76. Edwards says that though "God is really happy in loving his creatures, because in so doing he as it were gratifies a natural propensity in the divine nature," God does not do so because of an internal lack. On the contrary, God desires their returns of love and worship "because he loves them, not because he needs" (Edwards, "Miscellanies," no. 271, in *WJE* 13:374).

77. Scholars like Paula Cooey do not think that Edwards was either "a dualist or pantheist," since he conceived of nature as distinct from, subordinate to, but not separate from God. See Paula M. Cooey, *Jonathan Edwards on Nature and Destiny*, Studies in American Religion 16 (Lewiston, NY: Edwin Mellen, 1985), 3.

78. On Ezek. 1:4, Edwards notes that "The chariot of the world comes forth out of nothing" (Edwards, "Notes," no. 393, in *WJE* 15:388). See also, "All God's Methods Are Most Reasonable," in *WJE* 14:183; "Sermon Seventeen," in *WJE* 9:337.

79. Edwards, "Concerning the End," in *WJE* 8:420.

80. In Edwards's metaphysics of divine emanation, creation is a product of God's ontological "necessity" for temporal self-expression. See Patricia Wilson-Kastner, "God's Infinity and His Relationship to Creation in the Theologies of Gregory of Nyssa and Jonathan Edwards," *Foundations* 21 (October 1978): 314.

81. Although it may be argued that some creation is necessary for God's end to self-communicate, the actual world that is now in existence is not the best possible world *simpliciter*. It is only the best possible world in its own form and genus. See Oliver D. Crisp, "Jonathan Edwards' Panentheism," in *Jonathan Edwards as Contemporary: Essays in Honor of Sang Hyun Lee*, ed. Don Schweitzer (New York: Peter Lang, 2010), esp. 111–15.

82. "If we make no difficulty of allowing that God did immediately make the whole universe at first, and *caused it to exist out of nothing* . . . why should we make a difficulty supposing that he has still something immediately to do with things that he has made, and that there is an arbitrary influence still that God has in the creation he has made?" (Edwards, "Treatise on Grace," in *WJE* 21:177; emphasis mine).

83. Referring to the œconomical Trinity, Edwards notes that the divine persons "agreed to act in this order in all things appertaining to the glory of the Godhead. 'Tis not from the necessity of God's nature, not from any natural subordination, but 'tis the fruit of the will and pleasure of the persons of the Trinity." This includes "whether there should be any creation, and so whether any such thing as God's declarative glory" (Edwards, "Of God the Father," in *WJE* 25:147).

84. Thus, it is "not as if this nothing were a part of the substance of the thing made, but because the whole substance of a thing is produced by Him without anything else whatever presupposed" (Aquinas, *STh* I, q. 41, a. 3).

85. "There is no other way, but only for there to be existence; there is no such thing as absolute nothing" (Edwards, "Of Being," in *WJE* 6:207)

86. "There is such a thing as nothing with respect to this globe of earth, and with respect to this created universe. There is another way besides these things having existence. But there is no such thing as nothing with respect to entity or being, absolutely considered" (Edwards, "Of Being," in *WJE* 6:207). Edwards, like Barth, conceives of spatiality in God (Barth, *CD* II.1, 461ff.).

87. "Space is this necessary, eternal, infinite and omnipresent being. . . . But I had as good speak plain: I have already said as much as that space is God. And it is indeed clear to me, that all the space there is not proper to body, all the space there is without the bounds of the creation, all the space there was before the creation, is God himself" (Edwards, "Of Being," in *WJE* 6:203).

88. Edwards, "Miscellanies," no. 952, in *WJE* 20:213.

89. Eriugena's double affirmation of the created universe as simultaneously divine self-communication and *creatio ex nihilo* is both ingenious and self-consistent, since he made the principle of creation synonymous with God's nonbeing by eminence, viz., a nothingness by excess (*nihil per excellentiam*) but not a nothingness of deficiency (*nihil per privationem*). See Eriugena, *Periphyseon 3*, as cited by Dermot Moran, "John Scottus Eriugena," *The Stanford Encyclopedia of Philosophy (Fall 2008 Edition)*, ed. Edward N. Zalta, http://plato.stanford.edu/archives/fall2008/entries/scottus-eriugena. In Edwards's parlance, *nihil per excellentiam* is that "infinite, incomprehensible void or emptiness" in God (Edwards, "The Mind," in *WJE* 6:204–7).

90. Edwards, "Concerning the End," in *WJE* 8:451. See also, "Miscellanies," no. 1208, in *WJE* 23:137.

91. Edwards, "The Mind," in *WJE* 6:205. The universe, according to the young Edwards, "exists nowhere but in the divine mind" (ibid.). Edwards's "objective idealism" is derived from Henry More's identification of space with God, and his rejection of Descartes's *res extensa*. See Richard R. Niebuhr, "Being and Consent," in *The Princeton Companion to Jonathan Edwards*, ed. Sang Hyun Lee (Princeton, NJ: Princeton University Press, 2005), 35n4.

92. "Therefore the existence of created substances, in each successive moment, must be the effect of the immediate agency, will, and power of God" (Edwards, *WJE* 3:401). "This conservation is in very deed the same with Creation, differing only in reason, in that *Creation* includes a certaine newness which conservation excludes, & *Creation* excludes a precedent existence which conservation includes, so that that conservation is nothing else then as it were a continued *Creation*, and therefore it is joyned with *Creation*" (William Ames, *Marrow of Sacred Divinity Drawne Out of the Holy Scriptures, and the Interpreters thereof, and Brought into Method* [London: Henry Overton, 1642], ch. 9, 48). "For the being of every creature depends on God, so that not for a moment could it subsist, but would fall into nothingness were it not kept in being by the operation of the Divine power. . . . The preservation of things by God is a continuation of that action whereby He gives existence, which action is without either motion or time; so also the preservation of light in the air is by the continual influence of the sun" (Aquinas, *STh* I, q. 104, a. 1, responsio & ad 4). Edwards asserted that "we are anew created every moment" from as early as "Miscellanies," no. 18 (c. 1922) and continues this train of thought in his later writings, such as *Original Sin* (Edwards, *WJE* 3:397). On this point, see Harry Stout, "Editor's Introduction," in *WJE* 13:43.

93. "Where lies the great difficulty, if we own the being of a God, and that he created all things out of nothing, of allowing some immediate influence of God on the creation still?" (Edwards, "A Divine and Supernatural Light," in *WJE* 17:421). A physical entity or a "body," according to Edwards, "is nothing but an infinite resistance in some part of space caused by the immediate exercise of divine power." If original creation is God's first exercise of such divine power, then it follows that "preservation [is] only the continuation or the repetition of this power

every moment to cause this resistance." That being the case, preservation is nothing but "the universe [being] created out of nothing every moment" (Edwards, "Things to be Considered and Written Fully About," in *WJE* 6:241)

94. Edwards, *WJE* 3:402. Edwards's idealism, Chai suggests, corroborates with a conception of *creatio continua*, where God is pictured not only as "the foundation," but also as the "fountain of all being and beauty." Analogous to our thinking process, that "even after being formulated, they require constant thinking in order to remain in existence." See Leon Chai, *Jonathan Edwards and the Limits of Enlightenment Philosophy* (New York: Oxford University Press, 1998), 69. Chai goes on to say that Edwards's idealism is not only theological but also anthropological, and that reality is fundamentally constructed by our minds: "Since the dependence of existence on our thought applies universally in Edwards, however, it seems only reasonable to conclude that for him existence is identical to the process by which we form our conceptions" (Chai, *Jonathan Edwards and the Limits*, 70).

95. "For upholding the world in being and creating of it are not properly distinct works" (Edwards, "Miscellanies," no. 1349, in *WJE* 23:608). He echoes the Cartesian position where "the distinction between creation and conservation is solely a distinction of reason." See Rene Descartes, *The Philosophical Works of Descartes*, trans. Elizabeth S. Haldane and G. R. T. Ross (Cambridge: Cambridge University Press), 1:168.

96. Edwards, "Miscellanies," no. 346, in *WJE* 13:418. He goes on to cite the proof texts: "Job 9:9; Psalms 65:6, Psalms 104:4; Isaiah 40:22, Isaiah 44:24; Amos 5:8."

97. Lee has exegetical grounds in arguing that a "conception of reality as a dynamic network of dispositional forces and habits" is foundational to Edwards's thought (Lee, *PTJE*, exp. ed., 4). Chai posits an antithesis between immediate divine agency and Lee's dispositional interpretation of Edwards's ontology, particularly the law-like character of habits. He argues that "if all created substances are at each moment the effect of God's *immediate* agency, their existence cannot result simply from the operation of laws" since their "destruction at any moment must be equally possible" (Chai, *Jonathan Edwards and the Limits*, 144n8). Chai seems to be able to accept the idea of a dispositional notion of reality when construed as relationality.

98. "If any . . . shall insist . . . that there is no need of any immediate divine power, to produce the present existence of created substances, but that . . . the established course of nature is sufficient to continue existence, where existence is once given; I allow it: but then it should be remembered . . . [that] nature . . . and . . . the established course of nature is . . . [not] separate from the agency of God" (Edwards, *WJE* 3:401).

99. Paul Helm, "A Forensic Dilemma: John Locke and Jonathan Edwards on Personal Identity," in Helm and Crisp, *Philosophical Theologian*, 56–57.

100. Ibid. "Despite Edwards's very strong avowal of divine sovereignty it would seem that not even God can preserve in existence for more than a moment a being as a numerically identical being or as one that has numerical identical parts through that period of time" (ibid., 54).

101. Edwards, "Miscellanies," no. 136 (*151*), in *WJE* 13:295.

102. Edwards asks rhetorically: "Who can suppose that God made man to glorify Him so miserably as we are capable of in this life, and enjoy some little communion with Him for about sixty or seventy years, and then the man is annihilated, and the glory of God and the enjoyment of him is at an end forever? Who can think thus?" (Edwards, "The Importance of a Future State," in *WJE* 10:359).

103. Edwards, "The Torments of Hell Are Exceeding Great," in *WJE* 14:315. "If a man has to be to all eternity under the same agonies which he is under in the moments of death, it would be but an image of hell" (ibid.)

104. Edwards identifies all atomic bodies with solidity—a condition that defies division and annihilation. Working with the scientific presupposition of his time where "the parts of atoms cannot be torn asunder" by finite power, Edwards posits that an infinite power—God—must necessarily act continuously to preserve created being. As all created bodies are specific instances of God's immediate exercise of divine power, "the certain unknown substance, which philosophers

used to think subsisted by itself, and stood underneath and kept up solidity and all other properties, which they used to say it was impossible for a man to have an idea of" is, according to Edwards, nothing other than solidity (Edwards, "Of Atoms," in *WJE* 6:208–15).

105. Moreover, if one must insist on reality being conceptualized in terms of independent substances, Edwards logically concludes that created bodies are nothing except where True Substance—the Deity—acts. This position remained unchanged even in his later reflections in order to reject a crass materialism (Edwards, "Miscellanies," no. 1153, in *WJE* 23:39).

106. Edwards, "The Mind," in *WJE* 6:344.

107. Woodbridge Riley, "Jonathan Edwards," in Scheick, *Critical Essays*, 102. Or, as Jenson nicely summarizes Edwards's basic ontology: "to be is to pertain to the community of consciousnesses" (Robert W. Jenson, *America's Theologian: A Recommendation of Jonathan Edwards* [New York: Oxford University Press, 1988], 141).

108. Edwards, "Miscellanies," no. 3, in *WJE* 13:199. Very early on, Edwards opines that if the ultimate end of creation were merely "an understanding of the perfections of God" or the "declaring God's glory to others," it is "good for nothing" (Edwards, "Miscellanies," no. 3, in *WJE* 13:200). Schafer dates this entry to sometime between May and June 1723 when Edwards was in East Windsor ("Note on the Text of the 'Miscellanies'" in *WJE* 13:156). It is not the case that Edwards explicitly affirmed *esse est percepi* in his early metaphysics but could have modified this, based on his later *End for Which God Created the World*, into *esse est percepi et amari*. Holmes thinks that had Edwards continued to refine his metaphysics in tandem with his later theological reflections, he could have arrived at a "relational ontology . . . built finally on Trinitarian grounds" similar to what is transpiring within contemporary theological discourse (Stephen R. Holmes, *God of Grace and God of Glory: An Account of the Theology of Jonathan Edwards* [Edinburgh: T&T Clark, 2000], 87–92).

109. In fact, the soul and body may be described as two distinct substances united by the sheer power of God and the laws of nature constituted and upheld by God (Edwards, "Miscellanies," no. 313, in *WJE* 13:394). "For the soul is certainly [a] distinct substance from the body." There is "no reason or foundation in the separate nature of either substance why any motion in the body should produce any sensation at all in the soul, or any one more than another, or why any action in the soul should produce any motion in the body." However, their "union depends on his [God's] arbitrary efficacy alone, and the laws of it are such as he has established and he only upholds." Nevertheless, the essence of the soul "consists in power and habits," which are "[laws] that God has fixed, that such actions upon such occasions should be exerted" (Edwards, "Miscellanies," no. 241, in *WJE* 13:358). Aquinas's hylomorphism assumes a stronger body-soul relation. God acts as the life principle of the soul "in the manner of efficient cause" through the intermediary of the soul, the form of the body. Since nothing can come between form and matter, the soul or "the form, of itself, informs the matter or subject [the body]; whereas the agent [God] informs the subject, not by its substance, but by the form, which it causes in the matter" (Aquinas, *STh* I-II, q. 110, a. 1, reply obj. 2, 1133). Chai does not take into consideration this analogous relation between the soul and all reality when he critiques Lee for overinterpreting Miscellany no. 241 (*Jonathan Edwards and the Limits*, 144n8). As Edwards himself states, "laws . . . constitute all permanent being in created things, both corporeal and spiritual," and not merely created spirits ("The Mind," in *WJE* 6:391).

110. God knows things "as they exist in the knower," but wills things "as they exist in themselves" (Aquinas, *STh* I, q. 19, a. 3 ad 6, 105). In other words, the relation between the divine knowledge and its objects is absolutely necessary, while that between the divine will and its objects is not. Hence, all divine ideas are absolutely necessary insofar as they exist in God, but their actualization is contingent on the divine will and relatively necessary insofar as they are in existence.

111. Edwards, "Justification by Faith Alone," in *WJE* 19:158. Although this is quoted in reference to the *unio mystica*, the same logic applies to creation.

112. Hence, "spiritual unions—of the persons of the Trinity, of the two natures of Christ, of Christ and the minds of saints" (Edwards, "Miscellanies," no. 184, in *WJE* 13:330).

113. "And all communications, derivations, or continuation of qualities, properties, or relations, natural or moral, from what is past, as if the subject were one, depends on no other foundation," namely, "divine establishment" (Edwards, *WJE* 3:405).

114. Ibid., 403. The same language is evident for the hypostatic union, whereby "the Spirit of the Logos may dwell in a creature after such a manner, that that creature may become one person [with the Logos], and may be looked upon as such and accepted as such" (Edwards, "Miscellanies," no. 487, in *WJE* 13:528). With regard to the mystical union, "God in requiring this in order to an union with Christ as one of his people" constitutes "something really in them, and between them, uniting them, that is the ground of the suitableness of their being accounted as one by the Judge" (Edwards, "Justification by Faith Alone," in *WJE* 19:158).

115. Edwards admits that the production of the body in the "first creation of man" was "formed immediately by God," yet the production of the soul "was in a higher, more direct and immediate manner from God," so much so that God did "as it were communicate something of himself, something of his own Spirit of life or divine vital fullness" (Edwards, "Miscellanies," no. 1003, in *WJE* 20:328). "And though there be no such thing as any immediate creation since the beginning of the world in any other kind, unless perhaps in some rare instances of miracle, yet in this kind of creation, which is the greatest and most glorious being of the most perfect and exalted creature, immediate creation is continued, and is a thing that comes to pass in innumerable instances every day" (ibid.). Evidently, this constituted an argument against traducianism since the recurrent coming-into-existence of souls is akin to the immediacy of the first creation.

116. Edwards, "The Mind," no. 34, in *WJE* 6:354.

117. "It is not proper at all, nor doth it express the thing we would, to say, that 'bodies do not exist without the mind.' . . . But when I say, 'the material universe exists only in the mind,' I mean that it is absolutely dependent on the conception of the mind for its existence, and does not exist as spirits do, whose existence does not consist in, nor in dependence on, the conception of other minds. . . . [I]n a sense, the visible world is existent out of the mind, for it certainly, in the most proper sense, exists out of the brain" (Edwards, "The Mind," no. 51, in *WJE* 6:368–69).

118. "For we are to remember that the human body and the brain itself exist only mentally, in the same sense that other things do. And so that which we call place is an idea too. Therefore things are truly in those places, for what we mean when we say so is only that this mode of our idea of place appertains to such an idea" (Edwards, "The Mind," no. 34, in *WJE* 6:353).

119. Edwards's doctrines of continual creation and soft occasionalism are not meant to replace the older way of thinking and speaking: "Though we suppose that the existence of the whole material universe is absolutely dependent on idea, yet we may speak in the old way, and *as properly and truly as ever*: God in the beginning created such a certain number of atoms, of such a determinate bulk and figure, which they yet maintain and always will; and gave them such a motion, of such a direction, and of such a degree of velocity; from whence arise all the natural changes in the universe forever in a continued series" (Edwards, "The Mind," no. 34, in *WJE* 6:354; emphasis mine).

120. Genesis 1, passim.

121. "When I call this an arbitrary constitution, I mean, that it is a constitution which depends on nothing but the divine will; which divine will depends on nothing but the divine wisdom" (Edwards, *WJE* 3:403). For Edwards, "all the laws by which we are able to move so much as a finger, are nothing but so many methods of [God's] continual, immediate agency" (Edwards, "Controversies" Notebook, in *WJE* 27).

122. Delattre places the theme of participation as central to Edwards's theological ethics: "The Christian life is a life made new by cordial participation in the divine life overflowing into the world" (Roland André Delattre, "The Theological Ethics of Jonathan Edwards: A Homage to Paul Ramsey," *Journal of Religious Ethics* 19, no. 2 [Fall 1991]: 74).

123. Andrew Louth notes that the Augustinian tradition interprets the *imago Dei* within a more intellectual, Trinitarian framework while the Greek Fathers viewed the "image" christologically. The Greek Fathers and the early St. Augustine saw the human as being the image of the Image, the Son of God. In *De Trinitate*, St. Augustine moved away from this interpretation to see the rational soul of a human being as the image of the Trinity. This was to avoid a subordinationist reading of the Son, in which the Son is seen as the (lesser) image of the Father (Andrew Louth, *The Origins of the Christian Mystical Tradition from Plato to Denys* [Oxford: Clarendon Press, 1981], 146–47).

124. Edwards, *WJE* 2: 11; Edwards, "Essay on the Trinity," in *TG*, 104.

125. Edwards, "Miscellanies," no. 702, in *WJE* 18:287–88.

126. Edwards, "Charity, or Love, the Sum of all Virtue," in *Charity and Its Fruits: Christian Love as Manifested in the Heart and Life*, ed. Tryon Edwards (London: Banner of Truth Trust, 1969), 5.

127. Edwards, "Duty of Charity to the Poor," *WJE* 17:376.

128. "That only, therefore, is what I mean by true virtue, which, belonging to the heart of an intelligent being, is beautiful by a general beauty, or beautiful in a comprehensive view, as it is in itself, and as related to everything with which it stands connected" (Edwards, "True Virtue," in *WJE* 8:540).

129. Ibid., 545–47.

130. Jonathan Edwards, "Heaven is a World of Love," in *The Sermons of Jonathan Edwards: A Reader*, ed. Wilson H. Kimnach, Kenneth P. Minkema, and Douglas A. Sweeney (New Haven: Yale University Press, 1999), 249.

131. Edwards, "Miscellanies," no. 896, in *WJE* 20:155.

132. Edwards, "Miscellanies," no. 864, in *WJE* 20:96. "They are in the image of their Creator in that respect, that they have understanding and are voluntary agents, and can produce works of their own will, design and contrivance, as God does." Human beings "act in some imperfect manner like God, in disposing things, in things that they make and order—and no other" (ibid., 154).

133. "Upon these accounts, 'tis most reasonable to suppose these things more like the first cause than other things, especially if we consider that this is one instance of the First Cause's acting with design: that he has given intelligent creatures understanding and will to that end, that he might enable 'em to act for final causes, and have respect to that which is future" (Edwards, "Miscellanies," no. 896, in *WJE* 20:155).

134. Edwards, "Discourse on the Trinity," in *WJE* 21:117; "Miscellanies," no. 104, in *WJE* 13:272.

135. Edwards, "Miscellanies," no. 94, *WJE* 13:260.

136. According to Edwards, "man is as if he were two" as he is in constant "conversation with his own idea," experiencing either happiness or internal accusation, depending on whether there is agreement or discord between idea and person (Edwards, "Miscellanies," no. 94, in *WJE* 13:260). Natural conscience is for Edwards a relation within the self—that is, the self's relation to herself or the self's consciousness of himself.

137. Edwards, "The Importance and Advantage of a Thorough Knowledge of Divine Truth," in *WJE* 22:91.

138. "Divinity is commonly defined, the doctrine of living to God; and by some who seem to be more accurate, the doctrine of living to God by Christ. It comprehends all Christian doctrines as they are in Jesus, and all Christian rules directing us in living to God by Christ. There is no one doctrine, no promise, no rule, but what some way or other relates to the Christian and divine life, or our living to God by Christ" (Edwards, "The Importance and Advantage of a Thorough Knowledge of Divine Truth," in *WJE* 22:86).

139. The economic Trinity, in Edwards's understanding, reveals God's nature "as there is great reason to think it was, that his works should exhibit an image of himself their author, that it might brightly appear by his works what manner of being he is, and afford a proper representation

of his divine excellencies, and especially his *moral* excellence, consisting in the *disposition of his heart*" (Edwards, "Concerning the End," in *WJE* 8:422).

140. Since the Spirit is "the author" of this capacity for discerning natural evil, it belongs properly to the Spirit to assist the unregenerate through common, "legal illuminations" of sin and evil (Edwards, "Miscellanies," no. 732, in *WJE* 18:358–59).

141. "So that we see that a world without motion can exist nowhere else but in the mind either infinite or finite" (Edwards, "Of Being," in *WJE* 6:206).

142. Echoing Ames's distinction, God *in se* can only be called "causing power" since God is pure act, but in relation to creatures, God is experienced as "active power." "*Potentia, vel potestas causae,* A causing power yet properly active power doth not agree to God, as if in respect of himself, he were first idle, and after did put himself forth into act: for God is a most pure Act. *James* 1. 17" (Ames, *Marrow of Sacred Divinity*, ch. 6, 24).

143. Edwards, "Essay," in *TG*, 99. Augustine finally regarded memory, understanding, and love as three functions within the human mind directed toward God as the best analogy of the Trinity—Father, Son, and Holy Spirit. He saw his earlier analogy of mind, understanding, and love as inadequate because the latter two were relative to the former; as such, it is more properly an analogy that corresponds to God, Son, and Spirit (Edmund Hill, introduction to *The Trinity*, vol. 5 of *The Works of Saint Augustine*, ed. John E. Rotelle, intro. and trans. by Edmund Hill [Brooklyn, NY: New City, 1991], 53).

144. Edwards, *WJE* 2:96. While Augustine was not original in his attempt to posit an analogy between the Trinity and the human soul, his theological methodology has impacted much of Western Trinitarian discourse, including that of Edwards. Marius Victorinus's equation of the triad of *esse*, *vivere*, and *intelligere* (being, life, and thought) as an image of the Trinity arose from his cogitation upon the human soul. According to M. T. Clark, the origins of this triadic formula may be traced back to "the Chaldean Oracles or from Porphyry, or from commentators on Platonic dialogues or from Middle Platonists like Numenius." See Mary T. Clark, *The Saint Augustine Lecture 1969: Augustinian Personalism* (Villanova, PA: Villanova University Press, 1970), 14. With regard to the conspicuousness of the psychological analogy in Edwards's writings set against the background of the Reformed scholastics and Puritans who, by and large, avoided the use of created analogies, Pauw suggests that Edwards may have been influenced by Bartholomaeus Keckermann and Cotton Mather on account of the remarkably similar phraseology. Both Keckermann and Edwards spoke of God's "reflex act of knowledge", Mather's prominent references to the Father as "the fountain of the Godhead" and the Spirit as the Father's "love and delight in Himself" are also reflected in Edwards's theology (Pauw, "Supreme Harmony," 61–62).

145. Edwards, "Miscellanies," no. 370, in *WJE* 13:442. "And so you have a certain image of the trinity, the mind itself and its knowledge, which is its offspring and its word about itself, and love as the third element, *and these three are one* (1 Jn 5:8) and are one substance" (Augustine, *The Trinity*, bk. 9, ch. 3, 282). Subsequently, in Book X, Augustine saw a better analogy for the Trinity in the trio of mental acts—self-remembering, self-understanding, and self-willing. As Edmund Hill notes, the mind in the previous analogy is an absolute term while the understanding and will are relative to it; as such, the trinity of mind, understanding, and will corresponds more to God, Son, and Spirit than to Father, Son, and Spirit (Hill, introduction to Augustine, *The Trinity*, 53).

146. Inasmuch as Augustine's *Confessions* cannot be seen apart from *De Trinitate*, Edwards's assertion that "the soul of man" is one of the "more eminent and remarkable images of the Trinity" in his "Discourse on the Trinity" cannot be abstracted from his other claim in the *Religious Affections* that "holiness in man, is but an image of God's holiness" (Edwards, "Essay on the Trinity" in *TG*, 126; *WJE* 2:256). Cherry emphasizes Edwards's dependence on the Reformed tradition inasmuch as his "doctrine [of the Trinity] is modeled after his psychology of the faith-act" (Conrad Cherry, *The Theology of Jonathan Edwards: A Reappraisal* [Bloomington: Indiana University Press, 1990], 25). Nichols reminds us that Edwards's human psychology cannot be disassociated from his psychological model of the Trinity. See Stephen J. Nichols, *An Absolute Sort*

of Certainty: The Holy Spirit and the Apologetics of Jonathan Edwards (Phillipsburg, NJ: P&R, 2003), 28. Similarly, Augustine reminds us: "I wish that human disputants would reflect upon the triad within their own selves . . . being, knowing and willing. . . . The fact is certain to anyone by introspection. . . . It baffles thought to inquire whether these three functions are the ground which constitutes the divine Trinity, or whether the three components are present in each Person, so that each Person has all three, or whether both these alternatives are true." See St. Augustine, *Confessions*, trans., intro. and notes by Henry Chadwick, Oxford World Classics (Oxford: Oxford University Press, 1991), 13.9.12, 279.

147. Edwards, *WJE* 2:98. According to Stahle, Edwards uses soul, consciousness, person, spirit, and mind synonymously and interchangeably (Stahle, "Trinitarian Spirit," 132–33).

148. Edwards, "Miscellanies," no. 489, in *WJE* 13:533.

149. The human soul, as a psychological synthesis, images the Trinity; the human being is also a psychosomatic unity that images Christ, the perfect union of the material and spiritual (Stahle, "Trinitarian Spirit," 130).

150. Due to God's infinity, the divine attributes are properly incommunicable. "But if we will speak properly and exactly, we must needs say that all God's Attributes are *Incommunicable*, because they are all Infinite, as his knowledge is Infinite, so is his Power, his Goodness, his Justice, &c." This is because, in God, they are essential, original, and eminent, while in human beings, they are accidental, derivative, and imperfect. The *res significata* transcends the *ratio nomina* applied to us by a certain *modus*: "Thus the Divine Attributes cannot properly be said to be *communicated* to Men, but are spoken and meant of *God*, in a different way from what is found in us." Since human beings have only a participation of likeness in the divine attributes, John Edwards prefers to classify them as primary, or fundamental, and secondary attributes. "It is true some of these Excellencies, Knowledge, Goodness, &c. are in Men, but they are but shadows and resemblances of the like Perfections in God." See John Edwards, *Theologia reformata: or, the body and substance of the Christian religion* (London: Printed for John Lawrence, John Wyat, and Ranew Robinson, 1713), 44.

151. Edwards, "Miscellanies," no. 210, in *WJE* 13:342. Here, Edwards seems to be referring to the human conscience as spiritual image, which "is come to nothing." The indwelling Spirit is the renewal of this divine participation, which may be regarded as an addition of a new form or "soul" or a remaking of the original. "But the soule is the Image of the Essence of *God*, (as I may so speake) that is, it is a spirit immateriall, immortall, invisible, as he is; hath understanding and will, as he hath; he understands all things, and wills whatsoever he pleaseth." See John Preston, *Life eternall; or, A treatise of the knowledge of the divine essence and attributes. Delivered in XVIII sermons* (London: R. B. [Richard Badger?], 1631), 16.

152. "Those things are sometimes called divine in common use of speech that have any kind of resemblance or in which is any manifestation of any divine perfection." This even applies to nonanimate things: "So the sun for its brightness and glory which God has given it which is some faint shadow of the glory of its author may be called a divine work" (Edwards, 498. Sermon on 1 John 4:12 [undated], in *WJE* 53).

153. Edwards, "True Virtue," in *WJE* 8:591.

154. Ibid. "We never could have any notion what understanding or volition, love or hatred are, either in created spirits or in God, if we had not experienced what understanding and volition, love and hatred are in our own minds."

155. Ibid. Edwards reiterates that this "is the only way we come to be capable of conceiving of anything in the Deity" (ibid., 592).

156. As noted by Barth, the Thomistic *via negationis* and *via eminentiae*, corresponds to the *apophasis* and *kataphasis* of Ps.-Dionysius and is commensurable to the Reformed dialectic of incommunicable and communicable divine attributes. While avoiding the causal connotations of the *via causalitatis*, Barth was favorable to reconfiguring this third way as *via revelatus*—describing God's nature as revealed with appropriate corrections through the dialectic of negation and eminence. Following Schleiermacher, he interpreted the *via causalitatis* as the "epitome" of the

other two ways (Barth, "The Attributes of God," in *Göttingen Dogmatics: Instruction in the Christian Religion*, vol. 1, ed. Hannelotte Reiffen, trans. Geoffrey W. Bromiley [Grand Rapids, MI: Eerdmans, 1991], §17, 401). Palamas affirmed that union with God is a gracious and "real participation in divine things," not "simply an abstraction." Since these "possessions and gifts are ineffable," human speaking of God cannot be univocal but "must have recourse to images and analogies" (Gregory Palamas, *The Triads*, ed. with intro. John Meyendorff, trans. Nicholas Gendell, preface by Jaroslav Pelikan, Classics of Western Spirituality [Mahwah, NJ: Paulist, 1983], 36). In opposition to the nominalist tendency of Barlaam, Russo notes that Palamas "assumes the position of a critical realist." See Gerry Russo, "Rahner and Palamas: A Unity of Grace," *St. Vladimir's Theological Quarterly* 32, no. 2: 161. See Flogaus, 'Der Heimlich Blick nach Westen. Zur Rezeption von Augustins De Trinitate durch Gregorios Palamas,' *Jahrbuch der Österreichischen Byzantinistik* 46 (1996): 275–97; idem., *Theosis bei Palamas und Luther. Ein Beitrag zum ökumenischen Gespräch* (Göttingen, 1997), 50–284.

157. Edwards, 107. Sermon on Num. 23:19, in *WJE* 44.

158. "Such an inclination in men is called love. And therefore that inclination that is in the nature of God to beneficence, to do good, to creatures is called so too. Tho indeed God is without passions because all passions imply changeableness and imperfection. And therefore love can't be in God as it is in us. Because God is a being infinitely perfect" (Edwards, 52. Sermon on Luke 2:14[b], in *WJE* 42).

159. "But yet all that is excellent and denotes perfection in the love of creatures, is more eminently in God, is in him in a transcendent and infinite degree. But all that denotes imperfection in love is not in God" (ibid.).

160. Edwards, "Miscellanies," no. 135 (*150*), in *WJE* 13:295. "The difference is no contrariety, but what naturally results from his greatness and nothing else, such as created spirits come nearer to, or more imitate, the greater they are in their powers or faculties."

161. "So that if we should suppose the faculties of a created spirit to be enlarged infinitely, there would be the Deity to all intents and purposes, the same simplicity, immutability, etc." (ibid.) Schafer concludes that Edwards's identification of God and being implies Scotus's univocity, and the idea of God as highest being echoes Aquinas's analogical predication. In fact, Edwards does say that God is identical to Being itself, *ens entium*, only true substance. See Thomas A. Schafer, "The Concept of Being in the Thought of Jonathan Edwards" (Ph.D. diss., Duke University, 1951), 137–40.

162. Edwards, "The Mind," in *WJE* 6:381. For Edwards, "God . . . is the infinite, universal and all comprehending existence." Only *ad intra* (and not in comparison to created being) could the measure of being be used metaphorically of God: "He is in himself, if I may so say, an infinite quantity of existence." (ibid.)

163. Edwards, "Discourse on the Trinity," in *WJE* 21:113.

164. In God, however, there is no distinction between divine nature, predilection, and action, for the Father is united in "power and habit and act," the Son in "idea, and reasoning and judgement," and the Spirit in "will, inclination and love" (Edwards, "Essay," in TG, 99).

165. Edwards, "Essay on the Trinity," in *TG*, 99.

166. Edwards, 528. Sermon on Rom. 8:29–30, in *WJE* 54.

167. "But God's action is not distinct from His power, for both are His divine essence; neither is His existence distinct from His essence" (Aquinas, *STh* 1. 25. 1 ad 2).

168. For Edwards, human beings are intrinsically relational beings as "we are made to subsist by society and union, one with another, and God has made us with such a nature that we can't subsist without the help of another" (Edwards, "Duty of Charity to the Poor," in *WJE* 17:376).

169. Yet, the desire for happiness is intrinsic not only to human nature, but is "universal among all reasonable intelligent beings in heaven, earth or hell." It is "as universal as the very essence of the soul because it necessarily and immediately flows from the essence" (Edwards, 80. Sermon on Isa. 32:2 [1728], in *WJE* 43).

170. "The happiness of men consists in love and friendship. . . . There is no creature has that in himself alone that will fill the capacity and cravings of his nature; and especially man, who is so feeble and so imperfect a creature: while he is alone, he is empty and never can be happy, except it be in union with some other being" (Edwards, 131. Sermon on 1 Pet. 1:8[a] [Jul 1757], in *WJE* 44).

171. Ibid.

172. Yet, we can affirm that human beings image the divine in terms of a participation of likeness. Our goodness, as secondary and derivative, is a participation in God's goodness, though between the two there is a distinction of alterity (*unum ad alterum*). The description of such an asymmetrical but substantial relation between two ontologically distinct entities is similar to the Platonic notion of participation or *methexis*. The distinction between human and divine is not that of two or more species of beings under a third genus of Being (*multum ad unum* or *duorum ad tertium*). This weaker sort of relation of likeness of two things sharing something in common echoes the Platonic notion of *homoiosis*. See Norman Russell, *The Doctrine of Deification in the Greek Patristic Tradition*, Oxford Early Christian Studies (Oxford: Oxford University Press, 2004), 2.

173. Just as the Father "sees" and "loves" the divine essence in that two eternal processions or self-communications of God *ad intra*, the saints "see" and "love" God through the missions of the Son and the Spirit, in their self-communications of divine light (glory) and divine love (fullness) (Edwards, "Miscellanies," no. 1142, in *WJE* 20:517).

174. John of Damascus, following Ireneaus, posited a distinction between "image" and "likeness": "For the phrase 'after His image' clearly refers to the side of his nature which consists of mind and free will, whereas 'after His likeness' means likeness in virtue so far as that is possible" (John of Damascus, *Orthodox Faith*, bk. 2, ch. 12, 31 [*NPNF 9*]).

175. According to Preston, there "is a double Image of God in the soule, one in the substance of it, which is never lost; another is the supernaturall grace, which is an Image of the knowledge, holinesse, and righteousnesse of God, and this is utterly lost. But the soule is the Image of the Essence of God, (as I may so speake) that is, it is a spirit immateriall, immortall, invisible, as he is; hath understanding and will, as he hath; he understands all things, and wills whatsoever he pleaseth" (John Preston, *Life Eternall*, 16).

176. Edwards, "Miscellanies," no. 187, in *WJE* 13:331.

177. Edwards, "Concerning the End," in *WJE* 8:532.

178. "God intended when he created us that we should seek our own preservation and happiness he hereby obtains many wise ends. But God never intended that we should make our selves our chief end and our highest good and subject all other pursuits and aims to our own benefit or pleasure. Natural men they make themselves their first and their last, their Alpha and Omega" (Edwards, 40. Sermon on Luke 9:23[a] [1727], in *WJE* 42).

179. Edwards, "Miscellanies," no. 824, in *WJE* 18:536.

180. Edwards, "Miscellanies," no. 702, in *WJE* 18:288.

181. Edwards, "Miscellanies," no. 894, in *WJE* 20:153.

182. Ibid.

183. Ibid.

184. Edwards, "God Glorified," in *Sermons*, 205–6. As the first human beings were necessarily created holy in nature and functioned within an environment free from sin's dominion, their dependence on God was comparatively lesser. With regard to God's grace, "it would have been a disparagement to the holiness of God's nature, if he had made an intelligent creature unholy. But now when man is made holy, it is from mere and arbitrary grace" (ibid., 204). And as to God's power: "So 'tis a more glorious work of power to uphold the soul in a state of grace and holiness, and carry it on till it is brought to glory, when there is so much sin remaining in the heart, resisting, and Satan with all his might opposing, than it would have been to have kept man from falling at first, when Satan had nothing in man" (ibid., 206).

185. "Religion is life and spirit, which, flowing out from God, who is that underived existence that hath life in himself, returns to him again as into its own original, carrying the souls of good men up with it." See John Smith, *The Excellency and Nobleness of True Religion,* in *The Cambridge Platonists,* ed. Gerald R. Cragg (Lanham, MD: University Press of America, 1985; originally publ., New York: Oxford University Press, 1968), 101.

186. This is pithily stated by Augustine and elaborately laid out by Aquinas, both materially and architectonically, in his great *Summa.* The primary goal of Christian doctrine, so introduces St. Thomas, is "to know God in Himself, and as Alpha and Omega" ("non solum secundum quod in se est, sed etiam secundum quod est principium rerum et finis earum"), particularly in relation to intelligent creatures. Hence the threefold division of his *Summa Theologiae* expounds on the subject matter in this order: "(1) Of God; (2) Of the rational creature's advance towards God; (3) Of Christ, Who as man, is our way to God" ("tertio, de Christo, qui, secundum quod homo, via est nobis tendendi in Deum") (Aquinas, *STh* I, q. 2). "Now the only way that is infallibly secured against all mistakes, is when the very same person is at once God and man, God our end, man our way." See St. Augustine, "The City of God," in *St Augustin's City of God and Christian Doctrine,* vol. 2 of *A Select Library of the Nicene and Post-Nicene Fathers of the Christian Church, Series 1,* ed. Philip Schaff (Peabody, MA: Hendrickson, 1994), 11.2, 227.

187. In reference to the natures in Christ, Calvin, reiterating Augustine, notes that "the goal of faith" is that "namely, as God he is the destination to which we move; as man, the path by which we go" (John Calvin, *Calvin: Institutes of Christian Religion,* ed. John T. McNeill, trans. Ford Lewis Battles, Library of Christian Classics 20 [Philadelphia: Westminster, 1960], 3.2.1, 544).

188. Anri Morimoto, *Jonathan Edwards and the Catholic Vision of Salvation* (University Park: Pennsylvania State University Press, 1995), 150–51.

189. Edwards, "Concerning the End," in *WJE* 8:531.

190. "I need not run the parallel between this and the course of God's providence through all ages, from the beginning to the end of the world, when all things shall have their final issue in God, the infinite, inexhaustible, fountain whence all things come at first, as all the rivers come from the sea, and whither they all shall come at last: for of him and to him are all things, and he is the Alpha and Omega, the beginning and the end" (Edwards, "Images of Divine Things," no. 77, in *WJE* 11:79). This imagery was mediated to Edwards through the Puritan writings. Thomas Watson, for example, refers to God not only as the *summum bonum* but humanity's *terminus ad quem*: "God is not only our Benefactor, but our Founder; the Rivers come from the Sea, and they empty their Silver Streams into the Sea again." See Thomas Watson, "Man's Chief End to Glorifie God," in *The beatitudes: Or a discourse upon part of Christs famous sermon on the mount. . .* (London: Ralph Smith, 1660), 3.

191. Edwards, "Concerning the End," in *WJE* 8:467. Paul Ramsey notes this correspondence of the language of causality with the *exitus-reditus* idea in *WJE* 8:467n2. Of course, the development of this motif is not limited within the Eastern tradition; see Paul E. Rorem, "'Procession and Return' in Thomas Aquinas and His Predecessors," *Princeton Seminary Bulletin,* n.s., 13, no. 2 (1992): 147–63.

192. Edwards, "Miscellanies," no. 1142, in *WJE* 20:517.

193. Edwards, *WJE* 3:403.

194. Edwards, "Concerning the End," in *WJE* 8:535. Aquinas cannot be accused of a theology driven by Aristotelian ontology and rationalism, which provided the seedbed for Kantian agnosticism. Gunton sets up a straw man argument with claims like these: "The [negative, divine] attributes are those appropriate to a being who is the moving, efficient, material, formal and final cause of the cosmos." See Colin E. Gunton, *Act and Being: Towards a Theology of the Divine Attributes* (London: SCM, 2002), 52. For St. Thomas, besides efficient and final causation, the triune God is also the exemplary (as distinct from formal and certainly not material!) cause of matter.

195. "And if we proceed in the succession of existences till we come to the Supreme Being the other way, viz. to the end of the world—for though Proceeding thus from preceding to future

be according to a more common way of speaking descending, yet 'tis as truly ascending towards God as proceeding the other way, for God is the first and the last, the beginning and the end" (Edwards, "Miscellanies," no. 1263, in *WJE* 23:205–6). The return is the reverse motion of the procession viewed from the perspective of the creature. "Procession and reversion together constitute a single movement, the diastole-systole which is the life of the universe." See E. R. Dodds, *Proclus: The Elements of Theology*, rev. text with trans., intro., and commentary by E. R. Dodds (Oxford: Clarendon, 1963), 219. See also Adam G. Cooper, *The Body in St Maximus the Confessor: Holy Flesh, Wholly Deified* (Oxford: Oxford University Press, 2005), 81.

196. "God's providence . . . is . . . superior to the work of creation. . . . And that work of God's providence to which all other works of providence, both in the material and immaterial part of the creation, are subservient, is the work of redemption" (Edwards, "Miscellanies," no. 702, in *WJE* 18: 283–84). Stated differently, since "goodness is more excellent than creature greatness . . . therefore God is pleased to make goodness the end of greatness" (Edwards, "Miscellanies," no. 824, in WJE 18: 536). Elsewhere, "the work of redemption is the end and sum of all God's work: it was the end of the creation of the whole universe, and of all God's works of providence in it" (Edwards, "Miscellanies," no. 952, in *WJE* 20:220).

197. That Edwards assigns love and happiness/joy to the Spirit discounts Ramsey's interpretation that knowledge, love, and joy are distinctly appropriated to the three divine persons and that correspondingly "there is a threefoldness in the natural image (understanding, will, affections) as also in the spiritual image (knowledge of God, virtuous love or excellency, and joy or happiness)" (Ramsey, "Concerning the End," in *WJE* 8:529n4). Clearly, the Father has no *missio*, but is the divine person who sends the Word and Spirit in divine self-glorification.

198. "To rise above our selves and lose our selves in him by a total prefertion of self we must be enlightened inspired and animated by a superiour force continually descending upon us and investing us. As 'tis God alone that can enlighten us so 'tis he alone that can love himself in us. . . . But supernatural light and love their seeing God as he is and their loving him as he deserves are impressions that come from the immediate operation of the eternal Word and the holy Ghost" (Ramsay, *Principles* 1:309–15, as quoted by Edwards, "Miscellanies," no. 1254, in *WJE* 23:188–89).

199. Edwards, "Concerning the End," in *WJE* 8:531. "When God seeks his own glory, he does not so much endeavor after any thing without himself. . . . No: it is his own internal glory that he most loves, and the communication thereof which he seeks" (John Smith, *Excellency*, 112). Here, Edwards merely echoes John Smith's contention that the divine glory and human happiness meet when salvation is conceived in terms of participation in God. "I doubt we are too nice logicians sometimes, in distinguishing between the glory of God and our own salvation. . . . To love God above ourselves is not, indeed, so properly to love him above the salvation of our souls, as if these were distinct things; but it is to love him above all our sinful affections, and above our particular beings, and to conform ourselves to him. . . . And herein is God most glorified, and we made happy" (John Smith, *Excellency*, 114).

200. Ramsey, in Edwards, "Concerning the End," in *WJE* 8:532n1.

201. Edwards, "Concerning the End," in *WJE* 8:532.

202. Ibid., 531.

203. Ibid., 532.

204. Ibid., 531.

205. A reinterpretation of the Neoplatonic ontology of remaining (*mone*), procession (*proodos*), and return (*epistrophe*) (Dodds, *Proclus*, 38).

206. Edwards, "Miscellanies," no. 104, in *WJE* 13:273.

207. The union between Christ and the church, in some manner, reflects the eternal, mutual exchange of the Spirit of love between the Father and the Son since "the mutual joys between his bride and bridegroom are the end of creation" (Edwards, "Miscellanies," no. 271, in *WJE* 13:374).

208. "He is Christ, or the anointed, not only as he is anointed of God, but as he is anointed by the church, or by every believing soul, by the exercise of the grace of the Holy Spirit towards

him, and as it were pouring out his soul in divine love upon him, as Mary poured the precious ointment on Christ's head" (Edwards, "Blank Bible," note on Dan. 9:25, in *WJE* 24:768).

209. Edwards, 131. Sermon on 1 Pet. 1:8(a) (Jul 1757), in *WJE* 44.

210. According to Edwards, sincere love in general "is of a diffusive nature." In humans, it arises out of the natural principle of self-love, whereas divine love is a supernatural principle. In God, there is no such distinction. See Edwards, "Lecture VIII: The Spirit of Charity the Opposite of a Selfish Spirit," in *Charity and Its Fruits*, 172–74.

211. Edwards, "Lecture 1: Charity, or Love, the Sum of All Virtue," in *Charity and Its Fruits*, 2.

212. Edwards, "Miscellanies," no. 184, in *WJE* 13:330.

213. Edwards, "Miscellanies," no. 398, in *WJE* 13:463.

214. "But the Spirit that proceeds from the Father and the Son is the bond of union, as it is of all holy union between the Father and the Son, and between God and the creature, and between the creature among themselves" (Edwards, "Treatise on Grace," in *WJE* 21:186).

215. The Spirit is "the Divine essence being wholly poured out and flowing out in that infinitely intense, holy, and pure love and delight that continually and unchangeably breathes forth from the Father and Son, primarily towards each other, and secondarily towards the creature, and so flowing forth in a different subsistence or person in a manner to us utterly inexplicable and inconceivable, and that this is that person that is poured forth into the hearts of angels and saints" (Edwards, "Treatise on Grace," in *TG*, 63). Edwards would agree that it is most appropriate for the Spirit to be God's gift (*donum* or *datum*) since, as Ratzinger puts it, the Spirit "represents an opening to history and to man" (Ratzinger, "Holy Spirit as Communio," 330). The idea of the Spirit as the "surplus" of love between the Father and Son is seen in Walter Kasper's theology. See Gary D. Badcock, *Light of Truth and Fire of Love: A Theology of the Holy Spirit* (Grand Rapids, MI: Eerdmans, 1997), 158–59.

216. Edwards, "Miscellanies," no. 402, in *WJE* 13:466–67.

217. Edwards, "Lecture 1: Charity, or Love, the Sum of All Virtue," in *Charity and Its Fruits*, 19.

218. "The work of redemption, which the gospel declares unto us, above all things affords motives to love. . . . There is revealed how the Father and the Son are one in love, that we might be induced in like manner to be one with them, and with one another" (Edwards, "Charity and Its Fruits," Sermon 1, in *WJE* 8:144).

219. "And thus is the affair of our redemption ordered, that thereby we are brought to an immensely more exalted kind of union with God, an enjoyment of him, *both the Father and the Son*, than otherwise could have been. For Christ being united to the human nature, we have advantage for a free and full enjoyment of him, than we could have had if he had remained only in the divine nature. So, we being united to a divine person, as his members, can have a more intimate union and intercourse with the Father, who is only in the divine nature, than otherwise could be" (Edwards, "Excellency of Christ," in *Sermons*, 195–96).

220. What the Christian has in common with the Father and Son is the Holy Spirit, who is this "bond of perfectness"; as such, our relationship with God must necessarily include other believers because it is "in our partaking of the Holy Ghost that we have communion with the Father and Son and with Christians" (Edwards, "Miscellanies," no. 376, in *WJE* 13:448).

221. That is why Edwards could assert that happiness for both the Creator and the creature consists in communion and "the more perfect any creature is, the more strong this inclination" (Edwards, "Miscellanies," no. 96, in *WJE* 13:263–64).

222. As John of Damascus has argued, human beings are actually separated by spatial-temporal constraints and there can be no co-inherence; hence, their unity of essence is only a *distinctio ratio*. "For here indeed the subsistences do not exist one within the other . . . [and] dwell in one another but are separated." In relation to the Trinity, however, the case is "quite the reverse," for "there the community and unity are observed in fact." He goes to say that the divine persons are identical (and not similar) in essence and energy, and are factually or empirically

discerned. They are only distinct in persons, and this "difference" is recognized "by thought" (John of Damascus, *Orthodox Faith*, bk. 1, ch. 8, 10 [*NPNF* 9])

223. "Hence 'mission' [*missio*] and 'giving' [*datio*] have only a temporal significance in God; but 'generation' [*generatio*] and 'spiration' [*spiratio*] are exclusively eternal; whereas 'procession' [*processio*] and 'giving' [*exitus*], in God, have both an eternal and a temporal signification" (Aquinas, *STh* I, q. 43, a. 2).

224. Edwards, "Miscellanies," no. 1082, in *WJE* 20:466.

225. Edwards, "Miscellanies," no. 1151, in *WJE* 20:525.

226. Edwards, "Essay on the Trinity," in *TG*, 121. This proposition is a common theme running through the Puritan writings, influenced as it is by Augustinianism. "Now the highest faculties in man, are the *understanding* and *will; and their happiness consists in union with God, by knowledge and love." See William Bates, *The harmony of the divine attributes, in the contrivance and accomplishment of man's redemption by the Lord Jesus Christ* . . . (London: Nathaniel Ranew, Jonathan Robinson and Brabazon Aylmer, 1674), 10. William Bates (1625–1699) was a contemporary of Richard Baxter.

227. The "two ways of God's flowing forth and being communicated, that are the end of all things, are expressed, viz. manifesting God's name and communicating his love" (Edwards, "Miscellanies," no. 1084, in *WJE* 20:467).

228. Edwards, "Miscellanies," no. 1094, in *WJE* 20:483.

229. Edwards, "Miscellanies," no. 1142, in *WJE* 20:517.

230. Edwards, "Miscellanies," no. 1084, in *WJE* 20:467.

231. "So God glorifies himself toward the creatures also two ways: (1) by appearing to them, being manifested to their understandings; (2) in communicating himself to their hearts, and in their rejoicing and delighting in, and enjoying the manifestations which he makes of himself. They both of them may be called his glory in the more extensive sense of the word, viz. his shining forth, or the going forth of his excellency, beauty and essential glory *ad extra*. By one way it goes forth towards their understandings; by the other it goes forth towards their wills or hearts" (Edwards, "Miscellanies," no. 448, in *WJE* 13:495).

232. Edwards, "Discourse on the Trinity," in *WJE* 21:123.

233. Edwards, "Miscellanies," no. 1140, in *WJE* 20:517.

234. Edwards, "Miscellanies," no. 106, in *WJE* 13:277.

235. "The Holy Spirit seems to be called by the name of 'glory' in John 17:22" (Edwards, "Miscellanies," no. 1084, in *WJE* 20:467). "And here I might observe that the phrase 'the glory of God' is sometimes manifestly used to signify the second person in the Trinity" (Edwards, "Concerning the End," in *WJE* 8:513).

236. Edwards, "Miscellanies," no. 3, in *WJE* 13:200.

237. Edwards, "Lecture 1: Charity, or Love, the Sum of All Virtue," in *Charity and Its Fruits*, 21.

238. "The Holy Spirit is the harmony and excellency and beauty of the Deity, as we have shown; therefore 'twas his work to communicate beauty and harmony to the world, and so we read that it was he that moved upon the face of the waters [Gen. 1:2]" (Edwards, "Miscellanies," no. 293, in *WJE* 13:384).

239. Edwards, "On the Equality," in *WJE* 21:146.

240. Edwards, "Treatise on Grace," in *WJE* 21:188; "Miscellanies," no. 1151, in *WJE* 20:525.

241. Edwards, "Discourse on the Trinity," in *WJE* 21:134.

242. "As the supernatural light by which we know God is the emanation of the eternal Logos and a participation of that light by which he knows himself so the supernatural love by which we can love God is an emanation of the holy Ghost and a participation of that love by which he loves himself" (Edwards, "Miscellanies," no. 1254, in *WJE* 23:189).

243. Gilles Emery, *The Trinitarian Theology of Thomas Aquinas*, trans. Francesca A. Murphy (New York: Oxford University Press, 2007), 372–412. Aquinas took over this line of thought from Peter Lombard (*Sentences*, bk. 1, dist. 15, chs. 7–8; dist. 16, ch. 1; dist. 17, ch. 1). See Aquinas, *STh* I, q. 43, aa. 3–6.

244. "Or we see him in his Word, or voluntary signification of what is invisible in him, either internally speaking by impulses made on the mind, as in inspiration" (Edwards, "Miscellanies," no. 777, in *WJE* 18:429). There is an invisibility and mystery in relation to faith: "the nature and work of the received, he being a divine invisible Savior; the end for which he is received; the benefits, invisible; the ground on which he is received or closed with, the Word of God, invitations, promises; the circumstances of those things that are received, supernatural, incomprehensible, wonderful, difficult, unsearchable" (Edwards, "Faith," no. 89, in *WJE* 21:440). Faith involves "receiving a divine invisible Savior" (Edwards, "Faith," no. 92, in *WJE* 21:441)

245. "The new creature is a thing invisible, and no man knows what it is or can know but he that experiences it" (Edwards, "Saints Dwell Alone," in *WJE* 25:52).

246. In such occasions, there are intimations of the beatific vision. According to Edwards, "there are certain seasons in which this great Being, in some way or other invisible, comes to her and fills her mind with exceeding sweet delight, and that she hardly cares for anything, except to meditate on him—that she expects after a while to be received up where he is, to be raised up out of the world and caught up into heaven" (Edwards, *WJE* 4:68).

247. God "may be enjoyed in some measure now, viz., by the same knowledge begetting Likeness and Love, which will be answered with returns of Love." However, "this perfect freedom [is] never obtained till death," but when it is, it will be by "the same [means] by which it has obtained some likeness to, and fruition of, God in this world, viz., a clear manifestation of him" (Edwards, *WJE* 7:478). Thus, in "the Beatifical Vision of God, . . . the vision and fruition of God will be so intimate and clear as to transform the soul into the likeness of God" (Edwards, "The Value of Salvation," in *WJE* 10:324). According to Aquinas, "an end is possessed in two ways; perfectly and imperfectly. . . . Perfect enjoyment, therefore, is of the end already possessed: but imperfect enjoyment is also of the end possessed not really, but only in intention" (Aquinas, *STh* II-I, q. 11, a. 4).

248. Edwards, "Miscellanies," no. 702, in *WJE* 18:299.

249. Ibid.

250. Emery, *Trinitarian Theology of Thomas Aquinas*, 375. This again is a Franciscan inheritance. "Hence fruition seems to have relation to love, or to the delight which one has in realizing the longed-for term, which is the end" (Aquinas *STh* II-I, q. 11, a. 1).

251. Edwards, "Miscellanies," no. 1254, in *WJE* 23:188–89. "Just as the mode through which the Holy Spirit is referred to the Father is love, so the proper mode of reference of the Son to the Father is to be the Word who manifests him. And this is why, just as the Holy Spirit proceeds invisibly in the spirit through the gift of love, so likewise the Son [proceeds in the spirit] through the gift of wisdom, and this manifests the Father himself, the ultimate end to which we return" (Aquinas, I *Sent.* d. 15, q. 4, a. 1, as quoted in Emery, *Trinitarian Theology of Thomas Aquinas*, 376).

252. Edwards, "Miscellanies," no. 1218, in *WJE* 23:153.

253. "This one supreme end consists in two things, viz. in God's infinite perfection being exerted and so manifested, that is in God's glorifying himself, and second, his infinite happiness being communicated, and so making the creature happy" (Edwards, "Miscellanies," no. 1066, in *WJE* 20:446).

254. Edwards, "Miscellanies," no. 301, in *WJE* 13:387. Similarly, Irenaeus conceived of the *imago* as a tripartite union of "flesh, soul, and Spirit." The Fall is seen as a rejection of the Spirit of God, which resulted in the loss of freedom and participation in the divine life. Humankind, therefore, degenerated into a bestial condition. John Meyendorff, "Humanity: 'Old' and 'New'—Anthropological Considerations," in *Salvation in Christ: A Lutheran-Orthodox Dialogue*, ed. John Meyendorff and Robert Tobias (Minneapolis: Augsburg, 1992), 60.

255. "And whenever the Scripture speaks of the Spirit of God's dwelling in us, or our being filled with the Spirit, it will signify much the same thing if it be said, a divine temper or disposition dwells in us or fills us. Now the temper and disposition or affection of God is no other than infinite love" (Edwards, "Miscellanies," no. 396, in *WJE* 13:462). "But seeing spiritual beauty consists principally in virtue and holiness, and there is so little of this beauty to be seen now . . . on earth . . . we may certainly conclude that there has been a great fall and defection" (Edwards, "Miscellanies," no. 186, in *WJE* 13:330). See also, Edwards, "Miscellanies," no. 107(a), in *WJE* 13:277.

256. Edwards, "Lecture VIII: The Spirit of Charity the Opposite of a Selfish Spirit," in *Charity and Its Fruits*, 157. "And whenever the Scripture speaks of the Spirit of God's dwelling in us, or our being filled with the Spirit, it will signify much the same thing if it be said, a divine temper or disposition dwells in us or fills us. Now the temper and disposition or affection of God is no other than infinite love" (Edwards, "Miscellanies," no. 396, in *WJE* 13:462).

257. Edwards, *WJE* 2:256.

258. "Hence 'tis absolutely false, that there ever was, or can be a state of pure nature, wherein souls by their own inherent force could love God as he deserves, without any supernatural grace or immediate influence of the Holy Ghost: as it is impossible that there can be any state of pure nature wherein the soul can know God as he is, without any supernatural illumination or irradiation of the eternal Word. Men indeed may acquire by a successive comparison of their ideas a natural knowledge of God, but not the supernatural knowledge and love we are speaking of. If this were otherwise, the soul might beget within itself the eternal Logos, and the Holy Ghost; be its own light, and its own love; its own perfection, and its own happiness" (Ramsay, *Principles*, vol. 1, 309–15, as cited in Edwards, "Miscellanies," no. 1254, in *WJE* 23:189).

3

Trinitarian Action and Communication in Redemption and the Incarnation

The entry of sin into the world does not annul the œconomical purpose of God to communicate the Trinitarian fullness. But it does mean that the way to the end has to be modified through another eternal determination—the covenant of redemption. In this chapter, we shall look at how a consistent trinitarianism underlies Edwards's understanding of the *pactum salutis*, whereby God elects to redeem the church through the incarnation.

> Again it shows how much God designed to communicate himself to men, that he so communicated himself to the first and chief of elect men, the elder brother and the head and representative of the rest, even so that this man should be the same person with one of the persons of the Trinity. It seems by this to have been God's design to admit man as it were to the inmost fellowship with the deity.[1]

Ultimately, human participation in God is only arrived at through the Son's participation in human nature—a work that is carried out by the entire Trinity.

COVENANT OF REDEMPTION

As we have examined previously, the divine persons eternally order their operations *ad extra* in the œconomical Trinity toward the goal of expressing God's self-communicative nature. The *pactum salutis* determines the method and means to that end.[2] Included in this chosen means toward divine self-communication is the restoration of fallen humanity.[3] The *pactum salutis* is a temporary, though preeminent, agreement between the Father and Son in which the latter agrees to a new kind of subordination to the former.[4]

HEAD OF THE TRINITY: THE FATHER'S PREROGATIVE OF COMMAND

For Edwards, the covenant of redemption is logically posterior to the œconomical Trinity.[5] The Father must assume headship in the œconomical Trinity by mutual election before being able to personally appoint a Mediator in the *pactum salutis*.[6] Unlike the Trinitarian œconomy, then, the roles of the divine persons in determining the work of salvation cannot be by mutual election.[7] Why is this the case?

Since Edwards denies ontological subordinationism, a distinction between the economic and immanent trinities must be secured. A separate *pactum* is thus necessary since the incarnation involves the subjection of the Son to the Father far below the "œconomical station."[8] What is necessary to being the second divine person—the *proprietas personales* as the Son—must not be conflated with the second person's contingent election as Mediator.[9] But Edwards knows enough not to posit a simple contrast between an egalitarian ontology and a hierarchical perfomativity. To obtain a distinction-in-identity between the nature and work of the Trinity, a necessary, ontological *taxis* must be distinguished from a functional subservience by will.[10] As Edwards himself phrases it, "subordination is a very different thing from subjection."[11]

Although the Father, as the head of the œconomical Trinity, is naturally the *auctor* of this redemptive covenant, the Son voluntarily becomes subject to the Father by becoming incarnate.[12] Though their modes of action differ, inasmuch as it is the Father who appoints and the Son who is sent, this eternal covenanting is equally willed by both.[13] Being endowed with the "authority of the Godhead" through the œconomical Trinity, the Father "not only is higher in authority than [the other persons], but [their offices derive] all [their efficacy from him]" in the *pactum salutis*.[14] Strictly speaking, only the Son and Spirit are sent or have "offices" assigned by the Father in the redemptive economy.[15] But in a more general sense, all the persons may be considered to have "distinct offices" insofar as each one has a particular mode of operation in the work of redemption.[16] The modes and chronology of action stipulated in the *pactum salutis* are based on the antecedent œconomy of the Trinity, and both flow from the primal *taxis* of origination: Father, Son, and Spirit.[17]

Here, Edwards could affirm that the most glorious communication and manifestation of God's love to humanity was the Father's donation of Christ *pro nobis*.[18] It is also from God that we can have true virtue by the Holy Spirit, who, though eternally proceeding from and temporally sent by the Father, is the principle of grace.[19] Thus, it is from God the Father, who sends the Son and the Spirit as the mediator and the agent of salvation, respectively, that true participation in the divine life is made possible for the saints. All of Christ's benefits and the holiness we have are of the Father's grace, and every internal increase in holy disposition and each outworking of grace are dependent of the power that is of God the Father.[20] From the Father, the fountain and author of salvation, we receive all the benefits that Christ purchased. What is the character of Christ's mediatorship as defined by the *pactum salutis*?

<h3 style="text-align:center">ROLE OF THE MEDIATOR: PERMANENT OR TEMPORARY?</h3>

The role of mediator undertaken by the Son in the covenant of redemption involves his incarnation. However, the meritorious character of Christ's obedience comes about as the result of this covenant to be the mediator; it does not follow from the assumption of human nature per se. In this, Edwards distinguishes two kinds of contingent obedience in Christ. The first of these is an obedience that is "natural" to an incarnate Son in relation to a Father. This lies in the realm of *conveniens* and is a human expression of the eternal relation of Son to Father.[21] The second kind is a creaturely subjection to God's "commanding and legislative authority" as lawgiver and judge.[22] It is only in the latter that the Son covenanted with the Father to become "God's servant," thus meriting the reward of salvation *pro nobis*.[23] Strictly speaking then, the covenant of redemption is required in order for the "humiliation" of a mediator, "wherein he descends below the infinite glory of a divine person."[24] On this account, Christ's mediation before and after the incarnation is not supererogatory.[25]

The young Edwards, like Calvin, seem to regard the mediatorial role of Christ as a merely temporary affair to be ceded at the Parousia.[26] In his later writings, however, Edwards clarifies his position by insisting that "Christ's mediatorial kingdom never will be delivered up to the Father."[27] Like Owen, he wants to stress God's communication with the saints through Christ's human nature—this mediation is everlasting and permanent.[28] Here, he makes a distinction between the "representative kingdom" and "mediatorial kingdom" of the incarnate Son.[29] This is the "twofold dominion," in which the Son was invested through the covenant: "one vicarious, or as the Father's vicegerent, which shall be resigned at the end of the world; the other as Christ God-man, and head and husband of the church."[30]

While the œconomical *taxis* has an aesthetic and necessary correspondence to the ontological *taxis*, the roles of the divine persons in the covenant of redemption do not corroborate with the *proprietas personales*.[31] In addition to the usual way of considering appropriations, the Puritans advanced a novel interpretation whereby a temporary, dispensational office is attributed to a particular person of the Trinity as a result of the *pactum salutis*.[32] Here, then, it is the incarnate Son who takes over the title of Lord, which should, by appropriation, be the Father's.[33] Christ's temporary appropriation of the Father's authoritative office was "to put him under greater advantages to obtain the success of his labors and sufferings in the work of redemption."[34]

For Edwards, what would be terminated at the end of time is the representative kingdom of Christ, in which he acts as the Father's vicegerent, that is, in the Father's œconomical office as "lawgiver and judge."[35] Evidently, Christ's vicegeral role as God incarnate corresponds with Christ's character as the image of the Father, mirrored in a lesser way by human beings.[36] In accordance to the immanent and œconomical Trinitarian *taxeis*, Christ's representative economy could not be eternal since "that would amount to an overthrowing of the economy of the persons of the Trinity."[37] There will, however, only be a circumstantial change to Christ's mediatorial role in eternity, insofar as this includes the cessation of certain modalities of the *munus triplex*, especially as he is the *Christus Victor*.[38] In accordance with the œconomical Trinity, Christ will be "a middle person between the Father and the saints to all eternity, and as the bond of union with the Father, and of derivation from him, and all manner of communication and intercourse with the Father."[39]

In the end, the church's communion with both the Father and Son will be enhanced. No longer having to stand for the "Father's awful majesty" as appointed representative, ruler, and judge, the saints' enjoyment of Christ, the God-man, would be more intimate, as he will appear purely as "husband to his church," and the divine awe "shall be as it were laid aside, and be swallowed up in the gentleness and sweetness of the conjugal head."[40] The distinction here is between Christ's humiliation or "work under the Father" and his subsequent exaltation or "enjoyment of the Father," whereby "the state of reward is more glorious than a state of work."[41] As "the man Christ Jesus" is first perfected in beauty, happiness, and enjoyment of the Father, so the church shall participate in the divine glory as members of the *totus Christus*. The saints' communion with the Father "as the fountain of the deity" shall be closer since "Christ God-man shall now no longer be instead of the Father to them." They pass, so to speak, from diplomatic relations into an organic union with God through Christ—their "head" and organ of relish of the Father, so that "God will be all."[42]

A BIPERSONAL PACTUM SALUTIS: WHAT IS THE SPIRIT'S ROLE?

In becoming both the Father's vicegerent and God-man, Christ also acquires a double authority over the Spirit, one permanent and the other temporary.[43]

Christ's authority over the Spirit as cosmic sovereign and vicegerent will cease at the end of the redemptive economy.[44] In returning this borrowed appropriation to the Father at the Parousia, Christ also cedes the right to "the disposal" of the Father's "own divine infinite treasure, to dispense of it as he pleased to the redeemed," which had been received during the ascension.[45] In tandem with the perpetuity of the incarnation, however, the Spirit's subordination to the "husband and vital head of the Church" will continue eternally.[46]

Since the Holy Spirit is eternally received by the Son from the Father—a privilege that the Father rightfully exercises as Head of the Trinity, the Spirit's twofold subjection to Christ in the redemptive economy is only "circumstantially new."[47] As no additional kenosis is imposed upon the Spirit's person and work, there is no need to enter into a new covenant with the Father. The *pactum salutis*, though mutually consented to by the entire Trinity, is properly a bilateral pact between the Father and Son.[48] Now, if that is the case, what role is left for the Spirit within the *pactum salutis*?[49]

Here, the Augustinian mutual-love model of the Trinity comes to the fore. Being the *vinculum amoris* between Father and Son, the Holy Spirit "is the bond of union between the two covenanting persons."[50] Besides noting this unitive function, Edwards also correlates the Spirit's economic role to the Spirit's position in the *taxis* of origination. As the communicated fullness of God and "end of all procession," the Spirit "is the great good covenanted for, and the end of the covenant."[51] As outworked in the redemptive economy, the Spirit is the goal of the Father's electing as well as the Son's atoning work.[52]

On such an account, it may be said that Edwards's trinitarianism is not pneumatocentric but rather pneumatotelic.[53] Hence, this needs neither to compete with nor to supplant his christocentrism. Despite this laudable and consistent characterization of the Spirit as the unifying and telic principle, one may wonder whether Edwards accords any active role to the Holy Spirit within the *pactum salutis*.

By tapping into the Augustinian-Thomist tradition, Edwards capitalizes on the dynamic, volitional, and operative dimensions within the psychological analogy to counter a purely acquiescent pneumatology. In line with the Reformed tradition, Edwards insists that divine love was the moving cause of salvation, only to recast it on Trinitarian grounds.[54] At once pure act and subsistent operation *ad intra*, the Holy Spirit is suitably the "the internal spring" or immanent energy of the covenanting persons.[55] Here, the Father—as the "first mover"—is to be clearly distinguished from the Holy Spirit, who is "the love of the Father as its first spring."[56] Moreover, as the divine willpower who "wholly influences both the Father and the Son in all they do," the Holy Spirit exercises an elective preference and is thus the "moving cause" of the entire covenant.[57] As we have noted in the previous chapter, this is consistent with Edwards's characterization of the Spirit as the moving cause of creation and its end. In the redemptive economy, the "dying love of Christ" is thus "the internal moving cause" of the Son's sacrificial atonement.[58] As the moving cause and the aesthetic principle of the Godhead, the Holy Spirit is the art and beauty of the whole economy of salvation.[59] And this divine *oikonomia* of redemption is the motif we will now examine.

EX PATRE, PER FILIUM, IN SPIRITU SANCTI

Edwards characterizes the undivided activity of the Trinity in history as a reflection of the eternal *taxis* of origination—from the Father, through the Son, in the Holy Spirit.[60] His affirmation of Augustine's *filioque* as an ontological *per filium* allows him to maintain a consonance between the triune processions *ad intra* and redemptive operations *ad extra*.[61]

Notwithstanding such an ordering, Edwards states that no one person in the Trinity can be attributed "the greatest share" in the economy of redemption as "it's all from every one of them."[62] Using commercial language, "God the Father is the person of whom the purchase is made; God the Son is the person who makes the purchase, and the Holy Spirit is the gift purchased."[63] The atonement is therefore a Trinitarian work, where the Son, by self-giving, has bought our *summum bonum*—the Holy Spirit—from the Father. Elaborating on this elsewhere, Edwards describes the Father as the supplier of the client, cost, and commodity; the Son as the client and cost; and the Spirit as the commodity.[64]

In perfect correlation to the order of subsistence within the Trinity *ad intra*, the Father is "the cause and original" of all the saints' goodness; the Son "the medium"; and the Spirit "that good itself that is given and conveyed" in the work of redemption.[65] All the benefits of salvation come from the Father, through the Son, and in the Holy Spirit.[66] God is sovereign because every mode of salvific economy belongs to the Trinity: "We have all of God the Father through the Son and in the Holy Ghost, so that God is the Alpha and the Omega in this affair of redemption."[67]

As God the Father, Son, and Spirit are respectively the origin, medium, and completion of this redemptive work, the success of the entire endeavor is dependent on the effectiveness of each person's particular activity.[68] This is so that our worship of them is equal and that our dependence may be on the

Father, Son, and Spirit absolutely, with regard to the respective operation of each in the economy of salvation, both historically and existentially.[69] Not only does the believer rely on the Trinity in every *way* for her salvation, she depends on God for every *thing* in the gracious life. A person's being and well-being is *ad Patre, per Filium in Spiritu Sancti*.[70] Though every good comes from the Trinity, various roles in the economy and spiritual blessings given to the saints may be appropriated to the distinct persons according to their *proprietas personales* and *taxis*.[71] "Our having all *of* God, shows the fullness of his power and grace: our having all *through* him, shows the fullness of his merit and worthiness; and our having all *in* him demonstrates his fullness of beauty, love and happiness."[72] And while it is the Holy Spirit "by whom [the redeemed] nextly and most immediately have all spiritual blessings," the saints have all spiritual virtue and affections from the Father and through the Son. Edwards could claim that if one sought after the Spirit of charity in opposition to a self-seeking spirit, one would possess all things since "God himself will be yours, and Christ yours and the Holy Spirit yours."[73]

Not only is divine grace extended to sinners through the "monarchical" Trinitarian movement—from the Father, through the Son, in the Holy Spirit—all "their desires, their prayers and praises, their love, their trust and their obedience is offered to God [the Father] through Christ Mediator" in the reverse, "epicletic" Trinitarian dynamic "from the actings of the Holy Spirit in them."[74] The saint is led by the Spirit through the Son to know and love the Father.[75] In other words, in both the *exitus et reditus* movement of redemption, Christ is the medium of our salvation.

MEDIATION OF CHRIST

As the middle divine person between the Father and Spirit, there is fitness to Christ's mediating function in the economy between the Father and sinners, or "the Holy Ghost in them." Since the Father enjoyment's of the Spirit *ad intra* is through the Son (*per filium*), Christ is appropriately the "means or middle person by which holiness and happiness is purchased for them from the Father."[76] Christ acts as both the buyer and cost of our redemptive good—the *summum bonum* (Spirit), which is purchased from the seller (Father).[77] In this economic "transaction" between God and sinful humanity, Christ is both the Mediator "for them and from them with the Father": this is the emanation and remanation of divine good.

The economic role of the Son as the mediator of salvation and grace corresponds to the Son's position within the taxonomical ordering of the divine persons *ad intra*. "And it seems that the communication between God and the Church from the beginning of the world has not been immediate but through the Son."[78] The invisible church, "however small and obscure," already existed before the incarnation, yet not without the mediation of Christ: "And although it was long before Christ appeared in the world, yet all the benefits which they received were to receive were through him."[79] As Adam "was but a type of Christ, the second Adam," so the happiness procured in redemption transcends original happiness, "as antitypes are wont to exceed types."[80]

Edwards considers Christ's earthly history preresurrection as representing the greatest work done for the purchase of salvation.[81] In his mediatorial character as humanity's representative, Christ imparted to redeemed humanity all excellency in taking the suffering they deserved.[82] By Christ's suffering, satisfaction for our sin and freedom are obtained, and by Christ's obedience, happiness for us is merited.[83] Christ's death, by virtue of its holiness, "merited positive blessings" for humanity because of the infinitely holy love Christ had toward God, in protecting God's majesty and in obeying.[84] The Son did not satisfy the Father's wrath; rather, the awful and just glory of God was satisfied by the atoning punishment of Christ.[85]

What was the price that Christ paid in exchange for the Holy Spirit *pro nobis*? It was none other than death in the incarnation, that is, by "offering up of the flesh or human nature of Christ, all divine blessings are procured."[86] This is the basis of our vital union with Christ. Through Christ, we have all excellent, perfective, and satisfying spiritual blessings as "honey from the Rock."[87] The procession of the Holy Spirit *per filium* within the immanent Trinity is echoed temporally by the giving of the Spirit to the redeemed through Christ's economy. "The love of God the Father flows out toward Christ the head, and to all the members *through* him, in whom they were beloved before the foundation of the world, and in whom the Father's love was expressed toward them in time, by his death and sufferings, and is now fully manifested in heaven."[88]

Thus, it is through the Son that we are given the Spirit for sanctification and renovation after God's image.[89] The office of the Spirit in the work of redemption, in this Puritan schema, is primarily that of the agent or messenger of Christ.[90] By identifying the Spirit christologically, Edwards maintains the Reformed emphasis of the unity of Word and Spirit, thus affirming the christocentric nature of the work of redemption, "that Christ may be a complete savior."[91] As such, the eternal Love of the Father toward the Son, which is the foundation and end of God's love toward the saints, is historically mediated to them through Christ: "The love of God the Father flows out toward Christ the head, and to all the members *through* him, in whom they were beloved before the foundation of the world, and in whom the Father's love was expressed toward them in time, by his death and sufferings, and it is now fully manifested in heaven."[92]

In the end, there is but one work of God revealed in redemption: "'Tis all one scheme, one contrivance; and that is the scheme, contrivance and work of glorifying himself and his Son Jesus Christ, and gathering and uniting his creatures to himself, and making them happy in himself through Christ God-man by means of that glorious redemption that he has wrought out."[93] In this scheme of redemption, is the incarnation of the Son something necessary or accidental?

NECESSITY OR CONTINGENCY: THE FITNESS OF THE INCARNATION TO GOD THE SON

Thomas Aquinas thought that any, and even several, of the divine persons could have assumed one (or more) human nature(s) because of their indivisible and common essence, power, and operation.[94] Likewise, the medieval theologians insisted that God *de potentia absoluta* could have chosen various forms of assumption, even of irrational objects.[95] For Aquinas, the temporal sonship does not correlate with the eternal generation; any of the divine persons could become a human son. Any divine person could become incarnate (because of its contingency), but the logic of procession will determine the mission character of the enfleshment.[96] An incarnation of the Father would not constitute a mission, since he is unoriginate, and an incarnate Spirit would not be able to send the Son thereafter, since the Spirit completes the divine *taxis*.[97]

Affirming the correspondence principle, Puritan theologians, echoing John of Damascus, argued that it is the *proprietas personale* that determines who among the Trinitarian persons should be incarnate. Only the Son of God could properly be Son of Man without "losing the individuality of Sonship." [98] As Perkins put it different, only the Son could be incarnate as there cannot be more than one Son in the Trinity.[99]

On Thomist grounds, however, it is possible to argue that the *potentia absoluta* does not make the incarnation entirely arbitrary. Aquinas himself laid out aesthetic reasons for why the Son and not any other divine person actually became incarnate.[100] From Thomas's own writings, one might infer that it was solely the Son who could share the property of sonship or "filiability" to the Son's own humanity since this belongs properly to the Son and cannot be communicated to another person.[101]

Just as essentialism is not opposed to personalism, the Son's incarnation is both an act of divine power and is ordered. In light of this, Edwards adheres to the correspondence principle found in the Puritans while contending for a beautiful harmony in the Son's incarnation. This, of course, is based on his theological aesthetics.

THEOLOGICAL AESTHETICS: THE FITTINGNESS OF REALITY AND THE MEDIATOR

While beauty is a key theme in Edwards's theology, it is grounded in the more basic category of existence—not abstractly, but in the concrete reality of the Trinity.[102] For Edwards, the Trinity of Father, Son, and Spirit—"the supreme Harmony of all"—is the ontological foundation not only of all beauty but also of goodness and truth.[103]

Since beauty is a key theme in Edwards's theology, it is unsurprising that the Thomistic notion of "fittingness" or *convenientia* runs through his entire corpus.[104] As an aesthetic concept, the language of "fittingness" steers the *via media* between the purely necessary and the capricious.[105] Since there exists a "manifest analogy" between the soul's essence and the "nature of other things," Edwards uses "consent" as another manner of expressing "analogy": secondary beauty is but an analogue of primary beauty.[106] Evidently, his notion of *proportio* is similar to the medieval analogy of proportionality.[107]

God's glorious self-communication *ad extra* is a fitting reflection, in all its parts, of the internal goodness within God.[108] This unity of will within the divine society in this œconomical *taxis* toward diffusive self-communication arises from an ontological, aesthetic relationality in the Trinity. Though the order of acting "necessarily" flows from their order of subsistence, the divine persons are not coerced but freely agree on this beautiful order.[109] They freely embrace the *taxis* because of its irresistible beauty, as "they all naturally delight in what is in itself, fit, suitable and beautiful."[110] Hence, Edwards's use of the medieval grammar of *convenientia* is clearly evident: God's freedom is not capricious, but ordered, even in relation to the divine being and action.[111]

For Edwards, the complexity and beauty of the whole divine *oikonomia*, and the relation among its parts, points to a mutuality between divine freedom and fittingness, which otherwise would have been set aside were it based on God's *potentia absoluta*.[112] This idea links Edwards's thinking on primary (moral) and secondary (natural) beauty: the "most perfect exactness of proportion, harmony, equity and beauty" of nature's laws points to the "most strict and perfect justice in proportion and fitness" of God's moral laws.[113] There is an aesthetic harmony to God's primary, moral order just as (and much more so than) in the natural laws.[114] For Edwards, there is no contrariety or gap between the harmony of the *oikonomia* and God's freedom.[115] This idea runs from the cosmic right down to the personal insofar as God sees a "natural fitness" between a person's free acceptance of Christ and her actual union with Christ.[116] He thinks that had salvation depended on mere divine omnipotence or a "sovereignty" without "propriety," the Mediator and *oikonomia* would have been unnecessary.[117] How does Edwards apply the idea of *conveniens* to the incarnation of the Son?

MEDIATOR AS THE "MIDDLE PERSON" BETWEEN OTHER PERSONS

Using the psychological analogy, Edwards correlates the prophetic office of Christ with the person of the Logos. The Son thus fittingly takes on the role of "the great prophet and teacher of mankind, the light of the world and the revealer of God."[118] From the perspective of the taxonomy of processions, Christ stands as the "middle person" between the Father and Spirit, through which the Father has a telos and happiness.

Christ is the "middle person" not only between the Father and Spirit, but also between God and humanity; hence, Christ is fit to be the Mediator.[119] By middle person or mediator, Edwards does not mean a mere legal agent for one party, but rather a reconciler of two estranged parties.[120] Here, he stands within the Puritan tradition in which the incarnation may be seen as a sort of "middle union."[121] The Son, and neither the Father nor the Spirit, should be the Mediator, as the Father is the head of the Trinity and the Son is, in a sense, a mediator between the Father and Spirit in the divine–human relationship.[122] By *convenientia*, it is more consistent with their ontological and œconomical *taxeis* that that the Son should be functionally subordinated to the Father, and so incarnated.[123] By appropriation, the Son is suitably titled Redeemer.[124]

For Edwards, the names Christ, Anointed, and Mediator indicate the incarnational union mediated by the Spirit.[125] In the *pactum salutis*, there is the atonement already in anticipation just as Christ is eternally united to human nature as Logos *incarnandus*.[126] The beauty, excellence, and "worthiness" of Christ's divinity was itself the ground of Christ's election, while the divine freedom was the ground of Christ's human "worthiness."[127] The Son, as Creator and the prototype of creation, has a "natural inclination" to share happiness with humanity and is the divine person most suitable to be "the redeemer of men" and head of the church.[128]

In line with patristic thought, then, Edwards affirms that the Old Testament theophanies and appearances of the "angel of the Lord" to the "church of Israel" were christophanies.[129] As the "same person" with the coming Messiah, the preincarnate Son "used to appear in a human shape" and was God's very immanence to the Old Testament "church."[130] This was their immanent Head and Savior "dwelling with them on earth," who had "united himself to them in the strictest union" to be their "Mediator with God [the Father] in heaven."[131]

The mission of the Son *ad extra* corresponds to Christ's position in the ontological *taxis*. Accordingly, it is the "middle person of the Trinity" who should properly be the mediator between Father and the elect because the Son is "the intermediate between the Spirit and the Father" *ad intra*. In the redemptive economy, all transactions occur between the Father and the Spirit, who indwells the saints *per filium*. On the one hand, all goodness and grace that the saints have are "from the Father through the Son" and "terminates in the Spirit." On the other hand, it is "the Spirit in them that puts forth acts of faith in God," prays and praises "through a mediator."[132] Besides the role that *conveniens* plays in Edwards's musings on the incarnation, does he relate the Son's *proprium* to the role *ad extra*?

Event of the Incarnation: Common and Personal Modes of Operation

In this regard, how did Edwards's predecessors distinguish between the properties (*proprietas*) that are peculiar to the divine persons and the divine operations (*energeia*) that are held in common due to the identity of essence?[133] The Reformed-Puritan tradition generally followed Aquinas in this matter. While the act of uniting was seen as efficiently caused of the Trinity, peculiar modes of operations were assigned to the Father, Son, and Spirit, respectively: *auctoritas*, *assumptio*, and *conceptio*.[134] In the following subsection, we examine in detail the distinction between *unitio* and *assumptio*.

Is There a Distinction between the Common Act of Uniting and the Personal Act of Assuming?

Aquinas made a distinction between union and assumption: the Father and the Spirit unite the human nature to the Son, but they do not assume one themselves.[135] In other words, the *assumptio carnis* is a personal act.[136] In another place, however, he allowed the act of assumption to be also attributed to the divine nature, since person and essence in God are not really distinct.[137] Clearly, in Aquinas, the Augustinian *opera trinitatis ad extra sunt indivisa* stood in some tension with the Aristotelian *actiones sunt suppositorum*.[138] Now, if both assumption and unition are efficiently caused, this would imply that they are common, external divine operations.[139] How, then, is assumption proper to the Son alone and not just an appropriation?

CHRIST AS PRINCIPLE *AD EXTRA* AND TERM *AD INTRA* OF THE INCARNATION: AGAINST PROPRIETY AND IMPLICITLY NESTORIAN?

The resolution may be obtained through two related moves. Firstly, "the act of assuming" common to the Trinity is distinguished from "the term of assumption," which is proper to the Son alone.[140] Since only the Son is *both* the principle and term, assumption is thus properly attributed to the Son.[141] Secondly, while the incarnation is an act of efficient causality on the human nature *ad extra*, and therefore an *opera trinitatis*, it also ushers in a relation *ad intra* that is proper to the Son.[142] As a common divine operation, the act of assumption effects the union of an external nature to the Son, which results in an internal relation (of union) between the two natures, which is only proper to the Son.

However, this introduces another difficulty. If "principle" and "term" denote action and passion, respectively, the divine Logos, on Edwards's premise of a *creatio continua*, would be perpetually acting upon a passive human nature in the *unio hypostatica*.[143] On the temporal plane, the human Jesus would be continually created by the Spirit and repeatedly assumed by the Son. On this account, the Son qua God is an agent, but qua human is a patient.[144] In effect, the assumption resolves into a transitive action between the natures. Not only would this divide the person, the Son's temporal generation would not correspond to the eternal generation, whereby the Son's person is in a mode of passivity (in relation to the Father). In this construal of the incarnation, the Son would be both active and passive in se.

On Edwards's insistence on a *creatio continua* and the strict correspondence between *theologia* and *oikonomia*, the classical Christology he inherits must be modified. It is to this Christology reconstructed on Trinitarian grounds that we shall now turn.

EDWARDS'S TRINITARIAN DOCTRINE OF THE *ASSUMPTIO CARNIS*: THE BROAD OUTLINES

Without departing from the classical two-nature Christology, Edwards emphasizes a new relation inaugurated between God the Father and Jesus Christ in the incarnation. "The man Christ is united to the Logos these two ways: first, by the respect which God [the Father] hath to this human nature.

. . . And secondly, by what is inherent in this man, whereby he becomes one person."[145] The Logos-Jesus unity and Jesus-Father relation, in turn, are built upon a Spirit Christology in which the Father "incarnated him [the Son] by sanctification."[146] Edwards thus reintegrates the Father and Spirit into his christological thinking.

Clearly, there is no time gap between the sanctification of this human nature, its unity with the Son, and its participatory relation with the Father. But there is an order of nature and thought here. The habitation of Christ's human nature by the Holy Spirit causes the personal union by which the Father treats Jesus Christ as Son (see table 1.1).[147] Hence, "the Spirit of the Logos may dwell in a creature after such a manner, that that creature may become one person [with the Logos], and may be looked upon as such and accepted as such."[148] And for this human nature to enter in such relations with the Spirit, Son, and Father, that logically basic moment when this particular flesh comes into existence must first occur.

THE VIRGINAL CONCEPTION OF CHRIST BY THE FATHER'S SPIRIT

In patristic and medieval theology, the conception of Christ's human nature was regarded as a work of efficient causation *ad extra* and, hence, a common work of the Trinity.[149] However, the *conceptio* is specially appropriated to the Holy Spirit, in continuity with Scripture and tradition.[150] Edwards both continues and modifies this venerable tradition.

FATHER AS PRIMARY AGENT OF THE CONCEPTION OF CHRIST'S HUMAN NATURE

Although the Trinity is the *principium* of all creation, Edwards nuances the Augustinian axiom of *opera indivisa* to reflect the relations among the divine persons in their action *ad extra*.[151] The Father, as *principium* of the Son in the *actus personales*, fittingly acts as the aboriginal agent of the Son's generation in time. The Holy Spirit is the immediate agent of all created entities in accord with the Spirit's position as the *terminus* of the divine processions. However, the Son is the primary agent of all of creation except the Son's own human nature; the latter is appropriated to the Father.[152] "All universally are by the Spirit, but the human nature of Christ and what belongs to it is by the Spirit as the Spirit of the Father; but all the rest are by the Spirit as the Spirit of the Son."[153]

Respecting the unity of Christ's person, Edwards rejects the notion that the Son directly created Christ's own self in the incarnation.[154] In light of *creatio continua*, the *hypostatic union* is therefore a continuous assumption or act of unition, and, as such, the Son cannot be actively self-creating. This direct role of creating and sustaining the assumed human nature belongs to the Spirit.[155]

Nonetheless, although the creation of Christ's human nature was not an act of the Son, by virtue of the *opera indivisa* the Son both consented to and participated in Christ's *conceptio*.[156] What distinguishes the Holy Spirit as the Spirit of the Father from the Holy Spirit as the Spirit of the Son seems to be the fact that it is the Father's prerogative to possess the divine power of conception.[157] Since the Father conceives the Word in Love or Spirit, so it must be the Spirit of the Father who effects the *conceptio* "for it is the office of love to beget; generation is the work of love."[158] In fact, the human Jesus is denominated the Son of God by virtue of the Spirit being communicated.[159] The Spirit of the Father is therefore the prevenient grace of union.[160]

Contrary to Rahner, then, Edwards views the mode of incarnation—that is to say, the manner of origination—and not just the incarnation per se, as identity-constituting.[161] The virgin birth is thus crucial to the identity of the incarnate person as the absence of an earthly father reveals the eternal generation of the Son from the Father.[162]

EX PATRE: THE FATHER'S OBJECTIVE, TRANSITIVE ACTION UPON THE INCARNATE SON

Being the primary agent of the *conceptio* and in corresponding fashion, the Father continues to operate transitively and efficiently upon Jesus' entire historical existence. "All the works of God ad extra are wrought by Christ, excepting those that are immediately wrought upon or about Christ, or in which Christ himself is the effect or object, and these are more immediately from God the Father."[163] As the Father is the *principium sine principium ad intra*, so he is the primary agent of external acts of God upon the incarnate Son, beginning from Christ's conception.

Edwards emphasizes the Son's personhood as receptive and relational. Here, he does not emphasize the "in itself" dimension of personhood—that is, interiority and self-possession.[164] On this point, Edwards stands at the other end from Goodwin, who argued that the right of communicating "personality" to the assumed humanity belonged to the Son "for it is properly his own to bestow."[165] If the eternal Son derives subsistence and essence from the Father *ad intra*, it only makes sense that the Son should receive his reality as the incarnate Son from the Father. *Per conveniens*, Edwards therefore proposes a qualifying axiom: "It is meet that as the person [of the Son] is from the Father, so everything appertaining to him should be from the Father."[166]

As both *Logos asarkos* and *Logos ensarkos*, the Son is receptive in relation to the Father.[167] Every creative action that terminates in Christ and all identity by "nature and grace" is from the Father. As with the incarnation, Christ's resurrection "whereby he was born of the womb of the earth" has its cause in the Father as well.[168] As the *monogenes* and *eikon* of the Father, Christ reveals a derivative glory in transfiguration corresponding to eternal generation.[169] The Spirit constitutes the *conceptio carnis* as the Spirit of the Father, for in this, the Son does not cause temporal generation by the Son's own Spirit.[170] As the Son creates and perfects all creation by the Spirit, so the Father creates and perfects Christ in person and mystically.[171]

The hypostatic union comes into being when the human Jesus is included into the eternal Father-Son relation.[172] Still, the Father's regard for Jesus as Son flows from the prior *gratia unionis*.[173]

THE FATHER'S LOVE TOWARD THE SON

In Edwards's trinitarianism, the Father-Son relation does not exclude the Holy Spirit. Being the hypostatic Love of God, Jesus' immeasurable possession of the Spirit is identical with the Father's infinite love toward Jesus. Hence, the incarnation exists when "this man [Jesus] hath communion with the Logos, in the love which the Father hath to him as his only begotten Son. Now the love of God is the Holy Ghost."[174] Just as the *Logos asarkos* is the eternally Anointed One, so as *Logos ensarkos* he is also named the Christ in time.[175]

In this, Edwards favors the pneumatic Christology of Ireneaus rather than a more developed Logos Christology that describes the divinity as the ointment of Christ's human nature.[176] Not only in the divine nature alone is the Logos called Christ; the Logos is so in human nature as well: "In his human nature he is Christ, or the anointed, as the Spirit is given not by measure to him, as he was conceived by the power of the Holy Ghost, and the Spirit abode upon him, and dwelt in him from the first moment of his existence in that degree and measure as to be a bond of union with the eternal Logos so as to be the same person."[177] Ontologically, Christ is not only anointed with the Spirit qua God and human, but also operationally "in his office of mediator, for God the Father poured forth the Holy Spirit abundantly on him to consecrate him to and qualify him for this work."[178]

INCARNATION BY SANCTIFICATION: A SPIRIT-MEDIATED LOGOS CHRISTOLOGY

We have seen hints of how Edwards attempts to build a Spirit Christology that complements the classical two-nature account.[179] The *unio hypostatica* is the result of a communication of the Spirit to the assumed human nature.[180] In Edwards's pithy phrase, the Father sent the Son "or incarnated him by sanctification."[181]

In the classical Logos Christology, the relation and presence of the Holy Spirit to Jesus and to the saints is not different in kind.[182] There, the *gratia unionis* or hypostatic union ontologically and logically precedes the *gratia habitualis* or sanctification of the human nature.[183] Edwards inverts this ontological and rational ordering.

However, when Edwards claims that "Christ has so much of the Spirit, and hath it in so high" as to cause the incarnation, does he not reduce the *gratia unionis* to a *gratia habitualis per excellentiam*?[184] In other words, is sanctification no more than a deficient sort of incarnation?[185] Clearly aware of such a conclusion, Edwards insists that the incarnation is unique in kind, for Jesus possesses the Spirit "in a peculiar and inconceivable manner, and not by measure."[186] Edwards clearly regards Christ as more than just a Spirit-filled human.[187] But, if sanctification (whether in Christ or the saint) involves a self-communication of the Spirit no different from the Spirit's operation *ad intra*, how does Jesus have the Spirit in a "peculiar" manner? [188]

An incarnation, by Edwards's definition, "is not a union of contact or influence, but a personal union." Sanctification, which involves the Spirit's "indwelling and influence," may eventuate in but is certainly not identical to the incarnation.[189] So, the "Spirit of God did in such a manner dwell in his human nature, viz., so as to cause a personal union between him and the Godhead."[190] The indwelling or influencing union between the Spirit and Christ's human nature effected the hypostatic union.[191] Although Edwards affirms the chronological simultaneity of the sanctification, conception, and unition of the human nature, he regards the *gratia habitualis* as the cause of the *gratia unionis*.[192]

There is another objection that Edwards anticipates and directly addresses. Since the union of Christ's human nature to the Holy Spirit seems more direct than the relation of Christ's human nature to the Logos, would this not amount to an incarnation of the Holy Spirit? He dismisses this line of reasoning as absurd, since one could very well conclude that the Spirit's immediacy in Christ's *conceptus* and the saints' *unio mystica* would make him "the father of the man Jesus" or "their head" respectively.[193] What is behind Edwards's logic of making the Spirit's indwelling the logical and causal presupposition of the incarnation?

The Holy Spirit as Immediate Creator and Uniter of Christ's Human Nature

That the Spirit is the direct agent of the *conceptio* is indisputable on biblical and creedal grounds. In continuity with the theological tradition, Edwards reiterates that Christ "received his first being in this world by the Spirit of holiness."[194] However, he rejects the assignment of the act of assumption directly to the Son.[195] On this matter, he follows a minor strand within the Reformed–Puritan tradition that regarded the Holy Spirit as both the creating and uniting principle of Christ's human nature.[196] Referring to the Holy Spirit, he contends, "It was necessary that the same person that acted as the principle of union between the manhood of Christ and the person of the Son, should make the manhood of Christ."[197] But, we may ask, why was this necessary?

Presupposing *actiones sunt suppositorum,* Edwards insists that the *conceptio* and *unio* cannot be "two distinct acts" because that would imply "two distinct agents."[198] As the Holy Spirit is the immediate creator of Christ's human nature, it is this "same person" who brings about the *unio personalis*.[199] Otherwise, the agent of the conception would differ from the agent of union, which Edwards finds problematic in the classical Logos Christology.[200]

If Edwards ascribes action to a *supposit,* he is also aware that the divine persons cannot be made three principles of volition, consciousness, and operation.[201] The *opera indivisa,* including the acts of *conceptio* and *unio,* are to be terminated by the agency of the Spirit, who is God's direct, effective action in the world. This is consonant with Edwards's understanding of the Will and Act of God as the end of all procession.

A Single Principle of the Conceptio and Unitio of the Human Nature to the Logos

Ascribing action to nature or person is not the only driving factor in Edwards's consideration of the relationship between the *conceptio* and *unitio.* His deeper concern centers on the unity of the incarnational act. "If the making had been by one person and the unition by another," he reasons, "the humanity would not, by him that made it, be made out of nothing into the Son, nor could the person that made it, be properly said to make the Word flesh."[202] In other words, the Holy Spirit would only be Creator of a human, but not the incarnate Son. For Edwards, the *unio hypostatica* is not simply the production of Christ's human nature.[203] Following Leontius of Jerusalem, he regards the *assumptio carnis* as a single divine operation with a double outcome: the *caro* and the *unio*.[204] The *unitio personalis* is therefore "making and uniting in one act, or making in union."[205] And the conclusion of this single act must be assigned to the same divine person—the Holy Spirit.

To avoid the twin dangers of adoptionism and Nestorianism, Edwards's Spirit Christology must posit creation and unition as chronologically simultaneous.[206] But why must there be an operational unity as well, so that the *conceptio* and *unitio* happened "at the same time and by the same act"?[207] As we shall see in the next chapter, since Edwards conceives of the Holy Spirit as the *vinculum* and *vehiculum* between the human nature and the divine Logos in the *unio personalis*, the same Spirit must necessarily inaugurate such a state between the natures. With such an attenuated role given to the Holy Spirit in the incarnational act, how does Edwards construe the activity of the Son in the Son's own incarnation?

ROLE OF THE SON IN THE *UNITIO PERSONALIS*

In Aquinas, the meaning of *assumptio* as an act is quite elastic, for it may be interpreted either personally or essentially.[208] However, unlike the act of uniting (*unitio*), which is the conjoining of two extremes, *assumptio*, as regarded by Thomism, is a personal act of uniting something to oneself.[209] This definition, as we have previously observed, was asserted by the majority of Puritan thinkers. Similarly, Edwards opines that although the *assumptio carnis* comprehends the *unitio*, the two terms are not to be conflated because "assuming implies the uniting."[210] However, he modifies the mainstream Reformed-Puritan definition of the *assumptio carnis* as merely a direct assumption of the human nature by the Logos. For Edwards, the assumption is a twofold act by the Holy Spirit: the simultaneous creation of a human nature *ex novo* and its unification to the Logos. And this twofold act terminates in the Son: "Assuming is the making the human nature in the person of the Logos."[211]

HOW DOES THE SON PARTICIPATE IN THE ACT OF ASSUMPTION?

Edwards, with the tradition before him, agrees that the incarnation is proper to the Son of God; hence, the assumption terminates in the person of the Son.[212] In many instances, Edwards consistently refers to the assumption as belonging to the Son.[213] For example, Christ as Creator "became subject to nature as he assumed the nature of a creature and lived on earth a natural life."[214]

However, does that contradict Edwards's previous contention that the Logos is passive insofar as the Logos "is the effect or the object" of the incarnation and that all divine acts "wrought upon or about Christ" are to be attributed to the Father through the Spirit?[215] Even on this view that the Son does not assume humanity directly but by the Son's own Spirit, it would seem that Edwards implies a sort of mediated agency of the Son that is active.[216] Accordingly, "when something was to be assumed out of nothing into union to himself, the Logos or Word sent forth this constituent, or principle of assumption or unition, to assume it out of nothing to himself."[217] A few points are worth noting here.

Firstly, the Son is only passive in relation to the Father and the Father's Spirit, but is active in relation to the Son's own Spirit. This is possible because "contrary relations may belong to the same thing, at the same time, with respect to different things."[218] In other words, the incarnate Son is related to the Holy Spirit in two different modes—as the Spirit of Father and as the Son's own Spirit. Only in the first relation is the Son passive.

Secondly, the Spirit is not sent by the Son as an external efficient cause but as an internal bond of unition and union. Hence, "the Holy Ghost . . . was the bond of union that in descending from the divine nature of Christ which was in heaven, on the human which was on earth, anointed earth with heaven."[219] Insofar as the incarnational act is not merely *ad extra* but terminates in the *unio personalis*, this is proper to the Son alone as it happens *within* the person of the Son.[220] Therefore, the modality of unition/union (as distinct from creation) culminates "in the person of the Logos."[221] The human nature created *ex novo* by the Spirit of the Father may only be (logically) regarded as *ad extra* prior to its initial unition with the Word by the Son's own Spirit.[222] On Edwards's belief in a *creatio continua*, the *unitio* and *unio personalis* must be regarded as distinct only circumstantially.

This brings is us to the third point. Unlike a static *unio personalis* conceived of by the scholastics, Edwards's idea of the incarnation is that an ongoing active relation between the natures obtains.[223] In other words, the hypostatic union, as with the assumption, is an *event*. In Edwards's Christology, the *unio hypostatica* is not so much a state as a *unitio personalis ad infinitum*.[224] As the bond of unition and union, the Spirit of the Son inaugurates and sustains an ever-recurring act of internally relating the Word to the Son's human nature. Therefore, "that person that acted as the principle of union" is no different from the one who acted as the "principle of assumption or unition" in the *assumptio carnis*.[225] The incarnation, for Edwards, may be regarded both *in facto* and *in fieri* after the initial *unitio*.

Fourthly, the Spirit's *missio* from the Father and Son culminates in a new ontological reality—the God-man. The act of "being sanctified made him [the man Christ] God as it made him a divine person."[226] However, it is only the Spirit's *missio* from the Father that results in the *missio* of the Son.[227] The Son's "being sent into the world, i.e. upon the work and office that came upon, made [him] God by office."[228] Differently stated, the Son does not send the Son's own self by the Son's own Spirit.[229] On Edwards's strict definition of an "office," the Son cannot self-assign one; otherwise, the Son would then be simultaneously *auctoritas* and *subiectus*.[230] What implications can be drawn from Edwards's concept of the incarnation for his trinitarianism?

RECIPROCAL RELATIONSHIP BETWEEN THE MISSIONS OF WORD AND SPIRIT

In the immanent Trinity, being the eternal patient in relation to the Father, the Son's generation is not without the Spirit's primordial procession: the Son is the "Godhead being thus begotten by God's *loving* an idea of Himself and shewing forth in a distinct subsistence or person in that idea."[231] In God, the eternal generation of the Son and the procession of the Spirit from the Father are inseparable. Clearly, just as the divine processions are ontologically coincident in God, Edwards regards the divine missions of incarnation and sanctification in the virgin birth as "the *twofold* way of the Deity's flowing forth *ad extra*."[232] God the Father extends an eternal Anointing into space-time to effect the incarnation. Jesus is, therefore, united to the Logos in "the love which the Father hath to him as his only begotten Son."[233]

In the *oikonomia*, the Father, despite a status as the *fons deitatis*, cannot send the Son without the anointing of the Spirit upon Christ. Although the *processio ad intra* and *missio ad extra* of the Son is from the Father alone, the identity of the God-man is dependent on the reception of the Spirit of the Father. Edwards, as we have observed, affirms that "'tis by the Holy Spirit that Christ is the Son of God."[234] Since the Son is the Anointed both *ad intra* and *ad extra*, is it not logically consistent to conclude that Edwards's trinitarianism implies that the Son's eternal personhood must be dependent upon the reception of the Spirit from the Father?

Based on Edwards's strong correlation between the economic and immanent Trinities, the incarnation confirms that the *generatio* and *processio* from the Father *ad intra* are ontologically *simul*.[235] Insofar as the Father self-reflexively produces the beloved Son, the Love of the Father proceeds from the *principium sine principium* toward the Son. Put simply, the Father begets the Son *in* the procession of the Spirit. Similarly, in the *oikonomia*, the Father actively and "more immediately" constitutes the *unio hypostatica* by the Father's own Spirit (though the Son is involved as the term of the assumption).

On a different note, the Son's deity in eternity does not depend on the Spirit's *processio a patre*, but rather on the Son's own *generatione a patre*. However, the Son's consubstantiality with the Father is affirmed by the Spirit's *processio per filium*. On the premise of an eternal *communicatio essentiae*, an ontological *per filium* secures the coequality of the Father and Son. What gives the Son identity *ad intra* is not only procession from the Father, but also reception of the Spirit from the Father.

The Son's reception of the Spirit is not a reception of being or essence (as that happens in the Son's generation), but a reception of love or *koinonia*. As the Son's generation and Spirit's procession from the Father are simultaneous, the Son receives the divine essence, *koinonia* (the Father's love), and identity (individuality and a unique filial disposition). Yet this eternal, identity-constituting "movement" of the Spirit does not terminate in the Son: the Holy Spirit proceeds from the Father through the Son, who returns the Spirit to the Father.

In the procession of the Spirit *a Patre filioque*, the Spirit receives being from the Father and the Son. The Son, having received a disposition to sonship, exercises a pure act of filiation in returning the Spirit to the Father. Although the *filioque* makes the Son a secondary subject, the Father does not receive the Son's Spirit in the mode in which the Son receives the Father's Spirit. In receiving the perfect act of love from the Son, the Father receives *koinonia* but not the divine essence or the disposition to paternity. For as *principium sine principium*, the Father has the Godhead primordially as well as the disposition to fatherhood.

In time, then, both Father and Son are agents in the visible mission of the Spirit, yet only the Father acts immediately by the Father's Spirit as the creative cause *ad extra* of the incarnation, as this is commensurate with the Son's reception of essence, love, and identity *ad intra*. Similarly, the Son's action by the Son's Spirit to terminate the *assumptio* internally *ad extra* corresponds to the termination of the bond of *koinonia* with God *ad intra*—in the *filioque*.

In summary, the filiation of the Son is not only dependent on the Father as the source of deity; the eternal "resting" of the Spirit of the Father upon the Son also contributes to the Son's personhood. The Son's relation to the Father does not only constitute the Son as the Father's Son, but as a holy Son from eternity, eternally sanctified in the Spirit's procession *a patre*. For without the reception of the Father's Spirit, the Son would not have the disposition to return the Spirit to the Father. On such a close correlation between the Trinity *ad intra* and *ad extra*, how then does Edwards construe the relation of incarnate Son to the Son's own Spirit?

PERSONHOOD AS SUBJECTIVITY: CHRIST POSSESSING "THE SPIRIT OF THE ONLY BEGOTTEN OF THE FATHER"

In Owen's Christology, the Son's only immediate act on the human nature was the *assumptio carnis*.[236] Following that, "whatever the Son of God wrought in, by, or upon the human nature, he did it by the Holy Ghost."[237] In contrast to Owen's unqualified attribution of all divine acts to the Spirit, Edwards differentiates the objective from the subjective Spirit-mediated operations. On the one hand, the divine operations *upon* Christ's human nature were caused by the Father's Spirit. On the other hand, the Son acts by the Son's Spirit *through and in* the Son's own assumed nature.[238] Why is there the need to make this distinction between acts by the Father's Spirit and acts by the Son's Spirit?

According to Edwards, "action and passion are doubtless, as they are sometimes used, words of opposite signification." They are primarily relational terms, whereby action is "the activeness of something on another thing." Passion, when seen in polarity to action, is "used transitively" to signify "the relation of being acted upon."[239] It would be logically absurd if the same person were to be both simultaneously active and passive in relation to the self.[240] Were that the case, the Word and the human nature would stand in a transitive or transeunt relation that obtains between a subject and an object. From Edwards's point of view, then, Owen's assertion that "whatever the Son of God wrought . . . *upon* the human nature," even if Spirit-mediated, would tilt toward Nestorianism.[241]

For Edwards, the "man Jesus," unlike the saints, has a unique relation to the other divine persons. The human Jesus has the Holy Spirit as the divine Logos does—as Jesus' own Spirit, and not as "the Spirit of the Father."[242] As such, the assumed nature possesses the same relation to the Father as the Logos does, in having "the Spirit of the only begotten of the Father."[243] As the object of the incarnation, the Father acts by the Father's Spirit to constitute Christ; as the subject of the incarnation, Christ acts by Christ's own Spirit. Commensurable to the Son's status as derived *a patre*, the fullness and glory of Christ's human nature issues "from the glory of the Father." And in a manner analogous to the Son being *autotheos* with regard to divinity, the Son as God-man possesses the "glory of [his] human nature . . . though not as the cause of that glory, yet as the subject of it."[244] The constitution of the incarnate Son in time, in mirroring the eternal generation, is therefore passive in relation to the Father.[245]

Since personal characteristics are incommunicable, the Son's *proprium* of filiation cannot be transferred to the assumed human nature, yet there may be relational participation.[246] Rather than being a static property of the essence, the filial character of the Son consists in the Father's recognition and love of the Son. In the Father's gift of the Spirit to Jesus, the Son comes to possess the Spirit (of filiation), and is thus regarded by the Father as Son. Edwards adheres to the patristic dictum that the Son gives the Spirit as God, but receives the Spirit as human.[247] Christ receives the Spirit of the Father but possesses the Spirit as the Spirit of the Son. Saints, on the other hand, receive and possess the Spirit as the Spirit of God and Christ.[248] The Son does not have the Holy Spirit as the saints have, as "a filial spirit," but as "the Spirit of the only-begotten of the Father."[249] Hence, the "Spirit . . . dwells in Jesus not as the Spirit of the Father, but as the Spirit of the Son."[250] The human nature of Christ stands in a Father-Son relation commensurable to that which the Logos enjoys eternally. Jesus regards God "the Father as being his own Father in the manner that he is the Father of the Logos" because Jesus possesses the Holy Spirit in an utterly unique manner.[251] The Spirit of the Father is the Father's originating regard toward the Son, while the Spirit of the Son is the Son's returning regard toward the Father.

Yet, the eternal *processio* is both an emanation and remanation insofar as the Love of God proceeds and returns *a patre per filium*. Just as the Father and Son are eternally bound to each other by the circle of *vinculum amoris*, so the human Jesus in communion with the divine Logos is temporally united to the Father by the same bond of love. As the Love eternally conveyed between the Father and Son binds them together, so the Spirit of the Son acts as the means of conveyance between the divine and human natures and "faculties" and makes Christ a single ontological hypostasis and psychological subject. Since Christ has divine knowledge by virtue of the hypostatic union, "doubtless, this union was some union of the faculties of his soul."[252] Subjectively, Christ not only remembers in a human manner a self-identity as the divine Son as the Logos understands divinely to be so, but also has the spirit or disposition of the "only-begotten Son" of the Father, not merely a filial spirit like believers. This is the temporal correlate of the *filioque* where the human Son knows and loves the Father as a "natural" Father. Jesus knows by virtue of possessing the same "consciousness" as the eternal Son, in an appropriately human way, insofar as

Jesus is personally united to the Idea of God. This is the Son being subjectively aware of existence as Son in beholding the Father.

Yet, only by possessing the disposition or spirit of the Son could Jesus actively love the Father. As the eternal Son loves the Father by accepting the Father's Love and returning this Love to the Father, the human Jesus possesses the Spirit as Jesus's own Spirit "inherently," by which Jesus is disposed to act as true Son in a permanent response of love to the Father. By "the Spirit of the Logos . . . the man Jesus hath the spirit and temper of the only begotten Son of God."[253] The life of the incarnate Son is therefore an ongoing receptivity and activity in that the Son is acted upon by the Father's Spirit and, at the same time, re-acts toward the Father by the Son's own Spirit. This, therefore, makes the Son both patient and agent in time and in eternity—the one object of the divine emanation as well as subject of the divine remanation.

CONCLUSION

The Augustinian mutual-love model is clearly evident in Edwards's vision of the *pactum salutis*—the eternal compact between Father and Son. While the distinction of persons is reiterated at this level—the Father as head and the Son as mediator, Edwards creatively expands the role of the Spirit's participation in this divine counsel. As the central figure of the Trinitarian *taxis*, the Son is suitably and properly incarnated. In Edwards, the traditional Logos Christology is complemented not only by a Spirit Christology but also through a creative retrieval of the pre-Nicene emphasis on the Father-Son relation. The participation of the Son in human nature involves the Spirit's work of conceiving and sanctifying the human nature, unifying it to the Word and thus bringing Jesus into the Logos-Father relation. The actions of the Holy Spirit, as Spirit of the Father, are transeunt; those actions between the natures as the Spirit of the Son, however, are immanent within the person of the God-man. Jesus' participation in the Son's relation to the Father as well as in the being of the Logos is made possible by the Spirit, whose role is consistent with the Spirit's actions *ad intra*. In the following chapter, we will turn to the relation of the natures in the God-man and the role of the Spirit in establishing and sustaining this relation.

Notes

1. Edwards, "Miscellanies," no. 741, in *WJE* 18:367.

2. While "œconomy" is an eternal ordering of the divine persons toward Trinitarian self-communication *ad extra*, the covenant of redemption is a separate, subsequent, and specific "determination of wisdom intervening, choosing the means of glorifying that disposition of nature" (Edwards, "Miscellanies," no. 1062, in *WJE* 20:432). That is to say, Christ, as the wisdom of God, chooses to enter into this covenant to glorify the Father. Hence, "God's glory is the last end of that great work of providence, the work of redemption by Jesus Christ" (Edwards, "Concerning the End," in *WJE* 8:483–89).

3. The work of redemption or salvation represents the overall, unified design of the various economic activities of the Trinity from the fall of humanity to the *eschaton* (Edwards, "No. 1: Sermon 1" [Mar 1739], in *WJE* 9:116). Edwards broadly defines the salvation economy to includes "the preparation and the imputation and application and success of Christ's redemption" (ibid., 117).

4. The work of creation (which includes heaven and angelic beings) were "in order to the Work of Redemption" (ibid., 118). The œconomical Trinity is a permanent establishment; it is not only prior to the covenant of redemption but will remain even after the work of human salvation is completed.

5. The fact that "that economy, by which the Father is head of the Trinity, is prior to the covenant of redemption" is clearly scriptural (Edwards, "Miscellanies," no. 1062, in *WJE* 20:433).

6. "The Father is head of the Trinity, and is invested with a right to act as such before the Son is invested with the office of a mediator, because the Father, in the exercise of his headship, invests the Son with that office" (ibid., 433–34.)

7. Edwards rejects such a conflation: "If the Son were invested with the office of a mediator by the same establishment . . . of the Trinity by which the Father is invested with power to act as head of the Trinity, then the Father could not be said to elect . . . the Son to his office of mediator . . . anymore than the Son elects . . . the Father . . . head of the Trinity, or anymore than the Holy Ghost does [elect] both the Son and the Father to their several economical offices" (ibid., 434).

8. The Son as Mediator comes under a legal and natural subjection of the Father as a creature putting "himself in the proper circumstances of a servant" (ibid., 437).

9. He is resisting the "absurd" idea that the second person of the Trinity could have been simultaneously elected as Mediator and Son. The reality of the *Logos asarkos* and œconomical Trinity allows Edwards to keep the divine generation and the incarnation distinct. Hence, it cannot be that "the SONSHIP of the second person in the Trinity consists only in the relation he bears to the Father in his mediatorial character, and that his generation or proceeding from the Father as a Son consists only in his being appointed, constituted and authorized of the Father to the office of a mediator, and that there is no other priority of the Father to the Son but that is voluntarily established in the covenant of redemption" (ibid., 443). Pauw thinks that Edwards wrote this entry against Thomas Ridgley, who had "proposed a compromise between Arianism and orthodoxy" in order to explain the Son's subordination to the Father (Pauw, "Introduction," in *WJE* 20:31).

10. For Edwards, divine generation must be prior to and the ground of the incarnation; yet, they must be distinguished as acts of nature and will respectively. To confuse the constitution of the Mediator with the Mediator's ontological Sonship would mean "that there is no other priority of the Father to the Son but that is voluntarily established in the covenant of redemption" (Edwards, "Miscellanies," no. 1062, in *WJE* 20:443).

11. Edwards, 190. Sermon on John 15:10, in *WJE* 46.

12. Because of the Father's magisterial office, the Father is particularly "injured by sin"; therefore, the Father's wrath and sense of justice must be satisfied (Edwards, "Miscellanies," no. 1062, in *WJE* 20:433). That the Son, and not the Father, is the person fit to undertake the role of the Mediator is agreeable to the œconomy of the Trinity. See Jonathan Edwards, "Observations

Concerning the Scripture Oeconomy of the Trinity, and the Covenant of Redemption," in *Treatise on Grace and Other Posthumously Published Writings*, ed. Paul Helm (Cambridge, London: James Clarke, 1971), 86.

13. "The Son was as free to undertake [the Passion] as the Father was to propose it; it was as much by will of the Son himself that he suffered for sinners as it was by the will of the Father" (Edwards, 234. Sermon on Matt. 16:21-23 [1731], in *WJE* 47). "'Tis as much the act of God the Father as 'tis of the Son" (Edwards, 80. Sermon on Isa. 32:2 [1728], in *WJE* 43). Although the Father's role in the eternal covenant is primarily active and the Son's role receptive, the Spirit seems to play a silent, observational role in this.

14. Edwards, "Of God the Father," in *WJE* 25:148.

15. "And if we take 'office' in this sense, each person of the Trinity has not so properly a distinct office because the part that God the Father has in that affair is not under any other person, [as he] acts as head in the whole affair. But the part that the other two persons have [in our redemption] is properly called an office" (ibid., 145–46).

16. "Each one has a distinct part to act, [and] stands in a distinct place and capacity, and sustains a distinct character in the affair of man's redemption, and has a distinct care and work that more especially belongs to him rather than to either of the other persons" (ibid., 146).

17. Chronologically, the Father acts as the first mover and contriver; the Son, secondly, as redeemer; and finally, the Spirit, who makes us partakers of redemption (Edwards, "Threefold Work of the Holy Ghost," in *WJE* 14:378). The "Head of the Trinity," the Father is "the first mover and beginner," the work of Christ is for human beings, and the work of the Spirit is in human beings (Edwards, "Miscellanies," no. 1062, in *WJE* 20:436). And consistent with Edwards's affirmation of the *filioque*, the Father as eternal origin is the "first orderer"; the Son, who proceeds eternally from the Father, is sent by him; and the Spirit, who proceeds from both, is sent by both (Edwards, "Threefold Work of the Holy Ghost," in *WJE* 14:379).

18. Edwards, "Miscellanies," no. 197, in *WJE* 13:336.

19. This does not obviate the fact that it is directly *from* the operations and indwelling of the Spirit as "the Holy Ghost himself is God" (Edwards, "God Glorified in Man's Dependence," in *WJE* 17:203).

20. Ibid., 203–6. In fact, Edwards argues that humanity's dependence on God for grace and power is greater now than it was before the Fall. As the first human beings were necessarily created holy in nature and functioned within an environment free from sin's dominion, their dependence on God was comparatively lesser. With regard to God's character, "it would have been a disparagement to the holiness of God's nature, if he had made an intelligent creature unholy. But now when man is made holy, it is from mere and arbitrary grace" (ibid., 204). And as to God's power: "So 'tis a more glorious work of power to uphold the soul in a state of grace and holiness, and carry it on till it is brought to glory, when there is so much sin remaining in the heart, resisting, and Satan with all his might opposing, than it would have been to have kept man from falling at first, when Satan had nothing in man" (ibid., 206).

21. "Indeed, it would have been fitting and excellent in him, that his will and his actions should be conformed to the Father's will and be subject to him, as it is in itself fit and excellent that the Logos itself should love the Father, and that the Father should love the Son" (Edwards, "Miscellanies," no. 454, in *WJE* 13:499).

22. Ibid., 499.

23. "But it don't follow hence that Christ, merely because he had human nature, was the proper subject of God's commanding and legislative authority." That is, "he became properly God's servant, therefore, only by virtue of agreement or covenant" (ibid.). See also "Miscellanies," no. 1062, in *WJE* 20:439.

24. Edwards, "Miscellanies," no. 1062, in *WJE* 20:437. Otherwise, Christ's mode of operation as Mediator would come under the general purview of the œconomical Trinity, though a distinct decree or "consultation" among the divine persons would have been required to stipulate the kind of work—viz., creation or redemption.

25. "The obedience which the Son of God performs to the Father . . . as Redeemer or Mediator, before his humiliation, and also that obedience he performs as God-man after his humiliation . . . is no more than flows from his economical office or character, although it be . . . occasioned by the covenant of redemption." Hence, Christ's postresurrection obedience to the Father, being no more "than the obedience of the Holy Spirit," does not count for the justification of believers and "is no more imputed to them" (ibid., 438).

26. Edwards seems to allude to such a distinction in an earlier Miscellany. At this stage of his thinking, Edwards understands Christ's representational function, obeying and suffering "in man's stead" in order to merit acceptance for "Christ mystical," to be identical to the work Christ "performed as mediator" (Edwards, "Miscellanies," no. 496, in *WJE* 13:539), after which Christ's mediating function will end as "there will be no more need of a mediatorial government of the universe . . . and nothing will remain to be done that is proper to a Mediator." At the same time, Christ's union with the church is perfected, since Christ is "in some respects as Mediator more glorious . . . being now complete, being married to her [the church] who is the fullness of him who filleth all in all." Yet the church's dependence on and distinction from Christ remains, of course, as Christ is the "sovereign King of their souls" and "the eternal object" of their worship (Edwards, "Miscellanies," no. 86, in *WJE* 13:250–51). While it could be argued that Calvin distinguished the person and office of the Mediator, he was unequivocal regarding the temporary character of the mediatorial office, which is to be surrendered at the Parousia, whence the saints would enjoy a direct unmediated *visio Dei*. Sounding semi-Arian, Calvin could even say that the title "Lord," given to "the person of Christ" (emphasis mine), was temporary and "represents a degree midway between God and us" (John Calvin, *Calvin: Institutes of Christian Religion*, ed. John T. McNeill, trans. Ford Lewis Battles, Library of Christian Classics 20 [Philadelphia: Westminster, 1960],, 1.14.3, 485–86).

27. Edwards, "Miscellanies," no. 742, in *WJE* 18:373.

28. "What are, what will be, the glorious communications of God unto his saints for ever, in life, light, power, joy, rest, and ineffable satisfaction, (as all must be from him unto eternity,) I shall not now inquire. But this I say, they shall be all made in and through the person of the Son, and the human nature therein. That tabernacle shall never be folded up, never be laid aside as useless" (John Owen, *Christologia: Or, a Declaration of The Glorious Mystery of the Person of Christ, God and Man, to which are Subjoined, Meditations and Discourses on the Glory of Christ*, vol. 1 of *The Works of John Owen, D.D.*, edited by William H. Goold [New York: Robert Carter & Brothers, 1851], ch. 19, 271).

29. Edwards, "Miscellanies," no. 742, in *WJE* 18:373. As representative, Christ is both a "*natural* representative," as the perfect Image of the Father, and a "*constituted* representative," according to the Father's delegate as judge and lawgiver.

30. Edwards, "Miscellanies," no. 1062, in *WJE* 20:440.

31. Accordingly, "there is a particular covenant entered into about that very affair, settling something new concerning the part that some, at least, of the persons are to act in that affair" (ibid., 433).

32. Owen appropriates goodness, wisdom, and power exercised *ad extra* to the Father, Son, and Spirit respectively. See John Owen, *The Works of John Owen*, ed. William H. Goold, 16 vols. (London: Banner of Truth Trust, 1965–68; originally publ. Johnstone & Hunter, 1850–53), 1:182. See also appendix 3 below, "The Doctrine of Appropriations as Modified by the Reformed-Puritan Tradition."

33. This seems to be at odds with the traditional idea since such an appropriated office is no longer (even temporarily) consonant with the *proprium* of the person. "Yea, let me add this, that seeing to appropriate thus a work more especially to one person than to another is an act of God's will, hence it is that one person may have it for a time appropriated unto him, and afterward given up unto another person more properly" (Goodwin, *WTG* 1:503). We might term this an inappropriate appropriation.

34. Edwards, "Miscellanies," no. 1062, in *WJE* 20:439.

35. Edwards, "Miscellanies," no. 742, in *WJE* 18:373.

36. "Christ's having the image of God as God-man; as such, representing the person of God the Father as his vicegerent in governing and judging the world" (Edwards, "Miscellanies," no. 702, in *WJE* 18:287). According to Edwards, humankind was placed on earth as "God's vicegerent" to be "an image of God's authority and dominion" over the rest of "this lower world" (Edwards, "Blank Bible," note on Psalms 8:5-9, in *WJE* 24:478).

37. Edwards, "Miscellanies," no. 742, in *WJE* 18:373.

38. For example, "delivering the saints from the remains of sin, and interceding for them as sinful creatures, and conquering their enemies" (Edwards, "Miscellanies," no. 742, in *WJE* 18:373).

39. Ibid., 373–74.

40. Ibid., 375.

41. Ibid.

42. Ibid., 374. As the vital bond of union to the Father, Christ is, "as it were, the eye to receive the rays of divine glory and love for the whole body, and the ear to hear the sweet expressions of his love, and the mouth to taste the sweetness and feed on the delights of the enjoyment of God—the root of the whole tree planted in God to receive sap and nourishment for every branch" (ibid.).

43. The obedience of the Son to the Father prior to this covenant, and subsequently as God-man, is not supererogatory for it arises from the "natural" order of the œconomy. As the Son descends far below his œconomical office, he receives as reward an authority as ruler and vicegerent of the universe—a role that properly belongs to the Father's œconomical office—at the end of the mediatorial work. Christ not only is given universal dominion but also receives a new authority over the Holy Spirit—the Father's "own divine infinite treasure"—to be given to believers as Christ chooses (Edwards, "Miscellanies," no. 1062, in *WJE* 20:439).

44. So that "things will return to be administered by the Trinity only according to their economical order" (ibid.). Like Goodwin, Edwards thinks of this temporary lordship of Christ as a reward for *kenosis* but does not consider it a permanent appropriation. Thus, "the place and station that the Son attains to by this establishment is entirely distinct from that which he stands in by the economy of the Trinity, insomuch that by the covenant of redemption the Son of God is, for a season, advanced into the economical seat of another person, viz. the Father, ... as the Lord and Judge of the world in the Father's stead, and as his vicegerent. ... For by the economy of the Trinity it is the Father's province to act as the Lawgiver and Judge and Disposer of the world" (ibid., 435). In effect, what is appropriated to the Father—lordship—as corresponding to the Father's *proprium* as *principium sine principium* is, in the economy of redemption until the Parousia, a temporary *appropriatum* of the Son (Goodwin, *WTG* 1:503).

45. Edwards, "Miscellanies," no. 1062, in *WJE* 20:439.

46. The theandric nature of the Christ, as a result of the incarnation, shares in the eternal "œconomic" station of the Son as the second Person in the Trinity, with the Spirit's due deference to the Son in this regard (ibid., 440).

47. Ibid. This newness is acting under Christ as "God-man" and no longer under "the Son as God or divine person." As no humiliation is implied, this obedience of the Holy Spirit is neither meritorious for believers nor does the Holy Spirit receive a reward for it (ibid., 441).

48. Edwards, "Threefold Work of the Holy Ghost," in *WJE* 14:380. "Whatsoever is done concerning man's redemption, is done as it were by consultation and agreement amongst the persons of the Trinity ... and whatsoever is done by each person is done by the consent and concurrence of all." The *opera indivisa* is qualified: "there was a joint agreement of all, but not properly a covenant between 'em all" (Edwards, "Miscellanies," no. 1062, in *WJE* 20:442). All the three divine persons had as much concern in the salvation of humanity as they had in the creation (Edwards, "Threefold Work of the Holy Ghost," in *WJE* 14:378).

49. Cocceius only points to the roles of the Spirit directed *ad extra* in the *consilium pacis*, viz., as divine power (*potentia Dei*), love (*charitas*), and sealing (*obsignatio*). In other words, the Spirit only brings to reality what the Father and Son compacted in eternity. See Willem J. van Asselt,

The Federal Theology of Johannes Cocceius (1603–1669), trans. Raymond A. Blacketer (Leiden: Brill, 2001), 234.

50. Edwards, "Miscellanies," no. 1062, in *WJE* 20:443.

51. Edwards, "On the Equality," in *WJE* 21:146; "Miscellanies," no. 1062, in *WJE* 20:443. The Spirit with which the God-man is endowed is given by the Father and properly possessed by Christ. That which is given to the saints as the Spirit of the Father and the Son is purchased through Christ's atoning work.

52. For Barth, election pivots around Christ, but for Edwards, Christ's election is that the Spirit might be purchased *pro nobis*. "The end of the Father in electing is the Spirit. . . . His end in giving the Son [is] to purchase this" (Edwards, "On the Equality," in *WJE* 21:146–47).

53. It is at the same time centered in Christ and sourced in the Father. Edwards uses the divine *taxis* to parse the divine relations *ad intra* and to assert a divine coequality. It is the relational distinction and ordering that grounds their distinct "personal glory" or "dignity."

54. "Here is the only moving cause, or reason, why God bestows this great salvation . . . and that is his mere love and mercy." See Thomas Ridgley, *A Body of Divinity: Wherein the Doctrines of the Christian Religion are Explained and Defended Being the Substance of Several Lectures on the Assembly's Larger Catechism*, with notes, original and selected by James P. Wilson, 4 vols. (Philadelphia: Printed by and for William W. Woodward, 1815), 2:162. The moving cause of the atonement, as Berkhof notes, lies in God's love. See Louis Berkhof, *Manual of Christian Doctrine* (Grand Rapids, MI: Eerdmans, 2002; originally publ. 1933), 212.

55. Edwards, "On the Equality," in *WJE* 21:147; "Miscellanies," no. 1062, in *WJE* 20:443.

56. Edwards, "Blank Bible," note on 2 Cor. 13:14, in *WJE* 24:1078. Analogically, the human "will is the first spring of the voluntary exertions of active power in man, and the cause of it" (Edwards, "Miscellanies," no. 71, in *WJE* 13:240).

57. Edwards, "Miscellanies," no. 1062, in *WJE* 20:443. In connection with love and the Holy Spirit, Aquinas notes that a moving agent that grants form is more powerful than a mere efficient cause. "That is why the Holy Spirit, as it is a very powerful moving cause, when it moves us to loving, does so in such a way that it also endows us with the disposition of charity" (Thomas Aquinas, *Disputed Questions on the Virtues*, ed. E. M. Atkins and Thomas Williams, Cambridge Texts in the History of Philosophy [Cambridge: Cambridge University Press, 2005], "On Charity," art. 1, 112).

58. Edwards, "Miscellanies," no. 791, in *WJE* 18:494.

59. Frede reminds us that Aristotle (in his more theoretical passages) describes the art of sculpting, rather than the sculptor, as the moving cause. Hence, *causa movens* and *causa efficiens* may not be strictly identical (Michael Frede, *Essays in Ancient Philosophy* [Minneapolis: University of Minnesota Press, 1987], 126).

60. "And each person of the Trinity is equally glorified in this work. There is an absolute dependence of the creature on every one for all: all is *of* the Father, all *through* the Son, and all *in* the Holy Ghost. Thus God appears in the work of redemption, as all in all" (Edwards, "God Glorified," in *WJE* 17:212).

61. By capitalizing on Rom. 11:36, Edwards asserts that all our benefits are "of God and through God and in God" (Edwards, "Discourse on the Trinity," in *WJE* 21:137). Augustine made ample use of this formula in his writings (Augustine, *The Trinity*, vol. 5 of *The Works of Saint Augustine*, ed. John E. Rotelle, intro. and trans. Edmund Hill [Brooklyn, NY: New City, 1991], I: 12, 72; II: 25, 115; III: 9, 132; V: 9, 195; VI: 7, 209; VI: 12, 214).

62. Edwards, "Threefold Work of the Holy Ghost," in *WJE* 14:435.

63. Edwards, "Sermon Fourteen: Divine Love Alone Lasts Eternally," in *WJE* 8:353.

64. "Our dependence is equally upon each in this affair: the Father appoints and provides the Redeemer, and himself accepts the price and grants the thing purchased; the Son is the Redeemer by offering up himself, and is the price; and the Holy Ghost immediately communicates to us the

thing purchased by communicating himself, and he is the thing purchased" (Edwards, "Discourse on the Trinity," in *WJE* 21:136).

65. Edwards, "God Glorified," in *The Sermons of Jonathan Edwards: A Reader*, ed. Wilson H. Kimnach, Kenneth P. Minkema, and Douglas A. Sweeney (New Haven: Yale University Press, 1999), 68.

66. "All our good is of God the Father, 'tis all through God the Son, and all is in the Holy Ghost, as he is himself all our good" (Edwards, "Discourse on the Trinity," in *WJE* 21:191).

67. Edwards, "Threefold Work of the Holy Ghost," in *WJE* 14:150.

68. "We should look for life and holiness and comfort from the Father, through the Son and by the Spirit. So we should look for sanctifying influences, for supports under temptations and afflictions, for eternal life and heavenly glory from the Father, through the Son and by the Spirit" (ibid., 435).

69. "The Father manifests his glory by entertaining thoughts of mercy towards men after their rebellion, and that he should give his own Son, infinitely dear to him, for this end; and giving all the elect to him to be taken care of by him, and have their selection secured, and in accepting what Christ did, and justifying believers for his sake and taking them into favor. The Son, he is the Redeemer. He is he that actually procures salvation, that lays down his life; he redeems by merit, as he is the high priest, and by power, as he is the king of the church. The Holy Ghost is he that, after salvation is procured, immediately possesses them of it all. Though Christ procures all, he confers all; 'tis he that converts sinners, that brings him out of darkness; 'tis he unites to Christ. He gives holiness and he gives the happiness purchased; he enlightens [the] understanding and renovates the will, elevates and purifies the affections. He gives the heart all comfort and all spiritual blessing in this world; he preserves to the end and fits for glory" (ibid., 434–35).

70. Ibid., 435.

71. Though we are in utter need of each divine person "for all good," yet we are dependent upon the Son for "our wisdom, righteousness, sanctification, and redemption"; upon the Father for giving the Son; and upon the Spirit for uniting us to and giving us faith in Christ (Edwards, "God Glorified in Man's Dependence," in *WJE* 17:201).

72. Ibid., 211.

73. Edwards, "Lecture VIII: The Spirit of Charity the Opposite of a Selfish Spirit," in *Charity and Its Fruits: Christian Love as Manifested in the Heart and Life*, ed. Tryon Edwards (London: Banner of Truth Trust, 1969), 184–85.

74. Edwards, "Miscellanies," no. 772, in *WJE* 18:420. "The Spirit is the sum of all that which they have from the Father through the Son, all that to the Father doth through the Mediator, to and for the saints, terminates in the Spirit. And on the other hand, all that by which they come to the Father through the Mediator is the Spirit, and all that they do or transact through the Son, towards God, is by the Spirit" (Edwards, "Miscellanies," no. 733, in *WJE* 18:359).

75. "As no man can know the Father but by the Son so no man can love the Father but by the holy Ghost" (Ramsay, *Principles*, 1:309–15, as cited in Edwards, "Miscellanies," no. 1254, in *WJE* 23:188–89).

76. Edwards, "Miscellanies," no. 772, in *WJE* 18:419.

77. Ibid., 420. "The purchaser and the price are the intermediate between the person of whom the purchase is made, and the thing purchased of him."

78. Edwards, no. 37, John 15:5(a), in *WJE* 42.

79. Edwards, 118. Sermon on Song of Sol. 8:1, in *WJE* 44.

80. Edwards, "Miscellanies," no. 702, in *WJE* 18:309. On Edwards's use of typology, see Perry Miller, *Images or Shadows of Divine Things* (New Haven: Yale University Press, 1948); Mason I. Lowance Jr., *Language of Canaan: Metaphor and Symbol in New England from the Puritans to the Transcendentalists* (Cambridge, MA: Harvard University Press, 1980); and Mason I. Lowance Jr. and David H. Watters, "Editor's Introduction," in Edwards, *WJE* 11:3–48.

81. In Edwards's view, Jesus' propitiatory suffering and meritorious obedience was carried on throughout the entire period of his incarnation and was not limited only to his crucifixion

(though this was principal) (Edwards, "Sermon 15," in *WJE* 9:306–7). Christ purchased redemption during this period; what came before was preparatory to Christ's coming and what comes after is accomplishing the success of the purchase (ibid., 127–28).

82. Edwards, "Miscellanies," no. 496, in *WJE* 13:539.

83. Edwards, "No. 5: Sermon 14," in *WJE* 9:304–5.

84. Edwards, "Miscellanies," no. 452, in *WJE* 13:498.

85. "Though an admission to such a kind of fellowship with God perhaps could not be without God's own suffering, yet when a divine person has been slain, way is made for it, seeing that he has been dead. . . . The debt is all paid to the awful attributes of God; there is no need of any more" (Edwards, "Miscellanies," no. 741, in *WJE* 18:371)

86. Edwards, 932. Sermon on John 6:51 [June 1749], in *WJE* 67. Again, "all divine blessings are entirely through the giving of the flesh or human nature of Christ for Incarnation."

87. Edwards, "Honey from the Rock," in *WJE* 17:127–28.

88. Emphasis mine. Jonathan Edwards, "Heaven is a World of Love," in *Charity and Its Fruits*, 333.

89. Edwards, "Honey from the Rock," in *WJE* 17:135.

90. Edwards, "Threefold Work of the Holy Ghost," in *WJE* 14:377–81. "What the Holy Spirit doth in men's salvation, he doth as Christ's messenger. All that he doth amongst men since the Fall is as applying Christ's redemption, or some way in order to the application of it."

91. Ibid., 381.

92. Emphasis mine. Edwards, "Heaven is a World of Love," in *Charity and Its Fruits*, 333.

93. Edwards, "Miscellanies," no. 702, in *WJE* 18:296. Edwards declines to speculate on other possible worlds: "So that the work of God is but one, so far as the works of God are made known to us, for I would say nothing of possible unrevealed works with which we have nothing to do."

94. Aquinas, *STh* III, q. 3, a. 5–7, 2041–44.

95. The contention that God could have assumed a stone or fire (in Scotus) or an ass (in Occam) was an illustration *ad absurdum* against the *assumptus* theory of the incarnation, which argued that an incarnation was only possible on the supposition that the assumed human nature had its own prior *hypostasis*. The conclusion that God could have assumed any created form but did not in fact do so only served to enhance the "subsistence theory" of the incarnation. See Heiko Augustinus Oberman, *The Harvest of Medieval Theology: Gabriel Biel and Late Medieval Nominalism* (Cambridge, MA: Harvard University Press, 1963), 249–58. There were three different interpretations of the *henosis* in scholastic Christology: the Nestorian *assumptus* theory, the orthodox subsistence theory, and the docetic *habitus* theory (ibid., 252).

96. Bruce D. Marshall, "*Ex Occidente Lux?* Aquinas and Eastern Orthodox Theology," *Modern Theology* 20, no. 1 (January 2004): 42.

97. "It belongs to the Father to be innascible as to eternal birth, and the temporal birth would not destroy this." Yet, such an "Incarnation would not suffice for the nature of mission" (Aquinas, *STh* III, q. 3, a. 5, ad 3). See also Marshall, "*Ex Occidente Lux?*," 42–43.

98. John of Damascus, *Orthodox Faith*, bk. 4, ch. 4, 75 (*NPNF* 9).

99. "If either the Father or the H. Ghost should have been incarnate, the title of Son should have been given to one of them, who was not the Son by eternal generation: and so there should be more sons then one." See William Perkins, *A golden chaine: Or, the description of theologie, containing the order of the causes of salvation and damnation, according to Gods word . . .* (London: Printed by John Legatt, Printer to the Universitie of Cambridge, 1616), 24.

100. The incarnation of the Son, he continued, was "most fitting" in that the eternal Word and Wisdom should both repair the creation made in the Son's likeness and to perfect human wisdom. The incarnation is also a fitting antidote to the protological sin of "seeking knowledge" as it restores "true knowledge" to us. Moreover, it was appropriate that "the natural Son" should achieve the goal of the incarnation so that we could "share his likeness of sonship by adoption." (*STh* III, q. 3, a. 8, 2044–45).

101. In affirming Augustine's construal of Gift as the proper name of the Holy Spirit, Aquinas comments insightfully: "The word 'gift' conveys the idea of being givable" ("Dicendum quod in nomine doni importatur aptitudo ad hoc quod donetur"; Aquinas, *STh* 1, a. 38, q. 1). This notion has been fruitfully developed phenomenologically by Jean-Luc Marion in his *Being Given: Toward a Phenomenology of Givenness*, trans. Jeffrey L. Kosky (Stanford, CA: Stanford University Press, 2002), 107. In a similar manner, the notion of "being filiable" could be applied to the Son. See Earl Muller, "Real Relations and the Divine: Issues in Thomas's Understanding of God's Relation to the World," *Theological Studies* 56 (1995): 684–85. This move, on the one hand, seeks to counter Aquinas's appeal to the divine power in the incarnation, which logically entails that any of the divine persons could have assumed any number of human natures. On the other hand, however, it not only extends Aquinas's own argument of the appropriateness of the Son's incarnation (*conveniens*) but is also a faithful extension of his logic.

102. Undeniably, the concept of beauty is *one* of the more prominent motifs within Edwards's philosophical theology but it is certainly not *the* foundational category of his thought. The classical notion of beauty, with its emphasis on order and objectivity, though prominent in Edwards's reflections, is never elevated to the status of a regulating abstraction, as Delattre seems to argue. As the eternal being of the Trinity is more fundamental to Edwards's conceptualization than his theological aesthetics, existence must necessarily be the presupposition of all beauty. As Brand notes, Edwards's ontology is a more basic category than his aesthetics. See David C. Brand, *Beatific Vision, Benevolence and Self-Love: A Contextual Study of Jonathan Edwards with Special Reference to the Cartesian Revolution and the Arminian Triumph in Puritan New England* (New York: Oxford University Press, 1991). So, Edwards did not so much propound an aesthetic theology as propose a theological aesthetic, and specifically a Trinitarian aesthetic. See Robert W. Jenson, "A 'Protestant Constructive Response' to Christian Unbelief," in *American Apostasy: A Triumph of "Other" Gospels*, ed. Richard John Neuhaus (Grand Rapids, MI: Eerdmans), 60.

103. We may observe in Edwards the conception of divinity as the perfect unity of the Platonic triad of "the Good, the True and the Beautiful." God, Word, and Spirit, respectively, are the ultimate and personal synonymies of goodness, truth, and beauty themselves.

104. *Conveniens* is a Thomistic aesthetic concept, used interchangeably with terms like *proportio*, *analogia*, *ordinatio*, and *harmonia*. See Gilbert Narcisse, *Les Raisons de Dieu: Arguments de Convenance et Esthétique Théologique selon St. Thomas d'Aquin et Hans Urs von Balthasar*, preface by Jean-Pierre Torrell (Fribourg, Switzerland: Editions Universitaires, 1997). According to Paul Gondreau, "In Aquinas's vocabulary, conveniens signifies not only fittingness but also coherence, or even, in a more extended sense, ordered beauty." See Paul Gondreau, "The Humanity of Christ, the Incarnate Word," in *The Theology of Thomas Aquinas*, ed. Rik van Nieuwenhove and Joseph Wawrykow (Notre Dame, IN: University of Notre Dame Press, 2005), 259. See also John Milbank, "Forgiveness and Incarnation," in *Questioning God*, ed. John D. Caputo, Mark Dooley, and Michael J. Scanlon (Bloomington: Indiana University Press, 2001), 112–13. See Joseph P. Wawrykow's excellent article in *The Westminster Handbook to Thomas Aquinas* (Louisville, KY: Westminster John Knox, 2005), s.v. "fittingness," 57–60.

105. Narcisse, *Les Raisons de Dieu*, 165–80.

106. Edwards, "Miscellanies," no. 108, in *WJE* 13:278–79.

107. See "The Mind," no. 1, in *WJE* 6:332–39. The analogy of proportionality is founded on a proportion of proportion (e.g., intelligence is to mind as eye is to body) and is different from the analogy of proportion, whereby two things are directly related to each other (e.g., one's health is proportioned to the healthy antidote consumed).

108. Edwards, "Miscellanies," no. 1218, in *WJE* 23:152.

109. It is "that establishment that is founded in fitness and decency and the natural order of the eternal and necessary subsistence of the persons of the Trinity" (Edwards, "Miscellanies," no. 1062, in *WJE* 20:432).

110. "Though it is not proper to say decency *obliges* the persons of the Trinity to come into this order and economy, yet it may be said that decency requires it, and that therefore the persons

of the Trinity all consent to this order, and establish it by agreement" (ibid., 431). "Though it be from the free and voluntary agreement [of the persons of the Trinity], yet 'tis not arbitrary in such a sense as to exclude any fitness or wisdom appearing in such an established order of acting, agreeable to the order of subsisting" (Edwards, "Of God the Father," in *WJE* 25:147).

111. The notion of "fittingness" was a prevalent motif in Reformed scholasticism. For example, Sweeney names Adrian Heerebord's (1613–1661) *Meletemata philosophica* ("Editor's Introduction," in *WJE* 23:31n6).

112. Edwards, "Miscellanies," no. 1346, in *WJE* 23:381–82. "If God had not regarded fitness and propriety in the affair of man's salvation, the whole mediatorial scheme might have been set aside, or never have taken place. If free grace exercised in a way of mere sovereignty, without regard to propriety, was all that was requisite, there would have been no need of the means and methods provided for man's salvation in the admirable scheme which infinite wisdom hath contrived" (ibid., 381). Aquinas attempted to seek coherence in what has been revealed in God's economy, unlike later scholastics, who emphasized God's absolute freedom over against the contingency of the actual order such that the latter may be set aside by God's absolute power (Wawrykow, *Westminster Handbook to Thomas Aquinas*, s.v. "fittingness," 57).

113. Edwards, "Miscellanies," no. 1196, in *WJE* 23:118.

114. Edwards, "Miscellanies," no. 1007, in *WJE* 20:335–41.

115. Edwards, "Miscellanies," no. 1346, in *WJE* 23:382. "And God's insisting on this propriety is not in the least inconsistent with the highest possible freedom of his grace."

116. Ibid.

117. Ibid.

118. Edwards, "Discourse on the Trinity," in *WJE* 21:123.

119. "Christ God-man is a fit person for a mediator between God and man not only as he is a middle person between the Father and the Holy Ghost, but also between God and man. But as he is a middle person between God and men themselves, he is nearly allied to both; he is the Son of God and the Son of man" (Edwards, "Miscellanies, no. 772, in *WJE* 18:420).

120. Hence, the "business of a mediator is as a middle person between two parties, at a distance and at variance, to make peace between them" (ibid., 419). Elsewhere, Edwards contrasts "middle person" with mediator, the first "[acts] only for one of the parties," whereas the other "appears for both parties." Here, Edwards wants to draw a distinction between a "legal transaction," which any third party could carry out on behalf of God, and the "transaction of grace," where Christ mediates for God and human beings (Edwards, "Notes on Scripture," no. 423, in *WJE* 15:502)

121. For example, as the *unio hypostatica* lies between the essential union of the Trinity and the *unio mystica*, Goodwin appropriately termed it "the middle union." See Thomas Goodwin, "The Knowledge of the Father, and His Son Jesus Christ," bk. 2, in *WTG* 4:439.

122. Edwards, "Miscellanies," no. 614, in *WJE* 10:81.

123. "Thus if either the Father or the Son be brought into the subjection of a servant to the other, it is much more agreeable to the economy of the Trinity that it should be the latter, who by that economy is already under the Father as his head. That the Father should be servant to the Son would be contrary to the economy and natural order of the persons of the Trinity" (Edwards, "Miscellanies," no. 1062, in *WJE* 20:437).

124. "The Son, he is the Redeemer. He is he that actually procures salvation, that lays down his life; he redeems by merit, as he is the high priest, and by power, as he is the king of his church" (Edwards, "Threefold Work of the Holy Ghost," in *WJE* 14:434). Edwards describes the relation of the Trinity to the saints in heaven: "The God that dwells and gloriously manifests himself there, is infinitely lovely; gloriously lovely as a heavenly Father, as a divine Redeemer, and as a holy Sanctifier" ("Heaven is a World of Love," in *Charity and Its Fruits*, 328).

125. "Therefore I suppose the name of our Mediator, 'Messiah,' or 'Christ,' or 'Anointed,' signifies the union of the divine nature to the human. When Jesus is called Christ, or Anointed, it imports that he is a divine person and signifies the manner how he becomes so, viz. by the

communication of the Spirit of God, the true oil which was poured upon him without measure" (Edwards, "Miscellanies," no. 487, in *WJE* 13:530).

126. "Christ did, in effect, give himself to the elect to be theirs from eternity in the same covenant with the Father in which the Father gave them to him to be his. . . . Thus he from eternity gave himself to them, and looked on them as having so great a propriety in him, as amounted to his thus spending and being spent for them; and as he gave himself to them from eternity, so he is theirs to eternity" (Edwards, "Miscellanies," no. 741, in *WJE* 18:370). "But he has been pleased to unite himself to man . . . in some sort from eternity in the covenant of redemption by undertaking to be man's surety. Thus Christ speaks of himself as united to man before the world was created" (Edwards, 381. Sermon on Gen. 28:12 [Mar 1736], in *WJE* 51).

127. Edwards, "Miscellanies," no. 769, in *WJE* 18:415.

128. Edwards, "Miscellanies," no. 104, in *WJE* 13:274. In the self-communication of the Son, Edwards posits another Trinitarian image: "Wherein Christ is the everlasting father, and believers are his seed, and the Holy Spirit, or Comforter, is the third person in Christ, being his delight and love flowing towards the church. In believers the Spirit and delight of God, being communicated unto them, flows out toward the Lord Jesus Christ" (ibid., 273–74). Moreover, Turretin added, following Aquinas, that it was also fitting that the natural Son and Creator should undertake "to make us adoptive sons by grace" and "to recreate (*anaktizein*) whose it was to create" (Francis Turretin, *Institutes of Elenctic Theology*, trans. George Musgrave Giger, ed. James T. Dennison [Phillipsburg, NJ: P&R, 1992–94], vol. 2, topic 13, q. 4, para. 6, 305).

129. Edwards, "'Controversies' Notebook: Justification," in *WJE* 21:372. See also Edwards, "History," Sermon 2, *WJE* 9:131.

130. The "Angel of the Lord . . . went before 'em in the wilderness and dwelt with them in the tabernacle and temple, appearing in the cloud of glory" (Edwards, "'Controversies' Notebook: Justification," in *WJE* 21:395).

131. Ibid., 395, 383.

132. Edwards, "Miscellanies," no. 733, in *WJE* 18:359.

133. The *henosis* is brought about not by the operation of the Logos, but by the "substantial union" of the Logos with the created body—that is, total self-giving and inhabitation of the body by the Logos. See Aloys Grillmeier with Theresia Hainthaler, *Christ in Christian Tradition*, vol. 2, *From the Council of Chalcedon (451) to Gregory the Great (590–604)*, pt. 2, *The Church of Constantinople in the Sixth Century*, trans. Pauline Allen and John Cawte (Louisville, KY: Westminster John Knox, 1995), 229.

134. For Owen, while the whole divine nature is the principle of the incarnation, he appropriates "*authoritative designation*" to the Father, the creation of Christ's human nature to the Spirit, and the termination of the assumption to the Son (Owen, *Works*, 1:225).

135. "What unites and what assumes are not the same. For whatsoever Person assumes unites, and not conversely. For the Person of the Father united the human nature to the Son, but not to Himself; and hence he is said to unite and not to assume" (Aquinas, *STh* III, q. 2, a. 8, sc 2, 2035). Aquinas permitted that it could be improperly said the Father (or the Spirit) "takes human nature to the Person of the Word" (Aquinas, *STh* III, q. 3, a. 4,2040).

136. "Assumption determines with whom the union is made on the part of the one assuming, inasmuch as assumption means taking into oneself [*ad se sumptio*]" (Aquinas, *STh* III, q. 2, a. 8, ad 3, 2035).

137. He granted that "it may be said secondarily that the Nature assumed a nature to Its Person" (Aquinas, *STh* III, q. 3, a. 2, 2039). Because the divine essence and person are rationally distinct, "the Divine Nature is both that whereby God acts, and the very God Who acts" (Aquinas, *STh* III, q. 3, a. 2, ad 3, 2040).

138. Aquinas assigned causation to the divine essence and the three persons conjointly in different places. See Richard Cross, *Metaphysics of the Incarnation* (New York: Oxford University Press, 2002), 154n26. Bruce Marshall thinks that P. T. Geach's theory of relative identity (if philosophically sound), as applied specifically to the Trinity by Peter van Inwagen, sufficiently

deals with the issue of a numerically identical operation of the Trinity while accounting for distinct personal modes of action (Bruce D. Marshall, "What Does the Spirit Have to Do?" in *Reading John with St. Thomas: Theological Exegesis and Speculative Theology*, ed. Michael Dauphinais and Matthew Levering [Washington, DC: Catholic University of America Press, 2005], esp. 74–77).

139. Aquinas affirmed that "to assume is to act" (Aquinas, *STh* III, q. 3, a. 2) and that "the act of assumption proceeds from the Divine power, which is common to the three Persons" (Aquinas, *STh* III, q. 3, a. 4).

140. "Now to be the principle of the assumption belongs to the Divine Nature in itself, because the assumption took place by Its power; but to be the term of the assumption does not belong to the Divine Nature in itself, but by reason of the Person in Whom It is considered to be" (Aquinas, *STh* III, q. 3, a. 2). According to Turretin, "Although originally and principiatively as to efficiency the work of the whole Trinity, yet not subjectively and appropriately as to terminus (in which sense it belongs only to the Son)" (*Institutes* 2, topic 13, q. 4, para. 2, 304). So, Peter van Mastricht: "Sic incarnationis activae, quae tribus personis communis est, terminus, humana scil. natura, ad secundam personam assumentem, peculiariter refertur" (*Theoretico-practica theologia, qua, per singula capita theologica, pars exegetica, dogmatica, elenchtica & practica, perpetuâ successione coniugantur* [Traiecti ad Rhenum: Ex officinâ Thomae Appels, 1699], bk. 3, ch. 1, 306). "As regards the act, it is common to the three persons; for the Father and the Holy Spirit jointly effected the incarnation of Christ. But as regards the end, it is peculiar to the Son alone." See John Davenant, *An exposition of the Epistle of St. Paul to the Colossians . . .* (London: Hamilton, Adams, 1831), 414.

141. See Reginald Garrigou-Lagrange, *Christ the Saviour: A Commentary on the Third Part of Saint Thomas' Theological Summa*, trans. by Dom Bede Rose (St. Louis, MO: Herder [c1950]), ch. 5, q. 3. a. 2. Since the person of the Son is both the principle and term of the assumption, "a Person is primarily and more properly said to assume" (Aquinas, *STh* IIIa, q. 3, a. 2). The "*original efficiency*" of this "ineffable act" was an *opera Trinitatis ad extra*, whereas the "assumption was the only *immediate act* of the divine nature on the human nature in the person of the Son" (Owen, *Works*, 1:225). Owen cites the Damascene's authority when asserting that the *assumptio* was the "only singular immediate act of the person of the Son" (Owen, *Works*, 2:160).

142. The distinction between the *terminus* and *actio* as realities *ad intra* and *ad extra* respectively had already been made by Lutherans, such as Gerhard: "The work of incarnation is . . . called ad extra, and essential, or common, to the whole Trinity, as to the effect or production; but ad intra, and personal or proper to the Son, as to the termination, or relation" (Gerhard, as cited by Heinrich Schmid, "The 'Person of Christ,' according to the Older Theologians of the Evangelical Lutheran Church," *Mercersburg Review* 1 [1849]: 280n8). Or, as Mersch puts it, "If creation is the production of the order *ad extra*, the Incarnation is the taking of a creature to the Word *ad intra* so that it may subsist henceforth not in itself but in Him; it inaugurates what we have called the 'order of what is interiorized.'" See Emile Mersch, *The Theology of the Mystical Body*, trans. Cyril Vollert (St. Louis, MO: Herder, 1951), 417. Edwards alludes to this *ad intra* implication: "He was in the bosom of the Father from all eternity, but now he is in the bosom of the Father in our nature" (Edwards, 118. Sermon on Songs of Sol. 8:1 [1729], in *WJE* 44).

143. Aquinas paraphrases Aristotle: "For active power is the principle of acting upon something else; whereas passive power is the principle of being acted upon by something else, as the Philosopher says (*Metaph.* V, 17)" (Aquinas, *STh* I, q. 25, a. 1).

144. The assumption is an asymmetrical act of causation whereby the divine actively assumes a passive human nature (Aquinas, *STh* III, q. 2, a. 8, 2034–35).

145. "Miscellanies" no. 487, in *WJE* 13:529.

146. "Miscellanies" no. 709, in *WJE* 18:334.

147. For Edwards, personal identity is not merely mental or forensic on God's side but is founded on a real, ontological union of things or parts. We see this theme running through his cosmology and ecclesiology as well. Identity within the scheme of a continued creation is obtained

when God "so unites these successive new effects, that he treats them as one, by communicating to them like properties, relations, and circumstances; and so, leads us to regard and treat them as one" (Edwards, *WJE* 3:403). With regard to the mystical union, "God in requiring this in order to an union with Christ as one of his people" constitutes "something really in them, and between them, uniting them, that is the ground of the suitableness of their being accounted as one by the Judge" ("Justification by Faith Alone," in *WJE* 19:158).

148. "Miscellanies" no. 487, in *WJE* 13:528.

149. Leontius of Byzantium attributed the *ousiosis* to the common operation or *energeia* of the Trinity (Grillmeier, *Christ in Christian Tradition*, 2:229). "The work of the conception is indeed common to the whole Trinity; yet in some way it is attributed to each of the Persons. For to the Father is attributed authority in regard to the Person of the Son, who by this conception took to Himself (human nature). The taking itself (of human nature) is attributed to the Son: but the formation of the body taken by the Son is attributed to the Holy Ghost" (Aquinas, *STh* III, q. 32, a. 1, ad 1).

150. From the logic of *conveniens*, the work of creating Christ's human nature "befits" the Holy Spirit in three aspects. As "befitting to the cause of the Incarnation," (1) seen from the divine perspective, the Spirit appropriately brings about this act of divine love as the mutual love of Father and Son; (2) from the created perspective, since the human nature was assumed by grace and not merit, it is attributed to the Spirit of grace; and, (3) "befitting the term of Incarnation," as the Spirit regenerates and sanctifies the Christians, so the Spirit aptly makes the human Jesus "the Holy one and the Son of God" (Aquinas, *STh* III, q. 32, a. 1).

151. For Aquinas, "to create is not proper to any one Person, but is common to the whole Trinity," though an operational ordering corresponding to their *taxis* of origination (from the Father through the Son in the Spirit) and an appropriation of power, wisdom, and goodness are evident (Aquinas, *STh* I-I, q. 45, a. 6).

152. "And there is but one thing that is created that is more immediately the work of God the Father, and that is the human nature of Christ, and that both in its old and new creation" (Edwards, "Miscellanies," no. 958, in *WJE* 20:234). The nomenclature is Marshall's, which sums up Edwards's thought quite nicely: "Depending on the action—especially the actions of the divine persons in relation to one another . . . any of the persons might be the primary agent (the one with whose propria the action has the greatest likeness) or the immediate agent (the one whose role terminates the action)." See Bruce D. Marshall, *Trinity and Truth* (Cambridge: Cambridge University Press, 2000), 260.

153. Edwards, "Miscellanies," no. 958, in *WJE* 20: 234. Even in gracious operations (like illumination), "the immediate efficient cause is the Holy Spirit" (Edwards, "A Spiritual Understanding of Divine Things Denied to the Unregenerate," in *WJE* 14:88; see also Edwards, 26. Sermon on 1 Cor. 2:14 [Fall 1723–Winter 1724] in *WJE* 42).

154. While the Scriptures do refer to Christ as the universal Creator, "such expressions don't import that he made himself, or made that of himself which was made" (Edwards, "Miscellanies," no. 958, in *WJE* 20:237).

155. Thus, Edwards refers to the Spirit indifferently as the "principle of assumption or unition" or "principle of union" (Edwards, "Miscellanies," no. 709, *WJE* 18:335).

156. "Though the creation of the human nature of Christ ben't by Christ economically, or don't especially belong to him as a work appointed him in the order constituted among the persons of the Trinity, with respect to their operations and actions *ad extra*, yet 'tis true the creation of the human nature of Christ is not without the Son, as all the persons of the Trinity do concur in all acts *ad extra*" (Edwards, "Miscellanies," no. 958, in *WJE* 20:238). This was preached doctrine: "Indeed the whole Trinity is concerned in every work" (Edwards, "Of God the Father," in *WJE* 25:145).

157. Edwards, "Miscellanies," no. 1349, in *WJE* 23:423. "But the Holy Ghost is the Spirit of the supreme God and the Spirit of God the Father. For it was partly on this account that the virgin Mary's child is called the Son of God, because it was conceived by the power of the Holy Ghost

(Luke 1:35), which shows that the Holy Ghost, by whose power he was conceived, was the Spirit of the Father."

158. Edwards, "Miscellanies," no. 294, in *WJE* 13:385. Hastings accuses Edwards of conflating the *proprietas personales* of the Father and the Spirit based on the following entry (W. Ross Hastings, "'Honouring the Spirit': Analysis and Evaluation of Jonathan Edwards' Pneumatological Doctrine of the Incarnation," *International Journal of Systematic Theology* 7, no. 3 (July 2005): 293). "So it was the Spirit's work to impregnate the blessed Virgin, for it is the office of love to beget; generation is the work of love" (Edwards, "Miscellanies," no. 294, in *WJE* 13:385). Clearly, Edwards was aware of such a possible objection. If a correspondence between the Trinity *ad intra* and *ad extra* is assumed, then "generation" is the work of the Father's Spirit upon the incarnate Christ insofar as the Holy Spirit is the act or work of love of the Father toward the Son. This must account for the mutuality of the divine generation and spiration in Edwards's doctrine of the immanent Trinity.

159. Thus, the verbal *communicatio idiomatum* is founded on a real *communicatio Spiritum*. This shall be treated in greater detail in the next chapter.

160. Even before "the embryo of Christ in the womb of the Virgin Mary" was infused with a "spirit or soul," it was properly the Spirit's work to prepare it for sanctification (Edwards, "Miscellanies," no. 734, in *WJE* 18:359–40). Although there was "no proper holiness of nature, and nothing of the nature of the Holy Spirit" in the embryonic stage, yet this preparatory work is the Spirit's for it was "in order to an holy effect or production in her, for that was an holy thing that was born of her" (ibid.).

161. In fact, Rahner seems to think that the exteriorization of deity must, by necessity, result in human nature. "Now Christ's 'human nature' is not something which happens to be there, among many other things, which might equally well have been hypostatically assumed, but it is precisely that which comes into being when God's Logos 'utters' himself outwards" (Karl Rahner, *The Trinity*, trans. Joseph Donceel [London: Herder & Herder, 1970], 89). This finally resolves into an anthropological principle for, "if God wills to become non-God, the human being comes to be." See Karl Rahner, "Incarnation," *Theological Investigations*, iv, 116, as quoted in Dennis W. Jowers, *The Trinitarian Axiom of Karl Rahner: The Economic Trinity Is the Immanent Trinity and Vice Versa* (Lewiston, ME: Edwin Mellen, 2006), 117. See Thomas F. Torrance, "Toward an Ecumenical Consensus on the Trinity," in *Trinitarian Perspectives: Towards Doctrinal Agreement* (Edinburgh: T&T Clark, 1994), 89. Rahner's tacit appeal to the *anypostatos-enypostatos* dialectic cannot secure the case because *hypostasis* is not unique to the Son. Personal propriety only determines the *specific* human form a divine person might take in the event of an incarnation. Aquinas's supposition that any of the divine persons could be incarnate by virtue of their common divine power still holds. His argument from *conveniens* or "fittingness" of the Son's incarnation is transposed from the aesthetic to the ontological. In other words, the divine *Son* can come in the flesh only as the human *Son*. Does such taking of God's freedom as the hypothetical starting point turn "the incarnation [into] an unbelievable myth"? Surely not, as this position does not deny Rahner's axiom: "That which appears no longer expresses anything of the one who appears" (Rahner, *Trinity*, 90). As Marshall puts it: "Any divine person could become incarnate, but *this* incarnation, *this* history of salvation, could come about only by the enfleshment of the Son" (Marshall, "*Ex Occidente Lux?*," 42).

162. Temporally, "the Messiah [was to] be born of a woman, who shall be his mother, but not as begotten of a man, or having any man for his father." Hence, "the Messiah [was] . . . begotten not by any man, but by . . . his Father. And this generation of him, by . . . his Father, won't be then a new thing. It is an eternal generation; it has been already 'of old, from everlasting'" (Edwards, "Notes on Scripture," no. 501a, in *WJE* 15:589). Edwards's specificity would seem to discourage any notion of an incarnation of the Spirit or Father since this would be something novel, viz., noncorrespondence to their eternal *proprietas personales*.

163. Edwards, "Miscellanies," no. 958, in *WJE* 20:234.

164. As Clarke has argued, personhood is both "in-itself" and "toward others" substantial and relational. See W. Norris Clarke, "To Be Is to Be Substance-in-Relation," in *Metaphysics as Foundation: Essays in Honor of Ivor Leclerc*, ed. Paul A. Bogaard and Gordon Treash (Albany: State University of New York Press, 1993), esp. 174–79.

165. Goodwin, *WTG* 6:11.

166. Edwards, "Miscellanies," no. 958, in *WJE* 20:239.

167. Hence, creation is attributed to the whole Christ, except Christ's own self: "The things that are here spoken of Christ are spoken of him as God-man, either so actually, or so by constitution or immutable undertaking and appointment. All things are from him as God-man, but he him [self] as God-man is from the Father" (ibid., 238).

168. Ibid., 236. Edwards, like Owen, argues that it was the Holy Spirit who directly raised Christ's body from death. "And therefore that Spirit that is spoken of, by which Christ was raised, was without doubt the Holy Ghost, and not the divine Logos as is generally supposed" (Edwards, "Miscellanies," no. 487, in *WJE* 13:531). More accurately, it was the Spirit of the Father who resurrected the incarnate Son. Yet, Edwards did not deny Christ's immortal divinity a role. So, "it was impossible that Christ's body should be held by death, being a part of Christ" (Edwards, "Miscellanies," no. 155 [*145*], in *WJE* 13:304). The general resurrection, however, is the act of the Son by the Spirit.

169. In the transfiguration of Christ, a revelation of the eternal generation and divinity of the Son is given to the disciples. They thus saw Christ's external glory "as communicated from the glory in the cloud" (Edwards, "Notes on Scriptures," no. 265, in *WJE* 15:216). "The light in Christ's person appeared to them to be as it were lighted up, or begotten as it were, by that in the cloud, or the glory in the cloud appeared shining on Christ, and so communicating the same excellent brightness. This again declared him to be the Son of God, for it showed him to be the express image of the Father, and to be from the Father as begotten of him" (ibid., 216–17). Hence, there is a distinction between the creation as "a manifestation of the glory of the Son of God" and Christ's human nature issuing "from the glory of the Father" (Edwards, "Miscellanies," no. 958, in *WJE* 20:239).

170. "All [created things] universally are by the Spirit, but the human nature of Christ and what belongs to it is by the Spirit as the Spirit of the Father; but all the rest are by the Spirit as the Spirit of the Son. The incarnation of Christ was the work of the Father. He is not only the Son of God (i.e. of God the Father) by his eternal generation, but also by his generation in the womb of the virgin" (ibid., 234).

171. "All Christ's fullness is from the Father, although all the creatures' fullness be from him, and he filleth all in all, fills all things, both in heaven and in earth" (ibid., 239).

172. "The man Christ is united to the Logos . . . by the respect which God hath to this human nature. God hath respect to this man and loveth him as his own Son; this man hath communion with the Logos, in the love which the Father hath to him as his only begotten Son" (Edwards, "Miscellanies," no. 487, in *WJE* 13:529).

173. In Jesus, "the Spirit of the Logos may dwell in a creature after such a manner, that that creature may become one person [with the Logos], and may be looked upon as such and accepted as such" (ibid., 528). Edwards appropriates the classical two-nature Logos Christology but sets it within the Trinitarian context. "The man Christ is united to the Logos these two ways: first, by the respect which God [the Father] hath to this human nature. . . . And secondly, by what is inherent in this man, whereby he becomes one person" (ibid., 529).

174. Ibid.

175. "The name of the Son of God is Messiah and Christ." These names are not, Edwards asserts, "names proper to Christ only as man, or as Mediator: but God the Son from all eternity was Christ, or anointed with the Holy Spirit without measure, strictly speaking, or with the infinite love of the of the Father towards him" (Edwards, "Miscellanies," no. 225, in *WJE* 13:346). Elsewhere, Edwards reiterates that the Son "in his divine nature only . . . is Christ, or the anointed." He is so because "he is the object of the infinite love and delight of the Father, and as

the Father doth eternally pour forth the Spirit of love (which is typified in Scripture by oil) infinitely upon him" (Edwards, "Blank Bible," note on Dan. 9:25, in *WJE* 24:767).

176. On the name "Christ," or "anointed," Irenaeus gives a Trinitarian meaning: "The one who has anointed is the Father; the one who has been anointed, this is the Son; and the Unction is being in the Spirit" (*Adversus Haereses*, 3.18.3, as cited in Kilian McDonnell, *The Baptism of Jesus in the Jordan: The Trinitarian and Cosmic Order of Salvation* [Collegeville, MN: Liturgical Press, 1996], 118–19). The latter position can be found in Justin and is taken up by the Damascene: "For in His own person he anointed Himself; as God anointed His body with His own divinity, and as Man being anointed. For he is Himself both God and Man. And the anointing is the divinity of His humanity" (John of Damascus, *Orthodox Faith*, bk. 3, ch. 3, 47 [*NPNF* 9]).

177. Edwards, "Blank Bible," note on Dan 9: 25, in *WJE* 24:767.

178. Ibid. As we have seen, the first two senses are ontological; Christ is the Anointed as *Logos asarkos* and *Logos ensarkos*.

179. See Ivor Davidson's defense of the *anhypostaton-enhypostaton* Christology and his suggestion of the crucial role of the Holy Spirit in any attempt to reappropriate such a Christology for contemporary theology: "Theologizing the Human Jesus: An Ancient (and Modern) Approach to Christology Assessed," *International Journal of Systematic Theology* 3, no. 2 (July 2001): 129–53. Clearly, Edwards here transcends the simple polarity of emphases between an ontological Logos Christology and a functional Spirit Christology. Although one may not agree with Pinnock's distinction between person and work, we would agree that there is complementarity between Logos and Spirit Christologies. See Clark H. Pinnock, *Flame of Love: A Theology of the Holy Spirit* (Downers Grove, IL: InterVarsity, 1999), 91.

180. So, "the union of the man Christ Jesus to the divine Logos in the same person so as to be the same Son of God, is by communicating the Spirit of God" (Edwards, "Miscellanies," no. 709, in *WJE* 18:333).

181. Ibid., 334. Edwards thus logically reorders the traditional conception/incarnation/ indwelling schema to conception/indwelling/incarnation. Where Lutherans, such as Quenstedt, could posit the *unio personalis* as a result of the *communio naturarum*, Edwards considers the *unio* as arising from the Spirit's indwelling in the human nature. The natures in Christ are united such that "ut ex utraque sibi invicem communicante fiat unum incommunicabile, una sc. Persona." See Quenstedt, *Theol. Did. Pol.* [1685], III, 3, sect. 1, th. 36, as cited by Barth, *CD*, vol. 4, pt. 2, *The Doctrine of Reconciliation*, ed. G. W. Bromiley and T. F. Torrance, trans. G. W. Bromiley (Edinburgh: T&T Clark, 1958), § 64, 67.

182. "[The] Holy Ghost be to our bodies in a transcendent manner; though not by a personal union, yet by such an union as is between the human nature of Christ and the Holy Ghost: For, my brethren, though the Godhead of the second Person doth dwell in a personal manner in the human nature of Christ, yet the Holy Ghost doth not dwell personally in him; he is united unto the human nature but as he is unto us" (Goodwin, *WTG* 7:127).

183. For Aquinas, "the grace of union, precedes the habitual grace of Christ, not in order of time, but by nature and in thought" (Aquinas, *STh* III, q. 7, a. 13). This is rooted in the processions *ad intra*: "Now the mission of the Son is prior, in the order of nature, to the mission of the Holy Ghost, even as in the order of nature the Holy Ghost proceeds from the Son, and love from wisdom. Hence the personal union, according to which the mission of the Son took place, is prior in the order of nature to habitual grace, according to which the mission of the Holy Ghost takes place" (ibid.).

184. For Edwards was surely familiar with the axiom *gradus non mutant speciem*, that varying degrees do not change a nature. See Isaac Watts, *The Glory of Christ as God-Man Displayed in Three Discourses* (Boston: Printed by Manning and Loring for David West, 1795), § 2, 130. Or, as John Jewel stated it: "It is a common known rule in the schools: *Magis et minus non mutant speciem*." See John Jewel, *A defence of the apology of the Church of England*, in *The works of John Jewel, Bishop of Salisbury*, ed. John Ayre (Cambridge: The University Press, 1848; first published in 1567), 419.

185. Conversely, the incarnation is only the epitome of the mystical union.

186. Edwards, "Miscellanies," no. 487, in *WJE* 13:539. "For the creature is more or less holy according as it has more or less of the Holy Spirit dwelling in it; but Christ has so much of the Spirit, and hath it in so high and excellent a manner, as to render him the same person with him whose Spirit it is" (Edwards, "Miscellanies," no. 766, in *WJE* 18:413). The quantitative ("so high") marks Christ out as exemplary in sanctity, while the qualitative ("excellent a manner") as God incarnate and sui generis. See also Edwards, "Miscellanies," no. 1043, in *WJE* 20:383.

187. "Something more is doubtless intended than that he was an inspired person, and spake the Word of God as the prophets did" (Edwards, "Miscellanies," no. 764b, in *WJE* 18:411).

188. "But in the sanctifying work of the Holy Ghost . . . the Spirit of God . . . exerts its own proper nature; that is to say, it communicates and exerts itself in the soul in those acts which are its proper, natural and essential acts in itself *ad intra*, or within the Deity from all eternity" (Edwards, "Miscellanies," no. 471, in *WJE* 13:513).

189. Edwards, "Miscellanies," no. 487, in *WJE* 13:531–32.

190. The hypostatic "union is the consequence of God's communicating his Spirit without measure to [Christ's] human nature, so as to render it the same person with him that is God" (Edwards, "Miscellanies," no. 764b, in *WJE* 18:411).

191. "Christ may be by the indwelling and influence of the Holy Ghost personally united to the Son of God, and yet not be personally united to the Holy Ghost, through whose indwelling and influence it is" (Edwards, "Miscellanies," no. 487, in *WJE* 13:532).

192. While Jesus "was anointed as united to the divine nature when he first began to be" (ibid., 530), the incarnational "union [was] the *consequence* of God's [the Father] communicating his Spirit without measure to [Christ's] human nature" (Edwards, "Miscellanies," no. 764b, in *WJE* 18:411; emphasis mine). If one assumed a fundamental similarity between this idea of Christ's sanctification and the patristic notion of deification, Edwards is here reiterating the Damascene's insistence on the simultaneity of the *synousiosis*, *ousiosis*, and *theosis* in the hypostatic union. "For the Word Himself became flesh . . . [in] that these three things took place simultaneously, the assumption of our nature, the coming into being, and the deification of the assumed nature by the Word" (John of Damascus, *Orthodox Faith*, bk. 3, ch. 12, 56–57 [*NPNF* 9]).

193. See Edwards, "Miscellanies," no. 487, in *WJE* 13:531–32.

194. Edwards, "Miscellanies," no. 709, in *WJE* 18:334.

195. Echoing Aquinas's *gratia unionis/gratia habitualis* ordering, Goodwin asserted that "[t]he Holy Ghost was, 1. The immediate Former of the Humane Nature of Christ, in the Womb. 2. The Uniter of that Nature to the Son of God. 3. The Sanctifier thereof, with all Graces dwelling therein, above all measure" (Thomas Goodwin, *The Work Of The Holy Ghost In Our Salvation*, vol. 6 of *The Works of Thomas Goodwin, D.D. Sometime President of Magdelene College, Oxford* [Edinburgh: James Nichol, 1863], 43). Goodwin was not peculiarly ascribing the work of uniting the natures to the Spirit, since he regarded that as an *opera Trinitatis ad extra*. By special appropriation, the personal union belongs to the Son. "I have not found a ground why to attribute the personal union more particularly to the Holy Ghost; but rather . . . that action is more peculiarly to be attributed to the Son himself" (Goodwin, *Work Of The Holy Ghost In Our Salvation*, ch. 3, 8). Despite the *opera indivisa* caveat, Owen, like Goodwin, also insisted that the *assumptio* was the "only singular immediate *act* of the person of the Son on the human nature" and that the "immediate divine *efficiency*" of the *conceptio* "was the peculiar work of the Holy Ghost" (Owen, *Works*, 3:160, 163).

196. Among the Reformed-Puritan "divines," there were those who, as Goodwin put it, "ascribe unto this Spirit the special honor of tying that marriage knot, or union, between the Son of God, and that man Jesus, whom the Holy Ghost formed in the Virgin's womb" (Goodwin, *Work Of The Holy Ghost In Our Salvation*, ch. 3, 8). One example is Watson: "St. *Basil* saith, *It was the Holy Ghost's blessing the flesh of that Virgin whereof Christ was formed*. But there is a further mystery in it, the Holy Ghost having framed Christ in the Virgin's womb, did in a wonderful manner unite Christ's humane nature to his divine, and so of both made one person" (Thomas

Watson, *A body of practical divinity, consisting of above one hundred seventy six sermons on the lesser catechism . . .* [London: Thomas Parkhurst, 1692], 112).

197. Edwards, "Miscellanies," no. 709, in *WJE* 18:334–35.

198. Ibid., 335. Ascribing action to the agent would seem to be premised on Edwards's belief that "a person is that which hath understanding and will" (Edwards, "Discourse on the Trinity," in *WJE* 21:133). He is thus critical of the position, such as Owen's, which held that "this act of the Holy Ghost, in *forming of the body of Christ*, differs from the act of the Son in *assuming* the human nature into personal union with himself" (Owen, *Works*, 3:165). The axiom underlying Edwards's objection may be differently expressed as "divisis operibus dividitur persona" (Thomasius, *Christi Person und Werk* 1:604, as quoted by Wolfhart Pannenberg, *Jesus—God and Man*, trans. Lewis L. Wilkins and Duane A. Priebe [London: SCM, 1968], 309).

199. Edwards frames this rhetorically: "If 'tis by the Spirit of God that the human nature of Christ was conceived, and had life and being, why should we not suppose that 'tis also by the Spirit that he has union with the divine nature?" (Edwards, "Miscellanies," no. 487, in *WJE* 13:531).

200. As for Aquinas, "the principle of the union is the Person of the Son assuming human nature, Who is said to be sent into the world, inasmuch as he assumed human nature; but the principle of habitual grace, which is given with charity, is the Holy Ghost, Who is said to be sent, inasmuch as he dwells in the mind by charity." This would not be a problem if they were strictly appropriations. Aquinas, however, seems to describe the *assumptio* and *sanctificatio* as *propria* of Son and Spirit respectively. Thus the ordering of assumption-sanctification befits the ordering of *missio* and *processio*, which is to say, the Son precedes the Spirit (Aquinas, *STh* III, q. 7, a. 13).

201. "Here I would observe that divines have not been wont to suppose that these three had three distinct understandings, but all one and the same understanding" (Edwards, "Discourse on the Trinity," in *WJE* 21:133). The ascription of will and action to nature and not person had been decided in the Sixth Ecumenical Council in the face of the monothelite controversy.

202. Edwards, "Miscellanies," no. 709, in *WJE* 18:335.

203. "It was not properly the making the flesh of Christ that was sending Christ into the world, but *making the Word flesh*" (ibid., 334; italics original).

204. Ibid., 335. According to Grillmeier, for Leontius the *henosis* "consisted in an act of divine omnipotence which in one single action effected two things: the coming into existence (*ousiosis*) and the unification (*synousiosis*) of the human nature with the divine *hypostasis*" (Grillmeier, *Christ in Christian Tradition*, 2:509).

205. Edwards, "Miscellanies," no. 709, in *WJE* 18:335.

206. A purely miraculous conception without an assumption makes merely an inspirited person, while an assumption of an existing person would result in a union of two persons.

207. Ibid., 334.

208. In III *Sent.* d. 5, q. 2, a. 2, Aquinas outlines three senses in which the assumption may be taken: (1) the entire Trinity takes the human nature to the Son ("Uno modo communiter pro sumere, et sic tota Trinitas assumpsit humanam naturam filio"), (2) the divine nature in the Son takes to itself the human nature ("Secundo dicitur proprie quasi ad se: sumere ut sibi quocumque modo uniatur; et hoc modo natura divina in persona filii assumpsit humanam naturam"), and (3) only the Son properly takes to and into the Son's self the human nature ("Tertio dicitur propriissime, quasi ad se, et in se sumere; et sic convenit tantum personae, in qua facta est unio"). See R. J. Hennessey, ed., *Summa Theologiae*, 3a. 1–6, vol. 48, *The Incarnate Word: Latin Text, English Translation, Introduction, Notes, Appendices and Glossary*, 2nd ed., Blackfriars Translation (Cambridge: Cambridge University Press, 2006), q. 3, a. 2, 90–91n*b*.

209. Uniting or "union as an action implies only the conjunction of extremes" and not an interiorization of something external to oneself (Garrigou-Lagrange, *Christ the Saviour*, ch. 4, q. 2. a. 8). As *assumptio* signifies movement and action, *assumptio carnis* is the taking of an external human nature into the person of the Son. "And hence assumption determines the term whence

and the term whither; for assumption means a taking to oneself from another" (dicitur enim assumptio quasi ab alio ad se sumptio) (Aquinas, *STh* III, q. 2, a. 8).

210. Hence, "making is what belongs to assuming" (Edwards, "Miscellanies," no. 709, in *WJE* 18:335)

211. Ibid., 335.

212. "And if he had not actually assumed, married into one Person with himself, that which was formed in her Womb by the Holy Ghost, it had not been called the Son of God" (Goodwin, *Work Of The Holy Ghost In Our Salvation*, 386).

213. In the beatific vision, the saints shall "see that body, enlivened by that soul, which God had assumed into a personal union with himself, to be the same in person with him forever more" (Edwards, "Poverty of Spirit," in *WJE* 10:496; see also "Miscellanies," no. 460, in *WJE* 13:501). Others examples: "the human nature was to be assumed up into the second person" ("Miscellanies" no. 1261, in *WJE* 23:198); "he came down and became a dependent being; he assumed a weak and frail nature" (65. Sermon on 2 Cor. 8:9, in *WJE* 43); "the Son of God assuming human nature of the seed of Abraham." See Jonathan Edwards, "A Humble Attempt," in *The Works of Jonathan Edwards*, vol. 5, *Apocalyptic Writings*, ed. Stephen J. Stein (New Haven: Yale University Press, 1977), 309.

214. Edwards, "Miscellanies," no. 702, *WJE* 18:291.

215. Edwards, "Miscellanies," no. 958, in *WJE* 20:234.

216. "Whatever Christ assumes into union to himself must be by that person that acts as the principle of union" (Edwards, "Miscellanies," no. 709, in *WJE* 18:335).

217. Ibid.

218. Edwards, *WJE* 1:348.

219. Edwards, "Miscellanies," no. 487, in *WJE* 13:530.

220. The "external glory" appearing in Christ on earth corresponds to the eternal decision in the *pactum salutis* that "Christ should everlastingly be united to an external nature" (Edwards, "Notes on Scriptures," no. 266, in *WJE* 15:219).

221. Emphasis mine. Edwards, "Miscellanies," no. 709, in *WJE* 18:335.

222. As Mersch puts it, "It is *ad extra* by logical priority; in the mentally conceived instant that precedes it, the humanity, regarded in itself, is exterior to the divinity. . . . But . . . the Incarnation is *ad intra* by reason of its effect, by the personality it gives to this humanity" (Mersch, *Theology of the Mystical Body*, 417).

223. Aquinas, *STh* III, q. 2, a. 8, 2035. Or, more accurately, they stand in a relationship of "quasi-equivalence" (Garrigou-Lagrange, *Christ the Saviour*, ch. 4, q. 2, a. 8). "When motion is removed from action and passion, only relation remains" (Aquinas, *STh* I-a, q. 45, a. 3). The relation between the natures in Christ is not between that of agent and patient, as no movement is involved: "Transitive action is motion as coming from the agent, and passion is motion that is in the patient. Hence with the removal of action and passion, there is nothing left but a relation of real dependence" (Garrigou-Lagrange, *Christ the Saviour*, ch. 8, q. 6, n. 769).

224. On the contrary, the medieval scholastics systematized this distinction in terms of the assumption (*assumptio carnis* or *unitio personalis*) as dynamic event and union (*unio personalis* or *communio naturarum*) as static fact. "Hence the *first* and principal difference between assumption and union must be said to be that union implies the relation: whereas assumption implies the action" (Aquinas, *STh* III, q. 2, a. 8, 2035). In Aquinas's words: "For assumption implies *becoming* [*in fieri*], whereas union implies *having become* [*in facto*]" (*STh* III, q. 2, a. 8, 2035). Or, as Strauss puts it, *unitio personalis* is the "act of union" while *unio personalis* is the "state of union." See David Friedrich Strauss, *The Life of Jesus Critically Examined*, trans. Marian Evans (New York: Calvin Blanchard, 1860), 875. The Reformed and Lutherans also conceived the *unio personalis* and *communio naturarum* as states of perfection. It is not "as if the personal union or the personal indwelling of the whole fullness of the Godhead in the assumed nature of Christ became greater, closer, fuller, and more perfect as the years went by." See Martin Chemnitz, *The Two Natures in*

Christ, trans. J. A. O. Preus (St. Louis, Missouri: Concordia, 1971; originally published as *De Duabus Naturis in Christo*, Leipzig, 1578), 488. Edwards would only regard the incarnation as a *perfecting* event insofar as the humanity that is constantly united becomes perfect.

225. Edwards, "Miscellanies," no. 709, in *WJE* 18:335.

226. Edwards, "Miscellanies," no. 624, in *WJE* 18:154.

227. "By sending the Spirit, assuming his flesh into being and into the person of the divine Logos . . . the Father sent him into the world" (Edwards, "Miscellanies," no. 709, *WJE* 18:334).

228. Edwards, "Miscellanies," no. 624, in *WJE* 18:154. Edwards does not specify what this distinction between person and work entails, but it clearly inserts a gap between the eternal procession and mission of the Son. So, elsewhere, he closes this gap by characterizing the anointing as being the basis of both Christ's *persona* and *missio*. "Christ's anointing don't only mark out Christ as being our Mediator, but 'tis his anointing that qualifies and fits him for the work of Mediator; hence arises the value and efficacy of his sufferings and obedience" (Edwards, "Miscellanies," no. 487, in *WJE* 13:530). And elsewhere he posits a total unity: "But the giving such communion in the personality of the eternal Son to human [nature], was the very same as sending Christ into the world" (Edwards, "Miscellanies," no. 709, in *WJE* 18:334).

229. Or as Balthasar put it differently, "Jesus reveals God at the behest, not of the Trinity, but of the Father." See Hans Urs von Balthasar, *Theo-Drama: Theological Dramatic Theory*, vol. 3, *The Dramatis Personae: The Person in Christ*, trans. Graham Harrison (San Francisco: Ignatius, 1992), 225.

230. "And if we take 'office' in this sense, each person of the Trinity has not so properly a distinct office because the part that God the Father has in that affair is not under any other person" (Edwards, "Of God the Father," in *WJE* 25:145–46). This sense of self-sending implies a kind of nestorianizing of the natures.

231. Edwards, "Essay on the Trinity," in *TG*, 108.

232. "Miscellanies," no. 1151, in *WJE* 20:525. Since incarnation and sanctification are but "a kind of second proceeding of the same persons," the one cannot be without the other ("Miscellanies," no. 1082, in *WJE* 20:466).

233. Edwards, "Miscellanies," no. 487, in *WJE* 13:529.

234. Ibid., 530–31.

235. Yet, the eternal generation of the Son is logically prior to the double or mediated procession of the Spirit, whereas the temporal begetting of the Son is logically preceded by the Spirit's *missio*.

236. "The only singular immediate *act* of the person of the Son on the human nature was the *assumption* of it into subsistence with himself" (Owen, *Works*, 3:160).

237. Owen, *Works* 1:225. Since Owen presupposed that the "Holy Ghost . . . is the immediate, peculiar, efficient cause of all external divine operations," he concluded that "he [is] the immediate operator of all divine acts of the Son himself, even on his own human nature" (ibid., 3:160). Owen affirmed the indivisible *opera ad extra* and appropriated the perfecting mode of all divine operations to the Holy Spirit as corresponding to the divine *taxis*. So, "the immediate actings of the Holy Ghost are not spoken of him absolutely, nor ascribed unto him exclusively, as unto the other persons and their concurrence in them. It is a saying generally admitted, that *Opera Trinitatis ad extra sunt indivisa*" (ibid., 162). Yet, he thought of the operation of the Spirit upon Jesus as a *proprium*: "Yea, and there is such a distinction in their operations, that one divine act may produce a peculiar respect and relation unto one person, and not unto another; as the assumption of the human nature did to the Son, for he only was incarnate. And such are the especial actings of the Holy Ghost towards the head of the church, our Lord Jesus Christ, in this work of the new creation" (ibid.).

238. "'Tis manifest that the divine speeches that Christ uttered, and the divine works that Christ wrought, were by the Spirit of God. . . . When the man Christ Jesus said, 'I will; be thou clean,' or speaking in the name and person of the eternal Son of God, *spake* by the Holy Ghost,

then it will follow that it was by the Holy Ghost that the man Christ Jesus *was* in the name and in the person of the eternal Son of God. But he spake this by the Holy Ghost, for it was at the direction, motion, and influence of the Spirit of God on Christ's will that he wrought miracles" (Edwards, "Miscellanies," no. 766, in *WJE* 18:411, 413; italics original).

239. Edwards, *WJE* 1:347–48.

240. Ibid., 348. However, it is "no absurdity to suppose, that contrary relations may belong to the same thing, at the same time, with respect to different things."

241. If the Father is regarded as the source of the divine action, then the Son conjointly acts upon the human nature, though a step closer according to the divine *taxis*. Holmes's attempt to characterize Owen's idea that the *assumptio* was the only direct act of the Son upon his humanity as "asserting the positive . . . rather than the negative—that there are no other immediate acts of the Son" (Stephen R. Holmes, "Reformed Varieties of the *Communicatio Idiomatum*," in *The Person of Christ*, ed. Stephen R. Holmes and Murray A. Rae [London: T&T Clark International, 2006], 79–80) does not mitigate the crypto-Nestorianism of Owen's positive assertion—viz., that all acts of the Son of God "wrought in, by, or upon the human nature . . . he did . . . by the Holy Ghost" (Owen, *Works*, 1:225).

242. Edwards, "Miscellanies," no. 487, in *WJE* 13:529.

243. Ibid.

244. Edwards, "Miscellanies," no. 958, in *WJE* 20:239.

245. Ibid., 234–35. "He is not only the Son of God (i.e. of God the Father) by his eternal generation, but also by his generation in the womb of the virgin." Here, Edwards seems to depart from Aquinas, who, arguing for the incarnation of any divine person, reasoned that the temporal generation was not constitutive of personal identity. "The temporal sonship, whereby Christ is said to be the Son of Man, does not constitute His Person, as does the eternal Sonship; but is something following upon the temporal nativity" (*STh* III, q. 3, a. 5, ad 1, 2042).

246. If that were the case, the action would be transitive and the human nature would become an independent person. In short, this would be Nestorian. If Edwards allows for the saints' participation in the Son's filiation, what more of the Son's own human nature? "For being members of God's own natural Son, they are sort of partakers of his relation to the Father: they are not only sons of God by regeneration, but by a kind of communion in the sonship of the eternal Son" (Edwards, "Excellency of Christ," in *Sermons*, 195).

247. Affirming the *filioque*, he preached: "Christ as he is God is one person from whom the Spirit of God proceeds . . . and Christ as man and mediatour [*sic*] has the Spirit of God given by the Father not by measure." He receives the Spirit for himself (as *caput*) and for all the elect (*et membra*): "He has received the Holy Ghost not only for himself but for all that God has given him" (Edwards, 163. Sermon on John 1:14 [June 1752], in *WJE* 45).

248. "For these reasons he is called the Spirit of Christ, because he indeed as his Spirit; he proceeds from him, and because in all his work towards men he acts as his Spirit" (Edwards, Sermon on 2 Cor. 3:18 [a] [1728], in *WJE* 43).

249. Edwards, "Miscellanies," no. 487, in *WJE* 13: 529.

250. Ibid.

251. Ibid.

252. Edwards, "Miscellanies," no. 513, in *WJE* 18:57.

253. Edwards, "Miscellanies," no. 487, in *WJE* 13:530.

4

Hypostatic Union

Participation of the Human Nature in the Divine Person of the Logos

Previously, we looked at the *pactum salutis* as God's election to self-communicate *ad extra* in view of the Fall. Central to this Trinitarian decree was the incarnation of the Son, whose being was constituted through the specific *modus operandi* of the triune persons. In this chapter, we shift our focus to the relation between the divine Word and the Word's human nature.

> We have all reason to conclude that no degree of intimacy will be too much for the manhood of Christ, seeing that the divine Logos has been pleased to assume him into his very person; and therefore, we may conclude that no degree of intimacy will be too great for others to be admitted to, of whom Christ is the head or chief, according to their capacity: for this is in some sort an example of God's love to manhood, that he hath so advanced manhood.[1]

While Edwards's pneumatic Christology may not be set against the traditional Logos Christology, its basic Alexandrian character is refracted through specifically Reformed lenses. Again, the question of the divine self-communication surfaces. What is the relation between the Son and the *humanitas* that was inaugurated in the incarnation? How does the assumed human nature participate in the divine Word? What does this participation involve?

THE INCARNATION AS UNION-IN-DISTINCTION

"There is no distance of nature between man and man," Edwards states, "but between God and man there is an infinite distance of nature."[2] Reiterating the Cyrillian tradition, Edwards thinks of the incarnation as a sort of divine accommodation "in the *manner* of *existence*"—namely, God existing as a human being.[3] In the incarnation, then, the distance between the divine and human natures has been bridged.[4] But even so, this distance remains despite the incarnational crossing: the Creator willed to become a creature for the good of creation, without ceasing to be Creator.[5] Differently stated, the hypostatic union involves no confusion of essences.[6] What is God's goal in bringing the two natures together in Christ? It is to establish divine–human communion by way of a *commercium admiribile*: Christ's humiliation brings about human exaltation.[7] How, then, is this participation of existence and glory to be thought of?

UNITIO AND *UNIO HYPOSTATICA*: EVENT AND STATE
OF THE INCARNATION

The incarnation results from the coming into union of the divine and human natures in the Son. For John of Damascus, the *perichoresis* or interpenetration of the natures could be viewed as both unilateral and reciprocal.[8] The first unilateral uniting act is the divine nature permeating the human nature.[9] Although "it is impossible that the flesh should permeate through the divinity" on its own power and initiative, yet an ineffable power of penetration is granted to the human by the divine.[10] This reciprocal interpenetration of the natures thus constitutes the incarnation or state of union proper.[11] On the one hand, in terms of consequence and participation, the union is reciprocal; on the other hand, in terms of origin and power, it is asymmetrical.[12]

The Protestants appropriated the distinction between the *assumptio* as an immediate act and the *unio naturarum* as a mediate state.[13] In the state of union itself, however, a further distinction was made by the Reformed: *unio personalis* as an immediate union and *unio naturarum* as a mediate union.[14] In the asymmetrical concept of the act of uniting and its resultant state of union, the human nature is thought to be *enhypostaton*. This is a controverted motif to which we will turn.

EDWARDS'S APPROPRIATION AND MODIFICATION
OF THE *ENHYPOSTATOS-ANHYPOSTATOS* DIALECTIC

Without the technical language, Edwards adopts the ideas behind the medieval-Reformed *enhypostaton-anhypostaton* dialectic without denying the patristic *enypostatos* of Leontius of Byzantium.[15] For this Puritan thinker, the *enhypostaton* (derived existence and subsistence in another) includes the *enypostatos* (reality) and implies the *anhypostaton* (no independent subsistence).

Exegeting Luke 1:35, Edwards affirms that the flesh of Christ does not have its own separate personhood (*anhypostaton*): "'Tis said holy thing, not holy person or holy one; that holy thing is the human nature of Christ."[16] The *enhypostatos* was brought about by the *assumptio carnis*, which "was assuming flesh, or human nature, into the person of the Son."[17] This act of "giving communion of the divine personality to human nature" includes the *enypostatos*, "giving that human nature being."[18] Edwards sees the *enhypostaton* as the greatest intensification of divine-human intimacy.[19] This divine self-communication in Christ is finally soteriological, creating divine-human *communio* within God.[20]

"MAKING IN UNION": ENYPOSTATON AS COMPREHENDED IN THE ENHYPOSTATON

The *assumptio carnis*, as we have previously noted, is a twofold act of *unitio* and *conceptio* by the Holy Spirit. As a unifying act, that which is *anypostatos* becomes *enypostatos*, which is to say, "the uniting something out of nothing (i.e. something as yet unmade) to him."[21] As a creative operation, it involves the *enhypostatos* because "assuming is the making the human nature in the person of the Logos."[22] Simply stated, the assumption is a "making in union," an *ousiosis enhypostatos*, or an *enhypostaton* that includes the *enypostaton*.[23]

The Leontian *enypostatos*, when understood as "real," could very well be used of all existing persons. In other words, human *conceptio* results in the reality of a particular person. Applied to Christ, it serves to guarantee consubstantiality with the human species; it is an anthropological and generic notion. The *enypostatos*, however, secures the special dependence of the assumed nature in the person of the Son; its use is preeminently christological.

For Edwards, apart from the election to incarnation and the Spirit's actualization, the *ovum* assumed in the *assumptio carnis* could have had another reality through a natural conception (*enypostatos*).[24] He thus recapitulates Augustine in insisting that the *conceptio* of Jesus Christ is unlike any other on account of its simultaneity with the *unio*.[25] The assumption not only causes the reality of Christ's human nature—the *enypostatos*—it also is drawn into, shares in, and is sustained by the divine Word—the *enhypostaton*. As Edwards himself phrases it, the incarnation is the "assuming his flesh into being [*enypostatos*] and into the person of the divine Logos [*enhypostatos*], at the same time and by the same act."[26] On Edwards's idealism, however, the "*en*" is not to be understood as a localizing prefix in any spatial sense but indicates that the human nature depends wholly on the Word for its being and existence.[27]

HOLY SPIRIT AS THE PRINCIPLE OF THE CONTINUING IN-EXISTENCE OF CHRIST'S HUMAN NATURE

The *unio*, on Edwards's ontology, being a *unitio continua*, involves an ongoing moment-by-moment re-creation and re-assumption of the human nature into the person of the Son.[28] As the principle of the *assumptio carnis* or *unitio personalis*, the Spirit is also the principle of the *unio personalis*.[29] As the Spirit of the Father, the Spirit continually gives existence to Christ's human nature (*enypostaton*). As the Spirit of the Son, the Spirit ensures that this individual human nature has personhood in its perpetual in-existence in the Word (*enhypostaton*).[30]

In a static idea of the *unio personalis*, the *enypostatos* would have to exclude the *anypostatos*, but in a dynamic conception of the union, the case is quite different. Of itself, the *humanitas* has no *dispositio* to become and remain as the human nature of the Word; it has to be continuously occasioned by divine power. Christ's human nature is not self-perpetuating but is granted both reality and in-existence by the *Dispositio* of God moment by moment. The Holy Spirit must continually cause the incarnation as the Spirit of Father and Son, creating and uniting the human nature to the Word in one (twofold) act. "If the making had been by one person and the unition by another, the humanity would not, by him that made it, be made out of nothing into the Son."[31] Otherwise, Jesus would be a mere human by virtue of the Father's Spirit, who created but did not eventuate the *enhypostaton* of the human nature.

We may regard the role of the Holy Spirit in Edwards's Spirit Christology to approximate the actuating divine *esse* in St. Thomas's Christology.[32] Whether Aquinas's position is philosophically defensible need not detain us here, just as Edwards's metaphysics does not depend on the notion of the Son's uncreated *esse* as founding the *unio hypostatica*.[33] For the latter, the existence of the human Jesus is caused directly by the uncreated Spirit (of the Father).

SECOND ADAM: PARTICULAR AND REPRESENTATIVE HUMAN NATURE

While Edwards frequently refers to the hypostatic union as a reality between the Logos and the "man Jesus Christ," he also describes the latter as "this individual human nature."[34] Elsewhere, he points out that the "seed . . . in the womb of the virgin . . . was one of those seeds that had future humanity and that [had] individual humanity annexed to it by God's decree."[35] The notion of the assumption of a specific human nature is another way of parsing the *enhypostaton*. And Edwards stands in continuity with the Reformed-Puritan tradition in adopting this idea. For example, Owen claimed that the Son did not assume "*an individual person*."[36] On this account, the reality (*enypostatos*) of this individual human nature is included when it is granted dependent existence and personhood (*enhypostaton*) in the Word.[37]

Christ did "as it were appropriate human nature in general to himself," so as to become our substitute, representative, or "the head of those that had the human nature."[38] This is another expression of the *anhypostaton*. Not only are Christ and the church related as *caput et membra*, Christ is "more than our head, he is as the whole body"—the *totus Christus*.[39] Yet, within the particularism of Edwards's Calvinism, the idea of the assumption of "human nature in general" is only a synecdoche, hence the "as it were" qualifier. The *totus Christus*, while indicating the indivisibility of Christ mystical, is only *totum pro parte* in relation to the assumed humanity. In reality, Christ mystical is really "the head of all the *elect* creation."[40] Redemption was not potentially accomplished by Christ for humanity in general and, only then, to be actualized for particular persons through the Spirit's applicatory work. That is because the *assumptio* was not just the Word taking an *individuum* of the human genus or "one of this nature into a personal union with himself to be the head and king of the angels." It was also an act "as it were [of] assuming all *the elect* that were in that nature, who are all united to him as members to the head."[41]

Is the Incarnation an Incomplete or a Perfecting Union?

For Aquinas, the assumed nature lacks nothing essentially human although it is *enhypostaton* or an *individuum*.[42] Similarly, the Reformed tradition affirms that a complete, individual humanity has been assumed by the Son into a "complex person" since personhood is regarded as nonconstitutive of nature, "but is, as it were, the terminus which it tends."[43] What the assumed human nature lacks is self-existence, not psychological personality.[44] In fact, this individual human nature is more perfect than independent human subsistence due to the *enhypostaton*.[45] This christological principle is grounded in a more basic axiom of in-existence; namely, a thing is ennobled by its existence in a higher entity.[46]

Following St. Thomas, the Reformed-Puritan tradition affirmed that subsistence in a divine person is a greater dignity than independent subsistence.[47] And Edwards reiterates this insight: "The human nature of Christ was so honored as to be in the same person with the eternal Son of God."[48] Jesus is not only ennobled through in-existence in the divine Son but also exalted by the indwelling Spirit.[49] For Edwards, something of lesser dignity in itself as compared to another thing, for example, humans in comparison to angels, could be raised to a position of greater nobility through participation in something far nobler, such as divinity.[50] In all of created existence, the incarnate Son holds the preeminent place: "It was a great thing for God to make the creature, but not so great as for the Creator himself to become a creature. . . . When Christ was born, the greatest person was born that ever was or ever will be born."[51]

With regard to being, the *enhypostatos* was understood by the medieval and Reformed as the Son giving personal sustenance to the human nature not only in the assumption but in the very union itself.[52] Edwards expands the ontological idea of the human nature being sustained in the Logos in a more subjective manner. Christ's divinity psychologically upheld the humanity to freely endure the passion, without circumventing natural human mortality. "The divinity supported the humanity of Christ under his sufferings not as it kept his human nature from being annihilated or crushed in that respect, but as it kept him from sinking, and his courage from utterly failing, so as that he should have no command of himself; communicating such a degree of holiness to him, as to keep him from impatience and discontent, and that his love might be so great as to make him voluntary in it, in the midst of it."[53] The *enypostatos* does not make the flesh immortal, but made it permanently free and virtuous by participation in the Spirit. As Garrigou-Lagrange notes, this extends the in-existence axiom ethically for it "is a greater dignity for one . . . to act in conformity with God's will than to perform great acts by one's own choice."[54] Applied to the incarnation, this would veer toward Nestorianism, but the human volition in Christ is more dignified simply because it is the divine person who wills humanly.

DID THE SON OF GOD ASSUME A FALLEN OR UNTAINTED HUMAN NATURE?

From eternity Christ was elected to *enhypostatos* and sinlessness. "So that it was owing to this election of God that the man Jesus was not one of the corrupt race of mankind."[55] Edwards at times speaks of the hypostatic union as the assumption of fallen humanity: "But if he unites himself to guilty creatures, he of necessity brings guilt upon himself; if he unites himself to them that are in debt, he brings their debt on himself."[56] This is because the Son assumed human nature from a fallen Mary. "Christ was conceived . . . of the substance of a mother that was one of the corrupt race of mankind."[57]

However, since it was a sanctification par excellence that caused the conception, the created part of the *assumptio carnis* must necessarily be immaculate. "Christ, although he was conceived in the womb of one of fallen mankind, yet he was conceived without sin; because he was conceived by the Holy Ghost, which is divine love and holiness itself. That which infinite holiness and love immediately forms, it is impossible that it should have any sin."[58] For Edwards, then, there was only one immaculate conception in history—Christ's *conceptio*. Of course, this does not exempt Jesus from the weaknesses and attendant consequences of the Fall, even though the assumed nature is made impeccable in *assumptio carnis*.[59]

In sum, Christ obtains and maintains sinlessness by both election and sanctification, the first grounding the second.[60] The human nature of Christ is a *holy* thing, created and made impeccable by the agency of the Holy Spirit, as well as a holy *thing* without independent personhood.[61] The divine nature of the Logos (mediated by the Holy Spirit) not only sustained the existence of the human nature but also constituted and maintained Christ's impeccability.[62] If the incarnation brought about the exaltation and sanctity of the assumed human nature, does this union have any effect on the Logos?

REAL ENLARGEMENT IN GOD OR CHANGE IN THE ASSUMED HUMAN NATURE?

The hypostatic union does not "enlarge" the divinity of the Logos because such divine nature is (absolutely) infinite and must already comprehend all finite essences. In the *assumptus*, according to Aquinas, the Word "does not extend itself beyond the divine nature, but the greater receives what is beneath."[63] The Reformed tradition followed the patristic-medieval theologians in this.[64] As we have seen previously, it is the assumed human nature that is ennobled and sanctified by its union to the Logos.

Does Edwards contradict Aquinas when he asserts that God "as it were enlarges himself in a more excellent and divine manner"?[65] Clearly, this must mean that the divine enlargement is not properly *in se*, but *ad extra*. But how is it possible to speak of the immanent Trinity as fully actualized eternally and at the same time capable of being enlarged economically? The idea of self-repetition has been suggested as an interpretation.[66] God repeats or enlarges the divine self in a temporal mode. How does Edwards work out this notion in his Christology?

Edwards uses the twin notions of divine immutability and creaturely mutability to explain the social and reciprocal nature of love.[67] Inasmuch as God is triune, and thus perfect and self-sufficient in felicity, God's "natural" disposition to communicate happiness *ad extra* cannot be merely unilateral: an emanation cannot be without a remanation. If true happiness must be both communicated and received, how is it possible for God to be "the object of the creature's love" since infinite joy "cannot receive additions of happiness"?[68]

This is not only possible, Edwards answers, but has already been made actual in the incarnation: "But in the gospel God is come down to us, and the person of God may receive communications of happiness from us. The man Christ Jesus loves us so much, that he is really the happier for our delight and happiness in him."[69] The locus of the exaltation of the creature and the "enlargement" of God's happiness is finally, and foundationally, christological. Elaborating on this divine enlargement *ad extra*, Edwards notes that the human excellencies of Christ "are no proper addition to his divine excellencies. Christ has no more excellency in his person, since his incarnation, than he had before; for divine excellency is infinite, and can't be added to: yet his human excellencies are additional manifestations of his glory and excellency to us, and are additional recommendations of him to our esteem and love, who are of finite comprehension."[70]

On such an account, divine nature was not changed in the incarnation. To speak of the enlargement of God *in divina natura* is not proper, hence Edwards's qualifying "as it were." However, divine self-enlargement can be predicated concretely of God incarnate, in whom there is a double aspect. The capacity for glorification lies in both natures: the humanity as "the more immediate and proper subject" since only it is changeable, and the divinity insofar as it is "the especial ground" or condition of possibility of any human exaltation.[71] In contrasting the two natures, Edwards argues that Christ, as divine, was elected for God's "declarative glory"—that is, to reveal the essential and unchangeable "worthiness" of the divine nature, especially the divine wisdom.[72] As human, Christ was elected "to the highest degree of real glory and happiness of all creatures."[73] According to Edwards, Christ's human nature obtains an ontic and not merely a noetic enlargement, a point with which Isaac Watts would also agree.[74]

The human perfections of the incarnate Son are "*additional manifestations* of his glory and excellency"; that is to say, the Son's humanity represents a greater revelation of the divine perfections. Note Edwards's careful use of language here. The human attributes of Christ are not extensions of the divine because they are not directly identical to God's glory and excellency. The humanity of Christ is only a finite correlate to the deity to which it is united. Yet the human nature of Christ, being the *individuum humanum par excellence*, is capable of the greatest degree of enlargement and so is the most perfect finite vehicle for revealing God. The appropriation of humanity by the Logos is not to be seen as something reductive but rather as an amelioration, which far from curtailing the human essence brings about its perfection.[75]

The divine nature was not enlarged in the incarnation of the Word, but the human nature in Christ was—in Christ's own self (as *individuum*) and thus universally for us. Insofar as both natures are properly the Word's, enlargement can be really attributed to the Son, for the Trinity has elected that this capacity of enlargement would terminate in the person of Christ. The "enlargement" of God is possible christologically through the *communicatio idiomatum, in realis*, and, as such, *in verbum*.

NEW BUT REAL RELATION IN THE ASSUMED NATURE

The notions of divine immutability and creaturely mutability are expressed relationally by Edwards. When speaking of Christ being the Savior of elect humankind, Edwards points to the fact that "God sustains a relation entirely new, and distinct from the natural relation of a Creator."[76] This is another way of saying that the incarnation was a creative act *ad extra*.[77] With the Reformed scholastics, Edwards is again affirming that any change in Christ is to be attributed to the human nature assumed and not to the eternal Logos.[78] This is similar to Aquinas's notion of the "mixed" relation: real in the creature but rational in God.[79] The change on the divine side may be regarded as modal: God may exist as timelessly incarnate or nonincarnate.[80] As Rahner phrases it, "God can become something, he who is unchangeable in himself can himself become subject to change in something else."[81] A change from nonexistence to existence may be predicated of the individual human nature.[82] And through the incarnation, elect humans enter into a really new relation with God. They are now not merely creatures but are, in some sense, made participants in the relation the Son has to the Father.

What other changes—besides relations and properties of existence—accrued to the assumed nature of Christ? We move to the question now of how the assumed nature participates in the operations of the divine.

MEANS OF SALVATION: HUMAN NATURE AS THE *ORGANON* OF THE LOGOS

The Alexandrian conception of the instrumentality of Christ's human nature is found in the Reformed-Puritan writings, mediated through Thomas Aquinas.[83] Edwards adopts this doctrine as the operational correlate to the ontological *enhypostaton*.[84] Since the assumed human nature is granted an asymmetrical existence in the Word, the divine person functions appropriately as an actor (*principium quod*) operating through an instrument (*principium quo*).[85]

As with the order of existence, the body-soul analogy may be used to illustrate this order of operations.[86] However, the Reformed scholastics added a caveat: unlike the body-soul union, the hypostatic union is neither a coming together of two incomplete parts (insofar as the divinity is concerned) nor a *tertium quid*.[87] The human nature may be called an adjunct, not as an accident in a subject but insofar as it was added in time to the preexistent person of the Son.[88] Edwards elsewhere regarded the incarnation as a more plausible union "of two spirits . . . which are of natures more similar" than the body-soul union, "which are of natures so heterogeneous and opposite," being as it is a material-spiritual composite.[89] As Aquinas said, the relation of the natures is similar to the relation of actor-instrument but not to the relation of form-matter.[90] For Edwards, the soul is the animating principle of the body since "everything about a man besides the rational soul is not more than a house, ship or coach."[91] Like the human nature that is *enypostatos*, the principle of soul-body union lies in the soul. This, in effect, makes the body an adjunct of the soul and makes possible its participation in its union with Christ and Christ's resurrection.[92]

It is important to distinguish a proper (orthodox) usage of the *organon* concept from the Apollinarian or Nestorian construals.[93] This position has been judged, from the standpoint of modern (Leibnizian) logic, to be inadequate insofar as the human Jesus is not numerically identical to the divine Son.[94] On this critique, neo-Chalcedonian Christology functions on a part-whole schema, which relegates the assumed human attributes to merely second order, unlike the divine, first-order attributes.[95]

AGAINST OPERATIONAL NESTORIANISM: A CONJOINED INSTRUMENT OF THE PERSON

If "being is before action," the *enhypostaton* is the existential basis of the instrumentalization of the human nature, while the *hypostasis synthetos* is the ontological foundation of the communion of operations.[96] There are two modes of action of the one Logos incarnate, the human acting according to its manner in conformity to but yet subordinate to the divine.[97] However, agency is to be assigned to the Word incarnate as the sole subject of its twofold actions, and not to the natures.[98] The term *instrumentum Deitatis* must, therefore, be used concretely to refer to the incarnate Word.[99] As Edwards puts it, "The divine Logos is so united to the humanity of Christ that it spake and acted by it, and made use of it as its organ, as is evident by the history of Christ's life, and as it is evident he will do at the day of judgment."[100] The notion that Christ's humanity functions as an artisan's tool had already been rejected by Cyril in his disputations with Nestorius, since the union cannot be external.[101] Clearly, to avoid any such notion of an accidental union, a distinction has to be made between a conjoined instrument (*instrumentum coniunctum*) and a separated or "extrinsic instrument" (*instrumentum separatum*).[102] This means that Christ's human nature is a proper, permanent instrument of action and not a tool that may be picked up and laid aside episodically by any person.[103] Edwards, therefore, insists that the Logos does not act and speak through humanity "by occasional communication" (as though Jesus were merely an inspired human) but "constantly" due to the perpetuity of the hypostatic union.[104] Though Christ's human nature has its own human form and freedom like that of other human beings (hence the master and slave illustration), it is at the same time a proper and permanent instrument of the divine Word—just as a hand is conjoined to its body.[105] That the human nature is demeaned as the Logos's *organon* cannot be likened to the objectification of a person unless one presupposes a Nestorian relation between the two natures.[106]

AGAINST OPERATIONAL APOLLINARIANISM: A LIVING, SENTIENT, AND CONATIVE INSTRUMENT

Another common criticism against conceiving Christ's human nature as an "organ of divinity" is its purported reductionism.[107] Hence, the charge of Apollinarianism has even been leveled against Athanasius, who frequently applied the *organon* idea to the flesh of Christ.[108] And Edwards is not immune to such an accusation.[109] What can be said in defense of the orthodox tradition and Edwards in this regard?

First of all, the assumed humanity cannot be characterized as a lifeless object completed by the Logos in the incarnation. The orthodox theologians understood that Christ's humanity is not to be thought of as a totally passive "inanimate instrument" (*instrumentum inanimatum*) of the Godhead.[110] Rather, it is an *instrumentum animatum* or, in St. Thomas's words, "an instrument animated by a rational soul, which is so acted upon as to act."[111] Similarly, for Edwards, when Christ's human nature and other human beings act as functionaries of God, they are not *instrumentum inanimatum* but living instruments that God uses "in a manner that is agreeable to their nature, not as senseless, lifeless instruments."[112] Hence, the mode of assumption is important, as a thing can be taken up as a mere instrument (like a tool) or as something that is assumed personally and functions, *at the same time*, as a tool, akin to the relation of a hand to its body.[113] Since all living animals have their own proper energy, Christ's assumed human nature, though moved by a higher cause through efficient causality, possesses an operation corresponding to its own form.[114]

While the Apollinarian idea of the divine *energeia* acting instrumentally was appropriated by the orthodox tradition, they insisted that Christ's humanity is not only active but possesses a rational soul.[115] That is, it is not enough that the human nature should be an animated *organon*, it must have the full complements of humanity as distinguished from mere animality. If the metaphor of a helmsman steering a rudder is to be rejected, the idea of a rider guiding a horse is also inadequate because it signifies merely a living, sensible instrument.[116] To be human is to be rational and free. As Mascall notes, the notion of instrument is only repugnant if the paradox of divine and human volition is denied. Rather, the human will in greatest subjection to God is most free.[117] Though God occasionally uses inanimate or merely animate instruments to carry out the divine purposes, this is quite different from when "he makes use of intelligent, voluntary, spiritual creatures, or human souls or minds, to work miracles."[118] Similarly, Edwards's Christology is not anthropologically deficient: "Now 'tis manifest that the Logos, in thus acting by the humanity of Christ, did not merely make use of his body as its organ, but his soul, not only the members of his body, but the faculties of his soul."[119] Notwithstanding such an analogy that Edwards draws between human instruments and Christ's human nature as *organon*, how does he distinguish the two?

Word Incarnate and Human Prophets: Physical and Moral Instruments

In this communion and ordering of the natural wills, the Word appropriates the human nature as its vehicle to express the divine power.[120] Clearly, Edwards regards the human nature of Christ as more than a moral instrument in which divine power merely acts in concurrence with but not through it.[121] As both a physical and moral instrument, the flesh of Christ conveys and participates in the divine causality.[122]

This is clearly unlike normal prophets and miracle workers, who are merely moral instruments.[123] Human prophets act as "mere instruments" and are totally dependent on God as the author of supernatural works.[124] "Otherwise he don't really act in His name, but in his own name; he don't worship God in working the miracle, but makes a god of himself."[125] Edwards's idea of "mere instruments" in this case is similar to Thomas's concept of separate instrument. Hence, prophets differ from Christ, who worked miracles by the divine power and in the name of Christ's own self.[126] Among human beings, only the human Jesus is a divine person. In a manner analogous to the body-soul relation, the human nature of Christ is properly and uniquely the united instrument of God. In contrast, God exercises divine power improperly through a miracle worker just as a hand would wield an ax.[127] When speaking of saints, Edwards comments that "they cannot properly and in strictness of speech be instruments at all, for a miracle is wrought by the immediate power of God."[128]

The saints' minds are not instrumental causes but "antecedent and concomitant circumstances" or appendices to the production of miracles insofar as they are totally dependent on God.[129] Nonetheless, Edwards insists that God's miracles are "suspended" on human action. How then are prophets instruments of God's power? Only as moral instruments, whereby they exercise an inward faith expressed by an outward bodily act.[130]

In the end, Edwards claims as much as Aquinas does: that the operation of God and the operation of the human are distinct, but cooperate in a miracle. When the human soul and body are freely engaged in submission to the divine will, they act as an instrument. But they are not an instrument insofar as God's power may be exercised immediately—that is, nonsacramentally. Edwards wants to underline that God can perform miracles apart from instrumental mediation, a point with which Thomas would have no issue, since the divine power alone is the cause of both natural and supernatural effects. [131] Thomas would agree that there can be no instrumental causes, including human conception, in *creatio ex nihilo*.[132] Not only so, God may bring about both natural and supernatural effects apart from secondary causes. However, God acts instrumentally insofar as God has ordained it.[133]

In the case of Christ, however, the human nature cannot be a mere occasional cause but must exercise a causality that transcends its own form, as a brush participates in the creation of a masterpiece in the hands of a great artist.[134] And in being the instrument of the Word, the human nature is elevated.[135] From the perspective of freedom, the exaltation of human volition is supremely instantiated in Jesus Christ, the *theanthropos*.[136]

THEANDRIC ACTS OF CHRIST

John of Damascus made it clear that the Ps.–Dionysian term "one theandric nature" cannot be literal but is rather a verbal device to express the unity of the dual natures, or, more exactly, "a periphrasis, viz., when one embraces two things in one statement."[137] Using the analogy of the flaming sword, the Damascene points to the distinction of operations that are united "in theandric energy," just as fire and iron both retain their essential properties of burning and cutting, respectively, but together cause "the burnt cut" or "the cut burn."[138]

Similarly, Edwards states that the man Jesus "did not work miracles as other prophets, but as a divine person. It was a godlike way of working miracles."[139]

Nevertheless, it is not as if there are two distinct yet coordinated energies operating in parallel fashion in which the one composite person is merely a context or work site. Nor are all the distinct attributes of each nature necessarily corresponding, for while the human nature suffers, the divine also condescends or permits the humanity to suffer.[140] While the energies remain unconfused, the divine Word performs miracles through the human nature as its *organon*.[141] Thus, the seemingly monophysite Ps.-Dionysian notion of the "new theandric energy of Christ" was interpreted as the synergy of two natural operations with their corresponding distinct effects, which are yet united in purpose—one *apotelesma*.[142] There is such an identity of purpose that when the Logos wills to act through the human nature, it is the human Jesus who wills the miracles: "Christ's human nature had one will with the divine, and when he would, the divine power was exerted."[143] As Aquinas put it, the harmony of wills in Christ is not a simple numerical oneness but rather an ordered unity.[144] In being *enhypostaton*, the human nature as *instrumentum deitatis* entails the asymmetrical operation of the divine Word through it.[145] Since the divine Word acts sacramentally through the flesh in its miraculous operations, its distinct operations should not be reified.[146] "Both natures of Christ," according to Edwards, "are concerned [in] this exaltation of Christ because this manifestation that is made of the glory of the divine nature of Christ is not separate from the human nature but it shines forth through the human nature."[147]

HUMANITY AS MEDIUM AND MODERATOR OF THE DIVINE GLORY

Christ's humanity, rather than being "a fetter," is an instrument most fitting for manifesting the divine glory.[148] For Edwards, it is particularly the preeminently instrumental character of Christ's humanity that enables Christ to mediate salvation to others.[149] As Goodwin put it, Christ's humanity was the most appropriate *organon* because it was instrumental in the supreme work of salvation.[150] In the mystical union, the saints are "united to Christ as it were his body," and so become "the instruments of [God's] declarative glory."[151] This interchangeable use of instrumentality, means, and medium, while clearly delineating the functional and subordinate status of the humanity to its divine principle and term, points to its essential role in the glorification of God and humanity.

The human nature of Christ not only mediates and reveals the divine power but also acts as a buffer by which the divine *maiestas* is accommodated to human finiteness.[152] The human *instrumentum* is not merely the means to God's glory but is capacitated by the divine to be a suitable instrument for the divine *oikonomia*.[153] The divine accommodates; the human is elevated.[154] Like a crystal or lamp, the humanity of Christ makes the divine light bearable to humanity, and its darkened nature is transformed into a shining instrument.[155] Like Luther, Edwards also affirms that the *divine maiestas* was revealed *absconditas Dei sub contrario*.[156] God used a naturally "weak instrument" to defeat the devil and suffering so that "the power of God appears the more glorious in the victory."[157]

So far, we have observed that Edwards's understanding of this asymmetry between the Logos and the human nature means that the latter shares in the divine existence, power, and glory. In all this, the divine person of the Logos is the ground of life and action of the human Jesus as well as the unifying center of the divine and human modes of being.

One Personal Self-Consciousness in Two Modes of Knowledge

Edwards's affirmation of the *enhypostaton* of the Son's human nature allows him to construe an identity of consciousness in Christ that is effected by a Spirit-mediated *communicatio* between Christ's two minds.[158] "'Tis not [just] any communion of understanding and will that makes the same person; but the communion of understanding is such that there is the same consciousness."[159] The human Jesus is not merely a channel through which the divine Word speaks and acts. Jesus' speech and acts are none other than the divine Logos speaking in a human manner.[160] The affirmation of a single consciousness and double understandings was Edwards's way of securing the personal unity of the two natures in the incarnate Son without detriment to the integrity of the human nature.[161] "If the divine Logos speaks in and by the man Christ Jesus, so that the man Christ Jesus in his speaking should say, I say thus or thus, and his human understanding is made use of by the Logos, and it be the speech of his human understanding, it must be by such a communication between the Logos and the human nature as to communicate consciousness."[162]

Such an approach brings Edwards's psychological notion of identity in line with a classical ontology of Christ's person.[163] Edwards's christological ontology is classical in its characterization of personhood as modes of origin and operation: the Son, as both divine and human, exists from the Father and acts in a filial manner.[164] Nevertheless, there is a definite psychological turn toward the person as a self.[165] If the Logos is the reflex idea of God, it is not surprising that Edwards could affirm an identity of self-consciousness as a way of emphasizing the unity of person. Such a move brings about a convergence of Edwards's ontology, Christology, and theology because consciousness is essential to personal identity, particularly in this case to the personal identity of the one subject whose true nature is to be God's very self-consciousness.[166] Clearly, he conceives of Christ as possessing two distinct but commensurable understandings governed by a single Ego.[167]

Edwards was not original in suggesting a single personal consciousness within a dythelite Christology.[168] Like William Sherlock, Edwards locates this personal center in the divine mind, and this seems to be a psychologically appropriate way of interpreting Chalcedon's ontological "self-same Son," an emphasis clearly Cyrillian.[169] The fact that there is an "identity of consciousness" is not a speculative point for Edwards, though the specific manner and extent of the human consciousness "is uncertain."[170]

ANTIOCHENE MINOR KEY: CHRIST AS A MIXED PERSON

Throughout this chapter, we have examined Edwards's Christology, which displays a remarkable emphasis on the oneness and preeminence of the divine hypostasis. An Antiochene thread is an undertone to this major key. One important indicator of this minor key is Edwards's appropriation of the motif of Christ as a *hypostasis synthetos*. We look first at the how the tradition has drawn the boundaries for understanding the notion of the *hypostasis synthethos*.

The compound person is not inaugurating a new God–man species since the incarnation is sui generis.[171] To avoid any idea of an Apollinarian synthesis of parts, the compound person must not mean the union of two imperfect natures.[172] It cannot mean the literal compounding of all the properties of two distinct natures, for this could lead to a Nestorian conclusion, if person were defined as a catalog of properties.[173] The term *synthetos* is not to be used literally but rather metaphorically or analogically.[174] The accent, then, must not fall on the natures, for this would inevitably connote an essential union. If the emphasis is not on the *synthetos*, then it must be on the unchanged hypostasis of the Logos, who assumed a human nature to itself by divine fiat.[175] The compound person is not a physical coming together of two prior essences to produce one visible hypostasis, but the one person of Christ subsisting in two manners of existence.[176]

Edwards reiterates this Cyrillian assertion (with a pneumatological modification) that the two natures are none other than the modes of existence of the self-same Son. Thus it is the Spirit that "so unites the human nature of Christ with the divine . . . that the person of the one is the person of the other."[177] The distinction between subsistence and existence may be regarded as perspectival.[178] The *hypostasis synthetos* conceptualizes the incarnate Christ as one person subsisting in two natures, while the *enhypostaton* views the assumed nature as existing in the person of the Word. In short, its reality is no different from the *enhypostaton*.[179]

In the incarnation, Christ "partakes of the common nature of both" and acts accordingly.[180] As God, Christ's actions accord perfectly with the divine nature; as human, Christ's actions conform to "the divine law given to the reasonable creature." However, as Christ is *hypostasis synthetos* or "a mixed person . . . so his righteousness is of a mixed nature," which differs from human and divine righteousness "in its measure and formal nature."[181] This does not mean that Christ's personal righteousness is a *tertium quid*, but a theandric act. Correlating to the two natures, this righteousness of the Mediator "must be estimated by the same principles [of both natures]; that is, as it is a conformity to that which is the proper rule of it." Yet, since Christ is no mere human being, this human obedience was performed "under the influence of his divinity, and derived its value from thence."[182] Thus, the Antiochene *hypostasis synthetos* adopted by Edwards is quite consonant with his Alexandrian *enhypostatos* doctrine, as it emphasizes the distinction and asymmetry of the natures in the union. Since the human nature in-exists in the Word, the human righteousness is dignified by its union with the divine.

Although an Antiochene minor key can be detected, it would be a mistake to regard this as an incipient Nestorianism.[183] Nevertheless, such suspicions are aroused with statements like the following:

> In Jesus who dwelt here upon earth, there was immediately only these two things: there was the flesh, or the human nature; and there was the Spirit of holiness, or the eternal Spirit, by which he was united to the Logos. Jesus who dwelt among us, was as it were compounded of these two; the one from the earth, which he received of the Virgin Mary, the other from heaven, which descended on the Virgin at his conception.[184]

To grasp Edwards's view on the presence of the Logos in the incarnation, we will need to look briefly at his understanding of God's general and special presences to creatures.

Divine Omnipresence: The Relation between the Divine Essence and Creation

Does Edwards conceive of the divine omnipresence in a different way from the tradition before him? With the medieval–Reformed theologians, he believes that God's immensity is *per essentiam, praesentiam et potentiam*.[185] Just as Aquinas's *per essentiam* may be summed up as a causal presence, Edwards's concept of God's omnipresence presupposes omnicausality.[186] God immediately preserves all things through *creatio continua*.[187]

This omnipresence admits to no local variance, for God's "essential presence . . . is every where alike."[188] What secures this omnipresence is divine immutability since a God who changes locality is mutable.[189] God's general presence is thus repletive.[190] The divine omnipresence is "spatial" but not an infinite physical extension, just as there is infinite duration but not temporal succession in God's *aeternitas*.[191] The Trinity in eternal reciprocal indwelling both transcends and contains the created universe and is thus wholly present to creation.[192]

However, omnipresence is not identity, since God's spatiality includes distance.[193] For Edwards, God's uncreated "spatiality" means that God's essence is distinctly instantiated.[194] While the Trinity is indivisible in its *opera ad extra*, the omnicausality of God is exercised through the Spirit's direct agency.[195] As we have seen, the Logos creates and preserves the world through the immediate, causal agency of the Spirit. This economical role is consonant with the Spirit's position in the ontological taxis as the "end of all procession." Moving from Edwards's understanding of the divine presence in creation, we look next at how he sees the God's presence in the incarnation.

A Modified Communio Naturarum: The Relation between the Holy Spirit and Jesus

Unlike God's unvarying omnipresence, God's special presences on earth admit to "different kinds and degrees."[196] The two special presences of God *ad extra*, as delineated by medieval scholasticism, are the *unio hypostatica* and *unio mystica*.[197] Would it be accurate to say that Edwards affirms a *unio hypostatica* shorn of the *communio naturarum*?[198] If the *communio naturarum* amounts to just an asymmetrical intensification of the divine presence to the human nature, then Edwards's construal of the sanctification of Christ's nature is functionally identical.[199]

An incarnation, by Edwards's definition, "is not an union of contact or influence, but a personal union." Sanctification, which involves the Spirit's "indwelling and influence," may eventuate in but is certainly not identical to the incarnation.[200] Undoubtedly, the direct indwelling of the divine nature in Jesus is by the Spirit's immediate and infinite presence, which inaugurated the *unio personalis*.[201] With the *enhypostatos*, a mediated indwelling of Christ's person takes place.[202] Since the Spirit's inhabitation in Jesus is direct and infinite, it may be regarded as a communion of natures in a weak sense.[203] To be sure, there is no mutual, direct interpenetration of the natures properly belonging to the Son incarnate. Nonetheless, with the *enhypostatos* and indwelling Spirit, there is a reciprocal indwelling of the human and divine natures in the person of Christ.[204] In this sense, Edwards strongly insists on a *totus intra*, for the intensity of the divine presence in Christ is par excellence.[205]

From the perspective of the Logos Christology, does not such a Spirit-mediated union drive a wedge between the two natures?[206] On the contrary: when judged from an Augustinian standpoint, the Spirit's role as the *vinculum*, in fact, *guarantees* the intimacy between the natures.[207] Like Calvin, Edwards regards the Holy Spirit as the divine person who bridges distance.[208] Being sanctified "beyond measure" from the *conceptus*, this *gratia habitualis per excellentiam* is the cause of the *gratia unionis*. Undergirded by the bipersonal analogy, Edwards's construal of the Spirit as effecting the Logos's presence in Jesus is entirely self-consistent.[209]

In the *status exinationis*, the divinity is concealed under the veil of flesh, but in the *status exaltationis*, the majesty of God shines through a wholly transparent humanity.[210] While Edwards emphasizes the role of the Spirit in mediating between the natures of Christ, he apparently allows for a truly reciprocal interpenetration of the two natures in the *glorified* Christ.[211]

A RADICALIZED EXTRA CARNEM: THE RELATION BETWEEN THE LOGOS AND JESUS

At face value, Edwards's version of the Reformed *extra Calvinisticum* seems to differ from the patristic notion, which assumes a *communio naturarum* and thus an intimate indwelling, but not an imprisonment, of the Logos in the *sarx*.[212] As Athanasius argued, just as the divine omnipresence involves neither its containment nor confusion with other created essences, so the Logos, in the incarnation, is present in Christ's body yet is not confined by it.[213] The Reformed tradition appropriated the medieval *totus-totum* distinction to secure the immensity and unity of Christ's person while affirming the locality of the human nature.[214] From the texts cited, it would seem that Edwards conceives of the Holy Spirit as present on earth in Jesus while the Father and Son are situated in heaven—a corollary of his favored bipersonal analogy. Is there such a separation of the natures in Edwards's Christology?

Edwards echoes Turretin by not affirming a *communio naturarum* in a physical sense; the hypostatic union should not be regarded as "an union of contact."[215] But Turretin conceives of the *unio* in a much looser sense; the *enhypostaton* is merely sustenance of the assumed nature externally united to the divine.[216] Edwards, as we have seen, accepts the idea that the assumed human nature is pneumatically *enhypostaton*; that is to say, the assumed nature is metaphysically or, in scholastic terms, hyperphysically present in the Logos by the Spirit. This sort of mediated in-existence of the flesh in the Son must not be regarded as an external union or, worse still, a separation of the two natures. That Edwards's modified *communio naturarum* entails no physical interpenetration is, in one sense, not that far away from the understanding of certain Lutherans, who regarded the *communio naturarum* as metaphorical.[217]

However, if this in-existence is not to be thought of as local, then how is the Logos present to the assumed nature? Here, Turretin's distinction between presence and propinquity, or "distance of places," is useful.[218] There can be compresence and intimacy of the natures without the need for physical nearness or spatial proximity.[219] The mutual intimacy of the natures is, therefore, spiritual and not local.[220] Edwards clearly recognizes a kind of *communio naturarum* in the *enhypostaton*.[221] In summary, the intensification of the Logos's presence to the assumed nature in the incarnation is mediated by the Spirit, with no change made to the general omnipresence of the Trinity.

CONCLUSION

We have looked at Edwards's understanding of the character and relation of the assumed human nature to the Word. His Logos Christology carries on the Alexandrian thread running through the patristic, medieval, and Reformed traditions with its restatement of the *enhypostaton-anhypostaton* dialectic and the doctrine of the *instrumentum Deitatis*. However, his Chalcedonianism is clearly refracted through Reformed lenses with the modification of the *communio naturarum* and rather novel development of a Spirit-mediated Christology. The antagonism between these two traditions is evident in the rather eccentric construal of the *extra*. We will try to clarify some of these points of tension in the following chapter where we look at the *communicatio idiomatum*.

Notes

1. Edwards, "Miscellanies," no. 741, in *WJE* 18:368.

2. Edwards, 191. Sermon on Rom. 5:7-8 (Feb 1752), in *WJE* 46.

3. See Edwards, "Miscellanies," no. 763, in *WJE* 18:410. See Thomas G. Weinandy, "Cyril and the Mystery of the Incarnation," in *The Theology of Saint Cyril of Alexandria: A Critical Appreciation*, ed. Thomas G. Weinandy and Daniel A. Keating (London: T&T Clark, 2002), 38.

4. Although "there is an infinite distance between the human nature and the divine," yet "the meanness of our natures need be no hindrance" to our communion with God "for Christ is in our natures" (Edwards, "Miscellanies," no. 741, in *WJE* 18:366)

5. Echoing St. Cyril's notion of the *oikonomia*, Edwards speaks of the Creator of nature making himself subject "to the laws of nature" through the incarnation so that nature "might be subject to the good of the redeemed." While Christ chose to be subjected to nature's law by assuming a human nature for the good of human nature itself, "yet at the same time he appeared as the Lord of nature" (Edwards, "Miscellanies," no. 454, in *WJE* 13).

6. For Edwards, Christ's incarnation involved no essential confusion so that "neither the human nature [nor the divine] are changed into the other, though both are united in one person" (Edwards, "Images of Divine Things," no. 166, in *WJE* 11:110). Aquinas considered the mode of union per se as personal and not natural (*STh* III, q. 2, aa. 1–3, 2027–30). He restated this conclusion when considering the *assumptus*, viz., the mode of union from the perspective of the person: "unio facta est in persona, non in natura" (*ST* III, q. 3, a. 1, 2039). *Suppositum*, as used by Aquinas, is roughly equivalent to *hypostasis*—any nature that exists individually. When a *supposit* includes a rational nature, following Beothius's definition, it is a person (Aquinas, *STh* III, q. 3, a. 1).

7. "And this seems to be one glorious end of the union of the human to the divine nature, to bring God near to us; that even our God, the infinite Being, might be made as one of us . . . that Jehovah, who is infinitely distant from us, might become familiar to us" (Edwards, "Miscellanies," no. 81, *WJE* 13:248). In the context of the saints' being "admitted into . . . the infinitely sweet and glorious society of the persons of the Trinity," Edwards reiterates this idea: "There are two things that are wonderful in man's redemption: one, that is that Christ should be abased in coming down to us; and another is that man should be so exalted in ascending up with Christ to God" (Edwards, "Of God the Father," in *WJE* 25:153).

8. Harry Austryn Wolfson, *The Philosophy of the Church Fathers* (Cambridge, MA: Harvard University Press, 1956), 420. This position echoes the Maximian understanding, according to Thunberg's reading: "As soon as the union has taken place, the perichoresis is mutual." See Lars Thunberg, *Microcosm and Mediator: The Theological Anthropology of Maximus the Confessor*, 2nd ed., foreword by A. M. Allchin (Chicago: Open Court, 1995), 29. This was drawn from Pseudo-Cyril. See G. L. Prestige, *God in Patristic Thought* (London: SPCK, 1952), 295. Prestige's emphasis on the (Maximian) *perichoresis* as a unilateral, rotating, divine movement from a single point undermines the reciprocal human perichoretic movement, as Thunberg notes (*Microcosm and Mediator*, 27).

9. Wolfson, *Philosophy of the Church Fathers*, 423–24. This is based on Wolfson's exegesis of Pseudo-Cyril of Alexandria, *De Sacrosancta Trinitate* 24 (1165 C).

10. John of Damascus, *Orthodox Faith*, bk. 4, ch. 18, 91 (*NPNF* 9). This idea of reciprocity may be traced to the Stoic idea of unconfused "mixture" (*krasis*) of bodies already extant in Gregory of Nazianzen (Ep. 101) (Thunberg, *Microcosm and Mediator*, 28). Wolfson points out that the two Gregories, Augustine, and Nemesius of Emessa used the Stoic language of "mixture" to imply an Aristotelian "union of predominance," like that of form in relation to matter (Wolfson, *Philosophy of the Church Fathers*, 396). For John of Damascus, the mutual communion of wills and operations reveals the compenetration of natures in Christ: this is the hypostatic union. For Thunberg, this baseline notion of the incarnation as *perichoresis* is evident in Maximus's theology (*Microcosm and Mediator*, 26).

11. This movement represents the "humanation" or incarnation proper. Pseudo-Cyril actually refers to the second penetration as "union" (Wolfson, *Philosophy of the Church Fathers*, 424–25). For Barth, while there is "a mutual participation," the distinction remains as "the essence of the Son of God, is wholly that which gives," and the human, "that which receives" (Barth, *CD* IV.2, 72). This is the *communio naturarum*, a Lutheran favorite, which Barth affirmed and re-conceptualized. It is the divine essence imparting itself to the human essence (seen as the history of Jesus Christ) and the humanity of Christ receiving the divine (that is, elevated to fellowship with God) within the one person of Jesus Christ. The static Lutheran *genus maiestaticum* is rejected for a dynamic *communicatio gratiarum*, unique to the event of Jesus Christ. All this is actualized or operationalized, which led Barth to summarize the incarnation in its two states as "the *communicatio idiomatum et gratiarum et operationum*" (Barth, *CD* IV.2, 269). This "event" character of the incarnation is also observable in Edwards, though he affirms (contrary to Barth) an *et maiestaticum* in a modified sense.

12. John of Damascus, *Orthodox Faith*, bk. 4, ch. 18, 91 (*NPNF* 9).

13. "Assumption is the immediate act of the divine nature in the person of the Son on the human; union is mediate, by virtue of the assumption" (John Owen, *The Works of John Owen*, ed. William H. Goold [London: Banner of Truth Trust, 1965–68; originally publ. Johnstone & Hunter, 1850–53], 1:225–26). Owen appropriated this distinction in relation to the action of the divinity, "the nature assuming," and passion of the humanity, "the nature assumed" (ibid., 224). Owen's theology is less Scotistic than it is "a modified and eclectic Thomism." See Carl R. Trueman, *John Owen: Reformed Catholic, Renaissance Man* (Aldershot, UK: Ashgate, 2007), 24. "Hence this union . . . is usually termed, and distinguished to be two-fold: the one immediate, of the person assuming, and the humane nature assumed . . . the other mediate, of two natures, between themselves, wrought by means of the person, without any, either confusion of Natures, or division of person." See Lucas Trelcatius, *A briefe institution of the common places of sacred divinitie. . . .* (London: Francis Burton, 1610), 158.

14. Louis Berkhof, *Reformed Dogmatics*, 3 vols. (Grand Rapids, MI: Eerdmans, 1932), 1:321. The *unio naturarum* is a mediate union because the divine nature is said to be incarnate insofar as it is not regarded "absolutely and in itself, but in the Person of the Son" (ibid.). "Again, the manhood of Christ is first and immediately joined to the person of the Son himself, and by the person to the Godhead of the Son." See William Perkins, *An exposition of the symbole or creed of the apostles, according to the tenour of the scripture, and the consent of orthodoxe Fathers of the Church* (London: Printed by John Legatt, Printer to the Universitie of Cambridge, 1616), 181.

15. For a fuller background to the history of this idea, see appendix 4, "The *Enhypostaton-Anhypostaton* Dialectic: Faithful Appropriation and Elaboration of the Patristic-Medieval Tradition," infra.

16. Edwards, "Miscellanies," no. 958, in *WJE* 20:235. Edwards restates Goodwin: "The angel there speaks of Christ's human nature which was to be born of Mary, not as of a person but as of a thing, in the neuter gender, *That holy thing which shall be born of thee shall be called the Son of God*" (Goodwin, *WTG* 5:54). Aquinas regarded personhood as a positive addition to being, and in Christ's case, "His union hindered the human nature from having its personality" (Aquinas, *STh* III, q. 4, a. 2, ad 3, 2047). Elsewhere, he reiterates that "if the human had not been assumed by a Divine Person, the human nature would have had its own personality" (Aquinas, *STh* III, q. 4, a. 2, ad 2).

17. Edwards, "Miscellanies," no. 709, *WJE* 18:334.

18. Ibid. Similarly: "Assumption is properly an action by which the human nature is drawn into the subsistence of the Son, so that it may subsist by this subsistence. Hence this action not only produces in the human nature of Christ a relation of dependence on the Word, but communicates to it the personality of the Word" (Reginald Garrigou-Lagrange, *Christ the Saviour: A Commentary on the Third Part of Saint Thomas' Theological Summa*, trans. Dom Bede Rose [St. Louis, MO: Herder, (copyright 1950)], ch. 5, q. 3, a. 1).

19. "We have all reason to conclude that no degree of intimacy will be too much for the manhood of Christ, seeing that the divine Logos has been pleased to assume him into his very person" (Edwards, "Miscellanies," no. 741, in *WJE* 18:368).

20. "Again it shows how much God designed to communicate himself to men, that he so communicated himself to . . . the head and representative . . . [to] be the same person with one of the persons of the Trinity . . . [so as] to admit man as it were to the inmost fellowship with the deity" (ibid., 367).

21. Edwards, "Miscellanies," no. 709, in *WJE* 18:335.

22. Ibid.

23. Ibid. Puritan theologians, such as Davenant, thought that if the *conceptus* and *assumptus* were affirmed as *simul*, this would be sufficient to ensure the *enhypostatos* and *anhypostatos* of the human nature. "If they [the soul and flesh] had existed apart from the Logos, they would have had their own personality: but because they began to exist together, and to be united to the Word at the same time, there was a necessity that this human nature should draw its personality from the Word" (John Davenant, *An exposition of the Epistle of St. Paul to the Colossians* . . . [London: Hamilton, Adams, and Co., 1831], 420).

24. "That Christ was conceived by the power of the Holy Ghost was a fruit of his election. For that seed of the woman—those stamina and first principles of his human being that were in the womb of the virgin, that was one of those seeds that had future humanity and that [had] individual humanity annexed to it by God's decree—was as liable to be impregnated by man as any other seed of the woman whatsoever" (Edwards, "Miscellanies," no. 769, in *WJE* 18:417). "If 'tis by the Spirit of God that the human nature of Christ was conceived, and had life and being, why should we not suppose that 'tis also by the Spirit that he has union with the divine nature?" (Edwards, "Miscellanies," no. 487, in *WJE* 13:531).

25. "nec sic assumptus est ut prius creatus post assumeretur, sed ut ipsa assumptione crearetur." See Augustine, *Contra Sermonen Arianorum*, ch. 8, in *PL* 42, col. 688.

26. Edwards, "Miscellanies," no. 709, in *WJE* 18:334.

27. "For place itself is mental, and 'within' and 'without' are mere mental conceptions" (Edwards, "The Mind," no. 51, in *WJE* 6:368). Similarly: "And so that which we call place is an idea too" (Edwards, "The Mind," no. 34, in *WJE* 6:353).

28. Since it was axiomatic for Edwards that creation and preservation "are not properly distinct works," the conception and sustenance of Christ's human nature should be seen as two sides of the same coin. "For upholding the world in being and creating of it are not properly distinct works. For 'tis manifest that upholding the world in being is the same with a continued creation and, consequently, that creating of the world is but the beginning of upholding of it, if I may so say, the beginning to give the world a supported and dependent existence" (Edwards, "Miscellanies," no. 1349, in *WJE* 23:608).

29. As with created beings, which "wholly receive their being from him and are upheld in being by him . . . and perfectly dependent on him," so Christ's human nature is given existence, sustained and wholly reliant on God's Spirit (Edwards, "Miscellanies," no. 1156, in *WJE* 23:63).

30. The human nature is not deprived of a "first substance," yet it does not have personhood without the properties of "incommunicability" and independent subsistence (Francis Turretin, *Institutes of Elenctic Theology*, trans. George Musgrave Giger, ed. James T. Dennison [Phillipsburg, NJ: P&R, 1992–94], 2:316). Or, elsewhere, human personhood has "incommunicability with singularity" (ibid.).

31. Edwards, "Miscellanies," no. 709, in *WJE* 18:335.

32. Christ's human nature derives personhood solely through participation in the uncreated *esse* of the Word. Whether Aquinas affirmed a single or double *esse* in Christ is controverted. Based purely on textual evidence, Thomas goes with the single divine *esse* position in all his writings, with the exception of *Quaestio disputata De unione Verbi incarnati*, a. 4. See Joseph P. Wawrykow, "Hypostatic Union," in *The Theology of Thomas Aquinas*, ed. Rik van Nieuwenhove and Joseph Wawrykow (Notre Dame, IN: University of Notre Dame Press, 2005), 251n43.

Nieden regards the notion of a *humanitas* without its own *esse* as a weakness in Cajetan's Thomism. See Marcel Nieden, *Organum deitatis: Die Christologie des Thomas de Vio Cajetan*, Studies in Medieval and Reformation Thought 62 (Leiden: Brill, 1997), 87. Weinandy argues that if the human Jesus had a created soul that animated the body, he must have possessed a created *esse* (though secondary), which was actuated by its participation in the principal, divine *esse* of the Word. Weinandy demonstrates that this was Thomas's implicit stance in the four instances where he affirmed a single *esse* in Christ, which he stated explicitly in *De Unione Verbi Incarnati*. The created, real effect in Christ's assumed humanity (in the mixed relation) is this very same *esse secundarium* (ibid., 81). This makes sense of Aquinas's apparent contradiction, is consonant with the rest of his theology, and acquits him of being a crypto-monophysite (Thomas G. Weinandy, "Aquinas: God Is Man: The Marvel of the Incarnation," in *Aquinas on Doctrine: A Critical Introduction*, ed. Thomas G. Weinandy, Daniel A. Keating, and John P. Yocum [London: T&T Clark, 2004], 67–89). Unlike Scotus, who regarded the basis of the hypostatic union as a bare negation, Thomas (as interpreted by Cajetan) thought that a human nature required its own *esse* to gain independent personhood. For Cajetan Thomists, Christ's humanity could not have had a created *esse* actuated by its reception of the divine *esse*, as this would amount to Nestorianism. Extending Loofs's *enhypostaton* with Rahner's insights, Coffey sees the incarnation as a dynamic process in which the Word comes to subsist in the assumed nature. Aquinas, while affirming that humanity is capable operationally, by grace, of the divine, held to the classical *enhypostaton*. If the humanity of Christ is not ontologically capable of the divine, the *enhypostaton* cannot assure a union that is nonaccidental and intrinsic to the Word. Aquinas's position, in Coffey's assessment, is finally not only contradictory but also Nestorian. See David M. Coffey, "The Theandric Nature of Christ," *Theological Studies* 60, no. 3 (September 1999): 414–19.

33. Together with the communication of the divine *esse* to the human nature, a mode of subsistence is added, causing it to be incommunicable (Hans Urs von Balthasar, *Theo-Drama: Theological Dramatic Theory*, vol. 3, *The Dramatis Personae: The Person in Christ*, trans. Graham Harrison [San Francisco: Ignatius, 1992], 219). Hence, "person denotes a certain nature with a certain mode of existence. . . . [T]he mode of existence signified by the word person is most exalted, namely that a thing exists by itself." See St. Thomas Aquinas, *On the Power of God: Quæstiones disputatæ de potentia Dei*, trans. the English Dominican fathers (Eugene, OR: Wipf & Stock, 2004), 9.3. Cross notes that Aquinas held to a marginal position, which was rejected by most medievals save the staunchest Thomists. Furthermore, this position is not philosophically sustainable on Thomas's own grounds. On his mereological Christology, the assumed nature, which participates in the divine existence, would have to be either essential or accidental. If the human *individuum* were essential to the divinity, Thomas would be a monophysite. Yet, Aquinas explicitly denied that the union was accidental (Richard Cross, *Duns Scotus* [New York: Oxford University Press, 1999], 114–15).

34. Edwards, "Miscellanies," no. 766, in *WJE* 18:413.

35. Ibid., 414.

36. Owen, "A Brief Declaration and Vindication of the Doctrine of the Trinity; as also of the Person and Satisfaction of Christ . . ." in *Works*, 2:418; italics original. Owen held to the Scotistic position, in which the incarnation involved the mere negation of personhood, "preventing the personal subsistence of human nature in that flesh which he assumed." The human nature is both *enhypostaton* and *atomon*, as it is the "person of the Son of God" who "gave it [the human nature] subsistence in his own person; whence it hath its *individuation* and distinction from all other persons whatever" (ibid.). On Scotus's metaphysics, Jesus would exist as an independent human person if not united to the Word, for it would be absent of dependence on the divine person (Balthasar, *Theo-Drama* 3:218).

37. Davenant thought that "the human nature of Christ . . . is an individual or singular," but not personal in itself. However, had Christ's body and soul "existed apart from the Logos, they would have had their own personality: but because they began to exist together, and to be united

to the Word at the same time, there was a necessity that this human nature should draw its personality from the Word" (*Exposition of the Epistle of St. Paul*, 420).

38. Edwards, "Miscellanies," no. 385, in *WJE* 13:453.

39. Ibid., 454. This relates particularly to imputed righteousness, as we shall examine the subsequent chapter.

40. Edwards, "Miscellanies," no. 769, in *WJE* 18:415; italics mine.

41. Edwards, "Miscellanies," no. 702, in *WJE* 18:299; italics mine.

42. According to him, though the human nature of Christ is an individual thing (*individuum*), it "has not its own personality [*persona*], because it does not exist separately [*non per se separatim existit*], but in something more perfect [*in quodam perfectiori*], viz. in the person [*in persona*] of the Word" (Aquinas, *STh* III, q. 2, a. 2, ad 3, 2029). As *individuum*, "that Man was never a person of itself, but subsisted from the first in the personality of the second Person" (Goodwin, *WTG* 1:33).

43. Berkhof, *Reformed Dogmatics*, 1:318. "A person is a nature with something added to it, viz., independent subsistence, individuality." There must be a distinction between existence and personhood in creatures, insofar as what is assumed must be presupposed to the assumption. According to Garrigou-Lagrange, Aquinas distinguishes between "*quod est* and *esse*." According to Thomas, "In intellectual substances (and in every creature), there is a difference between existence and what is" (*Contra Gentes*, bk. 2, ch. 2, as quoted in Garrigou-Lagrange, *Christ the Saviour*, ch. 6. q. 4, a. 2, n. 704). That which is presupposed is, therefore, an individualized nature (*atomon*) and not a person. Otherwise, it would result either in the corruption of the person or two persons in the *unio hypostatica* (Garrigou-Lagrange, *Christ the Saviour*, ch. 6. q. 4, a. 2). That is why the person is the term of the assumption (Aquinas, *STh* III, q. 3, a. 4).

44. Barth, *CD* I.2, 164. As Barth comments, the Latin *impersonalitas* (sometimes used to translate *anhypostasis*) does not negate metaphysical *personalitas* or "existence or being" in Jesus, since the assumed nature has *individualitas* or psychological self-consciousness. Contemporary scholars misconstrue *non est persona* to mean the absence of a psychological personality (*impersonalitas*), when *anhypostaton* means that the human nature cannot (metaphysically) exist and subsist of itself. See Gerrit C. Berkouwer's defense of Barth's "anhypostasy" and "enhypostasy" in his *Studies in Dogmatics: The Person of Christ*, trans. John Vriend (Grand Rapids, MI: Eerdmans, 1954), 308–9.

45. "The human soul and body in Christ being drawn into the personality of the Word, and not constituting another person besides the person of the Word, does not mark a diminution of potency, but a greater excellence. Everything is better for being united to what is more excellent than itself, better than it was, or would be, if it stood by itself." See St. Thomas Aquinas, *Of God and His Creatures: An Annotated Translation (with Some Abridgement) of the* Summa contra gentiles *of Saint Thomas Aquinas*, trans. Joseph Rickaby (London: Burns and Oates, 1905), bk. 4, 40, 49.

46. "Now it is a greater dignity to exist in something nobler than oneself than to exist by oneself" (Aquinas, *STh* III, q. 2, a. 2, ad 2). By analogy, the human species is more perfect than animals because the sensitive part (which is itself the form in the animal) is united to and ennobled by the rational soul (the form in a human being).

47. "Proper personality is not wanting to the human nature, on account of the defect of any thing which is required to its perfection, but on account of the addition of something which far excels its nature, viz. its union to a Divine person. Christ, therefore, is not imperfect, but more eminent than other men; because our human nature subsists in us in its proper personality, but it subsists in Christ in that which is Divine; and it is much more noble and honorable to subsist in God by hypostatic union than to subsist by itself" (Davenant, *Exposition of the Epistle of St. Paul*, 419). The assumed human nature of Christ is "far more perfect" because it subsists in the uncreated *hypostasis* of the Word (Turretin, *Institutes*, 2:316).

48. Edwards, "Miscellanies," no. 791, in *WJE* 18:490. "As the same person exists in the human [and] as the human nature partakes of the same sonship, so it partakes of the same right of

inheritance" of the "natural Son of God." (Edwards, 412. Sermon on Rev. 14:14 [Oct 1736], in *WJE* 51). "The human nature of Christ was so honored as to be in the same person with the eternal son of God, that was equal with God" (Edwards, No. 6: Sermon 16 [June 17, 1739], in *WJE* 9:321).

49. "So the human nature of Christ is in itself a mean thing. . . . The human nature has no glory in itself; it is but a vessel that must receive its fullness from something else. . . . So the man Christ Jesus was exceeding excellent . . . endowed with . . . the divine good or fullness of God, his infinite holiness and joy. Christ is the person in whom is the Spirit of God, and therefore is called the Anointed" (Edwards, "Notes on Scriptures," no. 285, in *WJE* 15:243).

50. "Is it not a very improper thing that saints in some respects should be advanced above angels, seeing angels are of more excellent natural powers? I answer, no more improper than it is for the queen in some respects to be advanced above nobles and barons, of far nobler natural powers" (Edwards, "Miscellanies," no. ii, in *WJE* 13:186). "Believers are," therefore, "become immensely more honorable persons in God's esteem, by virtue of their relation to Christ, than man would have been considered as by himself; as a mean person becomes more honorable when married to a king" (Edwards, "Miscellanies," no. 627, in *WJE* 18:156).

51. Edwards, "No. 5 Sermon Fourteen," in *WJE* 9:299.

52. "The Word is united with the human nature by that whereby the Word terminates and maintains it" (Garrigou-Lagrange, *Christ the Saviour*, ch. 4, q. 2, a. 7).

53. Edwards, "Miscellanies," no. 728, in *WJE* 18:353.

54. Following Cajetan and applying Thomas's axiom operationally, Garrigou-Lagrange states that "it is better to be in a passive frame of mind as regards those superior to us, than to assume an active role as regards those inferior to us; and although it is better to give than to receive, it is better to receive from someone superior to us, than to give to someone inferior to us" (*Christ the Saviour*, ch. 4, q. 2, a. 9).

55. Edwards, "Miscellanies," no. 769, in *WJE* 18:417. Edwards makes a similar point with Barth here: the human essence of Christ is not only most divinely constituted but was so, and uniquely so, from the start. "He is totally unlike even the most saintly among us in the fact that His human essence alone is fully, because from the very outset, determined by the grace of God. This is the qualitatively different determination of His human essence, and of His alone as that of the One who as the Son of man is also and primarily the Son of God. But he is like us in the fact that His human essence determined in this way is in fact the same as ours" (Barth, *CD* IV.2, 89). John S. Macken makes this observation of Barth in his *The Autonomy Theme in the* Church Dogmatics: *Karl Barth and His Critics* (Cambridge: Cambridge University Press, 1990), 62. For Barth, Christ was perfectly and initially elect (and thus obedient) in Christ's humanity; for Edwards, Christ had the Spirit perfectly from the beginning of Christ's human existence. For Barth, the Son of Man was elected to be exalted (but not changed) in the human essence to be truly free. Christ assumed a sinful, and not Adamic, humanity but lived a sinless life through ethical determination.

56. Edwards, "Miscellanies," no. 764a, in *WJE* 18:410.

57. Edwards, "Miscellanies," no. 767, in *WJE* 18:414.

58. Edwards, "Miscellanies," no. 386, in *WJE* 13:454. "Though Christ was conceived . . . of the substance of a mother that was one of the corrupt race of mankind, . . . yet being conceived by the power of the Holy Ghost, which is the omnipotent holiness of God itself, that which was conceived and formed must needs be a perfectly holy thing" (Edwards, "Miscellanies," no. 767, in *WJE* 18:414).

59. In the incarnation, "Christ had his glory veiled by his conjunction, or union, with our nature in its low and broken state" (Edwards, "Notes on Scripture," no. 315, in *WJE* 15:291).

60. "That Christ was conceived by the power of the Holy Ghost was a fruit of his election" (Edwards, "Miscellanies," no. 769, in *WJE* 18:417).

61. "'Tis said holy thing, not holy person or holy one; that holy thing is the human nature of Christ" (Edwards, "Miscellanies," no. 958, in *WJE* 20:235).

62. "And that his human nature was not liable to sinful changes, as well as Adam or the angels, was not owing to any thing in his human nature but to its relation to the divine nature that upheld it" (Edwards, 470. Sermon on 1 Cor. 13:1-10 [b] [Apr 1738], in *WJE* 53).

63. "non se extendit ultra naturam divinam, sed magis accipit quod est infra." See St. Thomas Aquinas, *Quaestio disputata de unione Verbi incarnati*, trans. Roberto Busa (Taurini, 1953), a. 1, http://www.corpusthomisticum.org/qdi.html.

64. "By reason of this hypostatical union, though the Godhead receive nothing from the manhood, yet the manhood it self, which is assumed, is thereby perfected and enriched with unspeakable dignity" (Perkins, *An Exposition of the Apostle's Creed*, 181).

65. Edwards, "Excellency of Christ," in *The Sermons of Jonathan Edwards: A Reader*, ed. Wilson H. Kimnach, Kenneth P. Minkema, and Douglas A. Sweeney (New Haven: Yale University Press, 1999), 196; Edwards, "End of Creation," in *WJE* 8:461.

66. But, as Lee has pointed out, the temporal "becoming" of God (and the world) in some sense echoes the "becoming" that happens in the eternal, hypostatic differentiation within God (Lee, *PTJE*, 189).

67. Edwards, "Miscellanies," no. 97, in *WJE* 13:264. "Now the happiness of society consists in this, in the mutual communications of each other's happiness; neither does it satisfy in society only to receive the other's happiness without also communicating his own."

68. Ibid.

69. Ibid.

70. Edwards, "Excellency of Christ," in *Sermons*, 191–92.

71. Edwards, "Miscellanies," no. 722, in *WJE* 18:353.

72. Edwards, "Miscellanies," no. 769, in *WJE* 18:418. Since "the wisdom of any being is discovered by the wise choice he makes," God's divine wisdom is displayed in the election of the Son to the office of the mediator—the perfect "fitness" that only the divine could discern.

73. Ibid., 414.

74. "It is a *real* exaltation of Christ . . . and not merely a *manifestive* exaltation. It is an advancement to new degrees of knowledge, to a real increase in capacity, to new powers and advantages, which he had not on earth, as well as to new dignities. . . . Godhead cannot be any otherwise exalted. . . . [I]t must be therefore a creature, even the Man Jesus, who receives this real advancement" (Isaac Watts, *The Glory of Christ as God-Man Displayed in Three Discourses* [Boston: Printed by Manning and Loring for David West, 1795], § 2, 105).

75. It is instructive here to note that the term "deification" refers to the hypostatic union in relation to the human nature and, as John of Damascus points out, is used in conjunction with other similar terms: "assumption of the Word and exceeding exaltation and anointing" (John of Damascus, *Orthodox Faith*, bk. 31, ch. 18, 91 [*NPNF* 9]).

76. Edwards, "Miscellanies," no. 1304, in *WJE* 23:257.

77. Of real and rational relations in general, see Aquinas, *STh* I, q. 13, a. 7. Specifically, "the union of which we are speaking is not really in God, except only in our way of thinking; but in the human nature, which is a creature, it is really. Therefore we must say it [the union] is something created" (Aquinas, *STh* III, q. 2, a. 7, 2034).

78. Turretin is very cautious as he rejects any notion of ontological amelioration in the human nature, since the Son assumed a perfect humanity. Certainly, no change happened to the divine Logos in the incarnation; "the change (if there were any here) is in the human nature" (Turretin, *Institutes*, 3:317)

79. "Therefore there is no real relation in God to the creature; whereas in creatures there is a real relation to God; because creatures are contained under the divine order, and their very nature entails dependence on God. On the other hand, the divine processions are in one and the same nature" (Aquinas, *S.Th* 1, q. 28, a. 1, ad 3). Of course, Thomas is not denying here the reality of the incarnation from God's perspective. Since relations cannot be accidental in God, real relations within the divine nature can only be subsistent, and a subsistent relation is another term for a divine person.

80. Brian Leftow, "A Timeless God Incarnate," in *The Incarnation: An Interdisciplinary Symposium on the Incarnation of the Son of God*, ed. Stephen T. Davis, Daniel Kendall, and Gerald O'Collins (New York: Oxford University Press, 2002), 299.

81. Karl Rahner, *Theological Investigations*, vol. 4, *Most Recent Writings* (New York: Crossroad, 1982), 112.

82. "For change means that the same something should be different now from what it was previously" (Aquinas, *STh* Ia, q. 45, a. 2, ad 2).

83. The legitimate use by the Alexandrian theologians of the notion of Christ's humanity as the *organon, organum,* or *instrumentum* of the Word was taken over and married to the idea of Aristotelian causality by Thomas Aquinas. See Gilles Emery, *Trinity, Church, and the Human Person: Thomistic Essays* (Naples, FL: Sapientia, 2007), 198–202. Following the medievals, Scottish Puritan George Hutcheson acknowledged that "as God, [Christ] is a principal efficient, as man, he is the instrument of the Godhead, and as Mediator, he acts as the Father's servant." See George Hutcheson, *An Exposition of the Gospel of Jesus Christ according to John* (London: Ralph Smith, 1657), 226.

84. The relation of the human nature to the Logos "is ἐνυπόστατον, i.e. subsisting in the person, not as an equal part, but as an instrument pertaining to the unity of the hypostasis, as Damascenus expresses it; or as a thing subsisting in its principal" (Davenant, *Exposition of the Epistle of St. Paul to the Colossians,* 417).

85. Reformed theologians appropriated the medieval scholastic distinction—originally used to debate the Trinitarian processions—between the acting *suppositum* or "principle which" (*principium quod*) and the active nature or "principle by which" (*principium quo*) (Bonaventure, *Commentaria in Librum Primum Sententiarum,* English trans. Franciscan Archive, accompanied by Latin text of Quaracchi Edition, http://www.franciscan-archive.org/bonaventura/I-Sent.html, bk. 1, art. 1). "And though the human nature (which is in itself finite) be the *principium quo,* and the instrument by which, and in which the second Person does all that he does; and therefore answerably the physical being of those actions is but *finite in genere entis:* Yet all those articles being attributed to the person who is *principium quod,* the principle which does, and unto which all is to be ascribed (for *actiones sunt suppositorum,* actions are attributed to the persons, because that is said only to subsist) therefore the moral estimation of them is from the worth of the person that performs them" (Goodwin, *WTG* 5:105).

86. That is, the humanity/body being the instrument or *organon* of the deity/soul (Edwards, "Miscellanies," no. 1219, in *WJE* 23:153). Similarly, "though they may be in the soul as the *subiectum proximum & principium quo,* that is, as immediately proceeding from it, and subjected in it, yet they are properly in the whole compound, viz. the whole man or person, as the *subiectum ultimum,* and *principium quod*; and as that which receives the whole denomination from what belongs immediately to any part of it." See Robert South, *Tritheism charged upon Dr. Sherlock's new notion of the trinity . . .* (London: John Whitlock, 1695), 120. As the body stands in relation to the soul as its *organon,* the Catholic tradition has often viewed the *Logos-sarx* relation in similar terms (Aquinas, *STh* III, q. 8, a. 2). See Wolfson, *Philosophy of the Church Fathers,* 368–72.

87. Riisen, XI, 21, as quoted in Heppe, *Reformed Dogmatics Set Out and Illustrated from the Sources,* rev. and ed. Ernst Bizer, trans. G. T. Thomson (London: George Allen & Unwin, 1950), 430. Otherwise, the analogy moves toward the univocity underlying Apollinarian Christology—a synthesis of two natures (Aloys Grillmeier, *Christ in Christian Tradition,* vol. 2, *From the Council of Chalcedon (451) to Gregory the Great (590–604). Part 2, The Church of Constantinople in the Sixth Century,* trans. Pauline Allen and John Cawte [Louisville, KY: Westminster John Knox, 1995], 506).

88. Turretin, *Institutes,* 2:312; Martin Chemnitz, *The Two Natures in Christ,* trans. J. A. O. Preus (St. Louis, Missouri: Concordia, 1971; originally published as *De Duabus Naturis in Christo,* Leipzig, 1578), 31. Clearly, one needs to distinguish at least two senses of the *enypostatos* here: the Damascene and Palamite. The humanity must be regarded as truly and permanently existing in the

person of the Logos; it has real but not independent subsistence in the incarnation. Nevertheless, the assumed human nature cannot be thought of as inhering in another *accidentally* as does grace or in the way that the divine energies are *enhypostatic* in believers.

89. Edwards, "Miscellanies," no. 1233, in *WJE* 23:178.

90. Christ's human nature is related to the divine nature in "the way that the body is the instrument of the soul," though not "in the way that the soul is the form of the body." See St. Thomas Aquinas, *Disputed Question: Concerning the Union of the Word Incarnate*, trans. Jason Lewis Andrew West (Center Valley, PA: Aquinas Translation Project, DeSales University), a. 1, http://www4.desales.edu/~philtheo/loughlin/ATP/De_Unione/De_Unione1.html. Elsewhere, he explains that "inasmuch as the soul is its motor, the body serves the soul instrumentally" (Aquinas, *STh* III, q. 8, a. 2, 2070). "But whereas the rational soul is united with the body, (a) as form with matter, (b) as chief agent with instrument . . . this comparison cannot hold in respect of the former mode of union, for so we should be brought round to the [Eutychian] conclusion, that of God and man there was made one nature" (Aquinas, *Of God and His Creatures*, bk. 4: 41).

91. Edwards, "Miscellanies," no. *bb*, in *WJE* 13:178. This echoes patristic descriptions of the Logos's body as house, tabernacle, temple, or garment by Athanasius, John Chrysostom, Tertullian, Augustine, Hippolytus, and Clement of Alexandria (Wolfson, *Philosophy of the Church Fathers*, 368).

92. This inseparable soul-body relation makes the resurrection of the body "absolutely necessary in order to complete happiness." The happiness of the saints in heaven, as "separated souls," is not thwarted since "they have a certain hope, a certain knowledge of the resurrection, that completely satisfies this inclination during the separation" (Edwards, "Miscellanies," no. *bb*, in *WJE* 13:179).

93. Demetrios Bathrellos, *The Byzantine Christ: Person, Nature, and Will in the Christology of Saint Maximus the Confessor* (Oxford: Oxford University Press, 2004), 93. See, for example, Grillmeier's criticism of Athanasius's application of the Stoic *anima mundi* to the relation between the Word and the Word's instrumental human nature (Aloys Grillmeier, *Christ in the Christian Tradition*, vol. 1, *From the Apostolic Age to Chalcedon [451]* (London: Mowbrays, 1975), 310–18).

94. Evaluated from the axiom of the identity of indiscernibles, much of classical Christology would have to be construed on mereological terms. This has to be in order for opposing properties to be ascribed to (parts of) the same subject without contradiction. See Richard Cross, "Parts and Properties in Christology" in *Reason, Faith and History: Philosophical Essays for Paul Helm*, ed. Martin F. Stone (Aldershot, UK: Ashgate, 2008), 177–92.

95. The assumed human nature possesses its attributes as, for example, a hand has its weight, which, though predicable of the hand, is, nonetheless, not of the same order in which two hands are predicates of a human being. In other words, attributes in ordinary human beings are first-order (substantial) while human attributes in Christ are predicates of a predicate—an instrument united to a substance. See John Lamont, "The Nature of the Hypostatic Union," *Heythrop Journal* 47, no. 1 (2006): 16–17. For Cross, the difficulty of a part-whole Christology is "finding ways in which a nature could be part of any other substance." See Richard Cross, "A Recent Contribution on the Distinction between Monophysitism and Chalcedonianism," *Thomist* 65 (2001): 383. Such a criticism would not be entirely applicable if the natures were viewed by way of eminence. A noninstrumentalism, on the other hand, would move toward an equivalence of the natures bordering on a literal *hypostasis synthetos* or *tertium quid*.

96. In relation to created being, Edwards affirms the classical axiom *operari sequitur esse* (Edwards, "Miscellanies," no. 1129, in *WJE* 20:503). Turretin notes that the human nature is called the instrument of the Logos not with regard to the order of existence or being but of ethics or economic operations (Turretin, *Institutes*, 2, topic 13, q. 6, para. 6, 312).

97. Demetrios Bathrellos, "The Relationship between the Divine Will and the Human Will of Jesus Christ according to Saint Maximus the Confessor," in *Papers Presented at the Thirteenth International Conference on Patristic Studies held in Oxford 1999*, ed. M. F. Wiles and E. J. Yarnold

(Leuven: Peeters, 2001), 349. In order to avoid, on the one hand, the Nestorian position of turning the human nature into a willing subject and, on the other hand, an extreme Alexandrian stance of an overwhelming divinity, Barthrellos recommends Maximus's idea that "the Logos as God willed by his divine will, and the same Logos as man obeyed the divine will by the human will" (Barthrellos, "Relationship between the Divine Will," 351).

98. Maximus saw the Logos incarnate as the willing and acting subject, while the Sixth Ecumenical Council, followings Leo, spoke of the natures as subjects of action and volition. John of Damascus took on both emphases by alternating between the hypostasis and the natures as acting and willing subjects (Bathrellos, *Byzantine Christ*, 183–84). Rightly, there is only one actor and work, but two effects and operations arising from two natural principles: "Causa producens, persona θεάνθρωπος, ἐνεργῶν. 2. Principia duo, causae producentis ἐνεργγειτικὰ, duae in Mediatore naturae. 3. Duplex efficacia, pro numero duorum principiorum, seu duplex ἐνέργεια, divinae & humanae naturae. Denique 4. Opus unum, ἐνεργούμενον, seu ἀποτέλεσμα θεανδρικὸν, quod unus Mediator, pro duabus naturis, per cuique peculiarem efficaciam, producit" (Peter van Mastricht, *Theoretico-practica theologia, qua, per singula capita theologica, pars exegetica, dogmatica, elenchtica & practica, perpetuâ successione coniugantur* [Traiecti ad Rhenum: Ex officinâ Thomae Appels, 1699], 440). Though Chemnitz disavows the Nestorian notion of an *instrumentum* not anchored in the *enypostatos*, he seems to veer toward a kind of double agency within Christ: "For there is a rule in the schools which says, 'When two agents have one purpose (ἀποτέλεσμα), one is the principle and the other is the secondary, organic, or instrumental agent; for the action or ἀποτέλεσμα is rightly attributed not only to the principal agent but also the secondary or organic agent'" (Chemnitz, *Two Natures*, 254, 290).

99. Otherwise, it seems to signify the efficient agency of the Trinity, which either confuses the incarnate subject or reduces instrumental causality into secondary causality. The terminology is consistent with the indistinct attribution of the divine will and miracles of the Word incarnate to the Trinity. As Turretin put it, the person of Christ, being the "efficient cause," exerts a single power toward a single work, while Christ's natures, being a twofold "exciting cause," have a twofold operation (*energeia*) (Turretin, *Institutes* 2: 321). Note his careful designation of the natural operations as "twofold."

100. Edwards, "Miscellanies," no. 738, in *WJE* 18:364.

101. Uwe Michael Lang, *John Philoponus and the Controversies over Chalcedon in the Sixth Century: A Study and Translation of the* Arbiter, Spicilegium Sacrum Lovaniense: Études et Documents 47 (Leuven: Peeters, 2001), 45. He cites Cyril's *Epistula ad Monachos Aegypti*, 19–20.

102. Aquinas, *STh* III, q. 64, art. 3, ad 3, 2060. The minister, in relation to the mystical body of Christ, is an *instrumentum coniunctum*, while a sacrament is an *instrumentum separatum*. (Aquinas *STh* III, Q. 64, a.8, ad. 1). Citing Athanasius and Damascenus on this, Aquinas carefully insists that the assumed humanity is "not indeed an extrinsic and foreign instrument, but its own and a conjoined one [*non quidem extrinsecum et adventitium, sed proprium et coniunctum*]" (Aquinas, *De Unione*, a. 1).

103. Since the nature should be the content of the person, the humanity of Christ cannot be thought of as an instrument of the person. See Robert North, "Soul-Body Unity and God-Man Unity," *Theological Studies* 30, no. 1 (March 1969): 56. This comment was made in the context of Aquinas's notion of the *instrumentum coniunctum*, when loosely translated as a "tool hooked on," and Schillebeeckx's preference for the language of unity instead of union for describing the incarnation. On Aquinas's analogy, the assumed nature may be thought of as the addition of finite content to a preexisting person.

104. Edwards, "Miscellanies," no. 738, in *WJE* 18:364; see also "Miscellanies," no. 764b, in *WJE* 18:411. However, these "outward and inward" manifestations of divine knowledge and power were not, like those of "apostles and the prophets," done in another's name and power (Edwards, "Miscellanies," no. 766, in *WJE* 18:412). The human nature is unlike an ax, which, as an external instrument, may be used by many persons.

105. Michael R. Miller, "Freedom and Grace," in *Gathered for the Journey: Moral Theology in Catholic Perspective*, ed. David M. McCarthy and M. Therese Lysaught (Grand Rapids, MI: Eerdmans, 2007), 185–87. Miller points out that the illustration of a subordinate taking orders from a superior is descriptive of secondary causation.

106. John McIntyre, in *The Shape of Christology: Studies in the Doctrine of the Person of Christ*, 2nd ed. (Edinburgh: T&T Clark, 1998), 242, for example, appeals to Kant's castigation (in his *Second Critique*) of "the immorality of treating another person as a means to an end." Clearly, this confuses secondary with instrumental causation. See note above.

107. The critique of the instrumentalization of the human nature is found in many authors. For example, Louis Berkhof, *Systematic Theology*, new combined ed., with new preface by Richard E. Muller (Grand Rapids, MI: Eerdmans, 1996), 307. Brian O. McDermott calls it the "hegemony of the Logos" (*Word Become Flesh: Dimensions in Christology* [Collegeville, MN: Liturgical Press, 1993], 201, 251). If the atonement is to be regarded as the work of the entire God-man, and thus impossible even for the Logos per se, the humanity of Christ must not be thought of as a mere passive instrument of the divine but as "a causatively active humanity." This is the assumption that runs through the Christology of Dorner—an idea he considers to be true to the Lutheran emphasis on Christ's humanity, which he credits as "a striking observation of Schneckenburger's." See I. A. Dorner, *History of the Development of the Doctrine of the Person of Christ*, 5 vols., Clark's Foreign Theological Library, 3rd ser. (Edinburgh: T&T Clark, 1891), 2.2:434n42.

108. Gunton takes issue with Athanasius's reference to Jesus' body as the Word's "instrument," language he finds reminiscent of Apollinaris's. See Colin Gunton, *The Promise of Trinitarian Theology*, 2nd ed. (Edinburgh: T&T Clark, 1997), 69. Hanson accuses Athanasius of propounding a "Space-suit Christology." See R. P. C. Hanson, *The Search for the Christian Doctrine of God: The Arian Controversy 318–381 ad*, 1st paperback ed. (Grand Rapids, MI: Baker Academic, 2005; first published London: T&T Clark, 1988), 447–54. Grillmeier points out that Athanasius affirmed a dual *energeia* together with this doctrine of the *sarx* as *organon* (Grillmeier, *Christ in Christian Tradition*, 2.2:168n415). Anatolios faults Grillmeier for analyzing Athanasius's Christology within the framework of a parts Christology, which is found deficient without a mediating soul. Rather, we should interpret Athanasius as attempting to highlight the Creator-creator relation, explaining how the invisible God self-reveals through God's own visible body. See Khaled Anatolios, *Athanasius: The Coherence of His Thought* (London: Routledge, 1998), 71–72.

109. W. Ross Hastings, "'Honouring the Spirit': Analysis and Evaluation of Jonathan Edwards' Pneumatological Doctrine of the Incarnation," *International Journal of Systematic Theology* 7, no. 3 (July 2005): 298–99. Hastings attributes to Edwards and Jenson the error of substituting Jesus' human understanding and spirit with the Holy Spirit. Unfortunately, he fails to appreciate Edwards's insistence that the incarnate Son has two understandings and wills, in which the human nature is funded by a dichotomist anthropology. For Edwards, only pre-Edenic and regenerated human beings are properly spiritual, for they are soulish bodies by nature.

110. Aquinas, *STh* III, q. 7, a. 2, ad 3, 2060. Of the *instrumentum Deitatis*, Chemnitz asserts that "it is not a soulless instrument, like an ax, nor a brutish thing, like Balaam's ass which spoke, nor something inactive or without energy (ἀνενέργητον), as when the sun shines through a glass" (Chemnitz, *Two Natures*, 253).

111. Aquinas, *STh* III, q. 7, a. 2, ad 3, 2060. For extensive treatment of this, see Theophil Tschipke, *Die Menschheit Christi als Heilsorgan der Gottheit: unter besonderer Berücksichtigung der Lehre des heiligen Thomas von Aquin*, Freiburger theologische Studien 55 (Freiburg im Breisgau: Herder, 1940). See the recent French translation by Philibert Secrétan, *L'humanité du Christ comme instrument de salut de la divinité* (Fribourg: Academic, 2003).

112. Edwards, "Miscellanies," no. 1150, in *WJE* 20:521.

113. This is Aquinas's judgment of the Nestorian idea of union and instrument. "Not everything that is assumed as an instrument pertains to the hypostasis of the one who assumes, as is plain in the case of the saw or a sword; yet nothing prevents what is assumed into the unity of the

hypostasis from being an instrument, even as the body of man or his members" (Aquinas, *STh* III, q. 2, a. 6, ad 4, 2134). Aquinas's image of a slave obeying the master's command is a useful analogy for the *instrumentum* as *animatum* but not *coniunctum* (Aquinas, *STh* III, q. 18, a. 1, ad 2, 2120).

114. Aquinas, *STh* III, q. 19, a. 1, ad 2; q. 62, a. 1, ad 2. A modern-day analogy of instrumental causation is the automatic dryer, which has solar heat as its principal cause by which clothes are dried (like clothes on a washing line) but yet through its own unique form (unlike line drying). See Romanus Cessario, *Christian Faith and the Theological Life* (Washington, DC: Catholic University of America Press, 1996), 19. Edwards, however, does not go as far as Aquinas to assert that "Christ's humanity is both sanctified and sanctifier" (Aquinas, *STh* III, q. 34, a. 3, ad 3, 2195). Although it is Christ as God who grants the Holy Spirit and grace as efficient and meritorious cause, the humanity of Christ (and "even other saints") exercises instrumental causation in conferring grace (Aquinas, *STh* III, q. 8, art. 1, ad 1, 2070). For Edwards, as we have seen, Christ, as God, gives the Spirit but, as human and mediator, receives the Spirit of the Father. And as we will see later, Edwards's use of the *organon* concept does not extend to his ecclesiology.

115. See Grillmeier's interpretation of Apollinaris's *mia physis* concept in his *Christ in Christian Tradition*, 1:333. Chemnitz, echoing Aquinas and Damascus, though with a Nestorian tinge, described it as "an animated organ, living, intelligent, rational, which cooperates as a living and intelligent instrument, when the deity wills to accomplish divine activities through it" (Chemnitz, *Two Natures*, 253).

116. Aquinas, *STh* III, q. 18, a. 1, ad 2, 2120.

117. E. L. Mascall, *Christ, the Christian and the Church: A Study of the Incarnation and Its Consequences* (London: Longmans, Green, 1946), 232n1.

118. "God sometimes made use of brute creatures as instruments to do his work. . . . Sometimes he makes use of things without life" (Edwards, "Miscellanies," no. 1150, in *WJE* 20:521). God uses human persons, according to Edwards, as his instruments in performing miracles. "God is pleased often to make use of men as instruments in working miracles" (ibid.).

119. Edwards, "Miscellanies," no. 738, in *WJE* 18:364.

120. While the human nature is an instrument conveying the efficient causality of the divinity, through the action of the incarnate Word he communicates the excellency of its own form, "per formam suam," in the theandric act. Christ touches the world through his whole person, "per contactum suum," with both natures acting connaturally (Emile Mersch, *Theology of the Mystical Body*, trans. Cyril Vollert [St. Louis, MO: Herder, 1951], 229–30). See also Aquinas, *STh* IIIa, q. 50, a. 6.

121. A moral instrument acts in parallel with divine power without being a channel or participant itself. See Robert South, "Discourse V: The Scribe Instructed," in *Discourses on Various Subjects and Occasions Selected from the Complete English Edition* (Boston: Bowles and Dearborn, 1827), 103. Similarly, Goodwin envisions that, in the *unio mystica*, the Son's "human nature is not, nor was not the medium, or organ, much less the sole way or means by which the divine nature is united unto us." The divine is united to Christians by "his own immediate . . . act" and is not "mediately united; as the soul in the body takes hold of a thing by the hand only, immediately, but it self does not so much as touch it immediately" (Goodwin, "A Sermon on Ephesians 3.17: That Christ May Dwell In Your Hearts by Faith," in *Thirteen Sermons Preached on Diverse Texts on Scripture, upon Several Occasions*, in *The Works of Thomas Goodwin, D. D. sometime President of Magdalen College in Oxford*, ed. Thankfull Owen and James Barron (London: T. G. [Thomas Goodwin Jr.], 1681), 38; available at *The Digital Library of Classic Protestant Texts*; Goodwin, *Discourse of Christ the Mediator*, ch. 7, 55). In other words, Goodwin rejects the idea that the church is in any way an *instrumentum coniunctum* of God or Christ.

122. Christ's human nature, for the Reformed and Scotists, is only a moral instrument like a dollar note. The Thomists, however, regard it in both moral and physical terms (like an artist's paintbrush). See Reginald Garrigou-Lagrange, "De causalitate sacramentorum," in *De Eucharistia et Paenitentia*, q. 62 (Marietti, 1948), http://thomistica.net/storage/pdf-files/2007/Garrigou-

Lagrange other texts from De Eucharistia.pdf. The principles of causality in Thomas are not just moral, but "'physical,' or real; they show how the two natures are realized, fulfilled, and perfected precisely in their operations in the person of Christ, each working in relation with the other." See Paul G. Crowley, "*Instrumentum Divinitatis* in Thomas Aquinas: Recovering the Divinity of Christ," *Theological Studies* 52 (1991): 474.

123. Like human beings (Turretin, *Institutes*, 1:435), the humanity of Christ in its working of miracles was only a "moral instrument" (*Institutes*, 2:331). In a way analogous to the body-soul unity, the divinity of the Son acts immediately "as the soul doth many rational acts immediately itself whilst it is in the body . . . yet it uses not the body, as by which it doth them" (Goodwin, *WTG* 2:402). "It is one thing for one to do a thing by reason of another, and another to do it by the means and intervention of another's doing it, or as by the sole immediate act of another" (ibid.). There is here a sense of overemphasizing the *extra* to the point of hypostatizing the natures.

124. Edwards, "Miscellanies," no. 1150, in *WJE* 20:521.

125. Ibid.

126. Ibid. It is "suitable and highly requisite" that a prophet "should act as in the name of the Lord . . . and not take upon him to work miracles as of his own power and authority, as Christ did." Elsewhere, he expands upon this point with biblical illustrations, "The prophets don't used to preach as speaking their own word, but the word of another; and used to speak in such a style as this, 'Thus saith the Lord,' but Christ in such a style as this, 'I say unto you' thus or thus, 'verily, verily, I say unto you.' . . . He gave forth his commands, not as the prophets used to as God's commands, but as his own commands" (Edwards, "Sermon Fifteen," in *WJE* 9:316).

127. "This axe is not my own proper instrument as is this hand. With this axe many men may work: but this hand is set aside for the proper activity of this soul. Therefore the hand is a tool conjoined with and proper to him that works with it: but the axe is an instrument extrinsic to the workman and common to many hands. Thus then we may take it to be with the union of God and man" (Aquinas, *Of God and His Creatures*, bk. 4:41).

128. Edwards, "Miscellanies," no. 1150, in *WJE* 20:521.

129. "What they do has really no proper efficiency at all in the case, as tools have that men work with. . . . Created minds can be made use of as the instruments of miracles in no higher sense than that God should annex the miracle to proper acts of those minds towards him as the author, so that the mind shall as it were go to God for the effect and bring it down from him" (ibid., 522).

130. "If it were suspended on no acts of his, then he would not be in any respect an instrument in it. For therein does his instrumentality lie, viz. in the connection of the event on his acts. These acts of the instrument that the promise was suspended on were twofold: first, inward, or the act of the mind, which was in the exercise of dependence on God's sufficiency and faithfulness; secondly, those outward acts that he was to perform in signification of those acts of the mind, such as prayer or certain words to be spoken (as those of Peter, Acts 3:6, "In the name of Jesus Christ rise up and walk") or actions to be performed, as laying hands on the sick, anointing with oil, etc"" (ibid., 523–24).

131. Angus Paddison, *Theological Hermeneutics and 1 Thessalonians*, Society for New Testament Studies Monograph Series 133 (New York: Cambridge University Press, 2005), 88–89. Based on *SCG III*, 70, Paddison suggests that Thomas's notion of sacramental instrumentality is open to the reading that Christ's miracles could not have been achieved by divine power alone. Jesus' miracles and the general resurrection are synthetic effects—"something which neither God's power nor Christ's resurrection could achieve alone." However, Thomas here (in *SCG III*, 70) is contending for "how *natural effects* are attributable at once to God and to a natural agent" (italics mine), which clearly discounts divine miracles.

132. As there is nothing presupposed prior to creation, that is, preexisting matter, "therefore it is impossible for any creature to create, either by its own power or instrumentally—that is, ministerially" (Aquinas, *STh* Ia, q. 45, a. 5).

133. As first cause, God, by "natural necessity," cannot do things against the divine will and order, but God is free in regard to the divine relation to and ordering of secondary causes (*STh* I-I,

q. 105, a. 6, 519–20). Thus, "God can produce the effects of second causes, without these second causes," if God so chooses (*STh* I–II, q. 51, a. 4, 806). Applied christologically, "God's power is not tied to any particular second causes, but that He can produce their effects either immediately or by means of other causes. . . . In like manner according to the order appointed to human things by Divine providence, Christ's resurrection is the cause of ours: and yet He could have appointed another order, and then our resurrection would have had another cause ordained by God" (Aquinas, *STh* III, supp., Q. 76, a. 1, ad 2).

134. The issue, for Aquinas, "is not that a natural agent cannot cause a supernatural effect, but that a corporeal agent cannot cause a spiritual effect." See Philip Lyndon Reynolds, "Efficient Causality and Instrumentality in Thomas Aquinas's Theology of the Sacraments," in *Essays in Medieval Philosophy and Theology in Memory of Walter H. Principe: Fortresses and Launching Pads*, ed. James R. Ginther and Carl N. Still (Aldershot, UK: Ashgate, 2005), 71.

135. This does not abrogate the intrinsic, efficient causality of the human nature. Rather, insofar as the divine causality can be transferred or mediated through the instrument, the human nature participates in the divine power and so realizes (with the principal agent) the final cause that originates from the Logos. See Stephen M. Fields, *Being as Symbol: On the Origins and Development of Karl Rahner's Metaphysics* (Washington, DC: Georgetown University Press, 2007), 41.

136. Edwards titles Miscellany no. 205 "ΘΕΆΝΘΡΟΠΟς" (Edwards, "Miscellanies," no. 205, in *WJE* 13:340).

137. John of Damascus, *Orthodox Faith*, bk. 3, ch. 19, 68 (*NPNF* 9).

138. Ibid. This echoes Maximus (*Amb.* 5); see Thunberg, *Microcosm and Mediator*, 31. Though the analogy of fire and iron does highlight two distinct acts and a single agent, Owen, for example, does not think that it is particularly illuminating of the hypostatic union because heat seems to be accidental to, and separable from, iron. He terms this "an *artificial union*" and grants its application to the incarnational union "in the way of allusion" (Owen, *Works*, 1:230). While this may be inappropriate as a direct analogy for the *henosis*, it seems useful as a metaphor for the communication of works because something of the voluntary and existential character of *synergia* is pictured.

139. Edwards, "Blank Bible," note on Luke 7:13, in *WJE* 24:896. "It shows that the works were properly his own . . . that they were properly the effects of his own power as well as his own mercy and inclination."

140. "For it was with the permission of the divine will that He suffered by nature what was proper to Him" (John of Damascus, *Orthodox Faith*, bk. 3, ch. 18, 67 [*NPNF* 9]). The contemporary propensity to make humility and suffering divine attributes tends toward a dangerous anthropomorphism.

141. In the patristic, medieval, and Reformed authors, the mediation of the assumed nature in Christ's miracles is evident. Christ's "miracles, symbols of his divine nature" are, therefore, "performed by the divine activity *through* the activity of the flesh." See John of Damascus, *Three Treatises on the Divine Images*, trans. and intro. Andrew Louth (Crestwood, NY: St Vladimir's Seminary Press, 2003), 24. As an instrument, according to Aquinas, the humanity has a share in the divine agency of the Word: "Now, the power of an agent is in some way in the instrument, by which means the agent does something" (Aquinas, *III Sent.*, d. 5, q. 1, a. 2, resp. 6). Perkins affirmed that "by reason of this union, the godhead of Christ workes all things in the matter of our redemption, in and by the manhood" (Perkins, *Exposition of the Apostle's Creed*, 181).

142. Maximus interpreted Ps.-Dionysius's "new theandric energy" as an unconfused cooperation of the natures rather than a mixture of both forms in "one theandric energy" (a falsification that he attributed to Cyrus) (Thunberg, *Microcosm and Mediator*, 34). Aquinas interprets Ps.-Dionysius in this way as well. Coffey advances a novel interpretation, noting that Ps.-Dionysius refers to both the divine energy and the theandric energy as operations of the Logos, the one *asarkos* and the other *ensarkos* (Coffey, "Theandric Nature of Christ," 409–10). While he claims that this appropriation of Rahnerian Christology falls within the bounds of

orthodoxy, such an understanding seems to posit two personal wills in Christ, contradicting the Sixth Council.

143. Edwards, "Subjects of Inquiry," in *WJE* 28.

144. "Monotheletism" failed "to distinguish between what is absolutely one and what is one in subordination to another." See St. Thomas Aquinas, *Of God and His Creatures*, IV.36, 368. Christ's human will was in such perfect concord with the divine will (*ordine unum*) that it appeared to monothelites that there was only a single will (*simpliciter unum*). See Carlo Leget, *Living with God: Thomas Aquinas on the Relation between Life on Earth and "Life" after Death*, Publications of the Thomas Instituut te Utrecht, n.s., vol. 5 (Leuven: Peeters, 1997), 107.

145. Even though Barth rejected any construals of the *genus maiestaticum* and *communicatio gratiarum*, which in his view involve substantial change, he still conceived of the *communicatio operationum* asymmetrically. Consistent with his use of the *enhypostaton-enhypostaton* dialectic, he regarded the common actualization of the two natures to include the instrumentalization of the human nature. Hence, it is "where the divine rules and reveals and gives that the human serves and attests and *mediates*" (Barth, *CD* IV.2, 116; emphasis mine). Thus his frequent references to the "human essence" as the "organ of action" of the Son, empowered to obedience and witness to the divine will (Barth, *CD* IV.2, § 64, pp. 96–101).

146. Just as energy is an operation and not an operator, it "is energized rather than energizes." He cites Gregory of Nazianzus: "If energy exists, it must be manifestly be energized and will not energize: and as soon as it has been energized, it will cease" (John of Damascus, *Orthodox Faith*, bk. 3, ch. 15, 61 [*NPNF* 9]).

147. Edwards, 412. Sermon on Rev. 14:14 (Oct 1736), in *WJE* 51.

148. Mascall, *Christ, the Christian and the Church*, 49.

149. Edwards, "Miscellanies," no. 526, in *WJE* 13:70. "And Jesus Christ has this honor, to be the greatest instrument of glorifying God that ever was, and more than all other beings put together. Yea, he is so the great means or author of the glory of God, that what others do towards it is in a dependence upon what he does. . . . Agreeable to this, it was so ordered that Christ should be the great means of bringing the world from heathenism, to the knowledge of the true God and the true religion. . . . Therefore is Christ the grand medium of all communications of grace and happiness from God, by which especially God glorifies himself." See also "Miscellanies," no. 1156, in *WJE* 23:69.

150. "And indeed if for all other works God chooses out fit instruments, then surely for this great work of works else; and accordingly divines call his human nature *instrumentum Deitatis*, the instrument of the Godhead" (Goodwin, *WTG* 5:56). See also Chemnitz, *Two Natures*, 253.

151. Edwards, 905. Sermon on Eze. 28:22-26, in *WJE* 66.

152. God's bare glory is impossible to been viewed "immediately" as "our eyes will be dazzled." But in Christ, "the manifestation of the glory of God in the person of Christ . . . are as it were accommodated to our apprehensions." This is by virtue of the fact that he has "come to us in our nature" and has "as it were softened the light of God's glory and accommodated [it] to our view" (Edwards, 321. Sermon on Heb. 1:13 [1734], in *WJE* 49).

153. According to Chemnitz, without detriment to its own proper sphere of operation, the humanity is "formed, prepared, and made suitable and proper that it can be a useful (εὔχρηστον) instrument of the divine Logos" through the infused gifts (Chemnitz, *Two Natures*, 253).

154. As Thomas Watson put it, "Christ took our flesh, that he might make the *Humane Nature appear lovely* to God, and the *Divine Nature appear lovely* to Man" (Watson, "Christ's Humiliation in His Incarnation," in *A body of practical divinity, consisting of above one hundred seventy six sermons on the lesser catechism . . .* [London: Thomas Parkhurst, 1692], q. 17, 113).

155. "Upon our fall from God, our nature became odious to him. . . . As when the sun shines on the glass, it casts a bright luster, so Christ being clad with our flesh, makes the human nature shine, and appear amiable in God's Eyes. . . . The pure Godhead is terrible to behold. . . . Through the lantern of Christ's humanity, we may behold the light of the Deity shining. Christ

being incarnate, he makes the sight of the Deity not formidable, but delightful to us" (Watson, "Christ's Humiliation in His Incarnation," in *A body of practical divinity*, q. 17, 113).

156. The *doxa* is revealed precisely in the kenosis as "God is revealed hidden under his opposite (*absconditas Dei sub contrario*)." See Hans Küng, *The Incarnation of God: An Introduction to Hegel's Theological Thought as Prologomena to a Future Christology*, trans. J. R. Stephenson (Edinburgh: T&T Clark, 1987), 450.

157. Edwards, "Blank Bible," note on John 12:27-28, in *WJE* 24:948.

158. As it is the Holy Spirit that causes the human nature to be united to the Logos, so it is this same principle by which "the man Christ Jesus had his divine knowledge" (Edwards, "Miscellanies," no. 513, in *WJE* 18:57).

159. Edwards, "Miscellanies," no. 487, in *WJE* 13:529.

160. Similarly, "the human nature of Christ was conscious to all the actings of the divine Word in it" as in the miracles when "he felt the miraculous power of the divine Word working in him, as a man feels what is done in himself." See William Sherlock, *A vindication of the doctrine of the holy and ever blessed Trinity, and the incarnation of the Son of God. . . .* (London: W. Rogers, 1690), 270–71. Sherlock (1641–1707) wrote this treatise to counter the Socinianism of Stephen Ney but was accused of tritheism by Robert South. In contrast, Brian Hebblethwaite asserts that Christ's "human mind and will are the divine mind and will operative under human conditions." See Brian Hebblethwaite, *Philosophical Theology and Christian Doctrine* (Malden, MA: Blackwell, 2005), 65. Affirming an orthodox kenoticism, Hebblethwaite sides with Peter van Inwagen's "relative identity theory" in order to predicate human and divine properties to the one incarnate Son, countering the Leibnizian theory of the identity of indiscernibles.

161. Weinandy articulates a position very similar to that of Edwards: "When Jesus said 'I,' it was the Son of God saying 'I,' but he was saying 'I' in a human manner for it was as man that he was consciously speaking as an 'I,' as a subject, as a 'who.'" See Thomas G. Weinandy, "Jesus' Filial Vision of the Father," *Pro Ecclesia* 13, no. 2 (Spring 2004): 189–201.

162. Edwards, "Miscellanies," no. 738, in *WJE* 18:364.

163. Edwards includes in his definition of "a person that which hath understanding and will" (Edwards, "Discourse on the Trinity," in *WJE* 21:133). This idea of a Lockean psychological unity of personhood, as Jenson observes in Edwards, is certainly closer to our "modern understanding of personhood" than it is patristic (Robert W. Jenson, *America's Theologian: A Recommendation of Jonathan Edwards* [New York: Oxford University Press, 1988], 121). As Brian Daley has pointed out, while late patristic theology thought of the person as a denominated, irreducible individual, possessing the general properties of its species together with its own incommunicable characteristics, this should not be identified with the "*Fur-sich-sein*" of German idealism," in which the person is regarded as "an independent subject, constituted by a unique and unrepeatable focus of self-consciousness, practical autonomy, and some measure of psychological freedom." See Brian E. Daley, "Nature and the 'Mode of Union': Late Patristic Models for the Personal Unity of Christ," in Davis, Kendall, and O'Collins, *The Incarnation*, 193–94.

164. Personhood, for the post-Chalcedonian theologians, was defined not so much by any interior, psychological state and independent, self-possession as by a mode of being that is at once relational (mode of origin) and behavioral (mode of operation). As Brian Daley puts it, "*who we are* is revealed and actualized not only in *where we come from*, but in *how we act*" (Daley, "Nature and 'Mode of Union,'" 194). This metaphysical understanding of personhood—both divine and human—is evident in the Puritans, and Edward Leigh, for example, thinks that the divine persons are distinguished one from the other "by its personal property, and by its manner of working" (Edward Leigh, *A treatise of divinity consisting of three bookes. The first of which handling the Scripture or word of God. . . .* [London: William Lee, 1646], 129).

165. In continuity with the metaphysical construal within the Alexandrian-Thomistic Christology, Edwards assigns self-consciousness to person and not nature. See Walter Kasper's summary of this debate within modern Catholic Christology in his *Jesus the Christ* (Mahwah, NJ: Paulist, 1976), 243–45.

166. "And if we come even to the personal identity of created intelligent beings, though this be not allowed to consist wholly in what Mr Locke supposes, i.e. *same consciousness*; yet I think it cannot be denied, that this is one thing essential to it" (Edwards, *WJE* 3:398). See also Paul Helm, "A Forensic Dilemma: John Locke and Jonathan Edwards on Personal Identity," in *Jonathan Edwards: Philosophical Theologian*, ed. Paul Helm and Oliver D. Crisp (Aldershot, UK: Ashgate, 2003), 49.

167. Fundamentally, this assumes an Origenist emphasis on the *imago Dei* as *imago Christi* and the Athanasian-Cappadocian construal of the divine and human natures as noncompetitive. This emphasis of the person as a possessor of its nature or essence is contrasted with both the essentialism of the Apollinarian and Antiochene assumption of the incommensurability of God and humanity, which leaves one with either a truncation of the lesser or an operative union of the two. See Kenneth Paul Wesche, "The Union of God and Man in Jesus Christ in the Thought of Gregory of Nazianzus," *Saint Vladimir's Theological Quarterly* 28, no. 2 (2006): 84–88.

168. "To complete a personal union, it is necessary there be one consciousness in the whole. . . . But then we must observe, that where different natures are united into one person, this universal consciousness to the whole person, is seated only in the superior and governing nature." The Word is fully self-conscious as God and man not by omniscience of the common divine nature but by a personal self-consciousness—that is, "such a consciousness, as every person has of himself" (Sherlock, *A Vindication*, 268–69). Whether Edwards thought of this personal consciousness as located in the divine is debatable. However, the Cyrillian-Alexandrian emphasis would tend toward this direction.

169. Clearly, Sherlock's more Cartesian notion of the person comes closer to Edwards's idealism. Stephen Ney classifies Sherlock's trinitarianism as Cartesian in contrast with South's Aristotelian trinitarianism. Although both agree that body and soul make up the person, "South regards the body as an essential element of the person and argues that souls, when separated from their bodies, are not persons." On the other hand, "Sherlock maintains that the soul constitutes the person when united to a body, and is the (same) person when separated from the body." See Udo Thiel, "The Trinity and Human Personal Identity," in *English Philosophy in the Age of Locke*, ed. M. A. Stewart, vol. 3 of *Oxford Studies in the History of Philosophy* (London: Oxford University Press, 2000), 221. That Chalcedon's Christology represented very much a triumph of Cyril and the Alexandrian school of thought is a point well argued by John McGuckin in his *Saint Cyril of Alexandria and the Christological Controversy: Its History, Theology and Texts* (Crestwood, NY: St. Vladimir's Theological Seminary Press, 2004).

170. Edwards, "Miscellanies," no. 738, in *WJE* 18:364; "Miscellanies," no. 205, in *WJE* 13:341. This reality of Christ's unity "is no bold conjecture" and "must of necessity be." Edwards is attempting to explain, in this Miscellany, how it is that Scriptures speak of "a glorious created spirit, which was the Son of God, being created before the world was created" ("Miscellanies," no. 205, in *WJE* 13:341). Edwards did not regard this particular point as private speculation since he uses it in a sermon (Edwards, 526. Sermon on John 3:16, in *WJE* 54).

171. The term *hypostasis synthetos* does not mean a mixed nature, "not in the sense of one kind," as "there is no predicable form of Christlihood." It is in the unique "compound subsistence" of the incarnate Son, whereby the Son differs from all human and divine persons, in which the *perichoresis* and *antidosis* occur (John of Damascus, *Orthodox Faith*, bk. 3, ch. 3, 47 [*NPNF* 9]).

172. *Synthetos* does not imply a parts Christology (Davenant, *An Exposition of the Epistle of St. Paul to the Colossians*, 418). He cites Aquinas, *STh* III, q. 2, a. 4. The person is understood as "composite" not "properly" as the completion of a whole from two parts, but improperly "as that is said to be compounded which consists of different things" (Turretin, *Institutes*, 2:312).

173. One solution to this impasse would be to adopt an idea implicit in Leontius of Jerusalem: by the creative power of God, the human *idiomata*, both essential and accidental, were assumed into the preexisting personhood of the Logos before they could impart independent hypostatic character. According to Grillmeier, both Leontius of Byzantium and Leontius of Jerusalem worked with Basil's definition of hypostasis, which left them open to the Nestorian

critique, yet Leontius of Jerusalem could have avoided such a position had he realized this latent solution (Grillmeier, *Christ in Christian Tradition*, 2:290, 508).

174. A literalism would mean a "fusion of the human and the divine hypostasis" (McIntyre, *Shape of Christology*, 101). McIntyre adopts such an interpretation as a corrective to the supposedly docetic tendency of the *enhypostasia*, crediting it to Ephraim of Antioch. The implied Nestorianism is obvious when such a *synthetos hē hypostasis* is construed as a compound of "two *hypostaseis*" (ibid.)—that is, in the insistence of "the presence of the human *hypostasis* in the composite *hypostasis*" (ibid., 102). On the contrary, when "the ancient Fathers termed Christ a compound person, we must understand them not properly, but by proportion" and "only by analogy" (William Perkins, *A golden chaine: Or, the description of theologie, containing the order of the causes of salvation and damnation, according to Gods word . . .* [London: Printed by John Legatt, Printer to the Universitie of Cambridge, 1616], 25; idem., *An Exposition of the Apostle's Creed*, 181). The assumed humanity may even be metaphorically named a part of the God-man, as the *hypostasis synthetos* is not composed of two imperfect portions, but two complete things or natures. The perfection of nature is ruled by "matter, form and essential properties." Personhood does not enter into the definition of nature, "neither as an integral nor essential part" of it, but only "as it were the terminus" (Turretin, *Institutes*, 2:312).

175. "Thus it may be said to compose something with another not essentially, but personally; nor for its intrinsic perfection, but only for its extrinsic operation" (Turretin, *Institutes*, 2:312). The *synthetos* must not be thought of as a property accrued to the person from the two natures but as "a free act of the divine Person" (Balthasar, *Theo-Drama*, 3:223). Such an appeal to divine freedom (à la Leontius of Jerusalem) may work for actualistic Christologies like Barth's but is certainly not philosophically adequate for theologians like Cross ("A Recent Contribution," 383) and Swinburne. See Richard Swinburne, *The Christian God* (New York: Oxford University Press, 1994), 197.

176. The compound hypostasis must be regarded as the invisible basis or interior self—the *autos*—of the divine Word, who has assumed a human nature, and not as an exterior, visible product of the union. Nestorius's starting point of the hypostasis as the result of the union, and, therefore, two subjective identities, is contrary to the Justinian-Cyrillian interpretation of Chalcedon. See Kenneth Paul Wesche, "Introduction," in *On the Person of Christ: The Christology of Emperor Justinian*, trans. Kenneth Paul Weshe (New York: Saint Vladimir's Seminary Press, 1991), 17–21. On this point, one notes a similarity to Apollinaris's idea of the "*synthesis* of Logos and *sarx*," where the single hypostasis of Christ is thought to be the final product (*apotelesma*) of the *henosis* (Grillmeier, *Christ in Christian Tradition*, 2:506). Nestorius's use of *prosopon* is, therefore, quite different from Cyril's hypostasis. See McGuckin, *Saint Cyril of Alexandria*, 144. Aquinas sums up well the Cyrillian position: as the one incarnate person of Christ has a two different ways of subsisting ("*alia et alia ratio subsistendi*"), Christ is a *hypostasis synthetos* or composite (*composita*) person (Aquinas, *STh* III, q. 2, a. 4, 2031).

177. Edwards, "Miscellanies," no. 766, in *WJE* 18:413.

178. Thus, Christ "came into the world and subsisted in the human nature" (Edwards, 234. Sermon on Matt. 16:21-23 [1731], in *WJE* 47). Evidently, for Aquinas, the human nature exists in another (*existit in alio*)—in the person of the Word (*Quaestiones disputatae De unioni Verbi*, a. 2)—while the person of Christ subsists in two natures (*persona Christi subsistit in duabus naturis*) (*STh* III, q. 2, a. 4, 2031). Aquinas distinguishes existence from subsistence, since he affirms, on the one hand, that the human nature exists in the person of the Word but that, on the other hand, the Word subsists in the human nature (*verbum in ea subsistat*) (*STh* III, q. 2, a. 2, ad 1, 2029).

179. Certain Protestant theologians do not seem to have appreciated St. Thomas's subtlety. Ames elided the distinction between the divine person subsisting and human nature in-existing. In the *assumptus*, that the human nature comes to "subsist in the same person" is thus another way of stating "a twofold way of subsisting: one in the Divine nature from eternity, another in the humane nature after the incarnation" (William Ames, *The Marrow of Sacred Divinity Drawne Out of*

the Holy Scriptures, and the Interpreters thereof, and Brought into Method [London: Henry Overton, 1642], ch. 18, 81).

180. Edwards, "Miscellanies," no. 278, in *WJE* 13:377.

181. Ibid. Since *operari sequitur esse*, so "every worke of the Mediator is a compound worke, arising of the effects of two natures concurring in one and the same action." See William Perkins, *A reformed catholike, or, a declaration shewing how neere we may come to the present church of Rome in sundry points of religion: and wherein we must for ever depart from them* (London: Printed by John Legatt, Printer to the Universitie of Cambridge, 1616), 608.

182. Edwards, "Miscellanies," no. 278, in *WJE* 13:378.

183. Edwards seems to sharply distinguish the two natures when he describes the elevation of a human nature "in the person of Christ" as accomplished by the divine act of "making the man Christ Jesus Lord of all angels, in communion with the Logos" (Edwards, "Miscellanies," no. 702, in *WJE* 18:300). We need, however, to bear in mind that Edwards's frequent use of "God and Christ" or "God and Jesus" refers to the Father and Son, and not to the two natures in Christ. One may, at most, accuse Edwards of monopatrism, but not an incipient Nestorianism (pace Michael Bush, "Jesus Christ in the Theology of Jonathan Edwards" [Ph.D. diss., Princeton Theological Seminary, 2003], 125–28).

184. Edwards, "Miscellanies," no. 487, in *WJE* 13:532.

185. This could not be stated any more clearly by Edwards: "Even in hell God is present essentially and by his power and operation but it is in a dreadful tremendous manner that he is present there" (Edwards, 44. Sermon on Ps. 139:7-10 [n.d.], in *WJE* 42). "Therefore, God is in all things by His power, inasmuch as all things are subject to His power; He is by His presence in all things, as all things are bare and open to His eyes; He is in all things by His essence, inasmuch as He is present to all as the cause of their being" (Aquinas, *STh* I, q. 8, a.3). "If God is necessarily immense and if immensity is an essential property, then God is with us not only by his power and operation, but also in his very being" (Turretin, *Institutes*, 1, topic 3, q. 9, sec. 4).

186. For Edwards, divine presence follows divine causality: "God is omnipotent and therefore must be in every place. If God is omnipotent, he is able to do every thing in all places but if he be not in all places he cannot do this, for nothing can act where it is not" (Edwards, 44. Sermon on Ps. 139:7-10 [n.d.], in *WJE* 42). Cross limits definite presence—"the non-spatial presence of an unextended substance at a place"—as causal presence, which he claims was Aquinas's "usual" understanding. See Richard Cross, "Incarnation, Omnipresence, and Action at a Distance," *Neue Zeitschrift für Systematische Theologie end Religionphilosophie* 45, no. 3 (2003): 297.

187. "God is present everywhere where any other being is by his operation . . . for the same power that made things to be the first moment . . . is continually exercised to make them to be every moment that they are," the latter which is "nothing but a continued act of creation" (Edwards, 44. Sermon on Ps. 139:7-10 [n.d.], in *WJE* 42).

188. Ibid. Turretin affirmed the immensity of God "as the efficient and conserving cause of all things" (*Institutes*, 1:200), yet he also wished to assert an omnipresence "not only as to virtue and operation, but principally as to essence." However, this sort of transcendent intimacy was defined negatively where the divine essence is present neither by physical contact, extension, and diffusion nor by multiplication (ibid., 1:196–201). In Eastern theology, God's omnipresence is seen more positively as the divine energy that "penetrates everything" without confusion or division, since God is "wholly in everything and wholly above everything" (John of Damascus, *Orthodox Faith*, bk. 1, ch. 13, 15 [*NPNF* 9]).

189. "God is an unchangeable being and it follows from that that he is every where, for if he were in some places and not in others he would be changeable. For instance, if he were only in some finite place be would be capable of motion of moving from place to place which is change" (Edwards, 44. Sermon on Ps. 139:7-10 [n.d.], in *WJE* 42).

190. That is, God's "perfect comprehension of all things and the extendedness of his operation equally to all places" (Edwards, "Miscellanies," no. 194, in *WJE* 13:335). Edwards thus rejects the Cartesian *res extensa*; God as an extended substance "is a gross and an unprofitable idea."

See also John Webster, *Confessing God: Essays in Dogmatics II* (London: T&T Clark, 2005), 102.

191. "'Tis as improper, to imagine that the immensity and omnipresence of God is distinguished by a series of miles and leagues, one beyond another; as that the infinite duration of God is distinguished by months and years, one after another" (Edwards, *WJE* 1:386).

192. "God's own infinite and unchangeable glory . . . which may metaphorically be represented as heaven that was the eternal abode of the blessed Trinity, and of the happiness and glory they have one in another . . . is uncreated . . . from when God infinitely stoops to behold the things done in created paradise . . . is above and beyond the whole universe, and encompasses the whole" (Edwards, "Miscellanies," no. 952, in *WJE* 20:213). Elsewhere, he says that "God is where the world is and where the world is not and every where where the world is not" (Edwards, 44. Sermon on Ps. 139:7-10 [n.d.], in *WJE* 42).

193. This uncreated "abode of God" is "that which [we] conceive of as the infinite and unchangeable expanse of space" beyond and containing created space (Edwards, "Miscellanies," no. 952, in *WJE* 20:213). As Barth put it, "Presence as togetherness (as distinct from identity) includes distance. But where there is distance, there is necessarily one place and another place" (Barth, *CD* II.1, 468).

194. God's "relative being" as the three divine persons admits to being "here or there" (Edwards, "On the Equality," in *WJE* 21:147–48).

195. What was a marginal emphasis in Puritan writings, that "the Holy Spirit . . . is the immediate actor of all divine operations," seems to be pronounced feature in Edwards. So, in Owen, power is appropriated to the Spirit (Owen, *Works*, 1:182).

196. Edwards, 44. Sermon on Ps. 139:7-10 [n.d.], in *WJE* 42. It is only quantitatively perfect in heaven.

197. The one is "excellentius sc. per gratiam inhabitans in sanctis spiritibus et animis," and the other "excellentissime non per gratiam adoptionis, sed per gratiam unionis" (Lombard, *Sent*. I, dist. 37A, as cited in Barth, *CD* II.1, 484). Barth approvingly cites J. Gerhard: instead "of *excellenter* it is much better to say: *singulariter*" in reference to the hypostatic union (ibid.).

198. In his effort to affirm the nonenclosure of the Logos in the flesh (*numquam et nuspiam extra carnem*), Edwards seems to negate the copresence of the Logos and the flesh of the Logos (*totus totus intra carnem*). This confirms Edwards's predominantly asymmetrical Christology insofar as he reverses the Lutheran overturning of the *enhypostasis* by the simultaneous affirmation of the *communio naturarum* and denial of the *extra carnem* (as Barth so acutely observes in *CD* I/2, 166).

199. A unilateral notion of the *perichoresis* would be no different from the initial act of assumption or *unitio personalis*. Crisp regards the asymmetrical penetration of the divine nature as an intensification (but not a transference) of omnipresence to the human nature. See Oliver D. Crisp, *Divinity and Humanity: The Incarnation Reconsidered* (Cambridge: Cambridge University Press, 2007), 22–23. In his view, the "nature-perichoresis" in Christ should not be thought of as *inter*penetration and therefore reciprocal. Of course, the *enhypostatos* could very well be regarded as the reverse movement of penetration.

200. Edwards, "Miscellanies," no. 487, in *WJE* 13:531–32.

201. The Spirit-constituted *unio hypostatica* was such that "by the Spirit of God's dwelling in so high and transcendent a manner, the human nature is united to the divine in the same person" (Edwards, "Notes on Scripture," no. 285, in *WJE* 15:244). The incarnation involves "the communicating the divine personality from heaven to earth in giving being to Christ's manhood" (Edwards, "Miscellanies," no. 709, in *WJE* 18:334).

202. "So the human nature of Christ is only a repository or vehicle" where "the divine Logos dwelt in it by his Spirit" (Edwards, "Notes on Scripture," no. 285, in *WJE* 15:244). Passages that seem to imply a *communio naturarum* must thus be interpreted as Spirit-mediated: "The human nature of Christ had the Logos, or the Word of God, dwelling in it, as the divine eternal person of the Son is often called" (Edwards, "Notes on Scripture," no. 285, in *WJE* 15:245).

203. Thus Dorner concludes that, in Reformed Christology, the "'unctio spiritus sancti' is the surrogate of the Lutheran 'communicatio idiomatum'" (Dorner, *Person of Christ*, 2:341). By this he means the *genus maiestaticum*, which may be regarded as the consequence of the divine permeation of human nature in the *communio naturarum*.

204. Hastings (following Pauw) interprets Edwards's *unio personalis* as an immediate union, since the Holy Spirit is the *vinculum* for both the Trinitarian and christological *perichoresis* (Hastings, "'Honouring the Spirit,'" 295).

205. "So the human nature of Christ is . . . where God is present more than in any other part of the whole universe. It is, of all created things, the highest and most immediate seat of the divine presence, that in which God resides in a higher and more eminent manner than in any other part of the highest heaven itself" (Edwards, "Notes on Scripture," no. 285, in *WJE* 15:242).

206. If, in order for the flesh to "become entirely the personal body of the Word of the Father with no one else intervening," then the Spirit must not stand in the way. See St. Cyril of Alexandria, *On the Unity of Christ*, trans. and intro. John Anthony McGuckin (Crestwood, NY: St. Vladimir's Seminary Press, 1995), 133. The question to ask here is whether Edwards's rejection of the christological *perichoresis* of natures undermines the Trinitarian *perichoresis* of persons.

207. For the Holy Spirit constitutes and sustains all spiritual unions. As Caldwell has pointed out, because the Spirit is the agent of union, "his interposition between Christ's natures renders the unity of the God-man not less unified, but more unified" (Robert W. Caldwell III, *Communion in the Spirit: The Holy Spirit as the Bond of Union in the Theology of Jonathan Edwards* [Milton Keynes, UK: Paternoster, 2006], 90).

208. The Holy Spirit "was the bond of union that in descending from the divine nature of Christ which was in heaven, on the human which was on earth, united earth and heaven" (Edwards, "Miscellanies," no. 487, in *WJE* 13:530). According to Calvin, it is the role of the Holy Spirit as mediating bond to inexplicably transcend both spatial distance (*locorum distantia*) and disjunction (*locis disiuncta*): "What, then, our mind does not comprehend, let faith conceive: that the spirit truly unites things separated in space" (John Calvin, *Calvin: Institutes of Christian Religion*, ed. John T. McNeill, trans. Ford Lewis Battles, Library of Christian Classics 20 [Philadelphia: Westminster, 1960], 4.17.10, 1370).

209. The Holy Spirit is "the Divine essence being wholly poured out and flowing out . . . from the Father and Son, primarily towards each other, and secondarily towards the creature, and . . . is that person that is poured forth into the hearts of angels and saints" (Edwards, "Treatise on Grace," in *TG*, 63).

210. "The divine nature will then be manifest itself at that day in the person of Christ, and in and with his glorified human nature" (Edwards, "Like Rain upon Mown Grass," in *WJE* 22:302).

211. "It will be his human nature that will then be seen by men's bodily eyes. And his divine nature will then also be present, which is united to the human nature; and it will be by the wisdom of that divine nature that Christ will see and judge" (Edwards, "The Day of Judgment," in *WJE* 14:518). Notwithstanding a more "traditional" *communio naturarum* at the *status exaltationis* where there is no spatial distance between Christ's natures, the Spirit is still the bond between them.

212. Calvin considered it "mere impudence" to think of the Word as being "confined within the narrow prison of an earthly body." He continued, "For even if the Word in his immeasurable essence united with the nature of man into one person, we do not imagine that he was confined therein" (*Institutes*, 1, bk. 2, ch. 13, 481). For John of Damascus, even though the divinity of the Logos is located in the mind of the assumed nature, they are not united therein "as an inmate" (*Orthodox Faith*, bk. 3, ch. 6, 50 [*NPNF* 9]).

213. "Here is something marvelous: the Son of God descended from heaven in such a way that, without leaving heaven, he willed to be borne in the virgin's womb, to go about the earth, and to hang upon the cross; yet he continuously filled the world even as he had done from the beginning" (Calvin, *Institutes*, 1, bk. 2, ch. 13, 481; see also *Institutes*, 2, bk. 4, ch. 17, 1402). "The marvelous truth is, that being the Word, so far from being Himself contained by anything, He

actually contained all things Himself. . . . His body was for Him not a limitation, but an instrument, so that He was both in it and in all things, and outside all things, resting in the Father alone." See St. Athanasius, *On the Incarnation: The Treatise* De Incarnatione Dei Verbi, trans. and ed. by a Religious of C. S. M. V, intro. C. S. Lewis (Crestwood, NY: St. Vladimir's Seminary Press, 1998), bk. 3, sec. 17, 45–46. So writes John of Damascus: "So then He was both in all things and above all things and also dwelt in the womb of the holy Mother of God, but in it by the energy of the incarnation" (*Orthodox Faith*, bk. 3, ch. 7, 51).

214. The "whole Christ" (*totus Christus*) refers to the divine person in contrast to "the whole of Christ" (*totum Christi*), which refers to the natures that are in Christ (Calvin, *Institutes*, 2, bk. 4, ch. 17, 1403; Turretin, *Institutes*, 2, topic 13, q. 8, para. 17, 321). This relates to the distinction between concrete and abstract terms, person and nature: "The *totus Christus* is everywhere, but not the *totum Christi*, i.e. both the natures" (Johannes Wollebuis, *Christianae*, 66, as quoted in Heppe, *Reformed Dogmatics*, 443). In his article on Christ's literal descent into hell, Aquinas states that "Christ's Person is whole in each single place, but not wholly, because it is not circumscribed by any place." In death, then, Christ's soul was (essentially) in limbo (but not in the hell of the lost), his body in the tomb, his divinity everywhere. Though the body was separated from the soul in death, yet the whole Christ is affirmed to be (in limbo, on earth and) everywhere during that time due to the unity of Christ's person (Aquinas, *STh* III, q. 52, a. 3).

215. Edwards, "Miscellanies," no. 487, in *WJE* 13:532. Similarly, the *unio* is not sustained by "a local coexistence" (Turretin, *Institutes*, 2:329).

216. The human nature is only "sustained" by but does not in-exist the divine Logos (Turretin, *Institutes*, 2:317). The *unio personalis* is such that "only extrinsically was something [the human nature] adjoined to it [the Logos] for the work of redemption" (ibid.). Nonetheless, the Logos can in no wise be regarded as external to the human nature "by separation," yet it is such "by non-inclusion" (ibid., 2, topic 13, q. 8, 329). As already noted, Turretin wants to avoid any notion of the amelioration (and even ontological change) of the human nature in the hypostatic union. This results in his rejection of the *communio naturarum*. The position of seventeenth-century Dutch Reformed theologian Jacob Alting is more Lutheran: "The *unio personalis* in Christ was made αδιαιρέτως, indivisibly, in respect of place, so that the human nature is nowhere unsupported by the λόγος, the λόγος nowhere fails to support the human nature, nor is it outside the λόγος or the λόγος apart from it" (Jacobus Altingius, *Methodus Theologiae didacticae*, in *Opera* [Amsterdam, 1687], 100, as quoted in Heppe, *Reformed Dogmatics*, 434). Edwards's Spirit-mediated Christology occupies a *via media* between Alting and Turretin.

217. "Περιχώρησις . . . did not . . . [imply] locality, or quantity, as a bucket is said, to contain (χωρειν) water, but they employed it illocally and metaphorically" (Hollaz, as cited in Heinrich Schmid, "The 'Person of Christ' according to the Older Theologians of the Evangelical Lutheran Church," trans. C. P. Krauth, *Mercersburg Review* 1 [1849]: 288n2). Chemnitz's position seems to be much stronger, though the divine presence cannot be regarded as a circumscribed presence: "This hypostatic union, however, does not permit a separation or an absence of one nature from the other, as if one nature were separately located somewhere else; but it involves the most complete presence of the united natures with each other" (Chemnitz, *Two Natures*, 79).

218. Presence is opposed to absence and implies a relation of communion or enjoyment, whereas something may be absent although near. "What is near is not always present, and what is present is not always near" (Turretin, "Against Consubstantiation," in *Institutes*, 2, q. 28). However, Turretin surprisingly does not finesse his Christology with this distinction found in his sacramentology. "On this account, the Logos (*Logou*) existing on earth is most truly man and has the human nature personally and most intimately united with it, although it is not present on earth" (Turretin, *Institutes*, 2, topic 13, q. 8, 329).

219. *Propinquitas localis* and *praesentia* may be distinguished by Lonergan's illustration: stones may be spatially proximate to one another, but that does not imply that they are present to each other. See Bernard Lonergan, Collected Works of Bernard Lonergan, vol. 12, *The Triune*

God: Systematics, trans. Robert M. Doran and H. Daniel Monsour (Toronto: University of Toronto Press for Lonergan Research Institute of Regis College, 2007), 503.

220. The Son's indwelling presence in Jesus is more intense than the Son's general omnipresence and mystical presence to the church. "It is the Son of God whose delights are with the sons of men who all along dwelt with them and yet dwells with his Church in the execution of his kingly office" (Edwards, 37. Sermon on John 15:5 [a] [1726] in *WJE* 42).

221. "The man Christ Jesus being made in union with the divine nature, so as to be in the divine person. He was made in that person that was the essential image of God; and so had in a sense the Godhead communicated to him" (Edwards, "Miscellanies," no. 702, in *WJE* 18:287).

5

Communication of Properties, Works, and Grace in the Person of Christ as Mediated by the Spirit

We have seen how Edwards's Spirit-mediated Logos Christology functions primarily within an Alexandrian framework, refracted through Reformed lenses. From that foundational *Logos-sarx* relation, Christ's human nature participates in the personhood, existence, and operations of the divine Word and is thus made its salvific instrument. Yet there is also a minor Antiochene key that seems to be working against the ontological and operational unity of the two natures.

In this chapter, then, we shift our attention from the relation between the assumed human nature and the divine person to the mutual commerce between the natures. Clearly, the Word incarnate owns all the properties of Christ's human nature, but does this affect the divine nature directly? Is there a communication of divine properties to Christ's assumed nature? Is this even possible in the face of Edwards's rejection of the Lutheran *communio naturarum* and his radicalized *extra carnem*? Does Edwards differ from both the Lutherans and Reformed theologians on these issues? If so, in what ways?

In order to structure our investigation, we will use the types of christological *communicatio* developed by the sixteenth-century Reformed-Lutheran scholastics as heuristic backdrops to map Edwards's own position. What, then, does Edwards think of the *communicatio idiomatum* and its various genera?[1]

The *Genus Idiomaticum* in Edwards's Theology

In Edwards's single notebook entry, he considers the *communicatio idiomatum* a biblical, rational construct that is theologically grounded in the reality of the *unio hypostatica.*[2] It is also analogous to the body-soul union.[3] The *communicatio* encapsulates two ways of cross-predication between the natures and person. The first sort is founded on the distinction of natures within the one *hypostasis synthetos.* "When we say of him, that he suffered and died, we mean it of his human nature only; when we say of him, that he 'thought it no robbery to be equal with God,' that he is omniscient, omnipresent, etc., we mean it only with respect to his divine nature."[4] The second way of predication highlights the one hypostasis, who is the synthesis of the two natures.[5] Thus, "when we say of him, that he is the Mediator, the Redeemer and Savior of sinners, we mean it of his person constituted of both natures."[6]

Edwards, of course, does not understand the *genus idiomaticum* as something merely verbal, as such signification must stem from a real incarnation.[7] Hence, the *communicatio nomina* is based on the *communicatio idiomatum in concreto.*[8] This is beautifully and profoundly worked out in "On the Excellencies of Christ," where he sermonizes on the excellent attributes of humanity and divinity that "meet in the person of Christ."[9] It is in the person of the Mediator that the unity and distinction of the divine attributes and actions come to the fore. We look now at Edwards's understanding of the communication of works.

Divine Acts: The *Communicatio Operationum* as Coordinated and Inspirited

Under the rubric of Christ the Mediator involving the *munus triplex*, Calvin gave great attention to the *communicatio operationum.*[10] Reformed theology thereafter continued his emphasis: the Mediator's two distinct natural *operationes* united by a single *apotelesma* point to the dynamic and purposeful nature of the *unio hypostatica.*[11] That the Reformed referred to this genus as the *communicatio operationum* while the Lutherans referred to it as the *genus apotelesmaticum* indicates their respective biases toward distinction of actions and unity of purpose.[12]

In the previous chapter, we examined Edwards's conception of the human nature acting as the *organon* of the incarnate Word. That approach clearly highlighted the asymmetry of the acts in Christ. What does Edwards say regarding the reciprocity of the natural wills and actions in Christ?

Communion of Wills and Actions in the Hypostasis Synthetos

According to Edwards, the impeccability of Christ was not something inherent to the human nature, but came about through the Spirit-mediated *enhypostaton*.[13] The actuality of Christ's perfect obedience, therefore, implies no possibility of an imperfect moral choice, no option of sinning.[14] However, Edwards insists that Christ's human nature was not reduced to pure passivity, to being a "mere machine" animated by "natural necessity."[15] That Jesus had no "liberty *ad utrumlibet*," or libertarian freedom, does not contradict an ethical and supererogatory life.[16] If volitional indifference means the absence of a good disposition, Christ is the instantiation of the one with a plenitude of the divine disposition, who is the locus of true freedom.[17] Edwards's position thus echoes the patristic notion of an unclouded but nondeliberative will in Christ—a human will that is Godlike.[18] As he words it, "It is godlike freely to do good."[19]

Classical Christology also presupposed the perfect harmony of Christ's two wills, and Edwards reaffirms this line of thinking: "It was the will of God that [the passion] should be the act of Christ, both of the divine and human nature, that it might be a glorious manifestation of the love of both natures toward man, and it might be a more meritorious act of obedience."[20] He defends this dyothelitism on both christological and Trinitarian grounds. "[B]y reason of the personal union," Edwards maintains, "it was impossible that the divine nature of Christ should choose one thing and the human nature another."[21] The human nature always—and necessarily—acts in accord with the divine because there is one personal center of consciousness in Christ. Edwards's compatibilism, which asserts Jesus' necessary impeccability, is based upon both covenant and ontology.[22]

Firstly, by the *pactum salutis*, the same *Logos incarnandus* is made *incarnatus* in the economy of salvation. That is, what the divine Son, as mediator, compacted to do in eternity will undoubtedly see success in his mode of existence as man.[23] Not only did Christ choose the passion as God-to-be-incarnate in the *pactum salutis*, he consciously, wholly, and freely willed it as human, and especially so in Gethsemane.[24]

Secondly, and in a way related to the first point, Edwards points out that such a union of wills in Christ's person is based on a prior union between the Father and Son. While Edwards denies that humility can be predicated of the divine, Jesus' human obedience beautifully mirrors the eternal, responsive love of the Son toward the Father. "Indeed," Edwards postulates, "it would have been fitting and excellent in him that his will and his actions should be conformed to the Father's will and be subject to him, as it is in itself fit and excellent that the Logos itself should love the Father, and that the Father should love the Son."[25] Here, Edwards roots Christ's earthly subordination in the eternal Father-Son relation, without prejudice to the *homoousion*.[26]

Where is the place of the Spirit in all this? As the Spirit is the bond of unity between the Father and Son, so the Spirit is the bond of unity between Christ's wills.[27] Edwards weds the ethical to the ontological by characterizing the Holy Spirit as "the principle that as it were reigns over the Godhead and governs his heart, and wholly influences both the Father and the Son in all that they do."[28] Because the Spirit is had without measure in Christ, this divine principle not only constitutes the Son as God-man but aligns the human will of Christ to that of the Trinity. There can be no conflict between the divine and human wills in Christ. Christ's human will is truly free and, just so, is Godlike in its repetition of the divine freedom. What role does the Spirit play in mediating between the divine and human operations in Christ?

DOES THE HOLY SPIRIT UNITE OR SEPARATE THE TWO NATURAL ACTIONS?

The patristic and medieval theologians attributed the exercises of the divine power and will in Christ to the *opera Trinitatis*.[29] As we have seen, Edwards, following Owen, insists that "the divine works that Christ wrought, were by the Spirit of God."[30] This is apposite since he sees the Holy Spirit as "the divine nature [that] subsists in pure act and perfect energy."[31] Nonetheless, Edwards nuances Owen's indiscriminate attribution of all of Jesus' acts to the Holy Spirit.[32] The Father acts objectively upon Christ by the Father's Spirit and the Logos acts subjectively in and through the human nature by Christ's own Spirit.[33] By denying that the Logos acts upon Christ's own human nature, Edwards avoids the danger of Nestorianism or two agencies in Christ.

However, if both the "outward and inward divine" operations are attributed to the Logos incarnate and the Spirit, the issue of double agency still remains.[34] How does Edwards explain the fact that Christ is at once moved by the Spirit and self-moved? He replies that this state of affairs cannot be "otherwise than as the Spirit of God directed the human understanding, and moved the human will, as a bond of union between the understanding and the will of the divine Logos, and the understanding and will of the human nature of Christ."[35]

The miracles of the human Christ were not alternating operations of the Holy Spirit and the Logos as this would undermine the *opera indivisa*.[36] Neither is it the case that the Spirit singularly directed the miraculous works of the human Jesus. This Edwards rejects, as we have seen, for such a move would undermine the *vere homo*, resulting in a Nestorian and predominantly exemplarist Christology.[37] As *instrumentum coniunctum*, Jesus consistently performed miracles as self-willed and not as an inspired miracle worker.[38]

Pushing Edwards's Trinitarian and christological speculations to their logical conclusion would mean that the Holy Spirit at once unites and is united to the human faculties of Jesus. As the volitive principle in God, the Spirit, in uniting the divine will with Christ's human will, may be said to effectively be united to Christ's assumed humanity.[39] As the loving will and disposition in God, the Spirit exercises the same influence *ad extra* such that "a gracious man has [this] principle in his heart that directs and governs him."[40]

One criticism of Edwards's pneumatology is that the hypostasis of the Spirit seems to be reduced to an impersonal go-between. In the *unitio*, the Spirit functions as a principle of assumption between the Word and the assumed nature; in the *unio*, the Spirit acts as the permanent bond and conduit between the natures in sustaining the *unio* and enabling the *communicatio*. Of course, a uniting bond need not be impersonal: a child, for example, can act as a *vinculum amoris* between her parents.[41] On this account, the role of the Spirit as personally constituting and maintaining Jesus' singularly filial bond to the Father can be appreciated.

The *exitus-reditus* of the Spirit within the Trinity *ad intra* is replicated in time as the mutual love of the Father and the Son for each other. But as the one who causes the *creatio continua* of the human Jesus, the Spirit also sustains a *unitio continua* between the natures and wills in Christ. The incarnate Son is enabled to know and obey the Father by the Son's own Spirit. And in so doing, Christ is empowered by the Spirit to reveal the will of God definitively through a prophetic ministry and example par excellence.[42] This is the way that Edwards nuances the indivisible *opera ad extra* in the history of Jesus Christ to characterize the peculiar mode of action of the Spirit within an Augustinian-Calvinian paradigm.[43] Not only that, the Spirit mediates the participation of the human Jesus in the divine will and acts of the Logos and the Father.

If *theōsis* is interpreted as rooted in a communion of energies within Christ, both in terms of the reciprocity of the natural acts and an asymmetrical, theandric operation of the divine through an instrumental human nature, then *theōsis* is certainly present in Edwards's Christology. But what about the communication of majesty in Christ?

Does Edwards Advocate Any Kind of *Genus Maiestaticum*?

Edwards scholars present contradictory views on his use of the *communicatio idiomatum*. Robert Jenson thinks he advocates an undeveloped but nonetheless radical pseudo-Lutheran avowal of the *genera maiestaticum et tapeinoticum*.[44] Steven Holmes, on the other hand, suggests that Edwards advances an Owenite

Christology that does away with the *genus maiestaticum* altogether.[45] We will deal with these opinions in reverse order.

IS THE COMMUNICATIO IDIOMATUM THE NECESSARY RESULT OF THE UNITIO PERSONALIS?

In what sense is Edwards's Christology "Owenite"? For Owen, the single and necessary result of the *assumptio carnis* was the hypostatic union or the *enhypostaton* of the human nature in the Logos.[46] Whatever communication between the natures postassumption, he argued, was through the Spirit's free agency.[47] By making this move, Owen was trying to sever any presupposed causal link between the *communicatio idiomatum* and the *communio naturarum*.[48] Clearly, he thought this would undercut the Lutheran *genus maiestaticum*.[49] In other words, Owen denies that in the incarnation a communication of properties between the natures must follow (as a natural consequence) the communion of natures. That, however, does not obtain. Firstly, a Spirit-mediated union would still permit a willed, though not a mechanically necessary, *genus maiestaticum*. Secondly, no causal link exists to be broken if the *unio* is seen as identical to or an effect of the *communicatio*.[50]

On the latter point, then, Edwards follows Owen and the mainstream tradition in affirming that "Union always goes before communion" or communication.[51] But he denies Owen's assertion that the *assumptio carnis* results only in the *enhypostaton*. For Edwards, no *unio personalis* can exist without *communicatio realis*: "If there is no more communication between this individual human nature and the eternal Son of God than others, there is no more real union."[52] And on that premise, the intensity of communion or communication would be directly proportionate to the proximity of union.[53]

There cannot be, for Edwards, a bare union of in-existence without participation in the Word's dispositions and properties. Moreover, if the Spirit causes and upholds the *unio hypostatica*, the Spirit is also the communicative channel between the powers of the divine Word and the assumed nature. In the incarnation, "the Holy Ghost must . . . act as a means of conveyance of the understanding and will of the divine Logos, to the understanding and will of the human nature, *or* of the union of these understandings and wills."[54] Clearly, on such a dynamic pneumatology, the *communicatio operationum* is, for all intents and purposes, identical with the *communio naturarum*. That Edwards could dispense with the communion of natures on the principle of redundancy should come to us as no surprise. What sort of benefits does the assumed nature accrue from its communication or union with the divine nature?

Edwards follows the tradition in affirming a quantitative difference between Christ's *gratia capitis* and the saints' *gratia habitualis*.[55] Nevertheless, he rejects the idea of created grace.[56] Accordingly, Jesus' reception of the Spirit "without measure" cannot mean a superabundance of created graces.[57] This seems to indicate that Edwards must concede that *finitum capax infinitum* in some sense. Does this mean, then, that a back door is opened—through the *communicatio gratiarum*—for something like the *genus maiestaticum*?[58]

Although there is no direct *communio naturarum* in Christ, the infinite Spirit may be considered a substitute for the Logos's divine nature in Edwards's construct of the hypostatic union.[59] In this way, the human Jesus is capable of and exercises "divine power, and divine knowledge, and divine will, and divine acts" since these proceed from Jesus' own indwelling Spirit. "The union of the eternal Logos with the man Christ Jesus was doubtless by some communication or other, by that means some way peculiarly communicating with that divine Logos in what was his, or by having something dwelling in [him] that was divine, that belonged to the Logos."[60] This is not just the theandric operation of the God-man, whereby the Logos operates through Jesus, the *instrumentum deitatis*. More than just the instrumentalization of the human nature, this is about Jesus, in some sense, owning the divine attributes and operating supernaturally. But this does not mean the human instrumentalization of the divine attributes as distinct from the operations of the divine nature (as in Lutheran scholasticism). Rather, Edwards's point is that Jesus owns the Spirit of the Logos, and just so, is capable of divine acts by this very same Spirit.[61]

Edwards believes that in the hypostatic union the human nature of Christ was "infinitely dignified, and its fruit infinitely changed for the better."[62] As such, the human Jesus has every conceivable power except for God's "own incommunicable attributes"—this Edwards regards as an incontestable patristic insight. As it is possible for God to create finite creatures with greatly extended capacities, "what kinds of powers," Edwards surmises, "may we justly conclude his are, who is the firstborn of every creature and is personally united to the Deity! This seems to have been the universally received belief of the primitive church, which nobody ever thought of questioning."[63] What is this modified *genus maiestaticum* that Edwards speaks of?

Manifestive Glory: "The Mediator's Glory, Which Is Next to Divine"

Although the Reformed denied the Lutheran *genus maiestaticum*, they did not unanimously reject the notion of an exaltation of Christ's humanity (and derivatively that of the saints) above and beyond the *gratia habitualis* perfectly conferred on Christ in the incarnation. Other than the inherent human perfections and the *gloria Dei ad intra* of Christ, there is a strand within the Reformed tradition that conceived of a third category of glory—unique to the Mediator—which resulted from the incarnation.[64] Such a concept can be found in seminal form in Calvin and was subsequently expanded by writers such as Thomas Goodwin, whom Edwards cites favorably in many of his entries.

Double Image in Christ and the Notion of Christ's Manifestive Glory

One of Calvin's important teachings was his notion of the Mediator, whereby qualities that are attributed to Christ are "neither of deity or of humanity alone, but of both at once."[65] This idea, at first blush, appears to be the *genus operationum*.[66] On closer inspection, however, what Calvin introduces into his category of the Mediator is the idea that certain qualities or attributes, such as power to confer forgiveness, life, righteousness, holiness, and judgment, are to be predicated to the *Logos asarkos* and *Logos ensarkos* in different senses.[67] While no *genus maiestaticum* is spoken of here, these divine "prerogatives" possessed by the preincarnate Word were imparted to the incarnate Son in a new "manner or respect" in the incarnation.[68] They are qualities sui generis to Christ that "could not have been given to a man who was nothing but a man."[69] The Mediator, according to Christ's humanity, comes to own certain rights and qualities that are not strictly divine.[70]

Goodwin extended this undeveloped motif in Calvin. According to Goodwin, there is "a double image of God in Christ; The one *essential*, as he is second person; the other *manifestive*, as the glory of God shines in the face of the person of Jesus Christ, as man."[71] This "manifestive" glory, refracted through the human nature, results in an abridgment of the divine perfections.[72] Though they may be called the "many *Divine Attributes* of Christ, as God-man," they are not the *genus maiestaticum simpliciter*.[73] While creatures, in "subsisting by the Power of God," have dependent being, Jesus possesses life through an "Independentiam Similitudinariam" because the *enhypostaton* is a right permanently accorded to Jesus.[74] And though one cannot properly ascribe to Christ's humanity both omniscience and omnipotence, there is an "*omniscientia similitudinaria*, a similitudinary omnisciency" and "a similitudinary omnipotency."[75] Additionally, Jesus owns a "*Relative* Holiness" that is above and beyond "habitual Holiness."[76] There is, then, a kind of "illimitation" of the human nature, as Emile Mersch puts it, whereby "Christ's human nature must be adapted to the Omnipresent and must be omnipresent in its own way and in its own order."[77] As we shall see further on, Edwards echoes such language when he describes Christ's human nature as "in a sense omniscient."[78]

It was common practice for the Puritan writers to use "manifestive glory" or "declarative glory" interchangeably.[79] Similarly, for Edwards, Christ is "crowned with glory" insofar as it is spoken of economically—that is, as he is "God man and mediator." God's "declarative glory" shines forth through Christ, who is "this one grand medium that God communicates himself to all his elect creatures."[80] As the image or brightness of the Father, "all communicated glory to the creature must be by the Son of God . . . as God-man": Christ is the medium of communion between God the Father and the church.[81]

Echoing Calvin, Edwards affirms that such a glorification is to be attributed to Christ's humanity, "but yet Christ is not glorified merely as man."[82] Only through the hypostatic union with a divine person is the human nature made adequate for glorification, yet it is the human nature that has the capacity for change.[83] As human, Christ advances "to the highest degree of real glory and happiness of all creatures."[84]

Since immutability characterizes Christ's divine nature, the divine glory "can neither be added to or diminished," yet it is not uninvolved in the glorification of Christ incarnate.[85] "Though the divine nature be not properly exalted yet the divine nature is concerned in the exaltation, as this is the ground of the exaltation."[86] While no increase is attributed to the already infinite "essential glory or real happiness" in Christ's divine nature, there is "addition . . . to [his] great declarative glory."[87] The divine nature cannot and does not acquire any new perfections in the incarnation but is further exalted as it manifests itself through the organ of humanity.[88] In the incarnation, the transcendent distance between divinity and humanity has closed, and the divine *maiestas* shines "in our nature . . . so it should appear more lovely and amiable to us."[89] The "increase" in divine glory is the *exaltatio* of the humanity: the medium that once was *velatus* has become *revelatus*.[90] Edwards's construal of the manifestive glory stands as a kind of via media between the Lutheran *genus maiestaticum* and *gratia creata*.[91]

PARTICIPATION AND A DYNAMIC LIMITATION AXIOM: AD MODUM RECIPIENTIS

From what we have seen thus far, can one judge that Edwards has abandoned the Reformed *finitum non capax infiniti* axiom for the Lutheran *finitum capax infiniti non per se sed per infinitum*?[92] The answer is yes only insofar as the *per infinitum* is parsed as *per Spiritus infiniti*. This latent capacity for the divine is, as it were, hardwired into human nature by God and is (only) actualized by the indwelling Spirit. There is, therefore, an expansion of the human nature within the limits of its essence; that is to say, there is a (nonessential) transformation of humanity within the Chalcedonian paradigm.[93] Chalcedon's *atreptos* is not violated because the essence of being human is to change. But does this native dynamism lead to a confusion of essences, thereby annulling the *asunchutos*?

Edwards, citing Goodwin, points to a *communicatio* in Jesus Christ, where the "riches of glory" that belong to the divinity are communicated to the human nature "nearly and as was possible unto a creature."[94] Christ's humanity is "not deified" or made equal with divinity, but "is wonderfully glorified."[95] The question then is this: what sort of amelioration is the human nature capable of, save identity with the divine?[96] Since Christ's humanity is the storehouse of every grace, those graces are communicable to the saints. Yet grace in Christ differs comprehensively and quantitatively from the saints'; moreover, Christ's grace is the fount of theirs.[97]

What happens to the humanity of Christ in the *exaltatio*? Puritan writers were content to say that it "received all those perfections, which a created nature could take," being more concerned to deny the Lutheran *ubiquitas* or *multivolenspraesens*.[98] Edwards speculates that "the capacity of the man Jesus is so large" in the glorified state that if on earth right now, Jesus "would be perfectly acquainted with them [the saints] at first sight."[99] This is a rational conclusion since Jesus, even during the *exinanitio*, already "knew the thoughts of men . . . and knew things acted at a distance."[100]

Some scholars have argued that the christological controversy between the Reformed and Lutherans finally turned on the anthropological hinge: what are the limits of being human?[101] For Edwards, such boundaries are ultimately theological. *De potentia absoluta*, human essence is dynamic because God has made it essentially dilatable.[102] More than that, the "capacity of the man Jesus is so large" not only because of its essential dynamism but also "by reason of the personal union with the divine nature."[103] What does Edwards have to say about the capacity and operations of Jesus' mind in this regard?

JESUS' BEATIFIC, INFUSED, AND ACQUIRED KNOWLEDGE

In the preceding chapter, we cursorily surveyed Edwards's belief that Christ has a single psychological center or self-consciousness with regard to Christ's person. The Son, as divine and human, is self-aware as the same "I." At the same time, there are two psychological forms of life or consciousnesses located in the two natures: the Son knows the Son's own self in two ways.[104] Just as the Logos knows in a divine way that the Logos is the divine Son, Jesus knows in a human way that Jesus is the self-same divine Son.[105] We look now at how these two forms of knowledge, which correspond to his two natures, interact in the person of Christ.

PERSONAL KNOWLEDGE: DID JESUS HAVE THE BEATIFIC VISION?

The teaching that the earthly Jesus enjoyed an uninterrupted beatific vision has its roots in the Gospels: Jesus did not have to learn but always knew intuitively of an identity as the divine Son of the Father. Does Edwards believe, with Aquinas, that Christ possessed a beatific knowledge in the *status exinationis?*[106] Or does he adhere to the mainstream Reformed position that Jesus, as a *viator*, did not possess the beatific vision on earth?[107]

The answer depends on how the *visio beatifica* is defined. If one construes that as an objective vision of the divine essence, then the earthly Jesus had no *scientia beatifica*.[108] Edwards defines the "beatifical vision" as the saints' indirect vision of God the Father through Christ; this is markedly different from the medieval *scientia beatifica*, which is an essential or unmediated vision of God (the Trinity).[109] For Edwards, Jesus alone can and does possess a direct vision of God the Father.[110] In other words, the human Jesus does not have the beatific vision *per filium*. And to be able to perceive the Father as the Son does, Jesus must have direct perception of the Logos's mind. On this account, then, Edwards agrees with Aquinas that the assumed human nature possesses knowledge of "the Word, and things in the Word."[111] Strictly speaking, this is not so much a beatific vision of (the divine nature as) an Other but personal self-knowledge within a subject.

This subjective self-awareness is crucial to Jesus' self-identity. For Edwards, direct access to another's thoughts is no different from owning that person's ideas.[112] If direct perception is consciousness, it follows that "a spiritual, created being can't have an immediate view of another mind without some union of personality."[113] For two minds to be the same person without remainder, the intuitive perception by the one of the other would need to be total.[114] Personal union is thus proportioned to direct perception; a partial or temporary union would be commensurate with an incomplete or a transient perception.[115]

For Edwards, then, personal identity is synonymous with (self-)consciousness, since it is the mind's self-awareness of its immanent thoughts, feelings, and actions.[116] And since only the Logos has an immediate vision of the Father, Jesus is a participant in this. Accordingly, no created intellect can possess direct knowledge or consciousness of God, except Christ in the human nature.[117] "Jesus Christ, who alone sees immediately," is the unique mediator of divine revelation, "the grand medium of the knowledge of all others."[118]

What else does Jesus' consciousness include? While Edwards does not give a full definition, he agrees with Locke that it must involve memory or a continuity of ideas.[119] From this, he concludes that the human Jesus participates in the Logos's eternal knowledge *before* the incarnation. This comes to Jesus as a memory or "reminiscence or consciousness of what appertained to the eternal Logos, and so of his happiness with the Father."[120] That Jesus had such memories is no point of conjecture.[121]

Although Edwards claims "the things which he [the man Jesus] remembered were from all eternity in the Logos after the manner of God," in good Reformed fashion, he concedes that *finitum non capax infinitum*.[122] Accordingly, it is "impossible that the man Jesus Christ should remember this as it was in the Deity, for then the idea of the eternal mind could be communicated to a finite mind even as it is in the infinite mind."[123] Such knowledge, of course, is not memory in the Logos since there is no temporal succession in the Deity.[124] But to Jesus, this memory of "preexistence" as the self-same divine person is both virtual and *per modum recipientis*, "as if they had been after the manner of a creature."[125] This sort of memory is no figment of Jesus' imagination, for in Edwards's thinking, virtuality has a mode of reality apart from actuality.[126] Suppose the human Jesus had been in existence during the *pactum salutis*, he would have been party to all that transpired between Father and Son in the covenant of redemption in both the divine and human modes of being.

Clearly, the two modes of knowledge in Christ are not independent of each other. As the bond of union, "the Holy Ghost must in this act as a means of conveyance of the understanding . . . of the divine Logos, to the understanding . . . of the human nature."[127] This ongoing *unio personalis* or reiterative *unitio personalis* involves an existential communication of the Logos's knowledge to the human nature, which is received according to its own mode. Since this self-knowledge is translated from the Logos to the human mind of Jesus, the personal center is undoubtedly located in the divine Son.

JESUS' INFUSED AND ACQUIRED KNOWLEDGE

What about Jesus' knowledge of things in themselves—the *scientia infusa*?[128] Edwards surmises that Christ had actual knowledge of every elect individual, including his or her sins on the cross.[129] "'Tis not necessary for us here," he continues, "to inquire how far the human soul of Christ knew as to particulars: there was a very near union between the human soul and the divine nature, and therefore a free communication from the divine knowledge and the human."[130] Does this not imply more than a unilateral transference of knowledge from the divine?

In his "Subjects of Enquiry" on future scholarly projects, Edwards was to elaborate on what it means for Christ to have the "sameness of consciousness" as the divine Logos.[131] Echoing Goodwin, he opines that Christ's human nature, though not properly omniscient, can be considered "in a sense omniscient." By this Edwards would have us understand that the "human nature of Christ has the divine knowledge to be its own to use and to expatiate itself in at pleasure which way and about according to its capacity which way and about what subject it will."[132] This is no medieval *scientia infusa* since the divine knowledge is accessed just as one would refer to a comprehensive encyclopedia.[133]

However, this does not mean that the extent and intensity of Jesus' relative "omniscience" is static. In the state of humiliation, the "human mind of Christ" is much more limited in its access to the divine since it can only "expatiate itself according to its capacity."[134] With the exaltation of Christ, the human faculties are enlarged to enable increased possession of the divine knowledge, will, and power in human mode.[135] By virtue of the Logos's absolute omniscience and omnipresence, the glorified Jesus in heaven *virtually* enjoys a corporeal presence with the earthly saints. "And even the man Christ . . . being the same person with the divine Logos, has communion with them by the communion of this person, as much *as if* his human soul were present and suggested, and answered by suggestions, those sweet meditations; and there is the same delight in the man Christ *as if* he were bodily present with them, talking and conversing with them."[136] The glorified Jesus does share, in some sense, in the ubiquity of the divine nature, and can reach the saints through all times and places.

On the ignorance of the earthly Jesus, Edwards appeals to the both the distinction of natures and states.[137] *Per modus recipientis*, Jesus' access to and apprehension of this divine storehouse of knowledge must be grasped in a manner befitting human nature.[138] In the *status exinationis*, some limitation to the scope and depth of the divine omniscience must have been exercised by the Logos through the Spirit. Some things were hidden from the Jesus in the humbled human state.

Jesus, in the *status exinationis*, increased in all things including knowledge, except for perfect impeccability.[139] Jesus is like Adam in innocence, having no sinful tendency, though, like us, Jesus grew through acquiring knowledge.[140] Jesus' experiential knowledge is liable to improvement and so he knows not only who he himself is—the divine Son, but also what he himself is—a human being.[141]

Kenosis and the *Genus Tapeinoticum*

Does Edwards, as Robert Jenson claims, attribute passibility to the divine Logos and take as literal the assertion that Jesus Christ *as a creature* is Creator? Suffice it to say for now that Edwards most certainly did not insist on the latter proposition.[142] As we shall see, Edwards's conception of a Spirit-mediated *communicatio* in Christ opens up the way for a selective (albeit modified) *genus maiestaticum* without undermining the classical doctrine of divine impassibility.[143] How, then, does Edwards reinterpret the communication of majesty within the confines of the incarnate Son's kenosis?[144]

Genus Tapeinoticum: Does Edwards Allow for Any Form of Kenoticism?

Edwards, as with the entire theological tradition before the seventeenth-century Geissen and Tübingen Lutherans, rejects the communication of human attributes to the divine nature (the fourth *genus tapeinoticum* or *kenoticum*).[145] Adherence to an ontological kenoticism would not only demand the rejection of the ecumenical creeds but would also contradict the Lutheran *genus maiestaticum*.[146] Edwards has no doubt that from the creation of the world, the "same Word, the same Son of God" continues to preserve it.[147] When this same Christ, "in his humbled state" had "his strength . . . spent only with governing the motions of his own body," the question may be asked, "Who upheld and governed the world at that time?"[148] One answer, Edwards conjectures, may be "that God the Father took the world out of the hands of the Son for that time . . . and returned it into his hands again at his exaltation."[149]

However, he finds no biblical or theological grounds to justify such a functional, albeit temporary, kenoticism. For, on Edwards's theological logic, creation and preservation, as two modes of a single work, cannot be undertaken by two primary agents.[150] As creation is more directly the Son's work, the Son's role of preservation could not have been ceded to the Father during the *status exinanitio*.[151] Moreover, divine impassibility precludes any quiescent divinity during the period of Christ's humiliation, as this would imply change in God.[152] Additionally, a divine Word that is *passio* in the divine nature would mean the subversion of the *communicatio operationum*—a move away from Calvin's emphasis on Christ's mediation in both natures.[153]

One of the functions of the *extra-calvinisticum* in Calvin, it has been argued, was to exclude the *genus tapeinoticum*.[154] However, this does not abrogate the divine *compassio*. Divine immutability both ensures the integrity of and "reflect[s] glory upon" the other divine perfections, including compassion, which exists like "an ocean of love and pity in the heart of him" who is transcendent over all else.[155] Edwards clearly affirms that the divine nature is *apatheia*.[156] But what does Edwards mean when he says that the "love of God, as it is in the divine nature, is not a passion . . . but by the incarnation is really become passionate to his own"?[157]

COMPLEXIO OPPOSITORUM: PASSIBILITY AND IMPASSIBILITY IN CHRIST

Does Edwards countenance the divine nature literally becoming passionate in the incarnation, as Jenson claims? He thinks not, for this would mean that God is mutable and temporal. "Nothing is more impossible," Edwards insists, "than that the immutable God should be changed, by the succession of time."[158] Divine self-existence presupposes immutability, as any change in God would have to arise from dependence on some other cause.[159] Divine mutability based on God as *causa sui* is an inadequate explanation as well: "If you say that he causes the change himself, I answer that that supposes that there is some change already before he can desire to change his own nature."[160]

Clearly, Edwards, following the Alexandrian tradition, is predicating "passionate love" to the incarnate person of Christ.[161] Any change occurs in the human nature that is in union with the divine.[162] Such a passionate "love the human nature had to mankind, and by which he was prompted to undergo so much, it had only by virtue of its union with the Logos; 'twas all derived from the love of the Logos, or else they would not be one person."[163] In the hypostatic union, the love of the human Jesus has become relatively infinite: "Now this passionate love of Christ, by virtue of the union with the divine nature, is in a sort infinite."[164] In other words, Edwards's modified *genus maiestaticum/operationum* is at work here. With a Spirit-mediated *communicatio*, the way of a selective *genus maiestaticum* is opened up while retaining divine impassibilism.[165]

Edwards seems to intimate that the highest expression of love is self-giving, which is at the "expense of the beloved," as evidenced in Christ's self-sacrifice.[166] Yet the ground and agency of this voluntary self-sacrifice cannot be situated in the human nature per se, for it was the incarnate Logos that suffered humanly. No mere human being underwent the passion: it was a theandric operation. To be sure, Christ's *suffering* love was possible because of Christ's humanity, yet it is only suffering *love* as derived from the "great love of the eternal Logos."[167] Similarly, the "simple" divine Logos cannot die, but by virtue of the incarnation, the Logos did die as a human being.[168] While both possibility and impassibility are predicated of the two natures, Edwards does not allow them to be abstracted from the one divine-human person in whom they are realized. Thus, echoing Cyril's paradoxical language, Edwards admits that though the Son was "naturally infinitely above suffering . . . the second Person of the Trinity was willing to suffer for sinners."[169] God the Son is said to suffer only in virtue of the *communicatio idiomatum genus idiopoeticon*.[170] Through the suffering of one of the Trinity, the other two are revealed. The incarnation and the cross represent a "bright and glorious manifestation" of the Trinity, where the mutual love of Father and Son are expressed *ad extra*, by which forgiveness and glory *pro nobis* are obtained.[171] And this is the revelation of the triune God, who is love.

Edwards's impassibilism does not commit him to a God without an emotional life, since God is both disposition and act of love.[172] He is a God of affection, but not passion.[173] Again, Edwards reiterates that "God is without passions because all passions imply changeableness and imperfection."[174] God is positively affected—has real happiness—in self-communication to creatures.[175] This joy is in an independent self-giving *ad extra* and not dependent on creaturely response, though the latter is inevitably involved. God's *apatheia* is the natural ground for the incarnation, which necessarily oriented it toward the passion.[176] The thrust of passionate love is more about passiveness, or the relation of being acted upon, and less an irrational sort of reaction, though both are linked.[177]

TRANSFORMATION OF HUMAN PASSIBILITY IN CHRIST: SUFFERING MADE INFINITELY REDEMPTIVE

Not only did a divine person love in human manner, but the hypostatic union also enlarged the capacity of human affections.[178] As we have seen, Christ's love was "in a sort infinite."[179] This Edwards makes clear in another Miscellany where he argues that the glorified "man Christ Jesus," due to extended powers, is able to simultaneously think of every elect creature and exercise "a passionate love (such as we experience) to all of them in particular."[180] Nonetheless, Christ's passion "was not infinite suffering" that involved either divine passibility or the everlasting punishment of hell.[181] Christ's suffering in the human nature was finite but its union with the divine person gave it infinite value.[182]

WHAT GROUNDS ARE THERE FOR THE HUMILITY OF JESUS CHRIST?

Edwards gives a traditional answer to the question, *Cur Deus homo?* But how would he respond to Barth's *de iure* since humility could never be a divine attribute for Edwards?[183] While Jesus' human wisdom and holiness share the same *ratio nomina* with divine wisdom and holiness, Edwards regards humility or meekness as solely human properties.[184] Humility, therefore, cannot be attributed to the Father and the Spirit, since they are purely divine.[185] Neither can it be predicated of the Logos *simpliciter*.[186] Nevertheless, humility and meekness in human beings find their correlate in the "infinite grace and infinite condescension in the divine nature."[187] Because humility is the proper creaturely correlate to divine condescension, the incarnate Son possesses both of these perfections.[188] As we have noted previously, the obedience of the incarnate Son is not merely by covenant, but corresponds to the eternal love of the Son toward the Father *ad intra*.[189]

Edwards not only retains Cyril's paradoxical conjunction of opposing attributes in the union but also develops this notion of correlative properties that exist in the two natures.[190] Obviously, the medieval language of *convenientia* is used to highlight the fittingness and beauty of the union of attributes in Christ.[191] In doing so, would one have to reluctantly tolerate the *complexio oppositorum* of the divine attributes—namely, the unresolved conjunction of transcendence and condescension, love and grace, wrath and happiness in God? Edwards does not think so. Rather, the beauty of the divine attributes, even seemingly opposite ones like transcendence and condescension, he avers, are in fact enhanced by such a conjunction: "the divine perfections do sweetly kiss and embrace each other."[192]

DIVINE KRYPSIS ONLY? GLORY HIDDEN AND MANIFESTED IN HUMILIATION

As we have seen, there is a sense in which the divine *gloria* is veiled in the humanity of Christ, but there is a *terminus ad quem* to this *velatus*.[193] Does Edwards here intend the *exininatio* merely to be the means to the *exaltatio*? Not so, for the *doxa* is revealed as hidden in its contrary, *absconditas Dei sub contrario*: "There was a glory of Christ that shone forth in the stable and upon the cross."[194] Hence, the *divine gloria* as "awful majesty" and lovely beauty—wrath and love—was expressed in Christ's sufferings. Here, Edwards uses the *genus idiomaticum* to great effect:

> The awful majesty of God now won't be in the way to hinder perfect freedom and intimacy in the enjoyment of God, any more than if God were our equal, because that majesty has already been fully displayed, vindicated and glorified in Christ's blood. . . . Though an admission to such a kind of fellowship with God perhaps could not be without God's own suffering, yet when a divine person has been slain, way is made for it, seeing that he has been dead.[195]

In Christ's person, the contrast between the properties of both natures makes the divine more apparent.[196] In the divine economy, Christ "emptied himself in his humiliation" while remaining God.[197] There is no reduction of the divinity during the crucifixion just as there was no divine addition during Christ's exaltation.[198] Edwards's notion of Christ's kenosis as a space-time descent is figural with regard to divinity.[199]

Relative to the *statu exinationis* in which the divine glory is obscured, the revelation of divine glory in Christ's exaltation is now manifest, shining "forth without a veil." Nonetheless, it was not Christ's human nature *simpliciter* but its humiliated form that is the veil, since this glorious manifestation is now mediated through the exalted, resurrected body of Christ.[200] Clearly, like a solar eclipse, the earthly Jesus assumed a fallen nature with its attendant weaknesses and corruption, save for sin.[201] In other words, the human nature *in statu exinationis* both hinders and helps in the divine revelation. That is why Edwards argues elsewhere that the assumed body mediates—or, better, moderates—the *tremendum* of the divine glory to human beings, which otherwise would have had to remain hidden and inaccessible to creatures in its bare form.[202]

In the *exinanitio*, Edwards describes the divine *krypsis* as a sort of selective nonoperation of the divine power through the human nature.[203] To argue that Christ's divinity may have been predominantly veiled in the *exinanitio* (*krypsis*) is quite different from the postulate of a quiescent divine nature (functional kenosis).[204] If there was both a restraint and a veiling of the divine power in the earthly Jesus, what does Edwards think of the experience of divine joy in Christ's sufferings?

DID JESUS EXPERIENCE BOTH SUFFERING AND JOY ON THE CROSS?

Does Edwards, like Aquinas, affirm that Jesus simultaneously experienced both extreme suffering and an uninterrupted beatific vision on the cross?[205] The answer is no. Christ did not have at the same time spiritual joy and bodily pain in the passion but rather underwent simultaneous spiritual and physical suffering. Following Melchior Cano, Edwards distinguishes between the operations of knowledge and will whereby Jesus retained vision but not beatitude in extreme suffering.[206]

In the passion Jesus was denied a human cognate of the "happiness which he was originally in the possession of" as *Logos asarkos*.[207] In other words, the meaning of kenosis, for Edwards, is the incarnate Son's surrendering of the divine right to be born *in statu exaltationis*.[208] In fact, Jesus' awareness of the experiential gap between the actual *passio* and rightful *beatitudo* further intensified his psychological suffering on the cross.[209] Accordingly, it was "on account of his great love to God and his remembrance of God's love to him" that "rendered his sufferings as from God the greater trial" when the Father was hidden from Jesus in the crucifixion.[210] In fact, Christ was given a premonition of this experiential gap in Gethsemane.[211]

Jesus' access to the Logos's mind and cognitive knowledge of the Father's love cannot be diminished since a unified self-consciousness is needed to sustain the *unio*. Yet, Jesus' happiness was circumvented during the passion because the reciprocity of love between Jesus and the Father was temporarily short-circuited. The *status exinanitionis* involved a modulation and restriction of Jesus' reception of the Father's love. In other words, Christ did not lose objective knowledge of the Father's love but suffered the loss of the Father's subjective love—a sort of pain of loss (*poena damni*).[212] Jesus' suffering was "so much more grievous" than hell's torments since the disruption of the Father's infinite love toward Jesus was much greater compared to the loss of God's "lesser love" had Jesus been merely human.[213]

Moreover, Jesus positively suffered a kind of pain of sense (*poena sensus*), facing both "the fire of God's wrath" as well as "the fire of our sins" on the cross.[214] The experience of our sin and its deserved punishment was repugnant to Jesus' sanctity and humanity respectively.[215] Jesus did not experience the Father's personal anger but vicariously bore God's anger toward human sin.[216] Also, Christ did not suffer God's damning anger, but only redemptive anger, and so was not consumed by the divine wrath.[217] Through all of this, Christ's awareness of the ultimate blessedness that would arise from the atoning suffering was curbed.[218] Edwards thus extends Calvin's notion of Christ's descent to hell as a soulish suffering equivalent to hell's torments.[219]

What role does the Spirit play in the sufferings of Jesus? Even though Jesus was impeccable, Edwards argues that the agony "added to the finite holiness of the human nature of Christ."[220] As Jesus' revulsion toward sin deepened, a love of virtue increased and this "was done by the Spirit of God."[221] Besides the Spirit's role in Jesus' sanctity, what happened to Jesus' sense of self-identity in the passion?

If Jesus experienced a blackout of the Father's subjective love, "viz. the manifestation and enjoyment of the love of God," was the Spirit of God also temporarily withdrawn?[222] Could not the Spirit have self-restricted as a communicative channel of the divine affections during such occasions?[223] As we have seen earlier, there can be no lessening of Jesus' cognitive memory of the Father-Son relation as this would imperil Jesus' very own self-identity (as Word incarnate) and thus the hypostatic union. However, the Spirit's mediating role between the two minds of Christ, in its affective dimension, seems to have been restrained. And if that were the case, wouldn't the hypostatic union be imperiled by a kind of disabled *vinculum*, especially since Edwards characterizes the Spirit as the divine love and affection?

The *unio personalis* is safeguarded by a distinction between the Spirit's absolutely "sanctifying" but relatively "comforting" presence.[224] The *unio hypostatica* was inaugurated and maintained by the Spirit's permanent, sanctifying presence.[225] This is identical to Jesus' permanent possession of the Spirit of the Logos. However, the Son in the human nature suffered a diminishment of and even lost the Spirit's "comfortable" presence in the course of bearing humanity's sin and guilt.[226] This is synonymous with Christ's experience of the Father's hiddenness and loss of the divine joy. Jesus was conscious of a self-identity as Son even in the depths of the passion, particularly in suffering the loss of the Father's love.[227] Simply put, Jesus was holy (or more accurately, became holier) but not happy on the Cross.

Clearly, it is Edwards's commitment to divine impassibilism, which forces him to introduce an experiential cleavage between the Logos and the human nature in order to account for the *passio*. In light of Edwards's radicalized *extra carnem*, did Christ's self-identity move from one subject with two modes of consciousness to that of two distinct centers of self-awareness? If Jesus suffered the Father's absence while the Logos continued to enjoy the Father's love, the threat of Nestorianism looms.

Furthermore, it could be argued that the Logos only cognitively apprehends Jesus' suffering while Jesus cognitively perceives or remembers a past beatitude. Edwards's position in this is confirmed in his "Subjects of Inquiry," which we had examined earlier. Apparently, the earthly Jesus had access to "the divine omniscience" and "had one will with the divine and when he would the divine power was exerted"—all this in proportion to his finitude and humiliated state. However, it is only "Christ's *glorified* human nature [that] has the divine joy and divine happiness and God's love to the eternal Logos to expatiate itself in."[228] In other words, there is an affective dissonance between Christ's two natures in the state of humiliation.[229]

Of course, from the line of thought above, Edwards's Christ could be diagnosed as having dissociative identity disorder (a split personality), but this would be an imposition of psychoanalysis upon what is inscrutable. As Francis Hall reminds us, two modes of knowledge in Christ "does not mean that [Christ] has two *psychological* minds, both capable of emerging in human consciousness—whether by turns or in mutually confusing parallelism. The divine mind does not function psychologically at all, and its operations, by their very nature, must forever escape the attention and scrutiny of a really human mind."[230]

CONCLUSION

Edwards's Reformed heritage is evident in the amount of material he devotes to the *unio hypostatica* over the relation between the natures in Christ.[231] Just as the *unio hypostatica* is mediated pneumatically, the Spirit is accorded a fundamental role in the communication between the natures in Christ. In line with the patristic-Reformed theologians, suffering is not attributed to the divine nature or Logos *simpliciter* but to the Word incarnate according to Christ's humanity. Still, the suffering of Christ was salvific because the whole Christ is involved in the theandric acts. While Christ acts appropriately in both natures, the human nature participates in the divine action as an instrument but has access to the divine capacities through the mediation of the Spirit. Though there is not a bare communication of the divine attributes to the human nature, the human Jesus receives them in a form appropriate to its nature and potential. In all this, Edwards affirms that the suffering of the incarnate Christ as a divine person was for a purpose—to exalt humankind to divine fellowship through union with Christ.

> Christ will not descend lower, nor shall we ascend higher, in having Christ for us, and giving himself to us, in such a high degree of enjoyment, than to give himself to us to be our sacrifice, and to be for us in such a degree of suffering. . . . We may more easily conceive that God would go far in bestowing happiness on an inferior nature, than that he would go far in bringing suffering on an infinitely superiour divine person; for the former is in itself agreeable to his nature, to the attribute of his goodness, but bringing suffering and evil on an innocent and glorious person is in itself in some respect against his nature. If, therefore, God hath done the latter in such a degree for those that are inferior, how shall he not freely do the former? It will not be in any respect a greater gift for Christ thus to

give himself in enjoyment, than it was for him to give [himself] in suffering.²³²

For Edwards, then, Christology is intimately linked to soteriology, and in the next chapter we will look at how he bridges the hypostatic union to our union with Christ and examine in detail his understanding of the *unio mystica*.

Notes

1. See appendix 5, "*Genus maiestaticum*: A Communication of Action and Grace between Christ's Natures" below.

2. Edwards, "Miscellanies," no. 1219, in *WJE* 23:153. Of the thousand or so entries in his "Miscellanies," this is the only one on the *communicatio idiomatum* and is largely composed from a citation from Rawlins.

3. Ibid. This is similar to Calvin's use of the body-soul analogy (John Calvin, *Calvin: Institutes of Christian Religion*, ed. John T. McNeill, trans. Ford Lewis Battles [Philadelphia: Westminster, 1960], 2.xiv.1, 482–83). There are detractors and defenders of such a use. On the one hand, Thomas Weinandy has argued that such an application of the body-soul union to model the hypostatic union results in a *tertium quid* or "compositional union," which confuses the predication of attributes. See Thomas G. Weinandy, *Does God Suffer?* (Edinburgh: T&T Clark, 2000), 184. On the other hand, precisely because the *communicatio* is founded on a part-whole analogy, the nonmixture of the attributes is thus possible (Richard Cross, "A Recent Contribution on the Distinction between Monophysitism and Chalcedonianism," *Thomist* 65 [2001]: 371). The use of this analogy to illustrate the "how" of the union (and not merely the "fact") need not necessarily entail Nestorianism or monophysitism as it was frequently employed by the Fathers (Harry Austryn Wolfson, *Philosophy of the Church Fathers* [Cambridge, MA: Harvard University Press, 1956], 371–72). Charles Hodge, for example, introduces his Christology with this analogy (Charles Hodge, *Systematic Theology* [Grand Rapids, MI: Eerdmans, 1993; originally publ. 1872], vol. 2, pt. 3, ch. 2, 280–81).

4. Similarly, "we affirm that of the person, which agrees to one of the constituent principles of his nature considered by itself," viz., either body or soul (Rawlins, *Justification*, 240, as cited by Edwards, "Miscellanies," no. 1219, in *WJE* 23:154). This echoes John of Damascus, who asserted that one "can say of Christ . . . *This man is uncreated and impassible and uncircumscribed*," yet "it is not . . . as . . . man but as God." Likewise, although Christ can be "spoken of as God who suffers," yet it is "in respect of His being . . . man" (John of Damascus, *Exposition of the Orthodox Faith*, trans. S. D. F. Salmond [*NPNF* 9], bk. 4, ch. 4, 49).

5. Irrespective of whether the *hypostasis* of Christ is referred to by concrete terms of either one or both natures, "we still attribute to it the properties of both natures," since neither kind of attributes can be separated from the two natures, which is permanently united in the "one compound subsistence" (John of Damascus, *Orthodox Faith*, bk. 4, ch. 4, 49 [*NPNF* 9]).

6. As with the body-soul composite, there are times when "we affirm that of the person, which agrees to neither of the constituent principles of his nature considered alone, and is only true of the man as constituted of both" (Rawlins, *Justification*, 240, as cited by Edwards, "Miscellanies," no. 1219, in *WJE* 23:154).

7. The Mediator, as both divine and human, "partakes of the common nature of both" and conforms to their respective propriety (Edwards, "Miscellanies," no. 278, in *WJE* 13:377). The "*communicatio idiomatum* . . . did not intend just to prescribe a certain language, but to prescribe a certain language *cum fundamento in re*" (Hans Küng, *Incarnation of God: An Introduction to Hegel's*

Theological Thought as Prologemena to a Future Christology, trans. J. R. Stephenson [Edinburgh: T&T Clark, 1987], 444).

8. It is not "the conjunction of abstract and abstract." See Marcel Sarot, *God, Passibility and Corporeality* (Kampen, Netherlands: Kok Pharos, 1992), 93. For John of Damascus, then, the *antidosis* is both verbal/logical and realistic/ontological, the former based on the latter. Abstract terms, such as "divinity" and "humanity," can only refer to the respective natures, while the *hypostasis* can be denominated by concrete names of either nature, e.g., "God" or "man," or to both natures at once, e.g., "Christ" or "God Incarnate" (John of Damascus, *Orthodox Faith*, bk. 3, ch. 4, 49; ch. 5, 49 [*NPNF* 9]). Based on this realistic communication, there can be a synecdochic *communicatio idiomatum* where "the properties of the one nature may be predicated of the concretum of the other" (Heinrich Heppe, *Reformed Dogmatics Set Out and Illustrated from the Sources*, rev. and ed. Ernst Bizer, trans. G. T. Thomson [London: George Allen & Unwin, 1950], 441). "The *communicatio idiomatum* is nothing else than a synecdoche, by which what is *proper* to one nature in Christ is attributed the person itself, called by the name of the other nature" (Johannes Piscator, *Aphorismi*, 54, as quoted in Heppe, *Reformed Dogmatics*, 441).

9. "There do meet in the person of Christ, such really diverse excellencies, which otherwise would have been thought utterly incompatible in the same subject; such as are conjoined in no other person whatever, either divine, human, or angelical" (Edwards, "Excellencies of Christ," in *The Sermons of Jonathan Edwards: A Reader*, ed. Wilson H. Kimnach, Kenneth P. Minkema, and Douglas A. Sweeney [New Haven: Yale University Press, 1999], 166). He preached the *genus idiomaticum*: "the excellencies of his Godhead and of his manhood do illustrate one another when we see infinite greatness, and so great humility, infinite majesty and transcendent meekness meeting in the same person" (Edwards, 191. Sermon on Rom. 5:7-8 [Feb 1752], in *WJE* 46). The natures, as the Fifth Ecumenical Council has declared, are only to be distinguished *in theoria*. In keeping with this, St. John asserts that when the Christ "is called Man and Son of Man, he still keeps the properties and glories of the divine nature" (John of Damascus, *Orthodox Faith*, bk. 4, ch. 4, 49 [*NPNF* 9]).

10. Wolfhart Pannenberg, *Jesus—God and Man*, trans. Lewis L. Wilkins and Duane A. Priebe (London: SCM, 1968), 300.

11. Louis Berkhof, *Systematic Theology*, new combined ed., with a new preface by Richard E. Muller (Grand Rapids, MI: Eerdmans, 1996), 324. With the tradition, Berkhof notes that the outcome or *apotelesma* "bears a divine human character"; that is, it is theandric. However, he states that the "efficient cause" of Christ's salvific acts is Christ's Person, while distinguishing the divinity and humanity as the principal and instrumental causes respectively. This genus points to the Alexandrian emphasis on the dynamic and purposeful character of the incarnational union and is already noticeable in Apollinaris (albeit within a deficient Christology), clearly evident in Cyril of Alexandria, and appropriated by Severus of Antioch. See Iain R. Torrance, *Christology after Chalcedon: Severus of Antioch and Sergius the Monophysite* (Eugene, OR: Wipf and Stock, 1998), 65–67, 98–100.

12. Piotr Malysz, "Storming Heaven with Karl Barth? Barth's Unwitting Appropriation of the *Genus Maiestaticum* and What Lutherans Can Learn from It," *International Journal of Systematic Theology* 9, no. 1 (January 2007): 77.

13. That Jesus "was not liable to sinful changes . . . was not owing to any thing in his human nature but to its relation to the divine nature that upheld it" (Edwards, 470. Sermon on 1 Cor. 13:1-10 [b] [April 1738], in *WJE* 53). The "divine nature" need not be understood as either the Holy Spirit or the Logos, as Edwards used the same term for both.

14. According to Edwards, "'tis certain that the will of the man Christ Jesus was free, who was a man as well as we, one of the same faculties as we; yet as free as his will was, it was impossible that he should will sin" (Edwards, "Miscellanies," no. 31, in *WJE* 13:217). Edwards assumes that, as it would be unscriptural to deny that Christ *had* in fact willed perfectly, so it was equally impossible (and unscriptural) that he *could* have willed contrariwise.

15. Edwards, *WJE* 1:289–91.

16. This is in contrast to Scotus, who thought that Christ's human nature could choose either good or bad; in other words, Christ's impeccability did not arise from the hypostatic union, but flowed from the beatific vision (Richard Cross, *Duns Scotus* [New York: Oxford University Press, 1999], 122).

17. Thus, "acts which are done in a state of equilibrium, or . . . from perfect indifference . . . cannot arise from any good principle or disposition in the heart" (Edwards, *WJE* 1:321). It is the "antithesis" to real faith (Conrad Cherry, *Theology of Jonathan Edwards: A Reappraisal* [Bloomington: Indiana University Press, 1990], 194)

18. According to John of Damascus, Christ has two natural wills (*thelesis*) but not "opinion" (*gnome*)—"an inclination opposed to the divine will." Christ did not deliberate or "have counsel or choice" (*boule*) but had "knowledge of all things" through the hypostatic union. Deliberation is related to natural desire (*boulesis*) producing individual choice; habitual choice will result in an opinionated or gnomic will. A gnomic will entails a clouded vision of the good, for the natural will in perfect operation chooses effortlessly. A nondeliberative human will is therefore godlike, for "God does not deliberate, since that is a mark of ignorance, and no one deliberates about what he knows" (John of Damascus, *Orthodox Faith*, bk. 2, ch. 22, 37 [*NPNF* 9]). As Andrew Louth observes, this idea is inimical to post-Kantian moral philosophy in which only libertarian freedom is recognized. Hence, "freedom is not strictly exercise of the will, but rather the experience of accurate vision which, when this becomes appropriate, occasions action." See Iris Murdoch, *The Sovereignty of Good* (London: Routledge & Kegan Paul, 1970), 67, as cited in Andrew Louth, *St. John Damascene: Tradition and Originality in Byzantine Theology* (Oxford: Oxford University Press, 2002; reprint, 2004), 168; page references are to the reprint edition.

19. Here, Edwards is referring to the saints made in God's image: "He hereby makes them like the angels, who are ministering spirits to others' good; yea, he makes them like himself who is the fountain of goodness" (Edwards, "Charity and Its Fruits," sermon 4, in *WJE* 8:215).

20. Edwards, "Miscellanies," no. 621, in *WJE* 18:153.

21. Edwards, 234. Sermon on Matt. 16:21-23 (1731), in *WJE* 47. The communion of wills need not be predicated upon a *communio naturarum*, as a *mediate unio* is sufficient, viz., what the divine Word wills as human and as God are in conformity.

22. The divine mission was grounded in the Father's promises and divine constitution, and the Son's decision in the *pactum salutis* made it impossible to fail. Based on this prior predetermined character of Christ's sinlessness and holiness by the divine will, Christ's volitional acts in the economy "were necessarily so conformed" to the Father's will (Edwards, *WJE* 1:289).

23. Thus, "it was *impossible*" that there should be a contrariety of wills in the incarnate Christ because in the *pactum salutis*, the Logos, "who made the world," had already willed to obey as Mediator "before the world" (Edwards, *WJE* 1:287).

24. For the atonement to be properly a personal "act and choice" of the human Christ, an understanding of the extent of the suffering to be endured as well as the evil and sin that needed to be atoned was required (Edwards, "Miscellanies," no. 653, in *WJE* 18:193). In the garden and the crucifixion Christ experienced "two turns of suffering the wrath of God." In Gethsemane, the Father communicated to Christ "a clear and full idea" of his approaching suffering, for without such anticipatory knowledge and the "opportunity to flee," he could not have accepted the passion in "his own act as man" (Edwards, "Miscellanies," no. 621, in *WJE* 18:151–53).

25. Edwards distinguishes Christ's supererogatory obedience to the Father's "commanding and legislative authority" *pro nobis* and the incarnate Son's natural obedience to the Father: the first arises from covenant, the second from the propriety of the divine Son (Edwards, "Miscellanies," no. 454, in *WJE* 13:499). This point was to be robustly affirmed by Barth in terms of the language of correspondence: human autonomy is analogical to divine freedom. Whereas Edwards did not hesitate in applying necessity to the divine and human volition of Christ, Barth sees the correspondence in terms of humility—Jesus' obedience mirrors Christ's eternal obedience as divine

Son (John S. Macken, *The Autonomy Theme in the* Church Dogmatics: *Karl Barth and His Critics* [Cambridge: Cambridge University Press, 1990], 61).

26. "That the eternal Logos should be subordinate to the Father, though not inferior in nature—yea, that Christ, in his office, should be subject to the Father and less than he, though in his higher nature not inferior—is not strange" (Edwards, "Miscellanies," no. 1352, in *WJE* 23:640). It is not strange since such subordination is commonplace in earthly father-son relations.

27. As the principle of volition in God, the Spirit fittingly acts "as a means of conveyance of . . . [the] will of the divine Logos, to the . . . will of the human nature" (Edwards, "Miscellanies," no. 766, in *WJE* 18:412–13).

28. Edwards, "On the Equality," in *WJE* 21:147.

29. Since the Son is the proper subject of the incarnation, all acts as God-man are solely the Son's, with the exception of "the miracles, and in respect of good will and purpose," which involve the entire Trinity (John of Damascus, *Orthodox Faith*, bk. 3, ch. 11, 55 [*NPNF* 9]). Elsewhere, John states this exception as "approval and the working of inexplicable miracles" (*Orthodox Faith*, bk. 1, ch. 10, 12). This seems to be a reiteration of Pseudo-Dionysius (*PG* 3.644): the Father and Spirit are uninvolved in the theandric acts except for "the loving generosity of the divine counsels and in all that transcendent divine working of unutterable mysteries which were performed in human nature by Him who as God and as the Word is immutable." This was carried on by the medievals: "Jesus's miracles are performed by the Trinity, whether or not the human nature is used as an instrument" (Richard Cross, *Metaphysics of the Incarnation* [New York: Oxford University Press, 2002], 155)

30. Edwards, "Miscellanies," no. 766, in *WJE* 18:412.

31. Edwards, "Discourse on the Trinity," in *WJE* 21:122.

32. "Whatever the Son of God wrought in, by, or upon the human nature, he did it by the Holy Ghost" (John Owen, *The Works of John Owen*, ed. William H. Goold, 16 vols. [London: Banner of Truth Trust, 1965–68; originally publ. Johnstone & Hunter, 1850–53], 1:225).

33. "The divine Logos is so united to the humanity of Christ that it spake and acted by it" ("Miscellanies," no. 738, in *WJE* 18:364). In commending Owen for upholding the integrity of Christ's human nature, Gunton unnecessarily opposes Spirit Christology to Logos Christology. Accordingly, he asserts that the "freedom, particularity and contingency" of Jesus "are *enabled* by the (transcendent) Spirit rather than *determined* by the (immanent) Word" (Colin E. Gunton, *The Promise of Trinitarian Theology*, 2nd ed. [Edinburgh: T&T Clark, 1997], 69). Clearly, Gunton is thinking of a reified nature-to-nature relation here—the *deitas* overpowering the *humanitas* as if they were two subjects. If Christ is both human and divine, the incarnate Word must be free to act in two modes.

34. "Though he was directed by the Spirit of God when and how to work these works, and was moved by the Spirit to work them, yet he wrought them as of his own wisdom and his own will" (Edwards, "Miscellanies," no. 766, in *WJE* 18:412).

35. Ibid.

36. An incipient tritheism seems to underlie Walvoord's conclusion: "The final solution of the problem cannot be reached except to state that Christ performed His miracles in the power of the Spirit, and that he could if he wished and probably did exercise His own power as well" (John F. Walvoord, *The Holy Spirit: A Comprehensive Study of the Person and Work of the Holy Spirit* [Grand Rapids, MI: Zondervan, 1991], 97–98).

37. Chemnitz, citing Jean Gerson (*Sermo de 4 Dominibus*), points out that Christ's humanity must have an instrumental power of secondary causation in the performance of the miracles, unlike other saints (Martin Chemnitz, *The Two Natures in Christ*, trans. J. A. O. Preus [St. Louis, MO: Concordia, 1971; originally publ. as *De Duabus Naturis in Christo*, Leipzig, 1578], 255).

38. Christ's divinity is evident in the working of miracles, by will and constancy, in contrast to "other prophets," who merely performed them occasionally and by divine command (Edwards, "Miscellanies," no. 518[b], in *WJE* 18:63). "For those divine works that [Christ] wrought were his own works; they were not wrought by the Spirit, as the apostles and prophets wrought miracles by

the power and in the name of another, but as wrought in his own name and by his own power" (Edwards, "Miscellanies," no. 766, in *WJE* 18:412).

39. Edwards, "On the Equality," in *WJE* 21:147.

40. Edwards, "Blank Bible," note on Prov. 15:21, in *WJE* 24:559. In contrary fashion, "sin is the principle that has the dominion of over men[; it] is absolute Lord in his heart and governs all his powers and faculties" (Edwards, 237. Sermon on Luke 6:35 [1731–32], in *WJE* 47).

41. Another example is that of "one [person] introducing two people." See David T. Williams, Vinculum Amoris: *A Theology of the Holy Spirit* (Lincoln, NE: iUniverse, 2004), 19.

42. "Jesus Christ, the great prophet of God, when he came into the world to be 'the light of the world.' . . . In his doctrine he declared the mind and will of God, and the nature and properties of that virtue . . . more clearly and fully than ever it had been before . . . and he also in his own practice gave a most perfect example of the virtue he taught" (Edwards, *WJE* 7:89).

43. "And so, though it was the motion of the Spirit of God, yet it was of himself, because these motions of the Spirit themselves were of himself, i.e. of his divine person, the person of the Logos, conveying and uniting the divine understanding and will, and so of the divine nature with the human" (Edwards, "Miscellanies," no. 766, in *WJE* 18:412–13).

44. On whether the *communicatio idiomatum in abstracto et realis* was mutual, "neither Cyril or Luther dared say straight out that it does" since the Logos would become passible (Robert W. Jenson, *America's Theologian: A Recommendation of Jonathan Edwards* [New York: Oxford University Press, 1988], 118). Even though "Edwards was cautious" (118) generally, Miscellany z was a case "that might have seemed a bit unguarded even to Cyril of Alexandria or Martin Luther" (115).

45. Stephen R. Holmes, *God of Grace and God of Glory: An Account of the Theology of Jonathan Edwards* (Edinburgh: T&T Clark, 2000), 138. John Owen was more "radical" than Francis Turretin in his denial in toto of the *communicatio idiomatum* (Holmes, *God of Grace*, 138n42). For Turretin, the *unio personalis* does not entail any *communicatio idiomatum in abstracto*: "For although the union of the natures with each other is real, it is not necessary that the properties of the natures should be communicated to each other in turn" (Francis Turretin, *Institutes of Elenctic Theology*, trans. George Musgrave Giger, ed. James T. Dennison [Phillipsburg, NJ: P&R, 1992–94], vol. 2, topic 13, q. 8, para. 4, 322).

46. "That the only *necessary consequent* of this assumption of the human nature, or the incarnation of the Son of God, is the *personal union of Christ*, or the inseparable subsistence of the *assumed nature* in the person of the Son" (Owen, *Works*, 3:160–61; italics original).

47. Applying this to the death of Christ, Owen insisted that "here our preceding rule must be remembered,—namely, that notwithstanding the union of the human nature of Christ with the divine person of the Son, yet the communications of God unto it, beyond subsistence, were voluntary" (ibid., 180). This is appropriated to the Spirit in accordance to the divine *taxis* within the Trinity where "in every divine act, the authority of the Father, the love and wisdom of the Son, with the immediate efficacy and power of the Holy Ghost, are to be considered." Owen qualifies this statement by affirming the Augustinian axiom, "*Opera Trinitatis extra sunt indivisa*," thus denying that this work is either absolute or exclusive to the Spirit (Owen, *Works*, 2:162).

48. This assumption is clear in John of Damascus's definition of the *antidosis* as "either nature giving in exchange to the other its own properties through the identity of the subsistence and the interpenetration of the parts with one another." Since there is such an ordering, one deduces the "the manner of the mutual interchange arising from the ineffable union" (John of Damascus, *Orthodox Faith*, bk. 4, ch. 4, 49 [*NPNF* 9]). Thunberg thinks "that to Maximus *circumincessio* is the presupposition of *communicatio*, rather than the other way around." See Lars Thunberg, "'Circumincession' Once More: Trinitarian and Christological Implications in an Age of Religious Pluralism," in *Papers Presented at the Twelfth International Conference on Patristic Studies held in Oxford, 1995*, ed. Elizabeth A. Livingstone, Studia Patristica 29 (Leuven: Peeters, 1997), 366. On a purely Logos Christology, absent of a *communio naturarum*, no *genus maiestaticum* seems

possible. Berkhof rejects the notion of a *communio naturarum* as he identified it with a real *communicatio idiomatum in abstracto* (*Reformed Dogmatics*, 1:321).

49. "That all other actings of God in the *person of the Son* towards his human nature were *voluntary*, and did not necessarily ensue on the union mentioned; for there was no transfusion of the properties of one nature into the other, nor real physical communication of divine essential excellencies unto the humanity" (Owen, *Works*, 2:161).

50. Since Aquinas, medieval theology has generally worked on the basis that the *communicatio idiomatum* is the consequence of the hypostatic union and that it did not include abstract predication (Heiko Augustinus Oberman, *The Harvest of Medieval Theology: Gabriel Biel and Late Medieval Nominalism* [Cambridge, MA: Harvard University Press, 1963], 263). Lutherans like Jacob Andreae held that the *communicatio* was the result of the *unio personalis*, which was in opposition to the Reformed, like Theodore Beza, who thought that they were identical (Jill Raitt, *The Colloquy of Montbéliard: Religion and Politics in the Sixteenth Century* [New York: Oxford University Press, 1993], 117). Dorner points out that the *Formula of Concord* is self-contradictory as it treats, on occasion, the *unio personalis* as the ground of the *communicatio idiomatum* and in other instances reverses the relation (I. A. Dorner, *History of the Development of the Doctrine of the Person of Christ*, 5 vols. [Edinburgh: T&T Clark, 1891], 2:2, 231n1)

51. Oneness brings about sharing, for "union is such a nearness whereby they are no more two but one" (Edwards, 419. Sermon on John 13:23 [Jan 1736–37], in *WJE* 52) and "communion in or fellowship . . . is a common partaking of benefits" (Edwards, 103. Sermon on 1 Cor. 1:19 [1729], in *WJE* 44). Here, he reiterates Goodwin's axiom that "all communication depends upon an union." See Thomas Goodwin, *Of the Knowledge of God the Father, And His Son Jesus Christ*, ed. Thankfull Owen and James Barron, *The Works of Thomas Goodwin, D. D. sometime president of Magdalen College in Oxford* (London: [Thomas Goodwin Jr.], 1683); available at *The Digital Library of Protestant Texts*, 120.

52. Edwards, "Miscellanies," no. 766, in *WJE* 18:413.

53. "Now therefore by this rule, still, the nearer union, the nearer communication. And by the same proportion, the highest communication cannot be without the highest union." By "rule," Goodwin refers to another principle: "*Bonum est sui communicativum*; that is, that goodness is communicative: By the same also, *summum bonum est summè communicativum sui*; that is, the highest good is communicative of himself the highest way" (Goodwin, *Of The Knowledge Of God The Father, And His Son Jesus Christ*, 120). Edwards clearly agrees with Goodwin's "rule" because it is ultimately soteriological: As the incarnation is the most intimate union between God and humanity, "the nearest and fullest communications always follow upon the nearest union. To him therefore as man are communicated these riches of glory that are in the Godhead as nearly and as fully as was possible unto a creature and being thus communicated, must needs shine forth in him to us to the utmost that they ever could unto creatures" (Goodwin, "The Glory Of the Gospel," in *Works*, 1, pt. 3, 66, as quoted in Edwards, "Miscellanies," no. 1278, *WJE* 23:225).

54. Edwards, "Miscellanies," 766, in *WJE* 18:412. Italics mine.

55. "Now the whole body, head and members, have communion in Christ's righteousness; they are all partakers of the benefit of it; Christ himself, the head, is rewarded for it, and every member is partaker of the benefit and reward" (Edwards, "Miscellanies," no. 403, in *WJE* 13:468). For Edwards, Christ's "manhood" is fully actualized and transcends any ideal "human person" one could construct *via negationis* and *via eminentiae*. "Jesus Christ has in himself all human excellencies: everything that can possibly render any human creature amiable" (Edwards, 79. Sermon on Cant. 1:3 [a], in *WJE* 43).

56. "Yea, the grace of God in men's heart can hardly be called a creature" (Edwards, 72. Sermon on 2 Cor. 3:18 [a] [1728], in *WJE* 43). As we shall see later on, the Spirit is the divine *habitus* of Christ and of all saints.

57. While Barth reconceptualizes the *communicatio gratiarum* in primarily ethical terms to avoid any idea of a *gratia habitualis*—something that happens in the human essence of the

Son—Edwards sees the *communicatio gratiarum* as the Spirit given to Christ without measure (Barth, *CD* IV/2, 89–94).

58. Beza rejected Andreae's identification of "without measure" as "infinite" as if the entire uncreated divinity could be contained in created humanity. Only the divine Logos possesses the divine Spirit in its entirety, and through the union, the assumed humanity is granted the created gifts (Raitt, *The Colloquy of Montbéliard*, 123).

59. Edwards, "Miscellanies," no. 766, in *WJE* 18:413. Not surprisingly, Dorner could judge that, in Reformed Christology, the "'unctio spiritus sancti' is the surrogate of the Lutheran 'communicatio idiomatum'" (Dorner, *Person of Christ*, 2:341).

60. Edwards, "Miscellanies," no. 766, in *WJE* 18:413. Thus, "all that was divine in the man Christ Jesus is from the Spirit of God."

61. That is, Edwards is not referring to borrowed divine attributes; see appendix 5 *infra*, in the section entitled, "In What Way Does the Human Nature Participate in the Divine Attributes?"

62. Edwards, "Images of Divine Things," no. 166, in *WJE* 11:110.

63. Edwards, "Miscellanies," no. 81, *WJE* 13:248. Edwards would have read Louis Ellies Du Pin's *A New History of Ecclesiastical Writers* when he was at Yale. Du Pin notes the Cyrillian Christology of John Damascene in the *Orthodox Faith*, "There is in Christ an Incarnate Nature, a Theandrick Will, and a Human Nature Deified." See Lewis Ellies Du Pin, *A New History of Ecclesiastical Writers . . .* , 15 vols. in 7, 3rd ed. (London: Printed for Abel Smalle and Cim. Childe, at the Unicorn at the West-End of the St. Paul's Church-Yard, 1696), 6:103.

64. Muller, *PRRD* 3:548. "Our Divines distinguish between a glory merely divine, and a Mediator's glory, which is next to divine, far above all creatures" (Leigh, *Treatise*, II.xv (p. 115), as quoted by Muller, *PRRD* 3:548n399). See also Richard A. Muller, *Dictionary of Latin and Greek Theological Terms: Drawn Principally from Protestant Scholastic* Theology (Grand Rapids, MI: Baker Book House, 1985), s.v. "gloria," 129. The divine glory (*gloria dei*) considered as a divine attribute is intimately associated with the majesty of God (*maiestas Dei*).

65. This is the "key to right understanding," because it explicates Christ's "true substance most clearly of all"—a category neglected by unnamed "ancient writers," who muddied the clarity of John's Gospel and fell into error (Calvin, *Institutes*, 1.14.3, 485).

66. Tylenda thinks that Calvin does have an implicit *genus idiomaticum*, which Slater downplays based on a close textual reading of the *Institutes*. See Joseph N. Tylenda, "Calvin's Understanding of the Communication of Properties," *Westminster Theological Journal* 38 (Fall 1975–Spring 1976): 54–65. Slater is surely correct that "the overarching concern for Calvin in discussing the *communicatio* is the person and office of the mediator." However, Slater seems to imply that Calvin understood Christ's entire "role of mediation as temporary," which would seem to contradict the biblical portrayal of Christ as everlasting intercessor *pro nobis*. See Jonathan Slater, "Salvation as Participation in the Humanity of the Mediator in Calvin's *Institutes of the Christian Religion*: A Reply to Carl Mosser," *Scottish Journal of Theology* 58 (2005): 50.

67. Calvin, *Institutes*, 1.14.3, 484.

68. Ibid., 485.

69. Ibid. What is unclear here is whether the God-man was "endowed" with these *ex officiis* or *ex persona*, as Calvin clearly regarded "those things which apply to the office of the Mediator" as temporary. Clearly, while the atoning work of Christ does end, his intercessory work does not. Yet, Calvin could even say that the title "Lord," given to "the *person* of Christ" (emphasis mine) was temporary and "represents a degree midway between God and us." Obviously, some disjunction of person and work would have to be assumed here to avoid a *tertium officiis / nomina* from implying a *tertium quid* (ibid., 485–86).

70. The debate between Mosser and Slater seems to hinge on an either/or conceptuality. Though there are conceptual and metaphorical similarities, it cannot be concluded that "Calvin's understanding of deification is simply the patristic notion of *theōsis*" (Carl Mosser, "The Greatest Possible Blessing: Calvin and Deification," *Scottish Journal of Theology* 55 [2002]: 56). Mosser

simply asserts that Calvin held a realistic *communicatio idiomatum in abstracto* without proving his case (ibid., 46). Formally, Calvin's understanding of the *communicatio idiomatum* as no more than a mutual cross-predication between the natures—merely verbal—confirms this. Yet, to say that Calvin thought of our union with Christ as merely a participation "in what is Christ's according to his human *rather* than his divine nature" is also inexact (Slater, "Salvation as Participation," 41).

71. Goodwin, *Of the knowledge of God the father*, bk. 3, ch. 2, 103. Note his reference to Pareus's defense of Calvin's position with an appeal to the patristic and Reformed fathers like "*Ambrose, Martyr, Melancthon, Ursin &c.*"

72. These attributes are the *lumen*, shine, or rays of the Sun, "the Emissions and Effects of the Sun itself . . . and so inferior to that Essential Glory" of the Son as God. They are "a Resultance, and edition of the Godhead, in all the Perfections of it" (Goodwin, *Of the knowledge of God the father*, bk. 3, ch. 2, 104).

73. The "manifestive" glory is "not the bare communication of properties, so as only that which is said in the Godhead, is predicated of the manhood: Or that the manhood instrumentally useth the attributes of the Godhead, and so is omniscient with the omnisciency of the divine nature, and omnipotent with his omnipotency, (as the Lutherans fondly dream)" (Goodwin, *Of the knowledge of God the father*, bk. 3, ch. 2, 104).

74. "Yet there is this similitude in it, unto that which is in God; that this man can say, This power which I subsist by, is my own, by virtue of his relation unto the second Person; I being the Son of God, and one in Person with him, what is his, is mine, not originally, or essentially, but by gift; yet so, as there I have now an independent right to be and to subsist in that second Person forever, and can never be deposed" (Goodwin, *Of the knowledge of God the father*, bk. 3, ch. 2, 108).

75. By this wisdom, the glorified Christ "knows all that God hath done, or means to do: and so it is of as large extent, for the objects of it, as that knowledge in God himself is in that respect." By his human omnipotency, Christ can "both . . . do whatsoever he will, (his will pitching on the same design with God's in every thing) and in that all that God will ever pitch upon to be done, he is an instrument of." He attributes the nomenclature to the Reformed scholastic "Zanchy" (ibid., 109). This wisdom is neither God's own knowledge, "*per simplicem intelligentiam*," nor is it the Lutheran conception of Christ's "Human nature as omniscient with the omnisciency of the Divine Nature." Though they are incomparably inferior to the essential glories of the divine nature, yet these are "the completest image of them," truly inhering in Christ's humanity and incommunicable to any mere creature. These were the glories visibly manifested in the transfiguration, since the essential, divine attributes are invisible per se (ibid.).

76. Ibid., 108.

77. Emile Mersch, *The Theology of the Mystical Body*, trans. Cyril Vollert (St. Louis, MO: Herder, 1951), 232. Rejecting Lutheranism's ubiquitarianism and pantheism disguised as "panchristism," Mersch flatly denies that any finite nature—"not even the humanity assumed by the Son of God"—could possess the absolute omni-attributes of deity.

78. Edwards, "Subjects of Inquiry," in *WJE* 28.

79. "Christ Mediator is the brightness of the glory of God, in and through whom, his glorious attributes and nature was made conspicuous, and the declarative glory thereof had a more glorious lustre, than by all the works of Creation and Providence beside: upon the same account also Christ is called the *Image of the invisible God*, Col. 1. 15, because the glorious excellencies of God (otherwise invisible) are gloriously revealed by him, and to be seen in him" (Patrick Gillespie, *The ark of the covenant opened: Or, a treatise of the covenant of redemption between God and Christ, as the foundation of the covenant of grace . . .* [London: Tho. Parkhurst, 1677], ch. 2, 40). Linda Munk notes that Edwards spoke of divine glory as a metonymy for God's presence or Shekinah ("His Dazzling Absence: The Shekinah in Jonathan Edwards," *Early American Literature* 27, no. 1 [1992]: 1–30).

80. Edwards, "Approaching the End of God's Grand Design," in *WJE* 25:116.

81. Edwards, "Miscellanies," no. 952, in *WJE* 20:221.

82. Edwards, 257. Sermon on Heb. 12:29 (a), in *WJE* 47.

83. "'Tis Christ being a divine person that renders it fit in God's sight that Christ should be so exalted. . . . '[T]is being man that is the thing that makes him capable of being exalted but 'tis his being made God as well as men [*sic*] that makes it fit he should be so exalted and therefore he is exalted neither as man only nor as God only but as God man and mediatour [*sic*]" (Edwards, 412. Sermon on Rev. 14:14 [Oct 1736], in *WJE* 51).

84. Edwards, "Miscellanies," no. 769, in *WJE* 18:415.

85. Edwards, 51. Sermon on Luke 2:14, in *WJE* 42. "But Jesus Christ is and always was above want. 'Tis impossible he should stand in need of any thing. He had a fullness incapable of any addition. He possessed a treasure that could not be enlarged. He was from eternity perfectly in the enjoyment of the Father. Nothing that the creature can do can in the least add to his happiness. His blessedness is infinite and invariable" (Edwards, 191. Sermon on Rom. 5:7-8 [Feb 1752], in *WJE* 46). This divine glory is the common essential glory of the Son and the Spirit, viz. "the divinity that dwelt in him, and was in his person" (Edwards, "Notes on Scripture," no. 340, in *WJE* 15:325).

86. Edwards, 412. Sermon on Rev. 14:14 [Oct 1736], in *WJE* 51.

87. Edwards, "Miscellanies," no. 769, in *WJE* 18:415. As a consequence of the incarnation, there is "additional glory to God . . . a new manifestation of it" in both in heaven and on earth and in "a degree and manner inconceivable" to those on earth (Edwards, 51. Sermon on Luke 2:14, in *WJE* 42).

88. "But his exaltation was not limited to his human nature but appertains also to the divine nature not considered simply but as united to the human and manifestating [*sic*] itself in it. Not by conferring any new perfection or glory but by the manifestation of his Glory which was as it were hid and veil'd in his humbled state" (Edwards, 263. Sermon on Rev. 5:12, in *WJE* 47).

89. Edwards, 79. Sermon on Cant. 1:3 (a) (1728–29), in *WJE* 43. "'Tis an endearing consideration that all this divine excellency is *in* our nature; is united to humanity" (emphasis mine).

90. "The glory of the divine person was veiled in the meanness and sufferings of the human nature, but now shines forth gloriously in the exaltation of the human nature" (Edwards, "Miscellanies," no. 722, in *WJE* 18:351).

91. It is not surprising then that Reformed theologians, such as Bucan, regarded the *communicatio gratiarum* as a faithful appropriation of the patristic doctrine of *theōsis* and the medieval notion of *gratia habitualis* (Bucan II, 23, as quoted in Heppe, *Reformed Dogmatics*, 435). Hence, Barth rejected the notion of infused grace in Reformed dogmatics (citing Bucan specifically) as he deemed it a case of casting material "side-glances" at the Lutheran *genus maiestaticum* and on account of it possessing terminological similarities with the medieval *gratia habitualis*. In Barth's view, the Lutheran *genus maiestaticum* is the continuation of the patristic doctrine of *theōsis* pressed to its logical limits (Barth, "The Homecoming of the Son of Man," in *CD* IV.2, ch. 15, § 64, 2, 20ff.). Barth, according to Oh, rejected the *genus idiomaticum* and *gratiarum* due to their static and substantial ontology in favor of the relational *genus operationum* (Peter S. Oh, *Karl Barth's Trinitarian Theology: A Study in Karl Barth's Analogical Use of the Trinitarian Relation* [London: T&T Clark, 2006], 73–75).

92. According to Heron, the Lutherans ascribed the slogan *finitum non capax infiniti* to the Reformed theologians as a polemical contrast to their own *finitum capax infiniti*. See Alasdair Heron, "*Communicatio Idiomatum* and *Deificatio* of Human Nature: A Reformed Perspective," *Greek Orthodox Theological Review* 43, nos. 1–4 (Spring–Winter 1988): 368. Edwards would have encountered this scholastic dictum through his reading of Matthew Henry's works, particularly in his commentary on the Gospel of Luke. Henry explains the growth of graces in Christ as a progressive manifestation of the divine attributes, within and in proportion to the developing capacities of his human nature. "In the perfections of his divine nature there could be no increase; but this is meant of his human nature. . . . Though the Eternal Word was united to the human soul from his conception, yet the divinity that dwelt in him manifested itself to his humanity by

degrees, *ad modum recipientis—in proportion to his capacity*; as the faculties of his human soul grew more and more capable, the gifts it received from the divine nature were more and more communicated." See Matthew Henry, "An Exposition, with Practical Observations, of the Gospel according to St. Luke," ch. 2 of *Commentary on the Whole Bible*, vol. 5, *Matthew to John* (Grand Rapids, MI: Christian Classics Ethereal Library), ch. 2, 1067, http://www.ccel.org/ccel/henry/mhc5.html.

93. See Lars Thunberg, *Microcosm and Mediator: The Theological Anthropology of Maximus the Confessor*, 2nd ed. (Chicago: Open Court, 1995), 31; Vladimir Lossky, *The Mystical Theology of the Eastern Church* (Crestwood, NY: St. Vladimir's Seminary Press, 1997), 146; and, Hans Urs von Von Balthasar, *Cosmic Liturgy: The Universe According to Maximus the Confessor*, trans. Brian E. Daley (San Francisco: Ignatius Press, 2003), 254.

94. Goodwin, "The Glory of the Gospel," in *Thirteen Sermons, Works*, vol. 1, pt. 2, 66, as quoted by Edwards, "Miscellanies," no. 1278, in *WJE* 23:225. Since the incarnation is the "nighest kind of union" between Creator and creature, the communication between the natures must necessarily be the most intimate. The phrasing of the first citation is similar to that of John of Damascus, who thought that it was the "riches of the divine energies" that were communicated to the flesh of Christ "without entailing the loss of any of its natural attributes" (John of Damascus, *Orthodox Faith*, bk. 3, ch. 17, 66 [*NPNF* 9]). Other Puritans, like Watson, affirmed that the hypostatic union resulted in "a communication of all that glory from the deity to Christ as his human nature is capable of" (Thomas Watson, "Christ's Humiliation in His Incarnation," in *A body of practical divinity, consisting of above one hundred seventy six sermons on the lesser catechism . . .* [London: Thomas Parkhurst, 1692], q. 17, 119).

95. Watson, "Christ's Humiliation in His Incarnation," q. 17, 119.

96. Christ in his Humiliation descended so low, that it was not fit to go lower, and in his Exaltation he ascended so high, that it is not possible to go higher" (Watson, "Christ's Humiliation in His Incarnation," q. 17, 119).

97. "The Saints have no Grace to spare to others; but Christ diffuseth his Grace to others. Grace in the Saints is as Water in the Vessel, Grace in Christ is as Water in the Spring" (Watson, "Christ the Mediator of the Covenant," in *A Body of Practical Divinity*, 95).

98. Christ's exalted human nature goes through no essential change and so "can neither be every where, nor together in many places, nor in the same place with an other body *Penetrative*" (William Ames, *Marrow of Sacred Divinity Drawne Out of the Holy Scriptures, and the Interpreters thereof, and Brought into Method* [London: Henry Overton, 1642], ch. 23, 106).

99. Edwards, "Miscellanies," no. 81, in *WJE* 13:248.

100. Ibid.

101. If the earlier sacramental controversy centered on the cupola of the *hoc est corpus meum*, the later seventeenth-century Lutheran-Reformed debates over the constitution of Christ's body were finally anthropological disagreements. While both were united in rejecting the docetism of the medieval church, the Lutherans stressed the ultimacy and essential character of the ideal—the glorified body—in contrast to the Reformed emphasis on its present, empirical form, which awaits final spiritualization. For Dorner, the Reformed belief that "the body will assume spiritual qualities" can only be accidental to, and finally contradicts, its fundamental anthropology, which assumes actual, empirical conditions as its starting point (Dorner, *Person of Christ*, 2.2:246). Whether the Reformed tradition was guilty of advancing a natural, rather than biblical, anthropology is debatable. Clearly, they were intent on defending the *homoousios to anthropos* apart from the Alexandrian-Cyrillian soteriology that funded Chalcedon. The Lutherans, while extending the patristic idea of *theōsis*, speculatively advanced the idea of the transfigured humanity beyond its apophatic reserve and doctrinal elasticity.

102. "Could not those superior principles be in vastly greater strength at first, and yet be capable of endless improvement? And what should hinder its being so ordered by the Creator, that they should improve by vastly swifter degrees than they do?" (Edwards, *WJE* 3:203).

103. Edwards, "Miscellanies," no. 81, in *WJE* 13:248.

104. Edwards refers to these two forms of life as two "understandings," and not two *self*-consciousnesses (which Edwards terms "consciousness") in Christ, since the latter would be crypto-Nestorian. The dangers of monophysitism and monotheletism are present only on the premise of a single, divine center of consciousness, volition, and action. See Karl Rahner, *Foundations of the Christian Faith: An Introduction to the Idea of Christianity*, trans. William V. Dych (New York: Crossroad, 1978), 292. Clearly, Rahner's conception of a human Jesus adoring the Word makes the incarnation a union of two *egos*: "The human nature of Christ possesses . . . a human self-consciousness, which as creaturely faces the eternal Word in a genuinely human attitude of adoration, obedience, and a most radical sense of creaturehood." See Karl Rahner, "Current Problems in Christology," in *Theological Investigations*, vol. 1, *God, Christ, Mary and Grace*, trans. with intro. Cornelius Ernst, 2nd ed. (London: Darton, Longman & Todd, 1965), 158. Scotus's Christology, as developed by Cross, moves in this direction as well, since "the human Jesus and the second person of the Trinity can engage in dialogue and conversation" (Cross, *Metaphysics of the Incarnation*, 316).

105. Bernard Lonergan has suggested that Christ is not to be discerned as ontologically one and psychologically two, but both ontologically and psychologically one and two, in different senses. Christ is psychologically one as that identical Ego who is self-conscious as a divine person in both divine and human ways. At the same time, Christ is psychologically two as humanly aware of self-existence as human and also divinely aware of self-existence as God. See Bernard J. Lonergan, Collected Works of Bernard Lonergan, vol. 7, *The Ontological and Psychological Constitution of Christ*, trans. 4th ed. of *De constitutione Christi ontologica et psychologica* by Michael G. Shields (Toronto: University of Toronto Press for Lonergan Research Institute of Regis College, 2002), 221.

106. "And hence it was necessary that the beatific knowledge, which consists in the vision of God, should belong to Christ pre-eminently, since the cause ought always to be more efficacious than the effect" (Aquinas, *STh* III, q. 9, a. 2).

107. While Christ's *non posse peccare* is affirmed, the Reformed insistence on the *finitum non capax infiniti* and the real humanity of Christ compelled them to reject the attribution of omniscience and beatific knowledge to Christ in Christ's earthly state (Heppe, *Reformed Dogmatics*, 435–38).

108. Weinandy rightly characterizes any beatific vision of Jesus as falling within the Nestorian ambit: "It is an objective vision, a 'seeing' or 'contemplating,' of the divine essence that not only stands ontologically distinct from, but also then over against, the one 'seeing' or 'contemplating.'" See Thomas G. Weinandy, "Jesus' Filial Vision of the Father," *Pro Ecclesia* 13, no. 2 (Spring 2004): 190. Aquinas seems to lapse into a reification of the natures when he affirms that Jesus has an objective beatific vision, whereby "the soul of Christ . . . sees God in essence" (Aquinas, *STh* III, q. 9, a. 2). Yet, he elsewhere speaks of Jesus' preeminent (but not comprehensive) knowledge of things in subjective, not objective, terms, inasmuch as "the soul of Christ knows all things in the Word" (*STh* III, q. 10, a. 2). In Weinandy's attempt at securing an evolving filial vision in Jesus (from *viator* to *comprehensor*), his charge that the tradition posited an earthly Jesus who possessed "a comprehensive vision of the divine essence" is too sweeping (Weinandy, "Jesus' Filial Vision," 198).

109. "Hence that BEATIFICAL VISION that the saints have of God in heaven, is in beholding the manifestations that he makes of himself . . . in his Son" (Edwards, "Miscellanies," no. 777, in *WJE* 18:427). Not all the three divine persons are perceived: "There is to be seen a glorious heavenly Father, a glorious Redeemer; there is to be felt and possessed a glorious Sanctifier" (Edwards, "Sermon Fifteen: Heaven Is a World of Love," in *WJE* 8:370). Edwards's notion of the divine light is closer to the Eastern than to the Latin conception in his affirmation of the inaccessibility of the divine essence. Hence, the beatific vision of the saints is a "mediate," not an "immediate sight of God" (Edwards, "Miscellanies," no. 777, in *WJE* 18:428).

110. While the *visio Dei* can be had by the saints through the humanity of the Son, nonetheless it corresponds to the divine perception of the angels, and even of God, in its *per filium*

character. For, according to Edwards, the Father has self-knowledge *only* in viewing the Son (though the Father's self-perception is of the *Logos asarkos*). "Yea, 'tis by this image only that God sees himself, for he sees himself in his own perfect substantial idea" (Edwards, "Miscellanies," no. 335, in *WJE* 15:319).

111. Aquinas, *STh* III, q. 9, a. 3

112. Edwards, "Miscellanies," no. 777, in *WJE* 18:427. "An immediate and intuitive view of any mind, if it be consequent and dependent on the prior existence of what is viewed in that mind, is the very same with consciousness. . . . For there is no difference between immediate seeing ideas, and immediate having them."

113. Ibid.

114. However, for "two spirits" to constitute "the same individual person," the human nature will need to have a perfect, direct perception of another mind, "a full idea of all was necessarily constantly excited in the one consequent on its being in the other, and beheld as in the other." Ibid.

115. Suppose such an intuitive knowledge is had "not so constantly, but only for a season, there would be for a season an union of personality." And if this direct knowledge is "not fully perceived, but only in some degree," there will only be "an union of personality in some degree." Ibid., 427-28.

116. "Consciousness is the mind's perceiving what is in itself—its ideas, actions, passions, and everything that is there perceivable. It is a sort of feeling within itself. The mind feels when it thinks, so it feels when it desires, feels when it loves, feels itself hate, etc." (Edwards, "The Mind," in *WJE* 6:345). See also Richard R. Niebuhr, "Being and Consent," in *The Princeton companion to Jonathan Edwards*, ed. Sang Hyun Lee (Princeton, NJ: Princeton University Press, 2005), 36.

117. Edwards, "Miscellanies," no. 777, in *WJE* 18:427. "Therefore, there is no creature can thus have an immediate sight of God, but only Jesus Christ, who is in the bosom of God."

118. Ibid., 428.

119. "And if we come even to the personal identity of created intelligent beings, though this be not allowed to consist wholly in that which Mr. Locke places it in, i.e. same consciousness; yet I think it can't be denied, that this is one thing essential to it" (Edwards, *WJE* 3:398). His basic agreement with Locke was theologically modified to assert that the continuance of ideas did not so much lie in the person, but in God's free constitution of natural laws to establish such continuity. "Concerning IDENTITY," Edwards explains, "an old man has the same consciousness that he had in his youth, but that very consciousness itself depends on sovereign, arbitrary constitution" (Edwards, "Controversies" Notebook, in *WJE* 27). Since all creation exists anew moment by moment by *creatio continua*, this sameness of identity is also assured by "the arbitrary constitution of the Creator; who . . . so unites these successive new effects, that he treats them as one, by communicating to them like properties, relations, and circumstances" (Edwards, *WJE* 3:398). Otherwise, "if there were individual perceptions, the different, individual, created perceptions at individual moments could have no relation one to another: there would be no memory, no identity of person or consciousness at all" (Edwards, "Subjects of Inquiry," in *WJE* 28).

120. Edwards, "Miscellanies," no. 205, in *WJE* 13:340. "Therefore we often find Christ speaking as being very well acquainted with the Father before he came into the world, and speaking of the transactions betwixt him and the Father before he came, as if there were an agreement about the work of redemption, what he should teach, what he should do and who should be his."

121. With the caveat that "the particular manner of this consciousness, and how far the ideas of a creature can be after the manner of the divine, and how a creature may be said to remember what is in God, is uncertain" (Edwards, "Miscellanies," no. 205, in *WJE* 1:341).

122. Ibid., 341, 340. As the mode of reception is the understanding, so *quidquid percipitur ad modum percipientis percipitur.* This we shall look at more closely in the chapter on grace.

123. Ibid., 340.

124. Except, of course, if one uses "memory" in a broader sense to include a kind of eternal, tenseless knowledge of all times and places.

125. Edwards, "Miscellanies," no. 205, in *WJE* 13:340. Edwards echoes Sherlock here, who affirmed that Jesus was self-aware of an identity as the divine Word "as far as its nature is capable," yet it cannot be the case "that the human nature is conscious to all that is in the Word," for otherwise it would then be omniscient. "And therefore the human nature in Christ is in some measure, in such a degree, as human nature can be, conscious to the Word, feels its union to God, and knows the mind of the Word, not by external revelations, as prophets do, but by an inward sensation, as every man feels his own thoughts and reason; but yet the human nature of Christ may be ignorant of some things, notwithstanding its personal union to the divine Word, because it is an inferior, and subject nature" (William Sherlock, *A vindication of the doctrine of the holy and ever blessed Trinity, and the incarnation of the Son of God . . .* [London: W. Rogers, 1690], 269–70). This is similar to the position advocated by Coffey in his "The Theandric Nature of Christ," *Theological Studies* 60, no. 3 (September 1999): 419–20.

126. "In memory, in mental principles, habits and inclinations, there is something really abiding in the mind when there are no acts or exercises of them, much in the same manner as there is a chair in this room when no mortal perceives it. For when we say there are chairs in this room when none perceives it, we mean that minds would perceive chairs here according to the law of nature in such circumstances. So, when we say a person has these and those things laid up in his memory, we mean they would actually be repeated in his mind upon some certain occasions according to the law of nature; though we cannot describe particularly the law of nature about these mental acts, so well as we can about other things" (Edwards, "The Mind," in *WJE* 6:385). Lee has made much of this line of thought in Edwards in his *Philosophical Theology*, esp. 42–46. This motif of virtuality is evident in Edwards's doctrine of imputation and perseverance.

127. In other words, Edwards continues, the Spirit is the agent "of the union of these understandings" (Edwards, "Miscellanies," no. 766, in *WJE* 18:412–13).

128. According to Aquinas, "there is in [Christ's] soul . . . an infused or imprinted knowledge, whereby He knows things in their proper nature by intelligible species proportioned to the human mind" (Aquinas, *STh* III, q. 9, a. 3). This is knowledge of all that is actual, but not all all that is possible or all that is in the future.

129. "And it is certain that the person of Jesus Christ knew every particular believer when he laid down his life, had them in his actual view. He knew how many sins they had committed, or would commit, and what misery their sins deserved" (Edwards, 91. Sermon on Gal. 2:20 [1728], in *WJE* 43). Jesus knew of Judas's betrayal but treated him as an apostle until his betrayal came to light, as an example of pastoral ethics. Hence, "though Christ knew [Judas], yet he did not then clothe himself with the character of omniscient judge, and searcher of hearts, but acted the part of a minister of the visible church of God (for he was his Father's minister)" (Edwards, "The Distinguishing Marks," in *WJE* 4:245). Christ knew that Judas had neither saving grace nor "moral sincerity" (Edwards, "Lectures on the Qualifications for Full Communion in the Church of Christ," in *WJE* 25:421).

130. Edwards, 91. Sermon on Gal. 2:20 (1728), in *WJE* 43.

131. Edwards, "Subjects of Inquiry," in *WJE* 28.

132. Ibid.

133. So, "if we had all secrets recorded and clearly explained in a dictionary that we could turn to immediately we should not properly be infinite in knowledge. This may serve for a faint resemblance." Ibid. The same goes for the divine power and will. It is not divine knowledge transfused into and inhering in Jesus' mind. Instead of divine knowledge directed toward the human, it is Jesus' mind accessing the infinite mind within Jesus' own person.

134. Ibid.

135. If a normal human mind could hold together two different ideas in judgment, why should it be impossible for the glorified, enlarged mind of Jesus "to be exercised about millions of millions of ideas, with as great intenseness and clearness of apprehension" so as to simultaneously

"think on," and so love "all the saints in the world"? (Edwards, "Miscellanies," no. 777, in *WJE* 18:427).

136. Edwards, "Miscellanies," no. 81, in *WJE* 13:248; italics mine.

137. "Concerning the grand objection from that text, 'of that day and hour knoweth no man, nor the angels in heaven, nor the Son, but the Father' [Matt. 24:36; Mark 13:32], I would observe that even the Arians themselves, with regard to some things said of Christ, must make the distinction between his power or knowledge as to his inferior and superior nature. Or, if they don't allow two natures, then at least as to his humbled state, and his state both before and after his humiliation; as Mark 7:24, 'and would have no man know it: but he could not be hid.' This can't mean that the person who created the whole world, visible and invisible, etc., and by whom all consist and are governed, had not power to order things so that he might be hid" (Edwards, "Miscellanies," no. 1352, in *WJE* 23:634–36).

138. This would be similar to the manner in which Jesus remembers the eternal actions of the Logos. "His idea was finite, otherwise he could not pray that he might have the same glory again; for the man did not desire infinite glory, but he desired such glory as he remembered, that was the same as God the Son had, as near as the same could be communicated, either in conception or enjoyment, to Christ the creature" (Edwards, "Miscellanies," no. 205, in *WJE* 13:341).

139. Unlike "mere humans," Jesus had the divine nature to sustain it and so was "indefeatible and impeccable." But, like other human beings, "the human nature of Christ when he was upon earth was subject to many changes . . . not only with a change in his body by his increasing in stature but also in his mind" (Edwards, 470. Sermon on 1 Cor. 13:1-10 [b], in *WJE* 53).

140. Hence, "the principles of human nature should be so balanced, that the consequence should be no propensity to sin . . . in Adam, when first created, and also in the man Christ Jesus; though the faculties of the latter were such as grew by culture and improvement, so that he increased in wisdom, as he grew in stature" (Edwards, *WJE* 3:203–4). For Aquinas, Jesus had acquired knowledge as a knowledge by discovery, for as Teacher, Jesus was not taught (Aquinas, *STh* III, q. 9, a. 4). Thomas changed his mind on this (*III Sent.*, D, xiv, 3; D, xviii, 3), as he himself admits in this article.

141. "Though the man Christ Jesus knew that he was the most excellent and honorable of all men, yea, of all creatures, yet was he the most humble" (Edwards, "Miscellanies," no. 791, in *WJE* 18:489).

142. Commenting on Col. 1:15-19, Edwards is arguing for a distinction between the human nature of Christ and the rest of creation, viz., that the former was more immediately the work of God the Father and the latter, the Son (as examined in chapter 3):"Though the man Christ Jesus be a creature, the chief of all creatures, yet at the same time that 'tis asserted of him that he created all things visible and invisible, yet there is an evident distinction made between this firstborn of every creature that is the maker, and all things in heaven and earth, visible and invisible, that are made by him." Nonetheless, he makes it clear that: "The things that are here spoken of Christ are spoken of him *as God-man*, either so actually, or so by constitution or immutable undertaking and appointment. All things are from him *as God-man*, but he him [self] as God-man is from the Father" (Edwards, "Miscellanies," no. 958, in *WJE* 20:238; italics mine). Edwards, therefore, never intended to give "full shock value to the proposition" that Jesus *as creature* was the Creator, according to Jenson's contention that Edwards held to a mutual and real communication between the natures (Jenson, *America's Theologian*, 115).

143. The *communicatio* effects a unilateral transformation of the humanity, while the divinity remains "itself impassible and without participation in the affections of the flesh" (John of Damascus, *Orthodox Faith*, bk. 4, ch. 6, 52 [*NPNF* 9]).

144. "Kenosis" is used of the hypostatic union in relation to the divine nature and is correlated to other terms like "incarnation, becoming man, humility" (John of Damascus, *Orthodox Faith*, bk. 4, ch. 18, 91 [*NPNF* 9]). While these are necessary conditions of the union and "are

imposed on the Word and God through the flesh," Christ, nonetheless, "endured these things in person of His own free will."

145. *New Schaff-Herzog Encyclopedia of Religious Knowledge*, vol. 3.8, s.v. "The Scholastic Lutheran Christology." Luther affirmed a real ethical development in the life of Christ neither through a depotentiation of the Logos nor a voluntary restriction of the divine powers of the God-man, whose humanity was completely deified from conception (Dorner, *History of the Development*, 2.2:94–95).

146. The Giessen theologians, as is well-known, compromised on the divinity of the Logos in the *exinanitio*. They rightly asked, how could two sets of opposing attributes coexist in a single common nature? Thomasius, for example, affirmed a divestment of those divine attributes related *ad extra* at the *unitio* in order to preserve the humanity in the *unio*. On this account, as Baillie notes, the Trinitarian *opera indivisa* is abandoned, the *factum est* is but a literal mutation of the divinity, and the Chalcedonian double *homoousia* would not be simultaneous but successive. The first point Baillie attributes to William Temple's observation in *Christus Veritas*. As to the second point, what Baillie terms a "temporary theophany" is granting too much, since the earthly Christ is, at best, a partial and deficient revelation of the glorified Christ. See Donald M. Baillie, *God Was in Christ: An Essay on Incarnation and Atonement* (New York: Charles Scribner's Sons, 1948; reprint, Eugene, OR: Wipf and Stock, 2001), 94–98. The classical use of the term "theophany" as applied to Christ's baptism and transfiguration affirms a real, though temporary, self-revelation of the Trinity. These moments constitute a subjective, proleptic, noetic appropriation of Christ's divinity, veiled in the *exinanitio* but nonetheless ontically and fully present to the humanity at the *unitio*, perduring in the *unio*, and fully evident in the *exaltatio*. Moreover, *kenosis* as divestment of divine attributes makes the *genus maiestaticum* absurd. Surely, a divine essence emptied of its properties would have nothing to communicate to the assumed humanity! Yet, even in the kenoticists, the adherence to divine impassibility was still implicit although immutability can in no wise be predicated of the Logos with the depotentiation of its relative attributes. Not only does this contradict the Formula of Concord, but as Ritschl rhetorically put it: "For how can the incarnation of the Logos invest the human nature with those very attributes which the Logos in His union with the human nature no longer possesses?" See Albrecht Ritschl, *The Christian Doctrine of Justification and Reconciliation: The Positive Development of the Doctrine*, trans. H. R. Mackintosh and A. B. Macaulay (Continuum Books, 1966; reprint, Eugene, OR: Wipf and Stock, 2002), 410.

147. Edwards, "Miscellanies," no. 1358, in *WJE* 23:609.

148. Ibid.

149. Ibid. This presumes not an essential divine-human opposition, but a polarity between divinity and humanity *in via*, as the exalted Jesus assumes the role of Creator once again. Such a thesis assumes a nontimeless eternity.

150. Edwards, "Miscellanies," no. 1349, in *WJE* 23:608.

151. Edwards, "Miscellanies," no. 958, in *WJE* 20:234–39. "But is there any ground to suppose such a mighty change as this as to the Author of the universe, its having such different authors of its being and of all its properties, natural principles and motions and alterations and events, both in bodies and all created minds, for one, three, or four and thirty years, from what it had ever before or since? Have we any hint of such a thing?" (Edwards, "Miscellanies," no. 1352, in *WJE* 23:609).

152. Just as the divine glory cannot be increased, so "when Christ was in the greatest degree of his humiliation, the glory and happiness of the divine nature of Christ was not diminished" (Edwards, 412. Sermon on Rev. 14:14, in *WJE* 51).

153. During Calvin's and Vermigli's time, Stancaro argued that Christ was Mediator in human nature only. He drew this conclusion from his reading of Augustine, which found its particular interpretation in Lombard, Bonaventure, and Aquinas. See Stephen Edmondson, *Calvin's Christology* (Cambridge: Cambridge University Press, 2004), 16–39.

154. Slater, "Salvation as Participation," 46.

155. "All these receive glory from his unchangeableness. For if Christ were never so glorious, yet if he were changeable and he did not know how soon he might lose his glory, he would not be so worthy that creatures should entirely set their hearts on him" (Edwards, 79. Sermon on Cant. 1:3 [a] in *WJE* 43).

156. A divine person, being "infinitely worthy and glorious" as well as "happy and blessed," neither deserves to suffer nor should experience pain (Edwards, 195. Sermon on Ps. 108:4, in *WJE* 46). It is axiomatic for Edwards that "God is not subject to passion" (Edwards, "God Is Infinitely Exalted in Gloriousness and Excellency above All Created Beings," in *WJE* 10:432). Clearly affirming divine impassibility but with an Antiochene overtone, Edwards states that "the Logos felt nothing, no pain, and suffered no disgrace, but 'twas the human nature [that suffered]" (Edwards, "Miscellanies," no. 180, in *WJE* 13:327). Edwards is here referring to the divine nature *in concreto* and the human nature *in abstracto*. On Cross's analysis, Edwards uses a parts-Christology to affirm both possibility and impassibility in Christ. This, he thinks, is untenable because human properties must be attributed to the whole Christ *simpliciter*, since "a minimal requirement for the doctrine of the Incarnation is that the divine person possess human mental states and acts." To truly have experiences, Christ must not only have access to the human states but must own these properties without qualification (Richard Cross, "Parts and Properties in Christology," in *Reason, Faith and History: Philosophical Essays for Paul Helm*, ed. Martin F. Stone [Aldershot, UK: Ashgate, 2008], 191–92). Cross aligns the meriological approach to the body-soul analogy ("Incarnation, Omnipresence, and Action at a Distance," *Neue Zeitschrift für Systematische Theologie und Religionphilosophie* 45, no. 3 [2003]: 303n18). Edwards, following Aquinas, uses the reduplicative strategy to describe "the death of God himself in the human nature of the second Person in the Trinity" (Edwards, "The Importance of a Future State," in *WJE* 10:366). This use of "borrowed properties" is both logically and psychologically coherent. Christ, qua human, suffers, while Christ, qua divine, is impassible. See Eleonore Stump, *Aquinas*, Arguments of the Philosophers (London: Routledge, 2003), ch. 14, 407–26.

157. Edwards, "Miscellanies," no. z, in *WJE* 13:176–77.

158. Edwards, *WJE* 1:268. God "comprehends all things, from eternity to eternity, in one, most perfect, and unalterable view; so that his whole eternal duration is *vitae interminabilis, tota, simul*, and *perfecta possessio*." The idea of an omniscient and "infinite Eternal" implies immutability and "duration without succession" in God (Edwards, "Miscellanies," no. 1340, in *WJE* 23:371). Edwards emphasizes the utter mystery and apparent contradictions in our notion of the divine attributes in order to argue for the necessity of revelation (ibid.).

159. Edwards, 107. Sermon on Num. 23:19 (1729), in *WJE* 44.

160. Ibid.

161. On the contrary, far from affirming that divine, impassible love changed into possible love, Edwards uses "become" in the Chalcedonian sense of assumption without alteration. John of Damascus reminds us "that we say that God suffered in the flesh, but never that His divinity suffered in the flesh, or that God suffered through the flesh. For if, when the sun is shining upon a tree, and, nevertheless, the sun remains uncleft and void of passion, much more will the passionless divinity of the Word, united in subsistence to the flesh, remain void of passion when the body undergoes passion" (John of Damascus, *Orthodox Faith*, bk. 3, ch. 26, 71 [*NPNF* 9]).

162. The Damascene illustrates the point: just as water would extinguish the fiery heat in an incandescent iron without affecting it, the divine nature is similarly untouched by Christ's human suffering. Here, he reverses his usual application of the flaming sword metaphor (without forgetting to affirm the inadequacy of all metaphorical language), where fire "naturally suffers by water" and is "quenched, but the steel remains untouched" (John of Damascus, *Orthodox Faith*, bk. 3, ch. 26, 71 [*NPNF* 9]). This illustration was picked up by the Puritans: "*Damascen* expresseth it by this simile; If one pour water on iron that is red hot, the fire suffers by the water, and is extinguished, but the iron doth not suffer. So the human nature of Christ might suffer death, but the divine nature is not capable of any passion." See Thomas Watson, *The holy eucharist: Or, the*

mystery of the Lords supper. Briefly explained (London: Printed by E. M. for Ralph Smith, 1665), 13–14.

163. Edwards, "Miscellanies," no. 180, in *WJE* 13:327.

164. Edwards, "Miscellanies," no. z, in *WJE* 13:176–77.

165. The *communicatio* effects a unilateral transformation of the humanity, while the divinity remains "itself impassible and without participation in the affections of the flesh" (John of Damascus, *Orthodox Faith*, bk. 4, ch. 6, 52 [*NPNF* 9]).

166. Edwards, "Miscellanies," no. 180, in *WJE* 13:327. "How much soever the lover gives or communicates to the beloved, yet if he is at no expense to himself, there is not that high and noble expression of love, as if otherwise."

167. Edwards, "Miscellanies," no. 180, in *WJE* 13:327.

168. The wickedness of human beings, Edwards preaches, went so far as "even to kill God by their killing that person that was God. They could not kill the divine nature; but when God took flesh upon him and became man, that they could kill" (Edwards, 111. Sermon on Ps. 18:26 [1729], in *WJE* 44).

169. Not only did he suffer great physical pain and shame, he suffered death in its worst form and "was willing to suffer in his soul darkness and agony that was beyond all pain of body" (Edwards, 195. Sermon on Ps. 108:4, in *WJE* 46). Meyendorff points out that God is both essence, immutable and beyond participation, and person, taking on a new mode of existence and becoming passible. He notes a similarity between the Eastern emphasis on personhood as an "open" category and Karl Rahner's recovery of "a pre-Augustinian concept of God" and the openness of the human being. This is set in contrast to "the old Thomistic notion of God's immutability," which failed to secure "the real distinction" between essence and persons of the Trinity, since the latter were thought of as mere "internal relations in the divine essence." See John Meyendorff, *Christ in Eastern Christian Thought* (Washington, DC: Corpus, 1969), 164–66.

170. As Christ obeyed and suffered "in our nature," by virtue of the *communicatio idiomatum*, Edwards proclaims that, on the cross, "there is the Eternal God suffering for his own fallen creatures that they might be happy and not miserable" (Edwards, 79. Sermon on Cant. 1:3 [a] [1728] in *WJE* 43).

171. Edwards, "Miscellanies," no. 327 (a), in *WJE* 13:406. Thus the emanation of the "infinite love of the Father to the Son" is revealed in the Father's forgiveness of humanity's "infinite debt" and their exaltation to Christ's "mediatorial glory." And the remanation of the Son's love to the Father is manifested in Christ "infinitely abasing himself for the vindicating of his authority and the honor of his majesty" (ibid.).

172. For Edwards, "divine virtue, or the virtue of the divine mind, must consist primarily in love to himself" (Edwards, "Nature of True Virtue," in *WJE* 8:557).

173. Since "holy love" is both a "divine affection, and an habitual disposition to it," the Holy Spirit is the divine Affection in God (Edwards, *WJE* 2:107). Passion, in Edwards's definition, involves the sensitive and appetitive faculties and cannot be experienced by God (Edwards, "Miscellanies," no. 81, in *WJE* 13:247). He makes a clear distinction between affection and passion, similar to that of Augustine and Aquinas. See Anastasia Scrutton, "Emotion in Augustine of Hippo and Thomas Aquinas: A Way Forward for the Im/passibility Debate?" *International Journal of Systematic Theology* 7, no. 2 (April 2005): 169–77.

174. Edwards, 52. Sermon on Luke 2:14 (b), in *WJE* 42.

175. "[Y]et it don't hence follow, nor is it true, that God has no real and proper delight, pleasure or happiness, in any of his acts or communications relative to the creature; or effects he produces in them; or in anything he sees in the creature's qualifications, dispositions, actions and state" (Edwards, "Concerning the End," in *WJE* 8:446).

176. "It was needfull [*sic*] that he should be not only God but man for as he was God he was not capable of suffering. He became man that he might suffer and therefore as soon as he became man he began to suffer. He was born to this end that he might die and therefore he did as it were

begin to die as soon as he was born" (Edwards, 414. Sermon on Isa. 53:3 [b] [November 1736], in *WJE* 51).

177. Here, "passion" is that "which ordinarily signifies nothing absolute, but merely the relation of being acted upon" (Edwards, *WJE* 1:348). Being acted upon may result in "passions," which tend to be "more sudden, and whose effects on the animal spirits are more violent, and the mind more overpowered, and less in its own command" (Edwards, *WJE* 2:98). Similarly, John of Damascus defines passion as "a sensible activity of the appetitive faculty, depending on the presentation to the mind of something good or bad." Not all the activities that come from the passionate part of the soul are passions, only the "more violent ones," which cause sensation. However, passion is not self-moved and is "an irrational activity" of the disordered soul, whereas a nature true to itself has energy, or a "movement in harmony with nature" (John of Damascus, *Orthodox Faith*, bk. 2, ch. 22, 36 [*NPNF* 9]).

178. Edwards's definition of true affections as "the more vigorous and sensible exercises of the inclination and will of the soul" rules out mere feelings or choices that lack intensity or consistency (Edwards, *WJE* 2:98).

179. Edwards, "Miscellanies," no. z, in *WJE* 13:176–77.

180. Edwards, "Miscellanies," no. 81, in *WJE* 13:247. Since it is humanly possible to compare two ideas, Edwards argues, they need not be successive. If two ideas can exist simultaneously, then one could posit the simultaneity of "millions of millions of ideas" in Jesus' glorified mind.

181. Edwards, "The Sacrifice of Christ Acceptable," in *WJE* 14:452.

182. The suffering of the damned is quantitatively more than Christ's because Christ "had the divinity to support him" and "knew that his sufferings would soon be at an end and then he should enter into eternal joy and glory" (Edwards, 414. Sermon on Isa. 53:3 [b] [November 1736], in *WJE* 51). Yet Christ's suffering "was equivalent to infinite suffering for it was infinite expense," insofar as the human Jesus, who died, was God incarnate. Just as "his life was the life of that Person that was the eternal Son of God 'tho it was the life of the human nature," so "his blood which he spilled his life which he laid down was an infinite price because it was the blood of God" (Edwards, "The Sacrifice of Christ Acceptable," in *WJE* 14:452).

183. "We have not only not to deny but actually to affirm and understand as essential to the being of God the offensive fact that there is in God Himself an above and a below, a prius and a posterius, a superiority and a subordination." See Karl Barth, "The Obedience of the Son of God," § 59, in *Church Dogmatics*, vol. 4, pt. 1, *The Doctrine of Reconciliation*, ed. G. W. Bromiley and T. F. Torrance, trans. G. W. Bromiley (Edinburgh: T&T Clark, 1956), 200–201.

184. "Christ had some excellencies in his human nature of a different denomination from any in his divine, such as humility and meekness and the like. 'Tho they are from the communication of the same light and holiness; 'tis the same light reflected but as 'tis reflected it appears in a manner agreeable to the nature and state of a creature" (Edwards, 288. Sermon on Cant. 1:3 [b], in *WJE* 48).

185. Edwards defines humility as "a person's sense of his own comparative lowness and littleness before God or the great difference between God and the subject of this virtue" (Edwards, "The Excellency of Christ," in *WJE* 19:568).

186. "For Christ merely as God was not capable either of that obedience or suffering that was needful. The divine nature is not capable of suffering, for it is impassable and infinitely above all suffering; neither is it capable of obedience to that law that was given to man" (Edwards, "No. 5 Sermon Fourteen," in *WJE* 9:295–96).

187. Edwards, 406. Sermon on Rev. 5:5-6 (Aug 1736), in *WJE* 51. Similarly, the "wisdom and holiness that Christ hath in his human nature is but a participation of the wisdom and holiness of the eternal Word in the measure [of] and exercised after the manner of a creature" (Edwards, 288. Sermon on Cant. 1:3 [b], in *WJE* 48).

188. "And humility is the nearest and most proper conformity to the condescension of God that can be in a creature" (Edwards, "Charity and Its Fruits," sermon 3, in *WJE* 8:247). "Christ is

one who is God-man, and so has not only condescension which is a divine perfection, but also humility which is a creature excellence" (ibid.).

189. "Indeed, it would have been fitting and excellent in him, that his will and his actions should be conformed to the Father's will and be subject to him, as it is in itself fit and excellent that the Logos itself should love the Father, and that the Father should love the Son" (Edwards, "Miscellanies," no. 454, in *WJE* 13:499). He anticipates von Balthasar on this point; see Nicholas J. Healy, *The Eschatology of Hans Urs von Balthasar: Being as Communion*, Oxford Theological Monographs (New York: Oxford University Press, 2005), 107.

190. As Danaher correctly notes, "Edwards offers a new way to conceive of the *communicatio idiomatum*: The proper correlate to the love of the divine nature in the person of Christ is a human nature in which love is expressed in self-sacrifice." See William J. Danaher Jr., *The Trinitarian Ethics of Jonathan Edwards*, Columbia Series in Reformed Theology (Louisville, KY: Westminster John Knox, 2004), 82. Yet, as we have shown, Edwards did not abandon the patristic way of antinomically attributing passibility and impassibility of the two natures in Christ. Danaher interprets Cyril of Alexandria using Pope Leo's more Antiochene distinction of natures, thus minimizing Cyril's insistence on the incarnate Logos as the proper subject of all human and divine acts (and not the semi-Nestorian characterization of the two natures), and the philantrophic character of the divine *oikonomia*.

191. As to God's power, justice, wisdom, and mercy, "it is fit that the divine attributes should have exercise" (Edwards, "Miscellanies," no. 553, in *WJE* 18:97).

192. "So the mercy and love of Christ receive a great addition of glory from the greatness and infinite happiness. It is more wonderful and admirable to see one that is infinitely high, and mighty and happy; to be full of pity, full of love, of tender compassion, infinite in loving kindness and tender mercies" (Edwards, 288. Sermon on Cant. 1:3 [b], in *WJE* 48).

193. "Although Christ hereby humbled himself and veiled his glory with flesh, yet it issued in the more bright discovery of it" (Edwards, 118. Sermon on Cant. 8:1, in *WJE* 44).

194. Ibid.

195. Edwards, "Miscellanies," no. 741, in *WJE* 18:371. Edwards certainly considered the incarnation to be a greater mystery than spiritual regeneration, especially "that Christ, a heavenly and divine person, should die." These are "doctrines or truths" taught by Christ to Nicodemus (Edwards, "Miscellanies," no. 839, in *WJE* 20:55).

196. Grasped subjectively in faith, Christ's humiliation does not diminish but rather "illustrate his divine glory and make it appear in a stronger light" (Edwards, 79. Sermon on Cant. 1:3 [a], in *WJE* 43). "To see such infinite majesty and excellency, and such external meanness united in one person tends to fix the view of the mind with the more intenseness upon the two extremes and his divine brightness shine with the more strength if we compare it with his outward obscurity."

197. "He was, in some sense, cut off from the glory that he had with the Father before the world was, during his humbled state" (Edwards, "Images of Divine Things," no. 166, in *WJE* 11:110).

198. "Christ as God he is unchangeable in his glory. . . . When Christ was in the greatest degree of his humiliation, the glory and happiness of the divine nature of Christ was not diminished." (Edwards, 412. Sermon on Rev. 14:14 [Oct 1736], in *WJE* 51). "He is possessed of the same glory from eternity to eternity which can neither be added to nor diminished. . . . And so neither when he is exalted is the glory of the divine nature added to." Ibid.

199. "Christ did as it were leave his Father in order to obtain and be joined to the church; he came down from heaven, and did as it were leave the bosom of his Father" (Edwards, "Notes on Scripture," no. 232, in *WJE* 15:181). Edwards is implying a "descent without descending" with his "as it were" terminology.

200. The "glory of the divine nature of Christ is not separated from the human nature but it shines forth through the human nature, and the glory that Christ is exalted to is too great a glory for any mere creature" (Edwards, 412. Sermon on Rev. 14:14 [Oct 1736], in *WJE* 51). Christ's

"flesh, or the infirmity and imperfection of his human nature, was the veil that hid the glory of God" (Edwards, "Notes on Scripture," no. 340, in *WJE* 15:325).

201. "For as the sun has his light veiled by his conjunction with the moon in its darkness, so Christ had his glory veiled by his conjunction, or union, with our nature in its low and broken state. As the moon proves a veil to hide the glory of the sun, so the flesh of Christ was a veil that hid his divine glory" (Edwards, "Notes on Scripture," no. 315, in *WJE* 15:291).

202. "When Christ took the human nature upon him, he veiled his glory. The bright and strong light of the glory within, which otherwise would have been too strong for the feeble sight and frail eyes of men, was moderated, and as it were allayed and softened, to make it tolerable for mortals to behold" (Edwards, "Notes on Scriptures," no. 463, in *WJE* 15:553). "The great and awful majesty of God was at a great distance from us and his majesty did as it were forbid that intimate knowledge of him and acquaintance with him, but Jesus Christ, God-man is near. So he is one of us so that we may come to him boldly and behold all those glorious excellencies *in our nature*" (Edwards, 79. Sermon on Cant. 1:3 [a], in WJE 43; emphasis mine). In Christ, the divine perfections are more accessible because they not only are united to humanity but reside in it: "'Tis an endearing consideration that all this divine excellency is in our nature; is united to humanity" (Edwards, 79. Sermon on Cant. 1:3 [a], in WJE 43).

203. In the exaltation, the glory fully manifest is "by the excitation and use of that power and dominion which while Christ was in a state of humiliation did as it were lie unexercised . . . as to the exercise of it [and] in some respects as it were laid aside" (Edwards, 263. Sermon on Rev. 5:12, in *WJE* 47). This is akin to Chemnitz's position though he was not entirely clear in explaining the two states. On the one hand, Chemnitz distinguished between possession of the divine attributes and their temporary nonuse. Though he insisted that the divine power worked instrumentally through the assumed nature, he allowed for its operation through other "means and not always fully and openly" since the humanity acted as a veil. Nonetheless, he clearly denied a quiescent *divine* Logos by affirming a divine *krypsis*. Against the usual textbook reading of Lutheran Christology, Chemnitz did not reject the *extra calvinisticum*, since "the power and activity of the divine Logos were not at the time of humiliation in themselves entirely idle, but together with the Father and the Holy Spirit He administered all things everywhere powerfully and efficaciously" (Chemnitz, *Two Natures*, 490). This further strengthens the catholicity of the *extra* doctrine (E. David Willis, *Calvin's Catholic Christology: The Function of the So-Called Extra Calvinisticum in Calvin's Theology*, Studies in Medieval and Reformation Thought, vol. 2 [Leiden: Brill, 1966]).

204. The distinctions in parentheses are Crisp's terms; see his *Divinity and Humanity: The Incarnation Reconsidered* (Cambridge: Cambridge University Press, 2007), 119. The latter tendency has been argued to be incipient in Calvin's Christology. Based on an ambiguity in Calvin's writings, Slater concludes that "what we receive from [Christ] is what he has received *from* the Father according to his human nature, not what he possessed *with* the Father from all eternity" (Slater, "Salvation as Participation," 43). Having argued that our *beneficia* is in Christ's human qualities merited economically, Slater adduces Calvin's statement that Christ "died the same death as other men naturally die, and *received immortality* in the same mortal flesh which he had assumed" (Calvin, *Institutes* 2.16.13; emphasis mine) without exegeting the latter clause (Slater, "Salvation as Participation," 51–52). While this move may safeguard the finished character of Christ's earthly mediation, it would seem to introduce division into the divine nature or else imply a quiescent divinity in the earthly Christ. This is implied by Slater's interpretation of Calvin's doctrine of the atonement: "It is not that Christ ceased to be divine on the cross, however, but merely that his divinity was veiled and at rest" (ibid., 51). It is clear that Calvin says that what we have from Christ comes directly from the works he merited according to his human nature. Yet, he insists these are founded and flow "from the secret fountain of the Godhead" (Calvin, *Institutes* 3.11.12). On Slater's interpretation, Calvin's theology would not only tilt toward a Lutheran direction but would flatly contradict his insistence on the *extra*.

205. Though it was natural for the body to be affected by the soul, according to Aquinas, Jesus experienced the beatific vision in the higher regions of the soul while suffering was restricted to the flesh by the divine will (Aquinas, *ST* III, q. 14, a. 1, ad 2). Both Jean Galot and Thomas Weinandy reject Thomas's position, while Joseph White defends Christ's beatific knowledge on biblical and Chalcedonian grounds. According to White, Jesus' prayers and confident willing of the *dispensatio* are true expressions of the Son-Father relation. Otherwise, we would have a human Jesus exercising inchoate faith and increasing in self-identity as Logos. The beatific vision is personal insofar as Christ is Son of the Father, but it is also natural insofar as it is known in a human manner. The Son wills and prays as a human being, but it is not the case that Jesus obeys the Logos or adores the Trinity. Moreover, Jesus must be in possession of the beatific vision and not faith. Otherwise, some sort of *kenosis* of the divine nature would be required to contend for a Christ who needed faith without disparaging Christ's personal identity. See Thomas Joseph White, "The Voluntary Action of the Earthly Christ and the Necessity of the Beatific Vision," *Thomist* 69 (2005): 520n47.

206. Joseph Pohle, *Christology: A Dogmatic Treatise on the Incarnation*, ed. Arthur Preuss (Whitefish, MT: Kessinger Publishing, 2008), 258.

207. Edwards, "Miscellanies," no. 664b, in *WJE* 18:205.

208. "'Tis manifest the human understanding of Christ had some such union with the divine [understanding], from his history: knowing the hearts [of men], looking when he would into the hearts of any men, remembering what was before the world was. . . . So Christ's glorified human nature has the divine joy and the divine happiness, and God's love to the eternal logos, to expatiate itself in" (Edwards, "Subjects of Inquiry," in *WJE* 28).

209. "The degree of trial is not to be measured by the degree of distance of that suffering state from an indifferent state . . . as men are in when at ease, but by the distance from that state of happiness that he originally is in; or at least from that state of happiness that the human nature would have been [in], in such a participation of the happiness of the eternal Logos, as would have been answerable to its capacity and state, as being the same person with that eternal Logos" (Edwards, "Miscellanies," no. 664b, in *WJE* 18:205). It is tempting to read Edwards's "at least" here as an openness to conceding some form of eternal *kenosis* of the Logos. He is wavering between a comparison of Jesus' experienced passion and the Logos's divine beatitude, or the eternal beatitude in a human mode.

210. "That God should hide his face from him, and thus treat him as an enemy, was bitter and grievous to him. In proportion as he loved God and delighted in the manifestations of his favor, the loss or deprivation of these manifestations of his love were so much the more bitter. He remembered how he used to be in the enjoyment of his love, as appears by what he said to the Father in his prayer a little before his crucifixion" (Edwards, "Miscellanies," no. 664b, in *WJE* 18:205).

211. "When Christ was on earth, his human soul had communicated to it a kind of memory or consciousness of that happiness which his person had with God the Father before the world was, as far as an human mind was capable of it, and he reflected on this when he was going to shed his blood, as appears by what he says in the prayer he made the night before his crucifixion. . . . So that he had that happiness which he had with his Father from eternity to compare with the extreme sufferings that then were set before his eyes, which makes the self-denial infinitely greater than it otherwise would have been" (Edwards, "Christ's Sacrifice an Inducement to His Ministers," in *WJE* 25:662). Notably, Edwards does not consider this merely a point of private speculation but finds it fit for preaching.

212. "Though Christ knew the love of God to him, and knew that he should be successful in those sufferings, yet when God forsook him, those dismal views, those gloomy ideas, so fixed and swallowed up his mind, that, though he had the habitual knowledge of these, yet he could have comparatively but little comfort and support from them, for they could afford support no further than they were attended to, or were in actual view" (Edwards, "Miscellanies," no. 1005, in *WJE* 20:331).

213. "There were these things gave him a sense of the worth of the enjoyment of the Father's love: (1) He infinitely loved the Father; and the love of the man Christ Jesus was in some sort infinite, and proportionable was his desire of the love of the Father. (2) He had actually been infinitely happy in the enjoyment of the Father's love, so that he knew more by experience of the worth of it, than any angel or saint in heaven. And (3) the Father's love was infinite to him. It was a greater thing to have the expressions and manifestations of great love interrupted, than lesser love; the loss by the interruption was greater" (Edwards, "Miscellanies," no. 516, in *WJE* 18:62).

214. Edwards, "Miscellanies," no. 1005, in *WJE* 20:329.

215. Ibid. "For both the evil of sin and the evil of punishment are . . . infinitely disagreeable to Christ's nature: the former to . . . his nature as holy, the last to . . . his nature as man" (Edwards, "Miscellanies," no. 1005, in *WJE* 20:331).

216. Christ did not suffer God's anger "personally" because he objectively "knew that God did not hate him, but infinitely loved him." Rather, he perceived the "infinite wrath of God against the sins of men" (Edwards, "Miscellanies," no. 1005, in *WJE* 20:329).

217. Although Christ's "misery" on the cross was identical with ours, Christ did not "really" experience God's anger and hate as sinners do because Christ's misery was "accepted in him as satisfying." He uses the analogy of the effect that fire has on a "green tree"—Christ—in contrast to a sinner, who is like a "dry tree" (Edwards, "Miscellanies," no. 321b, in *WJE* 13:402).

218. Edwards, "Miscellanies," no. 1005, in *WJE* 20:330. In the *passio*, Christ was denied "an equal sight of good that comes by this evil [sin]." Christ was tormented by ideas of the punishment that the elect deserved for their sins but did not have the "pleasant ideas" of "the love of God, of a future reward, future salvation of his elect, etc." (Edwards, "Miscellanies," no. 1005, in *WJE* 20:331).

219. Christ had to have had "a perfectly clear and full idea of what the damned suffer in hell" for this was "perfectly equal to the thing itself" (Edwards, "Miscellanies," no. 1005, in *WJE* 20:331). Edwards, with Calvin and the Reformed tradition, wants to emphasize the spiritual suffering of Christ's soul. Calvin interpreted the creedal *descendus* as Christ's agony before death (Calvin, *Institutes* 2.16.10, 515).

220. Edwards, "Miscellanies," no. 1005, in *WJE* 20:332–33. If Jesus was anointed at the beginning of the incarnation with the Spirit without measure, what could Edwards mean by an increase of Jesus' finite holiness without the notion of uncreated grace? As we shall see in chapter 7, what increases is the operation of the Holy Spirit through and with the human nature of Christ in theandric and cooperative acts of holiness.

221. Through an increased awareness of the hideousness of sin, Christ's hatred toward sin increased, "and consequently of his inclination to the contrary, which is the same thing as an increase of the holiness of his nature." Thus, Christ's obedience or holiness at this point was at its greatest. "For though the furnace purged away no dross or filthiness, yet it increased the preciousness of the gold" (Edwards, "Miscellanies," no. 1005, in *WJE* 20: 332–33). Edwards's analogy seems to suffer a breakdown here as the value of gold is proportional to its purity.

222. Edwards, "Miscellanies," no. 516, in *WJE* 18:62.

223. Edwards's basic position here allows for the divided-minds Christology a la Swinburne and Morris (Richard Swinburne, *The Christian God* [New York: Oxford University Press, 1994], 199–209). Yet, he seems to permit a kind of mutual cognitive access between the two minds (mediated by the Spirit). Only affectively are the two minds of Christ divided, insofar as the Logos experiences the divine happiness, which is restricted to Jesus during the *exinanitio*. While the Spirit is the permanent bond of union, might it not be that the Spirit's role as the *vehiculum* or channel between the two minds of Christ is, in Owen's term, "voluntary"?

224. According to Edwards, "the sanctifying presence of God and his comforting presence are different things. Though they generally go together the saint always has the Spirit of God dwelling in his heart to sanctify him. He never leaves him in this respect but he may withdraw from him as to his comforting Presence and hide his face from him" (Edwards, 44. Sermon on Ps. 139:7-10 [undated], in *WJE* 42).

225. Since God's presence *per gratia unionis et adoptionis* are both mediated by the Spirit, the Father "incarnated [the Son] by sanctification" (Edwards, "Miscellanies," no. 709, *WJE* 18:334).

226. "God his heavenly Father had in a great measure forsaken him as to his comforting presence." This abandonment by God was not restricted to the cry of dereliction "but from the beginning of these his last sufferings" (Edwards, 93. Sermon on Isa. 53:3, in *WJE* 43). "And without doubt it was much more that the Son of God endured in his soul an effect of God's wrath against our sins. God had forsaken as to his comfortable presence but the absence of God from the soul is its greatest misery" (Edwards, 49. Sermon on Matt. 21: 5 [undated], in *WJE* 42). Edwards makes the distinction clear in reference to the church: "God as to his essential presence can't be driven away but you may grieve God by your sins so as to make him withdraw from you as to his comfortable presence" (Edwards, 44. Sermon on Ps. 139:7-10 [undated], in *WJE* 42). Again, he implies this distinction in reference to Christ's *exinanitio*: "Christ suffered the death of his body with extreme outward pains, and he suffered in his soul great darkness from God's withdrawing his comfortable presence and extreme agonies as the effects of God's wrath against our sins that were laid upon him" (Edwards, "The Sacrifice of Christ Acceptable, in *WJE* 14:452).

227. "Hence we may learn the wonderful humility . . . of Jesus Christ, although he knew at the same time that he was the eternal Son of God . . . yet he quietly and patiently took upon him all the ignominy and reproach that wicked men cast upon him" (Edwards, 49. Sermon on Matt. 21:5 [undated], in *WJE* 42). In this, the role the Holy Spirit plays in restricting the comforting presence of the Father to Jesus in Edwards's Christology mirrors the role of Christ's divinity in Aquinas's. From the psychological point of view, Aquinas's Jesus would seem to suffer from a kind of bipolarity on the cross, experiencing intense suffering in the lower nature while enjoying beatitude in the higher regions of Christ's spirit. But such a special restriction only happened by "the will of His Godhead," since "the natural relationship which is between the soul and the body" is one where "glory flows into the body from the soul's glory" (Aquinas, *ST* III, q. 14, a. 1, ad 2). One could use here the Freudian distinction between the unconscious and the conscious to explain the coexistence of beatitude and suffering in Aquinas's Christ, though in this case the unconscious mind would be acting as a reservoir of the positive and pleasant. Where Edwards's Christ gravitates toward Nestorianism, Aquinas' exhibits a kind of Docetism. Nonetheless, Thomas's position may have empirical warrant in the joy and suffering experienced by a Christian martyr.

228. Edwards, "Subjects of Inquiry," in *WJE* 28; italics mine.

229. Of course, such an analysis is only possible on a presupposition of two self-acting natures, as is evident from the grammar. On a reduplicative strategy, the unity-in-distinction is retained: the Logos incarnate, *qua* divine, is eternally blessed and, *qua* human, suffered on the cross.

230. See Francis J. Hall, *Theological Outlines*, rev. Frank Hudson Hallock, 3rd ed. (Eugene, OR: Wipf and Stock, 1933), 182.

231. Barth, *CD* IV.2, § 64, p. 66. Yet, Edwards pushes the boundaries of Reformed theology further by developing the Spirit Christology of Owen alongside the classical Logos Christology, and charted a Father Christology on his own. In other words, he pioneered a full-fledged Trinitarian christological ontology.

232. Edwards, "Miscellanies," no. 741, in *WJE* 18:369.

6

Unio Cum Christo
The Foundation of All Communion and Communication

Just as the *unio hypostatica* is central to Edwards's Christology, so the *unio mystica* is foundational to his soteriology. "By virtue of the believer's union with Christ, he doth really possess all things. . . . I mean that God three in one, all that he is, and all that he has, and all that he does, all that he has made or done—the whole universe . . . are as much the Christian's . . . because Christ, who certainly doth thus possess all things, is entirely his."[1] In this chapter, we will look at how Edwards uses the doctrine of the *unio cum Christo* as a synthetic, participatory category to embrace the various facets of salvation: regeneration, faith, justification, adoption, and sanctification. The chapter is organized based on his structuring of these aspects of salvation, with particular attention to justification. But before turning to those features, we will look at how Edwards relates the *unio mystica* to the *unio personalis.*

ANALOGY BETWEEN THE *UNIO HYPOSTATICA* AND *UNIO MYSTICA*

Despite resorting to negative definitions, the Reformed tradition has consistently insisted on a clear line between the *unio hypostatica* and the *unio cum Christo*.[2] In light of Edwards's Spirit-mediated Christology, which we have examined in detail in the previous chapters, does he end up confounding the two?

According to Edwards, the *unio hypostatica* is the *analogans* of the *unio mystica*, as there is between them a "likeness . . . though there be in the former great peculiarities."[3] In the incarnation, "the Logos dwelt in the human nature as in his body." In the mystical union, however, it is the whole "Christ [who] dwells in his church as in his body"—a body made up of distinct persons.[4]

231

In terms of likeness, both Christ's human nature and the church are recipients of the Holy Spirit.[5] Unlike the *unio hypostatica*, the Spirit's indwelling of Christ's human nature is, according to Edwards, a "union of contact or influence."[6] This presence of the Spirit in the incarnation differs from the *unio mystica*, for it is the "Spirit of the Logos [who is] dwelling in [Jesus] after a peculiar manner and without measure."[7] Edwards distinguishes the Spirit's indwelling between *caput et membra* as that of propriety and participation.

Firstly, there is a quantitative distinction, whereby Christ possesses the Spirit perfectly.[8] The saints, on the other hand, participate in the Holy Spirit by degree according to their individual capacities and states.[9] Evidently, on Edwards's suggestion that sanctification is of "everlasting duration," the distinction between the Head and its members would seem to collapse into the *totus Christus*. In spite of Edwards's insistence that "the time will never come when it can be said it has already arrived at this infinite" threshold, yet the infinite-finite distinction between Christ and the saints is occluded from the divine perspective. From God's point of view, the "whole of the creature's eternal duration, with all the infinity of its progress, and infinite increase of nearness and union to God . . . the creature must be looked upon as united to God in an infinite strictness."[10] That is why a peculiar manner of the Spirit's indwelling in Christ is asserted.

Appealing once again to the soul-body metaphor, Edwards points to a qualitative distinction.[11] Christ's human nature is related to the Spirit "as the head is the seat of the soul after a peculiar manner; 'tis the proper seat of the soul."[12] The Spirit is received by Jesus directly from the Father and is possessed as Christ's own Spirit. Edwards marks this distinction between the Spirit had by Christians as "a filial spirit, a spirit of adoption" and Christ's own Spirit as "the Spirit of the only-begotten of the Father."[13] Only Jesus Christ, as the Son of God, has received the Spirit from the Father.[14] In contrast, the church is gifted with the Spirit from God mediately or derivatively, *per filium*.[15] The filial Spirit that believers are given is the Spirit of the Son of the Father—that Spirit which first dwelled in the human Jesus.[16]

Not only must the Holy Spirit be received from and through the Son, it is had only in the incarnate Son.[17] Salvation cannot be laid hold of through a Spirit that is independent of the Son. "If we had the Spirit, yet if it was not in Christ Jesus, uniting of us to him, and as his Spirit, it would not have this virtue [of forgiveness and life]."[18] In short, the Holy Spirit is received by Jesus from the Father but indwells as Christ's own Spirit. The Christian, however, receives the Holy Spirit from the incarnate Son and cannot be said to possess the Spirit as her own spirit.

Furthermore, the *unio mystica* is not an incarnation of the Holy Spirit.[19] In the *union hypostatica*, the Logos assumes flesh, while in the *unio mystica*, the Spirit indwells other human persons.[20] Nonetheless, the *unio mystica* may be regarded as implied in the incarnation, insofar as the Son "took one of this nature into a personal union with himself . . . therein as it were assuming all the elect that were in that nature, who are all united to him as members to the head."[21] For sure, the *unio mystica* is the purpose of Christ's *unio hypostatica*.[22] In this sense, then, the *unio mystica* may be considered a *metaphorical* prolongation of the Son's incarnation. By this, Edwards is not confounding the *unio personalis* and *unio mystica*, but he is appealing to the Augustinian idea of the *totus Christus*.[23]

CHRISTUS TOTUS: THE PRIMACY OF UNION WITH CHRIST'S PERSON

Edwards's description of this Christo-ecclesiological reality is based in the Trinity. It is founded on the Father's eternal election of sentient creatures to be *en Christo* and outworked in time through Christ and the church. "As God determined in his eternal decrees to create a world, to communicate himself, and his Son might have an object for the object of his infinite grace and love, so God determined that this object should be one. His special aim in all was to procure one created child, one spouse and body of his Son for the adequate displays of his unspeakable and transcendent goodness and grace."[24] The Holy Spirit, as the *vinculum,* not only brings about an intimate relation between Christ and the church but makes them one mystical entity.[25] "Their union is such that the Church is Christ mystical. Christ and the Church are called Christ as if they were all but one person."[26] In Christ, and by Christ's Spirit, the saints have union with Christ, communion with God, regeneration, adoption, justification, sanctification, perseverance, and glorification.[27] We now examine how Edwards orders these aspects of salvation in the *unio mystica*.

Union with Christ as Hypernym for the Application of Salvation

In continuity with Calvin, Edwards looks to the *unio cum Christo* as the ground of the *beneficia christi*.[28] However, he denies that there is any preconversion, chronological *ordo salutis* since "God's Spirit is unsearchable and untraceable . . . in the method of his operations."[29] Nonetheless, with the scholastic Calvinists, he did not completely abandon a *logical* order of salvation.[30] For Edwards, then, the *unio cum Christo* serves as an umbrella concept or hypernym of the *applicatio salutis*.[31] The hyponyms, of course, stand in a particular order.

The most basic *unio* is a real and reciprocal union of hearts or love between Christ and the elect. "This union of hearts is the first thing, the foundation."[32] With this union of love in place, "another threefold union follows from [it]: A relative union. A legal union. A vital union."[33] It is from this tripartite union of kinship, law, and life to Christ that the benefits of adoption, justification, and sanctification/glorification are obtained.[34] "Relative blessings are more directly from the relative union. . . . Real blessings are by the real and vital union with Christ."[35] This placing of the real union of hearts before the benefits of adoption, justification, and sanctification indicates an ontological as well as causal priority of regeneration/faith.[36] Obviously, there is no chronological ordering of the relative, legal, and vital since they come under a single "threefold union," but Edwards, like the scholastic Calvinists, allows for a rational ordering of these subsidiary unions. At the same time, following Calvin, Edwards subsumes the benefits arising from these unions—the *triplex gratia dei* of adoption, justification, and sanctification—under the *unio mystica*.[37] This distinction between union in person and communion in benefits is common in the Reformed-Puritan writings, and we turn now to this motif.[38]

PRIORITY OF UNION OVER COMMUNION

Edwards states the axiom succinctly: "Union always goes before communion."[39] But what is *communio*? It is not just a simple sharing of ideas. "'Tis therefore a vulgar mistake," Edwards asserts, "that communion is nothing else but only society or conversation."[40] Rather, "mutual society" and communication is the result of communion.[41] What, then, is the primary constituent of communion? "That which is principally intended by communion in or fellowship in scripture," Edwards answers positively, "is a common partaking of benefits."[42]

Not only is such a definition biblical, it may be observed in relations among sentient beings. All happiness flows from love, for all intelligent beings must be united in love in order to participate in each other's happiness.[43] The clearest example is the sharing of property in marriage, and this serves as an apt illustration of Christ's relation to the church.[44] Our participation in Christ's benefits in the *unio mystica* comes from Christ's participation in our nature in the *unio hypostatica*.[45] Clearly, all this is rooted in election. God (logically) foreknows the saints in Christ before predestining them to salvific divine benefits.[46]

All the spiritual blessings that are the saints', including adoption, justification, sanctification, and glorification, are only had *en Christo*. "This relation or union to Christ . . . is the ground of their right to his benefits . . . our having Christ's merits and benefits belonging to us, follows from our having (if I may so speak) Christ himself belonging to us, or a being united to him."[47] This leads us to consider the most basic *unio cum Christo*—a real union of hearts—whereby every other union and communion is sourced.

Real Union of Hearts, Affection, or Love: The Foundation of All Other Unions

This foundational union of hearts is a reciprocal relation of Christ-in-us and us-in-Christ. Any intentional union between two persons, by definition, cannot exclude mutual consent of mind and heart.[48] Beginning from Christ's side, Christ's eternal love and will-to-union are historically actualized in the *unio hypostatica* and applied by the Spirit to each saint in regeneration.[49] When Christ graces the soul with the divine love, regeneration is inaugurated through the union of Christ's Spirit to the soul's faculties.[50] Regeneration is thus a kind of spiritual emanation whereby Christ initiates a union with the saint through Christ's indwelling Spirit. As a result, the believer responds to Christ in faith or repentance, thus completing this real union of love. Here, a remanation occurs whereby the soul's faith-act constitutes a return movement toward Christ. As with Christ's initiating love toward us, the basis of the believer's union with Christ must be through a free response of love befitting a sentient and conative being.[51] "There is a union with Christ, by the indwelling of the love of Christ, two ways: first, as 'tis from Christ, and is the very Spirit and life and fullness of Christ; and second, as it acts to Christ: for the very nature of it is love and union of heart to him."[52]

This mutuality of love is clearly ordered. Christ's love precedes ours. The divine love is prior to, and the ground of, the saints' response of love to God, both chronologically and ontologically.[53] Christ's eternal love to the church undergirds Christ's atoning work for the saints in time.[54]

> The first thing appertaining to this union between Christ and his people is the union of hearts. In this, Christ is first. . . . Christ from eternity set his love on them. He loved the church, and the fruit of his love to the elect church was his coming into the world to die for her. . . . And in consequence of this, believers have their hearts drawn to Christ, and henceforward there is a mutual complacence. This union of hearts is the first thing, the foundation.[55]

CHRIST'S UNION OF LOVE TOWARD THE CHURCH: ELECTION, INCARNATION, AND REGENERATION

Regeneration is but a culmination of God's election and Christ's eternal self-giving love to the saints. Edwards is insistent that election does not have a temporal ground: it is dependent neither on God's foreknowledge of our faith nor even on Christ's meritorious work for us.[56] Neither is the election of the saints simply identical with Christ's election or their union with Christ.[57] As all of God's determinations are christocentric, our election in Christ and to the divine *beneficia* is grounded in Christ's election. "So Christ's election is the foundation of ours, as much as his justification and glorification are the foundation of ours."[58] Put differently, God's glory and the happiness of the creature are summed up in Jesus Christ: "He being the end of all God's work *ad extra*, therefore the accomplishment of all was committed to him."[59]

The depth of Christ's love to the elect brought about both the incarnation and the substitutionary atonement.[60] The elect already, *per conveniens*, have a sort of right to the Logos *incarnandus* as a result of Christ's eternal love to them: "Thus he from eternity gave himself so to them that he looked on them as having so great a propriety on him as amounted to his thus spending and being spent for them."[61] In the incarnation, they come to possess "a full propriety" in Christ's twofold being, threefold office, and manifold benefits: "He has given them all that he is both in his divine and human nature. He has given them the perfections and glory of his divine nature; his power, wisdom; given his human nature his body his soul, his life, his blood. He has given himself to them in all his offices. He is their Priest, their Prophet and their King and so is their Redeemer and he has given them all that he has."[62] God's active love to the elect, therefore, is the cause of the incarnation, through which Christ made it possible for God to love the good in them in regeneration.[63]

In regeneration, there is a passive as well as an active reception of Christ: the prior impartation of a gracious spiritual principle efficaciously converts the will and causes faith in the human subject to both embrace Christ and repent.[64] In this spiritual regeneration, Word and Spirit function as agents of God the Father.[65] Regeneration, analogous to Christ's *conceptio*, is the communication of the Spirit or new disposition to the elect, which is an act of operative or efficacious grace.[66] In giving us the new principle it is, at the same time, Christ's act of closing with us or uniting to us.[67]

This infusion of divine love involves the conferral of a new, supernatural foundation whereby the soul is conformed to the divine.[68] This ontological transformation does not entail essential change whereby human faculties are mutated; it is fundamentally dispositional.[69] In this event, there is an initial purification of the soul from all sinful dispositions, a tending of the will toward obedience.[70] Following this, spiritual understanding is received prior to "any proper acts of the will," since the intellect is more basic than volition.[71] As Nichols points out, Edwards's doctrine of the new sense includes both regeneration and illumination; it thus involves both an ontological and epistemological transformation.[72] The divine emanation of spiritual light is perceived by the soul, bringing about a remanation of gracious acts.[73] As a result of this initial work of regeneration, the second mode—faith—arises, which is the "suiting," "according," and "symphonizing" of the human faculties toward salvation.[74]

THE SAINT'S ACTIVE UNION OF LOVE TO CHRIST: FAITH, CONVERSION, AND REPENTANCE

As we have seen in the previous subsection, regeneration, whereby the soul is passive, is only relatively distinct from conversion or repentance, where it is active.[75] Conversion, then, is a simultaneous turning away from sin and (re)turning to Christ.[76] Calling, or the offer of salvation, here becomes actual and effectual.[77] This initial faith-act is the saint's uniting response or "remanating" movement toward Christ's initiating love. In Edwards's terminology, it is the soul's "active uniting," "accepting," "closing with," "complying with," "coming to," "adhering to," or "falling in" Christ.[78]

From what we have seen so far, it is obvious that Edwards follows Calvin's understanding of the *unio cum Christo* as a Spirit-mediated reality.[79] However, he does not regard faith as something preceding and distinct from the *unio mystica*.[80] Rather, this initial faith-act by the saint is the secondary constituent of that fundamental union of love.[81] Hence "faith," as Edwards himself defines it, "is itself the very act of unition, on their part."[82]

Faith is an active receptivity; "faith is the soul's active uniting with Christ."[83] Stated differently, it is the God-ward response of love to Christ that closes the real union of heart.[84] Using bridal imagery not uncommon in the Puritan tradition, Edwards points out that "those conjugal motions of soul" that most characterize it as a spouse of Christ are an active, whole-person receptivity.[85] Since a person is regenerated as a psychosomatic whole and faith inevitably accompanies the new disposition, so Christian faith and practice must be acts of the whole person.[86] What are the elements of this holistic response of faith?

According to Edwards, faith cannot be merely notional but must include three elements: "assent of the soul and its consent and trust or reliance."[87] Firstly, there must be an assent of the mind to gospel truth or judgment.[88] But this belief in Christian truth cannot remain merely cognitive assent, for then it would not be spiritual but rather only natural.[89] Spiritual assent involves not only a recognition of the truths of the gospel but a perception of its beauty.[90] Secondly, only in this aesthetic perception of gospel truth is a person capable of consent.[91] Faith must also involve the volition because it would not be proper for "intelligent beings—capable of act and choice—as united to Christ that don't consent to it."[92] In this sense, salvation lies within our power but only if we could will it.[93] Finally, faith includes an element of trust whereby truth is personally appropriated.[94] Faith consciously acknowledges one's guilt and inability to merit righteousness except through the supererogatory work of Christ, and thus faith actively receives Christ as would a beggar.[95] This initial act of faith believes in Christ's economy of redemption and accepts that what Christ has done is *pro me*.[96] Does such an active, integral role for initial faith make salvation conditional on human action?

While the Reformed divines generally avoided calling faith an instrumental cause of justification, they did not object to the term "instrument of justification."[97] Edwards thinks that such a characterization leads to logical difficulties.[98] For him, justification is *iustitia aliena* insofar as it is not and cannot be self-wrought. Faith is not active in the sense that it becomes the condition for meriting Christ's righteousness, though faith may be called a *conditio sine qua non* of union with Christ and of actualizing the covenant of grace.[99] Strictly speaking, however, there is only a covenant of works between God and Adam, as well as a covenant of redemption between Christ and God, whereby conditions are attached. Through "perfect obedience and suffering," Christ has perfectly fulfilled the condition of the covenant of redemption.[100] Christ's offer of salvation is unconditional and faith cannot be termed conditional since it is more "the receiving [of the offer] itself."[101]

Union of Love as the Cause of the Threefold Union

As we have seen, there is a causal connection between the real union of hearts and the resultant threefold union—relative, legal, and vital. But what is their relation one to another?

Sanctification as Continuous Regeneration and Repentance

The foundational union of love is continuous with the vital union insofar as they are real, progressive, spiritual unions. In other words, sanctification is organically related to the regeneration-conversion couplet. Edwards frequently employs the nomenclature of regeneration, conversion, and repentance to signify the inception of sanctification.[102] In this usage, conversion is to be countenanced as an *ex novo* operation whereby a person is transitioned from a "state of total corruption and depravity into a state of grace."[103] Together with the tradition, Edwards affirms that sanctification, begun at regeneration, is gradualistic.[104]

However, this gradualism may be considered not only as an everlasting quantitative increase in holiness—a more and more—but also as a reiteration of that initial faith-act by which Christ is received again and again. "The obedience of a Christian . . . is but an expression of the soul's believing union to Christ . . . and every such act of obedience . . . is only a new effective act of reception of Christ."[105] In light of Edwards's doctrine of *creatio continua*, there is an analogous "circumstantial" distinction between initial faith and perseverance (see table 1.1).[106] Edwards's interchangeable use of regeneration, repentance, conversion, renovation, restoration, and sanctification to mean both the initial infusion of grace and the ongoing process from grace to glory is not merely nominal.[107] As the *unio cum Christo* is a kind of *unitio continua*, sanctification is truly a continual conversion. Sanctification is a *regeneratio continua*, so that "a new work of creation [must be enacted] on every heart, and this power must be continued [as] a kind of continual creation."[108]

NATURAL FITNESS BETWEEN THE ACT OF UNITION AND STATES OF UNION

From the domain of *conveniens*, Edwards insists that there must be a "natural fitness" among the parts and of the parts to the whole in the "admirable scheme" of salvation.[109] There is the requirement of a "natural fitness" between the union of love and the resultant relative and legal unions.[110] In other words, there is a proportionality between the initial *unitio mystica* and the ongoing *unio mystica*—that is to say, of "faith to a state of union with Christ."[111] What does he mean by a state of union?

In contrast to the process of sanctification, adoption and justification are completed states secured at regeneration and repentance. The legal and relative unions exist where persons are in "a justified state or freedom [from] guilt" and "state of sons," respectively.[112] "The relative union," in which adoption is found, "is both begun and perfected at once, when the soul first closes with Christ by faith."[113] Similarly, the legal union in which justification is obtained is perfect, as "there are no degrees of imputed righteousness."[114] What is this natural fitness that obtains between the real union and the relative and legal unions?

"Natural fitness," Edwards explains, "is not so properly a fitness of the subject to be in Christ."[115] Rather, it is "the fitness of God's act in looking on such an one as being in Christ."[116] A few points should be noted here. Firstly, this fitness does not rest in any moral quality in the human subject.[117] Hence, Edwards distinguishes moral from natural fitness. "A person is morally fit for a state, when by his excellency or odiousness commends him to it."[118] While moral fitness includes natural fitness, this equation is not reversible.[119] When such a natural fitness is present, God justifies the person not "out of love to the grace of faith itself" but from his "love of order."[120]

Secondly, and related to the previous point, God's "love of order" assumes a distinction between a person's "being in Christ" and "God's act in looking on such an one as being in Christ" or "Christ being looked upon as his."[121] The former is the real union of love while the latter refers to the subsidiary unions arising from it. Natural fitness is that condition God has ordained by which a relative union must accompany and follow a real union of hearts. Otherwise, "it would be naturally unfit that they should be looked upon as relatively in him or belonging to him if not really united to him."[122] Similarly, when a "rational voluntary agent is one with Christ by his own act," that person is "on that account much more fitly and suitably to be looked upon as [Christ's], and belonging to him, and legally one with him."[123] God's *potentia ordinata* is not capricious but is in harmony with nature and reason.[124]

If natural fitness is God's recognition of a natural congruity between the ontic and forensic forms of *unio*, then the justified cannot claim any *meritum de congruo* in justification.[125] Yet the faith-act is necessary to justification, not as a goodness in itself but as an active response or proper capacity.[126] Might faith then be regarded as a nonadequate condition for meriting real union with Christ? This Edwards denies, for faith itself is the act of our coming into union with Christ.[127] Hence, natural fitness presupposes the real union of love.

Imputation is based on our real union with Christ's person and, just so, in Christ's benefits: "Now believers are so closely united to Christ that they are the same in the Father's account; and therefore what Christ has done in obedience is the believer's, because he is the same."[128] Just as participation in Christ's person results in participation in Christ's benefits, so justification follows the believer's initial faith-act, which is none other than her act of uniting with Christ.[129]

Natural fitness admits that union with Christ and communion in the divine benefits are inseparable realities.[130] Human action is included in that natural fitness, which capacitates the person for the reception of Christ's benefits.[131] Edwards likens this to marriage, where a real union is entered into freely and mutually in order to receive a communion in benefits.[132] While there is a natural fitness between faith and union with Christ, this union is gracious and spiritual, not natural.[133] If this union were natural rather than spiritual, sanctification would be universally accomplished for all humanity and founded only on the personal union of the God-man with humanity rather than on Christ's work.[134]

Not only is faith regarded by God as a nonmoral quality, but Christ's benefits are not directly related to faith as would be in the case of works-righteousness; rather, they are mediated by "our interest in Christ or a communion in his benefits."[135] But this interest in Christ's benefits presupposes an interest in Christ's person. Accordingly, "the next benefit which the inherent qualification [faith] brings the person to is not justification or acceptance to eternal life itself, but an interest in Christ, a being looked upon as in him, united and belonging to him who has a valuable righteousness; and consequentially on this, and in the second step, that benefit is obtained of being interested in that acceptance to eternal favor and life, which is the reward of his righteousness."[136] Justification flows from a legal union grounded in a real union of hearts.[137] While faith engenders both adoption and justification, these two benefits are to be clearly distinguished and rationally ordered.

RELATIVE UNION AND THE BENEFIT OF ADOPTION

While the benefits of adoption flow directly from our relative union with Christ, the latter is grounded in the real union of regeneration and conversion.[138] This order is not reversible: "How unreasonable to be admitted into Family in order to be born into the Family."[139] We must have the nature of a child to then be granted the rights of a child. The two-sided reality of regeneration and repentance is the cause of the relative union, for the saints have to "be united to Christ, or be in Christ, in order to their being looked upon as his, belonging to him."[140] On the human side, that which precedes adoption is an active faith in the regenerate and thus a distinction "between accepting Christ and an having Christ," or reception and possession.[141] From the divine direction, adoption is God's consideration of the regenerate as being "relatively in [Christ] or belonging to him."[142]

What is the relation between the saint and the triune persons in adoption? The church is the child, friend, sibling, spouse, and body of Christ by covenant relation.[143] In regeneration, the Holy Spirit or "divine love is the bond by which the soul of the saint is united to God."[144] Unlike the real union of love whereby the Spirit is the *vinculum* between Christ/God and us, the saint's relative union to Christ "is immediate without any Person coming between."[145] There is a sort of identity between Christ and us because "he is as our selves."[146]

In this relative union, Christ functions as the "bond of union" between God the Father and the saint.[147] Christ "is next to us and the relation is immediate. Our relation to God the Father is not in the same sense immediate because 'tis by a mediatour."[148]

One needs to appreciate the distinction that Edwards posits between having a filial nature and being in a filial state, that is, between regeneration and adoption.[149] The real union of our hearts to Christ and God is having their Spirit in us. In regeneration, then, we participate on an entitative level in the "divine nature"—which is to say, the Spirit from the incarnate Son and the Father. Accordingly, when "we partake of the spirit of the Son, we are children by nature; that is, we have the nature of children."[150] The subjective, intuitive grasp of "the soul's relation to God" during its more lively occasions is the witness of the Spirit.[151] In adoption or the relative union, it is Christ mediating between God the Father and the saint. That is why our relative union to God the Father is perceived mediately through love, while the recognition of our real union to God is intuitive and immediate.[152] The relative union emphasizes relation and distinction, while the real union emphasizes ontology and identity.

How is adoption related to justification? Though justification is not the cause of adoption, Edwards insists that they should be clearly distinguished.[153] The one is forensic and the other relational.[154] Yet they are linked, for the person who is both regenerated and adopted by God is (naturally) unfit for condemnation but should rather be justified. "'Tis no way suitable that those who have the nature and state of sons should be condemned, but that they should have justification and life."[155] We turn now to the legal union, which Edwards places after the relative union in his *ordo salutis*.[156]

JUSTIFICATION AS THE BENEFIT OF LEGAL UNION

Like Luther, Edwards sees justification as part of the *unio mystica*.[157] It is more centrally related to faith than love. In regeneration, love fits the heart "to the nature of God," while faith involves suiting the mind to Christ.[158] The Spirit is the principle of faith, which brings an awareness that justification is in Christ alone.[159] Faith in the person of Christ includes embracing the *munus triplex* and all the benefits related to each of the offices.[160] Hence, even though faith is considered "no more immediately" than the reception of Christ "as a mediator for our justification," this involves the entitlement to sanctification.[161]

Edwards, like Calvin, applies the accounting and forensic metaphors to justification.[162] In the first place, if the benefit of justification is to be had, the person and Christ must be considered one legal entity.[163] "There is a legal union between them so that they are one in law and looked upon and accepted as one in what concerns the law by God the Judge of all."[164] In the second place, in the bookkeeping arena, "faith may be said to be imputed to us . . . as we are charged as debtors in the book of God's account, what Christ has done in fulfilling righteousness for us is charged as the grand balance of the account."[165]

While justification is considered after adoption, they are both grounded in regeneration/conversion. Hence, "what is real in the union between Christ and his people, is the foundation of what is legal."[166] With such a realist ontology, imputed righteousness is not legal fiction; it is not "a notion, but a reality."[167] Union with Christ includes the idea of mutual imputation—a *commercium admiribile*. And such a *commutatio mirifica*, or in Edwards's words "an interchanging or mutuation of righteousness," has both ontological and forensic *ratio*.[168]

God's justifies the church through Christ, and this is made possible by the incarnation and mystical union.[169] Ontologically, justification is grounded "in Christ's union with God, and his union with men," both of which are seen in relation to nature and love.[170] Firstly, Christ is united to God in two ways: (1) being God, Christ "has worthiness and merit sufficient for himself and for all others"; and, (2) having the Spirit or God's infinite love "gives an infinite value to Christ's sufferings and actions in God's account."[171] There is both infinite capacity for the believers' participation in Christ and infinite regard by the Father to both negative and positive imputation. Secondly, the believer participates in Christ's righteousness through union with Christ in two ways as well: (1) through the incarnation, Christ partakes of human nature, and through regeneration, believers are communicated Christ's Spirit or "divine nature"; and (2) through Christ's dying love in our stead Christ unites with us, and "on the believer's part is faith and love."[172] Inasmuch as justification is related to the *unio mystica* and *unio hypostatica*, its ultimate ground is the Holy Trinity.

JUSTIFICATION AS THE HOLY SPIRIT IN THE INCARNATE SON

How is justification, in the eyes of Edwards, a Trinitarian reality? Being primarily a forensic work, justification is appropriated to the head of the œconomy, God the Father.[173] Nonetheless, though Christ does not receive satisfaction in the office of mediator, he is involved as God, since justice is the prerogative of the divine nature.[174] This work of justification is appropriated to Christ since Christ's human righteousness is the material cause of our justification.[175] What, then, does the Holy Spirit do in justification?

As we have previously seen, the Spirit is not only the divine disposition in action in, with, and through the faculties of the saint expressed as faith toward

Christ, but also the bond that unites them both.[176] The Spirit causes the church to be united to Christ as the *unio* or *vinculum caritatis*, and the self-same Spirit is the self-communicative *communio* or *summum bonum* of the church.[177] In the legal union, God the Father "sends the Spirit to bring home the sinner to Christ that he may be justified through him, to impute that righteousness to him that is indeed in some respect the Spirit in the Son, the expressions of his influence and actings in him; and he justifies them that so they may have a right to the Spirit."[178]

As such, the imputed righteousness of the saint is, in a sense, the Spirit operative in the earthly Christ. In Edwards's words, the incarnate Son's righteousness "is in some sort his Spirit, and is applied by his Spirit" to sinners.[179] This case is especially so in the atonement, where the Spirit, who is "Christ's own love and his Father's love" has "its fountain in Christ's wounds" and flows to the saints "in the stream of his Blood."[180] In the *unio mystica*, the Holy Spirit liberates the Christian from guilt and death by uniting us to Christ, who has died for us and who is our life.[181] In short, Christ's sanctification is our justification. This righteousness, which is alien and imputed to us, is considered inherent in Christ.[182] This distinction between inherent and imputed righteousness is a theme we will now examine.

JUSTIFICATION AND SANCTIFICATION: IMPUTED AND INHERENT

That forgiveness and the holy life are inseparably united in Christ is an ecumenical touchstone for Protestants and Catholics.[183] Yet it was primarily the *distinctio* (and secondarily, the *ordo*), and not merely the *unio*, that the Reformers contended was insufficiently clarified within Thomist soteriology (as interpreted by Trent). As Edwards puts it, the issue is not whether faith justifies or not, but how it does so.[184] What marks the Reformed tradition is the distinction between righteousness that is inherent and that which is imputed.[185] For the Reformed, faith brings about not an infusion of justice into the saint but an imputation of righteousness.[186]

One could ask, what is the difference between the righteousness of justification and sanctification? Yet such a question is inappropriate since sanctification, and not justification (which has to do with a state or action), deals with grace itself; the one, infused *grace*, the other, *imputed* righteousness. "By the righteousness of faith," Edwards would have us understand, is not "*justitia*, but *justificatio*: not perfect holiness, but a justified state or freedom [from] guilt; and the imputation of righteousness, not so properly the righteousness imputed."[187]

In another place, Edwards defines "imputed righteousness [as] Christ's righteousness accepted for them, inherent holiness [as] Christ's righteousness communicated to them."[188] It is only through union with Christ that God "has complacency in him [the saint] for some excellency some way belonging to him, either inherent in him or imputed to him."[189] Justifying grace, as achieved by Christ, is wholly alien yet perfectly imputed to the sinner, who receives it passively by faith. Christ's righteousness is wholly and indivisibly imputed once and for all to every justified person.[190] This is entirely distinct from the quantitative nature of sanctifying grace in the soul of the regenerate, which is infused, habitual, partial, and incremental.

However, God cannot regard Christ's works as actually performed by us, for this would annihilate the notion of imputation.[191] Nor is imputation an infusion of Christ's righteousness into the believer's soul, as this is ontologically impossible.[192] Because Christ's righteousness belongs properly to the person of Christ, it is only imputed to us, as was Adam's sin. "This was personal and inherent in himself, and incommunicable to any other; the acts of righteousness were performed by him, and not by us; and in this sense 'tis his righteousness, and not ours; though the saving influence of it descends upon us, as did the malignant influence of Adam's sin."[193] By virtue of the saints' election in Christ, "the condition is as if it were performed by them."[194] The initial and inherent holiness in sanctification, which we have in germ and in part, is found whole and entire in Christ and will be never be ours *in via*. Yet, though the saint possesses perfectly both Christ's righteousness and Christ's holiness eschatologically, the one remains imputed and the other infused.[195]

As we are *in Christo*, God imputes Christ's righteousness to us as a garment covering us.[196] Edwards uses the imagery of justification as envelopment or "being clothed in Christ" in keeping with its *extra nos* (nonintrinsic or nonimparted) character and describes sanctification as "being engrafted into Christ," thus deriving life from the divine. In justification, the metaphor is aesthetic and the direction Christ-ward; we are in Christ and are clothed with Christ's beautiful righteousness. "Christ is more than our head, he is . . . as clothing to us; we are commanded to put him on, so that our deformity don't appear. Seeing we are clothed with him who is so beautiful, and for his beauty with which we are clothed, are we accepted and loved."[197] In sanctification, the metaphor is organic and the direction human-ward; Christ is in us and the divine holiness is infused into us gradually.[198] As Luther explained, then, justification and sanctification may be distinguished as "we in Christ" and "Christ in us."[199] Put differently, Christ is both our objective and our subjective good.[200] In a manner that echoes Calvin's textile imagery, Christ both hides our sins (negative imputation) and covers us with righteousness (positive imputation). This twofold imputation rests on Christ's twofold righteousness—positive and negative.

RIGHTEOUSNESS OF THE MEDIATOR: POSITIVE AND NEGATIVE

Edwards believes that justification, as negative and positive imputation, is connected to the atonement and incarnation.[201] Positive and negative imputation are merited by the life and death of Christ. Just as Adam's glorification did not merely depend on his remaining innocent or "not doing ill" but also on his active obedience or "doing well," so our salvation rests both on Christ's death and life, by which we are freed from guilt and active righteousness is procured for us.[202] Through substitution, Christ satisfies God's judgment of our sins by bearing our punishment and merits eternal life for us through obedience of the law.[203] Christ's positive righteousness takes the place of humanity's failed obedience, rightfully due God under the covenant of works. What was naturally and rightfully ours to perform has been done graciously by Christ.

As federal headship cannot be separated from the ontological, "Christ our second surety" is also the second Adam.[204] Since Christ, in both passive and active obedience, was neither acquitted nor rewarded "as a private person, but as a head," so "in his acquittance, [the elect] are acquitted" and "accepted in his acceptance."[205] On the one hand, Christ bore the punishment for humankind's sin, negatively imputed to Christ, thus restoring humans to the state of innocence in which they become "void of guilt."[206] On the other hand, the "whole mystical Christ" participates in Jesus' exaltation and glorification, merited by Jesus' active obedience to God: this is positive imputation.[207] Although both the negative and positive righteousness of Christ are indispensable to the work of Christ and our justification, this twofold imputation is ordered.

With the Reformed tradition, then, Edwards maintains the priority of positive imputation over nonimputation.[208] Strictly speaking, Edwards thinks that the term "pardon" is improperly used for negative imputation.[209] He elaborates: "Justification consists in imputing righteousness. To pardon sin is to cease to be angry for sin. But imputing righteousness and ceasing to be angry for sin are two things; one is the foundation of the other."[210] In the following, we will look at how Edwards connects Christ's righteousness to the two natures of Christ.

RIGHTEOUSNESS OF CHRIST: DIVINE OR HUMAN?

As we have seen, Edwards, with the Reformed tradition, is unequivocal that the material and meritorious cause of our justification is procured by the God–man through active and passive obedience.[211] Nonetheless, material and meritorious causation finds its foundation in efficient causation, for the incarnate Christ could only have purchased our salvation as the eternal God, its author and determiner.[212] In the economy of redemption, Christ's human righteousness *pro nobis* is rooted in being God.

Edwards points out two "great distinction[s]" between the righteousness of the covenant of works and that of the covenant of redemption.[213] Firstly, the distinction does not turn on a *iustitia aliena*; which is to say, in the covenant of redemption "we are not justified by our own righteousness but the righteousness of another."[214] For even if Adam had persevered in the covenant of works, justification would still have been obtained through "a surety or representative" and would not have been self-merited.[215] What is the difference then?

In the old covenant, Adam's representative righteousness, had he persevered, would have been that "of mere man" and "would have been properly an human righteousness." In the new covenant, however, the imputed righteousness of Christ is "by a divine person."[216] The value of Christ's righteousness is not intrinsic to the assumed human nature but derives its worth from the *enhypostaton*.[217] This efficacy of the obedience and death of Christ comes from the hypostatic union, which was effected by the Holy Spirit. "It was by the Holy Spirit that the human nature of Christ was united to the divine Logos, from which arises the infinite value of his blood and righteousness."[218]

Secondly, Christ's justifying righteousness is not derived from "any natural union . . . but a spiritual, active union."[219] Christ's imputed righteousness is recognized and appropriated only through faith, "the very bond of union."[220] Not only that, our dependence of God is enhanced because this response of faith is made possible by the Holy Spirit.[221] The Spirit forfeited by Adam in his probation was that which Christ purchased for us in blameless recapitulation of human history.[222] In both these ways, human beings are more dependent upon God (as Trinity) for their justification than they would have been under the old covenant.[223] Imputed righteousness is called "God's righteousness" in the Bible not only because Christ was a divine person "but rather as 'tis wholly and immediately received from God."[224] It is wholly imputed from God the Father and not self-merited.[225] Justification in the new covenant, for Edwards, is robustly Trinitarian.

However, as Christ is *hypostasis synthetos* or "a mixed person . . . so his righteousness is of a mixed nature," which differs from human and divine righteousness "in its measure and formal nature."[226] The Mediator, as both divine and human, "partakes of the common nature of both" and conforms to their respective propriety.[227] While Christ obeyed as human, the human righteousness was modified by the "mediatorial law" established and agreed upon in the *pactum salutis*.[228] We now move on from justification as a benefit of the legal union to Edwards's understanding of sanctification as flowing from the saint's vital union with Christ.

SANCTIFICATION AS VITAL UNION

Following the union of hearts, the other aspect of the real union is the vital union—sanctification that culminates in glorification.[229] This vital union follows the legal union, since God the Father "justifies them that so they may have a right to the Spirit."[230] Nonetheless, since true faith is inseparable from love, holy works must be its expression. "He is justified by faith alone, that is, 'tis faith that is all that has influence, but not by that faith that is alone."[231] Faith and obedience in believers are, therefore, acts of the "spirit of the Son" in believers that effect the ongoing, yet moment-by-moment *unitio cum Christo* in them.

Sanctification, as we have noted, is posterior to justification in both the "order of nature" and God's redemptive economy. Although Edwards admits that faith "is indeed something in man that is really and spiritually good, that is prior in the order of nature to justification," it is not considered as a good belonging to a person except after the fact.[232] For nothing in a person is accepted apart from union with Christ. Firstly, for God to regard a person as good and "yet remain separate from Christ" would annul the natural fitness of things.[233] Secondly, all human goodness is regarded as such by God "in consequence of justification." Sanctification, therefore, follows the union of hearts (regeneration and repentance) as well as justification.

Edwards distinguishes an Adamic works-righteousness from a personal righteousness *en Christo*. In the covenant of works, "the person was to be accepted and rewarded, only for the work's sake."[234] In the covenant of grace, however, "the work is accepted and rewarded, only for the person's sake; the person being beheld antecedently, as a member of Christ, and clothed with his righteousness."[235] Nonetheless, the legal union does away with guilt, covers our inherent sinfulness, and adds positive value to our inherent goodness.[236] Edwards is clear that God sees no moral value to human works before justification.[237] The works of the justified, however, are ennobled by a sort of secondary *enhypostaton* through the *unio mystica*.[238] This is a "secondary and derivative loveliness," in that Christ is the source of our continual sanctification and that the acceptance of this inherent holiness is founded on Christ's perfect and inherent righteousness.[239]

With the Reformed tradition, Edwards asserts that it is only Christ's work—not any act or quality of the regenerate—that has merited salvation.[240] Is it not contradictory to hold that salvation is *solus Christus* and, at the same time, to affirm a hierarchical scale of reward for good works? According to Edwards, Christ purchased perfect justification for all the elect, regardless of their potential for good works.[241] Christ merited eternal life or perfect happiness for all "in the general," which is qualitative insofar as it is relative to imperfect happiness.[242] But "it can't be said that Christ purchased any particular degree of happiness," for the capacity of our happiness is "left to God's sovereign pleasure."[243] The degrees of reward are not proportioned to the person's work but to the status and capability of the elect in the mystical body.[244] Christ is rewarded for obedience; the regenerate merely participate in the divine benefits. God "efficaciously" wills these varying stations and capacities in the elect and actualizes them by granting "different degrees of his Spirit."[245] The reward is thus founded on adoption as its proximate cause and the righteousness of Christ as its ultimate cause.[246] Believers must be weaned from this unstable, fleshly righteousness to Christ's righteousness. "We must be emptied of this fullness of the first Adam, as we would be filled with the fullness of the second Adam."[247] This fullness of Christ is the Holy Spirit.

GOD'S DECLARATIVE WORD IN JUSTIFICATION: MUST IT BE CREATIVE?

As we have seen, Edwards's forensic account of justification gives a prominent place to imputation. The overall tenor of his soteriology is clearly closer to Luther's (and Calvin's) than it is to Melanchthon's, which made justification the ground of sanctification.[248] Yet Melanchthon may be interpreted as faithfully extending Luther's belief in God's judicial declaration as a divine, creative act.[249] Such a Melanchthonian presupposition is likely to be funding Thomas Schafer's critique of Edwards's priority of the real (regeneration) over the legal (justification).[250]

However, this interpretation of justification as the cause of sanctification may not necessarily safeguard the distinction between the two. If God's declarative word were to be firstly forensic and secondarily transformative, then the line between imputation and infusion is blurred.[251] Although there is the *solus Christus, sola gratia*, and *sola fide* in Edwards's notion of justification, should there not also be a *solo verbo* by which God declares and makes the sinner righteous?[252]

Edwards no doubt affirms a *solo verbo*: "Justification is a sentence pronounced on a sinner pronouncing him in a state correspondent to the law."[253] Nonetheless, on his understanding, justification is not so much a transformative word but a judicial assertion; it does not make a person inherently righteous (even secondarily), but it is a divine judgment that simultaneously accomplishes its sentence.[254] Justification is God's judgment that a person is both righteous and not guilty.[255] In a word, justification justifies but does not sanctify. It is not so much a creative word of divine fiat that transforms the sinner as it is a legal judgment pronounced upon him or her based on evidential fact.[256] "There is a difference," Edwards states, "between declaration and evidence. The word declares, but the works are the proper evidence of what is declared."[257] There cannot be justification without justice wrought in and through Christ because if God forgave a sinner merely by divine fiat, this would be "no judicial act . . . but a pure act of sovereignty."[258]

As far as Edwards is concerned, such an arbitrary act like creation happens in regeneration, where an *ex novo* operation occurs.[259] To say that justification is declarative in a creative sense would overturn Edwards's notion of natural fitness. To create something out of nothing involves no preexisting conditions; that is, it involves the absence of any natural fitness of nonbeing to being.[260] Natural fitness, however, is based on *de potentia Dei ordinata*.[261] Christ's incarnation and atoning work are the foundation while the real and legal unions are the predisposing factors that must be in place for one to be fitly declared just.

In justification, the Judge must ascertain that there exists real righteousness that satisfies all legal requirements before the declaration or sentence of justification is pronounced.[262] Justification involves a judicial proceeding, which is finally demonstrated by a visible, rational, and public eschatological reckoning and declaration.[263] There is both a perfect, "invisible justification" following conversion that is subjectively appropriated and a declarative justification, that is publicly expressed eschatologically.[264] "To be justified is to be . . . approved and accepted in two respects; the one is to be approved really, and the other to be approved and accepted declaratively. Justification is two-fold; 'tis either the acceptance and approbation of the judge itself, or the manifestation of that approbation, by a sentence or judgment declared by the judge, either to our own consciences, or to the world."[265] There is, then, a second justification visible at final judgment and subjectively experienced again and again in repentance, which flows from the initial, perfect justification.[266]

Does this notion of a twofold justification move Edwards out of the Reformed fold?

DOUBLE JUSTIFICATION

If justification were to include an inherent process following operative, initial justification, the notion of meriting one's righteousness would enter the picture.[267] Clearly aware of the Roman distinction between initial and ongoing justification, Edwards accepts a double justification in a very qualified sense.[268] "I allow the distinction between the first and second justification, but then the second justification is no repetition of the first."[269] How is the second distinguished from the first?

Following a strand in Reformed thought, Edwards thinks that second justification is merely the ongoing manifestation of the perfect work of initial justification.[270] First justification is a *iustificatio impii* by which "the person justified is looked upon as (in himself) ungodly."[271] However, in line with Reformed orthodoxy, which located regeneration at the front of the *ordo salutis*, first justification is a justification of the *believing* sinner.[272] The second is a justification of the works of the godly—a *iustificatio pii*—subsumed under the *insitio in Christum*.[273] Just as our personal worth is enhanced solely *en Christo*, so our works derive their value wholly from and are thus rewarded as a result of Christ's dignity and merit.[274] Christ's inherent righteousness—imputed to us at first justification—remains *extra nos* and *pro nobis* in the second. This inherent righteousness is still Christ's, but the saint's inherent holiness (in Christ) has now acquired currency in God's eyes.[275]

First justification is real and perfectly enacted at conversion; faith makes us naturally fit for God's acceptance.[276] Second justification is proof that a saint has all other graces not limited to faith.[277] Edwards's construal of a double justification—which relies on the distinction between a primary imputation and a secondary declaration—is clearly indebted to Calvin.[278] On those who were contending against the apostle James, Edwards comments, "They did not distinguish between the first and second justification. The first justification, which is at conversion, is a man's becoming righteous, or his coming to have a righteousness belonging to him, or imputed to him. This is by faith alone. The second is at judgment, which is that by which a man is proved and declared righteous. This is by works, and not by faith only."[279]

St. James's justification of works is to be interpreted in light of St. Paul's justification without works: the former is to be understood as the assurance of our justification.[280] There is then a subjective justification included in second justification. Second justification includes a "cleaving to God in practice," in which our ongoing practical acts of faith are consequent on the initial dispositional act of "closing with" or union with Christ.[281] Our ongoing trust and obedience to Christ in Christ's threefold office is akin to a beggar stretching out his hand.[282] For Edwards, the merit of imputed righteousness is wholly and perfectly Christ's. However, God recognizes and rewards the inherent goodness of the saints, but only as they are in Christ and after they are justified.[283] One again hears echoes of Calvin's belief in the acceptability of works in Christ, by which an "absolute" justification by faith and imputation ground a "relative" works-righteousness.[284] As Luther put it, they are two kinds of *Christian* righteousness.[285]

In what sense then do human works condition justification? When Edwards speaks of works as a "condition" of justification, he does not mean the fulfillment of some prior act or thing that would merit or cause justification as its reward or effect. Rather, in continuity with Owen and other Puritan divines, he wants to maintain that the justified state, whether in its initiation or continuance, cannot be without sanctification.[286] For Edwards, just as works are the proof of faith, so faith is the "evidence" or "manifestation" of regeneration.[287] "The soul's act of faith" is the necessary "condition" of justification inasmuch as it must proceed from the new disposition—"the principle or being of faith."[288] And perseverance in faith is only to be understood as a condition of justification in that it will finally prove itself in the actual perseverance of the saint.[289]

PERSEVERANCE: ACTUAL OR VIRTUAL?

According to Edwards, during the initial act of faith or conversion, "the sinner is actually, and finally justified." However, perseverance, though not actual, is already in effect in first justification.[290] "The first act of faith gives a title to salvation . . . and so virtually contains perseverance."[291] This raises the question: how is first justification wholly actual while perseverance merely virtual at the point of conversion?

What is necessary for justification is, therefore, not (actual) perseverance but a disposition to perseverance.[292] None, except for infants, can be saved by pure disposition alone, since "the habit of grace is always begun by an act of grace in adult persons."[293] Our entitlement to eternal life is had through justification, which has been perfectly merited by Christ alone.[294] This right to eternal life acquired by Christ *pro nobis* includes perseverance.[295] Perseverance can be said to be a necessary "condition of justification" insofar as it maintains one's continual union with Christ.[296] Actual perseverance is thus necessary only as a sign of justification. Justification is had on account of "a persevering sort of faith."[297]

How, then, is the first act of true faith, which has perseverance virtually contained, distinguished from false faith? In reply to this question, Edwards states that "the proper evidence of its [true faith] being of that sort is actual perseverance."[298] If one's faith is only validated in the end, where is the assurance of salvation? And where is the ground of the saint's actual perseverance that is only virtual in first faith? The saint will persevere in the end because Christ has already persevered *pro nobis*.[299] Perseverance, though virtual in first faith, is not insecure, for its virtuality is a reliable *prolepsis* founded on Christ's finished work.[300] In this case, the virtuality of perseverance is not sourced in the saint's new disposition, but is grounded in the divine intention as realized in the history of the Mediator.[301]

If that were not the case, justification would not be the ground of perseverance. In Adam's case, justification was indeed conditional on works and "suspended" until its final accomplishment: it was probationary. What the elect in Christ receive is a complete and "confirmed" justification similar to what Adam would have had had he been perfectly obedient.[302] The saints are completely justified by faith because the work of righteousness, both active and passive, has been perfectly accomplished by Christ.[303] By participation in Christ's life, death, and resurrection, they "are justified in his justification."[304] Whereas Adam had to persevere in order to be justified, "the saints shall persevere because they are already justified."[305]

CONCLUSION

In summary, Edwards's vision of the *unio mystica* as a hypernym embracing a causal and rational *ordo* is his way of parsing human participation in the person and benefits of Christ. Regeneration and conversion, as a reciprocal reality, are the fundamental constituents of the *unitio mystica*—the real union of hearts between Christ and the believer. Flowing from this basic spiritual union, the benefits of adoption, justification, and sanctification are had from a threefold participation in Christ's person—relatively, legally, and vitally. A natural fitness comes about in which God recognizes the correlation between *unitio mystica* (the love-faith couplet) and relative/legal *unio*. With such a fitness in place, adoption and justification naturally follow. Moreover, there is a rational ordering of adoption before justification. Works before justification have no moral value, but they are ennobled through the *unio mystica* by virtue of union with Christ's person. Faith and works are crucial in the eschatological, second justification whereby God declares that the intrinsic sanctity of the Christian proves God's initial but perfect imputation of Christ's righteousness. These are broadly Reformed themes that Edwards integrates into his own soteriology. If his doctrine of justification by faith is seen as compromised by his notion of double justification, the criticism applies equally to Calvin and many along his trail.

Notes

1. Edwards, "Miscellanies," no. *ff*, in *WJE* 13:183–84.

2. Citing Wendelin, Riisen, and Wollebius, Heppe distinguishes the personal union (*unio hypostatica*) from the following: Trinitarian consubstantiality (*unio coessentialis*), divine repletive presence (*unio essentialis et virtus*), body-soul conjunction (*unio physica*), union of friendship (*unio relativa, consensus*), mystical union (*unio mystica*), sacramental union, and separate instrumental union (*per meram assistentiam*) (Heinrich Heppe, *Reformed Dogmatics Set Out and Illustrated from the Sources*, rev. and ed. Ernst Bizer, trans. G. T. Thomson, foreword Karl Barth [London: George Allen & Unwin, 1950], 431–32). *Unio mystica* is neither an essential nor a sacramental union; it is more than a natural or moral union; it is an organic, vital, spiritual, permanent, and mysterious union. See Augustus Hopkins Strong, *Systematic Theology: A Compendium and Commonplace Book Designed for the Use of Theological Students*, vol. 3, *The Doctrine of Salvation* (Philadelphia: Griffith & Rowland, 1909), 798–802.

3. Edwards, "Miscellanies," no. 487, in *WJE* 13:528.

4. Ibid.

5. "The Holy Spirit is given [to believers] much in the resemblance of its being given to Christ from the Father, as appears from *John 1:32-33*" (Edwards, "Miscellanies," no. 224, in *WJE* 13:346).

6. This, for Goodwin, was a matter of concern. Accordingly, the Spirit's union with us is "a nearer union than that of Christ within us; to which this limitation is added, He dwells in our hearts by faith. But of the Spirit, it is said, every where, that he dwells in us" (Thomas Goodwin, *Of the work of the Holy Ghost [the third person of the Trinity] in our salvation*, ed. Thankfull Owen and James Barron, vol. 5 of *The works of Thomas Goodwin, D.D., Sometime president of Magdalen College in Oxford* [London: T. G. (Thomas Goodwin [Jr.]), 1704], 35). Unlike Edwards, Goodwin thought that Christ has the priority in the order of action in establishing both unions. In the incarnation, it is "the Son of God the second Person dwelling first in, and possessing the human nature of Christ, as one Person with him; that then and thereupon the Spirit comes to dwell in that nature also." Similarly, in the mystical union, "Christ first dwells in us, and then sends his Spirit to dwell in us" (Goodwin, *WTG* 2:400).

7. Edwards, "Miscellanies," no. 487, in *WJE* 13:528.

8. "Christ's union with the Godhead is by the communication of the Holy Ghost not by measure to him" (Edwards, "Miscellanies," no. 624, in *WJE* 18:154). "The saints, on the other hand, participate in the Spirit by degrees through the mediation of Christ as their source of grace" (Edwards, "Notes on Scripture," no. 235, in *WJE* 15:185–86).

9. Edwards, "Miscellanies," no. 403, in *WJE* 13:468.

10. Edwards, "Concerning the End," in *WJE* 8:533–35.

11. "And, therefore, he chose one of that species to be the Head of the body, who should be also the Head of the whole creation, the first born of every creature, who should have the most transcendent union with the eternal Logos, even so as to be one person, and the rest to be strictly united to him" (Edwards, "Miscellanies," no. 1245, in *WJE* 23:180).

12. Edwards, "Miscellanies," no. 487, in *WJE* 13:528.

13. Edwards, "Blank Bible," note on Rom. 8:23, in *WJE* 24:1018; "Miscellanies," no. 487, in *WJE* 13:529.

14. Edwards, "Miscellanies," no. 529, in *WJE* 13:487.

15. Though the Spirit dwells in believers "as the soul also dwells in the members," this inhabitation is "by derivation from and participation with the head" (Edwards, "Miscellanies," no. 487, in *WJE* 13:528). Only unfallen human beings are fit to receive the Spirit of God unmediated. "So gospel holiness differs greatly from the holiness of man in innocency: man had the Holy Ghost then, as the Spirit of God; but now he must have it as the Spirit of the Son of God, the Spirit of a Redeemer, a Mediator between God and us, and a spiritual husband, etc." (Edwards, "Miscellanies," no. 894, in *WJE* 20:153). It was Christ who purchased the Holy Spirit from the Father for the church as a permanent, enduring principle, never to be lost. (Edwards, "Sermon Fourteen: Divine Love Alone Lasts Eternally," in *WJE* 8:353). In contrast to the experience of postlapsarian humanity, "the Spirit of God was communicated to our first parents in their state of innocence, and dwelt in them," but "they had no proper right or sure title to the Spirit" (ibid., 354).

16. "The Spirit therefore dwells in Jesus not as the Spirit of the Father, but as the Spirit of the Son" (Edwards, "Miscellanies," no. 427, in *WJE* 13:529).

17. "All this is 'in Christ Jesus,' as 'tis said in these Romans 8:1-2. 'Tis by their being in Christ that there is no condemnation to them, for 'tis by their being in Christ that they have the Spirit as a principle of life and action, or 'walk not after the flesh, but after the Spirit.'" (Edwards, "Blank Bible," note on Rom. 8:1–4, in *WJE* 24:1010).

18. Ibid.

19. "So in Christ dwells all the fullness of the Godhead bodily," yet in the saints, the Spirit "don't dwell in them bodily" (Edwards, "Miscellanies," no. 487, in *WJE* 13:529).

20. Like other Puritans, Edwards acknowledges the *unio hypostatica* as a substantial union. "By *bodily*, therefore, we ought to understand *personally* . . . by hypostatical union: so that the Λογος inhabiting or assuming, and the nature inhabited or assumed, should be one person, or one ὑφισταμενον, *one substance*" (John Davenant, *An exposition of the Epistle of St. Paul to the Colossians* . . . [London: Hamilton, Adams, and Co., 1831], 415). In Jesus, the Logos is "substantially dwelling in him, σωματιχως; that is, not only in a body, noting out the subject in which, but the manner, personally, bodily." See Thomas Goodwin, *A Discourse of Christ the Mediator*, ed. Thankfull Owen and James Barron, *The Works of Thomas Goodwin, D. D. Sometime President of Magdalen College in Oxford* (London: Thomas Goodwin Jr., 1692), 51; available at *The Digital Library of Protestant Texts.* So, "the entire fulness of the divinity dwells in Christ, not as in other holy men or angels, but bodily, as *in its own body*." See *The Book of concord . . .* ed. Henry Eyster Jacobs, trans. Charles P. Krauth and Charles F. Schaeffer (United Lutheran Publication House, 1911), "Solid Declaration," art. 8, 636.

21. Edwards, "Miscellanies," no. 702, in *WJE* 18:299.

22. "The assumption of that particular manhood of Christ was but as a means of the honor and advancement of the rest; and we may well argue the end from the means, and the excellency of the one from the excellency of the other" (Edwards, "Miscellanies," no. 741, in *WJE* 18:368).

23. Augustine understood Paul's corporeal image of the head and body to mean the entire Christ, the *Christus totus*, and not an analogy of the saints' relation to Christ as that between the head and members of its body. Citing *Sermo* 341.9.11 (*PL* 39, 1499), van Bavel points out that Augustine understood Jesus Christ in three senses: (1) as *Logos asarkos*, consubstantial with the Father; (2) as *Logos ensarkos*, the Mediator and Head of the church; and (3) *Christus totus*, the fulness of the church, both Head and Body. Augustine's threefold interpretation of the body of Christ in the Eucharist is (1) the historical flesh taken from Mary, (2) the eucharistic body given at the Last Supper, and (3) the body of believers. See Tarsicius van Bavel, "The 'Christus Totus' Idea:

A Forgotten Aspect of Augustine's Spirituality," in *Studies in Patristic Christology*, ed. Thomas Finan and Vincent Twomey (Dublin: Four Courts, 1998), 92.

24. Edwards, "Miscellanies," no. 1245, in *WJE* 23:179. Edwards describes the union and elevation of the human nature in the incarnation as Christ's individual nature, representative of all believers, and human nature in general. Firstly, the incarnation proper, in which the divine person assumed a particular human nature, its essence unchanged but its qualities are elevated. This is "Christ's incarnation, whereby his divine person . . . emptied himself in his humiliation . . . took the human nature," which was "not changed . . . though it be dignified and its fruit exceedingly changed" (Edwards, "Shadows of Divine Things," no. 166, in *WJE* 11:110). Secondly, "Christ's being ingrafted into the church of Christ, which was by his uniting himself with believers in his incarnation," whereby he becomes "a member of the church . . . a son of his mother, and a brother of believers." The result is that "the soul, by a vital union with Christ and by the faculties being as it were swallowed up in Christ, are altered, sanctified and sweetened" (Edwards, "Shadows of Divine Things," no. 166, in *WJE* 11:111). Thirdly, through the incarnation, which "feeds the world with its fruit."

25. Edwards articulates the distinction between relation and union: "Relation is such a nearness as that may be between two but union is such a nearness whereby they are no more two but one." Hence, "union is a word that signifies oneness." See Jonathan Edwards, 419. Sermon on John 13:23 [Jan 1736–37], in *WJE* 52. Edwards thus favors the image of Christ and the church as a single entity, and prefers the term *unio* over *relatio*. On a concessionary note, however, he is willing to accept "relation" and "union" as cognate terms. Commenting on the two words, he says, "[I]f any are disgusted at the word *union*, as obscure and unintelligible, the word *relation* equally serves my purpose." On the whole, however, he prefers to use "union" because it emphasizes unity rather than distinction (Edwards, "Justification by Faith Alone," in *WJE* 19:155).

26. Edwards, 180. Sermon on John 1:16 [c. 1729–31], in *WJE* 45.

27. The scope of the Spirit's work in the saint includes "the sanctification of our natures, our being made partakers of the divine nature, having the love of God shed abroad in our hearts, being united to the Son of God, being the children of God, having the presence of God, the light of his countenance and communion and fellowship with him, having divine peace and joy and living a divine life, and being hereafter possessed of eternal life and glory" (Edwards, "Praying for the Spirit," in *WJE* 22:217).

28. "Significantly, Edwards became the first major Reformed thinker since the Reformation era to place such a high premium on the doctrine of what scholastic (or academic) theologians called in Latin the *unio Christi*." See the introduction to *The Sermons of Jonathan Edwards: A Reader*, ed. Wilson H. Kimnach, Kenneth P. Minkema, and Douglas A. Sweeney (New Haven: Yale University Press, 1999), xliv. This theme was central in both the English episcopals and nonepiscopals alike. "Christ hath merited righteousness for as many as are found in him . . . for by faith we are incorporated into him." See Richard Hooker, *A Learned Discourse of Justification, Works, and How the Foundation of Faith Is Overthrown* (Grand Rapids, MI: Christian Classics Ethereal Library), 606, http://www.ccel.org/ccel/hooker/just.ii.html. "The foundation of the imputation is union . . . whereby the Lord Christ and believers do actually *coalesce into one mystical person*" (John Owen, *The Works of John Owen*, ed. William H. Goold [London: Banner of Truth Trust, 1965–68; originally publ. Johnstone & Hunter, 1850–53], 5:209). On its primacy in the Puritan tradition, see R. Tudur Jones, "Union with Christ: The Existential Nerve of Puritan Piety," *Tyndale Bulletin* 41 (November 1990): 168–208.

29. Neither "does the Spirit of God proceed discernibly in the steps of a particular established scheme, one half so often as is imagined." See Edwards, *WJE* 2:162. In this, he takes a position contrary to his grandfather, Solomon Stoddard.

30. Yet, even proponents of an *ordo salutis* did not abandon the idea of *participatio Christi*. Question 66 of the *Westminster Larger Catechism* sees union with Christ as effected by calling. See *The Westminster Larger Catechism* (Grand Rapids, MI: Christian Classic Ethereal Library), 11, http://www.ccel.org/ccel/anonymous/westminster2.pdf. Even though the Reformed scholastics

held to the *ordo salutis* of vocation, justification, and sanctification, they still regarded the *unio mystica* as foundational to the application of salvation. "At the root of the whole doctrine of the appropriation of salvation lies the doctrine of *insitio* or *insertio in Christum*, through which we live in him and him in us" (Heppe, *Reformed Dogmatics*, 511). Heppe cites Boquin, Zanchius, Olevian, Witsius, and Mastricht in this regard (ibid., 511–12). As compared to Calvin, Turretin has a logical *ordo* of calling, justification, and sanctification. Though the *unio mystica* is not separately treated, he regards faith, in terms of union and reception of Christ, as the "formal and principal act of justifying faith." From this *unio* "arises the participation in the blessings of Christ, to which (by union with him) we acquire a right (to wit, justification, adoption, sanctification and glorification)" (Francis Turretin, *Institutes of Elenctic Theology*, trans. George Musgrave Giger, ed. James T. Dennison [Phillipsburg, NJ: P&R, 1992–94], 2:563). Later scholars felt that this neglect was due to a fear of a "false mysticism," and they reiterated Calvin's emphasis by treating the *unio mystica* as a separate heading under the *applicatio salutis*, which logically precedes regeneration and justification, although, chronologically, all three come into existence simultaneously (Augustus Hopkins Strong, *Systematic Theology: A Compendium and Commonplace Book Designed for the Use of Theological Students*, vol. 3, *The Doctrine of Salvation* [Philadelphia: Griffith & Rowland, 1909], 795). Holding to a sublapsarian position, Reformed Baptist Augustus Strong lists his *ordo*: (1) preparatory: election and calling (redemption is prior to these two in God's eternal decree); (2) initial: union with Christ, regeneration, conversion, and justification (logical ordering); and (3) continuing: sanctification and perseverance.

    31. This is similar to Gaffin's interpretation of Pauline soteriology, where the *ordo salutis* is seen "not as distinct acts but as distinct aspects of a single act . . . the act of being joined *existentially* to Christ" (Richard B. Gaffin Jr., *The Centrality of the Resurrection: A Study in Paul's Soteriology*, Baker Biblical Monograph [Grand Rapids, MI: Baker Book House, 1978], 140). Edwards may be seen as anticipating "neoorthodoxy" and Westminster Calvinism in this regard. See A. T. B. McGowan, "Justification and the *ordo salutis*," in *Justification in Perspective: Historical Developments and Contemporary Challenges*, ed. Bruce M. McCormack (Grand Rapids, MI: Baker Academic; Edinburgh: Rutherford House, 2006), 156–62. It would be unhelpful here to classify Edwards's *ordo* as rational reduced to the "pedagogical" (as proposed by John M. Frame, "Salvation and Theological Pedagogy," *Act 3 Review* 14, no. 1 [2005]: 57–70).

    32. Edwards, "Sacramental Union in Christ," in *WJE* 25:585.

    33. Ibid. This threefold union finds a correlation in the *communio sanctorum*. "Being all so united to Christ, they must inevitably love [one] another. This is the natural consequence of their union of heart to Christ. . . . [As a] consequence of the relative union, [they are] nearly related one to another; [as a] consequence of the vital union, [they] have Christ's Spirit given them." And as legally espoused to Christ, "[they] must all be united as one holy society, subject to the same Lord, the same laws" (ibid., 585–86).

    34. This union of love "is the bond of union with Jesus Christ and the foundation of communion with him; it procures justification, adoption and glorification" (Edwards, 59. Sermon on Gal. 5:6 [a], in *WJE* 43).

    35. Edwards, 932. Sermon on John 6:51 (June 1749), in *WJE* 67.

    36. Edwards's overall logical order seems to follow van Mastricht's, if one assumes that (Edwards's notion of) adoption is commensurate with (van Mastricht's) *unio cum Christo*. For van Mastricht, his *ordo salutis* is based "at least in the order of nature if not of time": external call (offer of redemption), regeneration (receptive capacity imparted), conversion, faith or repentance (actualization of power to receive offer), union with Christ, justification, and sanctification (continual good works). See Peter van Mastricht, *A Treatise on Regeneration*, ed. Brandon Withrow (Morgan, PA: Soli Deo Gloria, 2002; first published as part of *Theoretico-Practica Theologia*, 1699, retypeset from 1769 ed.), 12.

    37. "By partaking of him, we principally receive a double grace (*duplicem gratiam*): namely, that being reconciled to God through Christ's blamelessness, we may have heaven instead of a

Judge a gracious Father; and secondly, that sanctified by Christ'a spirit we may cultivate blamelessness and purity of life" (Calvin, *Institutes* 3.11.1, 725). In this, Edwards's understanding displays a remarkable resemblance to Calvin's notion of *duplex gratia* (double grace), where justification and regeneration are conferred upon the saint as a single principle. See Paul Ramsey, appendix 4, "Infused Virtues in Edwardsean and Calvinistic Context," in *WJE* 8:746–49.

38. This is echoed by other Puritans: "The parts of application are two. Union with Christ, and communion of the benefits that flow from that union" (William Ames, *The Marrow of Sacred Divinity Drawne Out of the Holy Scriptures, and the Interpreters thereof, and Brought into Method* [London: Henry Overton, 1642], ch. 27, 123). "And although our redemption by Christ, as we are sinners, is an infinite benefit; yet his person thus given us, is more worth than all those his benefits, *Est aliquid in Christo formosius Salvatore.*" See Thomas Goodwin, *Of the Knowledge of God the Father, And His Son Jesus Christ,* ed. Thankfull Owen and James Barron, in *The Works of Thomas Goodwin, D. D. Sometime President of Magdalen College in Oxford* (London: Thomas Goodwin Jr., 1683),12; available at *The Digital Library of Protestant Texts.*

39. Edwards, 103. Sermon on 1 Cor. 1:9 [1729], in *WJE* 44.

40. Ibid. "To have communion with God, as many mistakenly understand it, is nothing else but to have spiritual conversation with God" (ibid.).

41. Edwards proposes a descending priority of the *unio mystica* based on an *ordo essendi*: being, having, and speaking. "A partaking together of the same enjoyments naturally begets mutual communication and society. . . . And where there is a common partaking in union there necessarily arises friendly communication and society" (ibid.). These realities are rooted in the beatitude of the Trinity, for "even the joy that God has in himself may be conceived of as the joy of union and society, the infinite joy and happiness in the eternal union and fellowship of the persons of the Trinity" (Edwards, 131. Sermon on 1 Pet. 1:8 [a] [Jul 1757], in *WJE* 44).

42. Edwards, 103. Sermon on 1 Cor. 1:9 [1729], in *WJE* 44. "COMMUNION is a common partaking of benefits, or of good, in union or society" (Edwards, "Miscellanies," no. 404, in *WJE* 13:468).

43. "There is no other way of intelligent minds being united as to cause happiness in each other, but love. 'Tis that by which two are as it were made one, and they have communion in each other" (Edwards, 131. Sermon on 1 Pet. 1:8 [a] [Jul 1729], in *WJE* 44).

44. Edwards points out the ascending degrees of relations that a believer stands to Christ: filial, fraternal, friendship, and marital. Edwards cites Heb. 11:12-13 to indicate Christ's relation to us as both Father and sibling. Yet, our relation to Christ is more immediate than to God the Father since "but there is no mediator between Christ and sinners to bring about a marriage union between Christ and their souls" (Edwards, "Miscellanies," no. 1091, in *WJE* 20:478)

45. Christ "is become our brother. So that he can communicate himself to us through that human nature more as we do one to another" (Edwards, 118. Sermon on Song of Sol. 8:1 [n.d.], in *WJE* 44).

46. Foreknowledge is God's choosing "us to be actually . . . in Christ, or being members of his Son," while predestination means that we are "elected in his election . . . to eternal life." Edwards distinguishes between election of the saints as foreknowledge, or "foreowning," and predestination, which is "consequent upon this foreknowledge" (Edwards, "Miscellanies," no. 769, in *WJE* 18:418).

47. Edwards, "Justification by Faith Alone," in *WJE* 19:156. Since participation of that which belongs to another flows from a prior union with the other, so it follows that none should "object against union to Christ's person being requisite to communion in his benefits" (Edwards, "Miscellanies," no. 1260a, in *WJE* 23:196).

48. "God sees it fit, that in order to an union's being established between two intelligent active beings or persons . . . that . . . there should be the mutual act of both . . . actively joining themselves one to another. God in requiring this . . . treats men as reasonable creatures, capable of act, and choice" (Edwards, "Justification by Faith Alone," in *WJE* 19:158).

49. "Christ is ingrafted into every believer . . . and every believer is a mother of Christ. Grace in the soul is the infant Christ there" (Edwards, "Shadows of Divine Things," no. 166, in *WJE* 11:112).

50. "The Spirit in us is that by which we are united to Christ, for by the Spirit of Christ being in us, we have Christ in us" (Edwards, "Blank Bible," note on Rom. 8:1–4, in *WJE* 24:1011).

51. Edwards, 131. Sermon on 1 Pet. 1:8 (a) (Jul 1757), in *WJE* 44. "And in order to the enjoyment of such an object, viz., of another mind, there must be union. There must be a suitable exercise of our wills towards the object, which is love, and answerable returns, which is by mutual love, and proper expressions of this love in society."

52. Edwards, "Treatise on Grace," in *WJE* 21:195.

53. "Therefore God, when he loved the saints before they actually love him, it is not upon a foresight of their love to him; but his love to them is previous in the order of nature, as well as time, to their love to him, because their love is a fruit of his love" (Edwards, 92. Sermon on 1 John 4:19, in *WJE* 43)

54. Edwards, "Sacramental Union in Christ," in *WJE* 25:585. "The first thing appertaining to this union between Christ and his people is the union of hearts. In this, Christ is first."

55. Ibid.

56. Edwards, "Miscellanies," no. 1245, in *WJE* 23:177–78. The meaning of election "cannot be a being chosen because it is foreseen we shall believe in Christ. Nor yet is it choosing us from foresight of his satisfactions and merits as our surety."

57. Ibid.

58. Edwards, "Miscellanies," no. 769, in *WJE* 18:418. "All things that God ever decreed he decreed for the sake of the beloved" (Edwards, "Miscellanies," no. 1245, in *WJE* 23:178).

59. Edwards, "Miscellanies," no. 1245, in *WJE* 23:178.

60. "That love that makes the lover willing to be in the stead of the beloved, even in the last extremity and where the beloved's utmost is concerned, even to perfect ruin and destruction, such love makes a thorough union" (Edwards, "The Threefold Work of the Holy Ghost," in *WJE* 14:404).

61. "And as he gave himself to them from eternity so he has so given himself to them as that he should be theirs to eternity" (Edwards, 419. Sermon on John 13:23 [Jan 1736–37], in *WJE* 52).

62. Ibid.

63. Edwards, 920. Sermon on 1 John 4:19, in *WJE* 67. "The love of benevolence is not purchased by Christ, for it was that that moved God to send Christ into the world; but God's love of complacency was purchased by Christ, purchased by his merits."

64. "This act of Faith doth depend partly upon a principle or habit of grace ingenerated, and partly upon the operation of God moving before and stirring up, John 6.44" (Ames, *The Marrow of Sacred Divinity*, ch. 27, 127).

65. "They are also immediately the children of the same Father. God hath begotten all by the same word and spirit. . . . Their Father of whom they are begotten is in heaven. The new nature and those principles that are infused, they are, as it were, sent down from heaven in that the Holy Ghost, whose immediate fruits those principles are, is from heaven. The Word of God, which is the seed by which they are begotten, is from heaven" (Edwards, "Christians a Chosen Generation," in *WJE* 17:288, 303).

66. The initial dispositional change whereby we are given a new nature, according to Edwards, is synonymous with first conversion for "what is done in conversion is nothing but the conferring of the Spirit of God" (Edwards, "Miscellanies," no. 241, in *WJE* 13:357–58). The Spirit's work of regeneration, "which is an ingenerating Christ in the heart," is analogous to the Spirit's role in the hypostatic union, "ingenerat[ing] the human nature of Christ . . . as that was an ingenerating Christ in the virgin's womb" (Edwards, "Miscellanies," no. 675, in *WJE* 18:236).

67. Edwards, "Miscellanies," no. 397, in *WJE* 13:462.

68. In contrast to faith making the soul capable for salvation, "love to God is rather a suiting or according of the soul to the nature of God" (Edwards, "Miscellanies," no. 507, in *WJE* 18:53).

69. In "the change made in man by regeneration . . . the same faculties [remain], the same human nature, that is as it were the substance or substratum of these properties, both old and new, and on which both old and new fruits do grow" (Edwards, "Shadows of Divine Things," no. 166, in *WJE* 11:112). Edwards would surely be familiar with Goodwin's insistence that the transformation at regeneration is not essential but dispositional. "It is a change, though not of the substance or faculties of the soul, yet of the temper, frame, and disposition of it." Using the example of a "dish being turned into a pot," Goodwin tries to illustrate a change in form but not of matter or substance (Goodwin, *Of the work of the Holy Ghost [the third person of the Trinity] in our salvation,* ed. Thankfull Owen and James Barron, vol. 5 of *The works of Thomas Goodwin, D.D. Sometime president of Magdalen College in Oxford* [London: T. G. (Thomas Goodwin [Jr.]), 1704], 363).

70. The purified faculties are "as the dross and scum useth to be in the melting of metals." God makes the soul pliable as one "softneth the good metal." Goodwin attempts a definition of such a transformation: "It is a universal frame and temper of all the Faculties of the Soul; whereby each, in their proportion, are respectively made suitable to the word in their inward several dispositions, and prepared and fitted to do what ever the Word commands" (Goodwin, *Work of the Holy Ghost in our salvation,* 363).

71. Edwards, "Miscellanies," no. 397, in *WJE* 13:463.

72. Stephen J. Nichols, *An Absolute Sort of Certainty: The Holy Spirit and the Apologetics of Jonathan Edwards* (Phillipsburg, NJ: P&R, 2003), 69. "Illumination," according to Nichols, "properly speaking, is the light seen by the one who is able, through regeneration, to see" (ibid.). It is more accurate, in our opinion, to say that illumination grants the light by which one can see the beauty of the Sun.

73. "There is not only the pleasure of seeing and beholding and receiving but there there is a great pleasure in acting and returning" (Edwards, 132. Sermon on 1 Pet. 2:2–3, in *WJE* 44).

74. As Caldwell observes, Edwards's "theory of excellency" or theological aesthetics is evidently at play here (Robert W. Caldwell III, *Communion in the Spirit: The Holy Spirit as the Bond of Union in the Theology of Jonathan Edwards* [Milton Keynes, UK: Paternoster, 2006], 131).

75. Edwards, "Fragment I," in *WJE* 54. "Regeneration may be signified this change as the mind may be passive [in] it and in the words conversion and repentance may signify the same as the mind is active in it." See also Edwards, *WJE* 3:362.

76. In Edwards's understanding, conversion is a single movement of repentance and faith. It is "the act of the soul turning from sin to God through Christ, as it respects the [object] from which the turning is, viz. sin, is called repentance. And as it respects the [object] to which, and the mediation by which [it turns], is called faith" (Edwards, "Charity and Its Fruits," Sermon 12, in *WJE* 8:331).

77. Like marital union, this covenant "between Christ and the soul" only becomes "proper covenant" at conversion. Prior to union with Christ and regeneration, the covenant of grace is no more than an "offer or invitation." (Edwards, "Miscellanies," no. 825, in *WJE* 18:537). "The revelation and offer of the gospel is not properly called a covenant till it is consented to" ("Miscellanies," no. 617, corol. 1, in *WJE* 18:149). See also Edwards, "Miscellanies," no. 825, in *WJE* 18:537.

78. Edwards, "Faith," nos. 75, 77, 82, 89, 92, in *WJE* 21:436, 437, 440, 444; "True Saints, When Absent From The Body, Are Present With The Lord," in *WJE* 25:231; *WJE* 2:397, 456; 510(a). Sermon on 1 Tim. 2:5, in *WJE* 54.

79. Hence, "the Holy Spirit is the bond of union by which Christ effectually unites us to himself" (John Calvin, *Calvin: Institutes of Christian Religion,* ed. John T. McNeill, trans. Ford Lewis Battles, Library of Christian Classics 20 [Philadelphia: Westminster, 1960], 3.1.1, 538). For Goodwin, the Son is immediately united to the saint, and, as such, the Father and Spirit indwell the saint mediately through the Son. From this *unio cum Christo* a threefold union ensues: relative, ontological, and operative. The relative union, like a marital union, grants that Christ and the saint may be spatially separated yet wholly united from the onset. The ontological union or "actual

inbeing of his person" in the saint is analogous to the soul-body relation. This is distinguished from "Christ dwelling in us by faith," which is "an operative dwelling" (Goodwin, *WTG* 2:404).

80. "It is true that we obtain this [union with Christ] by faith" (Calvin, *Institutes* 3.1.1, 537).

81. Although Caldwell does cite textual evidence that the *unio cum Christo* is mutual, he seems to emphasize the second half of the equation only when he claims that "faith is not logically distinct from a believer's union with Christ" (Caldwell, *Communion in the Spirit*, 131).

82. Edwards, "Justification by Faith Alone," in *WJE* 19:158.

83. Ibid. It is on this point that Edwards would agree with Aquinas: "Infused virtue is caused in us by God without any action on our part, but not without our consent. This is the sense of the words, *which God works in us without us*" (Aquinas, *STh* I-II, q. 55, a. 4, ad 6, 822). Of course, for Edwards, this only involves inherent or infused righteousness.

84. Caldwell describes faith as the instrument of union with Christ (Caldwell, *Communion in the Spirit*, 131).

85. "Now it is by faith that the soul is united unto Christ; faith is this bride's reception of Christ as a bridegroom." Christ, as husband, "naturally looks most at a soft and tender disposition of mind, and those virtues and affections . . . which he most naturally looks at in her, are a sweet and entire confidence and trust, submission and resignation" (Edwards, "Miscellanies," no. 37, in *WJE* 13:220).

86. "Indeed, the act [of faith] belongs to the being of faith; so indeed, considering the nature of man, as a being consisting of soul and body, the practice belongs to the nature of acceptance" (Edwards, "Miscellanies," no. 859, in *WJE* 20:84).

87. Edwards, 59. Sermon on Gal. 5:6 (a) (n.d.), in *WJE* 43.

88. "Judgment: Wherein an act of the judgment consists, or an assent to a thing as true, or a dissent from it as false. Shew it to be different from mere perception, such as is in the mere presence of an idea in the mind, and so not the perception of the agreement and disagreement of ideas" (Edwards, "Subjects to be Handled in the Treatise on the Mind," no. 28, in *WJE* 6:390).

89. "I suppose none will doubt but that some natural men do yield a kind of assent of their judgments to the truth of the Christian religion, from the rational proofs or arguments that are offered to evince it" (Edwards, *WJE* 2:295).

90. Therefore, "a spiritual conviction of the divinity and reality of the things exhibited in the gospel, which arises from a spiritual understanding of those things . . . is . . . a sense and taste of the divine, supreme and holy excellency and beauty of those things" (ibid.).

91. In Edwards's more philosophical description, a person "cannot actually will or act entirely unless his inclinations and consent to being have been made captive to the beauty of Being itself" (Edwards, *WJE* 1:51).

92. There must be a union of heart on the elect's side to Christ in order to "cordially receive him and cleave to him," and not "reject him" (Edwards, "Miscellanies," no. 1346, in *WJE* 23:382).

93. Edwards could assert that a "condition" of salvation lies "in our own power" (Edwards, "Miscellanies," no. 71, in *WJE* 13:238). Yet, it is equally impossible that we could save ourselves except by the Holy Spirit granting us a right disposition.

94. "Believing is the assent to any truth testified; trusting always respects truth that nearly concerns ourselves, in regard of some benefit of our own that it reveals to us, and some benefit that the revealer is the author of; it is the acquiescence of the mind in a belief of any person that by his word reveals or represents himself to us as the author of some good that concerns us" (Edwards, "Miscellanies," no. 329, in *WJE* 13:407).

95. Edwards rebuts the Arminian criticism of Luther's beggar metaphor—that human merit is implied in the act of receiving a gift. See Martin Luther, "The Last Written Words of Luther: Holy Ponderings of the Reverend Father Martin Luther" (16 Feb 1546), trans. James A. Kellerman, in *Dr. Martin Luthers Werke*, Band 85 (TR 5), 317–18 (Weimar: Hermann Boehlaus Nachfolger, 1909), http://www.iclnet.org/pub/resources/text/wittenberg/luther/beggars.txt.

96. "Therefore the first act of faith is . . . the soul's resting in him and adhering to him so far as his word does reveal him to all as a Savior for sinners, as one that has wrought out redemption,

as a sufficient Savior, as a Savior suited to their case, as a willing Savior, as the author of an excellent salvation, etc.; so as to be encouraged heartily to seek salvation of him, to come to him, to love, desire and thirst after him as a Savior, and fly for refuge to him. . . . That definition which we gave of trust before holds, viz. the acquiescence of the mind in the word of any person who reveals himself to us as the author of some good that nearly concerns us" (Edwards, "Miscellanies," no. 329, in *WJE* 13:408).

97. Calvin ascribes the efficient cause of salvation to the free mercy of God (the Father); the material cause to Christ and Christ's acquired righteousness; the formal or instrumental cause to faith; and the final cause to the glory of God. The first three may be read in a Trinitarian manner: the efficient is assigned to "the mercy of the Heavenly Father"; the material, "Christ, with his obedience"; and the formal, faith "whereby the righteousness of Christ is applied to us" since this is the principal work of the Holy Spirit. The final cause is God's glory, manifested "both in the proof of divine justice and in the praise of God's goodness." All four causes are *extra nos* and exclude cooperation or works-righteousness. Rome, Calvin thinks, would not dispute the efficient or final cause. However, "they falsely represent the material and formal cause, as if our works held half the place along with faith and Christ's righteousness" (Calvin, *Institutes*, III.xiv.17, 783–84). The final cause as "the glory of God and of Jesus Christ, and life everlasting" would be uncontroversial. The Reformed may agree with the agent of justification being "a merciful God" yet may take issue with the kind of divine operation subsumed under justification ("who washes and sanctifies gratuitously, signing, and anointing with the holy Spirit of promise." See J. Waterworth, trans., *The Canons and Decrees of the Sacred and Oecumenical Council of Trent Celebrated under the Sovereign Pontiffs, Paul III, Julius III, and Pius IV, to which are Prefixed Essays on the External and Internal History of the Council* (London: C. Dolman, 1848), Session VI, ch. 7, 34. Where Calvin uses formal and instrumental causation interchangeably in reference to faith in Christ, Trent deems God's justice to be the formal cause of justification in a differing sense. Clearly, Reformed scholastics cannot agree with Trent's idea of formal causation, even though it is ascribed to "God's justice," since it is not *extra nos*; this divine justice is "not that whereby He Himself is just, but that whereby He maketh us just." See Waterworth, *Council of Trent*, Session VI, ch. 7, 35. The Reformed tradition would distinguish Christ's righteousness as the formal cause from faith as the instrumental. See Peter Toon, *Justification and Sanctification*, Foundations for Faith (Westchester, IL: Crossway Books, 1983), 81.

98. Why is faith "the special condition" or instrument of justification? If one were to reply that it is "by virtue of God's appointing it to be a condition," this would amount to circular reasoning. This is like to saying "that God has appointed that faith should have something peculiar belonging to it, and the peculiar thing that he has appointed it shall have is that he has appointed it shall have something peculiar" (Edwards, "Miscellanies," no. 1092, in *WJE* 20:480).

99. The condition of the covenant of redemption "is all that Christ has done and suffered to procure redemption," while the "condition" of the covenant of grace "is that [Christ's people] should close with him and adhere to him" (Edwards, "Miscellanies," no. 617, in *WJE* 18:148). The covenant of redemption is an eternal pact between Father and Christ, who "as a public person" includes the church, while the covenant of grace is between Christ and the church (ibid.). We are party to both covenants as "one of the parties contracting" since, in the covenant of redemption, we are involved in the transaction "as being parts of Christ" and, in the other covenant, "as being distinctly and by ourselves" (ibid., 159).

100. Edwards, "Miscellanies," no. 2, in *WJE* 13:199.

101. Ibid., 198. In illustrating the "vast difference between a free offer and a covenant," Edwards likens the former to a "gift to a beggar . . . without any manner of preliminary condition." As such it cannot be properly said that the giver "makes a covenant with the beggar." In an earlier entry, Edwards refused to distinguish between a covenant of redemption and a covenant of grace, as this would "divide Christ and the church" and encourage works-righteousness and "neonomianism" (Edwards, "Miscellanies," no. 2, in *WJE* 13:198). Edwards admits that others may very well refer to the free offer of salvation as the covenant of grace and

faith as its condition, but in doing so, "it is much the more hard to think right, for speaking so wrong." In a later entry, however, he accepts the distinction between the covenant of redemption and covenant of grace, or "covenant of union," and insists on "rightly distinguishing" the subjects, conditions, and promises of the two covenants (Edwards, "Miscellanies," no. 825, in *WJE* 18:536–37; see also Edwards, "Miscellanies," no. 617, in *WJE* 18:148–51).

102. Edwards, *WJE* 3:361–71. Edwards identifies metanoia with these biblical images: being born again, circumcision of the heart, spiritual resurrection, having a new heart and spirit, putting on a new humanity, becoming a new creature. Van Mastricht, unlike Calvin and Edwards, used the term "regeneration" in the narrow sense: "The thing intended by regeneration is only that physical operation of the Holy Ghost whereby He begets in men . . . the first act or principle of spiritual life, by which they are enabled to receive the offered Redeemer" (Van Mastricht, *Treatise on Regeneration*, 13).

103. Edwards, "Treatise on Grace," in *WJE* 21:161.

104. Thus, "the real union, consisting in the union of hearts and affections, and in the vital union, is begun in this world, and perfected in the next" (Edwards, "Lectures on the Qualifications for Full Communion in the Church of Christ," in *WJE* 25:231).

105. Edwards, "Justification by Faith Alone," in *WJE* 19:20.

106. "And all the difference whereby the first act of faith has a concern in this affair that is peculiar, seems to be as it were only an accidental difference, arising from the circumstance of time, or its being first in order of time" (Edwards, "Justification by Faith Alone," in *WJE* 19:207).

107. Edwards, 564. Sermon on Luke 22:32, in *WJE* 56. "Sometimes regeneration is spoken of in a more limited sense as signifying only the first saving work of God upon the soul which is wrought in an instant. But sometimes regeneration is spoken of in Scriptures as a continued thing . . . both the beginning and the progress of the work are included in the word sanctification." Regeneration as first conversion is related to sanctification as continued conversion. "As it is with . . . first conversion . . . the progress of the work of grace in the hearts of saints, is . . . a continued conversion and renovation of nature" (Edwards, *WJE* 2:343). Clearly, Edwards would not have regarded his interchangeable use of regeneration and sanctification as sloppiness, but only as speaking scripturally (Conrad Cherry, *Theology of Jonathan Edwards: A Reappraisal* [Bloomington: Indiana University Press, 1990], 43).

108. Edwards, "Approaching the End of God's Grand Design," in *WJE* 25:126.

109. Edwards, "Miscellanies," no. 1346, in *WJE* 23:382.

110. Edwards's use of the phrase "natural fitness" is not without precedent within the tradition. For example, Reformed writers applied the term "natural fitness" sacramentally and vocationally. "There is a natural fitness and aptness in the outward things to express the inward." See James Ussher, *A body of divinity: or, the sum and substance of Christian religion . . .* (London: Printed by R. J. for Jonathan Robinson, 1702), 365. "Thus also as to all other callings, you must consider, not only the will of the child or parents, but their natural fitness of body and mind." See Richard Baxter, *A Christian directory: or, a summ of practical theology, and cases of conscience . . .* (London: Thomas Parkhurst, Jonathan Robinson, and John Lawrence, 1707), 358. Goodwin, who was closer to Edwards, used it in relation to the conforming of the soul to God's Word. Thus, "when there is an universal conformity of all faculties according to their several kinds and offices, and also their subordinations one to another, with a natural fitness and disposedness unto what the Law requires, then is the heart molded in the Word" (Goodwin, *Work of the Holy Ghost in Our Salvation*, 364).

111. Edwards, "Miscellanies," no. 1092, in *WJE* 20:481.

112. Edwards, "Miscellanies," no. zz, in *WJE* 13:197; "Blank Bible," Rom. 8:1-4, in *WJE* 24:1011.

113. Edwards, "Lectures on the Qualifications for Full Communion in the Church of Christ," in *WJE* 25:231. In regeneration, a person is transferred into "a state of grace, to an interest in Christ, and to be actually a child of God, is in a moment" (Edwards, "Treatise on Grace," in *WJE* 21:161).

114. Edwards, "Profitable Hearers of the Word," in *WJE* 14:266.

115. Edwards, "'Controversies' Notebook: Justification," in *WJE* 21:339.

116. Ibid. "A natural fitness for a state is when there is a good natural agreeableness, or accord, between the person or his qualifications and the state; or that there is a good capacity for a state" (Edwards, "Miscellanies," no. 647, in *WJE* 18:187).

117. "The moral fitness in this case is not in the act of faith but in the act of God with respect to the believer" (Edwards, "'Controversies' Notebook: Justification," in *WJE* 21:339).

118. Edwards, "Miscellanies," no. 647, in *WJE* 18:16. Elsewhere, he defines moral fitness as "the merit of the object of God's favor, or a moral qualification of the object attracting that favor and recommending to it" (Edwards, "'Controversies' Notebook: Justification," in *WJE* 21:339).

119. There is to be found both moral and natural fitness only in Christ, but only a natural fitness to salvation in the elect (Edwards, "Miscellanies," no. 647, in *WJE* 18:187–88).

120. Edwards, "Justification by Faith Alone," in *WJE* 19:159.

121. Ibid.; "'Controversies' Notebook: Justification," in *WJE* 21:339; and "Miscellanies," no. 877, in *WJE* 20:119. There is a "NATURAL FITNESS . . . between faith in Christ, and a being looked upon as united to Christ" (Edwards, "Miscellanies," no. 831, in *WJE* 18:544).

122. Edwards, "Miscellanies," no. 1260a, in *WJE* 23:196.

123. Edwards, "Miscellanies," no. 831, in *WJE* 18:544.

124. Ibid. Natural fitness is "a determination of the act of God's goodness to an object with certain qualifications to answer some wise design of his own" (Edwards, "'Controversies' Notebook: Justification," in *WJE* 21:339). Edwards will only allow that it is "by a sovereign" and "arbitrary" constitution that faith unites us to Christ if it is understood as God's "absolutely free grace, without any obligation by faith," but not "in that sense that it was by a constitution without any guidance of divine wisdom directing to that which was fit and suitable to be done" ("Miscellanies," no. 877, in *WJE* 20:119).

125. See Lee, "Editor's Introduction," in Edwards, *WJE* 21:1–106; Samuel T. Logan Jr., "The Doctrine of Justification in the Theology of Jonathan Edwards," *Westminster Theological Journal* 46 (Spring 1984): 26–52; Thomas A. Schafer, "Jonathan Edwards and Justification by Faith," *Church History* 20 (December 1951): 55–67; and George Hunsinger, "Dispositional Soteriology: Jonathan Edwards on Justification by Faith Alone," *Westminster Theological Journal* 66 (2004): 107–20.

126. "But *'tis* something that we do, that renders . . . it a meet thing in the sight of God that we in particular should be looked upon as united to the Saviour, and [as] having the merit of what he did and suffered (upon the account of which we are so justified) belonging to us" (Edwards, "Miscellanies," no. 416, in *WJE* 13:475–76). "The way in which the qualification appointed in the latter way, even faith in Christ, interests in its next immediate benefit, even an interest in Christ, is not on account of any moral value of faith in the sight of God, but only on account of a proper capacity which it implies for such a benefit." God has so determined that there must be "a proper capacity to receive, so that there should be a natural agreement between the qualification and capacity of the subject and the benefit that he is to be the subject of, that they may well consist together, and not be in nature repugnant one to another" (Edwards, "'Controversies' Notebook: Justification," in *WJE* 21:369).

127. "Indeed, neither salvation itself, nor Christ the Savior, are given as a reward of anything in man: they are not given as a reward of faith, nor anything else of ours: we are not united to Christ as a reward of our faith, but have union with him by faith, only as faith is the very act of uniting, or closing on our part" (Edwards, "Justification by Faith Alone," in *WJE* 19:200–201).

128. Edwards, "Miscellanies," no. s, in *WJE* 13:174. As John Brown put it: "Being insert into Christ glued & united unto him, he maketh what is his to be ours, he communicateth unto us his riches, he interposeth his Righteousness between the Father's judgment & our unrighteousness, and under it, as under a shield, he hideth, defendeth, & protecteth us from God's wrath, which we

had deserved; Yea at length giveth it to us, & maketh it ours; with which being covered & adorned, we may boldly & saifly sist ourselves before the Tribunal of God, and we not only appear Righteous, but also are Righteous." See John Brown, *The life of justification opened . . .* (Utrecht, 1695), 524.

129. According to Edwards, "our having Christ's merits and benefits belonging to us, follows from our having . . . Christ himself belonging to us, or a being united to him; and if so it must also be . . . that, in a person, that on his part makes up the union between his soul and Christ, should be the thing on the account of which God looks on it meet that he should have Christ's merits belonging to him" (Edwards, "Justification by Faith Alone," in *WJE* 19:156).

130. Edwards opines that those who oppose the idea of natural fitness in justification "might as well object against union to Christ's person being requisite to communion in his benefits" (Edwards, "Miscellanies," no. 1260a, in *WJE* 23:196).

131. Hence, the action of closing with Christ includes a "natural fitness or proper capacity for the benefit" (Edwards, "Miscellanies," no. 1070, in *WJE* 20:451).

132. "When a man offers himself and a joint possession of his estate to a woman whom he makes suit to, on condition she will receive him and unite herself to him as her husband, will any ever imagine that he . . . has [not] any respect to any fitness or propriety in her thus receiving him and uniting herself to him, in order to her being possessed of such a benefit . . . but that he is wholly arbitrary in requiring such terms?" (Edwards, "Miscellanies," no. 1092, in *WJE* 20:481).

133. "'Tis [not] by nature, by any natural union, dependence, or derivation from the person who wrought out righteousness, but a spiritual, active union" (Edwards, "Miscellanies," no. 1177, in *WJE* 23:94).

134. The source or "*treasury* and storehouse" of grace is not the human nature of Christ, but Christ as God-man. Hence, all graces are not "actually invested, or did reside and were in the human nature, and were from then really communicated to [the regenerate] by a participation in a portion of what did so inhere: but they are morally his, by a compact, to be bestowed by him as he thinks good, as he is mediator, God and man" (Owen, "On Communion," in *WJE* 2:68).

135. Edwards, "'Controversies' Notebook: Justification," in *WJE* 21:410.

136. Ibid., 368–69.

137. "God will neither impute Christ's righteousness to us [justification], nor adjudge his benefits to us, unless we be in him; nor will he look upon us as being in him [legal union] without an actual unition to him [real union], because he is a wise being and delights in order and not confusion" (Edwards, "Miscellanies," no. 712, in *WJE* 18:341).

138. "Relative blessings are more directly from the relative union; indeed this relative union is by a real union; a real union is the ground of it. But not properly a vital union" (Edwards, 932. Sermon on John 6:51 [June 1749], in *WJE* 67). Here, Edwards clearly distinguishes regeneration from sanctification, the former being the foundation of adoption.

139. Edwards, 932. Sermon on John 6:51 (June 1749), in *WJE* 67.

140. Edwards, "Miscellanies," no. 1260a, in *WJE* 23:196. This is analogous to the Father's regarding the human Jesus as the incarnate Son because of a real *unio hypostatica*. See chapter 4 and table 1.1.

141. Edwards, "Miscellanies," no. 1092, in *WJE* 20:489.

142. Edwards, "Miscellanies," no. 1260a, in *WJE* 23:196.

143. In the "relative union," believers "come to be nearly related to Christ. Their souls are brought to Christ as the King's daughter is led in unto a glorious prince to be united to him in spiritual wedlock. There is a covenant union between Christ and the soul of a Christian. They are united by the mutual bed of a covenant whereby he is theirs and they his. There is such an union that they have mutual propriety in Each other." Through the incarnation, Christ as consubstantial with us has "like relative capacities of a son, a neighbor, a friend and a brother" (Edwards, 233. Sermon on Matt. 11:29 [b] [Dec 1752], in *WJE* 47).

144. Edwards, "Miscellanies," no. 686, in *WJE* 18:249.

145. Edwards, 419. Sermon on John 13:23 (Jan 1736), in *WJE* 52.

146. Ibid.

147. "And again, as Christ unites mankind with the Father, by being the bond of union between them, as the third person in whom both are united (for the Father and he from eternity are one); and therefore, by making sinful men one with himself, as he does by three things, viz. by substituting himself in their stead from eternity, and by taking on their nature, and bringing them home to an union of hearts, and vital union" (Edwards, "Miscellanies," no. 781, in *WJE* 18:451).

148. Edwards, 419. Sermon on John 13:23 (Jan 1736), in *WJE* 52. This "mediety" of Christ brings God close to both human beings and angels (Edwards, "Miscellanies," no. 781, in *WJE* 18:450).

149. Revelation and grace are to see God in Christ by the Spirit. "To endeavor to get the knowledge of the excellency of God as it appears in the face of Jesus Christ or as he reveals himself in the Gospel. 'Tis the knowledge of this that begets a filial disposition. By seeing the Glory of God as the son reveals it we shall derive to our selves the spirit of the son" (Edwards, 130. Sermon on Eph. 5:1, in *WJE* 44). This filial spirit, or "Spirit of the Son of God," liberates believers from fear, bondage, and legalism as it imparts "in Christians a principle of love, of childlike confidence and hope" (Edwards, "Notes on Scripture," no. 196, in *WJE* 15:114).

150. Edwards, "Blank Bible," note on Rom. 8:1-4, in *WJE* 24:1010.

151. Edwards, "Miscellanies," no. 686, in *WJE* 18:249.

152. Edwards, *WJE* 2:239. "And though the sight of his relative union with God, and his being in his favor, is not without a medium, because he sees it by that medium, viz. his love; yet his sight of the union of his heart to God is immediate: love, the bond of union, is seen intuitively: the saint sees and feels plainly the union between his soul and God; it is so strong and lively, that he can't doubt of it. And hence he is assured that he is a child."

153. Edwards rebuts the idea that "all the privileges that appertain to adoption are among the benefits that are the reward of the righteousness . . . which is reckoned to him in his justification." He insists that "adoption is truly to be looked upon as properly diverse from justification, and not implied in it" (Edwards, "Miscellanies," no. 1093, in *WJE* 20:481). The seventeenth-century Protestant theologians regarded adoption as an effect of justification (Wolfhart Pannenberg, *Systematic Theology*, trans. Geoffrey W. Bromiley [Grand Rapids, MI: Eerdmans, 1998], 3:212).

154. In justification, human beings relate to God as universal judge under the law and covenant of works. In adoption, God becomes Father to the saints "by virtue of their special union with the only-begotten Son of God" under a new covenant of grace. As neither angel nor Adam could have obtained adoption by being righteousness, so adoption is "no privilege annexed by the law to righteousness" (Edwards, "Miscellanies," no. 1093, in *WJE* 20:481–82). In this, he differs from Ames: "This change of state is twofold; relative, and absolute or real," the first pertaining to "God's reputation" and including justification and adoption (Ames, *The Marrow of Sacred Divinity*, ch. 27, 129).

155. Edwards, "Blank Bible," Rom. 8:1-4, in *WJE* 24:1011.

156. In this regard, Edwards differs from his Puritan forebears, like John Ball, who placed adoption after justification. See Joel R. Beeke and Mark Jones, *A Puritan Theology: Doctrine for Life* (Grand Rapids, MI: Reformation Heritage Books, 2012), 486. Where justification rationally precedes adoption, one is declared to be no longer God's enemy in order to be legally pronounced a child. For adoption to precede justification, one needs to belong to Christ and regarded by God, in Jenson's terminology, as "one moral person" before being accounted righteous in God's sight (Robert W. Jenson, *America's Theologian: A Recommendation of Jonathan Edwards* [New York: Oxford University Press, 1988], 61).

157. "Through faith in Christ, therefore, Christ's righteousness becomes our righteousness and all that he has becomes ours; rather, he himself becomes ours. . . . [H]e who trusts in Christ exists in Christ; he is one with Christ, having the same righteousness as he." See Martin Luther, *Martin Luther's Basic Theological Writings*, ed. Timothy F. Lull, foreword by Jaroslav Pelikan (Minneapolis: Fortress Press, 1989), 156. Luther considered imputed righteousness as *extra nos*, and

even progressive. "For alien righteousness is not instilled all at once, but it begins, makes progress, and is finally perfected at the end through death" (ibid., 157).

158. Faith is the "suiting and according the soul to the Redeemer, and to his salvation and the nature of it," particularly its gratuity. It is "a suiting of judgment and sense and disposition of the soul," or an "according of the mind to a thing declared and proposed." (Edwards, "Miscellanies," no. 507, in *WJE* 18:53). Edwards makes this clear in asserting that "true faith arises from a spiritual sight of Christ" (Edwards, *WJE* 2:297). Echoing Luther, *caritas* is appropriated to the Spirit and *iustitia* to Christ. See Alister E. McGrath, *Luther's Theology of the Cross: Martin Luther's Theological Breakthrough* (Oxford: Blackwell, 1990), 85. We could call this a kind of "divine connaturality" whereby God makes our natural faculties fit to achieve their supernatural end. "For there is a connaturality in a spiritual heart to the Word of God, because this is the seed that did regenerate him." See Richard Baxter, *Gildas salvianus: The reformed pastor . . .* (London: Thomas Parkhurst, Jonathan Robinson, and John Lawrence, 1707), 360. See J. Budziszewski, "The Natural, the Connatural, and the Unnatural," unpublished paper presented at the conference "St. Thomas and the Natural Law," Jacques Maritain Center, University of Notre Dame, Notre Dame, Indiana, July 2004.

159. Elsewhere, Edwards reiterates that this "very bond of union, by which we are united to this divine person so as to be interested in his righteousness, is that principle and act of the soul by which we know that the righteousness is thus the righteousness, and by which we cordially and with all our hearts ascribe it wholly to him [Christ] and give him all the glory of it." Ibid.

160. Our "closing in" with the person of Christ includes the acceptance of Christ's kingly office and the benefits that come with it. Though rationally distinct, the royal and sacerdotal are not only united in the person of Christ, they are not ontologically separable realities, "for as a priest he procures a title to the benefits of his kingly office." As priest, Christ pays the price and purchases the Spirit *pro nobis*; as king, Christ receives this very same *summum bonum* as a reward from the Father. Faith in the royal office is "submitting to Christ" and involves accepting the prophetic office, that is to say, "yielding to Christ's teaching" (Edwards, "Miscellanies," no. 855, in *WJE* 20:82–83).

161. Edwards, "Miscellanies," no. 855, in *WJE* 20:83. This is sanctification broadly conceived, of course, since "the benefits of his kingly office" include "salvation from sin, and conformity to his nature and will, and actual salvation by actual deliverance from our enemies, and the bestowment of glory."

162. "'Tis absolutely necessary that in order to a sinner's being justified, the righteousness of some other should be reckoned to his account; for 'tis declared that the person justified is looked upon as (in himself) ungodly; but God neither will nor can justify a person without a righteousness; for justification is manifestly a forensic term" (Edwards, "Justification by Faith Alone," in *WJE* 19:188). Edwards concludes after a lengthy word study on "righteousness": "Hence the falseness of the opinion of those that deny the words justification and righteousness to be used as forensic terms by the apostles, but that some real change or inherent qualification was intended by these terms" (Edwards, "'Controversies' Notebook: Justification," in *WJE* 21:351).

163. "This relation or union to Christ, whereby Christians are said to be *in* Christ (whatever it be), is the ground of their right to his benefits. . . . First we must be in him, and then he will be made righteousness, or justification to us" (Edwards, "Justification by Faith Alone," in *WJE* 19:156). Edwards's parenthetical "whatever it be" does not indicate any agnosticism regarding the *unio mystica*; rather, he was not concerned to define what it is in this treatise. We could parse "whatever it be" as a hint of the multidimensionality of the *unio cum Christo*. Edwards's Christology is not more forensic than filial in its emphasis; rather, the forensic is distinct from the filial, but are both grounded in the agapic. See Michael Jinkins, *A Comparative Study in the Theology of Atonement in Jonathan Edwards and John McLeod Campbell: Atonement and the Character of God* (Lewiston, NY: Edwin Mellen, 1993). See also Hunsinger, "Dispositional Soteriology," 107–20.

164. Edwards, 549. Sermon on Heb. 12:22-24 [f] [1740], in *WJE* 55. "Righteousness," Edwards defines, "is a relative thing, and has always relation to a law" (Edwards, "Miscellanies," no. 278, in *WJE* 13:377).

165. Edwards, "Part IIa: Justification," in *WJE* 27. "Consider that if you are ingrafted into Christ," Edwards preaches, "your sins will be put on his account. As the debt of a woman after she is married is required of her husband so will your debts be answer'd by Christ" (Edwards, 308. Sermon on John 15:15 [Dec 1733], in *WJE* 48).

166. Edwards, "Justification by Faith Alone," in *WJE* 19:158. The *unitio mystica* is "the ground" of "a legal union between Christ and true Christians." Hence, the intimacy of these unions is placed by Edwards in an ascending order: legal, real, and spiritual. "Christ and believers are so one that they are one in law. Looked on as one by the Father, this legal union is founded in a real union . . . so one as the members and the Head are . . . but because this is not near enough still fully to represent the closeness of union . . . the Scripture bear a step further yet and represents Christ and believers . . . as . . . one Spirit" (Edwards, 419. Sermon on John 13:23 [Jan 1736], in WJE 52). Goodwin points out that the reality of Christ as "a mystical, spiritual head" transcends the ascending analogy of relations Christ has toward the saints—as their political, conjugal, and natural head. While Christ's conjugal (husband-wife) and natural (head-body) headship is only toward the church, his political headship (king-subject) includes the angels (Goodwin, *WTG* 1:546).

167. "Now in order to a sinner's being thus accepted with God, there must he some real righteousness that must be the sinner's. God don't look upon sinners as righteous for nothing, when they have no righteousness properly theirs; he don't look upon them to be or to have what they are or have not" (Edwards, "The Threefold Work of the Holy Ghost," in *WJE* 14:395)

168. "And what propriety can there be in accepting of that, as if we had performed, and looking upon us, because Christ performed those things, as if we performed them? This question may be divided into two questions: how this is consistent with the reason of things; and second, how it can be consistent with the law" (ibid., 14:401).

169. Through the incarnation, Christ is related to the church as "head of the whole," becoming our representative and substitute so that righteousness is imputed to "the whole." Thus, by virtue of the unity of *caput et membra*, "God loves and accepts the head for its holiness and amiableness," and the church is "accepted and beloved because [they] are in him who is beloved." Because God "won't separate head and members . . . he will accept and delight in the members for the sake of the excellency of the head" (Edwards, "Miscellanies," no. 385, in *WJE* 13:453).

170. Edwards, "The Threefold Work of the Holy Spirit," in *WJE* 14:401.

171. Ibid., 401–2. God's infinite love to Christ and his vicarious suffering "appeases and removes" his anger and imparts "value in God's account to his positive righteousness" (402).

172. This makes a "thorough union," by which "God is willing and sees proper to impute to them what he does and suffers for them" (Edwards, "The Threefold Work of the Holy Spirit," in *WJE* 14:403–4). Strong distinguishes Christ's union with humanity, which obtains their objective reconciliation, and Christ's union with the regenerate that secures their subjective reconciliation (Strong, *Systematic Theology* 3:802).

173. "Redemption belongs to the Son but justification peculiarly belongs to the office of God the Father. . . . Justifying and condemning are judicial acts or the acts of a Judge." In particular reference to the preached text, Edwards comments that "God the Father is the person spoken of and is here said to be the Judge of all; 'tis not the Son nor the Holy Ghost nor the deity as including all the persons but the Father particularly and this is manifest by the distinction that is used in the text between God the Judge and Jesus the mediator" (Edwards, 547. Sermon on Heb. 12:22-24 [d] [Apr–May 1740], in *WJE* 55).

174. "'Tis not properly [God the Son's] justice that is satisfied: 'tis the justice of his being and essence, but not properly of his person in his office" (Edwards, "Of God the Father," in *WJE* 25:151).

175. "Appropriation" is not used in the Thomistic sense of linguistic attribution, but in the sense that God the Father "assigns to the Son the office of justifying" (Calvin, *Institutes*, bk. 3, ch. 11, 734). Faith as the instrumental cause "for receiving righteousness" must not be confused with "Christ, who is the material cause" and source (efficient cause as God) (ibid., 735). Again, "the matter both of righteousness and of salvation resides in his flesh" (ibid., 736).

176. Edwards interprets that reality "between Christ and his people" (which is the foundation of the legal) as "something really in them, and between them, uniting them, that is the ground of the suitableness of their being accounted as one by the Judge" (Edwards, "Justification by Faith Alone," in *WJE* 19:158). Clearly, that which is both in and between Christ and the church is the Spirit. This can no wise be regarded as an intrinsic moral quality in the saint, unless a *tertium quid* conception of the *unio mystica* is assumed. Jeffrey C. Waddington highlights this dimension of Edwards's pneumatology in "Jonathan Edwards's 'Ambiguous and Somewhat Precarious' Doctrine of Justification?" *Westminster Theological Journal* 66 (2004): 357–72.

177. Edwards, 103. Sermon on 1 Cor. 1:9 [1729], in *WJE* 44. What the Father and Son gives to saints is "the communion of the Holy Ghost . . . but the blessing from the Holy Ghost is himself, a communication of himself" (Edwards, "Miscellanies," no. 341, in *WJE* 13:415). Calvin's idea of the Spirit as bond in the *unio mystica* was affirmed by the Puritan theologians, such as John Downame, who wrote that "the Spirit of God . . . [is] the bond of the spiritual union which we have with Christ . . . it maketh us to become one mystical body with Him." See John Downame, *The Christian warfare against the devill world and flesh wherein is described their nature, the maner of their fight and meanes to obtaine victory* (London: William Stansby, 1634), 1021.

178. Edwards, "Miscellanies," no. 706, in *WJE* 18:326. Edwards could conclude thus: "The righteousness of Christ, the thing given in justification, is in some respect the Holy Spirit in Christ, the expressions and fruits of his influence and actings in him" (Edwards, "Discourse on the Trinity," in *WJE* 21:142).

179. Edwards, "Miscellanies," no. 706, in *WJE* 18:326.

180. Edwards, 932. Sermon on John 6:51 (June 1749), in *WJE* 67.

181. "The Spirit, as 'tis the bond of union with Christ, frees us from condemnation, not only as it frees from obligation to suffer the condemnation of the law in that Christ has satisfied the law, but also renders it impossible that we should suffer the condemnation of the law, for they are hereby united to Jesus Christ, who is the Son of God and fountain of life, and therefore must live" (Edwards, "Blank Bible," Rom. 8:1-4, in *WJE* 24:1090).

182. Heppe, *Reformed Dogmatics*, 548. "All the virtue that Christ exercised in the human nature in any respect belongs to that righteousness which is imputed to believers for their justification" (Edwards, "Miscellanies," no. 791, in *WJE* 18:494).

183. Just as in Catholic theology, the forgiveness of sins (*gratia sanans*) and supernatural adoption (*gratia elevans*) do not divide divine grace, so justification and sanctification, for Calvin, are distinct but inseparably linked in Christ (Calvin, *Institutes*, III.xvi.1). See also Edward Yarnold, *The Second Gift: A Study of Grace*, Sarum Lectures (Slough, UK: St. Paul, 1974), 50–52. In fact, Puritans such as Thomas Watson describe grace as possessing both a "soul cleansing excellency" and a "soul-raising excellency." See Thomas Watson, "The Beauty of Grace," in *The beatitudes: Or a discourse upon part of Christs famous sermon on the mount . . .* (London: Ralph Smith, 1660), 518–20.

184. Edwards, "Miscellanies," no. 36, in *WJE* 13:219.

185. Here is how Hooker distinguishes the two: "That whereby we are justified is perfect, but not inherent. That whereby we are sanctified, inherent, but not perfect" (Hooker, *A Learned Discourse*). Certain Puritan writers distinguish justifying righteousness as in Christ, absolute and *extra nos*, as opposed to sanctifying righteousness that is imperfect and *intra nos*. See, for example, Thomas Adams, *A commentary or, exposition upon the divine second epistle generall, written by the blessed apostle St. Peter* (London: Jacob Bloome, 1633), 1378; and John Downame, *The summe of*

sacred divinitie first briefly & methodically propounded: and then more largly & cleerely handled and explaned (London: William Barret, 1620), 455.

186. Other Puritan writers assigned imputation to be the formal cause of justification as opposed to Rome's infused justice. "We do contrarily hold, that the material cause of mans justification, is the obedience of Christ in suffering & fulfilling the law for us: but as for the formal cause, that must needs be imputation, the which is an action of God the Father, accepting the obedience of Christ for us, as it were our own" (William Perkins, *A golden chaine: Or, the description of theologie, containing the order of the causes of salvation and damnation, according to Gods word . . .* [London: Printed by John Legatt, Printer to the Universitie of Cambridge, 1616], 101).

187. Edwards, "Miscellanies," no. zz, in *WJE* 13:197.

188. Edwards, "None Are Saved by Their Own Righteousness," in *WJE* 14:340. It is not an either/or case, as McDermott would have us think: "Martin Luther's salvation by faith *alone* becomes for Edwards salvation by faith *primarily*. While Luther emphasizes that in justification sinners are *counted as* righteous, Edwards insists that sinners are actually *made* holy in the act of regeneration" (Gerald R. McDermott, *Jonathan Edwards Confronts the Gods: Christian Theology, Enlightenment Religion, and Non-Christian Faiths* [New York: Oxford University Press, 2000], 136).

189. Edwards, 920. Sermon on 1 John 4:19, in *WJE* 67.

190. Hence, "there are no degrees of imputed righteousness; but that all saints are alike justified in the sight of God by the righteousness of Christ as there are no degrees in the same person with respect to this; but he is as much justified the first moment of his conversion as ever he is how much soever he may increase in holiness afterwards. So neither is there any difference in this respect in different persons" (Edwards, 84. Sermon on Matt. 13:23 [Jun 1756], in *WJE* 43).

191. "Not that he reckons we have wrought it out in our own persons, so that the individual obedience and sufferings of Christ are judged to be our obedience and sufferings; this destroys the imputation of that which is done by another for us, and is not according to the judgment of truth" (Rawlin, *Christ the righteousness of his people,* 72–73, as cited in Edwards, "'Controversies' Notebook: Justification," in *WJE* 21:342).

192. This perfect righteousness of the Mediator "was personal and inherent in himself, and incommunicable to any other," and could only be performed by God, though the salvific effects are communicable to sinners (Edwards, "Miscellanies," no. 278, in *WJE* 13:378). Citing Rawlins, Edwards notes that God does not lay hold of this righteousness "from Christ, and transposes it into us, so that we become the seat and subject of it by way of inherency, and this righteousness an inherent quality in us; that is impossible in the nature of things" (Rawlin, *Christ the righteousness of his people,* 72–73, as cited in Edwards, "'Controversies' Notebook: Justification," in *WJE* 21:342).

193. Edwards, "Miscellanies," no. 278, in *WJE* 13:378.

194. Edwards, "Miscellanies," no. 2, in *WJE* 13:199. While many things promised are identical in both the covenants (like eternal life, justification, and perseverance), in some cases some things are promises in one but conditions in the other (Edwards, "Miscellanies," no. 617, in *WJE* 18:149). Promises within the covenant of grace may be regarded as "between God the Father and believers" insofar as they are the revelation and renewal of the promises already made to believers in Christ in the covenant of redemption (Edwards, "Miscellanies," no. 919, in *WJE* 20:167). Thus regeneration and closing with Christ is one of the promises of the covenant of the Father with Christ but is the condition in the covenant of Christ with the saints. So, on the other hand, the incarnation, death, and sufferings of Christ are promises in Christ's covenant with the people, but they are the conditions of the covenant of the Father with the Son (Edwards, "Miscellanies," no. 617, in *WJE* 18:149).

195. On the day of judgment, "They shall now appear clothed with the glorious robe of Christ's righteousness. . . . And then also shall their inherent holiness be made manifest, all their good works be brought to light" (Edwards, "Sermon 9," in *WJE* 29:503)

196. The church is "clothed with imputed righteousness" (Edwards, *WJE* 2:347). Edwards uses his typologies to great effect: "The skins that Adam and Eve were clothed [in] were skins of

their sacrifices. God's clothing man with these was a lively figure of their being clothed with the righteousness of Christ" (Edwards, "Sermon 2," in *WJE* 9:136). Edwards uses the silkworm and sheep fleece as types of Christ (Edwards, "Shadows of Divine Things," nos. 35, 46, in *WJE* 11:59, 63).

197. Edwards, "Miscellanies," no. 385, in *WJE* 13:453–54. See also Edwards, "The Spiritual Blessings of the Gospel Represented by a Feast," in *WJE* 14:290–94. This is another place where he parts company with Newman, who regarded justification as Christ-in-us. "In like manner 'Christ in us' is said to be the 'hope of glory.' Christ then is our righteousness by dwelling in us by the Spirit; he justifies us by entering into us, he continues to justify us by remaining in us." See John Henry Newman, *Lectures on Justification* (London: J. G. & F. Rivington and J. H. Parker, 1838), 166. See also Toon, *Justification and Sanctification*, 117.

198. Edwards uses the engrafting metaphor to signify regeneration, conversion, and repentance. "The Scripture representations of conversion do strongly imply and signify a change of nature: such as . . . a being ingrafted into a new stock" (Edwards, *WJE* 2:340; see also 347). "Man must be as it were cut off from his own stock, and from that wood alike of which he is naturally a branch, in order to his being engrafted into Christ. He must be cut off as to that life that he lives by nature in order to the renewed life by Christ" (Edwards, "Like Rain upon Mown Grass," in *WJE* 22:307). Regeneration is the foundation of sanctification. Hence, "the union of the branches to the stock . . . is the ground of their partaking of the sap and life of the stock" (Edwards, "Justification by Faith Alone," in *WJE* 19:156). See also "Miscellanies," no. 862, in *WJE* 20:87; "Blank Bible," note on 2 Cor. 5:14-16, in *WJE* 4:1073; *Original Sin*, in *WJE* 3:405; "Concerning the End," in *WJE* 8:435; "Faith," no. 102, in *WJE* 21:444; and "True Saints, When Absent from the Body, Are Present with the Lord," in *WJE* 25:231.

199. Strong, *Systematic Theology*, 3:862. This presupposes justification as a consequence of union with Christ, "so Christ's righteousness is imputed to us, not because Christ is in us, but because we are in Christ." This, according to Strong, is Luther's "formula: "We in Christ = justification; Christ in us = sanctification.""

200. Edwards, 419. Sermon on John 13:23 (Jan 1736), in *WJE* 52.

201. Edwards exegetes the classic proof text: "This righteousness of God, which the Apostle so often speaks of in the matter of our justification, is in Christ. 2 Corinthians 5:21, 'He was made sin for us, that we might be the righteousness of God in him.' 'He was made sin,' i.e. sin was imputed to him. And what sin was it? Why, that sin that was in us. So we are made 'the righteousness of God.' But what righteousness of God is it that we are made? Why, that which was in Christ our Mediator" (Edwards, "Notes on Scripture," no. 318, in *WJE* 15:296).

202. Edwards, "Miscellanies," no. s, in *WJE* 13:174. Just as justification is not "merely negative" but includes the positive imputation of Christ's perfect obedience, so Adam would not have been justified by the mere innocence "at the first point of his existence" without a trial of obedience (Edwards, "Justification by Faith Alone," in *WJE* 19:150).

203. Ibid. On the satisfaction of Christ, Edwards notes: "That Christ indeed suffered the full punishment of the sin that was imputed to him, or offered that to God that was fully and completely equivalent to what we owed to divine justice for our sins" (Edwards, "Miscellanies," no. 1035, in *WJE* 20:375).

204. Edwards, "Justification by Faith Alone," in *WJE* 19:150. "And indeed the justification of a believer is no other than his being admitted to communion in, or participation of the justification of this head and surety of all believers; for as Christ suffered the punishment of sin, not as a private person, but as our surety, so when after this suffering he was raised from the dead, he was therein justified, not as a private person, but as the surety and representative of all that should be believe in him" (Edwards, "Justification by Faith Alone," in *WJE* 19:151).

205. Edwards, "Miscellanies," no. 118, in *WJE* 13:284.

206. Edwards, "Justification by Faith Alone," in *WJE* 19:187.

272 | Fullness Received and Returned

207. Edwards, "Miscellanies," no. 502, in *WJE* 18:51. See also Edwards, "Miscellanies," no. 532, in *WJE* 18:76–77.

208. McCormack points out that the priority and ordering of positive imputation vis-à-vis nonimputation is evident in Calvin and subsequently adopted in the Reformed confessions. See Bruce M. McCormack, "*Justitia aliena*: Karl Barth in Conversation with the Evangelical Doctrine of Imputed Righteousness," in McCormack, *Justification in Perspective*, 170–71.

209. Edwards, "Miscellanies," no. 812, in *WJE* 18:522–23. Edwards distinguishes "pardon" as used here from clemency, whereby a person is freed from punishment while remaining guilty. In justification the sinner is accepted as innocent in Christ and thus liberated. It is called "pardon" insofar it points to the gratuity of God.

210. Edwards, "Miscellanies," no. 812, in *WJE* 18:522.

211. Heppe, *Reformed Dogmatics*, 550. In Calvin and the Reformed tradition, Christ is seen both as the meritorious and material cause of our justification (Heppe, *Reformed Dogmatics*, 546). Calvin, in opposition to the Socinians, accepted the idea of Christ as meritorious cause insofar as principal causation is not set against subordinate causation. God's grace is to faith in Christ (together with Christ's merits) as principal is to secondary cause. "We see how God's love holds first place, as the highest cause or origin; how faith in Christ follows this as the second and proximate cause." God's love is the foundation of Christ's merits, and both of these are properly opposed to human works (Calvin, *Institutes*, 2.17.1, 529).

212. Efficiency, unlike the Arminian notion of permissive will, must be positively defined to include determination of consequence, says Edwards: "That efficient that so produces as to determine the effect, that only is properly said to give it, to procure, and this only can properly promise it, and to this the chief thanks and glory is due; that only is the proper foundation and author of it" (Edwards, "Efficacious Grace II," in *WJE* 21:232–33). That Christ's merits are entirely *pro nobis* is, for Calvin, beyond question. "What need was there for God's only Son to come down in order to acquire something new for himself?" (*Institutes*, 2.17.6, 534).

213. Edwards, "Miscellanies," no. 1177, in *WJE* 23:93.

214. Ibid.

215. Ibid.

216. Ibid. Elsewhere, he notes that the difference is "not that one is [his or her] own personal righteousness, and the other the righteousness of another" (Edwards, "Blank Bible," note on Rom. 10:3, in *WJE* 24:1024–26). Arguably, while Calvin's emphasis is on the "*origin* . . . rather than the *quality*" of our sharing in Christ's righteousness, it is not simply the case that what we participate in a mere human righteousness (Jonathan Slater, "Salvation as Participation in the Humanity of the Mediator in Calvin's *Institutes of the Christian Religion*: A Reply to Carl Mosser," *Scottish Journal of Theology* 58 [2005]: 43). As already pointed out in chapter 4, the quality of Christ's human righteousness is refracted through the hypostatic union; it is the unique righteousness of the God-man according to the human nature in which we have a share.

217. Christ merited righteousness for the saints not as "an human person by himself, but by a divine person," so that its value derives from the "dignity of the divine nature" (Edwards, "Miscellanies," no. 1177, in *WJE* 23:93).

218. Edwards, "Notes on Scriptures," no. 476, in *WJE* 15:575. Here, Edwards emphasizes the Spirit's role in the making the person and work of Christ "sweet and infinitely acceptable."

219. Edwards, "Miscellanies," no. 1177, in *WJE* 23:94. Otherwise, this would have been a passive affair, since the saints would be justified "without any knowledge or act of theirs."

220. Ibid.

221. "The glory of God in our justification is greatly secured and advanced . . . as the very bond of union, by which we are united to this divine person so as to be interested in his righteousness, is that principle and act of the soul by which we know that the righteousness is thus the righteousness, and by which we cordially and with all our hearts ascribe it wholly to him and give him all the glory of it." Ibid.

222. "But Christ the second Adam acts the same part for us that the first Adam was to have done, and failed in" (Edwards, "Miscellanies," no. 695, in *WJE* 18:279). Although the covenant of redemption is opposed and subsequent to the covenant of works, Christ and Adam are to be similarly considered in terms of their organic, representative, and communal character (Edwards, "Miscellanies," no. 825, in *WJE* 18:536–37).

223. In this way, God is glorified and humanity is humbled and made more dependent on God, which is why justification is called "the *righteousness of God*" in Scripture (Edwards, "Miscellanies," no. 1177, in *WJE* 23:93).

224. Edwards, "Miscellanies," no. 635, in *WJE* 18:165–66. This echoes Calvin's argument against Osiander's contention that Christ justified sinners through the divine "essential righteousness" (Calvin, *Institutes*, 3.11, 729–43). This imputed righteousness is merited by Christ through obedience and atonement according to the *oikonomia* and Christ's human nature. Nevertheless, the divine nature (or the Trinity) may be admitted as the "fountain" or efficient cause of justification and the whole Christ as the subject of this righteousness, for mere human nature cannot justify. "In this way and sense, I do not deny that Christ, as he is God and man justifies us; and also that this work is the common task of the Father and the Holy Spirit." With all these caveats, Calvin could concede that "that righteousness of which Christ makes us partakers with himself is the eternal righteousness of the eternal God" (ibid., 736).

225. Edwards, "Miscellanies," no. 635, in *WJE* 18:165–66. This divine righteousness is from the Father and incarnate Son insofar as it is "a righteousness of God's providing," and "a righteousness of God's working and inherent in God, i.e. in a divine person" (Edwards, "Miscellanies," no. 1271, in *WJE* 23:216).

226. Edwards, "Miscellanies," no. 278, in *WJE* 13:377.

227. Ibid.

228. Ibid., 378. "He consented to the terms which were fixed, and obliged himself to do whatsoever was necessary to the end proposed."

229. "The union of the heart of a believer to Christ is begun . . . at conversion; and consequent on this drawing and closing of his heart with Christ, is established a vital union with Christ; whereby the believer becomes . . . a member of Christ's mystical body, living by a communication of spiritual and vital influences from the head, and by a kind of participation of Christ's own life" (Edwards, "Lectures on the Qualifications for Full Communion in the Church of Christ," in *WJE* 25:231). Edwards had a robust understanding of the continuity between sanctification and glorification: "Eternal life is but the spiritual life brought to perfection. And the spiritual life here is but eternal life in embrio [*sic*] or an imperfect state" (Edwards, 37. Sermon on John 15:5 [a] [n.d.], in *WJE* 42).

230. Edwards, "Miscellanies," no. 706, in *WJE* 18:326.

231. Edwards, 59. Sermon on Gal. 5:6 (a) (n.d.), in *WJE* 43.

232. Edwards, "Miscellanies," no. 712, in *WJE* 18:341.

233. Ibid., 342.

234. Edwards, "Justification by Faith Alone," in *WJE* 19:214.

235. Ibid.

236. "Two things come to pass, relating to the saints' reward for their inherent righteousness, by virtue of their relation to Christ. First, the guilt of their persons is all done away, and the pollution and hatefulness that attends, and is in, their good works, is hid. Second, their relation to Christ adds a positive value and dignity to their good works, in God's sight" (ibid.).

237. "The acceptableness, and so the rewardableness of our virtue is not antecedent to justification, but follows it, and is built entirely upon it. . . . First, because till then we stand condemned before God, by his own holy law. . . . And, second . . . the loveliness of our virtue bears no proportion to our guilt. . . . And, third, because our good deeds . . . are in a sense corrupt . . . if we are beheld as we are in ourselves, or separate from Christ" (Edwards, "Justification by Faith Alone," in *WJE* 19:211–12).

238. "That little holiness . . . receive an exceeding value in the sight of God, by virtue of God's beholding them as in Christ . . . as persons of greater dignity on this account . . . because they are members of his own righteous and dear Son . . . and hence it follows, that he also sets a great value upon their good acts and offerings" (Edwards, "Justification by Faith Alone," in *WJE* 19:214). Thus *unio cum Christo* and *iustificatio* makes a person's "works" to be "accounted righteous above their worth" (Calvin, *Institutes*, 3.17.10, 813).

239. "When I speak of a derivative loveliness, I do not mean only, that the qualifications themselves, that are accepted as lovely, are derived from Christ, and are from his power and purchase; but that the acceptance of them as a loveliness, and all the value that is set upon them, and all their connection with the reward, is founded in, and derived from Christ's righteousness and worthiness" (Edwards, "Justification by Faith Alone," in *WJE* 19:215).

240. "God don't justify us . . . upon the account of any act of ours, whether it be the act of faith or any other act whatsoever, but only upon the account of what the Saviour did" (Edwards, "Miscellanies," no. 416, in *WJE* 13:475).

241. "The saints are as so many vessels, of different sizes, cast into a sea of happiness, where every vessel is full; this Christ purchased for all: but after all 'tis left to God's sovereign pleasure to determine the largeness of the vessel; Christ's righteousness meddles not with this matter" (Edwards, "Justification by Faith Alone," in *WJE* 19:219).

242. Edwards, "Miscellanies," no. 367, in *WJE* 13:437–38.

243. Ibid., 437.

244. As some parts of a human body possess more health than others even though the whole is healthy, "so in the mystical body of Christ, all the members are partakers of the benefit, of the righteousness of the head, but 'tis according to their different capacity and place they have in the body" (Edwards, "Miscellanies," no. 403, in *WJE* 13:468).

245. Ibid.

246. "The favor whence a believer's heavenly Father bestows the eternal inheritance, and his title as an heir, is founded in that relation he stands in to him as a child, purchased by Christ's righteousness; though he in wisdom, chooses to bestow it in such away, and therein to testify his acceptance of the amiableness of his obedience in Christ" (Edwards, "Justification by Faith Alone," in *WJE* 19:216).

247. Edwards, "Miscellanies," no. 862, in *WJE* 20:90.

248. Melanchthon already moved away from Luther's emphasis on the *unio cum Christo* and regarded sanctification as a result of justification (Pannenberg, *Systematic Theology*, 3:227). Without supplementing his strongly forensic emphasis on justification with the atonement, Melanchthon would not have avoided a thoroughgoing divine voluntarism: there is remission of sin, imputation of righteousness, and the acceptance by God by legal pronouncement *propter Christum*. See, for example, Philip Melanchthon, *Corpus reformatorum*, ed. Henricus Ernestus Bindseil (Brunsvigae: C. A. Schwetschke, 1854), 21:423: "Iustificamur per misericordiam promissam propter Christum; sed haec misericordia fide apprehendenda est. Hoc enim agit Paulus [Rom. 3], reconciliari homines fiducia alieni beneficii, non propter propriam dignitatem seu qualitatum seu operum." Hence, anything pertaining to the inhering qualification of the soul, whether created or uncreated grace, is denied in relation to justification. See Stephen Strehle, *The Catholic Roots of the Protestant Gospel: Encounter between the Middle Ages and the Reformation*, Studies in the History of Christian Thought (Leiden: Brill, 1995), 72.

249. It is the justification of the ungodly: "The love of God does not find, but creates, that which is pleasing to it" (Luther, *Heidelberg Disputation*, thesis 28, in *Luther's Works* [Philadelphia: Muhlenberg Press, 1957], 31:41, as quoted in Eberhard Jüngel, "On the Doctrine of Justification," *International Journal of Systematic Theology* 1, no. 1 [March 1999]: 41).

250. Schafer, "Jonathan Edwards and Justification by Faith," 55–67.

251. As appropriated by Newman, initial, perfect justification is only anticipatory of sanctification and thus only notionally distinguished by an eschatological gap. "He declares a fact, and makes it a fact by declaring it" (Newman, *Lectures on Justification*, 86). "In [justification], the

whole course of sanctification is anticipated, reckoned, or imputed to us in its very beginning" (ibid., 74). Where Newman differs from the Reformed here is the place he grants to sanctification where positive imputation should be. So, "justification is an announcement of fiat of Almighty God breaking upon the gloom of our natural state as the Creative Word upon chaos; that it *declares* the soul righteous, and in that declaration, on the one hand, conveys *pardon* for its past sins, on the other *makes* it actually *righteous*" (ibid., 90; italics original). See also Alister E. McGrath's analysis in his Iustitia Dei: *A History of the Christian Doctrine of Justification*, 3rd ed. (Cambridge: Cambridge University Press, 2005), 298.

252. Jüngel, "On the Doctrine of Justification," 42.

253. Edwards, 886. Sermon on Acts 26:18 (d) (Dec 1747), in *WJE* 65. Elsewhere: "Justification is a sentence passed by God as judge of the law." God, "in judging those that are the subjects of it passes a twofold sentence . . . a sentence of condemnation, which declares a person not right . . . and so liable to that punishment that the rule fixes; or secondly, a sentence of justification, judging the person right or strait according to the rule" (Edwards, "Miscellanies," no. 1093, in *WJE* 20:481–82),

254. "There is included in divine judging, executing the sentence; for the same person who passes sentence by his almighty power, executes the same. The sentence does as it were procure the execution. As God by his word created the world—he said, "Let it be," and it was so—by his word or sentence he will as it were procure the execution of it" (Edwards, 71. Sermon on Rom. 2:16, in *WJE* 43).

255. Accordingly, "justifying a man, as has been already shown, is not merely pronouncing him innocent or without guilt, but standing right, with regard to the rule that he is under, and righteous unto life; but this, according to the established rule of nature, reason, and divine appointment, is a positive perfect righteousness" (Edwards, "Justification by Faith Alone," in *WJE* 19:191).

256. The first case was proposed by Newman: "God's word, I say, effects what it announces. Thus in the beginning He said, 'Let there be light,' and there was light" (Newman, *Lectures on Justification*, 87).

257. Edwards, "Miscellanies," no. 1358, in *WJE* 23:607. This is similar to the reality of the resurrection as a factual attestation—one that "declared" Christ to be what Christ already was ontologically (Rom. 1: 4).

258. Edwards, "Justification by Faith Alone," in *WJE* 19:189.

259. To be regenerated is to be "born again, that they have been the subjects of this change which is so great, so wonderful, as it were, a coming out of nothing into being" (Edwards, "Born Again," in *WJE* 17:194)

260. Commenting on Isa. 41:18-20, Edwards wrote, "To 'create,' as the word is used in Scripture, is either to make out [of] nothing, or which is equivalent, to make out of that which has in itself no natural fitness, disposition, or preparation, or foundation for such an effect" (Edwards, "Notes on Scripture," no. 437, in *WJE* 15:521).

261. Without such "a peculiar beauty in his so ordering," a person's union with Christ would be based solely on *de potentia Dei absoluta*; that is, it would be based "solely and absolutely on God's mere good pleasure and sovereign and arbitrary will" (Edwards, "Miscellanies," no. 1042, in *WJE* 20:383; no. 1260a, in *WJE* 23:196)

262. "The judge's work is two-fold: it is to determine first what is fact, and then whether what is in fact be according to rule, or according to the law. . . . So that our Judge cannot justify us, unless he sees a perfect righteousness, some way belonging to us, either performed by ourselves, or by another, and justly and duly reckoned to our account. God doth in the sentence of justification pronounce a man perfectly righteous" (Edwards, "Justification by Faith Alone," in *WJE* 19:190).

263. Edwards, citing approvingly Dutch theologian Campegius Vitringa (1659–1722), observes, "that on the whole, as he argues, justification is not a phrase parallel to forgiveness, but refers to a judicial process, and carries in it the idea of acquittal, praise and reward. And indeed it

seems to me always ultimately to refer to the being pronounced and treated as righteous in the great day of God's universal judgment" (Edwards, "'Controversies' Notebook: Justification," note on Rom. 3:20, in *WJE* 21:412).

264. Edwards, "Miscellanies," no. 689, in *WJE* 18:252.

265. Edwards, "Justification by Faith Alone," in *WJE* 19:233.

266. There cannot be two kinds of justification, with two differing causes but a single "absolute justification" and its continuation, flowing from the same justifying faith, and works proceeding from this one justification as its effect or fruit. "All other works and duties of obedience do accompany faith in the continuation of our justified estate, as necessary effects and fruits of it, but not as causes, means, or conditions, whereon that effect is suspended." See John Owen, *Containing the Doctrine of Justification by Faith; and Gospel Grounds and Evidences of the Faith of God's Elect*, vol. 11 of *The Works of John Owen, with Memoirs of His Life and Writings by William Orme*, ed. Thomas Russell (London: Printed for Richard Baynes, 1826), 188. Or, as Goodwin put it, we "not only did rely upon that Righteousness wholly for our first Justification, (as the Papists distinguish)" but we are also "Justified continually all along the remainder of our Lives; for it is *Actus continuus* or *perpetuus*" (Goodwin, *The Work Of The Holy Ghost In Our Salvation*, 18).

267. Protestants reject the Thomistic construal of *gratia justificans* as a *qualitas quaedam supernaturalis*, as well as the notion of merit and good works associated with grace (W. J. Torrance Kirby, *Richard Hooker's Doctrine of Royal Supremacy*, Studies in the History of Christian Thought, v. 43 [Leiden, The Netherlands: E. J. Brill, 1990], 49). Hence, Owen denied the Roman position of initial justification with faith in Christ as it sole meritorious cause followed by a second and continuing justifying faith, which has "the intermixture" of faith in Christ and works as its cause (Owen, *Containing the Doctrine of Justification by Faith*, 187).

268. In this he follows Owen's rejection of the Roman doctrine of double justification. Trent's notion of first justification, in Owen's estimation, insists on the infusion of a habit of grace (*gratiam gratum facientem*), the elimination of original and habitual sins, faith as assent, Christ's atoning work as the meritorious cause, and largely avoids the notion of merit, excepting congruent merit. Second justification is understood as the effect of the first, its formal cause being good works flowing from that infused principle of charity, which merits eternal life for the just. First justification, therefore, resembles the Reformed notion of sanctification, and the second is nothing more than works-righteousness (Owen, *Works*, 5:137–38).

269. Edwards, "'Controversies' Notebook: Justification," in *WJE* 21:338. "Now the first act of God in the imputation of righteousness cannot be repeated" (Owen, *Containing the Doctrine of Justification by Faith*, 183).

270. "Men are justified in the sense wherein they are at first, viz. a being accepted as righteous but once and forever; the second justification is declarative only" (Edwards, "'Controversies' Notebook : Justification," in *WJE* 21:338). Theologians whom Edwards was familiar with worked with the notions of an essential and declarative justification. For Owen, there is a "continuation of our justification," so granting the distinction between justification as to its "nature or essence," and its continuity, which is a "declaration or manifestation" (Owen, *Works*, 5:139). Turretin highlights two biblical senses of justification: "Paul of justification *a priori* and constitutively; James of the same *a posteriori* and declaratively; Paul properly constitutes the former in faith alone; James rightly places the latter in works, by which the reality of our faith and justification is declared not only before men, but also before God" (Turretin, *Institutes*, 2, topic 16, q. 8)

271. Edwards, "Justification by Faith Alone," in *WJE* 19:188. "That justification respects a man as ungodly . . . can't imply less than that God in the act of justification, has no regard to anything in the person justified, as godliness, or any goodness in him; but that nextly, or immediately before this act, God beholds him only as an ungodly or wicked creature" (Edwards, "Justification by Faith Alone," in *WJE* 19:147). See also Edwards, "Miscellanies," no. 712, in *WJE* 18:342; no. 1161, in *WJE* 23:83–84; and *WJE* 3:295.

272. McGrath points out that the tradition after Luther departed from his belief in the justification of the unbelieving sinner (*Iustitia Dei*, 236). This thesis is taken up polemically by Carl E. Braaten, *Justification: The Article by Which the Church Stands or Falls* (Minneapolis: Augsburg Fortress, 1990), 21ff.

273. Following McGrath's reading, Bucer's (and Zwingli's) extrinsicism and "moral conception of justification," which is contrasted with Calvin's (and Luther's) intrinsicism, may be seen as reconciled in Edwards (McGrath, *Iustitia Dei*, 2nd ed., 224–25). This, of course, assumes that Calvin had no notion of a secondary justification.

274. "But he sets this value upon their persons purely for Christ's sake. . . . From the value God sets upon their persons, for the sake of Christ's worthiness, he also sets a high value on their virtues and performances" (Edwards, "Justification by Faith Alone," in *WJE* 19:215). "The acceptableness, and so the rewardableness of our virtue is not antecedent to justification, but follows it, and is built entirely upon it" (ibid., 211).

275. "This preciousness, or high valuableness of believers is a moral fitness to a reward, and yet this valuableness is all in the righteousness of Christ, that is the foundation of it. The thing that respect is had to, is not excellency in them, separately by themselves, or in their virtue by itself" (Edwards, "Justification by Faith Alone," in *WJE* 19:215). Like Calvin, God accepts our works only together with our persons in the *unio cum Christo* (Cornelis P. Venema, *Accepted and Renewed in Christ: The "Twofold Grace of God" and the Interpretation of Calvin's Theology* [Göttingen: Vandernhoeck & Ruprecht, 2007], 163–70).

276. In first justification, "only faith is concerned; because 'tis by that only in us, that we become fit to be accepted and approved" (Edwards, "Justification by Faith Alone," in *WJE* 19:233). Thus, first justification is perfect, for "justification is by the first act of faith, in some respects, in a peculiar manner, because a sinner is actually and finally justified as soon as he has performed one act of faith" (ibid., 202).

277. In second justification, "whatever is an evidence of our fitness, is alike concerned. And therefore take justification in this sense and then faith, and all other graces, and good works, have a common and equal concern in it: for any other grace, or holy act, is equally an evidence of a qualification for acceptance or approbation, as faith" (ibid., 233).

278. Of the justification in St. James, Calvin states, "[I]t is clear that he himself is speaking of the declaration, not the imputation, of righteousness" (Calvin, *Institutes*, 3.17.12, 816).

279. Edwards, "Blank Bible," note on James 2:14-26, in *WJE* 24:1171.

280. According to Edwards, "justification" in James 2:21, 25 "is of the same signification with that phrase of the apostle Paul, Hebrews 11:4, 'he obtained witness that he was righteous'" (Edwards, "Miscellanies," no. 1085, in *WJE* 20:468).

281. Edwards, "Miscellanies," no. 861, in *WJE* 20:85.

282. "Actually following Christ and practically cleaving to him, in hope of salvation from him, is actually accepting him and trusting in him as a savior" (Edwards, "Miscellanies," no. 856, in *WJE* 20:83).

283. Before effectual calling, "it is not meet that anything in us, should be accepted of God, as any excellency of our persons, until we are actually in Christ, and justified through him." Hence, "the saints are rewarded for their good works . . . for Christ's sake only, and not for the excellency of their works in themselves considered, or beheld separately from Christ." (Edwards, in "Justification by Faith Alone," in *WJE* 19:212–13).

284. "Accordingly, we can deservedly say that by faith alone not only we ourselves but our works as well are justified . . . this works righteousness [!] . . . depends upon faith and free justification, and is effected by this" (Calvin, *Institutes*, 3.17.10, 813). Steven R. Coxhead argues for a two-level justification in Calvin: the first an absolute justification by faith alone and the second, a works justification within union with Christ and the covenant of grace. See his "John Calvin's Subordinate Doctrine of Justification by Works," *Westminster Theological Journal* 71 (Spring 2009): 1–19.

285. "There are two kinds of Christian righteousness, just as man's sin is of two kinds. The first is alien righteousness, that is the righteousness of another, instilled from without. This is the righteousness of Christ by which he justifies through faith. . . . The second kind of righteousness is our proper righteousness, not because we alone work it, but because we work with that first and alien righteousness. This is that manner of life spent profitably in good works …" (Martin Luther, "Two Kinds of Righteousness," in *Luther's Works*, vol. 31, *Career of the Reformer I*, ed. J. J. Pelikan, H. C. Oswald, and H. T. Lehmann [Philadelphia: Fortress Press, 1957], 297–99).

286. "If this be that which is intended in this position, that . . . our own obedience and good works are the condition of the continuation of our justification,—namely, that God does indispensably require good works and obedience in all that are justified, so that a justified estate is inconsistent with the neglect of them,—it is readily granted" (Owen, *Containing the Doctrine of Justification by Faith*, 186).

287. Edwards, "Miscellanies," no. 859, in *WJE* 20:84. "Christian holiness" is the "effect, exercise and expression of faith" ("Miscellanies," no. 890, in *WJE* 20:152).

288. Edwards, "Miscellanies," no. 859, in *WJE* 20:84.

289. "PERSEVERANCE IN FAITH in one sense is the condition of justification; that is, the promise of acceptance is made only to a persevering sort of faith, and the proper evidence of its being of that sort is actual perseverance" (Edwards, "Miscellanies," no. 428, in *WJE* 13:480).

290. "Though perseverance be not an act performed, till after persons have finished their days; yet perseverance is looked upon as virtually performed in the first act of faith, because that first act is of such a nature as shows the principle to be of a persevering sort" (Edwards, "Persevering Faith," in *WJE* 19:601).

291. "Faith . . . is in its nature an actual unition of the soul to Christ. . . . The soul is saved no otherwise than in union with Christ . . . and in order to that, 'tis necessary that the soul should now be in him, even when salvation is actually bestowed, and not only that it should once have been in him. And there is the same reason why believing, or the quality wherein the unition consists, should remain in order to the union's remaining, as why the unition should once be in order to the union's once being" (Edwards, "Miscellanies," no. 729, in *WJE* 18:354–55).

292. Thus, "although it is not proper to say that perseverance is necessary in order to justification, yet a persevering principle is necessary in order to justification" (Edwards, "Persevering Faith," in *WJE* 19:601).

293. "But this don't conclude with respect to infants; for when Scripture tells us we are to be judged according to our works, it says it for our warning but don't say it of those that ben't capable of being warned by it" (Edwards, "Miscellanies," no. 289, in *WJE* 13:382). This Miscellany supports Bombaro's argument that Edwards's salvific inclusivism should not be extended from infants to "infidels" (John J. Bombaro, "Jonathan Edwards' Vision of Salvation,"*Westminster Theological Journal* 65 [2003]: 50–53).

294. "And so Christ's perseverance in perfect obedience, is the condition of our right to life by the second covenant. But 'tis not perseverance in our own personal, imperfect obedience that acquires a right to life. That can't be; for the saints' persevering in holiness is one of the benefits to which a right is acquired by that righteousness" (Edwards, "Persevering Faith," in *WJE* 19:600).

295. "'Tis necessary to salvation as a necessary consequence and evidence of a title to salvation. There never is a title to salvation without it" (ibid., 600–601).

296. Edwards, "Miscellanies," no. 808, in *WJE* 18:510–12. Since Scripture speaks of salvation as dependent on perseverance, "this implies that their being one, or their standing in a saving relation to him, and [in] union with his mystical body, depends on the perseverance of faith, even that union in which a title to all spiritual and saving benefits depends" (ibid., 511).

297. "Miscellanies," no. 428, in *WJE* 13:428.

298. Ibid.

299. "And thus the second Adam has persevered not only for himself, but for us" (Edwards, "Miscellanies," no. 695, in *WJE* 18:279).

300. "That the saints shall surely persevere will necessarily follow from that [Christ's perseverance], that they have already performed the obedience which is the righteousness by which they have justification to life, or it is already performed for them and imputed to them: for that supposes that it is the same thing in the sight of God as if they had performed it" (ibid.).

301. Creatively extending Edwards's own imagery in *The Mind*, virtual perseverance is not to be thought of as an imagined chair in an empty room. Christ's supererogatory life and death is analogous to a real chair etched in our communal memory, though not physically perceived by us in the here and now. Christ has obtained that "chair" of righteousness for us, which God has accounted to us.

302. Edwards, "Miscellanies," no. 711, in *WJE* 18:340.

303. "So Christ having done our work for us, we are justified as soon as ever we believe in him, as being through what he has accomplished and finished, now already actually entitled to the reward of life" (ibid.).

304. Ibid.

305. Ibid.

7

Self-Communication of the Holy Spirit as the Church's Participation in the Divine Nature

As we have seen, the saints' Spirit-mediated *unio cum Christo* enables their participation in the *beneficia Christi*. In this chapter, we look in greater detail at that real, progressive, and vital union in Christ whereby sanctification is wrought in a person by the Holy Spirit. Edwards regards the continuum of regeneration-sanctification-glorification as participation in the divine nature and grace:

> There is no gift or benefit that is so much in God, that is so much of himself, of his nature, that is so much a communication of the Deity, as grace is; 'tis as much a communication of the Deity, as light [is] a communication of the sun. 'Tis therefore fit that when it is bestowed, it should be so much the more immediately given, from himself and by himself.[1]

We have noted in passing that Edwards does not have a notion of created grace. If such is the case, how then could the Spirit be united to the saint without confusion? Also, how is the gradualistic nature of sanctification accounted for? And where is the place of human volition and action?

GRATIA UNCREATA AND GRATIA CREATA IN EDWARDS'S SOTERIOLOGY

Anri Morimoto has argued that Edwards inherited the idea of created grace as "an intermediary habit" from Thomas Aquinas through Edwards's Puritan forebears.[2] While it may look as if *gratia creata* and the intermediary habit are

281

cognates, we will need to examine the two in turn. Firstly, does Edwards think that there is a form of grace that is created?

GRACE AS CREATED OR UNCREATED?

The notion of *gratia creata* in Puritanism is unexceptional since it was already commonly held in the Western tradition. Founded on the christological *communicatio gratiarum*, Reformed theologians, such as Polanus, insisted that the "giftes given to the humanity of Christ, are created qualities: because his humanity is created."[3] Among Edwards's predecessors, there were those who explicitly affirmed the Thomistic notion of created grace.[4] John Owen, for example, described the habit of grace as a "virtue, a power, a principle of spiritual life and grace, wrought, *created*, infused into our souls."[5]

Edwards, however, explicitly and robustly rejects the idea that grace is something created.[6] He insists that "the grace of God in men's heart can hardly be called a creature . . . it is God himself."[7] In this, he disagrees with Goodwin, who claimed that regeneration brings about a new, created disposition distinct from the Spirit.[8] On the contrary, Edwards regards grace as "God's own beauty and excellency that is uncreated and eternal, which is not properly made but communicated," and is none other than "the Spirit" of God.[9] If there is no place for created grace in Edwards's soteriology, could he have countenanced something like an intermediary habit?

CAN GRACE BE THOUGHT OF AS AN INTERMEDIARY HABIT?

In their insistence on a direct communion between God and the saints, Eastern theologians have depicted the Latin idea of *gratia creata* as a "created supernatural," an "intermediary," or a *tertium quid* in the way of divine–human communion.[10] Protestant writers have advanced similar criticisms.[11] This is certainly a caricature of St. Thomas's doctrine of grace since the habit of grace cannot be a substance (*res*) or a thing but is rather an accidental quality that modifies a person's existence.[12] Because grace is not a substance but an accident, it "is also said to be created inasmuch as men are created with reference to it, i.e., are given a new being out of nothing, i.e., not from merits."[13] If grace is but a divine work effecting a wholly unmerited regeneration of the soul, Edwards may be said to advance a concept of *gratia creata* similar to Aquinas's.

Consequently, if grace as a *tertium quid* is a non sequitur on Thomistic premises, then Edwards could not have envisioned grace as an *intermediary* habit. Yet it would be inaccurate to conclude that he denied the *habitual* character of grace. What kind of via media between the Lombardian *gratia increata* and "the Thomistic emphasis upon grace as functioning in and through the natural powers of the regenerate" does Edwards propound?[14]

"After the Manner of a Natural Principle": Uncreated but Habitual Grace

There are numerous places where Edwards seems to distinguish the Holy Spirit from grace, or the new, divine principle in the soul. Like the *via moderna* theologians and Luther, Edwards rejects any idea of a *natural* habit, though he admits that the graced soul may be supernaturally habituated by "divine constitution and covenant."[15] The person of the Spirit who indwells the saints is described metaphorically, and in the singular tense, as operating like an inward, natural principle. However, there are new effects, such as "a new spiritual sense, and the new dispositions that attend to it."[16] Neither new faculties are given nor are the ordinary processes of the natural faculties changed or enhanced. What is given are "new principles of nature," or "a natural habit or foundation for action," whereby the saint now has a new capacity for new operations through the unmodified natural faculties, which "may be said to be his nature."[17]

Edwards seems to make contradictory claims about the manner of the Spirit's gracious operation. One the one hand, he states that "the Holy Ghost influences the godly as dwelling in them as a vital principle, or as a new supernatural principle of life and action."[18] In another place, however, he says that "the Spirit of God, united to human faculties, acts very much after the manner of a natural principle or habit."[19] How is it possible for the Holy Spirit to both indwell the saint as a new, *supernatural* principle and operate like a *natural* principle? Wouldn't this contradict the axiom that operation follows existence?[20]

In this, Edwards seems to countenance grace as uncreated but habitual. Thus, "special grace causes" gracious exercises "to be in the soul habitually, and according to such a stated constitution or law that lays such a foundation for a continued course of exercises, as is called a principle of nature."[21] This is the "general law" by which the Spirit operates in the regenerate. The free agency is only lawlike when the Spirit acts like a permanent, natural, living principle of action, yet the immanent movements upon a person's will are more sovereign and personal.[22]

Grace in the soul is a new communication in the regenerate. The new disposition is analogous to *creatio ex nihilo* insofar as it is a direct, free exercise of divine power.[23] But Edwards does not deny the operation of the indwelling Spirit as habit, which "as it were settles the soul in a disposition to holy acts."[24]

If the soul is a disposition to action, then the Spirit is the disposing disposition that rehabituates the soul toward gracious action.[25]

There are very clear instances where Edwards identifies the new disposition of the regenerate with the Holy Spirit.[26] Since grace is none other than divine self-giving, it must be efficaciously bestowed by God, "more immediately given, from himself and by himself."[27] The infusion of the regenerate disposition is no different from the indwelling of the Holy Spirit: "The Christian spirit is only the Spirit of Christ dwelling in the Christian, and acting there as a principle."[28]

However, Edwards was careful when speaking of the Christian's holy disposition to modulate his grammar from the personal to the operational. The new disposition is "the immediate fruit of his own Spirit . . . the effects of his own power and wisdom and the emanation of his own attributes."[29]

UNCREATED GRACE REQUIRES NO PRIOR PREPARATORY DISPOSITION TO RECEPTIVITY

With Edward's rejection of the idea of created grace, no place exists in his soteriology for conceiving *gratia increata* as a sort of "formal effect" of *gratia creata*—a line of thinking found in certain strands of medieval theology.[30] On this account, since the person must first be adapted by created grace in order to receive the indwelling Spirit, uncreated grace became somewhat secondary in the theology of grace.[31]

For Edwards, however, the entrance of divine love during regeneration brings about "a suiting or according of the soul to the nature of God."[32] Following that, the first act of faith is the suiting of the mind to receive Christ and, thereafter, Christ's benefits. For Edwards, then, it is uncreated grace that causes, and so precedes, the soul's new receptivity in relation to Christ.

The many expressions of Christian graces and virtues are unified and comprehended in that new supernatural disposition.[33] Edwards rejects the notion of acquired virtues, though natural affections may resemble virtues outwardly.[34] Only supernatural, infused virtue possesses any positive goodness.[35] In this, he differs from Aquinas, though they both use the language of infused dispositions and virtues.[36] Without a principle of grace distinct from the Holy Spirit, no notion of merit is possible within Edwards's theology of grace.[37]

In sum, Edwards sees grace as the uncreated Disposition continually operating with and in the saint. This means that, on the one hand, habitual grace grants the natural soul a new capacity to operate supernaturally.[38] On the other hand, habitual grace is the supernatural Spirit accommodating the divine operation to suit the natural—a motif we will now look at in closer detail.

DIVINE ACCOMMODATION: DIVINE KENOSIS AND CONDESCENSION OF THE SPIRIT

The modulation of the Holy Spirit's operation akin to a natural principle may be understood in light of the doctrine of divine condescension or accommodation (*synkatabasis*).[39] In this, Edwards follows Calvin's use of the concept of divine accommodation—that is, God's dispensational condescension to human behavior according to differing contexts.[40] Such a proportioning of God's self-giving is triune in scope. Ethically, God's demands do not exceed human limitation for "in everything [God] accommodates his commands to the capacity of the creature."[41] Epistemologically, God "accommodate[s] his revelation to our manner of thinking" without compromising the divine truth.[42]

The incarnation is an act of divine condescension on the Son's part.[43] In both the incarnation and illumination, Christ condescends for soteriological ends, engaging in divine accommodation *modus essendi* in the hypostatic union and *modus cognoscendi* in conversion.[44] In like manner, the Holy Spirit's work of grace in the regenerate falls under the rubric of the continuing *oikonomia* of God. This is rooted in the divine economy, where the Spirit serves the other two divine persons.[45] The Spirit not only accommodates ontologically, by indwelling and uniting with the human soul, but operationally as well.[46] Divine grace in its exercises is accommodated to each person's particularity in *via*.[47] Where Calvin speaks more of divine appropriation of external, human media and of divine revelation reaching us by external means of grace, Edwards emphasizes mediated divine operations—that is, the manner in which the Spirit (as divine Grace) works with us, in and through our faculties. The disposition is permanent but not continually in operation.[48]

While humility, for Edwards, is not a divine property, condescension is.[49] As humility is a human attribute, it is only improperly predicated of God the Father and the Spirit.[50] Only the incarnate Son, as both God and human, properly possesses the properties of condescension as well as humility.[51] But as humility is the most fitting human correlate to divine condescension, a Christian appropriately responds to the mercy of God in humble love.[52] But, if it is just this, then will not God's self-revelation be regarded as unreliable? Not so, for divine accommodation must not be regarded as God role-playing in the drama of salvation. Rather, it is a manifestation of God's glory in a mode of condescension.[53] Though it is partial and refracted, it is not an untrue revelation of the divine Being.

There is another sense in which the indwelling Holy Spirit—as grace—may be considered a constitutive principle of the human being in its natural state. To highlight this theme in Edwards, let us set it in the perspective of the larger Christian traditions.

GRACED NATURE VERSUS PURE NATURE?

Puritans before Edwards, including Goodwin, identified the new principle of life in the saint as the reconstituted *imago Dei*. It is to be regarded as a distinct reality from the uncreated Spirit, who is its original and renewing cause.[54] This is similar to the patristic construal of the *imago Dei*. In one sense, then, it is correct to say, with Palamas, that the gracious ontological change in human beings during the spiritual rebirth is "not itself supernatural" and that "man's co-operation with grace is natural."[55] Created grace, for the East, is no *donum superadditum* but is the restored *imago Dei* by which a human being recovers his or her natural capacity for divine communion through grace.[56] Due to the Pelagian heresy, however, the West had to emphasize that human nature in itself is incapable of divine communion, and therefore it construed habitual, created grace as a supernatural principle added to nature. As we have noted, for Edwards, the primal or "natural" state of humankind is also graced.[57] Yet the Spirit may be considered a *donum superadditum* inasmuch as this original grace was forfeited through sin and restored through redemption.[58] The concept of a pure nature, in Edwards's anthropology, can only mean fallen nature.

If the redeemed nature is uncreated grace dwelling in the saint, how does Edwards parse the language of spiritual growth?

SANCTIFICATION AS GRADUALISTIC: HOW CAN UNCREATED GRACE BE SAID TO GROW?

As we have observed, Edwards rejects the whole notion of *gratia creata* in his insistence that the new disposition is none other than the indwelling Holy Spirit. In other places, however, he seems to distinguish a *habitus* from the Holy Spirit: "Remember that grace grows by exercise. 'Tis in this way that the Spirit of God increases the principle and habit of grace and in this way he gives the experience of the sweetness and pleasantness of it."[59] This new, telic principle is elsewhere described as mutable, passible, "and as it were beats and struggles, thirsts after holiness."[60] Like fruit on a tree, "grace in the saints" exhibits development and exists "in a progressive state, growing in perfection."[61]

Correlative to this language of growth is Edwards's apparent quantitative description of the Spirit, who given in regeneration.

DERIVATIVE GRACE: THE SPIRIT AD EXTRA IS GIVEN IN DEGREES

In many instances, Edwards describes grace or the Spirit-given in quantitative terms: God is able to determine the individual capacities of the saints by "giving different degrees of his Spirit" to them.[62] The greatest saints, therefore, receive "the greatest share of the divine nature of the Spirit."[63] Christ received the *gratia capitis* immeasurably, and *gratia habitualis* flows from Christ to the saints proportionally.[64] Edwards, along with the Reformed-Puritan tradition, agrees with Aquinas that grace is not something essential to the human being.[65] However, this does not mean that saving grace is an "adventitious," external principle.[66] This accords with scriptural usage that Spirit-as-grace is denominated "a quality of the persons in whom it resides."[67] Grace, in this sense, may be said to belong to the saint.[68] But how can something divine be regarded as owned by a human being? Wouldn't this confuse the created with the Uncreated?

Edwards maintains the Creator-creature gap through a qualitative distinction: God is the origin of grace but human beings are merely participants. All three persons of the Trinity are the infinite source or fountain of grace.[69] As the Spirit is both source and grace, the Son receives the Spirit infinitely.[70]

What is communicated to us is not the divine essence of the Holy Spirit but the efflux of the divine glory.[71] The regenerate is not united to the divine essence per se, but participates in the divine act, "the essence of God flowing out in love and joy."[72] Thus human beings do not receive the divine essence nor are they origins of the streams of grace. Thus, the saints are merely mirrors or crystals who "shine by a reflected light as the moons and the planets do."[73] This participated glory consists in the reception of the Spirit and Word.

Edwards describes Christ, "the brightness of God's glory," as the "Sun [of] the spiritual world," whose "beams" denote Christ's self-revelation and self-communication.[74] More specifically, these beams of self-manifestation consists of Christ's "Word and ordinances," the fullness and influence of Christ's Spirit on human hearts, the operations of Christ's power or omnipotence, and the manifestation of the divine majesty, glory, and attributes in creation.[75] For believers, these spiritual beams serve to enlighten and manifest reality as well as to refresh, heal, mature, and beautify the soul.[76]

By the Spirit who reigns in the heart, Christ governs the saints, enabling them to freely obey the Word.[77] As the loving will and disposition in God, the Spirit exercises the same influence *ad extra* such that "a gracious man has

[this] principle in his heart that directs and governs him."[78] For Edwards, sanctification is human persons participating in the divine glory *ad extra*: "'Tis from [God's] glory as the cause to their glory as the effect, as when the sun's light is reflected from a jewel. There is one glory derived from another glory."[79] This participated light is God's glory revealed.

GRACE AS SPIRIT-GIVEN: DECLARATIVE GLORY AS ESSENTIAL GLORY EXISTING AD EXTRA

In continuity with the Reformed-Puritan tradition, Edwards appropriates the nomenclature of God's intrinsic glory (*gloria*) and declarative glory (*glorificatio*).[80] God's essential *gloria* is the two *actus personales* within God—the divine self-epiphany and delectation.[81] He distinguishes between the latent glory of God the Father, which is eternally manifested in the Son and communicated in the Spirit, and God's declarative glory, which is the believer's twofold reception of divine glory *ad extra*: the perception of the Son and enjoyment in the Spirit.[82] In other words, divine glory communicated and revealed to creatures is the Son and Spirit of God. God's essential glory cannot be added to as it proceeds from God's nature. God's declarative glory, however, is enlargeable and contingent, as it is an effect of the divine will.[83] In Edwards's perspective, the saints have a threefold happiness in God: "in seeing his essential glory, in his being glorified declaratively and in being the instruments of his declarative glory."[84]

Yet Edwards sees an overlap between the glory communicable and incommunicable, *gloria Dei* and *glorificatio*.[85] Just as divine glory *ad intra* is God's happiness in the divine idea, so *glorificatio* is the believer's enjoying the divine revelation.[86] Edwards is explicit that the divine happiness experienced by human beings is not qualitatively different from God's.[87] Their souls become God-oriented due to a kind of moral gravitas imparted by the divine glory.[88] Nonetheless, the essential glory of God cannot increase *ad intra* but is communicable *ad extra* as God's manifestive or declarative glory. What will be manifested universally is both God's glorious justice and mercy.[89] While the full scope of God's declarative glory will be revealed within created constraints, this will not equal the infinity of the divine, essential glory.[90] What sort of communication is this *glorificatio*?

SELF-COMMUNICATION OF THE HOLY SPIRIT

After ruling out the notion of *gratia creata*, is it not contradictory for Edwards to maintain at the same time that grace "*comes into existence* in the soul by the power of God in the influences of the Holy Spirit"?[91] The inconsistency vanishes, however, when such phraseology is compared to Aquinas's, for it means nothing more than the invisible, sanctifying mission of God toward the saint, whereby a divine person finds "a new way of existing in another."[92] In other words, it is another way of specifying God's self-communication to the regenerate.[93]

One may then ask: does the Holy Spirit indwell the soul as a divine person or the uncreated energies?[94] For Edwards, that question poses a false polarity. A person's "*relation of the Spirit*" is always twofold: the Spirit is both "the *operator* and . . . *operation itself.*"[95] The Holy Spirit exists in believers as an intrinsic, indwelling principle and operates in a spiritual manner. As such, the Spirit's action is self-communicative and brings about both supernatural and preternatural "qualifications, affections and experiences."[96]

With nonbelievers, however, the relation is as an extrinsic cause.[97] The operation of common grace is purely efficient and sporadic, producing "improvement, composition or management" of the natural, human faculties.[98] Hence, there are those divine operations in which the Spirit may "produce effects on many things to which it does not communicate itself."[99] In God's activity upon inanimate and natural things, the Spirit is not imparted, but in the divine action within persons, Edwards seem to posit a self-communication in qualitative terms: "the subject becomes a spiritual being, denominated so from the Spirit of God which dwells in him and of whose nature he is a partaker."[100] In the following subsection, we will examine in greater detail Edwards's elucidation of the Holy Spirit as both actor and act in the regenerate.

OPERATIVE GRACE: THE HOLY SPIRIT AS SOVEREIGN ACTOR AND PURE ACT

Along Augustinian lines, Edwards characterizes the Spirit as *donum*, though this does not apply *ad intra*.[101] Nonetheless, he does not press the bipersonal analogy to the detriment of the Spirit's personhood.[102] The Holy Spirit is both giver and gift, actor and act.[103] Though the Spirit functions as the Son's agent, this does not mean that the Spirit is less of a divine person.[104] Though an agent by reason of the Spirit's own personhood, the Spirit ordinarily remains hidden in the gracious divine operations, which mimic a natural principle.[105] However, in trying times, the Spirit's personal character as the divine Paraclete comes to the fore.[106]

For Edwards, grace is also a dynamic principle.[107] Like Gregory Palamas, he thinks that the Holy Spirit communicates "his own natural, essential and eternal act" when gracing the soul.[108] Here, Edwards freely mixes the Palamite language of *energeia* with the Thomistic *habitus*: the "habit of grace" is nothing less than "the exercises and operations" of God's Spirit in the human heart.[109] In other words, the divine *energeia* or *operatio* is the Holy Spirit in action as the uncreated *habitus*.[110]

This convertibility between the Spirit and the divine *energeia* is not a novel idea in the history of theology.[111] Human beings image God, who, as dispositional essence, is the coincidence of habit and act.[112] Sanctification, then, is the natural flowering of regeneration, just as God's nature is bountiful.[113] As an inward principle disposed to outward action, grace (re)integrates spirituality and ethics.[114] "As I have said, gracious affections have their exercise and fruit in Christian practice. . . . Christ lives in the heart and the Holy Spirit dwells there in union with the faculties of the soul as an internal, vital principle that exerts God's own proper nature. This is why true grace has such active power and efficacy."[115] Edwards's position is close to the Orthodox idea of the *unio mystica* as a kind of divine-human operational union.[116] The Holy Spirit, as the "principle that reigns over the Godhead and governs his heart," acts similarly *ad extra* as the "internal governing principle of life and practice" in the Adamic and regenerated heart.[117] As the Spirit is perfect action in God, Edwards likens glorified human beings to living verbs or *ekstasis*.[118] The saints become so because they mimic the Cause of their exaltation.

Grace as Infused: Quasi-Formal Causality

With the Western tradition in general, Edwards speaks of grace in terms of efficient causation.[119] God can only confer the grace promised if God is its cause. "For him to promise that has it not in his hands to dispose and determine is a great absurdity."[120] Hence, God must be the "efficacious cause or effectual cause" of "the benefit" as God is able to will, orchestrate, and produce it.[121] God's action *ad extra* is always purposeful and efficient "for 'tis not an ineffectual exertion that God aims at or inclines to."[122] The divine *energeia* is God's effectual working through, in, and with the human actor.[123] From this standpoint of efficient causality, the effect is to be regarded as fundamentally distinct from its cause.

However, although Edwards frequently refers to indwelling grace as an effect (as did his Puritan forebears), he identifies it with the Spirit, as we have noted at the start of this chapter.[124] On the former account, grace in the saints "is the effect of God's wonderful love to man through Jesus Christ."[125] This is akin to a kind of formal causation since "God's exercising his perfection to produce a proper effect is not distinct from the emanation and communication of his fullness."[126] This light is not of an ordinary sort; it is a *lux divina.*

A question arises: If Edwards does not understand grace to be *gratia creata,* how can the Spirit be classed as both cause and effect? And, if grace were to be considered a formal cause, must it not be a kind of created principle also?[127] To describe uncreated grace as the formative principle within the saint, something like the neo-Thomistic idea of quasi-formal causality would be required to secure the Creator-creature distinction.[128] In this regard, the term *formal* denotes the saint's assimilation to God, whereas *quasi* protects the divine transcendence.[129]

Echoing Lombard, Edwards separates the formal cause from its effect by differentiating the divine source from its emanation.[130] The divine communication is "something divine, something of God, something of his internal fullness."[131] This "something" is Edwards's way of saying "quasi," thus distinguishing God from the *lux.* Alternatively, expressed in Edwards's own metaphors, the creature receives the emanating sunbeams or water, and not the sun or fountain—the source itself.

When such a distinction is acknowledged, the communications from God can be regarded as "an increase, repetition or multiplication" of the divine goodness.[132] Clearly, Edwards's use of "repetition" *ad extra* is similar to his characterization of the divine processions *ad intra* as repetitions of the Deity: this cannot mean any real increase in God.[133]

Furthermore, one must note that quasi-formal causality, for Edwards, is distinct from but comprehends efficient causality.[134] Hence, he takes it as axiomatic that there is a likeness between an effect and its cause.[135] For instance, he insists that the divine glory "*existing ad extra*" is none other than "God's internal glory extant, in a true and just exhibition."[136] Grace involves God's informing and efficient action of union with and operation on the soul.[137]

How are God's efficacious operations toward the saints inclusive of a quasi-formal causality?[138] One way to picture this is as a relation between the stamp and its impress, of a seal upon wax—a biblical metaphor commonly adopted by the Puritan writers.[139] Accordingly "faith, or the mind's receiving or closing with Christ as Mediator" is not an instrumental cause but a receptive effect of the quasi-formal causation of union with Christ's person—regeneration.[140] "The soul by [faith] is suited as the socket for the jewel that is set in it; by this the soul admits it, as things transparent admit light when opaque bodies refuse it."[141] Regeneration and faith dispose the soul to become a suitable subject for salvation. The quasi-formal causality of uncreated grace activates existing potencies within the human nature in the *unio mystica.*[142] There is change in terms of an intensification of natural qualities, but this excludes an essential alteration or any addition of foreign attributes.[143] Of course, the new, supernatural, or spiritual disposition—uncreated grace—in the soul is not so much an addition but a reintroduction of that which had been lost in the Fall. Since grace "is as it were the life and soul of the soul," the Holy Spirit may be termed the quasi-form of the regenerate soul.[144]

In this Aristotelian analysis, God's action as both efficient and quasi-formal is inseparable from the final cause of creation.[145] God's self-operation *ad extra* is therefore the divine self-communication to the regenerate, and it constitutes the telos of the world.[146] The final form of the recreated creation is a beautiful one because its cause is Beauty itself.

GRACE AS AESTHETIC AND CRUCIFORM: SANCTIFICATION AS LOVELINESS AND HUMILITY

For Edwards, grace is an aesthetic principle that beautifies the human being.[147] In his understanding, there must be an ontological consent or correlation between the holy nature of the regenerated soul and the holy nature of God.[148] The believer is enabled to taste a measure of this Love between the Father and the Son in sanctification—an experience unique to the saint.[149]

While Edwards affirms this Augustinian-Calvinist sense of the heart, he recasts it in terms of Lockean sensationalist psychology as a Trinitarian, aesthetic response to divine perfection.[150] It is only when the Holy Spirit creates in the heart a "divine taste or sense" that the soul is thereby naturally inclined to love God.[151] The new spiritual sense is not only aesthetic but also rational.[152] Spiritual perception of the gospel includes an intuitive perception of divine glory and an indirect purification of the mind together with the enhancement of the cognition of truth.[153] There is a connaturality between divine sense and the *lux pulchra*, for Word and Spirit are always conjoined.

Clearly, God's infusion of the divine disposition from above creates a new sensibility in the human being: the saint is now enabled to respond heavenward. The *exitus et reditus* motif reappears in the trajectories of a theological descent and anthropological ascent: the new reality of the Spirit's immanence and the corollary recognition of God's transcendence. As a result of this spiritual elevation—disinterested perception and certainty of the beauty and glory of Christ and God—there is a corresponding evangelical humility.[154] In order to demonstrate through the divine economy that God "is all, and the creature nothing," the ascending movement of the saint's glorification is inextricably coupled with descending movement of evangelical humiliation. The saint's lightsomeness is proportioned to Christ's spiritual beauty.[155] And this mirrors the incarnate Son's *exinanitio* and *exaltatio*:

> And to prepare it [Christ's humanity] for its exaltation above all, it was first brought lowest of all in suffering and humiliation, and in some respects in office, in those parts of that office that were executed in his state of humiliation. And though the saints are exalted in glorious dignity, even to union and fellowship with God him[self], to be in some respects divine in glory and happiness, and in many respects to be exalted above the angels, yet care is taken that it should not be in themselves, but in a person that is God; and they must be as it were emptied of themselves in order to it.[156]

For the saint to possess humility is to have Christ's disposition, or "the lamblike, dovelike spirit and temper of Jesus Christ."[157] How does the saint participate in Christ's Spirit of humility?

The saints not only endure suffering for Christ as their Christian duty but are willing to suffer like him in bearing their crosses.[158] As Christ's virtuous life was more perfect and greater than that of any human or created being—in both degree and appearance—it is not only "the perfect example of true religion and virtue" for all to imitate, but also a standard "to try all other examples by."[159] The nature and exercise of Christ's love were relational: to God, self, and others.[160] With respect to self, Christ was the most humble and patient of all created beings in resisting pride and suffering abasement.[161] And in relation to others, Christ evidenced unparalleled meekness, love, and forgiveness.[162]

This threefold relational pattern of Christ's virtuous life is the basic model the Christian is to imitate and live by, enabled by the indwelling work of Christ's Spirit.[163] This mirroring of Christ by the Spirit is an expression of the Christian's participation in the divine nature—a theme we shall now examine in detail.

HUMAN PARTICIPATION IN GOD'S COMMUNICATED GRACE

With reference to grace, Edwards uses the terms "participation," "communication," and "communion" interchangeably.[164] He explicitly denies that "the saints are made partakers of the essence of God" in regeneration but explains instead that "they are made partakers of God's fullness."[165] Acquainted with the Puritans who rejected the mysticism of the Familists, Edwards clearly distances himself from the grammar of *apothēosis*.[166] Quoting James Lowde or John Flavel, Edwards rejects the "abominable and blasphemous language" of participation in God as being "'Godded' with God, and 'Christed' with Christ."[167] Nonetheless, he retains the grammar of participation in affirming that the saints have "something of the same nature with that Spirit"—that is, they share in the holy operations of the Spirit.[168] If by *thēosis* one means the goal of attaining (re)union with God and thereby participating in the divine actions and attributes, Edwards's theology clearly allows for it.[169]

Turretin, for example, interpreted the phrase "partakers of the divine nature" in 2 Pet. 1:4 not as formal but as analogical participation through the gifts of the Spirit.[170] Through the Cambridge Platonists, Edwards is familiar with the concept of human participation in the divine ideas, which are real relations of God *ad extra*.[171]

For Edwards, there is an identity-in-difference between grace and the Holy Spirit when he calls it "something of the same nature with that Spirit." On the one hand, it is of the "same nature" as brightness in a diamond is to the brightness of the sun, yet it is "something" that is only quantitatively different.[172]

According to Edwards, God does not create in order to receive anything from us, although there is an everlasting remanation of divine love to God. Rather, God's disposition is to self-communication, and that very reality makes God's self-communicative disposition the ground of creation. But if the Father can only enjoy the *summum bonum* or the Spirit through the Son, then it is only through Christ that the remanation of the Spirit is made possible in time.

Holiness is an essential property, by appropriation, assigned to the Holy Spirit. The self-communication of the Spirit comprehends the saints' participation in the communicable attributes of God.[173] Echoing St. Basil's notion of participation, Edwards describes the indwelling Holy Spirit as the saints' source of spiritual beauty and holiness inasmuch as a crystal becomes luminous because of the sunbeam.[174] "And as God delights in his own beauty, he must necessarily delight in the creature's holiness; which is a conformity to, and participation of it, as truly as the brightness of a jewel, held in the sun's beams, is a participation, or derivation of the sun's brightness, though immensely less in degree."[175] This distinction between the saints' participation in God's essence and the divine qualities is frequently illustrated with the metaphor of light.[176]

For Edwards, participation in the divine life is no different from sanctification.[177] Commenting of the classic deification proof text (2 Pet. 1:4), Edwards identifies with the Holy Spirit the divine nature in which the saints participate.[178] Sanctification is a qualitative, but not an essential, transformation.[179] The union of wills must be undergirded by a more fundamental ontological union.[180]

Like Aquinas, Edwards believes in a participation that is real and predicamental, whereby a substance partakes in its essential properties or accidents.[181] Grace is "called supernatural or divine," though it is neither essentially human nor accidental. This is not merely a logical, but a real, transcendental participation in God.[182] Using neo-Thomistic categories of participation, Edwards would agree that the believer is granted both a moral and physical participation in God.[183]

SPIRIT AS INCOMMUNICABLE AND COMMUNICABLE: DISTINCTION BETWEEN "ESSENCE" AND "NATURE"

The patristic notion of creaturely participation in the divine assumes a fundamental distinction of essences, since one cannot share in something one already has.[184] Both Athanasius and Cyril of Alexandria argued that the Holy Spirit is God because the divine essence is properly the Spirit's, while human beings only partake of God's nature. The Spirit deifies and gives life, while creatures are deified and receive life.[185]

In preaching about Christian participation in the divine life, Edwards is keen to emphasize the ontological distinction between God and human beings.[186] Using language Athanasius would have avoided, Edwards asserts that only "divine persons . . . do partake of the divine essence."[187] Solely the persons of the Trinity may be said to "partake of the divine essence" and thus to be God and divine persons.[188] Grace in saints cannot be called divine in this sense; they do not "partake of the divine essence or any part of the divine essence for the essence of God is not divisible nor communicable."[189]

Edwards attempts to forge a distinction between nature and essence in specifying human participation in God. "The nature of the Holy Spirit is love; and it is by communicating himself, or his own nature, that the hearts of the saints are filled with love or charity."[190] But does Edwards make a sufficiently clear distinction between essence and nature?[191]

Edwards, in a letter clarifying what he means by the Spirit's self-communication, or our participation in God's nature, gives both a negative and positive defense of his terminology in the *Religious Affections*. Negatively, God's "proper nature" does not mean "his essence"; positively, it means "something of his holiness."[192] Edwards alerts his correspondent to the polyvalent use of the terms *physis* and *natura*, which are sometimes used "to signify the essence of a thing."[193]

The Holy Spirit *ad intra* is the divine essence, while the Spirit indwelling and united to the saints *ad extra* is God's nature or disposition.[194] However, Edwards defines "nature" as that "property which is natural to anyone and is eminently his character . . . though [it] is not just the same with his essence."[195] Holiness is common yet appropriated to the Spirit and is communicable *ad extra*. According to Edwards, "holiness consists in having grace in the heart: grace and holiness are the same thing."[196] This ability to be attracted to the excellency of divine things is a particular Trinitarian reality of the Spirit because "the Spirit of God in the souls of his saints exerts its own proper nature; that is to say, it communicates and exerts itself in the soul in those acts which are its proper, natural and essential acts in itself ad intra, or within the Deity from all eternity."[197] Edwards, therefore, classes the *operatio* or *energeia* of the Spirit, both *ad intra* and *ad extra*, as the nature of God.

In addition to the fact that the ultimate oneness between God and the saints will never occur because of the distinction between infinite and finite, this oneness is a communal "union" of interest, respect, and distinction and not an identity of being.[198] The church's participation in divine glory is Trinitarian and, therefore, personal. The Son is not only the source of grace, since the Son is God, but is that source as the Father's image or eternal epiphany.[199] And Jesus Christ, as the possessor of the Spirit without measure, communicates to the saints this same grace by Christ's bond of union—the person of the Holy Spirit.[200] If one wishes to highlight an identity of "being" in terms of an entitative union, then it is the Holy Spirit existing *ad extra* and eschatologically—indwelling and operating in and through the church—that is identical to the Holy Spirit *ad intra*.[201] As the *vinculum* that unites without confusion the Father and Son in timeless eternity, this same Spirit will bind Christ to the church while retaining their personal distinction in sempiternal heaven.[202]

LIMITATION PRINCIPLE FOR THE HUMAN MODE OF RECEPTION

The anthropological corollary to the doctrine of divine accommodation (*synkatabasis*) is the notion of *per modum recipientis*. In other words, human participation in the divine is proportioned to divine communication. Edwards was aware, through Puritan sources, of the limitation principle used by the Fathers.[203] As encapsulated by the scholastics, the axiom goes thus: "Whatever is received into anything must be received according to the condition of the receiver."[204] As this is not a literal transference of the divine attributes, the axiom does not contradict the divine simplicity.[205]

Edwards is open to the possibility of more than a mere human participation in God's likeness. For "there is something of God actually communicated, some of that good that is in God, that the creature hereby has communion in, viz. God's happiness. The creature partakes of the happiness of God, at least an image of it."[206] Though Edwards concedes that human nature will be greatly augmented in glory, he rejects an unqualified (albeit Spirit-mediated) *genus maiestaticum*. "Though 'tis probable that men's capacities will be much greater than in their present state, yet they will not be infinite: though their understanding and comprehension will be vastly extended, yet men will not be deified."[207] However, the reception of God's goodness is adjusted according to their species-kind and individual capacity.

Edwards, with the Reformed tradition, affirms that human beings participate in the communicable attributes of God, not the incommunicable attributes like "eternity, infinity or infinite power."[208] While not "in the same degree," the saints do receive "every grace" that is in Christ through Christ "according to their measure."[209] Conformity to God includes the ethical, which is willing and acting as God would.[210] It is a participation in the divine justice, holiness, wisdom, and mercy.

Edwards thinks of regeneration as the Holy Spirit being united to the faculties of the person. With many Puritan writers, Edwards asserts that no new faculties are given, but a new divine foundation for their operations is created.[211] The saint possesses new dispositions insofar as the Holy Spirit acts as a foundation, causing supernatural dispositions and operations through the natural faculties.[212] Edwards, like his Puritan forebears, calls this new, inward principle a new spiritual sense, which grants the regenerate the capacity to taste and see the beauty of divine things.[213]

Two things need to be noted about this divine sense. In the first place, it is a passive capacity. The bestowal of grace, above and beyond the gift itself, includes the power to confer receptivity—namely "the determination of the inclination and will."[214] Like a natural principle, this new receptive capacity functions habitually in union with, and as mediated through, the soul's natural faculties.[215] Yet, this new receptive principle is supernaturally caused by and conformed to supernatural objects; in other words, both its source and content must be divine. The regenerate person is enabled to truly receive these divine *res* in a manner that does not abrogate the person's humanity since they are mediated through human faculties, which now operate in a mode commensurate to their divine objects.[216] The written Word is intellectually or "notionally" apprehended through the mind, yet its beauty is spiritually discerned through the new sense. It allows for a reception of Christ; it is faith acting as a receptive instrument.

In the second place, notwithstanding the receptive nature of this new sense, the natural, human faculties are not bypassed. Besides being the "subject" of special grace, they are "not merely passive, but active" in receiving the divine light.[217] The "propriety" of the salvation through the atonement and the saints' union with Christ must include their active human reception of him such that the "freedom of grace" is not contradicted.[218] This is based on Aquinas's epistemological distinction between primary and secondary cognition: knowledge of a thing per se and knowledge of a thing that is proportionate to the mode of its knower.[219] Our participation in the divine existence and attributes is not only in accordance to the kind of beings we are but is also governed by our individual capacities: "Esse autem participatum finitur ad capacitatem participantis."[220] This axiom was familiar to the Puritan writers: "Thus we are made one with God, *secundum modulum nostrum*, according to the capableness of our nature."[221]

Edwards's dynamic conception of human nature permits a quantitative dilation of its potency: "Humanity is in itself capable of being advanced to a great degree of amiableness."[222] The limitation principle is both christological and Trinitarian, for the church's telos is to apprehend and enjoy the triune beauty only with and through Jesus Christ.[223] The greater the capacity of a mind, the more it is able to appreciate complex beauties and so to intellectually apprehend the Trinity, "the supreme harmony of all."[224] Quantitatively, Christ possesses "the capacity of enjoyment" far greater than the saints, whether individually or collectively.[225] Even in heaven, the saints' *visio beatifica* will be measured to them "according to their capacity."[226]

WITHOUT SECONDARY CAUSES, WHERE THEN IS THE PLACE FOR HUMAN ACTION?

No charge of reductionism can be leveled at Edwards's theology of grace since he maintains the antinomy of "the *primacy of God . . .* and the *reality of regeneration*."[227] However, Edwards's so-called occasionalism would seem to obviate any role for natural causes in his cosmology.[228] Does he have a place for secondary causation?

SECONDARY CAUSATION IN NATURAL BUT NOT DIVINE ACTIVITY

It is clear that Edwards does allow for secondary causes to be operative in natural processes and acquired knowledge.[229] Mediate causation applies especially to creatures at the lower end of the chain of being and in the common, providential operations.[230] God, as the prime cause of all natural effects, correlates them with the natural laws that he has ordained.[231]

Edwards is keen to protect God's causal role in the miraculous, divine activity. He insists that the soul of every human being is a *creatio ex nihilo* resulting from "arbitrary" divine action, without any mediate cause.[232] As with the production of the human soul, human causation has no place in spiritual regeneration. While both grace and nature are characterized by a regularity underpinned by the immediate exercise of divine power, the new principle of grace is produced ex nihilo.[233] Christology is the only place where Edwards concedes a secondary, causative role to divine miracles. As we have seen, only the humanity of Christ is properly a united, animated, sentient, and instrumental cause of the divine action.[234]

THE ROLE OF CREATED MEANS IN EDWARDS'S DOCTRINE OF GRACE

Unlike Aquinas, however, Edwards does not carry his notion of instrumental causality over into his ecclesiology.[235] Divine power exercised through merely human agents does not make them proper instruments of the Godhead; only Jesus is the *instrumentum deitatis*.[236] Once again, Edwards's concern here is to safeguard the divine sovereignty.

Though ecclesial means of grace may not be instrumental causes, they are not occasions that merely coincide with grace's acting. Rather, they are fitting and appropriate "opportunities" for grace's acting.[237] Means of grace are not only "concerned in the affair of the production of grace," they "are necessary in order to it" as a kind of reactant in the combustion process.[238] Though there is no "absolute" connection between grace and its means, there is a suitability between the uncreated Spirit and created ordinances *de potentia ordinata*. Matter ordained for sacramental use, in a sense, mediates grace such that "the ordinances are conveyancers of the Spirit." In their own mode, they have a connaturality with the Holy Spirit, who is the *vehiculum aeternitatis*.[239]

Arguably, Edwards's sacramental position lies somewhere between Brian Gerrish's symbolic instrumentalism and symbolic parallelism.[240] It could be termed symbolic dispositionalism, insofar as sacraments are predisposed, by divine institution, to be fit occasions for the communication of grace. Without *materia* disposed to combustibility, so to speak, grace would have a less fitting context to ignite, to move from "virtuality to actuality."[241] The new disposition is not exercised in the saint without sacramental presence (occasion); rather, faith must be reignited continuously by Word and Spirit.

While Edwards is careful to assign all miraculous and *ex novo* action to God, means of grace are *conditio sine qua non* for the efficacy of grace. Means of grace supply content and move natural principles so that the soul may be provided with "matter that grace acts upon" in order that the workings of grace might be enhanced.[242] In fact, the Holy Scriptures as a means of grace is the necessary and fitting precondition for the existence of grace. Without the knowledge of key Christian doctrines, Edwards could not understand how "it is possible for God to infuse a principle of grace into the heart of a man."[243] That is, the Word must be present to ensure the Spirit's presence. Regeneration does not circumvent nature but capacitates the human faculties to exercise faith. All regenerate persons must exercise faith in Christ as the natural outworking of grace. An exception is in the case of children, who could be saved by disposition and union with Christ because they lack the capacity for faith without developed faculties.[244]

PLACE OF HUMAN ACTION IN ITS PARTICIPATION IN DIVINE GRACE

As we have noted, Edwards's denial of secondary and instrumental causation in the miraculous infusion of grace in regeneration asserts the divine-creaturely distinction.[245] Yet, in the continuing operation of grace, Edwards affirms the doctrine of concurrence between divine and human wills. As in natural operations, human beings exercise their faculties and powers "properly . . . with no more than that concurrence or influx where with God is present with every creature that he has made according to the natures that he has given them."[246] Divine concurrence operates such that upon every proper creaturely act, "the effect ever follows."[247] Both in nature and grace, human beings depend on God not only for their existence but for their operation as well.[248]

Acts of grace, unlike natural principles, are not governed by unchanging natural laws but are, nonetheless, linked to means by the *potentia ordinata*.[249] Insofar as the Spirit acts after the manner of a natural principle, gracious "exercises are excited by means, in some measure as other natural principles are."[250] But, we may ask, does not the characterization of the Spirit as both a "natural principle" and personal agency resolve into a single *gratia operans*? Let us pose the question differently: since Edwards does not allow for a *gratia creata*, how does he distinguish the act of the Holy Spirit or *gratia increata* from the human soul to which it is immediately united?[251]

Holy action is the "exercise of these Godlike tempers, wherein the soul acts in a kind of concert with God."[252] As grace becomes a principle intrinsic to the human person, there is no divine coercion as God enables the saint to exercise holy virtues.[253] That God continually produces *ex novo* a person's being and modes need not obviate the human power of action and free will. Edwards, with the Reformed tradition, regards free grace and human consent within a compatibilist framework. Such a compatibilism must mitigate any extreme occasionalism that would attribute positive causation of sin to God.[254] In grace, the concurrence of divine and human actions is not *partum-partum*, but *totum-totum*.[255] Hence, the human person is not "merely passive in it" but rather "in different respects wholly passive and wholly active."[256] In what respect then is humankind active in the operation of grace?

God is the true source of grace and of the human person, the real actor, so that it can be said that "God produces all and we act all."[257] Edwards, with Malebranche, thus distinguishes between (divine) production and (human) action.[258] As Edwards elaborates on this point in another place, "there may be as true and real a difference between *acting* and being *caused to act*, though we should suppose the soul to be both in the same volition, as there is between *living*, and *being quickened*, or *made to live*."[259] In other words, causation *ex novo* is not synonymous with action. If "author" means source, then God is the only author of our gracious actions.[260] If, however, the term "author" is applied to the person who acts immediately, then we can be said to be authors of our own gracious acts.[261] Edwards's dispositionalism lies midway between Aquinas's concurrentism and a pure occasionalism.[262]

CONCLUSION

Where the Latins qualify divine grace by predicating the term "created," the Palamite tradition qualifies the human subject with the "uncreated" predicate.[263] Edwards traces a via media between the doctrines of created grace and divine *energeia*.[264] On the one hand, grace as the indwelling Spirit operates as a natural *habitus*, is quantitatively described, and is liable to increase in the saint. On the other hand, grace as possessed by the saint imparts a new supernatural ontology for divine–human action. The Holy Spirit accommodates the divine operations according to the given capacity and limits of the human person. The saint participates dynamically in the divine workings or "nature," and not in God's essence. Our investigation highlighted Edwards's rejection of the idea of grace as a created entity superadded to the soul at regeneration. Rather, grace is uncreated, habitual grace in the saint. Divine communication is the indwelling Holy Spirit operating in and through the human being and modulating the divine actions to suit intrinsic human limitations. Human participation in the "divine nature" is the reception of a new supernatural disposition acting through (essentially) unchanged but dynamic human capacities. Divine condescension or accommodation is the counterpart of human glorification within the limitation principle. The Holy Spirit as pure act and beauty communicates the divine acts and form to sanctify Christians as their efficient, quasi-formal, and final cause. This conjunction of holy operations in sanctification does not abrogate human freedom since the Spirit does not replace or overwhelm human action but is the source of the saint's holy operations. In this sense, sanctity is theandric.[265]

Notes

1. Edwards, "Miscellanies," no. 537, in *WJE* 18:83.

2. For the argument that Edwards propounded the notion of an intermediary habit, see Anri Morimoto, *Jonathan Edwards and the Catholic Vision of Salvation* (University Park: Pennsylvania State University Press, 1995), 44ff. He cites Turretin, in particular, as Edwards's proximate source (50–54).

3. Amandus Polanus von Polansdorf, *The substance of Christian religion, soundly set forth in two bookes, . . .* (London: R. F. for John Oxenbridge, 1595), 67. In this, the Catholic emphasis on grace as *donum* to the created soul was not lost to the Reformed theologians. See appendix 5 below, "*Genus Maiestaticum*: Communication of Action and Grace between Christ's Natures," esp. the section, "The Reformed Insistence on the *Communicatio Gratiarum*."

4. Andrew Willet, *Hexapla: That is, a six-fold commentarie upon the most divine epistle of the holy apostle S. Paul to the Romanes . . .* (Cambridge: Leonard Greene, 1620), 283; Samuel Annesley, *Containing the first volume of the exercise at Cripplegate, and part of the supplement*, vol. 1 of *The morning exercises at Cripplegate, St. Giles in the Fields, and in Southwark . . .*, ed. James Nichols (London: Thomas Tegg, 1844), 612; and Patrick Gillespie, *The ark of the covenant opened . . .* (London: Tho. Parkhurst, 1677), 224. Even Palamas does not deny the concept of created grace, which is to be distinguished from the Holy Spirit, who is uncreated grace. "There is a created grace and another grace uncreated," he explains, but he then asks rhetorically, "since the gift which the saints receive and by which they are deified, is none other than God himself, how canst thou say that that too is a created grace?" (Palamas, *Against Akindynos* III, 8, Coisl. 98, folio 76v, as quoted in John Meyendorff, *A Study of Gregory Palamas* [Crestwood, NY: St. Vladimir's Seminary Press, 1998], 164). "There is nothing strange in using the word 'grace' both for the created and uncreated and in speaking of a created grace distinct from the created." See Gregory Palamas, *Letter to Athanasius*, Coisl. 98, fol. 14, in Meyendorff, *Study of Gregory Palamas*, 164.

5. Emphasis mine. The indwelling operation of the Spirit consists "partly by moving upon and stirring up the grace we have received; partly by new supplies of grace from Jesus Christ, falling in with occasions for their exercise, raising good motions immediately or occasionally within us" (John Owen, "On Communion," in *The Works of John Owen*, ed. William H. Goold [London: Banner of Truth Trust, 1965–68; originally publ. Johnstone & Hunter, 1850–53], 2:267). The "*habit of grace*" in the saint, as "*a created quality*, remains in us, as in its own proper subject, that hath not any subsistence" and is not identified with the indwelling Spirit, who is a "*free agent*" (273).

6. Though Edwards does not use the terms *gratia increata* and *gratia creata*, he very clearly rejects the latter here (pace Morimoto, *Catholic Vision*, 43). See Bombaro's critique of Morimoto on this point (John J. Bombaro, "Jonathan Edwards' Vision of Salvation," *Westminster Theological*

Journal 65 [2003]: 53–57). Yet, Morimoto is not incorrect in picking up Edwards's emphasis on grace as principle, though it is neither created nor an "intermediary."

7. Edwards, 72. Sermon on 2 Cor. 3:18 (a) (1728), in *WJE* 43.

8. Besides the destruction of the power of sin, there is, in regeneration, "a new principle created . . . here is spirit, a distinct thing from the Holy Ghost, that is the fruit of the second birth" (Goodwin, *WTG* 1:365).

9. Since only God can do the miraculous work of regeneration, that is one reason "why no creature works this work upon the hearts of men. . . . No, this is an honor that God reserves only for his beloved Son to work by his own Spirit" (Edwards, 72. Sermon on 2 Cor. 3:18 [a] [1728], in *WJE* 43).

10. Meyendorff, *Study of Gregory Palamas*, 163, 217. This is the usual Orthodox accusation as pointed out by Charles Mœller and Gérard Philips in their *The Theology of Grace and the Oecumenical Movement*, trans. R. A. Wilson (London: A. R. Mowbray, 1961), 2. In rejecting the idea of a supernatural, created grace, Palamas denies that grace could be reified in order to emphasize grace as the human being's direct existential encounter with the divine (Edward Yarnold, *Second Gift: A Study of Grace* [Slough, England: St. Paul Publications, 1974], 55–56). Ironically, the same accusation of the divine energies being an intermediate of essence and person has been leveled against Palamism.

11. "If grace is a relation of peace between Creator and creature, what is this *gratia creata* as a finite thing which brings about this reconciliation?" (Barth, *CD* IV.1, § 58, 84). Here, Barth adduces the frequent misunderstandings of *gratia creata* adduced by the Orthodox—that of a created supernatural—and the Protestants—a created "thing" in the possession and control of human beings (Mœller and Philips, *Theology of Grace*, 1–2). McGrath adopts a similar caricature of created grace "as a hybrid species, interposed as a created intermediate between God and man" (Alister McGrath, *Luther's Theology of the Cross: Martin Luther's Theological Breakthrough* [Oxford: Blackwell, 1990], 82). Does the very category of created, inherent, or infused grace conflate the divine and human, bringing about "an intolerable nostrification of the love and grace of God"? (Eberhard Jüngel, "On the Doctrine of Justification," *International Journal of Systematic Theology* 1, no. 1 [March 1999]: 43–44). In this article, Jüngel is concerned with justifying grace, *extra nos*, but he seems to reject the very idea of *gratia creata*, specifically that imparted as *gratia infusa* through the Roman sacramental system, as "an almost unsurpassably mischievous category mistake" (43).

12. Roger Haight, *The Experience and Language of Grace* (New York: Paulist, 1979), 62. Citing the authority of Boethius, Aquinas states that "no accident is called being as if it had being, but because by it something is; hence it is said to belong to a being rather than to be a being" (Aquinas, *STh* I-II, 110, 2, ad 2, 1133). Whether the Latin Scholastics after the thirteenth century were guilty of this shall not deter us here.

13. Aquinas, *STh* I-II, q. 110, a. 2, ad 3.

14. Lee, "Editor's Introduction," in *WJE* 21:52. Lombard identified the Holy Spirit with infused *caritas*, an idea that Luther clearly approved of. See Peter Lombard, *Quator Libri Sententiarium*, bk. 1, dist. 17, ed. Alexis Bugnolo (Franciscan Archive); available at http://www.franciscan-archive.org/lombardus/index.html. Lombard applied the terms *caritas*, *dilectio*, and *amor* interchangeably to the Holy Spirit (Philipp W. Rosemann, *Peter Lombard*, Great Medieval Thinkers [New York: Oxford University Press, 2004], 85). With Augustine in the background for both men, "Luther observes that the Master of Sentences came close to the truth: *habitus autem adhuc est spiritus sanctus*" (McGrath, *Luther's Theology of the Cross*, 85).

15. What Edwards wishes to reject is the idea of a "natural disposition to act grace" or "an abiding habit of grace for . . . future" acts of grace (Edwards, "Treatise on Grace," in *WJE* 21:196). According to McGrath, Scotus rejected Thomas's ontological causality (*ex natura rei*) with regard to *gratia creata* and justification (McGrath, *Luther's Theology of the Cross*, 83). While for Luther (and Scotus) the idea of sine qua non causality applied to justification, Edwards uses covenant causality in reference to regeneration and sanctification (McGrath, *Luther's Theology of the Cross*, 83–88).

See also Alister E. McGrath, *The Intellectual Origins of the European Reformation*, 2nd ed. (Malden, MA: Blackwell, 2004), 110.

16. Edwards, *WJE* 2:206. The new spiritual sense is defined as "a new foundation laid in the nature of the soul, for a new kind of exercises of the same faculty of understanding."

17. Ibid.

18. Edwards, "Miscellanies," no. 471, in *WJE* 13:512.

19. Edwards, "Treatise on Grace," in *WJE* 21:197.

20. "For the clearest indication of the nature of a thing is taken from its works." See St. Thomas Aquinas, *Commentary on the Gospel of John, Chapters 6–12*, trans. Fabian Larcher and James A. Weisheipl, intro. and notes by Daniel Keating and Matthew Levering (Washington, DC: Catholic University of America Press, 2010), ch. 10, 217. As formalized by the Latin Scholastics, the formula reads *operari sequitur esse* (E. L. Mascall, *Christ, the Christian and the Church: A Study of the Incarnation and Its Consequences* [London: Longmans, Green, 1946], 70). Of course, from the human perspective of an unfolding drama, one could affirm both that *agere sequitur esse* and *esse sequitur agere* are true of personal revelation. "Only the action itself will reveal who each individual is; and it will not reveal, through successive unveilings, primarily who the individual always was, but rather who he is to become through the action, through his encounter with others and through the decisions he makes." See Hans Urs von Balthasar, *Theo-Drama: Theological Dramatic Theory*, vol. 2, *Dramatis Personae: Man in God*, trans. Graham Harrison (San Francisco: Ignatius Press, 1990), 11, as cited in David C. Schindler, *Hans Urs von Balthasar and the Dramatic Structure of Truth: A Philosophical Investigation*, Perspectives in Continental Philosophy Series 34 (New York: Fordham University Press, 2004), 19. To prioritize existentialism over against essentialism for both divine and human seems to do away with Thomas's real distinction between essence and existence.

21. Edwards, "Miscellanies," no. 626, in *WJE* 18:155.

22. "For the actings of the Spirit of God in the heart are more arbitrary and are not tied to such and such means by such laws or rules, as shall particularly and precisely determine in a stated method every particular exercise and the degree of it; but the Holy Spirit is given and infused into the hearts of men only under this general law, viz. that it shall remain there and put forth acts there after the manner of an abiding, natural, vital principle of action, a seed remaining in us" (Edwards, "Miscellanies," no. 629, in *WJE* 18:157).

23. "If we make no difficulty of allowing that God did immediately make the whole universe at first, and caused it to exist out of nothing, and that every individual thing owes its being to an immediate, voluntary, arbitrary act of almighty power, why should we make a difficulty of supposing that he has still something immediately to do with the things that he has made, and that there is an arbitrary influence still that God has in the creation that he has made?" (Edwards, "Treatise on Grace," in *WJE* 21:177).

24. Ibid., 197.

25. This echoes John of Rochelle, who said that "the indwelling Spirit is a *forma transformans* and that it brings about in the soul a *forma transformata*" (*Summa Alexandri, pars tertia*, vol. IV, no. 609, sol., in Mœller and Philips, *Theology of Grace*, 16n3).

26. "So I suppose when we read of the Spirit of God, who we are told is spirit, it is to be understood of the disposition, temper or affection of the divine mind. . . . This is the divine disposition or nature that we are made partakers of (II Pet. 1:4); for our partaking or communion with God consists in the communion or partaking of the Holy Ghost" (Edwards, "Discourse on the Trinity," in *WJE* 21:122). This "godlike disposition" is that by which the regenerate has a "participation of the divine nature" (Edwards, 77. Sermon on Prov. 17:27 [1728], in *WJE* 43).

27. "There is no gift or benefit that is so much in God, that is so much of himself, of his nature, that is so much a communication of the Deity, as grace is; 'tis as much a communication of the Deity, as light [is] a communication of the sun" (Edwards, "Miscellanies," no. 537, in *WJE* 18:83).

28. Edwards, 133. Sermon on 1 Pet. 3:4, in *WJE* 44. Elsewhere in the sermon, Edwards asserts that "to have Christ's Spirit and to have the Christian spirit are the same thing."

29. Ibid.

30. Michael J. Scanlon, "The Ecclesial Dimension of Anthropology," in *The Gift of the Church: A Textbook on Ecclesiology in Honor of Patrick Granfield, O.S.B.,* ed. Peter C. Phan (Collegeville, MN: Liturgical Press, 2000), 207. The whole idea of created grace confuses the whole issue and may not be attributed to Aquinas himself. See Eberhard Jüngel, *Justification: The Heart of the Christian Faith,* trans. Jeffrey F. Cayzer, intro. John Webster [London: T&T Clark, 2006], 192–94). Although the notion of grace as created may be deduced from Aquinas, it was meant to point to the regenerate as a new creation ex nihilo and therefore not strictly created (Jüngel, *Justification*, 193n110). The idea of created grace as an intermediary and a thing, in germinal form, can be observed in St. Albert the Great's *Summa*, in which *gratia creata* was conceptualized as a static entity needed to bridge the infinite divine–human divide in regeneration. St. Thomas avoided this danger in his teacher's writings by denying that created grace is an object and that it is a dynamic, continuous disposition to action that follows uncreated grace (Mœller and Phillips, *The Theology of Grace*, 18–20).

31. Scanlon, "Ecclesial Dimension of Anthropology," 207. Created grace functions not only as the property of the soul that assimilates it to divine Goodness, but also grants to the finite nature a supernatural potency enabling it to receive uncreated grace—the Holy Spirit, who is inseparable and foundational to this created habit. See H. Daniel Monsour, "The Relation between Uncreated and Created Grace in the Halesian *Summa*: A Lonergan Reading" (Ph.D. diss., University of St. Michael's College, Toronto, 2000), 103–4, available at Theses Canada Portal, Library and Archives Canada, http://www.nlc-bnc.ca/obj/s4/f2/dsk2/ftp02/NQ54051.pdf. This, of course, makes uncreated grace the outcome of created grace, which seems to contradict the scriptural and patristic traditions. See Patrick Burke, *Reinterpreting Rahner: A Critical Study of His Major Themes* (New York: Fordham University Press, 2002), 48–49.

32. Edwards, "Miscellanies," no. 507, in *WJE* 18:53.

33. Just as St. Thomas regarded the theological virtues of faith, love, and hope to be inseparably linked (Aquinas, *STh* I-II, 65, 5 resp.), Edwards sees the saving virtues or gracious affections as "concatenated together." Though grace is a said to be a quality, Aquinas did not identify it with virtue; rather, the "disposition" or habitual grace is the "principle and root" of all infused virtue (Aquinas, *STh* I-II, a. 3, ad 3, 1134). In spiritual regeneration, a "new nature" is communicated to the saint, in which a unity of graces is manifest. While the Christian graces are "concatenated together," their one "common nature" ensures that the Christian life is "manifoldly diversified" (Edwards, "Charity," sermon 12, in *WJE* 8:332).

34. Drawing a clear line between common and saving grace, Edwards argues that "the notion of acquired habits is wrong," yet he does not deny the notions of natural affections, dispositions, and "kind instincts," which "have the appearance of benevolence, and so in some aspects resemble virtue" (Edwards, "Miscellanies," no. l, in *WJE* 13:169). Edwards wants to stress that true virtue cannot be acquired, but is infused ("Miscellanies," no. 73, in *WJE* 13:242). While affections could be natural or gracious, he does not use the term "natural virtues" for natural affections (Edwards, "Nature of True Virtue," in *WJE* 8:600–601). Natural affections are frequently confused with true virtue because they have "like effects" (Edwards, "Nature of True Virtue," in *WJE* 8:616). Aquinas ascribed the production of infused virtues to divine, efficient causality, thus distinguishing them from acquired virtues (Aquinas, *STh* I-II, q. 55, a. 4, 821–22). "Virtue," defined generally, "is a good quality of the mind, by which we live righteously, of which no one can make bad use." Infused virtue is qualified by the following clause: that "which God works in us without us." For Aquinas, God can infuse gracious habits and virtues that are beyond nature, as well as those that are natural, in order to demonstrate divine power (Aquinas, *STh* I-II, q. 51, a. 4, 806).

35. Edwards admits that natural affections and conscience have in them "a true negative moral goodness" insofar as they restrain sin and reduce moral evil and even "puts men upon seeking true virtue" (Edwards, "Nature of True Virtue," in *WJE* 8:613, 616). Yet, postlapsarian humanity, now bereft of the spiritual disposition and possessing merely the natural, inferior

principle of self-love, has none but "the source of all the wickedness that is in this world" (ibid., 616).

36. In as far as habitual grace is regarded as an innate principle, Edwards agrees with Aquinas, so uses the language of "infusion" (William J. Danaher, *The Trinitarian Ethics of Jonathan Edwards* [Louisville, KY: Westminster John Knox, 2004], 143); see also Paul Ramsey, Appendix 4, "Infused Virtues in Edwardsean and Calvinistic Context" in Edwards, *WJE* 8:739–51.

37. According to Hunsinger, Edwards affirms a sort of congruent merit in his theology of justification (George Hunsinger, "Dispositional Soteriology: Jonathan Edwards on Justification by Faith Alone," *Westminster Theological Journal* 66 [2004]: 108–9). Since *caritas* is the basis of merit, there must be in the believer a created habit of love that issues in true acts of charity, in order that both principle and operations belong to the human actor properly and not merely instrumentally (Irving Singer, *The Nature of Love*, vol. 1, *Plato to Luther*, 2nd ed. [Chicago: University of Chicago Press, 2009], 321–22). Edwards's rejection of *gratia creata* and his identification of the Spirit with uncreated grace would pose an issue for the Roman emphasis on free will and merit. "A person merits through free acts, and can be said to merit by habit, when regarded as a motive power" (Aquinas, *STh* II-I, q. 55, a. 1).

38. "But special grace causes the faculties to do that that they do not by nature; causes those things to be in the soul that are above nature, and of which there is nothing of the like kind in the soul by nature" (Edwards, "Miscellanies," no. 626, in *WJE* 18:155).

39. Stephen D. Benin traces the development of this idea in the Judeo-Christian tradition in his *Footprints of God: Divine Accommodation in Jewish and Christian Thought* (Albany: State University of New York Press, 1993). Aquinas happily took on the notion of divine accommodation through his readings of Maimonides, as Benin notes in "The 'Cunning of God' and Divine Accommodation," *Journal of the History of Ideas* 45, no. 2 (April–June 1984): 190.

40. Helm refers to Calvin's main conceptuality of divine accommodation as a "non-indexed sense of accommodation"—viz., the manner in which anthropomorphic and anthropopathic references to God are to be interpreted nonliterally in light of divine immutability. Calvin also construed divine accommodation as human adjustment in response to divine revelation. See Paul Helm, "Maimonides and Calvin on Divine Accommodation," in *Referring to God: Jewish and Christian Philosophical and Theological Perspectives*, ed. Paul Helm (New York: St. Martin's, 2000), 158–59.

41. Edwards, 307. Sermon on Eccles. 9:10 (b) (Dec 1733), in *WJE* 48.

42. This is a self-limitation as far as God "accommodates himself to our way of understanding in his manner of expressing and representing things, as we are wont to do when we are teaching little children" (Edwards, "Miscellanies," no. 583, in *WJE* 18:119). This echoes Calvin's notion of epistemological accommodation, viz., God adjusting to our level, speaking to us using human forms, as a nurse lisping to a child (Calvin, *Institutes* 1.13.1). See also Alister E. McGrath, *A Life of John Calvin: A Study in the Shaping of Western Culture* (Malden, MA: Blackwell, 1990), 130–32.

43. Matthew Henry, whose writings Edwards was no doubt familiar with, links divine *synkatabasis* to Christ's *kenosis*: "Herein Christ accommodated himself to his estate of humiliation, that, as he condescended to be an infant, a child, a youth, so the image of God shone brighter in him, when he grew up to be a youth, than it did, or could, while he was an *infant* and a *child*" (Henry, "An Exposition, with Practical Observations, of the Gospel according to St. Luke," ch. 2, in *Commentary on the Whole Bible*, vol. 5, *Matthew to John* [Grand Rapids, MI: Christian Classics Ethereal Library, (1721)], http://www.ccel.org/ccel/henry/mhc5.html). See Ford L. Battles's classic article on this: "God Was Accommodating Himself to Human Capacity," *Interpretation* 31 (1977): 19–28. With Calvin's manifold use of the divine accommodation (some of which imply grudging permission or compromise on God's part), Balserak opines that the incarnation cannot be thought of as the archetypal instance, though it could be understood as "the most magnificent act found amongst God's repertoire of accommodating deeds." See Jon Balserak, "'The Accommodating Act

Par Excellence?': An Inquiry into the Incarnation and Calvin's Understanding of Accommodation," *Scottish Journal of Theology* 55, no. 4 (2002): 408–23.

44. "God, in the manner of existence, came down from his infinite perfection, and accommodated himself to our nature and manner by being made man, as he was in the person of Jesus Christ. . . . So in like manner, . . . he comes down from his infinite perfection . . . in the manner of manifestation, and accommodates himself to our nature and manner, in the manner of expression" (Edwards, "Miscellanies," no. 763, in *WJE* 18:410).

45. As the "messenger" of the other two, the "Father and the Son principally stand in the place of lords, and the Holy Ghost is servant to them both, and commanding chiefly belongs to them" (Edwards, "On the Equality," in *WJE* 21:147).

46. "We ought to be filled with gratitude to the Spirit of God for his wonderful condescension and beneficence in coming to take up his abode in such and so honoring of us as to make us his temple and filling of us with such unspeakable riches, such glorious light and precious grace and sweet counsel. And we should glorify him abundantly upon the account of those more perfect degrees which we expect from him in another world when his light will be full and like the noon day sun" (Edwards, "The Threefold Work of the Holy Ghost," in *WJE* 14:436).

47. For now, the Spirit's operation is "accommodated to the imperfect circumstances of the present state"; it is only in glory that the indwelling Spirit or "the divine nature in them shall be in its greatest exaltation and purity" (Edwards, "Treatise on Grace," in *WJE* 21:170). Commenting on personal uniqueness, Edwards notes that "the special gifts of grace in the elect, when they are accommodated to the gifts of nature, everyone in this respect has his own proper gift, the gift that is suitable to his nature, and station, and circumstances in the world, or the station, use, office, and business God intends him for" (Edwards, "Blank Bible," note on Song of Sol. 8:8–9, in *WJE* 24:627).

48. Goodwin cites Basil, *De Spiritu Sancto*, cap. 26. The new principle is "always indeed present, but not perpetually operating" (Goodwin, *WTG* 6:194).

49. As we have noted in chapter 5, the incarnation—as divine accommodation—is not properly a functional *kenosis*, but it is a *krypsis*—namely, an intentional *incognito* that veils God's glory (Oliver D. Crisp, *Divinity and Humanity: The Incarnation Reconsidered*, ed. Iain Torrance [Cambridge: Cambridge University Press, 2007], 152). Similarly, the Holy Spirit is hidden in divine condescending action.

50. "The condescension of God is not properly humility. . . . And yet God, by his infinite condescension, shews his nature to be infinitely far from and hostile to pride, and therefore his condescension is sometimes spoken of as humility; and humility on our part is the most proper conformity to God's condescension that there can be in a creature" (Jonathan Edwards, "Charity, or Love, the Sum of all Virtue," in *Charity and Its Fruits: Christian Love as Manifested in the Heart and Life*, ed. Tyron Edwards [London: Banner of Truth Trust, 1969], 150).

51. "So the man Christ Jesus, who is the most excellent and glorious of all creatures, is yet meek and lowly of heart, and excels all other beings in humility" (ibid., 130–31).

52. "For there is no disposition of the creature more adapted to the condescension of the Creator than humility" (Edwards, "Charity and Its Fruits," sermon 3, in *WJE* 8:247). Because the gospel reveals the Father as "an infinitely condescending God," the proper and corresponding exercises of the new disposition in the believer issue in "humble acts of love." "The gospel teaches how God," Edwards continues, "who humbles himself to behold things in heaven, stooped so low as to take an infinitely gracious notice of poor vile worms of the dust, and to concern himself for their salvation, so as to send his only begotten Son to die for them that they might be honored and brought into eternal fellowship with him and the perfect enjoyment of him" (ibid.).

53. God the Father manifests "wonderful condescension . . . in making us his children and treating us as such in our privileges in his Church," despite human unworthiness (Edwards, 845. Sermon on Isa. 1:2 [Nov 1746], in *WJE* 64).

54. Why does Goodwin distinguish the new, vital principle of the regenerate from the Holy Spirit? "Because all his actions do not proceed from the Holy Ghost only, simply," he answers, "but

from the image of God which the Holy Spirit works in him, and acts and operates in him" (Goodwin, *WTG* 2:208). Here, we note that an incipient concept of an "intermediary principle" was already in Lombard in his distinction between charity, identified with the Spirit, and the other mediating theological virtues of hope and faith (Rosemann, *Peter Lombard*, 88–89). Goodwin, citing Aquinas favorably, did not hesitate to speak of the new principle as "a new form" and of grace as elevating. "Aquinas saith well, *elevat hominem*, saith he: when a man hath grace to aim at God, it raiseth a man up above all the being and power of nature. . . . [I]t is called, therefore, a 'divine nature'" (Goodwin, *WTG* 1:381).

55. Yarnold, *Second Gift*, 55–56.

56. For Palamas, like Athanasius, humanity in its natural, prelapsarian state possessed the faculties and powers of communion with God. Hence, Palamas takes the biblical terms "new heart," "new spirit," and "new creature" as synonymous with created grace. They are not supernatural principles added to nature upon regeneration, but gifts "recreated and renewed by the coming in the flesh of him who first created it" (Palamas, *Letter to Athanasius*, Coisl. 98, fol. 12–12v, as quoted in Meyendorff, *Study of Gregory Palamas*, 164). This should not be taken in a Pelagian sense in which human beings per se are capable of attaining God, but in the Athanasian sense: the original *logoi* in human beings are fulfilled by the Logos incarnate. In Meyendorff's summary statement of this insight in Maximian terms, "communion with the Logos is precisely the *natural state* (*lógos physikós*) of true humanity" (John Meyendorff, *Christ in Eastern Christian Thought* [Washington, DC: Corpus, 1969], 164).

57. As creation is God giving natural being or existence to humanity, so re-creation is God giving spiritual being to the saints. "And natural men are represented in Scripture as having no spiritual light, no spiritual life, and no spiritual being" (Edwards, *WJE* 2:204). In the first creation, the human soul was communicated to humanity "in a higher, more direct and immediate manner" as a kind of divine communication: "God did therein as it were communicate something of himself, something of his own Spirit of life and divine vital fullness" (Edwards, "Miscellanies," no. 1003, in *WJE* 20:328).

58. The impartation of the Spirit to the regenerate is akin to "a sort of adding a new soul to" or the "making a new soul of" human reason and conscience destroyed in the Fall (Edwards, "Miscellanies," no. 210, in *WJE* 13:342). This concept of a "second gift" beyond the first, created nature has been expressed in a variety of ways by the Fathers: *logos*, immortality, *pneuma, charis* (Yarnold, *Second Gift*, 16–24).

59. Edwards, 132. Sermon on 1 Pet. 2:2-3, in *WJE* 44.

60. Edwards, "Images of Divine Things," no. 190, in *WJE* 11:122–23.

61. Edwards, "Images of Divine Things," no. 171, in *WJE* 11:115.

62. Edwards, "Miscellanies," no. 403, in *WJE* 13:468.

63. Ibid. Hence, "the Spirit of God was given to the apostles in a large measure, and to Christ, the Author of the salvation, without measure" (Edwards, "Faith," in *WJE* 21:467).

64. "God gave Jesus Christ the Spirit without measure, but he gives the saints his Spirit by measure and in different proportion" (Edwards, "Profitable Hearers of the Word," in *WJE* 14:267)

65. Goodwin describes grace as a "new spiritual visive power," which is (in Thomistic terms) a "quality, and a super-additional accident introduced into the understanding" (Goodwin, *WTG* 6:192). "In a word, all the goodness that is in God, is essential unto him; our goodness, whatsoever we be, is but accidental unto us." Commenting on the classic deification proof text, Twisse reads the injunction as primarily ethical, whereby "it tends only to . . . set before us certain actions of God, as patterns and precedents to imitate him therein." See William Twisse, *A discovery of D. Jacksons vanitie . . .* (Amsterdam, 1631), 473. For Thomas Aquinas, grace is per se in God, but exists as a quality or *per accidens* in the human subject. "Now what is substantially in God, becomes accidental in the soul participating the Divine goodness imperfectly, as is clear in the case of knowledge" (Aquinas, *STh* I-II, q. 110, a. 2, 1133).

66. In comparison with ordinary, saving grace, "Extraordinary [common] gifts are nothing properly inherent in the man. They are something adventitious" (Edwards, "Charity and Its Fruits," sermon 2, in *WJE* 8:158).

67. Edwards, "Treatise on Grace," in *WJE* 21:197. "By his producing this effect the Spirit becomes an indwelling vital principle in the soul, and the subject becomes a spiritual being, denominated so from the Spirit of God which dwells in him and of whose nature he is a partaker [2 Pet. 1:4]" (Edwards, "Charity and Its Fruits," sermon 2, in *WJE* 8:158).

68. While Edwards undoubtedly emphasizes the Spirit's utter freedom or "arbitrary" operations, he is not afraid to use what A. N. Williams has termed "theotic" language as well: the Christian *possesses* grace. "It is an everlasting ornament and an everlasting spring of joy; 'tis a treasure in the heart of infinite worth to the person that possesses it" (Edwards, 133. Sermon on 1 Pet. 3:4, in *WJE* 44).

69. "Divine love is in him [the Father]," Edwards comments, "not as a subject which receives from another, but as its original seat, where it is of itself." The Son not only receives the Spirit's nature from the Father "without measure" and "infinitely," but is also the eternal recipient of the Spirit's essence, thus making the Son the mediating source of divine love: "The fountain does not only send forth large streams towards this object as it does to every other, but the very fountain itself wholly and altogether does go out toward him" (Edwards, "Charity and Its Fruits," sermon 15, in *WJE* 8:373). Elsewhere, Edwards preaches: "Christ as God is the Triune fountain and origin of holiness" (Edwards, 163. Sermon on John 1:14 [June 1752], in *WJE* 45).

70. The Holy Spirit is both divine grace itself as well as its source: "The Holy Ghost is given to us, and that is in the very nature of it divine love. 'Tis the infinite fountain" (Edwards, "Blank Bible," note on Rom. 5:5, in *WJE* 24:997).

71. "And God's love to us is only that fountain's flowing out to us, and our love to God is only something communicated from that fountain to our hearts" (ibid.). Edwards's language for the Spirit as an efflux from God is similar to pre-Nicene apologists such as Athenegoras. Athenagoras, according to Kelly, "even defined the Spirit as 'an effluence (ἀπόρροιαν) of God, flowing from and returning to Him like a beam of the sun'" (Athenagoras, *Supplic.* 10, 3, as quoted in J. N. D. Kelly, *Early Christian Doctrines* [New York: Harper & Brothers, 1958], 102).

72. Edwards, "Blank Bible," note on Rom. 5:5, in *WJE* 24:997.

73. Edwards, "Charity and Its Fruits," sermon 15, in *WJE* 8:373.

74. Edwards, "Christ the Spiritual Sun," in *WJE* 22:53. In an early Miscellany, which Edwards subsequently uses to pen his "Personal Narrative," he likens the soul to "a delightful field or garden." He goes on to say that "the sun is Jesus Christ; the blessed beams and calm breeze, the Holy Spirit; the sweet and delightful flowers, and the pleasant shrill music of the little birds, are the Christian graces" ("Miscellanies," no. a, in *WJE* 13:164).

75. Edwards, "Christ the Spiritual Sun," in *WJE* 22:54–55.

76. Ibid., 55–57. "Now things are seen as they be, in their proper forms and colors, in their true situations and relations." However, for unbelievers, these very same "influences of the Spirit of Christ" will be "as fire in their souls" at death and appear as a "dreadful majesty" in the Parousia of "an infinitely holy, just judge." At the last judgment, "every ray of that glory that Christ shall then appear in will be like a stream of scorching fire, and will pierce their hearts with a keener torment than a stream of fierce lighting" (ibid., 55–61).

77. "This power is a gracious, almighty influencer, whereby Christ guides and governs the inclinations and actions of the heart" (Edwards, "The Threefold Work," in *WJE* 14:422).

78. Edwards, "Blank Bible," note on Prov. 15:21, in *WJE* 24:559. In contrary fashion, "sin [as] the principle that has the dominion over men is absolute Lord in his heart and governs all his powers and faculties" (Edwards, 237. Sermon on Luke 6:35, in *WJE* 47).

79. Edwards, 72. Sermon on 2 Cor. 3: 18 (a) (1728), in *WJE* 43.

80. Reformed dogmatics prior to Edwards distinguished the internal, perfect, essential *gloria Dei* from the external, manifested, accidental *glorificatio*. These two distinctions were further categorized "either objectively or formally" (Muller, *PRRD* 3:547–48). For more of this, see

appendix 6 below, "God's Intrinsic and Declarative Glory in the Reformed-Puritan Tradition."

81. The incommunicable *gloria Dei* is objectively the natural excellence of God's own essence, formally and subjectively known and loved by Godself (Muller, *PRRD* 3:547–48).

82. In chapter 2, we looked at the invisible mission of the Son and Spirit as God's communication of divine grace to the elect creatures.

83. God's economy consists, in part, of "whether there should be any creation, and so whether any such thing as God's declarative glory," and, as such, does not arise "from the necessity of God's nature, not from any natural subordination, but 'tis the fruit of the will and pleasure of the persons of the Trinity" (Edwards, "Of God the Father," in *WJE* 25:147).

84. Edwards, 905. Sermon on Ezek. 28:22-26 (Aug 1748), in *WJE* 66.

85. Hence, "the happiness of the saints, will be very transcendent, as transcendent as the glory of God, seeing it is the same" (Edwards, "Miscellanies," no. 106, in *WJE* 13:276).

86. So, "glorifying of God . . . is nothing but rejoicing in the manifestation of him" (ibid.). Edwards refers to Miscellany no. 3 (*WJE* 13:199–200) as a summary of this idea. The position that Edwards outlines in the *End for Which God Created the World*, where the external glory of God in creatures manifests God's intrinsic glory, is quite consonant with the theological vision found in modern Eastern Catholic theology. For example, Bilaniuk speaks of divinization as glorification: "The intrinsic glory of God is His holiness, goodness, beauty and all the other attributes. The extrinsic glory of God is the true goal of creation, for it is a reflection and manifestation through creatures of the intrinsic and substantial glory that is God Himself. Therefore God necessarily ordered all things to His extrinsic glory. Consequently the intrinsic perfection of any creature is in reality the extrinsic glory of God." See Petro B. T. Bilaniuk, *Theology and Economy of the Holy Spirit: An Eastern Approach*, Placid Lecture Series 2 (Bangalore: Published for Centre for Indian and Inter-Religious Studies, Rome, by Dharmaram Publications, 1980), 192.

87. Of the saints in heaven, Edwards states, "Wherefore it may with equal evidence be argued that man's happiness, i.e. the happiness of the saints, will be very transcendent, as transcendent as the glory of God, seeing it is the same. . . . Again, that the saints will be full of happiness, will have as much happiness as they can contain (that is, they will have happiness completely adequate to their capacity), is evident, because happiness is nothing, as we have showed, but the perception and the possession of excellency" (Edwards, "Miscellanies," no. 106, in *WJE* 13:276–77).

88. Edwards, in a long biblical exegesis of the term "glory," describes it as a kind of weight, as opposed to lightness (Edwards, "Concerning the End," in *WJE* 8:513–14). He likens grace in the saint to "a kind of natural tendency and inclination in the heart: the weight of the soul, the verticity" (Edwards, 92. Sermon on 1 John 4:19, in *WJE* 43). It is a reestablishment of the original supernatural principle of love in human beings by which divine love, and no longer self-love, governs.

89. As no divine attribute should be unexercised for a "proper apprehension" of God, Edwards argues that God's glory must include "both the dreadfulness of his anger and the exceeding favor of his grace" (Edwards, 155. Sermon on Rom. 9:22 [a], in *WJE* 45). Corresponding to this, God's declarative glory will appear in the saints "actively and willingly, but in the wicked only eventually and against their wills" (Edwards, 905. Sermon on Ezek. 28:22-26 [Aug 1748], in *WJE* 66).

90. Although there must be a "compleat" communication of this declarative glory, which is not "equal in degree to his essential glory," nonetheless God is wholly revealed insofar as every divine perfection *ad intra* is "proportionably effulgent" *ad extra* (Edwards, 155. Sermon on Rom. 9:22 [a], in *WJE* 45). See also Edwards, "Miscellanies," no. 348, in *WJE* 13:419.

91. Emphasis mine. Edwards, "Treatise on Grace," in *WJE* 21:176. Edwards reiterates this in "Images of Divine Things," no. 190, in *WJE* 11:123: "And this principle, from its first existence, never ceases to exert itself, until the new creature be complete and comes to its proper perfection."

92. Aquinas, *STh* I, q. 43, a. 1. With respect to the destination of the sent, "The divine person is fittingly sent in the sense that He exists newly in any one" (Aquinas, *STh* I, q. 43, a. 3). See also Emery, *Trinity in Aquinas*, 161.

93. "'Tis God's own beauty and excellency that is uncreated and eternal, which is not properly made, but communicated" (Edwards, 72. Sermon on 2 Cor. 3:18 [a] [Jul 1727], in *WJE* 43). Aquinas links friendship with sanctifying grace: "Accordingly, since there is a communication between man and God, inasmuch as He communicates His happiness to us, some kind of friendship must needs be based on this same communication. . . . The love which is based on this communication, is charity: wherefore it is evident that charity is the friendship of man for God" (Aquinas, *STh* II-II, q. 23, a. 1). Divine love, as Owen outlined, includes love of union and enjoyment, assimilation, complacence, and benevolence, as well as friendship. See John Owen, *Christologia: Or, a Declaration of The Glorious Mystery of the Person of Christ, God and Man, to which are Subjoined, Meditations and Discourses on the Glory of Christ*, vol. 1 of *The Works of John Owen, D.D.*, ed. William H. Goold (New York: Robert Carter & Brothers, 1851), 203–8.

94. A question first posed by Yves Congar to Gregory Palamas. See "A Note on the Theology of Gregory Palamas," in Yves Congar, *I Believe in the Holy Spirit*, trans. David Smith (New York: Crossroad, 1983), 3:63. Palamas notes that "grace is therefore uncreated and it is what the Son gives, sends and grants to his disciples; it is not the Spirit himself, but a deifying gift which is an energy that is not only uncreated, but also inseparable from the Holy Spirit." See St. Gregory Palamas, *Dialogue between an Orthodox and a Barlaamite*, trans. Rein Ferwerda, intro. Sara J. Denning-Bolle (Binghamton, NY: Global Publications / CEMERS, 1999), ch. 8, 51.

95. Edwards, *WJE* 2:202.

96. Ibid. In the Christian, the Spirit will "communicate itself in its nature in the soul" (Edwards, "Miscellanies," no. 471, in *WJE* 13:513). However, not all acts of the Spirit are self-communicative: "The Spirit of God may act and not, in acting, communicate itself" (ibid., 514). The intrinsic agency of the Spirit "not only *assists* them in doing better what they ordinarily do, it also *restores* them to the original purposes for which they were created" (Morimoto, *Catholic Vision*, 30).

97. Edwards, *WJE* 2:205. The Spirit acts upon the mind of the unregenerate only to "produce effects in it" (Edwards, "Miscellanies," no. 471, in *WJE* 13:513).

98. Edwards, *WJE* 2:205. The "praeternatural" are enhanced natural powers, not new gifts, and do not raise the creature beyond the order of the natural (Yarnold, *Second Gift*, 29–30).

99. Edwards, "Charity and Its Fruits," sermon 2, in *WJE* 8:158. "So the Spirit of God moved on the face of the waters, but not so as to impart himself to the waters."

100. Ibid.

101. "Grace signifies a free gift. Now the holiness of the divine nature is not a gift. 'Tis only communicated holiness that is a gift" (Edwards, 163. Sermon on John 1:14 [June 1752], in *WJE* 45). There is no direct communication of holiness to the saints, which would amount to an essential communication, but only through the Trinitarian *oikonomia* and the incarnation. "But holiness as it is in Christ considered only as God is not called grace. Holiness is called grace only as derived from God and communicated by him through his Spirit" (ibid.)

102. Believers should extend hospitality to the Spirit not only as "the most precious and desirable of all gifts," descending from the Father and the Son, but as "the most glorious guest." As the indwelling and transforming Spirit of Christ, Edwards exhorts his listeners "to entertain him as a welcome guest" (Edwards, 72. Sermon on 2 Cor. 3:18 [a] [1727], in *WJE* 43). So, while Edwards was well aware that "the word person be rarely used in the Scriptures," he affirmed "that we have no word in the English language that does so naturally represent what the Scripture reveals of the distinction of the Eternal Three,—Father, Son, and Holy Ghost,—as to say they are One God but three persons" (Edwards, "Treatise on Grace," in *WJE* 21:57). If personalist conceptions of the Trinity, as defined by O'Carroll, may be understood within philosophical (as incommunicability and independence of being), social (as relational effects on other beings), and psychological

(identity circumscribed within a psychosomatic unity) categories, Edwards has certainly left to posterity a profoundly holistic view of the personalness of God. See Michael O'Carroll, s.v. "personality," in *Trinitas: A Theological Encyclopedia of the Holy Trinity* (Wilmington, DE: Michael Glazier, 1987), 181.

103. The Spirit is no mere divine act but also an Actor who "doth something in the soul" (Edwards, "Miscellanies," no. p, in *WJE* 13:171). In this, Edwards echoes Goodwin, who emphasized the unhindered operation of the Holy Spirit, who is "*agens liber*"—a free agent. "The Holy Ghost is not as a natural agent that works *ad ultimum virium* . . . as fire that burneth as much as it can burn" (Goodwin, *WTG* 1:386). For Goodwin, the Spirit does not dwell in the human nature of Christ "by his graces and operations only," but also personally; so it is with the Spirit's indwelling in the saints (Goodwin, *WTG* 2:400).

104. "You ought to entertain him for Christ's sake, whose [S]pirit he is and in whose name he comes, and you should entertain him upon his own account" (Edwards, 72. Sermon on 2 Cor. 3:18 [a] [1727], in *WJE* 43.).

105. Saving grace in the regenerate acts "*both* after the manner of a natural principle or seed" and "*also* as a voluntary agent manifesting care of that heart that it is in" (emphasis mine). In one sense, the "continuance of its actings" resembles nature in its stability, and yet it also points to God's covenant faithfulness (Edwards, "Miscellanies," no. 818, in *WJE* 18:528–29).

106. Especially in times of extraordinary trial, the perseverance of grace manifests its supernatural character "more than a natural necessary principle," viz., the Spirit acting as a voluntary agent. The supernatural character is evident in its origin as divine, efficient causality that is "immediate and arbitrary." Its effects are supernatural as it transcends both human operation and every law of nature (Edwards, "Miscellanies," no. 818, in *WJE* 18:529).

107. "Grace consists very much in a principle that causes vigorousness and activity in action" (Edwards, "Miscellanies," no. p, in *WJE* 13:171).

108. Edwards, "Miscellanies," no. 471, in *WJE* 13:513–14.

109. Edwards, "Miscellanies," no. 818, in *WJE* 18:528–29. This is an echo of St. Basil, who variously described the Holy Spirit, the Spirit's operation, and grace as the form, power, and habit in the soul. "*Form* is said to be *in Matter*; *Power* to be *in* what is capable of it; *Habit* to be *in* him who is affected by it. . . . Therefore, as much as the Holy Spirit perfects rational beings, completing their excellence, He is analogous to Form. . . . And as the power of seeing in the healthy eye, so is the operation of the Spirit in the purified soul. . . . And as the art in him who has acquired it, so is the grace of the Spirit in the recipient ever present, though not continuously in operation" (italics original). See St. Basil the Great, *The Treatise De Spiritu Sancto*, ch. 26, trans. Blomfield Jackson, *NPNF* 8:38. Here the language corresponds to Aristotle's distinction between potentiality and operation (David Bradshaw, *Aristotle East and West: Metaphysics and the Division of Christendom* [Cambridge: Cambridge University Press, 2004], 172–73).

110. On this, see appendix 7 below, "Divine *Energeia* in the Eastern and Western Traditions."

111. Nicolas of Methone, for example, refers to the person of the Holy Spirit as "a natural, essential and enhypostatized energy." See A. Dimitrakopoulos, *Ekklisiastiki Vivliothiki* (Leipzig, 1866), 213, as quoted in Gabriel Patacsi, "Palamism before Palamas," *Eastern Churches Review* 9 (1977): 66.

112. As the "first supreme and universal principle of things," God is "a principle of action" (Edwards, "Miscellanies," no. 383, in *WJE* 13:451–52).

113. The principle of grace in the regenerate soul or "Spirit Life" cannot lie dormant, but is outwardly active, since the "divine nature that is pure act [is] not an unfruitful thing." See Jonathan Edwards, 723. Sermon on Deut. 5:27-29 (Nov 1743), in *WJE* 61. Since, grace, by definition, is a "principle of holy action," it must tend toward practice as a root brings forth a plant. "Principles and acts are correlates which necessarily have respect one to another. . . . So it is absurd

to talk of a principle that it does not tend to practice" (Edwards, "Charity and Its Fruits," sermon 10, in *WJE* 8:298).

114. The Spirit exerts the holy nature "as an internal vital principle" of grace in the heart, which is "all life, all power, all act" (Edwards, *WJE* 2:392–93). It holds together inward experience and outward practice: "To speak of Christian experience and practice, as if they were two things, properly and entirely distinct, is to make a distinction without consideration or reason" (ibid., 450–51).

115. Ibid., 169.

116. Note the essence-person-energy distinction in their grammar of unions: "Our union with God is neither substantial (the unity of the divine Persons) nor hypostatic (the unity of Christ's natures), but energetic" (Vladimir Lossky, *The Mystical Theology of the Eastern Church* [Crestwood, NY: St. Vladimir's Seminary Press, 1997], 87).

117. Edwards, "On the Equality," in *WJE* 21:147; "Efficacious Grace," in *WJE* 21:301. The Spirit, as we have seen, "wholly influences both the Father and the Son in all that they do" (Edwards, "On the Equality," in *WJE* 21:147). "Man was made at first with a principle of love to God as his governing principle" (Edwards, 92. Sermon on 1 John 4:19, in *WJE* 43). This superior principle ruled over self-love, but self-love became the "sole governing principle" after the Fall (Edwards, "Miscellanies," no. 534, in *WJE* 18:78).

118. "The Holy Spirit is . . . pure act . . . because that which acts perfectly is all act, and nothing but act. There is an image of this in created beings that approach to perfect action: how frequently do we say that the saints of heaven are all transformed into love, dissolved into joy, become activity itself, changed into mere ecstasy" (Edwards, "Miscellanies," no. 94, in *WJE* 13:260–61).

119. Yves Congar suggests that the East and West have different emphases on grace. The one looks to the order of being (ontology) and formal or exemplary cause; the other to the order of doing (ethics) and efficient cause. See Michael A. Fahey, "Trinitarian Theology in Thomas Aquinas: One Latin Medieval Pursuit of Word and Silence," in *Trinitarian Theology East and West: Saint Thomas Aquinas–Saint Gregory Palamas*, ed. Michael A. Fahey and John Meyendorff, Patriarch Athenagoras Memorial Lectures (Brookline, MA: Holy Cross Orthodox, 1977), 5–23.

120. "If God is not the disposing author of virtue, then he is not the giver of it. The very notion of a giver implies a disposing cause of possession of the benefit" (Edwards, "Efficacious Grace, Book III," in *WJE* 21:242–43).

121. Ibid., 246–47. Mere willing does not necessarily imply efficient causation, since it may just be permissive: "A being may be determiner and disposer of . . . the futurity of the event, yet there is no positive efficiency or power of the cause that reaches and produces the effect, but only a withdrawing or withholding of efficiency or power."

122. Edwards, "Miscellanies," no. 1218, in *WJE* 23:153.

123. Hence, "as we in Ephesians are said to believe according to the efficacious working of God, the word energeia is also used here in Colossians," where "God is said to be the author" (Edwards, "'Controversies': Efficacious Grace," in *WJE* 21:304). According to John of Damascus, energy is an activity and not a capacity (which is the nature). In created essences, it is life itself, "the primal energy of the living creature," and "the perfect realization of power" (John of Damascus, *Exposition of the Orthodox Faith*, trans. S. D. F. Salmond [*NPNF* 9], bk. 3, ch.15, 61).

124. For example, van Mastricht distinguished between "the Spirit giving" and "spirit given" to contrast the operation from the effect of regeneration (Peter van Mastricht, *Treatise on Regeneration*, ed. Brandon Withrow [Morgan, PA: Soli Deo Gloria, 2002; first published as part of *Theoretico-Practica Theologia*, 1699, retypeset from 1769 ed.], 19–20).

125. Edwards, 52. Sermon on Luke 2:14 (b) (1727), in *WJE* 42.

126. Hence, the *gloria Dei ad extra* is "the exercise of God's perfections to produce a proper effect, in opposition to their lying dormant and ineffectual" (Edwards, "Concerning the End," in *WJE* 8:527).

127. For Aquinas, then, grace as an infused *habitus* is not an efficient cause but a kind of formal cause. "Grace, as a quality," Thomas avers, "is said to act upon the soul after the manner of a formal cause, as whiteness makes a thing white, and justice, just" (Aquinas, *STh* I-II, q. 110, a. 2, ad 1, 1133).

128. Rahner reiterated the primacy of uncreated grace within the terms of scholastic theology with the notion of quasi-formal causality. See Karl Rahner, "Some Implications of the Scholastic Concept of Uncreated Grace," in *Theological Investigations*, vol. 1, *God, Christ, Mary and Grace*, trans. and intro. Cornelius Ernst, 2nd ed. (London: Darton, Longman & Todd, 1965), 319–46. He based it on Thomas's notion of the "light of glory" (*lumen gloriae*) that renders the saint fit for the *visio beatifica*. God's presence (uncreated grace) in the *visio* through the *lumen gloriae* (created grace) is analogous to the relation of form to matter (Haight, *Experience and Language of Grace*, 122–23). In God's act of "informing" the soul after the manner of a quasi-formal cause, the *lumen gloriae* exists as the effect or "material cause" of the beatific vision. In Rahner's own words, if our relation with God is not one of "efficient causality (a production *out* of a cause)," it must then come under a kind of "formal causality (a taking up *into* the ground)" (Rahner, "Zur scholastischen Begrifflichkeit," Schriften 1:357–58, as quoted in Burke, *Reinterpreting Rahner*, 50).

129. Burke, *Reinterpreting Rahner*, 50.

130. Lombard posed an objection: How could the Spirit as *caritas* be said to be less or more in a person if God is immutable? To this, he replied: "As God is said to be exalted in us [*in nobis*], and not in himself [*in se*], so the Spirit could be said to increase or decrease in the saints" (Lombard, *Quator Libri Sententarium*, bk. 1, dist. 17, ch. 5).

131. Edwards, "Concerning the End," in *WJE* 8:531.

132. Ibid., 433. According to Edwards, "so far as the communication or external stream may be looked upon as anything beside the fountain, so far it may be looked on as an increase of good."

133. If the repetition *ad extra* adds to God's being, then God would be less than infinite. The second "real" reading would make Edwards a tritheist, as Helm has charged.

134. As expressed by Coffey, this is Rahner's insight "that in any instance of formal causality, efficient causality will be contained in it as its 'deficient mode'" (David M. Coffey, "Quaestio Disputata: Response to Neil Ormerod, and Beyond," *Theological Studies* 68 [December 2007]: 909). This, of course, is a restatement of Aquinas, echoing the Aristotelian idea of formal causation. In arguing that all created excellencies are found in God, Aquinas reasons that "whatever perfection exists in an effect must be found in the effective cause: either in the same formality, if it is a univocal agent—as when man reproduces man; or in a more eminent degree, if it is an equivocal agent—thus in the sun is the likeness of whatever is generated by the sun's power" (Aquinas, *STh* I, q. 4. a. 2). Efficient causality as presupposed in quasi-formal causality may be pictured as "the anointing to the ointment of the uncreated act." See Ralph Del Colle, *Christ and the Spirit: Spirit-Christology in Trinitarian Perspective* (New York: Oxford University Press, 1994), 69–70. Mersch's proposal that the action *ad extra* of the Trinity is subsumed within de la Taille's theory of "created actuation by uncreated act" is adduced here. See also Emile Mersch, *The Theology of the Mystical Body*, trans. Cyril Vollert (St. Louis, MO: Herder, 1951), 208.

135. Thus, "every effect has in some respect or another the nature of its cause" (Edwards, "Treatise on Grace," in *WJE* 21:180). He heartily agrees with Samuel Clarke that any perfection of an effect must necessarily be found in its cause. A cause has priority over its effects in the order of nature. "'Tis impossible" (as Dr. Clarke observes) "that any effect should have any perfection, that was not in the cause: for if it had, then that perfection would be caused by nothing" (Samuel Clarke, *A Demonstration of the Being and Attributes of God* [London, 1705], 104, as cited in Edwards, "Treatise on Grace, in *WJE* 21:164–65). This is nothing but the *via causalitatis* (or in Barthian nomenclature, "way of revelation") understood as embracing and transcending the *viae eminentia* and *negationis*. "As regards the third way, the way of causality . . . it simply means that the effect bears witness to the cause and its perfection, but starting with the same effect we can describe this perfection of the cause either positively or negatively" (Barth, "The Attributes of

God,' in *Göttingen Dogmatics: Instruction in the Christian Religion*, ed. Hannelotte Reiffen, trans. Geoffrey W. Bromiley [Grand Rapids, MI: Eerdmans, 1991], vol. 1, § 17, 401).

136. Edwards, "Concerning the End," in *WJE* 8:527.

137. It is "an immediate infusion or operation of the Divine Being upon the soul" (Edwards, "Treatise on Grace," in *WJE* 21:165).

138. Yet, God cannot be regarded as an efficient cause that is extrinsic to and substantially different from the effect, for in reality it is "God's exerting himself in order to the effect" (Edwards, "Miscellanies," no. 1218, in *WJE* 23:153). In fact, the final cause is commonly regarded as extrinsic to the efficient cause. Clearly, for Aquinas, the *imago Dei* finds its Aristotelian equivalence in the relation between efficient and formal causality. "And as every agent produces its like [*omne agens agat sibi simile*], the principle of action can be considered from the effect of the action" (Aquinas, *STh* I. 45. 6).

139. On goodness in the soul, Goodwin opines that "God's power must work it . . . as take a piece of soft Wax, and another of hard, the soft is no more able of it self to work the image and impression of any thing upon it, than the hard; but a Hand and Seal must stamp the one, as well as the other" (Thomas Goodwin, *Of the work of the Holy Ghost [the third person of the Trinity] in our salvation*, ed. Thankfull Owen and James Barron, vol. 5 of *The works of Thomas Goodwin, D.D. Sometime president of Magdalen College in Oxford* [London: T. G. (Thomas Goodwin [Jr.]), 1704], bk. 9, ch. 5, 418). See also, Thomas Watson, "Prayer," in *A body of practical divinity, consisting of above one hundred seventy six sermons on the lesser catechism . . .* [London: Thomas Parkhurst, 1692], 430; Richard Baxter, *A saint or a brute . . .* (London: Thomas Parkhurst, Jonathan Robinson, and John Lawrence, 1707), 673. One need not abandon causal grammar for the personal for fear of confusing the Creator-creature distinction. These are, after all, analogies, and there is scriptural warrant for both anthropomorphic and cosmomorphic language. (For example, the image of a seal is found in John 6:27; 2 Cor. 1:22; and Eph. 1:13, 4:3.) The organic metaphor is central to *unio cum Christo*. Barth thought that a conflation of the Spirit and the human life force in us (like the Bergsonian *élan vital*) would reduce the divine-human distinction to one of degree. Not only that, "God must confront us in a relation of Creator and creature, that is, as person and not merely basis or cause. . . . His work . . . can have nothing in common with an event of nature. Relevant here is neither a mechanical relation of cause and effect, of pressure and impress, of a great and small quantity, nor the organic one of growth in its various stages or of life in its various forms" (Barth, "Faith and Obedience," in *Göttingen Dogmatics*, § 7, 179).

140. "The mind don't receive as the body receives, by taking with [the] hand or by opening the door; mental or spiritual reception can be nothing else but the suiting or according of the mind to a thing declared and proposed" (Edwards, "Miscellanies," no. 507, in *WJE* 18:53).

141. Ibid.

142. Mersch is quick to concur with Chalcedon's assertion of the consubstantiality of Christ's human nature. The perfection of Christ's human nature in the incarnation cannot and must not be "an accretion of new qualities," for, in the process of being made much more perfect, Christ would be made the much more different. Quasi-formal causality is thus "a transcendent actuation brought about by union with the Pure Act . . . nothing else than a pure adaptation, a pure assimilation and participation" of the human in the divine (Mersch, *Theology of the Mystical Body*, 214).

143. Ibid.

144. Edwards, "Miscellanies," no. 541, in *WJE* 18:89. Here, Edwards faces the same objection that was posed to Lombard: does the Spirit as *caritas* become nothing more than a part of human being? (Wolfhart Pannenberg, *Systematic Theology*, trans. Geoffrey W. Bromiley [Grand Rapids, MI: Eerdmans, 1998], 3:193).

145. "The exertion and the effect ought not to be separated as though they were two ends. One is so related to the other, and they are so united, that they are most properly taken together as

one end and the object of one inclination in God" (Edwards, "Miscellanies," no. 1218, in *WJE* 23:153).

146. "And God, in aiming at these, makes himself his end. 'Tis himself exerted and himself communicated. And both together are what is called God's glory. The end, or the thing which God attains, is himself, in two respects: he himself flows forth; and he himself is pleased and gratified. For God's pleasure all things are and were created" (ibid.).

147. Hence, "a Christian spirit is a real excellency of the person, which renders his soul—which is indeed the man—more beautiful and lovely." This is no different from the *imago Dei* (Edwards, 133. Sermon on 1 Pet. 3:4, in *WJE* 44).

148. Edwards, *WJE* 2:261–62. "An holy nature must needs love that in holy things chiefly, which is most agreeable to itself. . . . [H]oly nature must be above all things agreeable to holy nature; and so the holy nature of God and Christ . . . must be above all other things, agreeable to the holy nature that is in the saints."

149. This feeling of *suavitas* is the saint's perception of divine beauty present in this reality and in Ultimate Reality—the latter is the Trinitarian, aesthetic perfection of consent found in the eternal love "between the Father and the Son which is the Holy Spirit." See Terrence Erdt, *Jonathan Edwards: Art and the Sense of the Heart* (Amherst: University of Massachusetts Press, 1980), 42; see also his "The Calvinist Psychology of the Heart and the 'Sense' of Jonathan Edwards," *Early American Literature* 13, no. 2 (Fall 1978): 165–80. While the unregenerate may have a cognitive perception of the natural and even the moral attributes of God, the aesthetic apprehension of God's moral attributes remains hidden from them (Edwards, *WJE* 2:263–64). In this regard, Delattre highlights the important epistemological distinction Edwards uses to designate three levels of our perception of God: "the knowledge of his natural perfections, the knowledge of his moral perfections, and finally the knowledge of his beauty." Therefore, Edwards accords to beauty the primary rank in relation to God's perfections, followed in turn by goodness and power. See Roland André Delattre, "Beauty and Theology: A Reappraisal of Jonathan Edwards," *Soundings* 51, no. 1 (Spring 1968): 72–73.

150. As Delattre has noted, while Edwards uses the language of faculty psychology in the *Religious Affections*, the understanding and will are used to denote the aesthetic-affectional self's engagement with reality. The understanding is, therefore, the self's encounter with reality as being, and the will is the self's engagement with actuality as good or evil (Roland André Delattre, *Beauty and Sensibility in the Thought of Jonathan Edwards: An Essay in Aesthetics and Theological Ethics* [New Haven: Yale University Press, 1968], 7–8).

151. Edwards, "Treatise on Grace," in *TG*, 49. As Erdt shows, the conception of the regenerate's sense of the heart is not unique to Edwards; it can be traced back to the sense of divinity that Calvin and Augustine spoke of in their writings (Erdt, *Art and the Sense of the Heart*, 8–20). This notion of sweetness, termed *suavitas* by Calvin, became typical vocabulary in the voluntarism of Puritans who preceded Edwards, such as John Wollebius, Richard Baxter, and Thomas Hooker. Within the Calvinist understanding, this perceptive ability is a Trinitarian experience as it arises from the work of the Holy Spirit transforming the heart's disposition, thereby allowing the regenerate to taste the divine sweetness of the Father's mercy in Christ. The grammar of "the heart" and the capacity for spiritual taste can be found in the writings of St. Macarius the Great, as noted by John Meyendorff in his introduction to *The Triads*, by Gregory Palamas, ed. and intro. John Meyendorff, trans. Nicholas Gendell [Mahwah, NJ: Paulist, 1983], 3.

152. This spiritual sense of the heart is necessarily instructive as it involves an aesthetic perception of divine holiness "together with all that discerning and knowledge of things of religion, that depends upon, and flows from such a sense" (Edwards, *WJE* 2:272).

153. Edwards continues the Augustinian tradition of asserting that the basis of faith is intrinsic to the gospel itself, and he advances the original notion that this object of divine beauty is to be subjectively grasped via the new sense of the heart (Smith, "Introduction," in *WJE* 2:35). It is Edwards's category of aesthetic consent that allows him to posit this subjective-objective

correlation; God-in-us must recognize God-without-us for the Spirit is the immanent beauty of God within the saint and also the basis of God's and Christ's objective, transcendent beauty.

154. These two movements are balanced and create that aesthetic proportionality in one's life.

155. This double knowledge of the divine beauty and human deformity is powerfully transformative, as the sight of divine *gloria* capacitates the saint to reflect the beauty of Christ. The Spirit of God, who enables "the soul of a saint [to receive] light from the Sun of Righteousness," transforms the nature of the saint into the image of Christ. Believers become like Christ, the perfect image of God, as "they also become little suns, partaking of the nature of the fountain of their light" (Edwards, *WJE* 2:343). Saints will reflect the aesthetically balanced, harmonious image of Christ, the true Icon of God, so that "there is something of the same beautiful proportion in the image, which is in the original" (ibid., 365). John Smith traces an Augustinian influence (as in *De ordine*) in Edwards's stress on order and proportion (Miller, "Editor's Introduction," in Edwards, *WJE* 2:38). So, the spiritual appetite of the saint for God's beauty increases in proportion with the saint's taste and relish of "this excellent, unparalleled, exquisite, and satisfying sweetness" (Edwards, *WJE* 2:379). There is consent between the saint's spiritual sense and appetite with its aesthetic object: "But undoubtedly the same sweetness that is the chief object of a spiritual taste, is also the chief object of the spiritual appetite."

156. Edwards, "Miscellanies," no. 681, in *WJE* 18:241.

157. Edwards, *WJE* 2:344.

158. Edwards, "Charity and Its Fruit," sermon 11, passim, in *WJE* 8:313–26. To have the Holy Spirit, the spirit of love, is synonymous with "a suffering spirit." Edwards subsumes the theme of suffering as imitation (like Christ) under the notion of suffering as obedience (for Christ). "It is given as the character of true followers of Christ, that they follow the Lamb withersoever he goeth, Rev. 14.4. They who are willing to follow Christ only to the crown and not to the cross, or who follow him only through prosperity and not through adversity, or who have a spirit to follow him only through some sufferings and not through all, cannot be said to follow him whithersoever he goes" (ibid., 320).

159. Edwards, *WJE* 2:111; *WJE* 7:91–96. Although Edwards regards Christ as the only perfect example of the religious life, he nevertheless counted Brainerd as "a remarkable instance of true and eminent Christian piety in heart and practice" save his "imperfections" of a chronic melancholy and extreme activism (*WJE* 7:91–96). Christ's virtues appear great because of enduring the greatest sufferings: "Strict virtue shines most when most tried, but never any virtue had such trials as Christ's had" (Edwards, "No. 6: Sermon 16," in *WJE* 9:320).

160. Edwards, "No. 6: Sermon 16," in *WJE* 9:320. The basic triple relational structure that Edwards uses in this sermon is clearly seen outworked in greater depth and subtlety in the *Treatise on the Religious Affections*. If true love is to love what the Other loves, then the love of God is the highest love. It is axiomatic for Edwards that "the necessary consequence of the true esteem and love of any person or being (suppose a son or a friend) that we should approve and value others' esteem of the same object, and disapprove and dislike the contrary." Since God views and values the divine perfections and glory infinitely and supremely, God's desire for the human being's good is that she would have "a supreme regard to God" in participating in the divine goodness and glory (Edwards, "Concerning the End," in *WJE* 8:533). As Ramsey puts it, this is "complacence in complacent being (delight or esteem of another's delight or esteem)" (Paul Ramsey, *WJE* 8:533n3).

161. Edwards, "No. 6: Sermon 16," in *WJE* 9:321–22. The human Christ did not self-elevate despite being "the same person with the eternal Son of God," performing great miracles, and knowing that the Father would grant the title king of the universe. Christ's humility was great as a result of descending far lower than any slave from a position far higher than any angel and doing so for others in a free and cheerful assent. Also, Christ exercised great virtue in patient lamblike suffering and disregard of earthly, temporal glory.

162. Christ's meekness was considerable in all the abuses endured, both in nature and in unreasonableness. Christ withstood all this provocation without harboring a revengeful

disposition, but instead maintained a most forgiving spirit. Christ not only demonstrated on the cross the greatest outworking of this other-centered love, but the life of self-donation "exceeded the love of all other men as the ocean exceeds a small stream" (ibid., 322–23).

163. The indwelling and leading of the Spirit results in true godliness that is Christlike.

164. George S. Claghorn, Introduction to "Unpublished Letter on Assurance and Participation in the Divine Nature," in *WJE* 8:631. Claghorn refers to Edwards, in *WJE* 2: 200–204, 233, 236–37, 296, and 392.

165. Edwards, *WJE* 2:203.

166. For a comprehensive study of the Dutch sixteenth-century founder of Familism, Henry Nicolas, and its English offshoot, with which the English Puritans were familiar, see Alistair Hamilton, *The Family of Love* (Cambridge: James Clarke, 1981). For another study, which relies primarily on translated sources, see Jean Dietz Moss, *"Godded with God": Hendrik Niclaes and His Family of Love* (Philadelphia: American Philosophical Society, 1981). With regard to terminology, *theosis* must be differentiated from *apotheosis*, which was specially used for elevating a living emperor or dead ordinary citizens, and *ektheosis*, favored by the Neoplatonists, who applied it to the descent of divine power that elevated lower-level beings through participation. See Norman Russell, "Appendix 2," in his *Doctrine of Deification in the Greek Patristic Tradition* (Oxford: Oxford University Press, 2004), 333–44, where he presents a comprehensive word study on the various terms for deification. *Theopoēsis* was first appropriated by Athanasius and taken up by Cyril of Alexandria, while *theosis* was used by Gregory of Nazianzus, followed by Ps.-Dionysius and Maximus the Confessor. *Apotheosis*, which gained pejorative connotations after the Nestorian controversy, was seldom used by Christian writers, and *ektheosis* was even rarer.

167. John Flavel, Sermon 5, "Of Christ's Wonderful Person," in *The Works of John Flavel*, vol. 1, *The Fountain of Life Opened Up* (Carlisle, PA: Banner of Truth Trust, 1968, 1982; first published by W. Banes and Son, 1820). "They are not christed into Christ, or godded into God, as blasphemous Familists speak." Augustus Strong attributes this phrase to "Lowde, a disciple of Malebranche . . . and Jonathan Edwards in his Religious Affections, quotes it with disapprobation" (Augustus Hopkins Strong, *Systematic Theology: A Compendium and Commonplace Book Designed for the Use of Theological Students*, vol. 3, *The Doctrine of Salvation* [Philadelphia: Griffith & Rowland, 1909], 800).

168. Edwards, *WJE* 2:202.

169. Although the technical term for deification, *theosis*, was first employed by Clement of Alexandria, its primarily metaphorical usage was given conceptual clarity by Dionysius the Areopagite in the sixth century: "And divinization consists of being as much as possible like and in union with God." See Ps.-Dionysius, *Ecclesiastical Hierarchy*, 1.3, as quoted in *Pseudo-Dionysius: The Complete Works*, trans. Colm Luibheid, foreword, notes, and translation collaboration by Paul Rorem, preface by Rene Roques, intro. Jaroslav Pelikan, Jean LeClercq, and Karlfried Froehlich (Mahwah, NJ: Paulist, 1987), 198. Russell outlines three senses in which *theosis* was used in early patristic theology: (1) the nominal, where the human beings were referred to as "gods" in a titular sense; (2) the analogical, where Christians, by grace, become children and gods in their relation to Christ, who is Son and God, by nature; and (3) the metaphorical, in ethically attaining godlikeness or *homoiosis*, as well as, realistically, by participation in God or *methexis* (Russell, *Doctrine of Deification*, 1). Deification, in a sense, is a reestablishment of the original human constitution of "impassibility par excellence," in which the human will is in total conformity to its nature and therefore to the divine will (Meyendorff, *Christ in Eastern Christian Thought*, 125). This theological point is, therefore, crucial to the ascetical tradition, where the constant struggle against the passions aims toward acquiring a godlike impassibility.

170. Turretin, *Institutes*, 2, topic 13, q. 8, para. 9, 324.

171. Because of the infinity and perfection of the divine essence, one cannot participate in God, who "cannot be perfectly imitated by anything outside of himself." Only the Logos, "who is the Brightness of his Glory, and the express Image of his Substance," is capable of imaging God

perfectly." However, since the divine essence necessarily include all degrees of being and perfection, God "must be conceived in various degrees to be imitable and participable, even ad extra." Norris goes on to specify that that which is participable in God in none other than the divine "ideas of them [created things] as he is imitable by them." The divine simplicity is not compromised because ideas in God are neither modes nor real things in God, but are synonymous with the divine essence in relation to things *ad extra* (John Norris, *Philosophical and Theological Writings*, ed. Richard Acworth [Bristol: Thoemmes, 2001], 6:246–47, 294).

172. The holiness we have is "of the same nature with the divine holiness, as much as 'tis possible for that holiness to be, which is infinitely less in degree" (Edwards, *WJE* 2:202).

173. Thus, he describes holiness, which "may, without absurdity, be said to be the proper nature of the Holy Spirit" as that which saints' can partake of "and therefore is called by divines in general a communicable attribute" (Edwards, "Unpublished Letter on Assurance and Participation in the Divine Nature," in *WJE* 8:639).

174. "Just as when a sunbeam falls on bright and transparent bodies, they themselves become brilliant too, and shed forth a fresh brightness from themselves, so souls wherein the Spirit dwells, illuminated by the Spirit, themselves become spiritual, and send forth their grace to others" (Basil, *On the Holy Spirit* 23, 15–16 [*NPNF* 8]).

175. Edwards, "End of Creation," in *WJE* 8:442.

176. On 2 Pet. 1:4, Willet comments: "That essential and infinite honour and glory which is in God, is not communicated unto any other: but yet there are certain influences and bright beames of that glory, which in Christ are imparted to his members" (Willet, *Hexapla*, 108).

177. Edwards echoes Athanasius here: "Spiritual life is a participation of the life of God. . . . This divine life is the spirit of God living and acting in the soul." This is no different from partaking "of his Nature 2 Pet 1,4 that by these ye might be made partakers of the divine nature have escaped the corruption that is in the world through lust" (Edwards, 52. Sermon on Luke 2:14 [b] [1727], in *WJE* 42).

178. Edwards, "Miscellanies," no. 396 in *WJE* 13:462. "This Holy Spirit of God, the divine temper, is that divine nature spoken of, 2 Peter 1:4, that we are made partakers of through the gospel." Thomas Watson, in his commentary on 2 Pet. 1:4, understood partaking in the "Divine Nature" to mean participation in the "Divine Qualities" (Watson, "God is a Spirit," in *A body of practical divinity*, q. 4, 24). "We are made Partakers of the Divine Nature, not by Identity or Union with the Divine Essence, but by a transformation into the Divine Likeness." The doctrine of the *imago Dei* is to be seen primarily as a spiritual conformity: a likeness to Christ through the reception of the Spirit. "The essence of God is incommunicable, but the motions, the presence and influences of his Spirit. When the sun shines in a room, not the body of the sun is there, but the light, heat, and influence of the sun" (Watson, "God is a Spirit," in *A body of practical divinity*, q. 4, 26).

179. While the deified human being is "changed" through "participating in the divine glory," this transformation does not involve a "change into the divine being" (John of Damascus, *Orthodox Faith*, bk. 2, ch. 12, 31 [*NPNF* 9]).

180. Patacsi points out that scholastic theologians failed to recognize that a more foundational entitative union underlies each intentional union. "All knowledge and all love," he avers, "are in fact the fruit of a certain 'touching' or of a mutual influence which, without leading to confusion of essences, happens on the level of objective being" (Patacsi, "Palamism before Palamas," 66).

181. For Edwards, some properties "properly" belong to the essence of a thing, such as reason in human beings. These natural endowments are like conscience tied to understanding and the principle of self-love (or happiness) tied to the will. Some effects or "produce" of a thing's essence, like "acquired gifts . . . don't belong to their nature or essence . . . and are not properly parts of their nature." Hence, they may be lost, but this does not change the essence of an entity (Edwards, 498. Sermon on 1 John 4:12 [Dec 1738], in *WJE* 53).

182. Fabro lists three different sorts of participation in Aquinas: (1) logical, as man participates in the species "animal"; (2) real and predicamental, as matter participating in its form or substance in accidents; and (3) real and transcendental, as an effect participates in its cause (for example, created participation in God's *esse*). These are summarized in John F. Wippel, *Metaphysical Themes in Thomas Aquinas II*, Studies in Philosophy and the History of Philosophy 47 (Washington, DC: Catholic University of America Press, 2007), 285.

183. Reginald Garrigou-Lagrange, *Grace: Commentary on the* Summa theologica *of St. Thomas, Ia IIae, q. 109–14*, trans. the Dominican Nuns, Corpus Christi Monastery, Menlo Park, CA (St. Louis, MO: B. Herder Book, 1952), ch. 3, q. 110, a. 2.

184. This, of course, is based upon the Platonic metaphysical idea of participation as a thing deriving its reality by virtue of another. See David C. Schindler, "What's the Difference? On the Metaphysics of Participation in a Christian Context," *Saint Anselm Journal* 3, no. 1 (Fall 2005): 1. "If a being participates in the superior substance and distinct class of another being, then it must itself be different in nature from the being in which it participates." See St. Cyril of Alexandria, *Commentary on the Gospel according to St. John*, bk. 10, as quoted in J. Patout Burns and Gerald M. Fagin, *The Holy Spirit*, Message of the Fathers of the Church (Eugene, OR: Wipf and Stock, 1984), 164. This is quite different from contemporary notions of participation, such as Tillich's, which is premised on a primordial divine-human unity. This "essential" divine-human unity is actualized and made concrete for the first time through Christ's entry into the conditions of existence and perfect overcoming of existential estrangement.

185. "He who does not partake of life but is himself partaken and gives life to creatures, what kinship can he have with things originated? . . . If the Holy Spirit were a creature, we should have no participation of God in him." See St. Athanasius, *To Serapion*, para. 22, 24, as cited in Burns and Fagin, *Holy Spirit*, 103–4. This was Cyril's contention for the deity of the Spirit: "If the Spirit is himself created or made, then what would remain in which the creation could participate? Certainly not part of itself. Being created would be common to both" (St. Cyril of Alexandria, *Commentary on the Gospel according to St. John*, bk. 10, as cited in Burns and Fagins, *Holy Spirit*, 64).

186. Hence, the Son is "the principle and independent possessor of life" in contrast with creatures, who "all have life derivatively and dependently" (Edwards, 498b. Sermon on 1 John 4:12, in *WJE* 53). Edwards also describes degrees of existence, Christ as God being the "chief or highest in life." "There are various degrees of Life among the creatures. The life of a [brute] creature is more perfect than the Life of a tree. The life of a rational creature is more . . . but the life of Christ is infinitely above all, more perfect and glorious than all." Note the terminology of degrees of perfection similar to the language of Gregory of Nyssa.

187. Edwards, 498b. Sermon on 1 John 4:12, in *WJE* 53. Athanasius championed the uncreated/created distinction to exclude any mediate category of created divinities. Origen confessed three divine persons, yet held "nothing to be uncreated but the Father." The Holy Spirit is "the most excellent and the first in order of all that was made by the Father through Christ." He depends on Christ for "his essence" and has existence and wisdom, like rational beings, "by participation of the character of Christ" (Origen, *Commentary on John*, bk 2, ch. 10, as cited in Burns and Fagins, *Holy Spirit*, 73).

188. Edwards, 498b. Sermon on 1 John 4:12 [n.d.], in *WJE* 53.

189. Ibid. Consistent with what we have seen in chapter 2, Edwards is denying any *communicatio essentiae ad extra*. Of the incommunicability of the Godhead, or "absolute subsistence," and divine personality, or "relative subsistence," Garrigou-Lagrange helpfully clarifies: "The first incommunicability is not within the Trinity, but only external to it. The second incommunicability is both internal and external to the Trinity. Common and absolute subsistence does not formally attribute incommunicability internally to the Deity, for the Deity is communicated to the Son and to the Holy Ghost. On the contrary, the personality of the Father is not communicated to the Son" (Reginald Garrigou-Lagrange, *Christ the Saviour: A Commentary on the Third Part of Saint Thomas' Theological Summa*, trans. by Dom Bede Rose [St. Louis, MO: Herder, (copyright 1950)], ch. 5, q. 3, a. 3). Puritan writers, such as Thomas Watson, refuted

Osiander's and Servetus's contention that the divine essence could be communicated to humankind (Watson, "God is a Spirit," in *A body of practical divinity*, q. 4, 24).

190. Edwards, "Charity," sermon 1, in *WJE* 8:132.

191. Pauw thinks that Edwards failed to consistently maintain the distinction between "God's being or essence, and God's mode of being, or nature" (Amy Plantinga Pauw, *The Supreme Harmony of All: The Trinitarian Theology of Jonathan Edwards* [Grand Rapids, MI: Eerdmans, 2002], 156) in statements like these: the Spirit as divine love that "is poured forth into the hearts of angels and saints" is conflated with "the Divine essence being wholly poured out and flowing out" (Edwards, "Treatise on Grace," in *TG*, 63).

192. Edwards, "Participation in the Divine Nature," in *WJE* 8:638. Other Puritan writers also drew such a distinction: "The Holiness of God is the intrinsick Purity of his Essence. He who hath God for his Father, partakes of the Divine Nature; though not of the Divine Essence, yet of the Divine Likeness" (Watson, "Prayer," in *A Body of Practical Divinity*, 430). Even Palamas permitted, in a nontechnical sense, the idea of participation in God's nature or essence as equivalent to the divine energies. Citing Ps.-Dionysius, the term "essence" may denote an intimate, real, ontological union of "essences" without confusion, provided one recognizes a mode of divinity that is beyond participation, viz., the superessence. Similarly, Symeon the Theologian made infrequent assertions that human beings can partake of God's essence (Patacsi, "Palamism before Palamas," 66).

193. Edwards, "Treatise on Grace," *WJE* 21:197.

194. Edwards distinguishes a twofold meaning for the term "spirit" when applied to spiritual beings: "when it is not put for a spiritual substance itself (angel, or human soul, or divine essence), it is put for the disposition, temper, inclination, or will of that spiritual substance." Accordingly, this distinction of noun and genitive case applies to the divine essence, "as when we read that God is a Spirit," or the "holy temper, or disposition or affection of God, as when we read of the Spirit of God." The indwelling Spirit or the divine nature in the saint is, therefore, to be regarded genitively as "a divine temper or disposition dwells in us or fills us." So, "Spirit of God" and "the Spirit of Christ" refer to the disposition in God and Christ, respectively (Edwards, "Miscellanies," no. 396, in *WJE* 13:462).

195. Edwards, "Participation in the Divine Nature," in *WJE* 8:639.

196. Edwards, "Charity and Its Fruits," sermon 2, in *WJE* 8:158.

197. Edwards, "Miscellanies," no. 471, in *WJE* 13:512–14.

198. "And as the happiness will be increasing to eternity, the union will become more and more strict and perfect; nearer and more like to that between God the Father and the Son; who are so united, that their interest is perfectly one. . . . If by reason of the strictness of the union of a man and his family, their interest may be looked upon as one, how much more one is the interest of Christ and his church" (Edwards, "Concerning the End," in *WJE* 8:533–35).

199. "All communicated glory to the creature must be by the Son of God, who is the brightness or shining forth of his Father's glory" (Edwards, "Miscellanies," no. 952, in *WJE* 20:221).

200. "That Jesus Christ is the fountain of grace argues that he has all grace on himself. . . . If he is the fountain of all that heavenly excellency that is bestowed upon men, it argues that there is an ocean of it in him. . . . But then he yet the more deserves our love in that he not only has all grace, all holiness in himself, but is communicative of it. He communicates it to us by his spirit; is continually sending forth streams down upon his people here on earth" (Edwards, 72. Sermon on 2 Cor. 3:18 [a], in *WJE* 43).

201. "The image [of God in the saints] is more and more perfect, and so the good that is in the creature comes forever nearer and nearer to an identity with that which is in God" (Edwards, "Concerning the End," in *WJE* 8:443).

202. This "infinitely strict and perfect nearness, conformity, and oneness" between God and the church "will forever come nearer and nearer to that strictness and perfection of union which there is between the Father and the Son" (ibid.).

203. The communicability of the divine energy is "in proportion to the fitness and receptive power" of its object (John of Damascus, *Orthodox Faith*, bk. 1, ch. 13, 15 [*NPNF* 9]). Matthew Henry also applied this axiom explicitly to the efficacy of grace in relation to the disposition of its recipient. "The success was to be different, according to the different dispositions of those whom they preached to and prayed for. . . . *Recipitur ad modum recipientis—The quality of the receiver determines the nature of the reception*" (Henry, Luke 10, in *Commentary on the Whole Bible*, vol. 5).

204. "omne quod recipitur in aliquo, est in eo per modum recipientis" (Aquinas, *STh* I, q. 76, a. 2, sc 3). He repeats the principle and applies it epistemologically: "Quod enim recipitur in aliquo, recipitur in eo secundum modum recipientis" (*STh* I, q. 79, a. 6). More succinctly stated: "quidquid recipitur, recipitur ad modum recipientis" (Mersch, *Theology of the Mystical Body*, 207). See also David M. Coffey, "The Theandric Nature of Christ," *Theological Studies* 60, no. 3 (September 1999): 419. Jüngel thinks that this rule "is indisputable" (Eberhard Jüngel, *God as the Mystery of the World: On the Foundation of the Theology of the Crucified One in the Dispute between Theism and Atheism* [Grand Rapids, MI: Eerdmans, 1983], 254). On this limitation axiom in Aquinas, see esp. ch. 4 in Wippel, *Metaphysical Themes*, 2:113–22.

205. Strauss notes that the Lutheran effort to mitigate the *genus maiestaticum* using the axiom *uti per suam indolem potest* would invalidate the whole notion of participation (David Friedrich Strauss, *The Life of Jesus Critically Examined*, trans. Marian Evans [New York: Calvin Blanchard, 1860], 876). Presumably, the divine attributes, if they can be communicated, must be wholly and not partially communicated.

206. Edwards, "Miscellanies," no. 1218, in *WJE* 23:152.

207. Edwards, "A Farewell Sermon Preached at the First Precinct in Northampton, after the People's Public Rejection of Their Minister . . . On June 22, 1750," in *WJE* 25:464.

208. These being "inimitable and incommunicable attributes" (Edwards, "Way of Holiness," in *The Sermons of Jonathan Edwards: A Reader*, ed. Wilson H. Kimnach, Kenneth P. Minkema, and Douglas A. Sweeney [New Haven: Yale University Press, 1999], 5). They participate in all of Christ's "communicable divine excellencies" but not the "excellencies Christ hath as God [that] are incommunicable" (Edwards, 180. Sermon on John 1:16 [June 1752], in *WJE* 45). In contrast, compare Maximus's grammar of "participated beings" for uncreated Goodness, Life, Simplicity, and Infinity and "participating beings" in reference to created beings who become good, living, simple, and infinite through participation. See Torstein Tollefsen, "Did Maximus the Confessor Have a Concept of Participation?" in *Papers Presented at the Thirteenth International Conference on Patristic Studies held in Oxford, 1999*, ed. M. F. Wiles and E. J. Yarnold, with the assistance of P. M. Parvis, Studia Patristica 37 (Leuven: Peeters, 2001), 619. God created and preserves sentient beings by giving them participation in four divine attributes: being and well-being in relation to essence, together with goodness and wisdom in relation to their wills. Maximus appropriated the Proclan triad of the unparticipated, the participable, and the participant. See Maximus, *The Four Hundred Chapters*, 3.25, as quoted in Tollefsen, "Did Maximus the Confessor Have a Concept of Participation?," 622.

209. Edwards, 180. Sermon on John 1:16 [June 1752], in *WJE* 45.

210. "Holiness is . . . [not only] conformity to his will, whereby he wills things that are just, right, and truly excellent and lovely . . . but also a doing as he doth: in acting holily and justly and wisely and mercifully" (Edwards, "Way of Holiness," in *Sermons*, 5). It is the soul of a human being, which obeys commands, whether from God or human beings. Prescriptions are "directly and properly" related to "the disposition and acts of the will of that intelligent being that is commanded." This is no different from stating that "any command given to an intelligent, voluntary substance is directly and properly the thing commanded and required of that substance but such acts of its will" (Edwards, "Miscellanies," no. 1153, in *WJE* 23:39).

211. St. Thomas rejected St. Albert's distinction between *virtus divina increata* and *virtus divina creata*; the former denied the notions of *virtus divina creata* and *liberum arbitrium* as a third faculty, even in his early *Commentary on the Sentences*. See Bernard J. Lonergan, *Grace and Freedom:*

Operative Grace in the Thought of St. Thomas Aquinas, ed. J. Patout Burns, intro. Frederick E. Crowe (London: Darton, Longman & Todd; New York: Herder & Herder, 1971), 141. Like Edwards, Goodwin thinks that the new disposition is "not a faculty, as the understanding is essentially inherent in the soul; yet as it is planted in the soul in order to receive and take in things spiritual . . . so this new divine and heaven-born power, elevating and empowering the soul to discern them, hath justly the name of being enstyled a 'new understanding'" (Goodwin, *WTG* 6:192).

212. "Hence we learn that the prime alteration that is made in conversion, that which is first and the foundation of all, is the alteration of the temper and disposition and spirit of the mind for what is done in conversion, is nothing but conferring the Spirit of God, which dwells in the soul and becomes there a principle of life and action" (Edwards, "Miscellanies," no. 397, in *WJE* 13:462).

213. Goodwin, *WTG* 6:192. The new principle is "a new bodily eye, or a new endowment of it with a new power of seeing."

214. Edwards, "Efficacious Grace, Book III," in *WJE* 21:248.

215. As Baxter notes, "holy Desires" toward God "are our *Receptive disposition*," and our reception of God's grace is commensurate to our moral receptivity. See Richard Baxter, *The poor man's family-book. . . .* (London: Thomas Parkhurst, Jonathan Robinson, and John Lawrence, 1707), 172–73.

216. "And if you have any philosophy, you know that *recipitur ad modum recipientis*, and what a wonderful variegation of effects there is in the world, from the same beams or influxes of the sun, by the great variety of receptive dispositions. . . . There is a sweet and admirable co-operation between the bountiful communications of God, and the holy and constant desires of the soul" (ibid.).

217. Edwards, "Divine and Supernatural Light," in *Sermons*, 130.

218. Edwards, "Miscellanies," no. 1346, in *WJE* 23:382. God's insistence "on this propriety is not in the least inconsistent with the highest possible freedom of grace" since it is entirely consistent that human persons "capable of act and choice" must "cordially receive [Christ] and cleave to him" in order to have union with Christ's person and participate in the divine benefits.

219. This is a correction of the Platonic idea that knowledge of material objects is impossible for immaterial entities, while retaining the Aristotelian idea of like knowing the like (*simile simili cognoscitur*) (Aquinas, *STh* I, Q. 84, a. 1, 421–22). See also Aristotle, *De anima* 1.5. Using this axiom, Aquinas was able to secure the ontological difference between the (knowing) subject and (known) object while retaining a realistic conception of knowledge. See Matthew Schumacher, *Knowableness of God: Its Relation to the Theory of Knowledge in St. Thomas* (Notre Dame, IN: University Press, 1905), 43–46. This appears already in Ps.-Dionysius: "Divine things are revealed into each created spirit in proportion to its powers." See Pseudo-Dionysius the Areopagite, *On the Divine Names and the Mystical Theology*, I.1, in *Pseudo-Dionysius: The Complete Works*, 52.

220. "Now participated existence is limited by the capacity of the participator; so that God alone, Who is His own existence, is pure act and infinite" (Aquinas, *STh* Ia, q. 75, a. 5, ad 4, 367).

221. Thomas Adams, *A commentary or, exposition upon the divine second epistle generall, written by the blessed apostle St. Peter* (London: Jacob Bloome, 1633), 70. Adams, exegeting 2 Pet. 1:4, railed against the dual error of the "*Maniches*," who claimed "*Nos ex traduce Dei ortos*, that we came by traduction from the nature of God himself," and the "*Familists*," who taught that "there is *Transfusio divinae essentiae in hominem, infinitae in circumscriptam*: a transfusion of the divine being into man."

222. Edwards, 79. Sermon on Song of Sol. 1:3 (a), in *WJE* 43.

223. Christ admits the elect, so says Edwards, into the "utmost degree and Intimacy of Communion with him" through participation in the "Spirit of communion . . . as fully as . . . their capacities or desires can reach" (Edwards, 419. Sermon on John 13:23 [Jan 1736–37], in *WJE* 52). The saints' capacity for enjoying God is enlarged insofar as they are united to "Christ their head," who "is as it were their organ of enjoyment" (Edwards, "Miscellanies," no. 1072, in *WJE* 20:455)

224. "Then, also, our capacities will be exceedingly enlarged, and we shall be able to apprehend, and to take in, more extended and compounded proportions. We see that the narrower the capacity, the more simple must the beauty be to please" (Edwards, "Miscellanies," no. 182, in *WJE* 13:329).

225. Edwards, "Miscellanies," no. 1072, in *WJE* 20:455.

226. Edwards, "Miscellanies," no. 1089, in *WJE* 20:469. They not only see God "in their measure," but they participate in Christ's perception of "the Church of God on earth," and "of his enemies in hell" (ibid.).

227. This is the *complexio oppositorum* which any theology of grace must hold onto (Mœller and Philips, *The Theology of Grace*, 4).

228. "In metaphysical strictness," Edwards claims, created things "are not proper causes of the effects [of natural operations], but only [their] occasions" (Edwards, "Miscellanies," no. 629, in *WJE* 18:157). This is consistent with his insistence elsewhere that the laws of nature "are not so properly laws by which the creature acts as fixed rules according to which God acts with respect to the creature" (Edwards, 107. Sermon on Num. 23:19 [1729], in *WJE* 44).

229. "Mortal men are capable of imparting the knowledge of human arts and sciences, and skill in temporal affairs. God is the author of such knowledge by those means: flesh and blood is made use of by God as the mediate or second cause of it; he conveys it by the power and influence of natural means" (Edwards, "A Divine and Supernatural Light," in *WJE* 17:409). This is highlighted as contrasting with spiritual knowledge, which Edwards attributes solely to divine causation. While God may grant secondary causation a role in the production of the "meaner gifts, qualifications and attainments," divine holiness imparted through regeneration is effected through the direct, efficacious agency of the Spirit. The Christian spirit is the greatest glory of the human being because it is God's greatest imparted or communicated glory *ad extra*. If such is the case, could God, Edwards asks rhetorically, "leave to the power of second causes, or honor any arm of flesh or created power or faculty to be the proper instrument of" the believer's regeneration? (Edwards, "Miscellanies," no. 1003, in *WJE* 20:328).

230. For Edwards, the higher a created entity is within the hierarchy of being, the more immediate is the divine operation and the less is the need for secondary causation. The human soul, being "the crown and the end of all the rest" of creation, is created immediately by God and "communicated directly from him without the intervention of instruments or honoring second causes" (Edwards, "Miscellanies," no. 1003, in *WJE* 20:327; see also "The Great Concern of a Watchman for Souls," in *WJE* 25:64).

231. Only in this sense are "natural means the causes of the exercises of natural principles" (Edwards, "Miscellanies," no. 629, in *WJE* 18:157).

232. And while human beings exist through the course of natural reproduction except "the first creation of man, when his body was formed immediately by God not in a course of nature," one observes that for every human soul after Adam "immediate creation is continued, and is a thing that comes to pass in innumerable instances every day" (Edwards, "Miscellanies," no. 1003, in *WJE* 20:328).

233. Edwards, "Miscellanies," no. 481, in *WJE* 13:523–24. Comparing nature and grace "as to the exercise of power," Edwards comments that "they are both alike immediately from God." Yet "there is this difference: common benefits are statedly connected with preceding things in the creature, so that they are in a sense dependent on the creature; but this excellency and blessedness of the soul is connected only with the will of God, and is dependent on nothing else." This applies preeminently to regeneration. If the human soul exists apart from secondary causation, less still would God allow the new, regenerated nature to be effected instrumentally since it is "the crown and glory of the human, and that by which he is nearest to God and does partake of his image and nature, and is the highest beauty and glory of the whole creation, and is as it were the life and soul of the soul" (Edwards, "Miscellanies," no. 541, in *WJE* 18:89).

234. From an occasionalist standpoint, because human beings are not secondary causes with intrinsic causal powers, the construal of Christ's human nature as *instrumentum* does not abrogate

Christ's essential humanity, as it would seem to do in Aquinas's Christology (Richard Cross, *Duns Scotus* [New York: Oxford University Press, 1999], 56). Of course, the issue of the heteronomy, for Edwards, is located in his anthropology and cosmology.

235. The realistic or "physical" idea of union, in which the hypostatic union (and the *communicatio idiomatum*) are inseparably tied to our spiritual and sacramental union with Christ and one another through the Spirit and the Eucharist, finds its fullest expression in Cyril of Alexandria (Kelly, *Early Christian Doctrines*, 405). Thomas's system of instrumental causality is an extension of this Cyrillian realism using Aristotelian categories.

236. Hence, "they cannot properly and in strictness of speech be instruments at all, for a miracle is wrought by the immediate power of God" (Edwards, "Miscellanies," no. 1150, in *WJE* 20:521).

237. For Edwards, the Word and sacraments are "means of grace" insofar as they are not "adjuvant causes or instruments" but act as only under those occasions for "grace's acting suitably in the nature of things" ("Miscellanies," no. 539, in *WJE* 18:84).

238. He gives the example of Elijah "laying fuel upon the altar," thereby giving occasion for the fire of grace to burn. This, of course, depends on "when God should send it down from heaven" (ibid.).

239. Edwards, "Miscellanies," no. 689, in *WJE* 18:253.

240. Edwards thinks that in divine illumination "the Word of God is no proper cause of this effect," yet it is the natural cause of the "subject matter" or doctrine of the divine light. Scripture "conveys to our minds these and those doctrines; it is the cause of the notion of them in our heads, but not of the sense of the divine excellency of them in our hearts" (Edwards, "Divine and Supernatural Light," in *Sermons*, 130). Based on "Miscellanies," no. 1138, Jenson thinks that the later Edwards changed his mind about the Word's causal role in grace: "Now, revelation as *word* is precisely not mere evidence; and this character is its authenticity" (Robert W. Jenson, *America's Theologian: A Recommendation of Jonathan Edwards* [New York: Oxford University Press, 1988], 192). Brian A. Gerrish includes Zwingli's "symbolic memorialism" as the third option within Reformed sacramentalogy. See his *The Old Protestantism and the New: Essays on the Reformation Heritage* (Chicago: University of Chicago Press, 1982), esp. 5.

241. Lee, *PTJE*, 106.

242. As to the *materia*, Edwards emphasizes the cognitive value of Word and sacrament in supplying "the mind with notions or speculative ideas, about the things of religion." Thus, grace is given "greater opportunity to act" through "Scriptures, instructions of parents and ministers, sacraments, etc." in proportion to the accuracy, quantity, intensity, and frequency of doctrinal input. The effects are merely preparatory in that they augment the work of grace by assisting our natural reason and affection (Edwards, "Miscellanies," no. 539, in *WJE* 18:85–86).

243. "But the acting's of grace will be very unsuitable to the nature of things; it must act very lamely or monstrously, and so unsuitably, that I believe God ordinarily don't see meet that it should be, where there is no opportunity for it to act no better" (ibid., 84).

244. "The infant that has a disposition in his heart to believe in Christ—if he had a capacity and opportunity—is looked upon and accepted as if he actually believed in Christ, and so is entitled to eternal life through Christ" (Edwards, "'Controversies' Notebook Original Sin," in *WJE* 27). Clearly, Edwards's aesthetics comes into play here with the ideas of *convenientia* and fitness. *Opportunitas* includes convenience and fitness, or the ordered, lawlike character of a dispositional ontology.

245. Those who deny infused grace, Edwards argues, do not thereby reject the subjective operation of the Spirit in toto. The issue is not whether "the Spirit doth something in the soul," but "how much is infused" (Edwards, "Miscellanies," no. p, in *WJE* 13:171). He argues that those who hold to cooperating grace, whereby it is thought that "the Holy Spirit assists the man in acquiring the habit," cannot be wholly Pelagian because such a *partum-partum* synergy must assume to some extent the Spirit's operation "how so little ever that be."

246. Edwards, 307. Sermon on Eccles. 9:10 (b) (Dec 1733), in *WJE* 48.

247. Ibid.

248. "In strictness we can do nothing of our selves as we han't our being of our selves so neither are we capable of acting of our selves but are immediately dependent on God every moment to enable us to perform any act at all. We can do nothing without the influx of the divine power. Without this we can't eat or work or walk or breathe or stir hand or feet. God must uphold man in being and not only so but 'tis God that upholds the life and upholds the power of action" (ibid.). As Ames puts it, the creation is not only dependent upon God for "its *fieri* . . . but also its *esse, existere, permanere & operari*," such that if he were to cease sustaining the creature's being, existence, continuance, and operation, the world would return to nonbeing (William Ames, *Marrow of Sacred Divinity Drawne Out of the Holy Scriptures, and the Interpreters thereof, and Brought into Method* [London: Henry Overton, 1642], ch. 9, 48).

249. "Though grace ben't in the saints as a mere natural principle, but as a sovereign agent, and so its exercises are not tied to means by an immutable law of nature, as in mere natural principles; yet God has so constituted that grace should dwell so in the hearts of the saints, that its exercises should have some degree of connection with means, after the manner of a principle of nature" (Edwards, "Some Thoughts Concerning the Revival," in *WJE* 4:454).

250. Ibid.

251. So, Cooey's suggestion that "for Edwards every human being is potentially an incarnation of the Holy Spirit" is not totally unfounded (Paula Cooey, *Jonathan Edwards on Nature and Destiny* [Lewiston, NY: Edwin Mellen, 1985], 99).

252. Edwards, *WJE* 7:444.

253. "[Christ] don't only live without [the soul], so as violently to actuate it; but he lives in it; so that that also is alive" (Edwards, *WJE* 2:342).

254. That God is the "author of sin" does not mean that he is "the sinner, the agent, or actor of sin, or the doer of a wicked thing." It means "the permitter, or not a hinderer of sin; and at the same time, a disposer of the state of events, in such a manner, for wise, holy and most excellent ends and purposes, that sin, if it be permitted or not hindered, will most certainly and infallibly follow" (Edwards, *WJE* 1:311).

255. It is not that "God [does] some and we do the rest, but God does all and we do all" (Edwards, "Efficacious Grace, Book III," in *WJE* 21:251).

256. Ibid. Passivity or receptivity is not a bad thing in itself; so Mascall reminds us that there is a vast distinction between "passive capacity and a positive repugnance" (Mascall, *Christ, the Christian and the Church*, 50).

257. Edwards, "Efficacious Grace, Book III," in *WJE* 21:251.

258. "There are in the soul two different powers or activities. The first is properly only the action of God . . . [who] continually creates the soul with the invincible desire to be happy, or continually moves it toward the good in general. But the second . . . which is the essence of freedom, . . . consists in a true power, not to produce, by its own efficacy, new modifications in itself, that is, new interesting perceptions or new movements in the will, but . . . a true power of the soul to suspend or to give its consent to the movements that follow naturally upon interesting perceptions." See Nicolas Malebranche, *Oeuvres complètes de Malebranche*, ed. André Robinet (Paris: Vrin, 1958–84), 16:46–47.

259. Italics original. Edwards, *WJE* 1:348.

260. "God is the only proper author or fountain; we only are the proper actors" (Edwards, "Efficacious Grace, Book III," in *WJE* 21:251).

261. "As the phrase, 'being the author,' may be understood, not of being the producer by an antecedent act of will; but as a person may be said to be the author of the act of will itself, by his being the immediate agent, or the being that is acting, or in exercise in that act; if the phrase of 'being the author,' is used to signify this, then doubtless common sense requires men's being the authors of their own acts of will, in order to their being esteemed worthy of praise or disparise on account of them" (Edwards, *WJE* 1:342)

262. As Stephen A. Wilson has recently argued, Edwards's affirmation of secondary causes within an Aristotelian virtue ethics lies within the ambit of the Protestant scholasticism he inherited together with an allegedly consistent and strong occasionalism (Stephen A. Wilson, *Virtue Reformed: Rereading Jonathan Edwards's Ethics*, Brill Studies in Intellectual History 132 [Leiden: Brill, 2005], 174–89). Secondary causes are, after all, not incompatible with *creatio continua*, as evidenced in Aquinas's concurrentism.

263. This corresponds to the Eastern theology of grace, which emphasizes eschatology and the divine *oikonomia*, in contrast to the West's tendency to regard grace in terms of the individual human response to God. See Gerald O'Collins and Mario Farrugia, *Catholicism: The Story of Catholic Christianity* (Oxford: Oxford University Press, 2003), 203.

264. That the Thomistic and Palamite options are the only two conceptual schemas available in the Christian tradition seems to be suggested by Duncan Reid, in what he characterizes as the Latin "identity principle" and the doctrine of energies of the Eastern church (Duncan Reid, *Energies of the Spirit: Trinitarian Models in Eastern Orthodox and Western Theology* [Atlanta, GA: Scholars Press, 1997], passim).

265. More accurately, humano-divine or materially theandric, as distinct from the divine action of the Word through his assumed humanity, which is formally theandric. These distinctions are taken from John Chapman, "Monothelitism and Monothelites," in *The Catholic Encyclopedia*, vol. 10 (New York: Robert Appleton Company, 1911); available at <http://www.newadvent.org/cathen/10502a.htm>.

8

Conclusion of Salvation
Participation in God as the End without an End

In the order of time, Edwards acknowledges that grace precedes glory.[1] Although human friendship or communion is "one of the highest sorts of pleasures," Edwards regards our eternal happiness or glorification, in enjoying and loving God, as infinitely greater.[2] But more than that, sanctification is assimilation to God in the highest.[3] This is because conformity to God *is* union with God.[4] For to be like God is more excellent than to merely enjoy God, since union is greater than mere relation. "Sanctification," when regarded as distinct from glorification, "is as great, yea, a greater favor done to the creature, than glorification."[5] If, however, it is seen as an aspect of glorification, "Man's highest happiness consists in holiness."[6] Glorification, in the broader sense, includes both conformity and communion.[7] The love and yearning of the regenerate is for holiness—this is the unceasing business of heaven.[8]

Eschatological Participation in God as Everlasting Expansion and Progress

Eschatological perfection, according to Edwards, is not a static concept since there is such a thing as "degrees of perfect happiness."[9] Like Aquinas, Edwards thinks that the growth of grace is unlimited because human capacity is increased with the influx of grace.[10] However, Edwards believes that progress and hope does not cease in the *Eschaton*, for "the state of perfection . . . is a growing state."[11] The glorification of the saints is an eternally dynamic state whereby the saints' participation in the knowledge, love, and joy of God is ever increasing; as such, the "happiness of heaven is progressive."[12] Human beings, as we have seen, are essentially mutable, and this dynamism is unlimited.[13] From the perspective of the creature, the creation does not terminate in static perfection but in everlasting progress in heaven: the end of creation is, so to speak, an end without an end.[14]

From the infinite perspective of God, whose omniscience is both comprehensive and nonsuccessive, being "vitae interminabilis, tota, simul, et perfecta possessio," the divine goodness in God and in us is one.[15] For Edwards, the glorification or happiness of the creature, which consists in "the perception and possession of excellency," is never deficient in relation to its source, medium, and stability.[16] According to Edwards, from the perspective of "the whole of the creature's eternal duration, with all the infinity of its progress . . . the creature must be looked upon as united to God in an infinite strictness."[17] Though Edwards pushes the logic of human participation in God through the doctrine of eternal progression to its logical limits, he nonetheless retains the Creator-creature distinction not by an unbridgeable chasm but "a genuine distance."[18] He does so by affirming a temporal gap whereby "there will never be any particular time when it [our union with God] can be said already to have come to such a height."[19] God is absolutely infinite—that is, infinite in an infinity of modes—whereas sanctification makes a human person only relatively infinite, infinite in one dimension—temporally.[20] And such a relative infinity is never reached because of an infinitely receding horizon. Moreover, it is a relative infinity only in its futurity, as creaturely time has a starting point.

It is only Christ, who is not only the true image of the self-communicative, creative Father but is also the perfect human, who possesses the love of God without measure.[21] The filial spirit in Christians, then, is both attitudinal and conditional, as they are in "a state of imperfection" or "a growing state" that continually desires for God and further increases in holiness.[22] Thus, the happiness of the saints—which is desire for God and holiness—both on earth and in heaven is at once immediately satisfying yet never ultimately satisfied. While Edwards does not have a corresponding apophaticism, as in Gregory's vision, he speaks with a certain eschatological reserve regarding human *glorificatio*: "We therefore may be without doubt, that man shall be exceeding happy beyond conception."[23]

What else does Edwards say regarding the character of this final beatitude of the human person? Is it a static, intellectual vision or contemplation of the divine Being? Not so, for in his construal, the beatific end of the church is a perfect contemplation that comprehends a perfect action: "The most perfect rest is consistent with being continually employed."[24] Human persons become, like the Spirit of God, action itself as they are full of divine love. "Now the hearts of the saints in heaven are all, as it were, a pure flame of love."[25] This is to be like God, who is an eternal object of reception and pure act (*actus purus*).[26] The saints, therefore, are not just passive participants in God's glory and goodness, for heaven is the preeminent place where contemplation (emanation) and action (remanation) occurs. "They do not merely enjoy God passively, but in an active manner. They are not only acted upon by God, but they mutually act towards him, and in this action and re-action consists the heavenly happiness."[27]

DIVINE SELF-ENLARGEMENT IN HUMAN GLORIFICATION

With Edwards's doctrine of the everlasting progress of the saints, the *tantum-quantum* formula is enabled in the eschatological enlargement of the saints' capacity to receive and return the glory of God.[28] Insofar as the church comes to participate in the divine life, Edwards thinks that God "as it were enlarges himself in a more excellent and divine manner."[29] On the one hand, the mode by which the saints will know and love God remains finite ontologically and temporally; on the other, the human capacities will be able to enjoy God in infinite duration.[30] For God's glory is infinite, the saints' power to perceive it is perfect "as far as their capacity allows," and their "possession" of it is eternal.[31]

Our capacity for eternal and progressive glorification is based on Christ's human nature as its prototype: "The man Christ Jesus became immortal and eternal at his resurrection, but yet that was no impediment in the way of his being as it were further glorified, as it were in infinitely higher degrees, as in his first and second ascension."[32] Through the redemptive work of the Son, the true image of God, and in union with Christ, we participate in the divine nature by the Spirit, the love of God. The negative aspect of glorification—mortification—will increase in this life with the presence of sin; in heaven, though sin will be no more, the saints' glory will increase in everlasting duration as their capacities enlarge with the reception of more life, happiness, and knowledge in the Spirit.[33] Thus, the church regains the image of the Father's self-expansive ontology as God redeems the "selfish spirit" of fallen humanity: "And so Christianity restores an excellent enlargement, and extensiveness, and liberality to the soul, and again possesses it with that divine love or charity that we read of in the text, whereby it again embraces its fellow creatures, and is devoted to and swallowed up in the Creator."[34]

Originally, "the soul of every man craves a happiness that is equal to the capacity of his nature."[35] Since the intellect is an "exceeding extensive faculty," the soul's desire for happiness must be proportional to the expansion of its understanding.[36] While God operates in accordance with a thing's mode and not against it, this "does not hinder God from doing what nature cannot do."[37] Though our capacity for understanding and love is limited, as is our nature, "man is of such a nature that he is capable of an exceeding great degree of happiness."[38] The human desire for happiness is increased in accord with a craving for knowledge, which is not only natively dynamic but also potentially spacious:[39]

> 'Tis more especially by reason of that faculty of understanding that the soul is capable of so great a happiness and craves so much. The understanding is an exceeding extensive faculty. It will extend itself beyond the limits of earth, yea beyond the limits of the creation. We are capable of understanding immensely more than we do understand. Who can tell how far the understanding of man is capable of stretching itself; and as the understanding enlarges, the desire will enlarge with it.[40]

Echoing Augustine, this profound restlessness of the soul can only be satisfied by that which is an infinitely beautiful object. "Every creature is restless till it enjoys what come up to the capacity of its nature. . . . It must therefore be an incomprehensible object that must satisfy the soul."[41] And it only in Jesus Christ that such human longing is met:

> But Christ Jesus has true excellency and so great excellency that when they come to see it they look no further, but the mind rests there. It sees a transcendent glory and an ineffable sweetness in him. It sees that till now it has been pursuing shadows, but that now it has found the substance that before it had been seeking happiness in the streams, but that now it has found the fountain; has found the ocean. The excellency of Christ is an object adequate to the natural cravings of the soul and enough to fill the capacity. It is an infinite excellency: such an one as the mind desires in which it can find no bounds and the more the mind is used to it the more excellent it appears. Every new discovery this beauty appears more and ravishing and the mind sees no end. Here is room enough for the mind to dive deeper and deeper and never come to the bottom.[42]

While the saints will enjoy the fullness of divine love and knowledge in heaven, this future state will be one of progressive perfection, as the experiential capacity of the human spirit will increase in an eternal duration before God, that infinite fountain of knowledge, holiness, and joy, through the God-man.[43]

GOD GLORIFIED IN HEAVEN AND HELL

Where is this eternal progress located? This *epektasis* of the saints takes place within an external, created heaven of "eternal duration," while the uncreated Trinity *ad intra*, at its deepest level, occupies a "metaphorical" heaven that is immutable and infinite.[44] In heaven, the Father and the Son will grant "more abundant manifestations of [their] glory," which is none other than an even greater communication of their Spirit.[45] This glory may be regarded as a common *vinculum* shared by the Father, the Son, and the saints.[46] If all creation, as we have seen, is located in the perichoretic "space" in God, how do the elect and reprobate differ in terms of divine participation?

Clearly, the damned continue to possess the natural image of God but not the spiritual. This means that they exist in God but that God, by the Son and Spirit, does not indwell them.[47] The "final disposal of mankind" will have a twofold end in order for God "to glorify himself in their eternal state."[48] Just as the saints' eternal beatitude must be communicated without end in order to "satisfy [God's] infinite grace and benevolence," so infinite punishment of the damned meets God's "satisfying justice" in a similar manner.[49] The glorification of the saints not only includes the *visio beatifica*, but also a *visio damnata*.[50] God remains the *mysterium tremendum et fascinans* in the saints' perception of the "lovely" as well as "awful" attributes of the divine.[51]

In the end, Edwards's robust and vivid double predestinarianism seems to introduce a kind of tension, if not conflict, into God's very being, since wrath and hell are merely the shadow side of love and heaven, both of which fall under the umbrella of God's glory.[52] The "eternal flame" of hell and the "eternal light" of heaven are two modes of God's singular glory: the one, "the glory of his anger" toward the damned, the other, "the glory of his grace" toward the saints.[53] God's eschatological glory of beatitude and punishment will be manifested through the "glorified humanity of Christ," and both the wicked and the saints will perceive this "external light" in its duality through transformed "bodies and organs of senses."[54] Eternal suffering and joy are thus experienced bodily.

HUMAN PARTICIPATION IN GOD AS A CORPOREAL REALITY

Edwards's emphasis on the aesthetic is clear when he affirms that "the sense of seeing," and not hearing, as one would suppose, "is the noblest of all external senses."[55] In his view, the goal of the incarnation is that Christians, in their *whole* persons, might enjoy this heavenly vision: "This end is obtained by Christ's incarnation, viz. that the saints may see God with their bodily eyes as well as by an intellectual view. They may see him in both ways of seeing which is their natures, being body and spirit, are capable of; they may see him as they see one another, which shall not only be spiritually but outwardly."[56] In heaven, the elect shall behold more clearly Christ's visible and external, human glory as well as spiritual, divine glory.[57] As such, this divine light or wisdom, "most excellent" and pleasurable, is the sole cause of *every* Christian's ontological transformation into Christlikeness and every Christian's moral-ethical life; it is not the reward of the select few.[58] God the Father is the source of the *lumen gloriae* "which will be given [to] the souls of the glorified saints."[59] Yet, together with the spiritual apprehension of the light of glory is a physical apprehension through Jesus Christ.

> And besides these there will doubtless after the resurrection be a light of glory to be seen with bodily eyes which probably will be the light that shines forth from Christ's glorious body. A visible glory, exceeding that which appeared in his body and countenance at his transfiguration, and the bodies of the saints also, will then probably shine with a glorious brightness, but only with a derived and communicated light, so that God is still the Father of lights.[60]

The saints in heaven have an immediate sight of Christ whereas the regenerate on earth see the glory of God "by a medium, by an intervening looking glass."[61] These "intermediations" or "mirrors" of God's glory include "Christ's ministers, and the gospel which they preach, and his ordinances which they administer."[62] However, our mediated knowledge of God excels that glory of God perceived "under the law" or in Old Testament times, as in Moses' face, where the "reflected glory of God" was then veiled.[63]

The saints do not participate "with Christ . . . of the life that he lived before his death" but rather "in his resurrection life."[64] This is identical to participation in Christ's purchased Spirit.[65] This personal glorification of the saints is to be understood together with the notion of the *Christus totus*, for even now the "glorified saints in heaven . . . are in some sense the glorified body of Christ."[66] What kind of participation in Christ's resurrected body do the resurrected saints acquire?

They will longer be susceptible to mortality and corruption. Firstly, the saints "partake of the nature of the Son, which is an immortal nature."[67] Secondly, all bodies in the new creation, Edwards speculates, will be spiritualized or "changed into quite another kind of substance" and natural laws will be reconfigured so that "there shall be a great and inward universal transformation . . . in order to fix it in an incorruptible state."[68] Adam's body before the Fall was glorious and beautiful, no doubt due to the Spirit.[69] Just as Christ's body was glorified together with Christ's soul, so "the bodies of the saints shall be glorified as well as their souls."[70] And if the mystical body of Christ is glorified, the external heavens, as the garment and temple of Christ, shall also be renewed.[71]

As such, Edwards eschatological vision of heaven is that of "a world of love" where believers, participants by grace in the "glorious society" of the Trinity, contemplate and enjoy the beatific vision of God: "The God, who dwells and gloriously manifests himself there, is infinitely lovely. There is to be seen a glorious heavenly Father, a glorious Redeemer; there is to be felt and possessed a glorious Sanctifier. All the persons who belong to that blessed society are lovely. The Father of the family is so, and so are all his children. The Head of the body is so, and so are all the members."[72]

Such a glorious end of redemption far exceeds any "natural" end of creation: "Hence we may learn something how vastly greater the glory and happiness the elect are brought by Christ than that which was lost by the fall, or even than that which man would [have] attained to if he had not fallen."[73] The resurrection of the saints, the glorification of their bodies, and their ascension into heaven, reign, and union with God is, from one perspective, personal, since Christ is already the exemplar or "forerunner" in the first resurrection, glorification, ascension, reign, and enjoyment of God.[74] "None ever ascended to heaven but mystical Christ, and there is no way of any others' ascending to heaven but by being members of him."[75]

EMANATION AND REMANATION: THE SAINTS' DESCENT AND ASCENT IN CHRIST

The Trinitarian *emanation-remanation* theme is echoed by a christological *descent-ascent* motif.[76] "Christ has so descended for that very End that we might ascend."[77] Edwards characterizes the "natural" lightness of the divine nature, which descended in the *exininatio* and in so doing raised the sinking human nature in his *exaltatio*.[78] For him, the crucial consideration was that Christ's humanity has spatially ascended to heaven in the *status exaltationis*, though he was content to affirm a metaphorical descent of the Logos in *status exinationis*.[79] God descends in the incarnation, in our regeneration, and in the Parousia; we ascend at Christ's ascension, our biological death, and final resurrection.

First, he came into this world and brought God or divinity down with him to us; and then he ascended to God and carried up humanity or man with him to God. He brings God to dwell with their souls on earth in their conversion, and he brings their souls to dwell with God in heaven at their death. The time will come when he will come down again from heaven in person, and will bring God with him and to man a second time, and will a second time ascend to carry up man with him.[80]

In Christ's first coming, the descent is metaphorical as it refers to the divine nature alone.[81] This is unlike the second coming, which is the literal descent of the Word incarnate with a glorified human nature.[82] For, at the Parousia, Christ's "human nature . . . with his glorified body shall come down from heaven," unlike the incarnation, where "his human nature never had been in heaven . . . but then began to have its being."[83]

In the manner of Christ's "first ascension," we shall ascend in Christ as "his glorified and complete mystical body" and with "his natural body" in the *Eschaton*.[84] Just as Christ first ascended with "our nature" after the resurrection, so Christ will ascend again with "our persons" in the general resurrection.[85] Thus, through the incarnation, "Christ brings God and man to each other, and actually unites them together. This he does by various steps and degrees, which terminate in the highest step, in the consummation of actual union, which he will accomplish at the end of the world."[86]

Yet human *exaltatio* is always *in Christo*, and, as such, kenosis is inseparably implied in *thēosis*:

And though the saints are exalted to glorious dignity, even to union and fellowship with God him[self], to be in some respects divine in glory and happiness, and in many respects to be exalted above the angels, yet care is taken that it should not be in themselves, but in a person that is God; and they must be as it were emptied of themselves in order to it.[87]

The kenosis is not spiritually expressed in terms of asceticism but rather as a way to show God's glory and sovereignty.[88] Humility is, therefore, a mark of the movement of emanation and remanation in the life of a Christian—a child of God.

HUMAN PARTICIPATION IN THE INCARNATE SON: ITS FILIAL CHARACTER

The filial spirit implies a posture of humility before God, as Christians gain a self-understanding of their limited love, gratitude, and knowledge of the

Father.[89] Humility, as an absolute distinction between God and humanity, includes the corollary concept of a relative humility before others, as " a little child is modest before men."[90] This also begets a tender heart, as that of a child who approaches the Father in holy reverence.[91] The child of God will have the lamblike, dovelike disposition of the Son of God—the character of "love, meekness, quietness, forgiveness and mercy"—by the indwelling of the Spirit of Christ.[92]

Christians' filial relation to God is a corollary of their union with Christ: "For being members of God's own natural Son, they are sort of partakers of his relation to the Father."[93] This disposes the saint to have true gratitude to God, which arises from a prior disinterested love that has its foundation in the very nature of the Father, primarily in moral perfection.[94] This love of the Father cannot be separated from our knowledge of the divine, for the "child of God is graciously affected, because he sees and understands something more of divine things than he did before."[95] This love of God, as Edwards points out, is a category that includes love of others.[96] Union with Christ brings about a communion between angels and human beings.[97]

It is a permanent inclusion in the family of God as believers have been "made nigh by the blood of Christ, and that were no more strangers and foreigners, but fellow citizens with the saints, and of the household of God."[98] In this eschatological "household of God," the church becomes "the spouse" of the natural Son of the Father.[99] "The church is the daughter of God, not only as he hath begotten her by his word and spirit, but as she is the spouse of his eternal Son. So we being members of the Son, are partakers in our measure, of the Father's love to the Son, and complacence in him."[100] The saints have a "higher manner" of filiation than through regeneration and an adoptive parent-child relationship, "for being members of God's own natural Son, they are partakers of his relation to the Father, or of his sonship."[101] That personal communication of the Spirit of adoption to the saints enables their participation, in measure, in the Son's ontological filiation to the Father: "they are not only sons of God by regeneration, but by a kind of communion in the sonship of the eternal Son."[102] This leads to a spiritual and rational conviction of the gospel, which is the revelation of the eternal sonship of Jesus Christ. In Edwards's understanding, the gospel as mediated through the written word of God is fundamentally christocentric.[103] Thus faith in believers involves a spiritual sight of the person (as the Son of God), the work of Christ (as the Savior of the world), and the revelation of the Father.[104]

In the believers' union with Christ, they not only enjoy the love of God the Father as adopted children through rebirth in the Spirit, but they also become inexplicably related to God "in a higher manner," as they are "partakers in [their] measure, of the Father's love to the Son, and complacence in him."[105] Divine love, given to the church, has its source in God's love of the Son and the members of Christ's body: "When Christ says to his Father (John 17:26) that he would declare his name to his disciples, 'that the love wherewith thou hast loved me may be in them,' I can understand nothing else by [it] but that the Holy Spirit might be in them and dwell in them, which *is the love of the Father to the Son*."[106]

The Spirit is the *vinculum* who unites the Father, the Son, and "the daughter of God"—"They all have communion in the same spirit, the Holy Ghost."[107] The Father's infinite, immanent, and eternal love of joy and love toward the Son—the Spirit himself—is purchased by Christ from the Father in the work of redemption in order that this gift may be conveyed to the saints.[108] The saints' conformity to the Son is universal because they have the "whole image of Christ"; "there is every grace in them, which is in Christ."[109] The Holy Spirit, as the "spirit of adoption" or "spirit of love" in the saint, grants him the sense that "he stands in a childlike relation to God" so that he "as it were, naturally and necessarily cry, 'Abba, Father.'"[110] This spiritual understanding consists in the leading of the Spirit of God, "a distinguishing mark of the sons of God."[111] This participation in the Son's relation to the Father is to be partakers of the Spirit or divine nature, which is included in God's life of communion.

"PARTAKERS IN THE DIVINE NATURE" AS INCLUSION INTO THE TRINITARIAN KOINONIA

The incarnation satisfies two "natural inclinations" within the human person as *homo adorans* and *homo philia*: worship and friendship.[112] Christ becomes our object of adoration in the divine nature and an object of friendship in the human nature; the Spirit as the holy principle enhances these two natural desires.[113] The purpose of the incarnation was that the Father, Son, and saints may become "as it were one society, one family."[114] It not only reverses the Fall but enhances the communion between uncreated and created being, angels included.[115] The Puritan stress on a communal, corporeal paradise is implicit in Edwards's idea of a relational Trinity:

> God must have perfect exercise of his goodness, and therefore must
> have the fellowship of a person equal to himself. . . . No reasonable
> creature can be happy, we find, without society and communion, not
> only because he finds something in others that is not in himself, but
> because he delights to communicate himself to another. . . . So that

we may conclude, that Jehovah's happiness consists in communion, as well as the creature's.[116]

According to Edwards, the saints are "in a sort admitted into that society of the three persons in the Godhead"; this participation is construed not within the social, tripersonal imagery, but as a familial, bipersonal analogy.[117] Of course, the divine persons of the Trinity are not multiplied, but remain three.[118] The "divine society" remains triune and does not increase numerically, as the saints are included as members of the Son, not as though the historical Christ were imperfect but rather "to render him complete in his station."[119]

Edwards's eschatological vision includes the saints' participation in that eternal, affective relationality among the persons of the Trinity, made possible through the mediation of Christ: "Christ has brought it to pass, that those that the Father has given him, should be brought into the household of God; that he, and his Father, and his people, should be as it were one society, one family; that the church should be as it were admitted into the society of the blessed Trinity."[120] In the end, for Edwards, God will be all in all and we will be in God.[121]

> The emanation or communication of the divine fullness, consisting in the knowledge of God, love to God, and joy in God, has relation indeed both to God and the creature: but it has relation to God as its fountain, as it is an emanation from God; and as the communication itself, or thing communicated, is something divine, something of God, something of his internal fullness. . . . In the creature's knowing, esteeming, loving, rejoicing in, and praising God, the glory of God is both exhibited and acknowledged; his fullness is received and returned. Here is both an emanation and remanation. . . . So that the whole is of God, and in God, and to God; and God is the beginning, middle and end in this affair.[122]

Concluding Summary

In chapter 1, we looked at Edwards's conception of the perpetual self-communication of essence within God, by which the persons of the Son and Spirit proceed from the Father as their primal source. At the heart of this is his appropriation of Augustine's mutual-love model of the Trinity, which is parsed in psychological terms. God the Father—in one eternal act—produces the Son by self-ideation and their Holy Spirit through self-love. Edwards interprets the *filioque* as an ontological *per filium* and subsumes it within the framework of a mutual-love model. This is the eternal ground for the emanation and remanation of the Spirit in God. And as the modes of generation and spiration in God are simultaneous, the Word is never excluded from the *exitus-reditus* of the Spirit.

This eternal movement of procession and return is mirrored in the Trinitarian operations *ad extra*, which we have investigated in chapter 2. The œconomical Trinity is the mutual agreement by the divine persons to order their external actions with the goal of self-communication *ad extra*. The creation of the world is an analogical procession of creatures from God, by which human beings image the Trinity in their psychological structure. The ex nihilo, for Edwards, is a contingent moment by moment coming-forth of creature distinct from but comprehended by the infinite perichoretic spaciousness of God. The end of human beings or the church is to be receptors of a real self-communication of divine knowledge and love—the Son and Spirit. The entrance of sin, however, inaugurated the covenant of redemption.

As we note in chapter 3, Edwards uses the mutual-love Trinitarian analogy to highlight the communion of will of the Father and Son to redeem human beings, although he does not neglect the active role of the Spirit. This *pactum salutis* is actualized in the incarnation of the Son. In the communication of a new mode of existence to the Son, the entire Trinity is mutually involved. The Father acts as the primary agent through the immediate agency of the divine Spirit in all objective acts upon the Son. The Son as incarnate acts subjectively through the Son's own Spirit.

In chapter 4, we examined the participation of the assumed human nature in the divine Word. Edwards develops a Spirit Christology on the base of an Alexandrian Logos Christology, in both ontological and operational terms. This is evident in his appropriation of the *enhypostasis-anhypostasis* dialectic and the human nature as the *organon* of the Word. In all of this, Edwards affirms that the divine Logos, by the divine Spirit, has appropriated and ennobled a full individual human nature in the *unitio personalis*. By the mediation of this very same Spirit, the Logos continues to sustain and operate theadrically through the human nature in the *unio personalis*, which may be considered a perpetual *unitio personalis*. An Antiochene undercurrent seems to stand in variance with his Alexandrianism. But, as we have seen, the apparent "separation" of the divine Word from the assumed human nature is entirely consistent with Edwards's overall pneumatology, by which the Spirit operates causally and immediately on earth both as God's omnipresence and in the incarnation. This Augustinian-Calvinist interpretation of a Spirit who bridges distances, in fact, allows

Edwards to affirm a modified *communio naturarum* (of the divine nature of the Spirit and the human nature of the Logos) and the *extra carnem*.

In chapter 5, we investigated the doctrine of the *communicatio idiomatum* in Edwards's Christology. Edwards's christological ontology, shorn of a *communio naturarum*, will not allow a Lutheran *genus maiestaticum*. Yet, if deification is parsed as a theandric act, then Edwards's construal of the Spirit as *actus purus* and the instrumentalization of Christ's human nature is certainly consonant with *thēosis* understood as a communication of divine energies in Christ. Thus, the incarnate Son exercises divine power by the Holy Spirit, through and with the Son's own human nature. Hence, this Spirit-mediated Christology opens the way to an exercise of the divine attributes through the human nature. No divine powers or properties are transferred to the human nature via a *communio naturarum* and *genus maiestaticum*; it is thus *finitum non capax infinitum*. Yet, since the infinite Spirit is present in the assumed nature to mediate the exercise of the divine powers, the human Jesus is *capax infinitum*.

However, Edwards's impassibilism precludes any kenoticism, whether ontological or functional. His Antiochene leaning is therefore a crucial component in securing a two-minds Christology. In this way, the human mind of Christ has a cognitive recollection and access to the divine mind, and thus has a unity of self-consciousness in two modes. But the Holy Spirit, as a personal *vinculum* and *vehiculum* between the natures, not only enables but also restricts the commerce of operations between Christ's natures. As such, the Father's silence toward Jesus on the cross is brought about by the Spirit's restraint of God's comforting but not sanctifying presence (which would jeopardize the *unio personalis* itself). On this account, though, a polarity is introduced between the eternal *beatifica* of the divine Logos and Jesus' human cognition, but interrupted experience, of such joy in the passion.

We looked at Edwards's understanding of the *unio cum Christo*, which encompasses a causal and rational *ordo salutis*, in chapter 6. Basic to his schema is an emphasis on the regeneration-conversion couplet as closing the *unitio mystica*—the real union of hearts between Christ and the believer. From this, the benefits of adoption, justification, and sanctification are had from a threefold participation in Christ's person—relatively, legally, and vitally. There is a natural fitness in God's recognition of a correlation between the real union and relative/legal unions, or love/faith and adoption/justification. Morever, there is a rational ordering of adoption to justification. From this regard, justification follows. Works before justification have no moral value, but they are ennobled through the *unio mystica* by virtue of union with Christ's person. Faith and works are crucial in the eschatological, second justification whereby God declares that the intrinsic sanctity of the Christian proves God's initial but perfect imputation of Christ's righteousness. Participation in Christ's perfect righteousness is through imputation and not through organic transference as it is with sanctification.

Finally, in chapter 7, our investigation highlighted Edwards's rejection of the idea of grace as a created entity superadded to the soul at regeneration. Rather, grace is uncreated, habitual grace restored to the saint. Divine communication is the indwelling Holy Spirit operating in and through the human being, who accommodates divine actions to suit intrinsic human limitations. Human participation in the divine "nature" is, for Edwards, the reception of a new supernatural disposition acting through (essentially) unchanged but dynamic human capacities. Divine condescension or accommodation is the counterpart of human glorification within the limitation principle. The Holy Spirit as pure act and beauty communicates the divine acts and form to the believer; the Spirit is thus the efficient, quasi-formal, and final cause of the believer's sanctification. This conjunction of operations in sanctification does not abrogate human freedom because the Spirit does not replace or overwhelm human action but is the source of the saint's holy acts. In this sense, human sanctity is theandric.

This process of sanctification, as we examined briefly at the start of this chapter, is everlasting. While sanctification is a greater privilege than communion with God, they both constitute humankind's glorification. Sanctification is a participation in Christ's bodily resurrection and includes a corporeal assimilation to Christ and a bodily (as well as intellectual) *visio Dei* through Christ. Participation in the incarnate Son is finally entrance into fellowship with and assimilation to the triune God.

WHAT ABOUT THE GRAMMAR OF THĒOSIS IN EDWARDS'S CORPUS?

The Christian doctrine of human participation in God has been expressed through the patristic and Byzantine tradition in terms of deification, or *thēosis*.[123] Although Edwards's doctrine of participation in God is not to be equated with *thēosis* but represents his own unique soteriological vision built upon Reformed-Puritan sources, it has material similarities to this venerable patristic construal of salvation. While Edwards makes no distinction between an essential and energetic procession of the divine persons *ad intra*, his effort to draw a line between the communication of the divine nature and the essence of the Spirit *ad extra* approximates the *hyperousia-energeia* distinction in Orthodoxy. And his language overlaps with theirs as well.

As an example, Edwards echoes the Irenaean *recapitulatio* in saying that Christ "acted Adam's part all over again," and he calls this "a great doctrine of Christianity."[124] Our final enjoyment of God through Christ will certainly excel what we otherwise would have experienced had Adam not sinned.[125] Thus the salvation of humanity is not merely a restoration of the creation but also its exaltation "to a state of excellency and glory vastly greater than their original excellency."[126] That is, mere "happiness of men" in Adam has become, in Christ, participation in "a sort of the very happiness of God himself."[127] In this, the divine wisdom is apparent in "how God hath confounded Satan, in actually fulfilling that which was a lie in him, wherewith he deluded poor man and procured his fall, viz. that they should be as gods."[128] Not only that, this happy fault (*felix culpa*) has resulted in a sort of *thēosis*: "Little did the devil think of any such thing as this being the consequence of man's fall when he said, 'Ye shall be as gods.'"[129]

Sanctification for Edwards is not identical to the Orthodox teaching on *thēosis*.[130] Nonetheless, sanctification as glorification is, to be sure, human participation in God enabled by God's very own self-communication. Edwards can thus describe this reality as "the glory of divine grace, God's own image, and that which is infinitely God's most excellent, gracious and glorious gift, and man's highest honor, excellency and happiness, whereby he is partaker of the divine nature and becomes a godlike creature . . . [and is] so high an endowment . . . by which man becomes like God."[131]

Notes

1. "Man's chief end is to enjoy God for ever; before this plenary fruition of God in heaven, there must be something previous and antecedent, and that is, our being in a state of grace: We must have conformity to him in grace, before we can have communion with him in glory. Grace and glory are *inter se connexae*, link'd and chain'd together; grace precedes glory, as the morning-star ushers in the sun" (Watson, "Man's Chief End to Glorifie God," in *A body of practical divinity .. .* [London: Thomas Parkhurst, 1692], q.1, 10).
2. Edwards, "God's Excellencies," *WJE* 10:428–29.
3. "Holiness is the very beauty and loveliness of Jehovah himself. 'Tis the excellency of his excellencies, the beauty of his beauties, the perfection of his infinite perfections, and the glory of his attributes" (Edwards, "God is Infinitely Exalted in Gloriousness and Excellency Above All Created Beings," in *WJE* 10:430).
4. "One part of that divine fullness which is communicated, is the divine knowledge. . . . This knowledge in the creature is but a conformity to God" (Edwards, "Concerning the End," in *WJE* 8:442). And so it is with God's holiness and happiness.

5. The *imago* is greater than the *fructio*, since "the creature is more honored by being made like unto God in holiness, than in happiness; the image and likeness of God upon the creature exalts it and honors it more, than the fruition of him" (Edwards, "God is Infinitely Exalted in Gloriousness and Excellency Above All Created Beings," in *WJE* 10:430).

6. Edwards, "Charity and Its Fruits," sermon 2, in *WJE* 8:158.

7. Goodwin distinguished between the saints' happiness and communion with God, the latter being foundational. "Now of the two, communion with God is the greater. There is *beatitudo objectiva*, the thing possessed, which is God himself; and there is *beatitudo formalis*, which is the fruition of him; the happiness by enjoying God, and by knowing God" (Goodwin, "Sermon 20," in *The Works of Thomas Goodwin, D.D. Sometime President of Magdalene College, Oxford*, vol. 1, *Containing an Exposition of the First Chapter of the Epistle to the Ephesians* [Edinburgh: James Nichol, 1861], 297).

8. Edwards, *WJE* 2:97–103.

9. Edwards, "Miscellanies," no. 367, in *WJE* 13:438.

10. As *viator*, there is no limit to the acquisition of grace since its principle is infinite. Not only so, the capacity of the subject is potentially limitless "because whenever charity increases, there is a corresponding increased ability to receive a further increase" (Aquinas, *STh* II-II, q. 24, a. 7, 1274).

11. Edwards, "Miscellanies," no. 371, in *WJE* 13:443. "Their having of perfect happiness don't exclude all increase, nor does it exclude all hope; for we don't know but they will increase in happiness forever." On the contrary, for Aquinas, "infinite progress is repugnant." Only the *viator* can progress infinitely since "merit and progress belong to this present condition of life" (Aquinas, *STh* I, q. 62, a. 9).

12. Edwards, "Miscellanies," no. 777, in *WJE* 18:427–34.

13. "It seems to be quite a wrong notion of the happiness of heaven, that it is in that manner unchangeable, that it admits not of new joys upon new occasions" (Edwards, "Miscellanies," no. 372, in *WJE* 13:444).

14. Union with God is asymptotic: "Let the most perfect union with God be represented by something at an infinite height above us; and the eternally increasing union of the saints with God, by something that is ascending constantly towards that infinite height . . . to continue thus to move to all eternity . . . though the time will never come when it can be said it has already arrived at this infinite height" (Edwards, "Concerning the End," in *WJE* 8:534). Ramsey, while urging that Edwards's converging lines ought to be viewed in asymptotic terms, nonetheless concludes that this imagery is, "for all its vividness, still a gross one" (Ramsey, *WJE* 8:534n8). Gregory of Nyssa's notion of an eternal *epektasis* describes man's ascent to God as a progression of "constantly realized hope" in relation to God's inexhaustibility (Meyendorff, "Humanity: 'Old' and 'New'—Anthropological Considerations," in *Salvation in Christ: A Lutheran-Orthodox Dialogue*, ed. John Meyendorff and Robert Tobias [Minneapolis: Augsburg, 1992], 63).

15. What exists before the world is but "the eternity of God's existence . . . which is nothing else but his immediate, perfect and invariable possession of the whole of his unlimited life, together and at once" (Edwards, *WJE* 1:368; Edwards cites Andrew Baxter here). "If God has respect to something in the creature, which he views as of everlasting duration, . . . then he has respect to it as, in the whole, of infinite height" (Edwards, "Concerning the End," in *WJE* 8:534).

16. Edwards, "Miscellanies," no. 106, in *WJE* 13:276–77. There is an implicit trinitarianism here, as the Father is the perfect source of the divine glory, the Son our means of perception insofar as the Spirit becomes our permanent "possession."

17. Edwards, "Concerning the End," in *WJE* 8:534. Edwards continues further on, "But if strictness of union to God be viewed as thus infinitely exalted; then the creature must be regarded as infinitely, nearly and closely united to God" (8:535).

18. Hart states this beautifully with regard to Gregory of Nyssa, but the same could be said of Edwards: "the entire thrust of the theology of eternal progress is precisely to show how it is possible to speak intelligibly of deification, despite the ontological distance between God and

creation: by showing that it is not an uncrossable abyss but a genuine distance, reconciled and yet preserved in the incarnate Logos, crossed from the divine side so that it may be crossed forever from the side of the creature; and by showing that the God who is infinite, for this reason, cannot be made absent by any distance" (David Bentley Hart, *The Beauty of the Infinite: The Aesthetics of Christian Truth* [Grand Rapids, MI: Eerdmans, 2003], 199).

19. Edwards, "Concerning the End," in *WJE* 8:534.

20. One of Edwards's many conceptions of infinity is a mathematical infinity, which may be applied relatively to finite things. Hence, "mathematicians conceive of greater than infinite in some respects, and of several infinites being added one to another; but 'tis because they are in some respect finite: as a thing conceived infinitely long may not be infinitely thick, and so its thickness may be added to" (Edwards, "Miscellanies," no. 697, in *WJE* 18:282). In contrast, the divine infinity must be absolute or comprehensive since there cannot be two infinites. "Infinity and omneity, if I may so speak, must go together" (18:281). For an excellent summary and analysis of Edwards's notions of infinity, see Don Schweitzer, "Jonathan Edwards' Understanding of Divine Infinity," in *Jonathan Edwards as Contemporary: Essays in Honor of Sang Hyun Lee*, ed. Don Schweitzer (New York: Peter Lang, 2010), 49–65.

21. As "head of the moral world" and "the chief of God's servant," Jesus Christ is suitably the "chief and most perfect pattern and example of goodness," who desires after that which God desires in "the spirit of true respect and friendship to God." As such, Christ's (and the saints') ultimate desire is for the glory of God and the good of the creature, which is the participation of the creature in the life of God (Edwards, "Concerning the End," in *WJE* 8:474).

22. Edwards, *WJE* 2:377–83. Edwards insists that the saint's primary object of desire, consistent with the aim of his new spiritual sense, is "God and Christ . . . and holiness, for its own sake," and not merely for spiritual benefits or "any manifestation of God's love and favor" (Edwards, *WJE* 2:382–83).

23. Edwards, "Miscellanies," no. 106, in *WJE* 13:277. See esp. Vladimir Lossky, "Apophasis and Trinitarian Theology," in *Eastern Orthodox Theology: A Contemporary Reader*, ed. Daniel B. Clendenin (Grand Rapids, MI: Baker Academic, 2003), 149–62; Lossky, "The Divine Darkness," ch. 2 of *The Mystical Theology of the Eastern Church* (Crestwood, NY: St. Vladimir's Seminary Press, 1997), 23–43. Unlike the Eastern Orthodox tradition, Edwards does not have an apophatic theology, based on an unknowable divine super-essence (*hyperousia*), in delineating his divine ontology (God's transcendence and immanence) and epistemology (God's unknowability and knowability). Nonetheless, Edwards recognizes the limits of rationality and affirms the divine mysteries. See Edwards, "Discourse on the Trinity," in *WJE* 21:139–40. See also William J. Wainwright, "Jonathan Edwards and the Hiddenness of God," in *Divine Hiddenness: New Essays*, ed. Paul K. Moser and Daniel Howard-Snyder (Cambridge: Cambridge University Press, 2002), 98–119. For works on Edwards's broader epistemology, see Leon Chai, *Jonathan Edwards and the Limits of Enlightenment Philosophy* (New York: Oxford University Press, 1998). Stephen H. Daniel highlights Edwards's dependence on Ramist logic and uses poststructuralist discourse to illuminate his theology; see *The Philosophy of Jonathan Edwards: A Study in Divine Semiotics* (Bloomington: Indiana University Press, 1994).

24. Edwards, 344. Sermon on Rev. 14:2 (Nov 1734), in *WJE* 49.

25. Ibid. Similarly, "the angels are blessed spirits, and yet they are exceedingly active in serving God. They are as a flame of fire, which is the most active thing that we see in this world" (ibid.).

26. "God himself enjoys infinite happiness and perfect bliss, and yet he is not inactive, but is himself in his own nature a perfect act, and is continually at work in bringing to pass his own purposes and ends" (ibid.).

27. Ibid.

28. In Maximus's thought, the "reciprocity of natures between God and man," as Thunberg calls it, is effected christologically by the *tantum-quantum* formula, where the gracious deification of humanity is effected in proportion to the humanization of God in the incarnation. See Lars

Thuberg, *Man and the Cosmos: The Vision of St. Maximus the Confessor*, foreword by A.M. Allchin (Crestwood, NY: St. Vladimir's Seminary Press, 1985), 52ff. Russell calls it the "exchange formula," citing Ireneaus's axiom that the Son "became what we are in order to make us what he is himself" (Norman Russell, The *Doctrine of Deification in the Greek Patristic Tradition* [Oxford: Oxford University Press, 2004], 106).

29. Edwards, "Excellency of Christ," in *The Sermons of Jonathan Edwards: A Reader,* ed. Wilson H. Kimnach, Kenneth P. Minkema and Douglas A. Sweeney (New Haven: Yale University Press, 1999), 196; Edwards, "Concerning the End," in *WJE* 8:461. That God is eternally immutable yet temporally "enlarged" seems to be a perspectival notion for Edwards. In commenting on the human excellencies of Christ, Edwards notes that "these, indeed, are no proper addition to his divine excellencies. Christ has no more excellency in his person, since his incarnation, than he had before; for divine excellency is infinite, and can't be added to: yet his human excellencies are additional manifestations of his glory and excellency *to us*, and are additional recommendations of him to our esteem and love, *who are of finite comprehension*" (Edwards, "Excellency of Christ," in *Sermons*, 191–92; emphasis mine). But, as Lee has pointed out, the temporal "becoming" of God (and the world), in some sense, echoes the "becoming" that happens in the eternal, hypostatic differentiation within God. See Lee, *PTJE*, 189.

30. Edwards speaks of the enlargement of our capacities, like John Smith. "The *first* property and effect of true religion whereby it expresseth its own nobleness is this: *that it widens and enlarges all the faculties of the soul, and begets a true ingenuousness, liberty and amplitude, the most free and generous spirit, in the minds of good men*" (John Smith, *The Excellency and Nobleness of True Religion*, in *The Cambridge Platonists*, ed. Gerald R. Cragg [Lanham, MD: University Press of America, 1985], 102; italics in original).

31. Edwards, "Miscellanies," no. 106, in *WJE* 13:277.

32. Edwards, "Miscellanies," no. 952, in *WJE* 20:214.

33. Edwards, *WJE* 2:376–83.

34. As the Son is defined in relation to the Father as his image or idea, the church recognizes its significance as Christ in the world—the image of the Son (Daniel, *Philosophy of Jonathan Edwards*, 129). Edwards, "Lecture 8: The Spirit of Charity the Opposite of a Selfish Spirit," in *Charity and Its Fruits: Christian Love as Manifested in the Heart and Life* (London: Banner of Truth Trust, 1969), 158–59.

35. Edwards, 80. Sermon on Isa. 32:2 [n.d.], in *WJE* 43.

36. Ibid.

37. Aquinas, *STh* I–II, q. 51, a. 4, ad 2, 806. The opposite of the limitation axiom is that "an act that exists in nothing is limited by nothing (*actus igitur in nullo existens nullo terminatur*)" (Wippel, *Metaphysical Themes in Thomas Aquinas II* [Washington, DC: Catholic University of America Press, 2007], 131). Thus, God as *actus purus* is unlimited.

38. Edwards, 80. Sermon on Isa. 32:2, in *WJE* 43. In Thomistic terms, the obediential power of the human intellect and will are unlimited as to their capacity for the beatific vision. "The obediential power of our intellect is in itself unrestricted, because our intellect by God's absolute power, can always be raised to a higher degree of the light of glory, and our will to a higher degree of charity" (Reignald Garrigou-Lagrange, *Christ the Saviour: A Commentary on the Third Part of Saint Thomas' Theological* Summa, trans. Dom Bede Rose [St. Louis, MO: Herder, 1958], ch. 6, q. 4, a. 1).

39. The affection of desire, as Edwards defines it, is the exercise of the will toward that which is not present (Edwards, *WJE* 2:97).

40. Edwards, 80. Sermon on Isa. 32:2, in *WJE* 43. In this, Edwards echoes Aquinas and Aristotle that the human spirit can become all things—*quodammodo omnia* (Aquinas, *S.Th* I, q. 84, a.2, ad 2). If the human spirit, in particular, the intellect, has the ability to relate to the totality of being, then its capacity is unlimited. "The intellectual soul as comprehending universals, has a power extending to the infinite" (Aquinas *S.Th* I, q. 76, a. 5, ad 4).

41. Edwards, 80. Sermon on Isa. 32:2 [n.d.], in *WJE* 43.

42. Ibid.

43. Paul Ramsey, appendix 3, "Heaven is a Progressive State," in *WJE* 8:706–38.

44. That which is "unalterable is the state of God's own infinite and unchangeable glory . . . which may metaphorically be represented as heaven that was the eternal abode of the blessed Trinity, and of the happiness and glory they have one in another; and is an heaven that is uncreated" (Edwards, "Miscellanies," no. 952, in *WJE* 20:213).

45. Edwards, "Miscellanies," no. 371, in *WJE* 13:444.

46. Edwards, "Miscellanies," no. 376, in *WJE* 13:448. "'Tis our partaking of the Holy Ghost that we have communion with the Father and Son and with Christians . . . this is the bond of perfectness, by which they are one in the Father and the Son, as the Father is in the Son and the Son in the Father."

47. This point is noted by Oliver D. Crisp, "Jonathan Edwards' Panentheism," in *Jonathan Edwards as Contemporary: Essays in Honor of Sang Hyun Lee*, ed. Don Schweitzer (New York: Peter Lang, 2010), 119.

48. Edwards, "Miscellanies," no. 930, in *WJE* 20:175. *Heaven is a World of Love* and *Sinners at the Hands of an Angry God* typify the two polarities in Edwards's vision of humankind's telos, as is evident in the final paragraphs of the *End for which God Created the World*. As heaven is a world of love, so "hell is a world of hatred" (Edwards, "Heaven is a World of Love," in *WJE* 8:390).

49. Edwards, "Concerning the End," in *WJE* 8:536.

50. "So I believe the saints in heaven are made perfectly holy and impeccable by means, viz. by the beatific vision of God in Christ in glory, by experiencing so much the happiness of holiness, its happy nature and issue, by seeing the wrath of God on wicked men, etc." (Edwards, "Miscellanies," no. 442, in *WJE* 13: 490–91). Just as "means of grace" such as the natural revelation of God's judgment can, in this life, serve to augment the regenerate's sense of God's glory, so "the awful spectacle" of God's unrestrained punishment of sinners in hell will cause "the glorious inhabitants of heaven" to "fall down and adore that great power and majesty" (Edwards, "Sinners in the Hands," in *WJE* 22:415).

51. Mircea Eliade in all probability coined the phrase in *The Sacred and the Profane: The Nature of Religion* (New York: Harcourt, 1959). Rudolph Otto concentrates more on the *tremendum* aspect of the divine in *The Idea of the Holy: An Inquiry into the Non-Rational Factor in the Idea of the Divine and Its Relation to the Rational*, trans. John W. Harvey (London: Oxford University Press, 1950).

52. Pauw's view is that Edwards's relational trinitarianism contradicts his Calvinistic double predestinarianism. Riley contends that Edwards Augustinian-Calvinist dualism and determinism stands in tension with his mystical pantheism (Woodbridge Riley, "Jonathan Edwards," in *Critical Essays on Jonathan Edwards*, ed. William Scheick [Boston: G. K. Hall, 1980], 109). Unlike Riley, who posits a duality between Edwards's metaphysics and theology, Stephen thinks that Edwards's philosophical monism is entirely consistent with his theology: "The love of 'Being in general' is the love of God." Yet, he is guilty of logical inconsistency with his doctrines of original sin and hell (Leslie Stephen, "Jonathan Edwards," in Scheick, *Critical Essays*, 75).

53. Edwards, "Miscellanies," no. 926, in *WJE* 20:171. "The sun is the greatest image of God [of] any inanimate creature in the whole universe (or at least it is so to us), in these two things, viz. as a fountain of light and life and refreshment, and also in being a consuming fire, an immense fountain as it were of infinitely fierce and burning heat. And since it is abused by wicked men in the former sort of influences, they shall suffer the latter" (Edwards, "Miscellanies," no. 931, in *WJE* 20:180).

54. Edwards, "Miscellanies," no. 926, in *WJE* 20:169–70.

55. Edwards, "Miscellanies," no. 721, in *WJE* 18:350.

56. Edwards, "Miscellanies," no. 460, *WJE* 13:501.

57. Edwards, "Miscellanies," no. 721, in *WJE* 18: 350–51. Edwards does not equate this "spiritual glory . . . wherein his [Christ's] divinity consists" with the "outward glory of his transfiguration," which was but "a remarkable image or representation of that spiritual glory" (Edwards, "A Divine and Supernatural Light," in *Sermons*, 134).

58. "It assimilates the nature to the divine nature, and changes the soul into an image of the same glory that is beheld" for "[t]his light, and this only, has its fruit in an universal holiness of life" (Edwards, "A Divine and Supernatural Light," in *Sermons*, 139–40). Of the uncreated light, Palamas states, "It is a light bestowed [by the Spirit] in a mysterious illumination, and recognized only by those worthy to receive it" (Palamas, *The Triads*, III.i.9, 71).

59. "God is the author of the light of glory, of that light that enlightens heaven, that shines in that world of light where there is no night, nor darkness nor shadow" (Edwards, 66. Sermon on James 1:17 [1727–28], in *WJE* 43).

60. Ibid.

61. Edwards, "Miscellanies," no. 335, in *WJE* 15:321.

62. Ibid., 320.

63. Ibid., 320–21.

64. Edwards, "Miscellanies," no. 823, in *WJE* 18:534.

65. "This spiritual resurrection and life is procured and purchased for Christ's members by Christ's suffering obedience, in the same manner as his own resurrection and life is purchased by it" (ibid.).

66. Edwards, "Miscellanies," no. 1089, in *WJE* 20:469.

67. Edwards, "Blank Bible," note on Rom. 8:1-4, in *WJE* 24:1010.

68. Edwards, "Miscellanies," no. 926, in *WJE* 20:171.

69. "Whether man's body before the fall shone or no, I believe his flesh looked glorious, and appeared with a beautiful cast and a sort of splendor, which was immediately lost upon the transgression" (Edwards, "Miscellanies," no. 174, in *WJE* 13:325).

70. Edwards, "Miscellanies," no. 952, in *WJE* 20:215. "All must be altered [in] proportion, for Christ is the glory of heaven, the beauty and ornament, life and soul of all; and there is no glory there, but only the reflection of his glory, and the emanation of his brightness and life, and the diffusion of his sweetness" (ibid., 216).

71. Ibid., 215.

72. Edwards, "Heaven is a World of Love," in *Sermons*, 246.

73. Edwards, "Miscellanies," no. 571, in *WJE* 18:110–11.

74. Edwards, "Miscellanies," no. 1126, in *WJE* 20:496. "They are with him as it were in all things, being partakers of him in all his exaltation and glory . . . Christ with his glorified mystical body being but one mystical person" (ibid.).

75. Edwards, "Miscellanies," no. 809, in *WJE* 18:514.

76. What was crucial to Edwards was Christ's sole mediatorship, for "no man even ascended [to heaven] in his own right but [Christ]. But he came down from Heaven that all that are his might ascend thither" (Edwards, 381. Sermon on Gen. 28:12, in *WJE* 51). Edwards uses this motif of ascent and descent in "The Excellency of Christ." See William J Scheick, "Breaking Verbal Icons," in *Design in Puritan American Literature* (Lexington, KY: University of Kentucky Press, 1992), 89–119. This ascent-descent motif reiterates the Athanasian/Irenean axiom: God became human so that humans can become divine.

77. Edwards, 419. Sermon on John 13:23 (Jan 1736/7), in *WJE* 52.

78. In a typological reading of 2 Kgs. 6:6, Edwards likened Christ's divinity to a stick, which by nature, "tended not to sink, but to ascend in the water." This is contrasted to the human soul weighed down by "sin and guilt," and like iron, it is drowning in the "deep waters" of "destruction, and . . . misery." While Christ descended into the depths of human "affliction, misery, and death" in the economy, these could not overcome the "buoyancy" of Christ's divinity. Christ's resurrection redeems us from our justly deserved condition: "The stick, when that rose,

brought up the iron with it; so Christ, when he rose, he brings up believers with him." (Edwards, "Notes on Scriptures," no. 170, in *WJE* 15:99).

79. In the incarnation, "he united himself to man by taking on him man's nature. He who is the owner of heaven and who dwells in heaven, he came down from heaven and was made flesh and dwelt amongst us, John 3: 13. . . . Christ since his resurrection is gone into heaven and taken possession of it in his people's name. He ascended into heaven in our nature. The man Christ Jesus is gone to heaven and he is gone in our name as well as nature" (Edwards, 381. Sermon on Gen. 28:12, in *WJE* 51). With reference to the comings of God, the Reformed tradition distinguished between a metaphorical and literal descent. "Nor if it is said metaphorically of the Logos (*Logō*) that he came from the Father and came down from heaven, is there the same relation of leaving the world as to the flesh (which is properly attributed to him)" (Turretin, *Institutes of Elenctic Theology*, trans. George Musgrave Giger, ed. James T. Dennison [Phillipsburg, NJ: P&R, 1992–94], vol. 2, topic 13, q. 8, 326)."There is one descent local, another metaphorical, another of nature, another of dispensation, another according to substance, another according to evacuation; Christ descended [*exinanitionem*] according to the manner of dispensation and evacuation, and not locally" (Trelcatius, *A briefe institution of the common places of sacred divinitie* [London: Francis Burton, 1610], bk. 2, ch. 6, 172). Lucas Trelcatius (1542–1602) was professor of theology at Leiden.

80. Edwards, "Miscellanies," no. 772, in *WJE* 18:422.

81. Edwards understood Christ's descent from heaven in four senses: (1) the *unio hypostatica*; (2) the *Parousia*; (3) the "great dispensations of providence," where divine power is manifested on behalf of the church; and (4) *the unio mystica*, where Christ is present to the saint in regeneration and sanctification. As expected, Christ descends in the third and fourth senses figuratively (Edwards, "Like Rain Upon Mown Grass," in *WJE* 22:303). Edwards rightly does not construe the incarnation to be a literal and thus a circumscription of the Logos, in which "the divine nature left heaven, so that heaven was empty of the divine nature of Christ." For Edwards, heaven is the "proper place" of abode for the divine nature of the Son, and Christ's descent in the incarnation meant "he did as it were come down and tabernacle with us" (ibid.).

82. Ibid.

83. Ibid., 302.

84. Edwards, "Miscellanies," no. 1126, in *WJE* 20:496–97.

85. Edwards, "Miscellanies," no. 772, in *WJE* 18:422,

86. Ibid.

87. Edwards, "Miscellanies," no. 681, in *WJE* 18:241–42. As exemplar in both person and mission, "the man Jesus Christ himself, who is the very highest and most exalted of all creatures, and the head of all . . . descended the lowest of all." In fact, "none . . . ever descended so low as Christ did, who descended as it were into the depths of hell" (ibid.).

88. "The design of God in thus ordering things is to teach and show that he is all, and the creature nothing, and that all exaltation and dignity belongs to him; and therefore, those creatures that are most exalted shall in other respects be least and lowest" (ibid., 241). This echoes Maximus's notion yet has its own Reformed twist.

89. "Because they look on themselves as but little children in grace, and their attainments to be but the attainments of babes in Christ, and are astonished at, and ashamed of the low degrees of their love, and their thankfulness, and their little knowledge of God" (Edwards, *WJE* 2:322).

90. Ibid., 338. Edwards defines humility, not unlike Soren Kierkegaard, primarily as "a sense of our meanness as compared with God, or as sense of the infinite distance there is between God and ourselves" and secondarily as a "comparative meanness" to the humbler creature. This gulf between God and humanity includes the "natural meanness" of a creature and the "moral meanness" of the sinner. The ethical correlate of the epistemological aspect of humility necessarily implies obedience to God and lowliness before others. See Edwards, "Charity, or Love, the Sum of all Virtue," in *Charity and Its Fruits*, 131–36.

91. Edwards, *WJE* 2:360–61. The filial spirit of obedience to the Father contains the gracious affections enumerated in signs II, VI and IX: "So there are these three graces implied in a gracious, childlike submission to the will of God, viz. love, and humility and reverence" (Edwards, "Charity and Its Fruits," Sermon 12, in *WJE* 8:331).

92. Edwards, *WJE* 2:344–57.

93. Edwards, "Excellency of Christ," in *Sermons*, 195. The saints, in some way, participate in Christ's "child-like relation to the Father" or "his filial relation to God" (Edwards, "True Saints, When Absent from the Body, are Present with the Lord," in *WJE* 25:234).

94. Edwards concisely defines gratitude elsewhere as a subset of disinterested love to God: "True thankfulness is no other than the exercise of love to God on occasion of his goodness to us." See Edwards, "Charity and Its Fruits," Sermon 12, in *WJE* 8:331.

95. Edwards, *WJE* 2:266.

96. The motivational thrust of true Christian love to God and humanity, which arises from the activity of the Spirit, is identical: "for holiness' sake." So, the Christian loves others "either because they are in some respect like God, in the possession of his nature and spiritual image, or because of the relation they stand in to him as his children or creatures" (Edwards, "Charity, or Love, the Sum of all Virtue," in *Charity and Its Fruits*, 5). More foundational is the fact that humans are ontologically relational beings as "we are made to subsist by society and union, one with another, and God has made us with such a nature that we can't subsist without the help of one another" (Edwards, "Duty of Charity to the Poor," in *WJE* 17:376).

97. Edwards, "Miscellanies," no. 120, in *WJE* 13:284. "He is the head of all the rational creation; saints and angels are united in Christ, and have communion in him."

98. Edwards, *WJE* 2:344.

99. Edwards, "Miscellanies," no. 571, in *WJE* 18:110.

100. Edwards, "The Excellency of Christ," in *WJE* 19:593.

101. Edwards, "Miscellanies," no. 571, in *WJE* 18: 109.

102. Edwards, "Excellency of Christ," in *Sermons*, 195.

103. "'Tis only the godly that have any understanding of the excellency and fullness of Christ which is taught in the Word. *Jesus Christ is the sum and substance of the gospel*; he is the main subject of revelation since the Fall" (Edwards, "Profitable Hearers of the Word," in *WJE* 14:250; emphasis mine).

104. Edwards, *WJE* 2:292. As all gracious affections are linked together and imply one another, Edwards instructs one to "try one grace by another." The test of true love to God is the presence of true faith in Christ: "Herein is one great difference between false affections and true affections: false affections and [a delusory] saving love to God and Christ are not accompanied with this conviction; they do not withal see truth and reality of divine things" (Edwards, "Charity and Its Fruits," Sermon 12, in *WJE* 8:336).

105. As the Giver of being and life, the Spirit as Given (*datus*) connects filiation (*natus*) to that which is created (*factus*) (Ratzinger, "Holy Spirit as Communio: Concerning the Relationship of Pneumatology and Spirituality in Augustine," *Communio: International Catholic Review* 25 [Summer 1998]: 330). Augustine, *On the Trinity*, bk. 5, ch. 3, 197–200. For Augustine, in these three different senses: The Father is the origin of the Son, the Father and Son is the one origin of the Spirit, and the created world has God the Trinity as their origin. Yet, in spiritual regeneration, as Edwards notes, we are made partakers of the Son's "natural" filiation, in some sense, in being made children of God by the gift of the Spirit of adoption.

106. Edwards, "Miscellanies," no. 98, in *WJE* 13:265; italics mine. In heaven, the saints are with Christ "in his pleasures; they are with him in his enjoyment of the Father's love, the love wherewith the Father loves him is in them, and he in them [John 17: 22]" (Edwards, "Miscellanies," no. 1089, in *WJE* 20:470).

107. Edwards, "Miscellanies," no. 571, in *WJE* 18:110.

108. "Christ purchased for us that we should enjoy the love: but the love of God flows out in the proceeding of the Spirit; and He purchased for them that the love and joy of God should dwell in them, which is by the indwelling of the Holy Spirit" (Edwards, "Treatise on Grace," in *TG*, 67–68).

109. Edwards, *WJE* 2:365.

110. All Christian graces are "concatenated together" as they arise from the same person and work of the Holy Spirit, and have their *arche* and telos in "the knowledge of God's excellency." All graces are different modalities of love, the "sum of them all," for "[t]hey are but so many diversifications, and different habitudes and relations and manners of exercise of the same things. See Edwards, "Charity and Its Fruits," Sermon 12, in *WJE* 8:333; *WJE* 2:230–39.

111. Edwards, *WJE* 2:279. Here Edwards cites Rom. 8:14: "For as many as are led by the Spirit of God, are the sons of God."

112. "One design of God in the gospel, is to bring us to make God the object of our undivided respect . . . that whatever natural inclination there is in us, he may be the center of it. . . . Thus there is a natural inclination in the creature, not only to the adoration of a glorious being infinitely superior, but to friendship" (Edwards, "Miscellanies," no. 510, in *WJE* 18:54).

113. Ibid., 54–55.

114. Edwards, "Miscellanies," no. 571, in *WJE* 18:110.

115. Edwards believes that the incarnation of Christ was not only "for our sakes (though chiefly for ours), but also for the sake of the angels." That is why he united "himself to a created nature . . . [through] a personal union . . . [in order that] all elect creatures hereby have opportunity for a more free and intimate converse with God, and full enjoyment of him than otherwise could be" (Edwards, "Miscellanies," no. 744, *WJE* 18:389). He adds that "though Christ is not the Mediator of the angels in the same sense that he is of men, yet he is a middle person between God and them, through whom is all their intercourse with God and derivations from him." Edwards even says that the incarnation brought about "reconciliation" between God and angels, excepting any "alienation." The ontological distance between God and angels that did "in some measure forbid that intimate enjoyment" was bridged in Christ's kenosis. This reconciliation was brought about by love's "natural propensity" for union. Hence, Christ "is the head of all the rational creation; saints and angels are united in Christ, and have communion in him" (Edwards, "Miscellanies," no. 120, in *WJE* 13:284–85).

116. Edwards, "Miscellanies," no. 96, in *WJE* 13:263–64. See Amy Plantinga Pauw, "'Supreme Harmony': Jonathan Edwards and the Trinity" (Ph.D. diss., Yale University, 1990), 396. Edwards proposes a heavenly dynamism where our knowledge, love, and enjoyment of God increase to the expansion of God's glory. This view, according to Plantinga, is Edwards's most novel reflection of heaven—one that departs from his Augustinian-Calvinist-Puritan tradition.

117. Edwards, "Miscellanies," no. 571, in *WJE* 18:110. "As the society is by divines compared to a family, so God the Father acts as head of the whole family. . . . The church is now as it were brought into this family—adopted into it, though naturally far off—of the household of God. Thus she is said to have fellowship with the Father and the Son (1 John 1:3), and to have the communion of the Holy Ghost" (Edwards, "God the Father," in *WJE* 25:147).

118. "Though the church be brought in, yet it don't properly add to the divine society: still there are but three in the society. The church is brought in as belonging to one of the eternal members of the society, to render him complete in his station" (Edwards, "God the Father," in *WJE* 25:148).

119. Ibid.

120. Edwards, "The Excellency of Christ," in *Sermons*, 196.

121. The notions of God as Infinite and of *infinitum capax finiti* are integrated into the idea of God as Shekinah and of *finitum capax infiniti*. See Jürgen Moltmann, "The World in God or God in the World," in *God Will Be All in All: The Eschatology of Jürgen Moltmann*, ed. Richard Bauckham (Edinburgh: T&T Clark, 1999), 35–42.

122. Edwards, "Concerning the End," in *WJE* 8:531.

123. For brief essays on this, see John Meyendorff, "Thēosis in the Eastern Christian Tradition," chap. 16 in *Christian Spirituality: Post-Reformation and Modern*, ed. Louis Dupré, Don E. Saliers, and John Meyendorff (New York: Crossroads, 1989), 470–76; and Christoforos Stavropoulos, "Partakers of Divine Nature," in Clendenin, *Eastern Orthodox Theology*, 183–94. In relation to patristic thought, see, for example, Jules Gross, *The Divinization of the Christian according to the Greek Fathers*, trans. Paul A. Onica and intro. Kerry S. Robichaux and Paul A. Onica (Anaheim, CA: A&C, 2002), which was originally published as *La divinisation du chrétien d'après le perès grecs: Contribution historique à la doctrine de la grâce* (Paris: J. Gabalda, 1938). For the classic twentieth-century study of this theme by an émigré Russian Orthodox theologian, see Lossky, *Mystical Theology*, esp. chs. 10 and 11; Paul Negrut mounts a Western appraisal of Lossky's neo-Palamism in his article "Orthodox Soteriology: *Theōsis*," *Churchman* 109, no. 2 (1995): 154–70. With the rising interest in this topic, scholars situated within the Western theological tradition have recently produced comparative and evaluative works on this doctrine. Anna N. Williams, *The Ground of Union: Deification in Aquinas and Palamas* (New York: Oxford University Press, 1999), attempts to find common ground between the Thomistic and hesychastic traditions. For a Protestant appraisal of a major Romanian Orthodox theologian, see Emil Bartos, *Deification in Eastern Orthodox Theology: An Evaluation and Critique of the Theology of Dumitru Stăniloae* (Carlisle, UK: Paternoster, 1999). For a sympathetic article about this doctrine by an evangelical Protestant, see Robert V. Rakestraw, "Becoming Like God: An Evangelical Doctrine of Thēosis," *Journal of Evangelical Theology* 40, no. 2 (June 1997): 257–69.

124. Edwards, "Miscellanies," no. s, in *WJE* 13:174.

125. "The happiness that is by Christ is much above what would have been by Adam, as heaven is high above the earth" (Edwards, "Miscellanies," no. 809, in *WJE* 18:515).

126. Edwards, "Miscellanies," no. 952, in *WJE* 20:211

127. Edwards, "Miscellanies," no. 809, in *WJE* 18:515. Citing Goodwin, Edwards notes that the divine love to Adam, which we would have experienced had he not fallen, is qualitatively different from the divine love for the elect in Christ, for the latter is "that love of God by which God loves his own dear Son" (Edwards, "Miscellanies," no. 1274, in *WJE* 23:217).

128. Edwards, "Miscellanies," no. 571, in *WJE* 18:111. As one Orthodox writer puts it, the original transgression of humans was also a vocational sin for, instead of dependence on God, Adam chose the way of self-reliance in trying to fulfill his divine calling to deification, that is, to "become a god without God." See Maximos Aghiorgoussis, "Orthodox Soteriology," in Meyendorff and Tobias, *Salvation in Christ*, 38.

129. Edwards, "Miscellanies," no. 809, in *WJE* 18:515. What Satan intended as a "mere illusion" in the end "proves an occasion" whereby humans "are taken in his room" in their exaltation to heaven.

130. McClymond (with McDermott) has recently reiterated (and quite rightly) the parallels in Gregory Palamas and Edwards, such as the divine light and energies, concluding boldly that "Edwards taught a doctrine of divinization," save the "word itself." See Michael J. McClymond and Gerald R. McDermott, *The Theology of Jonathan Edwards* (New York: Oxford University Press, 2012), 416–19. Nonetheless, we must note the discontinuities as well, that Edwards denies that the divine light could be physically perceived and does not have the concept of an unknowable *hyperousia*, as did Palamas.

131. Edwards, "'Controversies' Notebook: Efficacious Grace," in *WJE* 21:298–99.

Appendix 1

TABLE 1.1 EDWARDS'S OBJECTIVE IDEALISM

CREATION	CHRIST	CHURCH
Creatio ex nihilo	*Unitio personalis / assumptio carnis*	*Unitio mystica*
Communication of being and relations to the creation	Creation and union of human nature to the Word	a. Real union of love—Christ unites Christ's self to the soul in regeneration
Creatio continua	*Unio personalis*	*Unio mystica*
Preservation as reiterative communication of being and relations to the creation	Continual communication of divine power through the human as *instrumentum Deitatis* Continual communication of divine knowledge and happiness from the Logos to the human nature	b. Vital union—continual sanctification as Christ continually imparts the Spirit to the soul as it responds in continual faith to Christ
Identity in creation	*Identity of Jesus Christ*	*Identity in Christ*
1. Divine perspective		
God treats entities in seriatim as genidentical	The Father treats the human Jesus as only-begotten Son	c. Relative union and adoption—God treats us as sons and daughters in the Son

| | | d. Legal union and justification—God accepts us as without sin and perfectly righteousness in and due to Christ |

2. Human perspective

Human minds perceive the identity and continuity of entities	Jesus relates to the Father as would the Logos in a human manner	a. Loving one another
		b. Sharing Christ's Spirit
		c. Being related to one another
		d. Being legally bound to the same Lord, by the same laws

TABLE 1.2 EMANATION AND REMANATION MOTIF

LOCUS	EMANATION	REMANATION
A. Immanent Trinity		
1. Generation of the Son	Simultaneous with the procession of the Spirit from the Father	Returns with the Spirit to the Father
2. Procession of the Spirit	Love of the Father to the Son	Love of the Son to the Father
B. Economic Trinity	Creation	End of creation / redemption
	Natural image—human mind and will	Spiritual image—divine knowledge and love
C. Christology	Descent of God	Ascent of humanity

1. Virginal conception	Spirit of the Father	*Enypostatos*—derivation of being
2. *Unitio personalis*	Spirit of the Son as *vinculum*	*Enhypostaton*—derivation of existence and personhood
3. *Unio personalis*	Spirit of the Son as *vehiculum*	*Instrumentum*—theandric operation

D. Pneumatology

1. *Unitio mystica*—real union of hearts	Regeneration / Spirit's descent / Christ's love for us	Faith / Soul's ascent / Loving response to Christ
2. *Unio mystica*		
a. Relative union / adoption	Related to the Father / made sons and daughters in the Son	Relating to the Father / acting as sons and daughters in the Son
b. Legal union / justification	Accepted and declared righteous by God	Faithful perseverance in Christ
c. Vital union / sanctification	Dying to self / mortification	Rising in Christ / vivification

Appendix 2: The Doctrine of *Autotheos* in Calvin and the Reformed Tradition

John Calvin introduced the idea that though the Father is the ultimate origin of the subsistences of the Son and Spirit, nonetheless all three persons possess the divine essence of themselves.[1] What prompted this novel move? He was trying neither to pit Western against Eastern trinitarianism nor to set one Cappadocian father against another, as has been suggested.[2] He did this to reconcile the apparent tensions within the patristic writings in response to his semi-Arian contemporaries.[3] In a sense, it was Calvin's way of restating the Nicaean *homoousion*.[4]

Though Calvin insisted that the divine persons and essence are not to be separated, he seems finally to have rejected the Nicene notion of the *communicatio essentiae*.[5] In eschewing the idea that the Father communicated different essences to the Son and Spirit, Calvin discounted the idea that their being is in any way derived.[6] This is corroborated by his dismissal of the notion of the Son's generation as an eternally perfect yet perpetual communication of essence from the Father to the Son.[7] Without reservation, therefore, Calvin contrasts the *autotheos* with any derivation of the divine essence.[8]

The positions taken up by various Reformed writers were varied. A few, like Francis Cheynell, went further than Calvin by insisting that the divine persons are *autotheos* even as to subsistence in light of the *perichoresis*.[9] Others attempted to reconcile the Nicene *communicatio essentiae* with Calvin's *autotheos*. Thomas Cartwright, for example, restated Calvin's distinction between person and essence: when the divine person of the Son is regarded in relation to the Father, the Son is derived; when the divine essence is considered *in se*, all three divine persons are *autotheos*.[10]

Puritans closer to Edwards, such as Thomas Goodwin, recapped Nicaea: the Father is the *Fons Deitatis* and the communication of the divine essence coincides with the divine processions.[11] Francis Turretin affirmed the *communicatio essentiae* without denying Calvin's *autotheos* completely.[12] The divine essence, being given to the Son by the Father, is absolute and *autotheos*, for it is independent, undivided, and underived.[13] Turretin's mediating position is the one Edwards chooses to adopt.

Notes

1. "Therefore we say that deity in an absolute sense exists of itself; when likewise we confess that the Son since he is God, exists of himself, but not in respect to His Person; indeed, since he is the Son, we say that he exists from the Father. Thus his essence is without beginning; while the beginning of his person is God himself" (John Calvin, *Calvin: Institutes of Christian Religion*, ed. John T. McNeill, trans. Ford Lewis Battles, Library of Christian Classics 20 [Philadelphia: Westminster, 1960], 1.13.25, 154). Gunton, quoting Wolfson approvingly, traces this distinction to Augustine: "For him the other two persons do not derive their Godhood from the Father (they derive only their existence, not their divinity, from him)" (Wolfson, *Philosophy of the Church Fathers*, [n.p.], as cited in Colin E. Gunton, *The Promise of Trinitarian Theology*, 2nd ed. [Edinburgh: T&T Clark, 1997], 54).

2. Warfield contends that Calvin was in favor of a more egalitarian and Western, specifically Augustinian, doctrine of the Trinity against the more subordinationist Eastern or Athanasian account (B. B. Warfield, "Calvin's Doctrine of the Trinity," *Princeton Theological Review* 7, no. 4 [1909]: 553–652). Neither was Calvin's intent to pit the Cappadocians against one another: Basil and Gregory of Nyssa did not think of the Father as the "essentiator," and Gregory of Nazianzen did not anticipate Calvin's *autotheos* argument (Thomas F. Torrance, "Calvin's Doctrine of the Trinity, in *Trinitarian Perspectives: Towards Doctrinal Agreement* [Edinburgh: T&T Clark, 1994], 60–61). Cleenewerck points out that Gregory of Nazianzus clearly affirmed the Father as the cause of the other Two; see Laurent A. Cleenewerck, *His Broken Body: Understanding and Healing the Schism between the Roman Catholic and Eastern Orthodox Churches* (Washington, DC: Euclid University Consortium Press, 2007), 326n2.

3. Calvin, *Institutes*, 1.13.19, 143–44. Calvin thinks that "the opinions of the ancients are to be harmonized" through the *autotheos* doctrine (ibid.). Hence, both the divine essence and the Father may be called "unbegotten" (Calvin, *Institutes*, 1.13.25, 153). Calvin himself points out that Cyril affirmed that the Son has a nature *a se ipso* (Calvin, *Defense against the Calumnies of Peter Caroli*, vii, 322, as cited in Warfield, "Calvin's Doctrine of the Trinity," 606).

4. Warfield, "Calvin's Doctrine of the Trinity," 617–18, 652. Put differently, Calvin merely restates the classical *alius-aliud* distinction. "*Pater, Filius & Spiritus Sanctus sunt* αὐτόθεος. *The Father, Son & Holy Spirit are one and the self-same God* . . . the best way to avoid [Sabellianism] (saith judicious Calvin) is to say *That there is a Trinity of Persons in one and the same essence of God*" (Francis Cheynell, *The divine triunity of the Father, Son, and Holy Spirit* . . . [London: Samuel Gellibrand, 1650], 267). "Master *Calvin* confutes certain blasphemous heretics of our age . . . granting that these two persons come from the Father as from a fountain, denies it to be true, that they had no essence or being of themselves." See Thomas Cartwright, *A confutation of the Rhemists translation, glosses, and annotations on the New Testament, so farre as they containe manifest impieties, heresies, idolatries, superstitions, prophanesse, treasons, slanders, absurdities, falsehoods, and other evills* . . . (New York: Theatrum Orbis Terrarum, Da Capo Press, 1971), 211.

5. Despite Calvin's affirmation that "we do not separate the persons from the essence, but we distinguish among them while they remain within in" (Calvin, *Institutes*, 1.13.25, 153–54), Warfield is of the opinion that Calvin ultimately denies "begetting and procession as involving any communication of essence" (Warfield, "Calvin's Doctrine of the Trinity, 624).

6. Calvin's main opponent was Valentinus Gentilis, "who [denied] the Son and Spirit to be coessential with the Father, but saith the Father did essentiate the Son with . . . a created and produced essence" (Cheynell, *Divine Triunity*, 232–33). On this account, Calvin rejected "a

Trinity of . . . Essence, Son and Spirit." He also condemned Servetus's idea that "the Father . . . in forming the Son and the Spirit, infused into them his own deity" (Calvin, *Institutes*, 1.13.25, 154).

7. "Indeed, it is foolish to imagine a continuous act of begetting, since it is clear that three persons have subsisted in God from eternity" (Calvin, *Institutes*, 1.13.29, 159). See also Warfield, "Calvin's Doctrine of the Trinity," 613–14; and Thomas Torrance, "Calvin's Doctrine of the Trinity," 63.

8. "For whoever says that the Son has been given his essence from the Father denies that he has being from himself" (Calvin, *Institutes*, 1.13.23, 150).

9. "Every single person is αὐτόθεος and . . . these three persons . . . perfectly subsist by themselves, though in one another; for they have one . . . nature, which is of it self, and is complete in it self, . . . and therefore contains all absolute and relative perfection in it self" (Cheynell, *Divine Trinunity*, 87–88)

10. "But for further explaining of this truth by Master *Calvin* . . . that where the persons are noted, there he confesses the Son of God to be of the Father touching his eternal essence. But when the eternal Essence and simple Nature is considered in it self, without relation of persons, there the essence is the same in all three persons. . . . so that the Word is the Son of the Father, but God of himself" (Cartwright, *Confutation of the Rhemists*, 211). Cheynell lists "*Beza, Viret, Farrell, Simler, Volanus, Gualter, Bullinger, Lavater*, the Orthodox Helvetians" as Reformed writers who followed Calvin in this matter (Cheynell, *Divine Trinunity*, 233).

11. As "the fountain of glory, of the deity itself," the Father "communicated that Deity to the Son and unto the Holy Ghost." See Thomas Goodwin, *An Exposition of the First, and Part of the Second Chapter, of the Epistle to the Ephesians*, in *The Works of Thomas Goodwin, D. D., Sometime President of Magdalen College in Oxford*, ed. Thankfull Owen and James Barron (London: T. G. [Thomas Goodwin (Jr.)], 1681], 285; available at *The Digital Library of Protestant Texts*. Elsewhere: "For, the Father communicates all and the whole of himself unto the Son, giving him by his eternal generation of him, the fullness of the deity" (Goodwin, *WTG* 9:139–40).

12. "As all generation indicates a communication of essence on the part of the begetter to the begotten . . . so this wonderful generation is rightly expressed as a communication of essence from the Father" (Francis Turretin, *Institutes of Elenctic Theology*, trans. George Musgrave Giger, ed. James T. Dennison [Phillipsburg, NJ: P&R, 1992–94], 1:292–93).

13. "Although the Son is from the Father, nevertheless he may be called God-of-himself (*autotheos*), not with respect to his person, but essence; not relatively as Son but absolutely as God inasmuch as he has the divine essence existing from itself and not divided or produced from another essence (but not as having that essence from himself)" (Turretin, *Institutes*, I.xxviii.40).

Appendix 3: Doctrine of Appropriations as Modified by the Reformed-Puritan Tradition

Appropriations may be applied nonexclusively to the indivisible work of the Trinity *ad extra*, in which some likeness is perceived between that work and the *propium* of a particular divine person. A common role or attribute may be appropriated in a threefold manner to the divine persons, but chiefly to one, according to their *propria* and *taxis*.[1] Of course, appropriations of God's attributes evident in creation presuppose the revealed knowledge of the divine persons.[2] In the Puritan tradition, the Latin hermeneutical strategy for appropriations was transposed into the covenantal, where the divine persons are understood to eternally agree to distribute work among themselves.[3] Appropriations are not so much what we assign to the divine persons, but divine self-assignment.

However, God's tripersonality ought to be manifest in the undivided action of the divine persons.[4] As the *communicatio essentiae* and *actus personales* do not undermine their consubstantiality and coequality, the *opera ad extra* is certainly undivided but not undifferentiated. The Augustinian *opera indivisa* is just the half of it, since "servato discrimine et ordine personarum."[5] Hence, the Greeks and Latins agree that the *opera ad extra* is a concerted work.[6] Edwards, with the Reformed-Puritan tradition, parses the indivisibility of the divine *opera ad extra* as mutual concurrence.[7]

How can appropriations be distinguished from proper divine modes of action? A proper mode of action is an exclusive relation between divine persons in their work *ad extra*, which corresponds to their internal relations. Edwards follows Calvin in ascribing particular modes of activity to each person in the divine economy.[8] Hence, "their particular glory" is manifested in the economy in accord with "their particular manner of subsistence."[9]

And seeing God subsists in three persons that are the same in essential glory, it was seen meet that in this great work they should all of them have their particular glory manifested with a brightness and luster answerable to their equal, essential glory; that not only the perfections of the divine essence common to all might be manifested therein, but that glory of God be shown which consists in the deity's subsistence in three persons and their particular manner of subsistence.[10]

While appropriations are grounded in God's being *ad intra*, they must nonetheless be distinguished from the *actus personales*.[11] While what is *per appropriationem* corresponds to the *actus personales*—the divine self-communication *ad intra*—it should not be confused with other willed, contingent divine *propria* or *missio*—the divine self-communication *ad extra*.[12] The incarnation of the Son and the Spirit's outpouring at Pentecost are proper divine acts, which God has assigned *ad intra* solely to a particular mode of the divine being in eternity to be effected *ad extra*.[13] They are thus nonessential, are permanent, and may not be interchanged among the divine persons.[14] For Aquinas, *missio* indicates how the sent is related to its origin and term, and the divine missions denote the triune modes of procession *ad extra*.[15] Under proper modes of action, God's *missio* are the *processio* expressed in space-time and are used of the Son and Spirit in relation to the Father, who has no unique and separate *missio*.

Notes

1. Put simply, appropriations are a way of "counting agents without counting actions" (Bruce D. Marshall, *Trinity and Truth*, Cambridge Studies in Christian Doctrine [Cambridge: Cambridge University Press, 2000], 254–55). Aquinas says that "appropriation may be made on the grounds that what is common nevertheless has a greater resemblance to what is proper to one person than it has to what is proper to another." See Thomas Aquinas, *Questiones Disputatae de Veritate*, qq. 1-9, trans. Robert W. Mulligan (Chicago: Henry Regnery Company, 1952), q. 7, a. 3; available at http://dhspriory.org/thomas/QDdeVer.htm, and Eric Luitjens, *Sacramental Forgiveness as a Gift of God: Thomas Aquinas on the Sacrament of Penance*, Thomas Institut Utrecht 8 (Nijmegen: Peeters, 2003), 127.

2. Timothy Smith, "The Context and Character of Thomas' Theory of Appropriations," *Thomist* 63 (1999): 584. Barth was to emphasize Scripture as the regulative principle to anchor the revealed in the real: the *ratio cognosendi* flows from the *ratio essendi*. See Karl Barth, *Church Dogmatics*, vol. 1, pt. 1, *The Doctrine of the Word of God*, ed. G. W. Bromiley and T. F. Torrance, trans. G. T. Thomson and Harold Knight, paperback ed. (London: T&T Clark International, 2004), 349, 373–75. Hence, appropriations "are authentic when they are taken

literally or materially or both from Holy Scripture, when they are a rendering or interpretation of
the appropriations found there" (Barth, *CD* I/1, 349, 374).

3. "They not only are all concerned as joint actors and co-workers in an affair of common
concern, but each one has his distinct part in the affair assigned him, as what more especially
belongs to him, rather than to either of the other persons of the Trinity" (Edwards, "Of God the
Father," in *WJE* 25:145).

4. In *STh* 3, 32, 1, Aquinas states an objection: "It would seem that the accomplishment of
Christ's conception should not be attributed to the Holy Ghost, because as Augustine says (*De
Trin.* i), "The works of the Trinity are indivisible, just as the Essence of the Trinity is indivisible
[*indivisa sunt opera Trinitatis, sicut et indivisa Trinitatis essentia*]." Yet, he qualifies the axiom: "The
work of the conception is indeed common to the whole Trinity; yet in some way it is attributed to
each of the Persons [*modum aliquem attribuitur singulis personis*]."

5. Emil Brunner refers to the Latin phrase as the "Augustinian Clause"; see his *Dogmatics I:
The Christian Doctrine of God*, Library of Theological Translations (Cambridge: James Clarke,
1949), 234. Augustine states the axiom: "as Father and Son and Holy Spirit are inseparable, so do
they work inseparably" without confounding the persons. Hence it was not "this same three" that
was incarnated, died, resurrected, and ascended "but the Son alone." So it was "the Holy Spirit
alone" that descended "in the form of a dove at his baptism" and at Pentecost, and the Father "who
spoke from heaven" during Christ's baptism and transfiguration (Augustine, *The Works of Saint
Augustine, Part I, Vol. 5: The Trinity*, Publications of the Augustinian Heritage Institute, ed. John E.
Rotelle, intro., trans., and notes Edmund Hill [Brooklyn, NY: New City, 1991], bk. 1, ch.2. §7,
69–70).

6. It is a "*mutually* single act," as Jenson calls it. See Robert Jenson, *Systematic Theology*, vol.
1, *The Triune God* (New York: Oxford University Press, 1997), 111. This reiterates Gregory, for
"every operation which extends from God to the Creation . . . has its origin from the Father, and
proceeds through the Son, and is perfected in the Holy Spirit. For this reason the name derived
from the operation is not divided . . . but whatever comes to pass . . . comes to pass by the action
of the Three, yet what does come to pass is not three things" (Gregory of Nyssa, "On 'Not Three
Gods' to Ablabius," trans. William More and Henry Austin Wilson [*NPNF* 5], 334.

7. Modified to suit a *pactum* theology, Edwards affirms that "all the persons of the Trinity do
concur in all acts *ad extra*" (Edwards, "Miscellanies," no. 958, in *WJE* 20:238). The language of
joint action is commonly employed by the English Puritans. Goodwin, for example, was well
aware that the "rule . . . *opera Trinitatis ad extra sunt indivisa*" affirms the reality of the "one being,
one essence" of the persons "so they have but one work." This, he continues, needs to be qualified:
"yet as they have three several subsistences, so they have three several manners of working"
(Goodwin, *WTG* 1: 461). Sweeney places Thomas Goodwin (1600–1680) fifth among Edwards's
sources (Douglas Sweeney, "Editor's Introduction," in *WJE* 23:18–19).

8. Gerald L. Bray, *The Doctrine of God* (Downers Grove, IL: InterVarsity, 1993), 202–3.
Calvin assigned particular modes of action to each person of the Trinity within the entire scope of
economic roles they shared: Father: beginning, Son: arrangement, and Spirit: efficacy.

9. Edwards, "Threefold Work," in *WJE* 14:434. The Latin doctrine of appropriations is a
hermeneutical tool by which an essential title, property, or act common to God is assigned to a
particular divine person by way of similarity or dissimilarity to the *propria personae*. Timothy
Smith, "The Context and Character of Thomas' Theory of Appropriations," *Thomist* 63 (1999):
579–612; Thomas F. Torrance, *The Christian Doctrine of God: One Being, Three Persons* (Edinburgh:
T&T Clark, 1996), 200; and, William J. Hill, *The Three-Personed God: The Trinity as a Mystery of
Salvation* (Washington, DC: Catholic University of America Press, 1982), 282–84. "The divine
person can be manifested in a twofold manner by the essential attributes; in one way by similitude,
and thus the things which belong to the intellect are appropriated to the Son, Who proceeds by
way of intellect, as Word. In another way by dissimilitude; as power is appropriated to the Father .
. . because fathers by reason of old age are sometimes feeble" (Aquinas, *STh* I, q. 39, a. 7).

10. Edwards, "The Threefold Work of the Holy Ghost," in *WJE* 14:434.

11. Jüngel extends the *ratio essendi* to include appropriations as grounded in God's self-constitution as triune: "Attribution is that process in which, in the concrete harmony of his modes of being, God assigns to himself his being *as Father, as Son* and *as Spirit.*" See Eberhard Jüngel, *The Doctrine of the Trinity: God's Being Is in Becoming*, trans. Horton Harris (Grand Rapids, MI: Eerdmans, 1976), 51. Here, the divine processions are thus regarded as a volitional *opera ad intra* that includes a reference to the world as object.

12. As Bruce Marshall puts it, not all *propria* (viz., features "by which we pick out or identify its possessor"), such as the incarnation and Spirit's outpouring, constitute a person or identity, since these are contingent acts of God (Marshall, *Trinity and Truth*, 263n30).

13. Barth regarded his triad of "Creator, Reconciler and Redeemer" as appropriations. Creator is appropriated to the Father since he is the principle of "origination." Although all three persons are the one Subject of reconciliation and redemption, nonetheless "certain statements about the work of the Son and the Spirit cannot be appropriated to the Father." The titles of Reconciler and Redeemer are not synonymous with the divine *missio*, and just so, it is "improper to say that God the Father died." Yet, he fudges the distinction between *appropriatum* and *proprium* when he states that "we ascribe creation as a *proprium* to the Father and that we regard God the Father *peculiariter* and specifically as the Creator." Clearly, he saw the difficulty in all this for it "is impossible to draw an absolutely unambiguous line between what is commanded and what is forbidden" (*CD* I/1, 397).

14. Roman Catholic scholastic theology has traditionally affirmed the incarnation as a *proprium* of the Son, but the indwelling of the Spirit as an *appropriatum*. Matthias Scheeben has instituted a degree of pneumatic emphasis with his mediating category of "non-exclusive proprium theory" (Ralph Del Colle, *Christ and the Spirit: Spirit-Christology in Trinitarian Perspective* [New York: Oxford University Press, 1994], 60n38). The distinction is not made in regard to the Son and Spirit. The difference is between the visible missions of the Son (incarnation) and Spirit (at Jesus' baptism, Jesus' transfiguration, and Pentecost), which are proper to the divine persons, and the invisible missions of the Son (sending of Wisdom in the OT) and Spirit (regeneration), which are appropriations (Luitjen, *Sacramental Forgiveness*, 137–38). In sanctification, both the Son and Spirit—and not the Father—are invisibly sent to the soul, though the Father comes to indwell the saint. The likening of the soul and spiritual gifts pertaining to the intellect and love are, therefore, respectively appropriated to the Son and Spirit (Aquinas, *STh* I, q. 43, a. 5).

15. Insofar as the "notion of mission includes two things: the habitude of the one sent to the sender; and that of the one sent to the end whereto he is sent," a divine mission indicates "in one way the procession of origin from the sender [*processionem originis a mittente*], and . . . a new way of existing [*novum modum existendi*] in another" (Aquinas, *STh* I, q. 43, a. 1).

Appendix 4: The *Enhypostaton-Anhypostaton* Dialectic

Much scholarly debate has been generated over Friedrich Loofs's misinterpretation of the notion of *enypostatos* in his seminal study of Leontius of Byzantium.[1] Apparently, Loofs thought of it as an ontological process of "insubsistence" (*enhypostaton*) whereby a human nature without personhood (*anhypostaton*) is "hypostasized" in the person of the Logos in the *unio personalis*.[2] This seems to be a process that had occurred in the *assumptio carnis* or *unitio personalis*.

Critics of this position contend that Leontius was no theological innovator, as his understanding of the *enypostatos* was without Loofs's metaphysical implications.[3] Originally, *enypostatos* simply meant "subsisting" or "possessing reality," which points more to the state of union (*unio personalis*) than *anypostatos*, which meant "not subsisting" or "without reality."[4] Suppose it is conceded that Leontius's notion of *enypostatos* means "real"; it still does not follow that the *anhypostasis-enhypostasis* couplet is a theological *novum* without patristic antecedents or, worse still, "a dubious christological formula."[5] Defenders of Leontius castigate this Loofsian interpretation as an invention of Protestant scholasticism, famously formalized by Barth's *enhypostasis-anhypostasis* dialectic.[6] That being the case, it is crucial to establish the patristic-medieval antecedents of this dialectic.

ENYPOSTATOS OR *ENHYPOSTATON*: REAL OR EXISTING IN?

Firstly, the term *enypostatos*, in patristic orthodox usage, has a semantic field that certainly cannot be limited to Leontius of Byzantium's usage. For example, *enypostatos* could be taken as that which does not exist independently, but as something recognized in a *hypostasis*, as Gregory Palamas asserted of the divine energies.[7] In other words, an accident in a substance may be termed *enypostaton*.[8]

Uwe Lang has argued persuasively that though the Protestant scholastics used the *enypostatos* adjectivally and not nominally, they did not carry on the Leontian usage (as "real").[9] This alternate meaning of *enhypostaton*, whereby the flesh finds its subsistence in the person of the Logos ("in-existence") is, nonetheless, neo-Chalcedonian in its origins.[10] John of Damascus synthesized this doctrine of christological in-existence with the term *enypostatos*, thus legitimating the use of the *en-* as a "localizing prefix."[11] Although the "enhypostatic [*enypostatos*] Wisdom and Power of the most high God, the Son of God . . . was not made one with flesh that had an independent pre-existence," yet in the assumption, this flesh "found existence in Him."[12] Here, John clearly extended the meaning of the Leontian *enypostatos* from mere existence.

The reading of *enypostatos* as in-existence in the Logos, if not already in the Damascene, was certainly mediated through medieval Christology in order to clarify what *assumptus* means. While Aquinas, following John of Damascus, acknowledged that accidents are commonly said to exist in something else, he acknowledged that individual human nature also comes to in-exist in another (*in alio*), namely the Word, neither accidentally nor essentially, but hypostatically (or substantially) and mysteriously.[13]

No Protestant scholastic would have thought of the human nature of Christ as having "its subsistence or hypostasis in the hypostasis of another nature" as if the union were external.[14] Such phrasing is found, for example, in John of Damascus.[15] The Protestant scholastics surely understood the significance of Chalcedon's Cyrillian emphasis on a single Subject: the flesh assumed is not another's but belongs to the "one and the same" Word.[16] For example, Chemnitz defined *enypostaton* as that which "subsists in another person."[17] Inasmuch as the flesh is the Son's by virtue of the incarnation, this human nature can no longer be recognized as existing in a *hypostasis* that is foreign to it.[18] Neither would they have allowed a reversal of the *enypostaton* to assert that the Logos subsists in the person of the human Christ.[19]

It was this use of the *enypostatos*, Lang reminds us, that was subsequently assimilated by the seventeenth-century Protestant scholastics.[20] Turretin, for example, understood it both in the Leontian and medieval sense: in the incarnation, "the flesh is not a hypostasis, but real [*enypostatos*]; not existing separately, but sustained in the Logos [*enhypostaton*]."[21] Others understood it as in-existence. Goodwin clearly excluded the Nestorian idea of the assumption of an *independent*, human person. It is an *assumpsit ad*, whereby the Word took on flesh "to subsist in himself, not of itself."[22] The preexistent Son is thereby the principle of existence of divine humanity since "the second person becomes a foundation of subsistence to the human nature of Christ, as an oak is to the ivy."[23]

The expanded meaning of *enhypostaton* as an ontological event was already contemplated by Puritan writers. For Davenant, the incarnation could be described "(if it may be permitted to frame a word) by a new personation of human nature."[24]

Unreal or Dependent Human Nature: *Anypostatos* or *Anhypostaton*?

Leontius is correct to deny that Christ's human nature is *anypostatos* if all natures, created and uncreated, can only exist in the concrete. This meaning is carried across from Trinitarian usage and is clearly reiterated by John of Damascus.[25] In the incarnation, since the natures "both . . . have one and the same subsistence," they cannot be "without subsistence" (*anypostaton*).[26] The assumed nature is not unreal.

However, the later application of *anhypostaton* should not be discredited insofar as its significance was modified.[27] The *anhypostasis*, when referring to Christ's human nature after the *egeneto*, cannot obviously mean unreal or nonexistent but, rather, without independent subsistence.[28] It must be acknowledged that *anypostaton* had a very elastic if not plainly confusing usage even in John of Damascus.[29]

Aquinas affirms the *anhypostaton* within his own metaphysic. A created entity has both its own essence and "act of existence" (*esse*) from God. The case of the hypostatic union, however, is unique.[30] The human nature is given its own essence and receives the divine *esse* of the Word by which it becomes actuated.[31] Hence, the human nature of Christ has neither existence without the *communio naturarum* nor personhood apart from the *unio hypostatica*.[32] For Aquinas, the human Jesus is personal only as it is in the person (*in aliqua persona*) of the Son; on its own account, it is not a person (*non est persona*).[33]

The Protestant tradition took the cue from Aquinas. They parsed the *anhypostaton* in terms of the *non est persona*.[34] Reformation theologians like Beza and Olevian simply affirmed Aquinas's phrasing without further qualifications.[35] Later, John Gerhard spelled out the difference between *anypostatos* and *anhypostaton* in their absolute and relative senses. Echoing Leontius's use, Christ's human nature is not "absolutely" *anhypostaton* (that is, *anypostatos*); otherwise it would have no positive content or reality.[36] However, it may be regarded as "relatively" *anhypostaton*—that is to say, not possessing independent subsistence apart from subsistence in another.[37] "In this sense, the flesh of Christ is said to be *anhypostatos*, because it is *enhypostatos*, subsisting in the *logos*."[38]

THE *ENHYPOSTATOS-ANHYPOSTATOS* DIALECTIC IN PROTESTANT THEOLOGY

As Gerhard so clearly put it, the *anhypostaton* in its relative sense implies the *enhypostaton*.[39] This is what the *enhypostaton-anhyposaton* dialectic seeks to convey: that which has dependent personhood cannot have independent personhood. For the Protestant scholastics, that dialectic is a faithful appropriation, restatement, and extension of the Catholic tradition. This was precisely how Martin Chemnitz interpreted John of Damascus through the eyes of Aquinas:

> Damascenus also applies to the subject the terms "not subsisting *in itself*" (ἀνυπόστατον) and "subsisting in something else" (ἐνυπόστατον). For although elsewhere the term ἀνυπόστατον indicates something which simply does not exist and ἐνυπόστατον something which either exists of itself or inheres in another, as an accident in a subject, yet Damascenus is quite correct in his belief that the human nature in Christ can be called ἀνυπόστατος inasmuch as it does not subsist in itself and according to itself, in its own personality, as the Scholastics say, but is ἐνυπόστατος. It subsists in another person, namely, the Logos, who has become the hypostasis for it.[40]

While Chemnitz's reading of Damascenus may not be wholly accurate, he has a full grasp of the semantic range of the dialectic.[41] Thus, the later use of *anhypostaton,* as mediated through Maximus, Damascenus, and Aquinas, cannot be seen simply as a flat contradiction of Leontius's *anypostatos* because it is always a conjunctive of *enhypostaton*.[42]

The Puritans, in continuity with the Anglican theologians, stated the *enhypostaton-anhypostaton* pairing frequently and simply, without the technical terminology of the scholastics.[43] If subsistence means independence of being, *anhypostaton* negates self-subsistence.[44] Yet this does not deny essential completeness, for when paired with *enhypostaton*, the human nature of Christ is acknowledged as possessing personhood that is derived.[45] This does not mean that personhood and existence are transferred from the Word to the human nature.[46]

In summary, the *enhypostaton* (derived existence and subsistence in another) includes the *enypostatos* (reality) and implies the *anhypostaton* (without independent subsistence). This line of thinking continues in Edwards.

Notes

1. This reading is appropriated by Harry Austryn Wolfson, *The Philosophy of the Church Fathers* (Cambridge, MA: Harvard University Press, 1956), 414.

2. The Loofsian "insubsistence" characterizes Leontius's *en-* prefix as a conceptual *novum* as if "two independent substances are brought together in an existential relationship." Loofs also claimed that Leontius did not posit an asymmetry between that which assumed (*hypostasis*) and that which was assumed (*enhypostatos*). Aloys Grillmeier, *Christ in Christian Tradition*, vol. 2, *From the Council of Chalcedon (451) to Gregory the Great (590–604)*, part 2, *The Church of Constantinople in the Sixth Century*, trans. Pauline Allen and John Cawte (Louisville, KY: Westminster John Knox, 1995), 195.

3. See also Andrew Louth's summary of the controversy in his *St. John Damascene: Tradition and Originality in Byzantine Theology*, ed. Gillian Clark and Andrew Louth (Oxford: Oxford University Press, 2002; repr. 2004), 160–61. Gerrit Berkouwer has outlined this debate well in chapter 12 of his *Studies in Dogmatics: The Person of Christ*, trans. John Vriend (Grand Rapids, MI: Eerdmans, 1954), 305–28.

4. This is one instance of a Greek adjective "in which the prefix ἐν- is joined to a substantive to signify the possession of some thing or quality, as opposed to an *alpha privative*, which would signify its absence" (Brian E. Daley, "The Christology of Leontius of Byzantium: Personalism or Dialectics," in *Papers from the Ninth Conference on Patristic Studies 1983, Oxford, England, Patristic Monograph Series*, Philadephia Patristic Foundation [typescript], as quoted in Grillmeier, *Christ in Christian Tradition*, 2:194) In a published article, Daley points out that "one of Loofs' most influential mistakes" was to construe the *en-* as a "localizing prefix" ("A Richer Union: Leontius of Byzantium and the Relationship of Human and Divine in Christ," *Studia Patristica* 24 [1993]: 241).

5. F. LeRon Shults, "A Dubious Christological Formula. From Leontius of Byzantium to Karl Barth," *Theological Studies* 57 (September 1996): 431.

6. Shults, "Dubious Christological Formula," 431–46. Shults does not deny that "Leontius, most of the Protestant Scholastics, and Barth" affirm the doctrine "that the human nature of Jesus does not subsist except in its union with the Logos in the one person of Christ" (433). What he is critical of is the use of the *anhypostasis-enhypostasis* formula—an invention of Protestant scholasticism (that Barth appropriated)—to describe that christological assertion. The *enhypostasis* overlays a metaphysical baggage not extant in Leontius's conception of the *enypostatos*, and the Protestant *anhypostasis* flatly contradicts the patristic notion of *anypostatos*.

7. The divine energy "is 'enhypostatic,' not because it possesses a hypostasis of its own, but because the Spirit 'sends it out into the hypostasis of another,' in which it is indeed contemplated. It is then properly called 'enhypostatic,' in that it is not contemplated by itself, nor in essence, but in hypostasis" (Gregory Palamas, *The Triads*, ed. with intro. John Meyendorff, trans. Nicholas Gendell [Mahwah, NJ: Paulist, 1983], 3.1.9, 71). He cites Maximus who affirmed that the divine energies are not only "enhypostatic, but also . . . unoriginate (not only uncreated), indescribable and supratemporal" (Palamas, *Triads*, 3.3.31, 86). Meyendorff points out that "enhypostatic" could mean both "what exists in another hypostasis" and "what really exists," attributing the first sense to Leontius of Byzantium and the second to Mark the Monk (Meyendorff, in Palamas, *Triads*, 137–38n4).

8. More properly, an accident is "*heterohypostaton*, or something which subsists in another." See John of Damascus, "Fount of Knowledge," in *St John of Damascus: Writings*, trans. Frederic H. Chase Jr., Fathers of the Church 37 (Washington, DC: Catholic University of America Press, 1958), ch. 44, 68.

9. Lang argues that the *anhypostasis-enhypostasis* formula is not traceable to the Lutheran and Reformed scholastics but belongs to Barth. They affirmed a non-Leontian notion of the *enypostatos* (which Barth subsequently assimilated into his dogmatics) without asserting that the humanity of Christ was *anhypostasis*. We argue that Barth's "formula" is not novel as its basic form is already extant in Aquinas, if not earlier.

10. As examples, see John of Caesarea's interpretation of the Cyrillian *henosis kat' hypostasin* as *enypostatos henosis*; Leontius of Jerusalem's notion that the two natures of Christ exist concretely (*enypostatos*) in one *hypostasis*; and Anastasius I of Antioch's insistence that the human nature of Christ has a no separate *hypostasis* but "subsists in the Logos." See Uwe Michael Lang, "Anhypostatos-Enhypostatos: Church Fathers, Protestant Orthodoxy and Karl Barth," *Journal of Theological Studies* 49, no. 2 (1998): 636–48. Grillmeier thinks that the Loofsian *enhypostaton* as a *via media* between *hypostasis* and *anhypostatos* (unreal) cannot be found in Leontius of Jerusalem's more sophisticated thought. As with Leontius of Byzantium, *enypostatos* also means "real," for "Christ is only one hypostasis in the real two natures." Both the natures of Christ, for the later Leontius, are "*enhypostata*" (Grillmeier, *Christ in Christian Tradition*, 2:285–86). However, Cross contends that the Loofsian idea of in-existence is already implicit in the later writings of Leontius of Byzantium (Richard Cross, "Individual Natures in the Christology of Leontius of Byzantium," *Journal of Early Christian Studies* 10, no. 2 [Summer 2002]: 245–65).

11. Lang, "Anhypostatos-Enhypostatos," passim.

12. John of Damascus, *Orthodox Faith*, bk. 3, ch. 2, 46 (*NPNF* 9). Wolfson makes this clear in his translation of Damascus's *Dialectica*: "Again enhypostatos is said to be a nature which is assumed by another hypostasis and which has its existence in that hypostasis" (John of Damascus, *Dialectica* 44 [PG 94, 616B], in Wolfson, *Philosophy of the Church Fathers*, 416).

13. Accordingly, "since the human nature in Christ does not subsist separately through itself but exists in another, i.e. in the hypostasis of the Word, [*existit in alio, id est in hypostasi verbi Dei*] (indeed not as an accident in a subject, nor properly as a part in a whole, but through an ineffable assumption)" (Aquinas, *Quaestiones disputatae De unioni Verbi*, trans. Roberto Busa. Taurini, 1953, a. 2, available at http://www.corpusthomisticum.org/qdi.html).

14. F. LeRon Shults, "A Dubious Christological Formula: From Leontius of Byzantium to Karl Barth," *Theological Studies* 57 (September 1996): 440. Shults's criticism is such a "localization" of one nature *in* another would not only imply the destruction of the assumed human nature but "would [also] require that the divine nature was in the hypostasis of the human nature." According to him, what Leontius meant by *enypostatos* was that "the natures share a common subsistence that is constituted by their relationality." There is a twofold rebuttal here. Firstly, no Protestant orthodox would have countenanced any sort of diminution of Christ's human nature in the *enhypostatos* as if some confusion of essences were presupposed. Secondly, the great tradition (with the possible exception of a school of Reformed scholastics) clearly affirmed that the two natures in Christ do share a common subsistence by means of a mutual in-existence of the natures in the union, viz., the christological *perichoresis*. This is the way they parsed the "relationality" of the natures in the incarnation, which Edwards modified with his construal of a Spirit-mediated *enhypostatos*.

15. "For the flesh of God the Word did not subsist as an independent subsistence, nor did there arise another subsistence besides that of God the Word, but as it existed in that it became rather a subsistence which subsisted in another [*allo en aute hypostasa, enypostatos mallon*], than one which was an independent subsistence" (John of Damascus, *Orthodox Faith*, bk. 3, ch. 9, 53 [*NPNF* 9]). The Latin translation: "sed cum in ea subsisteret, facta est potius ἐνυπόστατος, id est, in

alio substans, quam scorsim in seipsa substans hypostasis" (*PG* 95, col. 1017). See also John of Damascus, "Fount of Knowledge," ch. 44, 68.

16. John McGuckin, *Saint Cyril of Alexandria and the Christological Controversy: Its History, Theology and Texts* (Crestwood, NY: St. Vladimir's Theological Seminary Press, 2004), 237–38. Since the Logos and human nature "both . . . have one and the same subsistence," they cannot "have subsistences that differ from each other [*heterohypostatous*]" (John of Damascus, *Orthodox Faith*, bk. 3, ch. 9, 53 [*NPNF* 9]).

17. Martin Chemnitz, *The Two Natures in Christ*, trans. J. A. O. Preus (St. Louis, MO: Concordia, 1971; originally published as *De Duabus Naturis in Christo*, Leipzig, 1578), 31. Thomas states with greater precision: "The Word subsists in the human nature." For that which subsists is the very Word and not the human nature (Reginald Garrigou-Lagrange, *Christ the Saviour: A Commentary on the Third Part of Saint Thomas' Theological Summa*, trans. Dom Bede Rose [St. Louis, MO: Herder, (copyright 1950)], ch. 4, q. 2, a. 2). Hence, the Son subsists in both natures (Aquinas, *STh* III, q. 2, a. 4, 2031). More will be said on this below.

18. This is the Cyrillian insight ratified by the Fourth and Fifth Ecumenical Councils: the union (*henosis*) of the natures in the one Christ means that the natures could only be distinguished in thought (*en theoria*), since they are united not merely by conjunction, will, relation, and the like, but in person (*kat'hypostasin*) (McGuckin, *Saint Cyril of Alexandria*, 239–40).

19. Shults thinks this would obtain if one overlaid the meaning of the Protestant *enhypostaton* onto the Leontian *enypostatos*. Since every essence cannot be without *hypostasis*, the incarnate Son, who is *enypostatos*, would have to be conceived as insubsisting in another person as well. This sort of double *enhypostasis* is observed even in Luther's *communio naturarum* without the *extra carnem* (Barth, *CD* I/2, 166–67). Aquinas clearly rejects this: "But the Word of God has not its subsistence from its human nature, but rather draws that human nature to its own subsistence or personality: for it does not subsist through it, but in it" (Aquinas, *Of God and His Creatures: An Annotated Translation [with Some Abridgement] of the Summa contra gentiles of Saint Thomas Aquinas*, trans. Joseph Rickaby [London: Burns and Oates, 1905], bk. 4, 40, 49).

20. Lang traces John of Damascus's influence on the Wittenberg theologians Calov, Quenstedt, and Hollaz. He notes that Calov is particularly dependent on the Reformed divine Alting as well. However, Lang's thesis is dismissed by Louth as "unpersuasive."

21. Francis Turretin, *Institutes of Elenctic Theology*, trans. George Musgrave Giger, ed. James T. Dennison (Phillipsburg, NJ: P&R, 1992–94), 2:317. Connected to the *enypostatos* is the notion of that the human nature is continually given existence by the Logos through the union "as an instrument and adjunct personally joined to it" for the *oikonomia*.

22. Goodwin, *WTG* 5:51. "He not only took on him, but to him, επιλαμζάνεται, *assumpsit ad. Assumpsit non hominem personem, sed hominem in personem.*"

23. Ibid., 52. Perkins uses the same analogy: "As the plant called *Missell* or *Misselto* . . . lives in the stock or body of the oak . . . so the human nature having no proper subsistence, is, as it were, ingrafted into the person of the Son, and is wholly supported and sustained by it so, as it should not be at all, if it were not sustained in that manner" (William Perkins, *An exposition of the symbole or creed of the apostles* . . . [London: Printed by John Legatt, Printer to the Universitie of Cambridge, 1616], 181). One could fault this horticultural analogy for being both christologically and botanically deficient. While the ivy-oak relation may seem too incidental, from a christological perspective this metaphor has the advantage of conveying the *asynchytos* natures in the incarnation—clearly a Reformed concern. Because the ivy does not draw life from the oak, the metaphor may fail to convey the idea that the assumed nature has derivative existence and subsistence, yet plant biology would define nutritive dependence as a parasitic trait. Certainly, his concern was to point out that the human nature has a dependent existence in the Word.

24. John Davenant, *An exposition of the Epistle of St. Paul to the Colossians. Translated from the original Latin; with a life of the author, and notes . . . by Josiah Allport. To the whole is added, a*

translation of Dissertatio de morte Christi *by the same prelate* (London: Hamilton, Adams, and Co., 1831), 419.

25. The patristic notion of *anypostatos* was borrowed from Trinitarian terminology. For John of Damascus, every essence must be concretely instantiated (*enypostatos*), and every particular entity must have an essence (*enousia*) (Louth, *St. John Damascus*, 159). In Trinitarian use, person cannot be empty of essence (*hypostasis enousia*) and essence cannot be without concrete existence (*ousia enypostaton*).

26. John of Damascus, *Orthodox Faith*, bk. 3, ch. 9, 53 (*NPNF* 9).

27. Donald Macleod, *The Person of Christ*, Contours of Christian Theology (Downers Grove, IL: InterVarsity, 1998), 200–201.

28. Owen, in reference to the human nature, says: "In itself it is ἀνυπόστατος,—that which has not a subsistence of its own, which should give it individuation and distinction from the same nature in any other person. But it hath subsistence in the person of the Son, which thereby is its own" (*Works* 1:233). Berkhof thinks it proper to speak of the humanity of Christ as "in-personal rather than impersonal" but grants that impersonality "is true only in the sense that this nature has no subsistence of its own" (Louis Berkhof, *Reformed Dogmatics* [Grand Rapids, MI: Eerdmans, 1932], 1:319).

29. Other than "non-existence," *anypostaton* may mean "that which does not have its being in itself but exists in another." An example John cites is "the accident," which he previously categorizes as *enypostaton* (!) as well as *heterohypostaton* (John of Damascus, "Fount of Knowledge," ch. 45, 69).

30. "The eternal being of the Son of God, which is the Divine Nature, becomes the being of man, inasmuch as the human nature is assumed by the Son of God to the unity of Person" (Aquinas, *STh* III, q. 17, a. 2, ad 2).

31. On this account, supposing that *esse* is a predicate of the person instead of the nature, Aquinas would have been guilty of tritheism (Joseph P. Wawrykow, "Hypostatic Union," in *The Theology of Thomas Aquinas*, ed. Rik van Nieuwenhove and Joseph Wawrykow [Notre Dame, IN: University of Notre Dame Press, 2005], 242). Piet Schoonenberg thinks that this position falls into docetism since the human nature is unreal. Yet, as Richard Sturch rebuts, this position only amounts to locating the reality of the human nature in the divine, and not in itself (Richard Cross, *Metaphysics of the Incarnation* [New York: Oxford University Press, 2002], 312).

32. For it "does not exist of itself apart from the Divine Nature [*non est per se seorsum existens a divina natura*]" and "is not of itself a person apart from the Person of the Son of God [*non est per se seorsum a persona filii*]" (Aquinas, *STh* III, q. 16, a. 12, 2116).

33. Thomas suggests two legitimate ways to parse the reduplicative phrase "Christ as Man is a hypostasis or person." Firstly, and unqualifiedly, "Man" can be identified with the *hypostasis*. Secondly, if "Man" refers to the nature, "Christ as Man" is a person insofar as "it belonged to human nature to be in a person [*in aliqua persona*]," viz., *enhypostaton*. If, however, "proper personality" is thought to be "caused by the principles of a human nature," then "Christ as Man is not a person [*non est persona*]" (Aquinas, *STh* III, q. 16, a. 12, 2116).

34. As evident from the preceding footnotes, "non est persona" is just shorthand for "non est per se seorsum a persona filii," which implies "non est per se seorsum existens a divina natura," since person and nature in God are not really distinct. Gockel notes that Aquinas does not use *anhypostaton* but suggests that *impersonalitas* was his way of asserting the same. However, Gockel provides no textual proof. See Matthias Gockel, "A Dubious Christological Formula? Leontius of Byzantium and the Anhypostasis-Enhypostasis Theory," *Journal of Theological Studies* 51 (October 2000): 527.

35. "Idcirco humana natura in Christo non est persona, sed humanitas subsistit in persona Verbi." See Theodore Beza, *Adversus sacramentariorum errorem pro vera Christi praesentia in coena domini, homiliae duae*, auctore *Nathanaele Nesekio* (Geneva, 1574), 8. "At humana natura in Christo non est persona nec per se subsistit, neque fuit homo sive persona humanitas illa, cum assumeretur

à λόγῳ in unitatem suae personae." See Caspar Olevian, *In Epistolas D. Pauli Apostoli ad Philippenses & Colossenses, notae, ex Gasparis Oleviani concionibus excerptae, & a Theodoro Beza editae: cum praefatione eiusdem Bezae* (Geneva: Apud Eustathium Vignon, 1580), 127.

36. "*Anhypostaton* has a twofold meaning. Absolutely, that is said to be *anhypostaton*, which subsists neither in its own *hypostasis*, nor in that of another, which has neither essence nor subsistence, is neither in itself, nor in another, but is purely negative. In this sense, the human nature of Christ cannot be said to be *anhypostaton*." See John Gerhard, *Loci Theologici* III, 421, as quoted in Heinrich Schmid, *The Doctrinal Theology of the Evangelical Lutheran Church*, trans. Charles A. Hay and Henry E. Jacobs, 3rd rev. ed. (Minneapolis: Augsburg Publishing House, 1899), pt. 3, ch. 2, §32, 223.

37. "Relatively, that is said to be *anhypostaton*, which does not subsist in its own, but in the *hypostasis* of another; which indeed has essence, but not personality and subsistence peculiar to itself" (John Gerhard, *Loci Theologici* III, 421, as quoted in Schmid, *Doctrinal Theology*, pt. 3, ch. 2, §32, 223).

38. John Gerhard, *Loci Theologici* III, 421, as quoted in Schmid, *Doctrinal Theology*, pt. 3, ch. 2, §32, 223. Thus, not only in Barth, but in the eyes of the Protestant scholastics (pace Lang), the *anhypostatos* and *enhypostatos* are mutually implicative.

39. Though it has no independent personhood, it derives it by existing in the Logos (*enhypostaton*). Thus, the Protestant *anhypostaton* serves to contradict the Nestorian *idiohypostatos*, whereby Christ's flesh is said to have its "own *hypostasis*" (Grillmeier, *Christ in Christian Tradition*, 2:284).

40. Chemnitz, *Two Natures*, 31. His references to the texts (with editorial updating) are *Dialectica* (Migne, *PG* 94, 589) and *De Fide Orthodoxa* 3.9 (Migne, *PG* 94, 1017).

41. For Chemnitz, *anhypostaton* should not be taken to mean "unreal," and *enhypostaton*, when understood as subsisting in another, cannot be thought of as mere accidental existence—for example, the presence of habitual grace in the Christian.

42. Balthasar opines that Barth's (so-called) "*anhypostasis-enhypostasis* formula" is not without precedent in Maximus's thought. Lang notes that Maximus, while borrowing from Leontius of Byzantium, "exactly reverts the sense of terminology in Leontius and can—*mutatis mutandis*—even be said to have anticipated the Loofsian misreading" (Lang, "Anhypostatos-Enhypostatos," 643n60). Daley himself admits that Maximus does "lend himself to this kind of reading" because of his commitment to "questions of ontology, and in the metaphysics of the Person of Christ" (Daley, "Translator's Foreword," in Hans Urs von Balthasar, *Cosmic Liturgy: The Universe According to Maximus the Confessor*, trans. Brian E. Daley [San Francisco: Ignatius, 2003], 18). Eric Perl makes this a cornerstone in Maximus's thought (Eric Perl, "Methexis: Creation, Incarnation, Deification in Saint Maximus the Confessor" [Ph.D diss., Yale University, 1991], 190–220). Törönen thinks that Maximus's use of the *enhypostatos* comes close to that of *individuum* (Melchisedec Törönen, *Union and Distinction in the Thought of St Maximus the Confessor*, Oxford Early Christian Studies [Oxford: Oxford University Press, 2007], 103–4). Louth rejects this line of interpretation for a Leontian understanding of Maximus's *enypostatos* (Andrew Louth, *Maximus the Confessor* [London: Routledge, 1996], 170n5).

43. "For the divine nature . . . of the Son, is . . . actually subsisting in it self: the human nature . . . does neither subsist in it self, nor by it self" (William Perkins, *A golden chaine: Or, the description of theologie, containing the order of the causes of salvation and damnation, according to Gods word. . . .* [London: Printed by John Legatt, Printer to the Universitie of Cambridge, 1616], 25). In a seventeenth-century work, Jean Gailhard affirmed that "Christ's human nature hath no personality, but is upheld by the divine person." See Jean Gailhard, *The blasphemous Socinian heresie disproved and confuted, wherein the doctrinal and controversial parts of those points are handled, and the adversaries scripture and school-arguments answered: with animadversions upon a late book called, Christianity not mysterious* (London: R. Wellington and J. Hartley, 1697), 301.

44. Since "subsistence must be by it self, neither the part of another thing, nor sustained of another thing . . . so we rightly say, that the humanity of Christ, consisting of a reasonable soul and body, as all other men do, yet in him makes not a person . . . because it subsists not alone, but in the Deity which supports it" (John Downame, *The summe of sacred divinitie first briefly & methodically propounded: and then more largly & cleerely handled and explaned* [London: William Barret, (1620?)], 28). "In itself it [the human nature] is ἀνυποστατος, that which hath not a subsistence of its own, which should give it individuation and distinction from the same nature in any other person" (John Owen, *Christologia: Or, a Declaration of The Glorious Mystery of the Person of Christ, God and Man . . .* , vol. 1 of *The Works of John Owen, D.D.*, ed. William H. Goold [New York: Robert Carter & Brothers, 1851], 306). On this, Owen merely appropriated existing tradition (Carl R. Trueman, *John Owen: Reformed Catholic, Renaissance Man* [Aldershot, UK: Ashgate, 2007], 93).

45. "Hence . . . the manhood of Christ . . . is a nature only and not a person: because it does not subsist alone, as other men . . . do: but wholly depends on the person of the Word, into the unity whereof it is received" (Perkins, *An exposition of the symbole or creed of the apostles*, 181).

46. Turretin rejected the idea of a "transitive" communication of the *hypostasis* of the Logos to the human nature as "the flesh would formally subsist in the subsistence of the Logos (*Logou*) and thus be truly a person." The flesh has communion with the Logos neither "effectively," for that would be Nestorian, nor "transitively," which in Turretin's view amounts to heresy, but "assumptively." Presumably, an effective relation amounts to a union of the Logos to a human nature that remains external, while a transitive relation implies a separation between the Logos-subject and human nature (Turretin, *Institutes*, 2:328). Furthermore, this is not possible based upon a Victorine definition of person, viz., that it is incommunicable. Similarly, Goodwin thought that neither the personal property of begottenness nor independent subsistence could be communicated to the human nature in the *enypostaton*. "God is the *principium* of subsistence to all, but in Christ he is the *terminus subsistendi*, yet not so as if the personal property were communicated that is incommunicable, as to be begotten of God, and to subsist of itself." However, it may be said that "the Son of God communicates his personality, his subsistence, to the man Christ Jesus" (Goodwin, *WTG* 5:52). Elsewhere, Goodwin asserts that "the Man Christ Jesus was capable of being one Person" of the Trinity, which, differently stated, "the Personality, or to be one in Person, might be communicated unto a Creature." See Thomas Goodwin, *Of the Knowledge of God the Father, And His Son Jesus Christ*, ed. Thankfull Owen and James Barron, in *The Works of Thomas Goodwin, D. D. Sometime President of Magdalen College in Oxford* (London: T. G. [Thomas Goodwin (Jr.)], 1683), 50; available at *The Digital Library of Protestant Texts*.

Appendix 5: *Genus Maiestaticum*

Largely a development of Cyrillian Christology, the doctrine of the *communicatio idiomatum*, variously termed the communication of idioms, attributes, or properties, serves to clarify the relations between the natures in the person of Christ.[1] While the subsequent Western tradition took over the patristic *antidosis idiomata* via John of Damascus under the term *communicatio idiomatum*, distinctive emphases among the Latin, Reformed, and Lutheran traditions are evident despite their common lineage.

POSTMEDIEVAL ELABORATION OF THE *COMMUNICATIO IDIOMATUM*

Thomas Aquinas worked out precise, second-order linguistic rules of predication for the one hypostasis of Christ.[2] The sixteenth- and seventeenth-century Lutherans systematically expanded the *communicatio* into three genera.[3] Firstly, the attributive genus (*idiomaticum or idiopoieticon*) attributes the properties of both natures to one person. Secondly, in the majestic genus (*auchematicum or maiestaticum*) the divine attributes are directly communicated to the human nature. Thirdly, the official (*operationum or apoteslematicum*) understands the two natures to operate distinctly but in communion with each other in the *oikonomia*.[4] To this triad, the seventeenth-century Giessen and Tübingen Lutherans would add a fourth kenotic genus (*tapeinoticum or kenoticum*), where human properties are communicated to the divine nature.

Since the divine *apatheia* was axiomatic for both the earlier Lutheran and Reformed scholastics, the *genus tapeinoticum* was denied. The Reformed theologians embraced the attributive and official genera but rejected the *genus maiestaticum*.[5] With the medievals and the Lutherans, they also affirmed the communication of gifts (*communicatio gratiarum or charismatum*). Under this doctrine, Jesus received the grace of headship (*gratia capitis*), and was thus eminently and uniquely exalted; through Jesus, the saints are in turn proportionally glorified.[6] This, however, was not listed as a genus under the *communicatio idiomatum* by the Lutherans since no real communication of inherent properties was involved, but only an infusion of created gifts into the assumed human nature.[7]

What Does the *Genus Maiestaticum* Mean?

In continuity with Chalcedon, Reformed and Lutheran theologians confessed that the natures underwent no essential change in the incarnation.[8] Even so, both parties were adamant that the human nature was elevated and received some form of communication from the deity.[9] The crux of the controversy was the kind of communication received by the assumed nature. For the Lutherans, this meant the *genus maiestaticum*, to which the Reformed countered vociferously.

Both parties invoked the Fathers, particularly John of Damascus, for the justification or rejection of this genus.[10] Scholastic Reformed theologians accepted the *communicatio idiomatum* as interpreted *in concreto*, but not *in abstracto*, as did the Lutherans.[11] Yet, it cannot be denied that the Fathers spoke concretely of the deification of the Word's flesh.[12] Still, what is communicated to the human nature?

In What Way Does the Human Nature Participate in the Divine Attributes?

If the *communio naturarum* is regarded as mutual fellowship (*koinonia*) between the natures that results in the *genus maiestaticum*, the latter may then be conceived of as a unilateral penetration (*penetratio*) of the human nature or the mutual action between the natures.[13] The idea of *penetratio*, however, seems to posit a distinction without difference, as *perichoresis* is none other than in-existence or interpenetration.[14] But if reciprocal penetration is read as mutual action upon each other, this would tend to nestorianize the natures. It is no wonder that a stream within the Reformed tradition emphasized a mediate union and downplayed the iron-fire analogy.[15]

If, however, the notion of the penetration of nature includes the permeation or diffusion of a nature's properties, the *genus maiestaticum* is nothing else but one side of the *communio naturarum*.[16] Of course, if the *communio* is no different from the *communicatio*, then human attributes should be transferred to the divine as well, since the interpenetration of natures is reciprocal.[17] But if the divine cannot undergo *passio*, there is no mutual *communicatio*, just as fire heats iron without undergoing change.[18] In this case, the *communio naturarum*—being identical to the *genus maiestaticum*—becomes meaningless shorn of the idea of joint participation.

Furthermore, this notion of the *communicatio* as diffusion does not seem to be supported by the Lutherans since they, following the Fathers, rejected any notion of a physical infusion of the divine attributes into the human nature.[19] Tied to this is the denial that the humanity of Christ could own the divine attributes essentially or naturally.[20] For, if two essences were to share properties, this would result in either their essential merger or multiplication into two divinities.[21] This conclusion was denied by the Lutherans. There is no double divinity, they said, the one original and the other derivative, but "only one divine omnipotence, power, majesty, and glory, which is peculiar to the divine nature alone."[22] If the divine attributes could be received but not owned by the human nature, what sense might one make of this?

It could mean that the divine attributes were given to the human nature for its use only.[23] But the notion of borrowed attributes seems unthinkable as this would separate the divine essence from its attributes.[24] In fact, the very idea that the divine attributes could be communicated to the human nature without thereby implying ownership jettisons the doctrine of divine simplicity.[25] Moreover, a single human nature would, on this account, have two kinds of operation, only one of which is proper to itself.

If the *genus maiestaticum* does not mean the instrumentalization of the divine attributes by the human nature, then it can only mean instrumentalization of the human nature by the divine. This was what Aquinas thought of as included in the *deificatio*, which was affirmed by the Lutherans.[26] On this interpretation, this is but the *communicatio apotelesmaticum* seen asymmetrically as a theandric act.

ARE THE DIVINE ATTRIBUTES WHOLLY OR SELECTIVELY COMMUNICATED?

If the *genus maiestaticum* were total and complete at the point of the *unitio personalis*, the glorification of Christ would be simply identical to the incarnation.[27] This notion of a total *genus maiestaticum* is clearly untenable. The Lutherans had to explain the *exinanitio* as a voluntary restriction of the use or manifestation of the divine attributes by Christ. During Christ's "exinanition," it was held that these divine properties were largely "concealed and withheld," but they are "fully, powerfully, and publicly" manifest in the glorified Christ.[28] Now, if this meant the divine Logos restricting the operation of the divine attributes through the humanity but not *extra carnem*, then this would be no different from the Reformed position.

This, however, was not the case because the Lutherans rejected the idea of a passive humanity, yet there was no common consensus among them.[29] There were those who said that the divine attributes were potentially possessed at the incarnation. But if, at the *unitio*, the *communio naturarum* were perfect and actual, how could the *genus maiestaticum* be only in potency? Others thought that Christ, as human, while possessing the divine attributes in full, nonetheless restrained their use. Yet this cannot be, as the human nature would then be in possession of a single will but two energies. Still others judged the kenosis as an act of the God-man manifesting divine perfection on occasion. If this precludes Christ acting *extra carnem*, then this would be the precursor of seventeenth-century German kenotic theology.

For the patristic theologians, however, the communication of divine properties to the human is real but highly selective. Cyril, for example, thought of it as principally a communication of life.[30] The Lutherans extended this to include divine attributes like omnipresence but denied a real communication of the divine immensity and eternity to the human nature.[31] Clearly, the notion of the *ubiquitas* of Christ's human nature is a Lutheran theological *novum*.[32] In rejecting the *genus maiestaticum*, Turretin asserted that Christ's humanity did not become omnipresent, omniscient, and omnipotent and even denied the patristic notion that Christ's humanity was made life giving.[33]

The Reformed charged that the idea of selective communication was inconsistent with divine simplicity since the *genus maiestaticum* must happen to either none or all of the divine properties.[34] In response, the Lutherans qualified the divine simplicity with a double distinction: between God *in se* and *ad extra* and between the divine essence and the divine attributes.[35] On this distinction, negative divine attributes are affirmed as immanent to the divine essence, inoperative, and incommunicable, while the positive ones operate *ad extra* and are thus communicable.[36]

This absolute and relative enumeration of the divine attributes, as Chemnitz noted, has been dogmatized as the communicable and incommunicable attributes by both Reformed and Lutheran theologians.[37] Reformed scholastics, such as Turretin, rejected the distinction between operative and inoperative, but retained the distinction between communicable and incommunicable.[38] Divine simplicity is then secured by a notion of analogical, but not formal (that is, proper and real) participation.[39] How are the supernatural virtues different from natural endowments except quantitatively, based on Turretin's notion of analogical participation for sanctifying grace, since human goodness is merely ectypal of divine goodness?[40]

What is communicated in the *genus maiestaticum* is to be strictly distinguished from the *communicatio charismatum/gratiarum*: they are infinite, essential attributes exercised through the assumed nature, which, nonetheless, cannot be said to possess them.[41] Understood in such an existential sense, would the Reformed have objected to this particular construal of the genus of majesty, since it approximates the neo-Chalcedonian idea of the theandric operation? Puritan theologians, such as John Owen, rejected the *genus maiestaticum* and *communicatio in abstracto* as both Nestorian and unintelligible.[42] With Calvin, Owen interpreted the tradition's affirmation of the *communicatio idiomatum in abstracto* as merely hermeneutical and argued for a communication of works (*operationum*) and grace (*gratiarum*).[43]

REFORMED INSISTENCE ON THE *COMMUNICATIO GRATIARUM*

Reformed theologians remained wary of—if they did not reject outright—the *genus maiestaticum*, primarily to ensure the integrity of Christ's humanity.[44] Yet they did not deny that Christ's human nature was exalted through a communication of gifts or graces (*communicatio gratiarum/charismatum*).[45] Both the Lutherans and Reformed traditions, together with the medieval, conceded that Christ possessed created, habitual graces.[46] Due to the grace of union (*gratia unionis*), Jesus was imparted the created graces in superabundance as the grace of headship (*gratia capitis*).[47] Although the incarnation is sui generis, these habitual graces are understood as only quantitatively different from the saints' because they flow from Christ's human nature.[48]

Contrary to the medieval scholastics who regarded Jesus as both *comprehensor* and *viator*, the Reformed and Lutherans agreed that these gifts were gradually imparted to Jesus.[49] Lutherans were keen to distinguish the *gratia habitualis* from the *genus maiestaticum*, and they did not classify the former as a separate genus.[50] In fact, for Chemnitz, the *gratia habitualis* rendered Jesus fit to be the *instrument Deitatis* such that the divine majesty may operate through it.[51] Thus, the *gratia habitualis* were preparatory for the *genus maiestaticum* in Christ firstly, and the saints nextly.[52] In fine, the *gratia capitis* in Christ, though supereminent, is nonetheless not different in kind from the saints' *gratia habitualis*.[53] They are created graces and gifts.[54]

Notes

1. The practice was already implicit in Ignatius (J. N. D. Kelly, *Early Christian Doctrines* [New York: Harper & Brothers, 1958], 143). Since the incarnate Word is one *prosopon*, "we attribute to him all the human characteristics . . . and all the divine characteristics" on account of both natures (Cyril of Alexandria, "Explanation of the Twelve Chapters," in John

McGuckin, *Saint Cyril of Alexandria and the Christological Controversy: Its History, Theology and Texts* [Crestwood, NY: St. Vladimir's Theological Seminary Press, 2004], 287).

2. Francis Turretin, *Institutes of Elenctic Theology*, trans. George Musgrave Giger, ed. James T. Dennison (Phillipsburg, NJ: P&R, 1992–94), vol. 2, 13.6.21, 316. The *communicatio* is a secondary way of describing the "*unum suppositum.*" See Henk J. M. Schoot, *Christ the "Name" of God: Thomas Aquinas on Naming Christ* (Leuven: Peeters, 1994), 147–52.

3. Martin Chemnitz formally distinguished and systematically treated these three genera in his *De Duabis Naturis in Christo*. His place among the sixteenth-century Lutheran scholastics was already recognized in the century after, judging from this well-worn motto: "'If Martin [Chemnitz] had not come, Martin [Luther] would hardly have stood' (*Si Martinus non fuisset, Martinus vix stetisset*)" (J. A. O. Preuss, "Translator's Preface," in Martin Chemnitz, *The Two Natures in Christ* [St. Louis, MO: Concordia, 1971], 9). Chemnitz lists the *genus maiestaticum* third for the sake of teaching because it is the controverted category.

4. Bernhard Erling, "Communicatio Idiomatum Re-Examined," *Dialog* 2 (1963): 140. See Heinrich Schmid, *The Doctrinal Theology of the Evangelical Lutheran Church*, trans. Charles A. Hay and Henry E. Jacobs, 3rd rev. ed. (Minneapolis: Augsburg, 1899), 331–60. Heron classifies the three genera as the *genus maiestaticum, genus tapeinoticum,* and *genus idiomaticum* or *apotelesmaticum*, the first two regarded as "strictly speaking, improper," while the attributive and official genera are conflated in the last (Alasdair Heron, "*Communicatio Idiomatum* and *Deificatio* of Human Nature: A Reformed Perspective," *Greek Orthodox Theological Review* 43, nos. 1–4 [Spring–Winter 1988]: 372).

5. As Turretin puts it, "the question concerns communication in the abstract or of nature to nature—whether the properties of the divine nature were really and truly communicated to the human nature by the hypostatical union. This the Lutherans hold; we deny" (Turretin, *Institutes*, vol. 2, topic 13, q. 8, para. 6, 322–23). The communication to the person happens on three levels: (1) the *communicatio idiomatum* of natures to person; (2) the *communicatio apotelesmaticum* or "communication of office and of effects," where the redemptive works of the God-man are ascribed to both natures; and (3) the communication of honor and worship (*latria*) due to the *theanthropos* (322).

6. There is, according to Turretin, a twofold communication to the human nature: (1) the grace of eminence, which makes the humanity of Christ elevated beyond any other creatures because this human nature alone is properly God's, and (2) habitual grace, which, while an excellent gift, is created, not infinite, and proportionate to one's capacity (Turretin, *Institutes*, vol. 2, topic 13, q. 8, para. 6, 321).

7. Chemnitz, *Two Natures*, 247–55.

8. There is "no conmingling, conversion, equating, or abolition of the natures and their essential properties" (Chemnitz, *Two Natures*, 288). "For we affirm his divinity so joined and united with his humanity that each retains its distinctive nature unimpaired" (Calvin, *Institutes of Christian Religion*, ed. John T. McNeill, trans. Ford Lewis Battles [Philadelphia: Westminster, 1960], 2.14.1, 482).

9. The *asynchytos* is "certainly not a satisfactory, sufficient, or valid reason" to deny the testimony of Scripture "that certain things have been given or communicated to Christ according to his human nature" (Chemnitz, *Two Natures*, 288). See also, I. A. Dorner, *History of the Development of the Doctrine of the Person of Christ*, Clark's Foreign Theological Library, 3rd ser. (Edinburgh: T&T Clark, 1891), 2.1, 128. Since the dual natures of Christ include two corresponding wills and energies, the human volition and operation are deified "without transgressing their own limits," just as "the flesh was deified without undergoing change in its own nature" (John of Damascus, *Orthodox Faith*, bk. 4, ch. 15, 61 [*NPNF* 9]).

10. In favor of the Reformed, John rejected any direct, mutual, cross-ascription of properties between the natures, as this would confuse them. Verbally, "When . . . we speak of His divinity we do not ascribe to it the properties of humanity . . . Nor, again, do we predicate of . . . His

humanity the properties of divinity." For in reality, one nature cannot have two opposing sets of properties: "For the created remaineth created, and the uncreated, uncreated." Additionally, a *communicatio in abstracto* would mean an incarnation of the entire Trinity or the assumption of all humankind (John of Damascus, *Orthodox Faith*, bk. 3, ch. 3, 48 [*NPNF* 9]). The last point is moot because the *genus maiestaticum* is a unilateral communication to a particular or individual human nature. The affirmation of the *genus maiestaticum* does not mean that all three divine persons are incarnate by reason of the divine attributes and operations being essential and common to the entire Trinity, for the *communicatio idiomatum* is a consequence of the *unio personalis*, unique to the person of the Son (Chemnitz, *Two Natures*, 305).

11. For Turretin, a *communicatio idiomatum in abstracto* cannot be the consequence of the "real union," since it would obliterate the distinction of the natures (Turretin, *Institutes*, vol. 2, topic 13, q. 8, para. 22, 328). The Reformed claimed to interpret the terms *abstracto* (in reference to nature) and *concreto* (to person) in accordance with the patristic tradition, as opposed to "the abusive sense of the Lutherans," where *abstracto* was taken to mean that the human nature was separated from the divinity, and *concreto* to signify its union with the Logos (Turretin, *Institutes*, vol. 2, topic 13, q. 8, para. 5, 322). Of course, the Lutherans denied this.

12. Clearly, the *communicatio* does not apply to the divine nature but "the Word appropriates to Himself the attributes of humanity: for all that pertains to His holy flesh is His." Yet, what exactly does Damascus mean when he affirms that "the Word . . . imparts to the flesh His own attributes"? (John of Damascus, *Orthodox Faith*, bk. 3, ch. 3, 48 [*NPNF* 9]). Presumably, this could mean either the essential, common divine attributes, the Son's *proprietas*, or both. If a person is its nature, then the Lutherans are justified in seeing the *genus maiestaticum* in John. At the very least, there is in Damascus's writings a tension between his denial of a real, mutual communication between natures and his affirmation of a limited *genus maiestaticum*. See especially ch. 4 in Grzegorz Strzelczyk, *Communicatio Idiomatum: Lo scambio delle proprietà; Storia, status quaestionis e prospettive* (Rome: Pontificia Università Gregoriana, 2004).

13. Thus, Leontius of Byzantium advances a direct, reciprocal *koinonia* of substances (*ousiai*), but he conceived of the permeation (*penetratio*) occurring from the divine side only (Grillmeier, *Christ in Christian Tradition*, trans. Pauline Allen and John Cawte [Louisville, KY: Westminster John Knox, 1995], 2:209). Of course, if the Christological *perichoresis* is taken beyond compresence, it would lead the hypostatizing of the natures.

14. John of Damascus clarified the Chalcedonian Christology by correlating its grammar with the nomenclature already stabilized within Trinitarian theology. Thus, he could affirm that just as the three divine *hypostases* have a simple essence and nature, and are inseparably joined to each other without confusion and interpenetrating one another without alteration, so the two natures in Christ are united distinctly and interpenetrate each other without change (John of Damascus, *Orthodox Faith*, bk. 3, ch. 5, 49 [*NPNF* 9]). While its use in Christology moved from one of "*perichoresis* to" (Maximus), signifying an alternation or rotation of action, to "*perichoresis* in" (Cyril), or interpenetration, the former usage was never applied to the Trinitarian *perichoresis*, thus emphasizing that the divine persons were "coterminous and co-extensive," and not "equivalent or alternative" (G. L. Prestige, *God in Patristic Thought* [London: SPCK, 1952], 298).

15. In fact, John is keen to emphasize not only that the deification of the flesh leaves "the natures . . . unconfused and their properties unimpaired," but that the flaming sword analogy "points most expressly and most directly" to the distinction of natures and wills in Christ. Citing *Orations* 42, John comments, "Gregory the Theologian, indeed, says, 'Whereof the one deified, the other was deified,' and by the words 'whereof,' 'the one,' 'the other,' he assuredly indicates two natures" (John of Damascus, *Orthodox Faith*, bk. 3, ch. 17, 66 [*NPNF* 9]). Ames, like the Reformed theologians, regarded the illustrations of form-matter, soul-body, and fire-iron as insufficient analogies of the incarnation, much less proof of the *genus maiestaticum* (William Ames, *The Marrow Of Sacred Divinity Drawne Out of the Holy Scriptures, and the Interpreters thereof, and Brought into Method* [London: Henry Overton, 1642], ch. 18, 83–84). They object that the

analogy signifies two created realities, whereas, in Christ, the divine nature is uncreated and infinite and only the human nature created and finite (Jill Raitt, *The Colloquy of Montbéliard: Religion and Politics in the Sixteenth Century* [New York: Oxford University Press, 1993], 123). An incarnational union that turns primarily on a *communio naturarum* (and not the *enhypostatos*) tends to devalue the person of Christ (Barth, *CD* IV/2, 51–91). For Barth, any alteration of human nature by *apothēosis* conceals a hidden divinity within human nature. The *genus maiestaticum*, in his opinion, also dissolves the preeminence of the Subject since the asymmetrical *assumptio* of the humanity (of the *unitio personalis*) is deemphasized in favor of the consequential *perichoresis* of natures. See Piotr Malysz's summary of this in his "Storming Heaven? Barth's Unwitting Appropriation of the *Genus Maiestaticum* and What Lutherans Can Learn from It," *International Journal of Systematic Theology* 9, no. 1 (January 2007): 75–76.

16. Dorner has suggested that the second-generation Calvinists (Beza, Sadeel, and Ursinus) would have accepted the *genus maiestaticum* had it been conceived along the lines of a *perichoresis* (or fellowship) rather than a transference of attributes (Dorner, *Person of Christ* 2:234).

17. This logical conclusion was made by the kenotic theologians of the eighteenth century. Brian Hebblethwaite allows for a mutual communication of attributes with this qualification: "Thus, on a kenotic view, the *communicatio idiomatum* is not a one-way process, but the human expression of divine attributes requires self-limitation in a way in which the divine awareness of the human experience does not." See Brian Hebblethwaite, *The Incarnation: Collected Essays in Christology* (Cambridge: Cambridge University Press, 1987), 164.

18. Appealing to the authority of patristic writers, the Lutheran theologians recounted the analogy whereby iron is said to shine and emit heat not by itself (*kat' eauton*) but by another (*kat' allo*): a communion (*koinonia*) and interpenetration (*perichoresis*) is admitted (Chemnitz, *Two Natures*, 290).

19. Though the *genus maiestaticum* is not merely verbal ("verbalis communicatio") but real ("de reali communicatione"), this implies no physical or substantial transference ("physica communicatio vel essentialis transfusio") (*Formula of Concord*, 8:63). This is an obvious reference to the Damascene, who asserts that the flesh of Christ was suffused with and manifests the divine energy on account of the hypostatic union, but is not "endowed in a physical way" (John of Damascus, *Orthodox Faith*, bk. 3, ch. 17, 66 [*NPNF* 9]). The Lutherans, however, speak of a communication of attributes and not energy. Strictly speaking, there is no *genus maiestaticum* in John of Damascus's writings (George D. Dragas, "Exchange or Communication of Properties and Deification: *Antidosis* or *Communicatio Idiomatum* and *Theosis*," *Greek Orthodox Theological Review* 43, nos. 1–4 [Spring-Winter 1988]: 377–99).

20. Dorner, *Person of Christ*, 2:1, 128.

21. Oliver D. Crisp, *Divinity and Humanity: The Incarnation Reconsidered*, Current Issues in Theology, ed. Iain Torrance (Cambridge: Cambridge University Press, 2007), 9. If the human properties are either obliterated (e.g., mortality by immortality) or absorbed (e.g., finite knowledge into omniscience) in the *communicatio*, this would result in one god on the axiom of the identity of indiscernibles. If, however, some essential or accidental human properties are retained despite the *communicatio*, there would then be two gods; the one original and the other a *tertium quid*, essentially divine with some additional human properties.

22. *Formula of Concord*, 8:66.

23. Schmid summarizes well this tendency when he classes "the apotelesmatic genus" as including the fact "that the human nature is to be regarded as active, not alone by means of the attributes essentially its own, but that to these are added, by virtue of the second genus of the communicatio idiomatum, the divine attributes imparted to it, with which it operates" (Schmid, *Doctrinal Theology*, 232). The language here tends toward a construal of the human nature as an operating subject.

24. The idea that the divine attributes could be thought of as merely borrowed is absurd (Dorner, *Person of Christ*, 2:239).

25. Or, to put it more positively: That the divine attributes communicated do not become the *proprium* of the humanity, but are predicated of the divinity *ex se* and *per se*, presupposes a distinction between the essence and attributes of God. Such a distinction is admissible anthropologically but contradicts the notion of divine simplicity and "plainly leads to coarse representations" (Dorner, *Person of Christ*, 2:2, 235).

26. The attributes of the divinity radiate "in, with, and through" the humanity of Christ as fiery and heated iron (*Formula of Concord*, 8:66). For St. Thomas, deification does not mean that the flesh changes into the divine essence, but that it receives the *gratia unionis* and *gratia capitis* and acts as the *instrumentum Deitatis* of salvation (Aquinas, *III Sent.*, d. 5, q. 1, a. 2, resp. 6).

27. Donald Macleod, *The Person of Christ*, Countours of Christian Theology (Downers Grove, IL: InterVarsity, 1998), 198. The Lutheran theologians of the sixteenth century conceived of a total *genus maiestaticum* at the *unitio*. If the humanity of Christ were omnipotent, omniscient, omnipresent, and incorruptible from conception, the *unio hypostatica* would be nothing but a farce—this was just another form of Aphthartodocetism!

28. *Formula of Concord* 8:64.

29. Charles Hodge, *Systematic Theology* (Grand Rapids, MI: Eerdmans, 1993; originally publ. 1872), 2:418.

30. That is, through the reception of the Spirit in baptism and the blood and body of Christ in the Eucharist. See Daniel A. Keating, "Divinization in Cyril: The Appropriation of Divine Life," in Weinandy and Keating, *The Theology of Saint Cyril of Alexandria*, 165. For John of Damascus, following Cyril, deification involves the flesh becoming life giving not *per se*, but by reason of the hypostatic union (John of Damascus, *Orthodox Faith*, bk. 3, ch. 18, 66 [*NPNF* 9]).

31. Dorner points out that "a lower, mediated form of 'Communicatio'" was posited here (which could be easily have been admitted by the Reformed), where all divine attributes are affirmed as "*communicated*," but not all are "*predicated*" of the human nature (Dorner, *Person of Christ*, 2:2, 231n2).

32. There is unanimity in the scholarly opinion here: Heron, "*Communicatio Idiomatum*," 375; Marilyn McCord Adams, "Biting and Chomping Our Salvation: Holy Eucharist, Radically Understood," in *Redemptive Transformation in Practical Theology: Essays in Honor of James E. Loder, Jr.*, ed. Dana R. Wright and John D. Kuentzel (Grand Rapids, MI: Eerdmans, 2004), 88; Louis Berkhof, *Systematic Theology*, new combined ed., with a new preface by Richard E. Muller (Grand Rapids, MI: Eerdmans, 1996), 325; and Francis J. Hall, *Theological Outlines*, rev. Frank Hudson Hallock, 3rd ed. (Eugene, OR: Wipf and Stock, 1933), 176.

33. Turretin, *Institutes* 2:327. The flesh is not vivifying because only the divine essence (which was not communicated to the human nature) is. Furthermore, to assert that the flesh is life giving would either mean that Christ could not die or that the hypostatic union was "dissolved."

34. Turretin, *Institutes* 2, topic 13, q. 8, para. 11, 324; Louis Berkhof, *Reformed Dogmatics* (Grand Rapids, MI: Eerdmans, 1932), 1:326.

35. Lutherans like Chemnitz, Selnekker, and Kirchner—but not the Würtembergers—admitted a distinction between the divine essence and its attributes (Dorner, *Person of Christ* 2:233). Chemnitz granted that when the divine essence is considered *per se*, there is an absolute identity between the divine essence with the divine attributes, and the divine properties are indistinct from each other. But when viewed in relation to the world, there is "a certain distinction between His essence and His attributes," and "a certain degree of distinction among the divine attributes" (Chemnitz, *Two Natures*, 307). These should be accurately termed attributes, but not "peculiarities (*idiomata*)" (Chemnitz, *Two Natures*, 307). According to John of Damascus, the nonenergetic attributes—those that "remain within the essence and do not go outside of it into creatures by special activities (*energeia*)"—include "the eternity, immeasurability, infinity and the spiritual qualities of the essence." A summary of John of Damascus's *De Fide Orthodoxa*, bk. 3, ch. 15, is found in Chemnitz, *Two Natures*, 307.

36. On this point, in a way reminiscent of Gregory Palamas, Chemnitz distinguishes "spiritual" attributes immanent to the divine essence, like "eternity, immeasurability, infinity," and the divine *energeia* that are manifested "outside" the divine essence, like "His justice, His goodness, His power, majesty, glory, wisdom and life," which operate upon and affect created things. Here, he appeals directly to John of Damascus's *De Fide Orthodoxa* (Chemnitz, *Two Natures*, 307). Aquinas states that communicable divine attributes can be predicated to the human nature but incommunicable ones, like being "uncreated and omnipotent," cannot. With the logic in reverse, human properties cannot be predicated of the divine nature since the latter cannot receive anything "by participation from the human nature" (Aquinas, *STh* III, q. 16, a. 5, 211).

37. Chemnitz, *Two Natures*, 308. Early Reformed orthodox theologians distinguished between the essence and operations of God using various cognate distinctions like incommunicable/communicable and primary/secondary—"essential" properties and attributes of the *vita dei*.

38. Turretin, *Institutes* 2, topic 13, q. 8, para. 11, 325.

39. Turretin, *Institutes* 2, topic 13, q. 8, para. 11, 325. Similarly, see Willem J. van Asselt, *The Federal Theology of Johannes Cocceius, (1603–1669)*, trans. Raymond A. Blacketer (Leiden: Brill, 2001), 164–65. Placher charges Turretin with advancing a crypto-univocity not unlike Suarez's; see William C. Placher, *The Domestication of Transcendence: How Modern Thinking about God Went Wrong* (Louisville, KY: Westminster John Knox, 1996), 79.

40. There is no communication of the divine life to Christ's humanity since Turretin, in opposition to the Lutherans, rejected this under the *genus maiestaticum* with other divine attributes of omnipotence, omniscience, and omnipresence (Turretin, *Institutes* 2:327).

41. The question as to whether the Logos (and in the saints, the Holy Spirit) operated directly through and with the human nature or by the mediation of the infused gifts was a sorely debated point in medieval scholasticism (Chemnitz, *Two Natures*, 252). Edwards would have affirmed the former since he rejects the notion of created grace (as was examined in ch. 8, *supra*).

42. "For that which some have for a long season troubled the church withal, about such a *real communication of the properties of the divine nature unto the human*, which should neither be a *transfusion* of them into it, so as to render it the subject of them, nor yet consist in a reciprocal denomination from their mutual in-being in the same subject,—it is that which neither themselves do, nor can any well understand" (John Owen, *The Works of John Owen*, ed. William H. Goold [London: Banner of Truth Trust, 1965–68], 1:234; italics original).

43. What he affirms as "a threefold *communication* of the divine nature unto the human" in Christ amounts to the *enypostaton*, habitual grace, and dignity of the mediatorial office (Owen, *Works* 1:233). Calvin's *communicatio operationum* is parsed under his concept of the Mediator (Calvin, *Institutes* 2.14.3, 484).

44. Owen was willing to allow for the exaltation of Christ's humanity insofar as the perfections communicated are not "inconsistent with [Christ's human] essence," which otherwise would amount to "a destruction of its being" (Owen, *Works* 1: 239–40). Whatever divine attributes that could be communicated to Christ's humanity, the saints would never be participants: "The way of the communications of the divine nature unto the human in his person is what we cannot comprehend; we have no notion of it,—nothing whereby it may be illustrated. . . . [W]e know it not. But whether they be of life, power, light, or glory, they are of another kind than that whereby we do or shall receive them" (Owen, *Works* 1:240). The *genus maiestaticum* reduces the *kenosis* "to the most Pickwickian sense." See Sarah Coakley, *Powers and Submission: Spirituality, Philosophy and Gender* (Oxford: Blackwell, 2002), 15.

45. There was an elevation of the human nature as a result of the communication of gifts of excellence by the "Logos-person" (Heinrich Heppe, *Reformed Dogmatics Set Out and Illustrated from the Sources*, rev. and ed. by Ernst Bizer, trans. G. T. Thomson [London: George Allen & Unwin, 1950], 434). Louis Berkhof lists two subsets under the *communicatio charismatum*: (1) the "*gratia unionis cum persona tou Logos*," which he identifies with the "*gratia eminentiae*," by which

Christ becomes the object of adoration, and (2) the *gratia habitualis* (which includes *posse non peccare*). While it is true that by both these graces Christ is "elevated high above all creatures," the grace of union must surely be a qualitative distinction. And if that is the case, then the grace of eminence is sui generis (Berkhof, *Systematic Theology*, 324). The distinction is further made between the complex person as the object of adoration and the divine Logos, its ground (Berkhof, *Reformed Dogmatics* 1:322).

46. Aquinas considered the possession of habitual grace as gracious participation in the divine nature, viz., *deificatio* (Aquinas, *STh* III, q. 7, a. 1).

47. The *enypostatos* is none other than the grace of union that results in the sanctification of the human nature: "For the grace of union is the personal being that is given gratis from above to the human nature in the Person of the Word, and is the term of the assumption. Whereas the habitual grace pertaining to the spiritual holiness of the man is an effect following the union" (Aquinas, *STh* III, q. 6, a. 5). Goodwin notes that "the school-men do exceedingly well in" their elaboration of the grace of union, habitual grace, and grace of headship in Christ (Goodwin, *WTG* 1:536). According to Owen, the unusually termed "grace of union" (*gratia unionis*) should not be understood as habitual grace intrinsic to the human nature of Christ, but another term for the hypostatic union. It signifies the gracious predestination of the hypostatic union (in order to remove any meritorious cause in the human nature of Christ), the uniqueness and dignity of Christ's humanity not shared with any other human being, and the fitness and capacity granted to the incarnate Christ to undertake the mediatory functions (Owen, *Works* 1:227–28).

48. Christ's anointing was, first of all, as God-man, so as to be equipped for the *triplex munus*: this relates to the *communicatio operationum*. Secondly, because *finitum non capax infinitum*, Christ did not receive the "essential properties of the Godhead" but only "certain created gifts and qualities." Yet, the *gratia creata* was "not conferred in small scantling or measure," for as grace of headship, they were given to Christ eminently—"far more both in number and degree, than all men or angels have or shall have." Perkin's argument for created grace was not only Chalcedonian, viz., that Christ's assumed nature was consubstantial with ours, it was also soteriological, for "otherwise we should not have any participation of them" (William Perkins, *An exposition of the symbole or creed of the apostles . . .* [London: Printed by John Legatt, Printer to the Universitie of Cambridge, 1616], 169).

49. Aquinas, *STh* III, q. 3, a. 4. The infused gifts were restrained from birth so that they "might gradually and little by little increase and advance before God and men" (Chemnitz, *Two Natures*, 490).

50. Chemnitz agrees with Owen's definition of *gratia habitualis* as finite, created gifts infused into the human nature of Christ and remaining there "formally, habitually, and subjectively." For example, Chemnitz distinguishes the habitual graces and infused gifts of Christ from the "essential attributes of the divine nature" communicated to Christ's humanity according to the *genus maiestaticum*. Following the medieval scholastics, these are effects of the divine operations by which "created and finite gifts" are infused into the human nature (ibid., 248).

51. The infused gifts prepare the humanity "so that it can be an instrument characteristic of, suitable for, and properly disposed for the deity, through which and in communion with and in cooperation with which the divine power of the Logos can exercise and carry out the workings of His divine majesty." (ibid.). The authority of John of Damascus is cited here (ibid., 253).

52. Ibid., 247.

53. In Christ, the *gratia capitis* and *gratia habitualis* admit only a rational distinction: "Hence the personal grace, whereby the soul of Christ is justified, is essentially the same as His grace, as He is the Head of the Church, and justifies others; but there is a distinction of reason between them" (Aquinas, *STh* III, q. 8, a. 5).

54. For Owen, the fullness of communicable grace in Christ, though including "all kinds . . . and all degrees of grace, . . . is created grace." He defines created grace as "grace inherent in a created nature, not infinite," and thus it can be spoken of quantitatively (Owen, "On

Communion," in *Works* 2:66). "He communicates of himself unto us, in the effects of his goodness, grace, and mercy, by the operations of his Spirit in us. Of the same kind will all the communications of the divine nature be unto us, unto all eternity" (Owen, *Works* 1:240). See also Chemnitz, *Two Natures*, 250.

Appendix 6: God's Intrinsic and Declarative Glory in the Reformed-Puritan Tradition

The Reformed-Puritan tradition distinguished *gloria* from *glorificatio*.[1] Furthermore, *glorificatio* is distinguished in both its objective and subjective aspects as divine revelation and human participation in God.[2] In Owen's distinction, there is a real manifestation of the divine essential glory, which results from God's action, and a declarative glory, which is worship.[3] Owen gives a definition of essential glory: "It is the being of God, with that respect which all creatures have unto it."[4]

The glory given to the Mediator, by whom the saints have a participation in glory, is not something that could add to God.[5] Rutherford was attempting to refute Suarez's assertion of God's passibility.[6] God of necessity loves the divine essential glory, and so the divine essence, persons, and attributes.[7] This is similar to Aquinas's distinction between necessary and contingent willing in God, which correlates to a distinction between *ad intra* and *ad extra*. Yet, God could have willed to hide the divine declarative glory by not creating the world.[8] Although Edwards did posit that some of God attributes would have been unexercised apart from creation, he, unlike Gillespie, did not shy away from insisting that the goal of God's creating the world was the emanation of God's essential glory.[9]

Notes

1. Thomas Watson refers to them respectively as the "intrinsical Glory . . . essential to the Godhead," and the "Glory which is ascribed to God, or which his Creatures labour to bring to him" (Watson, "Man's Chief End to Glorifie God," in *A body of practical divinity . . .* [London: Thomas Parkhurst, 1692], 1). According to Samuel Rutherford, "There is a declarative glory, which is not essential to *God*, . . . that shines *ad extra*. And this glory is not essential to *God* as so declared, for he was infinitely glorious from eternity, and should eternally be essentially glorious, though neither world, nor man, nor Angel, had been created." See Samuel Rutherford, *The covenant of life opened; or, a treatise of the covenant of grace* (Edinburgh: Printed by A. A. for Robert Broun, 1655), 29. Edward Leigh succinctly defines this "twofold glory" in God. The one is "essential, infinite, everlasting . . . is called *gloria*" and "receives neither addition nor diminution by

any created power." The other is "accidental, finite, temporary, called *glorificatio*; this ebbs or flowes, shines, or is overshadowed, as goodness or gracelesness prevailes in the world" (*A treatise of divinity consisting of three bookes . . .* [London: William Lee, 1646], 115–16).

2.   There is both "contemplation" as well as "enjoyment" of God, which consists "not only [in] *inspection,* but *possession. . . .* To *behold* God's glory, there is glory revealed to us; but to *partake* of his glory, there is glory revealed in us" (Watson, "Man's Chief End," 12). Muller's twofold distinction of *glorificatio* is this: objectively, as seen in its created effects, and formally, as human subjective recognition of God—that is to say, "the creatures' glorification of their creator" (Richard A. Muller, *Post-Reformation Reformed Dogmatics: The Rise and Development of Reformed Orthodoxy, ca. 1520 to ca. 1725*, vol. 3, *The Divine Essence and Attributes* [Grand Rapids, MI: Baker Academic, 2003], 548–50).

3.   "The manifestation of the glory of God consists really in the effects of his infinite wisdom, goodness, grace, and power;—declaratively, in the express acknowledgement of it with praise" (John Owen, *Christologia: Or, a Declaration of The Glorious Mystery of the Person of Christ, God and Man, to which are Subjoined, Meditations and Discourses on the Glory of Christ*, vol. 1 of *The Works of John Owen, D.D.*, edited by William H. Goold [New York: Robert Carter & Brothers, 1851], ch. 20, 256).

4.   Owen, *Christologia*, ch. 20, 262.

5.   Leigh, *Treatise of Divinity*, 115. Christ had glory communicated to his human nature "in decree and predestination, and that was not God's essential glory, which is a property, for he requires he may have it now, which could not be if he had it from eternity. We glorify God not by putting any excellency into him, but by taking notice of his excellency, and esteeming him accordingly, and making manifest this our high esteem of him."

6.   "Yea this is that which misjudging *Suarez* saith, that the creature may do a real injury to *God*, and take away from *God ius Dei ad gloriam*, his right to glory, but the truth is, the creature by sin darkeneth or overcloudeth his declarative glory, but can take away no essential glory, nor any real right or real good from *God*" (Rutherford, *Covenant of Life Opened*, 27).

7.   "What by necessity of nature *God* wills, that certainly, and by necessity of nature is and existeth, as he loveth himself, and his Son by necessity of nature, and begets, his Son by necessity of nature, so also by necessity of nature *God* is loved, and the Son of God is loved, and the Son is by necessity of nature, begotten of the Father" (ibid., 27).

8.   "For by necessity of nature he loves himself, and cannot but love himself. But he might, if so it had pleased him, never have intended to show forth his own glory, and does not show it forth by necessity of nature as he loves himself. Yea he might never have created the world, never have acted without himself: For he was sufficient within himself and stood in need of no declarative glory" (ibid., 31).

9.   "The supreme end, to glorify his mercy and justice; I mean his declarative glory, that shines *ad extra*; not the essential glory of God, whereby he was infinitely glorious from eternity, and should eternally be essentially glorious, though neither Man nor Angel, nor any other object of his glory had been created" (Gillespie, *The ark of the covenant opened . . .* [London: Tho. Parkhurst, 1677], ch. 2, 35).

Appendix 7: Divine *Energeia* in the Eastern and Western Traditions

Duncan Reid traces two contrasting interpretations of Aristotle's notion of *energeia*. In the East, the Aristotelian categories were developed to distinguish between *ousia* and *energeia*, by interpreting *dunamis* and *energeia* as virtually identical.[1] The terms *energeia* and *energein* were transmitted to the West largely through the Latin Vulgate as *operatio* and *operari*, respectively, and could not convey the idea of divine dispositional powers in which human activity could participate.[2] Since the writings of Iamblichus and Proclus were not translated into Latin during the Middle Ages, the West failed to appreciate the thick description of *energeia* as "the fusion of activity and actuality."[3] "That is why," Bradshaw notes, "when the works of Aristotle were translated in the twelfth and thirteenth centuries, *energeia* had to be rendered in different contexts by three different terms: *operatio*, *actus*, and *actualitas*."[4] In the West, Aristotle's notion of an essence with its power/potentiality (*dunamis*) and energy/actuality (*energeia*) developed into the identification of *energeia* and *ousia* in God as pure actuality (*actus purus*), and into the corollary distinction in creatures between act and potency.[5] This is based on the assumption that eternal things exist of necessity and, therefore, do not include potency with regard to their existence.[6]

Gregory of Palamas and the Notion the Divine *Energeia*

St. Basil emphasized that though God's essence is inaccessible to creatures, God can be known through the divine energies.[7] The distinctions between the essence (*ousia*) and the energies (*energeiai*) of God, made initially by the Cappadocians, were systematically elaborated by Pseudo-Dionysius and fully formulated by Gregory Palamas.[8] For example, Gregory of Nyssa uses a particular causal sequence of nature-power-activity to show that while activity reveals its originating power, nature remains apophatic.[9]

Palamas makes a clear distinction between the uncreated, eternal divine energy from "the effects of the divine energy [which] are creatures."[10] While the divine energetic operations appear as multiple in their temporal manifestations, they are, simultaneously, singular since they proceed from the simple superessentiality of God.[11] As Thomas Anatos has pointed out, the essence-energy distinction in Palamas represents a radicalization of both sides of the transcendence-immanence polarity within God's being.[12] According to Georges Florovsky, the essence-energies dialectic distinguishes (but does not separate) the divine nature from the divine will and corresponds to the necessity-freedom distinction within God.[13]

Furthermore, it is in the uncreated energies surrounding the superessentiality of God where the attributes of God are placed, and where "God's pretemporal but contingent idea of creation is located."[14] The existence of the *uncreated* energies is not dependent upon creation, but neither is the actualized creation coeternal with the energies.[15] Hence, the divine essence (in its three hypostatic modalities), the uncreated energies of the Trinity, and the created world are respectively characterized by eternity, aeonic eternity, and temporality.[16] According to Reid, Georges Florovsky has "reintroduced the Aristotelian distinction between potentiality and actuality" by positing a distinction between the divine idea of creation, which is located in God's aeonic eternity, and actual space-time creation.[17]

CRITIQUE OF THE PALAMITE ESSENCE-ENERGY DISTINCTION

Accordingly, the rejection of the essence-energies distinction, in favor of a Thomistic notion of an active divine essence, can only allow for the explanation of the God-world relation based on a cause-and-effect schema.[18] Paul Negrut has further highlighted a few weaknesses of Palamite trinitarianism. Firstly, while the energies are enhypostatic and only express but are not identical to the divine persons, it follows that "the latter is forced to occupy a kind of intermediary level between the essence and energies," thus distancing *theologia* from *oikonomia*. Secondly, by asserting that the *ousia* is totally impenetrable and incommunicable, Palamas has reified the divine essence altogether beyond the divine persons, departing from the Cappadocians, who identified the personal existence of Father, Son, and Spirit as the *ousia*.[19] In this way, the loyalty of Palamite theology to the Cappadocian contribution of the ontology of divine personhood to theology, and hence the primacy of person over essence, is questioned.[20]

It has been alleged that Palamas's doctrine of the essence-energy distinction threatens the doctrine of divine simplicity. Using such a rationalistic critique, the West has often charged Palamas of separating God into an undefined essence and unreal attributes.[21] In reply to such a charge, Palamas asserts that no composition is introduced into the unity of God, since it is "being acted upon and . . . passivity," and not activity, that makes something mutable and composite.[22]

Palamas denies this and insists on the simultaneous unity and distinction of the divine essence and energies.[23] The essence-energy distinction does not compromise the divine simplicity: "For the distinction in the divinity is not contrary to its unity."[24] On the other hand, the distinction between the essence (superessentiality) and existence (persons and energies) of God, it is argued, concurrently secures the idea of divine transcendence and enables an existentialist conception of God.[25] The *energeiai*, as "powers that inhere," are located in the one essence of God analogous to the human "powers of the senses."[26] The *energeia*, though distinct from the *ousia*, proceeds from it as the essential operation of nature: the essence is not equivalent to, but possesses, the energies.[27] The divine energy reveals, and is thus distinguished from, the divine substance according "to the fact of its existence but not as to what it is."[28]

Latin scholars concede that the Cappadocians distinguished the essence and operations of God *ad extra* but contend that Palamas's distinction between real divine essence and energies *ad intra*, which he inherited from Maximus, is a theological *novum* in relation to early patristic theology.[29] Accordingly, some contend that the essence-energies distinction would not have been worked out as a theological statement had mystical experience not been central to Orthodox theology.[30] If innovation and tradition are not regarded as antithetical in all cases, Palamas should neither be simply regarded as a theological maverick nor a regurgitator, but rather "a traditional innovator."[31]

Moreover, it has been argued that the textual ambiguity in Palamas's writings warrants contrasting interpretations of the distinction between essence and energies as either nominal or real.[32] The doctrine of the divine energies is, in a sense, a *via media* between the static theology of a narrow Thomism and the dynamism of process theology.[33]

Notes

1. Duncan Reid, *Energies of the Spirit: Trinitarian Models in Eastern Orthodox and Western Theology* (Atlanta, GA: Scholars Press, 1997), 15. Here, the notion of movement and mutability (*kinesis*) toward an external telos is removed from *energeia* so that the latter becomes a kind of operation that has its own intrinsic goal. David Bradshaw, *Aristotle East and West: Metaphysics and the Division of Christendom* (Cambridge: Cambridge University Press, 2004), 24.

2. Bradshaw, *Aristotle East and West*, 153.

3. Ibid.

4. Ibid.

5. Reid, *Energies of the Spirit*, 11. The earlier *energeia-dunamis* distinction was later expanded by Aristotle: "As Aristotle broadens *dunamis* to encompass all types of potency, he correspondingly broadens *energeia* to encompass all types of actuality" (Bradshaw, *Aristotle East and West*, 24).

6. Bradshaw, *Aristotle East and West*, 24.

7. "For His energies descend down to us while His essence remains inaccessible." St. Basil, *Epistle of Amphilochius*, as cited in George A. Maloney, *A Theology of "Uncreated Energies,"* 1978 Pere Marquette Theology Lectures (Milwaukee, WI: Marquette University Press, 1978), 63.

8. Georges Florovsky, *Collected Works of Georges Florovsky*, vol. 3, *Creation and Redemption* (Belmont, MA: Nordland, 1976), 62–71. The major primary sources in translation are found in *Gregory Palamas: The Triads* (trans. Gendell). The classic scholarly work on Palamas is John Meyendorff's *A Study of Gregory Palamas* (Crestwood, NY: St. Vladimir's Seminary Press, 1998). For a critique of Meyendorff, see John S. Romanides, "Notes on the Palamite Controversy," *Greek Orthodox Theological Review* 6, no. 2 (Winter 1960–61): 186–270.

9. Lewis Ayres, *Nicaea and Its Legacy: An Approach to Fourth-Century Trinitarian Theology* (Oxford: Oxford University Press, 2004), 354–63.

10. Gregory Palamas, *The One Hundred and Fifty Chapters*, ed. and trans. Robert E. Sinkewicz, Studies and Texts 83 (Toronto: Pontifical Institute of Mediaeval Studies, 1988), ch. 140, 245.

11. St. Maximus the Confessor points out that the human voice is analogous to the energies, in which being one is participated in by many, and not swallowed up by the multitude. Hence, the voice represents the energy of the essence of reason—the former shared by all (its hearers), but yet the reason is one and undivided. See Christos Yannaras, "The Distinction between Essence and Energies and Its Importance for Theology," *St. Vladimir's Theological Quarterly* 19, no. 4 (1975): 236–37, citing Maximus, Scholia on *On the Divine Names* (PG 4, 332CD).

12. Hence, the "energies" serve to secure the intimacy of the union between Creator and creature, while the essence is "elevated" to a superessence that is utterly apophatic and inaccesible to human comprehension and contact. See Thomas L. Anastos, "Gregory Palamas' Radicalization of the Essence, Energies, and Hypostasis Model of God," *Greek Orthodox Theological Review* 38, no. 14 (1993): 335–49.

13. Florovsky, *Works*, 3:69.

14. Reid, *Energies of the Spirit*, 102. This idea of "aeonic eternity" has been suggested by modern Orthodox theologians like Dumitru Stăniloae and Georges Florovsky.

15. Lossky, *The Mystical Theology of the Eastern Church* (Crestwood, NY: St. Vladimir's Seminary Press, 1997), 74–75.

16. Edwards's description of God in immanent (the processions), œconomic (the divine counsels and decrees), and economic (creation and redemption) terms seems to show similarities with this distinction between eternity, aeonic eternity, and temporality. The first is the realm where the "necessity" of the processions and God's knowledge of all possibilities are located; the second, the divine volition at work in virtualizing possibilities through election and decision; and the third, the spatio-temporal creation where the divine decisions are actualized.

17. Reid, *Energies of the Spirit*, 62.

18. Yannaras, "Distinction between Essence and Energies," 239. The Latin conceptuality cannot account for "the ontological reality of the world, the formation of matter and its essential character."

19. Paul Negrut, "Orthodox Soteriology: Theosis," *Churchman* 109, no. 2 (1995): 166–67.

20. John D. Zizioulas, in *Being as Communion: Studies in Personhood and the Church* (Crestwood, NY: St. Vladimir's Seminary Press, 1997), argues that the Cappadocian fathers are to be credited with bequeathing to posterity an ontology of personhood.

21. The critique that there are "two distinct divine spheres," of a formless divine essence and attributes without being, rests on a misunderstanding of Palamas's position (Barth, *CD* II.1, 331–32). Barth compares Gilbert of Porree, charged by the Synod of Reims (1148) for teaching a real distinction between the essence and attributes of God, with Gregory Palamas's doctrine of the uncreated light. He defends Barlaam's contention of the inseparability of the essence and attributes, and charges Eastern hesychasm of maintaining an abstract doctrine of divine simplicity while desiring direct mystical experience.

22. Palamas, *One Hundred and Fifty Chapters*, ch. 145, 251.

23. both the uncreated essence (*aktistos ousia*) and uncreated energy (*aktistos energeia*) are inseparably united and represent, for Palamas, the "one uncreated divinity [*aktistos theotes*] of the Father, the Son and the Holy Spirit." He cites Maximus, Gregory of Nyssa, and Cyril of Alexandria as authorities here (Gregory Palamas, *Dialogue between an Orthodox and a Barlaamite*, trans. Rein Ferwerda. [Binghamton, NY: Global Publications / CEMERS, 1999], ch. 16, 57). Though Palamas acknowledges that there is, in God, "both what is substance and what is not substance," he denies that the divine energy should then be regarded as either nonexistent or accidental: it is real, eternal and immutable. He admits that that the divine energy could be called "a quasi-accident," insofar as it is not substantial (Palamas, *One Hundred and Fifty Chapters*, ch. 135, 241).

24. Palamas, *Dialogue*, ch. 16, 58.

25. "The originality of the Palamite response to the essentialist concept of God does not consist in adding another element—the energies—to the Divine being, but in thinking of God Himself in existentialist terms, while holding to His absolute transcendence" (John Meyendorff, *Palamas and Orthodox Spirituality*, 126, as cited by Reid, *Energies of the Spirit*, 85).

26. Palamas, *Triads*, 93.

27. Ibid.

28. Palamas, *One Hundred and Fifty Chapters*, ch. 141, 247.

29. Gerry Russo, "Rahner and Palamas: A Unity of Grace," *St. Vladimir's Theological Quarterly* 32, no. 2 (1988): 162n17.

30. Roland D. Zimany, "The Divine Energies in Orthodox Theology," *Diakonia* 11, no. 3 (1976): 284.

31. George Mantzarides, "Tradition and Renewal in the Theology of Saint Gregory Palamas," *Eastern Churches Review* 9 (1977): 1.

32. A. N. Williams, *Ground of Union: Deification in Aquinas and Palamas* (New York: Oxford University Press, 1999), 172. Williams's final judgment is that of "a nominal distinction, at least as far as the *Triads* and the *Capita* are concerned," and "a complete lack of clarity on this point" must be minimally recognized.

33. Petro B. T. Bilaniuk, *Theology and Economy: An Eastern Approach* (Bangalore: Published for Centre for Indian and Inter-Religious Studies, Rome, by Dharmaram Publications, 1980), 60. "Thus, God in His essence is *primus motor immobilis*, but in His uncreated energies He is *primus motor mobilissimus*."

Selected Bibliography

Adams, Marilyn McCord. "Biting and Chomping Our Salvation: Holy Eucharist, Radically Understood." In *Redemptive Transformation in Practical Theology: Essays in Honor of James E. Loder, Jr.*, ed. Dana R. Wright and John D. Kuentzel, 69–94. Grand Rapids, MI: Eerdmans, 2004.

Adams, Thomas. *A commentary or, exposition upon the divine second epistle generall, written by the blessed apostle St. Peter.* London: Jacob Bloome, 1633.

Aghiorgoussis, Maximos. "Orthodox Soteriology." In Meyendorff and Tobias, *Salvation in Christ,* 35–40.

Ames, William. *The Marrow of Sacred Divinity Drawne Out of the Holy Scriptures, and the Interpreters thereof, and Brought into Method.* London: Henry Overton, 1642.

Anastos, Thomas L. "Gregory Palamas' Radicalization of the Essence, Energies, and Hypostasis Model of God." *Greek Orthodox Theological Review* 38, no. 14 (1993): 335–49.

Anatolios, Khaled. *Athanasius: The Coherence of His Thought.* London: Routledge, 1998.

Annesley, Samuel. *Containing the first volume of the exercise at Cripplegate, and part of the supplement.* Vol. 1 of *The morning exercises at Cripplegate, St. Giles in the Fields, and in Southwark: being divers sermons, preached A.D. MDCLIX–MDCLXXXIX. By several ministers of the Gospel in or near London.* Edited by James Nichols. London: Thomas Tegg, 1844.

Aretius, Benedictus. *A short history of Valentinus Gentilis the tritheist, tryed, condemned, and put to death by the Protestant Reformed city and church of Bern in Switzerland, for asserting the three divine persons of the Trinity, to be three distinct, eternal spirits, &c.* London: E. Whitlock, 1696.

Asselt, Willem J. van. *The Federal Theology of Johannes Cocceius (1603–1669).* Translated by Raymond A. Blacketer. Leiden, Netherlands: Brill, 2001.

Athanasius, Saint. *On the Incarnation: The Treatise* De Incarnatione Dei Verbi. Translated and edited by a Religious of C. S. M. V. With an Introduction by C. S. Lewis. Crestwood, NY: St. Vladimir's Seminary Press, 1998.

Augustine, Saint. "The City of God." In *St Augustin's City of God and Christian Doctrine.* Select Library of the Nicene and Post-Nicene Fathers of the

Christian Church, ser. 1, vol. 2. Edited by Philip Schaff. Peabody, MA: Hendrickson, 1994.

———. *Confessions.* Translated with an introduction and notes by Henry Chadwick. Oxford World Classics. Oxford: Oxford University Press, 1991.

———. *The Works of Saint Augustine, Part I, Vol. 5: The Trinity.* Publications of the Augustinian Heritage Institute, ed. John E. Rotelle. Introduction, translation, and notes by Edmund Hill. Brooklyn, NY: New City, 1991.

Ayres, Lewis. *Nicaea and Its Legacy: An Approach to Fourth-Century Trinitarian Theology.* Oxford: Oxford University Press, 2004.

Baillie, Donald M. *God Was in Christ: An Essay on Incarnation and Atonement.* New York: Charles Scribner's Sons, 1948. Reprint, Eugene, OR: Wipf and Stock, 2001.

Badcock, Gary D. *Light of Truth and Fire of Love: A Theology of the Holy Spirit.* Grand Rapids, MI: Eerdmans, 1997.

Balserak, Jon. "'The Accommodating Act Par Excellence?': An Inquiry into the Incarnation and Calvin's Understanding of Accommodation." *Scottish Journal of Theology* 55, no. 4 (2002): 408–23.

Balthasar, Hans Urs von. *Cosmic Liturgy: The Universe According to Maximus the Confessor.* Translated by Brian E. Daley. San Francisco: Ignatius, 2003.

———. *Theo-Drama: Theological Dramatic Theory.* Vol. 3, *The Dramatis Personae: The Person in Christ.* Translated by Graham Harrison. San Francisco: Ignatius, 1992.

Barnes, Michel R. "Augustine in Contemporary Trinitarian Theology." *Theological Studies* 56 (June 1995): 237–51.

———. "De Regnon Reconsidered," *Augustinian Studies* 26 (1995): 51–79.

Barth, Karl. *Church Dogmatics.* Vol. 1, pt. 1, *The Doctrine of the Word of God.* Edited by G. W. Bromiley and T. F. Torrance. Translated by G. T. Thomson and Harold Knight. Paperback ed. London: T&T Clark International, 2004.

———. *Church Dogmatics.* Vol. 1, pt. 2, *The Doctrine of the Word of God.* Edited by G. W. Bromiley and T. F. Torrance. Translated by G. T. Thomson and Harold Knight. Paperback ed. London: T&T Clark International, 2004.

———. *Church Dogmatics.* Vol. 2, pt. 1, *The Doctrine of God.* Edited by G. W. Bromiley and T. F. Torrance. Translated by T. H. L. Parker and J. L. M. Haire. Edinburgh: T&T Clark, 1957.

———.*Church Dogmatics.* Vol. 4, pt. 1, *The Doctrine of Reconciliation.* Edited by G. W. Bromiley and T. F. Torrance. Translated by G. W. Bromiley. Edinburgh: T&T Clark, 1956.

———. *Church Dogmatics*. Vol. 4, pt. 2, *The Doctrine of Reconciliation*. Edited by G. W. Bromiley and T. F. Torrance. Translated by G. W. Bromiley. Edinburgh: T&T Clark, 1958.

———. *The Göttingen Dogmatics: Instruction in the Christian Religion.* Vol. 1. Edited by Hannelotte Reiffen. Translated by Geoffrey W. Bromiley. Grand Rapids, MI: Eerdmans, 1991.

Bartos, Emil. *Deification in Eastern Orthodox Theology: An Evaluation and Critique of the Theology of Dumitru Stăniloae.* Paternoster Biblical and Theological Monographs. Carlisle, UK: Paternoster, 1999.

Basil the Great, Saint. *The Treatise De Spiritu Sancto.* Translated by Blomfield Jackson. In Schaff and Wace, *Nicene and Post-Nicene Fathers*, vol. 8.

Bates, William. *The harmony of the divine attributes, in the contrivance and accomplishment of man's redemption by the Lord Jesus Christ. Or discourses, wherein is shewed, how the wisdom, mercy, justice, holiness, power and truth of God are glorified in that great and blessed work.* London: Nathaniel Ranew, Jonathan Robinson and Brabazon Aylmer, 1674.

Bathrellos, Demetrios. *The Byzantine Christ: Person, Nature, and Will in the Christology of Saint Maximus the Confessor.* Oxford Early Christian Studies. Edited by Gillian Clark and Andrew Louth. Oxford: Oxford University Press, 2004.

———. "The Relationship between the Divine Will and the Human Will of Jesus Christ according to Saint Maximus the Confessor." In Wiles and Yarnold, *Papers Presented at the Thirteenth International Conference on Patristic Studies*, 346–52.

Battles, Ford L. "God Was Accommodating Himself to Human Capacity." *Interpretation* 31 (1977): 19–28.

Bauckham, Richard, ed. *God Will Be All in All: The Eschatology of Jürgen Moltmann.* Edinburgh: T&T Clark, 1999.

Baxter, Richard. *A Christian directory: or, a summ of practical theology, and cases of conscience. Directing Christians, how to use their knowledge and faith; how to improve all helps and means, and to perform all duties; how to overcome temptations, and to escape or mortifie every sin. In four parts. I. Christian ethicks (or private duties.) II. Christian oeconomicks (or family duties.) III. Christian ecclesiasticks (or church duties.) IV. Christian politicks (or duties to your rules and neighbours.).* London: Thomas Parkhurst, Jonathan Robinson, and John Lawrence, 1707.

———. *Gildas salvianus: The reformed pastor. Shewing the nature of the pastoral work; especially in private instruction and catechizing. With an open confession of our too open sins. Prepared for a day of humiliation kept at Worcester, Decemb. 4. 1655. by the ministers of that county, who subscribed the agreement for catechizing and personal instruction, at their entrance upon that work.* London: Thomas Parkhurst, Jonathan Robinson, and John Lawrence, 1707.

———. *The poor man's family-book. I. Teaching him how to become a true Christian. II. How to live as a Christian towards God, himself, and others, in all his relations; especially in his family. III. How to die as a Christian in hope and comfort, and so to be glorified with Christ for ever. In plain familiar conference between a teacher and a learner. With a form of exhortation to the sick; two catechisms; a profession of Christianity; forms of prayer for various uses, and some psalms and hymns.* London: Thomas Parkhurst, Jonathan Robinson, and John Lawrence, 1707.

———. *A saint or a brute. The certain necessity and excellency of holiness, &c. So plainly proved, and urgently applyed, as by the blessing of God may convince and save the miserable, impenitent, ungodly sensualists, if they will not let the Devil hinder them from a sober and serious reading and considering. To be communicated by the charitable, that desire the conversion and salvation of souls, while the patience of God, and the day of grace and hope continue.* London: Thomas Parkhurst, Jonathan Robinson, and John Lawrence, 1707.

Beeke, Joel R., and Mark Jones. *A Puritan Theology: Doctrine for Life.* Grand Rapids, MI: Reformation Heritage Books, 2012.

Benin, Stephen D. "The 'Cunning of God' and Divine Accommodation." *Journal of the History of Ideas* 45, no. 2 (April–June 1984): 179–91.

———. *Footprints of God: Divine Accommodation in Jewish and Christian Thought.* Albany: State University of New York Press, 1993.

Berkhof, Louis. *Manual of Christian Doctrine.* Grand Rapids, MI: Eerdmans, 2002. Originally published in 1933.

———. *Reformed Dogmatics.* 3 vols. Grand Rapids, MI: Eerdmans, 1932.

———. *Systematic Theology.* New combined edition, with a new preface by Richard E. Muller. Grand Rapids, MI: Eerdmans, 1996.

Berkouwer, Gerrit C. *Studies in Dogmatics: The Person of Christ.* Translated by John Vriend. Grand Rapids, MI: Eerdmans, 1954.

Beza, Theodore. *Adversus sacramentariorum errorem pro vera Christi praesentia in coena domini, homiliae duae, auctore Nathanaele Nesekio.* Geneva, 1574.

Bilaniuk, Petro B. T. *Theology and Economy of the Holy Spirit: An Eastern Approach.* Placid Lecture Series, no. 2. Bangalore: Published for Centre for Indian and Inter-Religious Studies, Rome, by Dharmaram Publications, 1980.

Boff, Leonardo. *Trinity and Society.* Translated by Paul Burns. Theology and Liberation Series. Maryknoll, NY: Orbis Books, 1988.

Bombaro, John J. "Jonathan Edwards' Vision of Salvation." *Westminster Theological Journal* 65 (2003): 45–67.

Bonaventure of Bagnoregio, Saint. *Commentaria in Librum Primum Sententiarum.* English translation by the Franciscan Archive. Accompanied by the Latin text of the Quaracchi Edition. http://www.franciscan-archive.org/bonaventura/I-Sent.html.

The Book of concord: Or, the symbolical books of the Evangelical Lutheran Church. Translated from the original languages, with analyses and an exhaustive index. Edited by Henry Eyster Jacobs. Translated by Charles P. Krauth and Charles F. Schaeffer. United Lutheran Publication House, 1911.

Braaten, Carl E. *Justification: The Article by Which the Church Stands or Falls.* Minneapolis: Augsburg Fortress, 1990.

Bradshaw, David. *Aristotle East and West: Metaphysics and the Division of Christendom.* Cambridge: Cambridge University Press, 2004.

Brand, David C. *Beatific Vision, Benevolence and Self-Love: A Contextual Study of Jonathan Edwards with Special Reference to the Cartesian Revolution and the Arminian Triumph in Puritan New England.* American Academy of Religion Series. New York: Oxford University Press, 1991.

Bray, Gerald L. *The Doctrine of God.* Downers Grove, IL: InterVarsity, 1993.

Brown, John. *The life of justification opened. Or, a treatise grounded upon Gal. 2. 11. Wherein the orthodox doctrine of justification by faith, & imputation of Christ's righteousness, is clearly expounded, solidly confirmed, & learnedly vindicated from the various objections of its adversaries. Whereunto are subjoined some arguments against universal redemption.* Utrecht, 1695.

Brunner, Emil. *Dogmatics I: The Christian Doctrine of God.* Library of Theological Translations. Cambridge: James Clarke, 1949.

Budziszewski, J. "The Natural, the Connatural, and the Unnatural." Unpublished paper presented at the St. Thomas and the Natural Law conference, Jacques Maritain Center, University of Notre Dame, Notre Dame, Indiana, July 2004. Available at http://maritain.nd.edu/jmc/ti04/budz.htm.

Burke, Patrick. *Reinterpreting Rahner: A Critical Study of His Major Themes.* New York: Fordham University Press, 2002.

Burns, J. Patout, and Gerald M. Fagin. *The Holy Spirit.* Message of the Fathers of the Church. Eugene, OR: Wipf and Stock, 1984.

Bush, Michael. "Jesus Christ in the Theology of Jonathan Edwards." Ph.D. diss., Princeton Theological Seminary, 2003.

Bush, Randall B. "Trinitarian Conflict: A Re-assessment of Trinitarian Analogies in the Light of Modern Psychological and Sociological Conflict Theories." *Perspectives in Religious Studies* 19, no. 1 (Spring 1992): 9–12.

Caldwell, Robert W., III. *Communion in the Spirit: The Holy Spirit as the Bond of Union in the Theology of Jonathan Edwards.* Studies in Evangelical History and Thought. Milton Keynes, UK: Paternoster, 2006.

Calvin, John. *Calvin: Institutes of Christian Religion.* 2 vols. Edited by John T. McNeill. Translated by Ford Lewis Battles. Library of Christian Classics 20. Philadelphia: Westminster, 1960.

Cartwright, Thomas. *A confutation of the Rhemists translation, glosses, and annotations on the New Testament, so farre as they containe manifest impieties, heresies, idolatries, superstitions, prophanesse, treasons, slanders, absurdities, falsehoods, and other evils. . . .* New York: Theatrum Orbis Terrarum, Da Capo, 1971.

Cessario, Romanus. *Christian Faith and the Theological Life.* Washington: Catholic University of America Press, 1996.

Chai, Leon. *Jonathan Edwards and the Limits of Enlightenment Philosophy.* New York: Oxford University Press, 1998.

Chapman, John. "Monothelitism and Monothelites." In *The Catholic Encyclopedia*, vol. 10. New York: Robert Appleton Company, 1911. http://www.newadvent.org/cathen/10502a.htm.

Chemnitz, Martin. *The Two Natures in Christ.* Translated by J. A. O. Preus. St. Louis, MO: Concordia, 1971. Originally published as *De Duabus Naturis in Christo*. Leipzig, 1578.

Cherry, Conrad. *The Theology of Jonathan Edwards: A Reappraisal.* Bloomington: Indiana University Press, 1990.

Cheynell, Francis. *The divine triunity of the Father, Son, and Holy Spirit: or, the blessed doctrine of the three coessentiall subsistents in the eternall Godhead without any confusion or division of the distinct subsistences, or multiplication of the most single and entire Godhead.* London: Samuel Gellibrand, 1650.

Clark, Mary T. *The Saint Augustine Lecture 1969: Augustinian Personalism.* The Saint Augustine Lecture Series, ed. Robert P. Russell. Villanova, PA: Villanova University Press, 1970.

Clarke, Samuel. *A Demonstration of of the Being and Attributes of God, and Other Writings.* Edited by Ezio Vailati. Cambridge Texts in the History of Philosophy. Cambridge: Cambridge University Press, 1998.

Clarke, W. Norris. "To Be Is to Be Substance-in-Relation." In *Metaphysics as Foundation: Essays in Honor of Ivor Leclerc*, edited by Paul A. Bogaard and Gordon Treash, 164–83. Albany: State University of New York Press, 1993.

Cleenewerck, Laurent A. *His Broken Body: Understanding and Healing the Schism between the Roman Catholic and Eastern Orthodox Churches*. Washington, DC: Euclid University Consortium Press, 2007.

Clendenin, Daniel B., ed. *Eastern Orthodox Theology: A Contemporary Reader*. Grand Rapids, MI: Baker Academic, 2003.

Coakley, Sarah. *Powers and Submission: Spirituality, Philosophy and Gender*. Oxford: Blackwell, 2002.

Coffey, David M. *Deus Trinitas: The Doctrine of the Triune God*. New York: Oxford University Press, 1999.

———. "The Holy Spirit as the Mutual Love of the Father and the Son." *Theological Studies* 51, no. 2 (June 1990): 193–229.

———. "The 'Incarnation' of the Holy Spirit in Christ." *Theological Studies* 45 (1984): 466–80.

———. "*Quaestio Disputata*: Response to Neil Ormerod, and Beyond." *Theological Studies* 68 (December 2007): 900–15.

———. "The Roman 'Clarification' of the Doctrine of the Filioque." *International Journal of Systematic Theology* 5, no. 1 (March 2003): 3–21.

———. "The Theandric Nature of Christ." *Theological Studies* 60, no. 3 (September 1999): 405–31.

Congar, Yves. *I Believe in the Holy Spirit*. Translated by David Smith. New York: Crossroad, 1983.

Cooey, Paula M. *Jonathan Edwards on Nature and Destiny*. Studies in American Religion 16. Lewiston, NY: Edwin Mellen, 1985.

Cooper, Adam G. *The Body in St Maximus the Confessor: Holy Flesh, Wholly Deified*. Oxford: Oxford University Press, 2005.

Cousins, Ewert. Introduction to *The Soul's Journey into God; The Tree of Life; The Life of St. Francis*. Translated and introduction by Ewert Cousins. The Classics of Western Spirituality. Mahwah, NJ: Paulist, 1978.

Copan, Paul. "Jonathan Edwards's Philosophical Influences: Lockean or Malebranchean?" *Journal of the Evangelical Theological Society* 44, no. 1 (March 2001): 107–24.

Coxhead, Steven R. "John Calvin's Subordinate Doctrine of Justification by Works." *Westminster Theological Journal* 71 (Spring 2009): 1–19.

Cragg, Gerald R., ed. *The Cambridge Platonists.* Lanham, MD: University Press of America, 1985. Originally published, New York: Oxford University Press, 1968.

Crisp, Oliver D. *Divinity and Humanity: The Incarnation Reconsidered.* Current Issues in Theology. Cambridge: Cambridge University Press, 2007.

———. "Jonathan Edwards on Divine Simplicity." *Religious Studies* 39 (2003): 23–41.

———. "Jonathan Edwards' Panentheism." In Schweitzer, *Jonathan Edwards as Contemporary,* 107–25.

Cross, Richard. "Divine Monarchy in Gregory of Nazianzus." *Journal of Early Christian Studies* 14, no. 1 (Spring 2006): 105–16.

———. *Duns Scotus.* Great Medieval Thinkers. New York: Oxford University Press, 1999.

———. *Duns Scotus on God.* Ashgate Studies in the History of Philosophical Theology. Burlington, VT: Ashgate, 2005.

———. "Gregory of Nyssa on Universals." *Vigiliae Christianae* 56 (2002): 372–410.

———. "The 'Incarnation' of the Holy Spirit in Christ." *Theological Studies* 45 (1984): 466–80.

———. "Incarnation, Omnipresence, and Action at a Distance." *Neue Zeitschrift für Systematische Theologie end Religionphilosophie* 45, no. 3 (2003): 293–312.

———. "Individual Natures in the Christology of Leontius of Byzantium." *Journal of Early Christian Studies* 10, no. 2 (Summer 2002): 245–65.

———. *Metaphysics of the Incarnation.* New York: Oxford University Press, 2002.

———. "On Generic and Derivation Views of God's Trinitarian Substance." *Scottish Journal of Theology* 56, no. 4 (2003): 464–80.

———. "Parts and Properties in Christology." In *Reason, Faith and History: Philosophical Essays for Paul Helm,* edited by Martin F. Stone, 177–92. Aldershot, UK: Ashgate, 2008.

———. "*Quid tres?* On What Precisely Augustine Professes Not to Understand in *De Trinitate* 5 and 7." *Harvard Theological Review* 100, no. 2 (June 2007): 215–32.

———. "A Recent Contribution on the Distinction between Monophysitism and Chalcedonianism." *Thomist* 65 (2001): 361–83.

———. "The Roman 'Clarification' of the Doctrine of the Filioque." *International Journal of Systematic Theology* 5, no. 1 (March 2003): 3–21.

Crowley, Paul G. "*Instrumentum Divinitatis* in Thomas Aquinas: Recovering the Divinity of Christ." *Theological Studies* 52 (1991): 451–75.

Cyril of Alexandria, Saint. *On the Unity of Christ.* Translated and with an introduction by John Anthony McGuckin. Crestwood, NY: St. Vladimir's Seminary Press, 1995.

Daley, Brian E. "The Christology of Leontius of Byzantium: Personalism or Dialectics." In *Papers from the Ninth Conference on Patristic Studies 1983, Oxford, England, Patristic Monograph Series.* Philadephia Patristic Foundation [typescript]. As quoted in Grillmeier, *Christ in Christian Tradition,* 2:194.

———. "Nature and the 'Mode of Union': Late Patristic Models for the Personal Unity of Christ." In Davis, Kendall, and O'Collins, *The Incarnation,* 164–96.

———. "A Richer Union: Leontius of Byzantium and the Relationship of Human and Divine in Christ." *Studia Patristica* 24 (1993): 239–65.

Danaher, William J., Jr. *The Trinitarian Ethics of Jonathan Edwards.* Columbia Series in Reformed Theology. Louisville, KY: Westminster John Knox, 2004.

Daniel, Stephen H. *The Philosophy of Jonathan Edwards: A Study in Divine Semiotics.* Indiana Series in the Philosophy of Religion, ed. Merold Westphal. Bloomington: Indiana University Press, 1994.

Davenant, John. *An exposition of the Epistle of St. Paul to the Colossians. Translated from the original Latin; with a life of the author, and notes . . . by Josiah Allport. To the whole is added, a translation of* Dissertatio de morte Christi *by the same prelate.* London: Hamilton, Adams, and Co., 1831.

Davidson, Ivor J. "Theologizing the Human Jesus: An Ancient (and Modern) Approach to Christology Assessed." *International Journal of Systematic Theology* 3, no. 2 (July 2001): 129–53.

Davis, Stephen T., Daniel Kendall, and Gerald O'Collins, eds. *The Incarnation: An Interdisciplinary Symposium on the Incarnation of the Son of God.* New York: Oxford University Press, 2002.

———. *The Trinity: An Interdisciplinary Symposium on the Trinity.* New York: Oxford University Press, 2002.

Delattre, Roland André. *Beauty and Sensibility in the Thought of Jonathan Edwards: An Essay in Aesthetics and Theological Ethics.* New Haven: Yale University Press, 1968.

———. "Beauty and Theology: A Reappraisal of Jonathan Edwards." *Soundings* 51, no. 1 (Spring 1968): 60–79.

———. "The Theological Ethics of Jonathan Edwards: A Homage to Paul Ramsey." *Journal of Religious Ethics* 19, no. 2 (Fall 1991): 71–102.

Del Colle, Ralph. *Christ and the Spirit: Spirit-Christology in Trinitarian Perspective.* New York: Oxford University Press, 1994.

de Prospo, R. C. *Theism in the Discourse of Jonathan Edwards.* Newark: University of Delaware Press, 1985.

Descartes, René. *The Philosophical Works of Descartes.* 2 vols. Translated by Elizabeth S. Haldane and G. R. T. Ross. Cambridge: Cambridge University Press, 1911–12.

Dietz Moss, Jean. *"Godded with God": Hendrik Niclaes and His Family of Love.* Philadelphia: American Philosophical Society, 1981.

Dodds, E. R. *Proclus: The Elements of Theology.* A revised text with translation, introduction and commentary by E. R. Dodds. Oxford: Clarendon Press, 1963.

Dorner, I. A. *History of the Development of the Doctrine of the Person of Christ.* 5 vols. Clark's Foreign Theological Library, 3rd ser. Edinburgh: T&T Clark, 1891.

Downame, John. *The Christian warfare against the devill world and flesh wherein is described their nature, the maner of their fight and meanes to obtaine victory.* London: William Stansby, 1634.

———. *The summe of sacred divinitie first briefly & methodically propounded: and then more largly & cleerely handled and explaned.* London: William Barret, [1620?].

Dragas, George D. "Exchange or Communication of Properties and Deification: *Antidosis* or *Communicatio Idiomatum* and *Theosis*." *Greek Orthodox Theological Review* 43, nos. 1–4 (Spring–Winter 1988): 377–99.

Du Pin, Lewis Ellies. *A New History of Ecclesiastical Writers: Containing an Account of the Authors of the Several Books of the Old and New Testament; and the Lives and Writings of the Primitive Fathers; an Abridgement and Catalogue of all their Works; Censures Determining the Genuine and the Spurious, a Judgment upon their Style and Doctrine, and the Various Editions of their Writings: to which is added, a Compendious History of the Councils; and many necessary Tables and Indexes.* 15 vols. in 7. 3rd ed. London: Printed for Abel Smalle and Cim. Childe, at the Unicorn at the West-End of the St. Paul's Church-Yard, 1696.

Edmondson, Stephen. *Calvin's Christology.* Cambridge: Cambridge University Press, 2004.

Edwards, John. *Theologia reformata: or, the body and substance of the Christian religion.* London: Printed for John Lawrence, John Wyat, and Ranew Robinson, 1713.

Edwards, Jonathan. *Charity and Its Fruits: Christian Love as Manifested in the Heart and Life.* Edited by Tryon Edwards. London: Banner of Truth Trust, 1969.

———. *Treatise on Grace and Other Posthumously Published Writings.* Edited by Paul Helm. Cambridge: James Clarke, 1971.

———. *The Sermons of Jonathan Edwards: A Reader.* Edited by Wilson H. Kimnach, Kenneth P. Minkema, and Douglas A. Sweeney. New Haven: Yale University Press, 1999.

———. *The Works of Jonathan Edwards.* Vol. 1, *Freedom of the Will.* Edited by Paul Ramsey. New Haven: Yale University Press, 1957.

———. *The Works of Jonathan Edwards.* Vol. 2, *Religious Affections.* Edited by John E. Smith. New Haven: Yale University Press, 1981.

———. *The Works of Jonathan Edwards.* Vol. 3, *Original Sin.* Edited by Clyde Holbrook. New Haven: Yale University Press, 1970.

———. *The Works of Jonathan Edwards.* Vol. 4, *The Great Awakening.* Edited by C. C. Goen. New Haven: Yale University Press, 1972.

———. *The Works of Jonathan Edwards.* Vol. 5, *Apocalyptic Writings.* Edited by Stephen J. Stein. New Haven: Yale University Press, 1977.

———. *The Works of Jonathan Edwards.* Vol. 6, *Scientific and Philosophical Writings.* Edited by Wallace E. Anderson. New Haven: Yale University Press, 1980.

———. *The Works of Jonathan Edwards.* Vol. 7, *The Life of David Brainerd.* Edited by Norman Pettit. New Haven: Yale University Press, 1984.

———. *The Works of Jonathan Edwards.* Vol. 8, *Ethical Writings.* Edited by Paul Ramsey. New Haven: Yale University Press, 1989.

———. *The Works of Jonathan Edwards.* Vol. 9, *A History of the Work of Redemption.* Edited by John F. Wilson. New Haven: Yale University Press, 1989.

———. *The Works of Jonathan Edwards.* Vol. 10, *Sermons and Discourses 1720–1723.* Edited by Wilson H. Kimnach. New Haven: Yale University Press, 1992.

———. *The Works of Jonathan Edwards.* Vol. 11, *Typological Writings.* Edited by Wallace E. Anderson, Mason I. Lowance Jr., and David H. Watters. New Haven: Yale University Press, 1993.

———. *The Works of Jonathan Edwards.* Vol. 13, *The "Miscellanies" (Entry Nos. a–z, aa–zz, 1–500).* Edited by Thomas A. Schafer. New Haven: Yale University Press, 1994.

———. *The Works of Jonathan Edwards.* Vol. 14, *Sermons and Discourses: 1723–1729.* Edited by Kenneth P. Minkema. New Haven: Yale University Press, 1997.

———. *The Works of Jonathan Edwards*. Vol. 15, *Notes on Scripture*. Edited by Stephen J. Stein. New Haven: Yale University Press, 1998.

———. *The Works of Jonathan Edwards*. Vol. 17, *Sermons and Discourses, 1730–1733*. Edited by Mark Valeri. New Haven: Yale University Press, 1999.

———. *The Works of Jonathan Edwards*. Vol. 18, *The "Miscellanies" (Entry Nos. 501–832)*. Edited by Ava Chamberlain. New Haven: Yale University Press, 2000.

———. *The Works of Jonathan Edwards*. Vol. 19, *Sermons and Discourses, 1734–1738*. Edited by M. X. Lesser. New Haven: Yale University Press, 2001.

———. *The Works of Jonathan Edwards*. Vol. 20, *The "Miscellanies" (Entry Nos. 833–1152)*. Edited by Amy Plantinga Pauw. New Haven: Yale University Press, 2002.

———. *The Works of Jonathan Edwards*. Vol. 21, *Writings on the Trinity, Grace, and Faith*. Edited by Sang Hyun Lee. New Haven: Yale University Press, 2002.

———. *The Works of Jonathan Edwards*. Vol. 22, *Sermons and Discourses, 1739–1742*. Edited by Harry S. Stout and Nathan O. Hatch, with Kyle P. Farley. New Haven: Yale University Press, 2003.

———. *The Works of Jonathan Edwards*. Vol. 23, *The "Miscellanies" (Entry Nos. 1153–1360)*. Edited by Douglas A. Sweeney. New Haven: Yale University Press, 2002.

———. *The Works of Jonathan Edwards*. Vol. 24, *The "Blank Bible."* Edited by Stephen J. Stein. New Haven: Yale University Press, 2006.

———. *The Works of Jonathan Edwards*. Vol. 25, *Sermons and Discourses, 1743–1758*. Edited by Wilson H. Kimnach. New Haven: Yale University Press, 2006.

———. *The Works of Jonathan Edwards Online*. Vol. 27, *"Controversies" Notebook*. New Haven: Jonathan Edwards Center at Yale University, 2008.

———. *The Works of Jonathan Edwards Online*. Vol. 28, *Minor Controversial Writings*. New Haven: Jonathan Edwards Center at Yale University, 2008.

———. *The Works of Jonathan Edwards Online*. Vol. 42, *Sermons, Series II, 1723–1727*. New Haven: Jonathan Edwards Center at Yale University, 2008.

———. *The Works of Jonathan Edwards Online*. Vol. 43, *Sermons, Series II, 1728–1729*. New Haven: Jonathan Edwards Center at Yale University, 2008.

———. *The Works of Jonathan Edwards Online*. Vol. 44, *Sermons, Series II, 1729*. New Haven: Jonathan Edwards Center at Yale University, 2008.

———. *The Works of Jonathan Edwards Online*. Vol. 45, *Sermons, Series II, 1729–1731*. New Haven: Jonathan Edwards Center at Yale University, 2008.

——. *The Works of Jonathan Edwards Online.* Vol. 46, *Sermons, Series II, 1731–1732.* New Haven: Jonathan Edwards Center at Yale University, 2008.

——. *The Works of Jonathan Edwards Online.* Vol. 47, *Sermons, Series II, 1731–1732.* New Haven: Jonathan Edwards Center at Yale University, 2008.

——. *The Works of Jonathan Edwards Online.* Vol. 48, *Sermons, Series II, 1733.* New Haven: Jonathan Edwards Center at Yale University, 2008.

——. *The Works of Jonathan Edwards Online.* Vol. 49, *Sermons, Series II, 1734.* New Haven: Jonathan Edwards Center at Yale University, 2008.

——. *The Works of Jonathan Edwards Online.* Vol. 51, *Sermons, Series II, 1736.* New Haven: Jonathan Edwards Center at Yale University, 2008.

——. *The Works of Jonathan Edwards Online.* Vol. 52, *Sermons, Series II, 1737.* New Haven: Jonathan Edwards Center at Yale University, 2008.

——. *The Works of Jonathan Edwards Online.* Vol. 53, *Sermons, Series II, and Undated, 1734–1738.* New Haven: Jonathan Edwards Center at Yale University, 2008.

——. *The Works of Jonathan Edwards Online.* Vol. 54, *Sermons, Series II, 1739.* New Haven: Jonathan Edwards Center at Yale University, 2008.

——. *The Works of Jonathan Edwards Online.* Vol. 55, *Sermons, Series II, January–June 1740.* New Haven: Jonathan Edwards Center at Yale University, 2008.

——. *The Works of Jonathan Edwards Online.* Vol. 56, *Sermons, Series II, July–December 1740.* New Haven: Jonathan Edwards Center at Yale University, 2008.

——. *The Works of Jonathan Edwards Online.* Vol. 61, *Sermons, Series II, 1743.* New Haven: Jonathan Edwards Center at Yale University, 2008.

——. *The Works of Jonathan Edwards Online.* Vol. 64, *Sermons, Series II, 1746.* New Haven: Jonathan Edwards Center at Yale University, 2008.

——. *The Works of Jonathan Edwards Online.* Vol. 65, *Sermons, Series II, 1747.* New Haven: Jonathan Edwards Center at Yale University, 2008.

——. *The Works of Jonathan Edwards Online.* Vol. 66, *Sermons, Series II, 1748.* New Haven: Jonathan Edwards Center at Yale University, 2008.

——. *The Works of Jonathan Edwards Online.* Vol. 67, *Sermons, Series II, 1749.* New Haven: Jonathan Edwards Center at Yale University, 2008.

——. *The Works of Jonathan Edwards Online.* Vol. 72, *Sermons, Series II, 1754–1755.* New Haven: Jonathan Edwards Center at Yale University, 2008.

Eliade, Mircea. *The Sacred and the Profane: The Nature of Religion.* New York: Harcourt, 1959.

Elwood, Douglas J. *The Philosophical Theology of Jonathan Edwards.* New York: Columbia University Press, 1960.

Emery, Gilles. "The Doctrine of the Trinity in St Thomas Aquinas." In Weinandy, Keating, and Yocum, *Aquinas on Doctrine: A Critical Introduction,* 45–66.

———. *The Trinitarian Theology of Thomas Aquinas.* Translated by Francesca A. Murphy. New York: Oxford University Press, 2007.

———. *Trinity, Church, and the Human Person: Thomistic Essays.* Naples, FL: Sapientia, 2007.

———. *Trinity in Aquinas.* Ann Arbor, MI: Sapientia, 2006.

Erdt, Terrence. "The Calvinist Psychology of the Heart and the 'Sense' of Jonathan Edwards." *Early American Literature* 13, no. 2 (Fall 1978): 165–80.

———. *Jonathan Edwards: Art and the Sense of the Heart.* Amherst: University of Massachusetts Press, 1980.

Erling, Bernhard. "Communicatio Idiomatum Re-Examined." *Dialog* 2 (1963): 139–45.

Estwick, Nicolas. *Pneumatología: Or, a treatise of the holy ghost. In which, the Godhead of the third person of the Trinitie is strongly asserted by Scripture-arguments. And defended against the sophisticall subtleties of John Bidle.* London: Ralph Smith, 1648.

Fahey, Michael A. "Trinitarian Theology in Thomas Aquinas: One Latin Medieval Pursuit of Word and Silence." In *Trinitarian Theology East and West: Saint Thomas Aquinas—Saint Gregory Palamas,* edited by Michael A. Fahey and John Meyendorff, 5–23. Patriarch Athenagoras Memorial Lectures. Brookline, MA: Holy Cross Orthodox Press, 1977.

Fields, Stephen M. *Being as Symbol: On the Origins and Development of Karl Rahner's Metaphysics.* Washington, DC: Georgetown University Press, 2007.

Fiering, Norman. "The Rationalist Foundations of Edwards' Metaphysics." In *Jonathan Edwards and the American Experience,* edited by Nathan Hatch and Harry Stout, 73–101. New York: Oxford University Press, 1988.

Flavel, John. *The Works of John Flavel.* Vol. 1, *The Fountain of Life Opened Up.* Carlisle, PA: Banner of Truth Trust, 1968, 1982. First published by W. Banes and Son, 1820.

Florovsky, Georges. *Collected Works of Georges Florovsky.* Vol. 3, *Creation and Redemption.* Belmont, MA: Nordland, 1976.

Fortman, Edmund J. *The Triune God: A Historical Study of the Doctrine of the Trinity.* Philadelphia: Westminster, 1972.

Frame, John M. "Salvation and Theological Pedagogy." *Act 3 Review* (formerly *Reformation and Revival Journal*) 14, no. 1 (2005): 57–70.

Frede, Michael. *Essays in Ancient Philosophy.* Minneapolis: University of Minnesota Press, 1987.

Gaffin, Richard B., Jr. *The Centrality of the Resurrection: A Study in Paul's Soteriology.* Baker Biblical Monograph. Grand Rapids, MI: Baker Book House, 1978.

Gailhard, Jean. *The blasphemous Socinian heresie disproved and confuted, wherein the doctrinal and controversial parts of those points are handled, and the adversaries scripture and school-arguments answered: with animadversions upon a late book called, Christianity not mysterious.* London: R. Wellington and J. Hartley, 1697.

Garrigou-Lagrange, Reginald. *Christ the Saviour: A Commentary on the Third Part of Saint Thomas' Theological* Summa. Translated by Dom Bede Rose. St. Louis, MO, Herder, [copyright 1950].

———. "De causalitate sacramentorum." In *De Eucharistia et Paenitentia.* Marietti, 1948. http://thomistica.net/storage/pdf-files/2007/Garrigou-Lagrange%20other%20texts%20from%20De%20Eucharistia.pdf.

———. *Grace: Commentary on the* Summa theologica *of St. Thomas, Ia Iiae, q. 109–14.* Translated by the Dominican Nuns, Corpus Christi Monastery, Menlo Park, CA. St. Louis, MO: B. Herder, 1952.

Gebauer, Gunter, and Christoph Wulf. *Mimesis: Culture, Art, Society.* Translated by Don Reneau. Berkeley: University of California Press, 1992.

Gerrish, Brian A. *The Old Protestantism and the New: Essays on the Reformation Heritage.* Chicago: University of Chicago Press, 1982.

Gerstner, John H. *The Rational Biblical Theology of Jonathan Edwards.* 3 vols. Powhatan, VA: Berea Publications; Orlando, FL: Ligonier Ministries, 1991–[1992].

Gibson, Michael D. "The Beauty of the Redemption of the World: The Theological Aesthetics of Maximus the Confessor and Jonathan Edwards." *Harvard Theological Review* 101, no. 1 (2008): 45–76.

Gillespie, Patrick. *The ark of the covenant opened: Or, a treatise of the covenant of redemption between God and Christ, as the foundation of the covenant of grace. Wherein is proved, That there is such a covenant. The necessity of it. The nature, properties, parties thereof. The tenor, articles, subject-matter of redemption. The commands, conditions, and promises annexed. The harmony of the covenant of suretyship made with Christ. . . . Grounds of comfort from the covenant of suretyship.* London: Tho. Parkhurst, 1677.

Gockel, Matthias. "A Dubious Christological Formula? Leontius of Byzantium and the Anhypostasis-Enhypostasis Theory." *Journal of Theological Studies* 51 (October 2000): 515–32.

Gondreau, Paul. "The Humanity of Christ, the Incarnate Word." In Van Nieuwenhove and Wawrykow, *Theology of Thomas Aquinas*, 252–76.

Goodwin, Thomas. *A Discourse of Christ the Mediator.* Edited by Thankfull Owen and James Barron. In *The Works of Thomas Goodwin, D. D. Sometime President of Magdalen College in Oxford.* London: T. G. [Thomas Goodwin Jr.], 1692. Available at *The Digital Library of Protestant Texts.*

_____. *An Exposition of the First, and Part of the Second Chapter, of the Epistle to the Ephesians.* In *The Works of Thomas Goodwin, D. D., Sometime President of Magdalen College in Oxford.* Edited by Thankfull Owen and James Barron. London: T. G. [Thomas Goodwin Jr.], 1681. Available at *The Digital Library of Protestant Texts.*

_____. *Of the Knowledge of God the Father, And His Son Jesus Christ.* Edited by Thankfull Owen and James Barron. In *The Works of Thomas Goodwin, D. D. Sometime President of Magdalen College in Oxford.* London: T. G. [Thomas Goodwin Jr.], 1683. Available at *The Digital Library of Protestant Texts.*

_____. *Of the creatures, and the condition of their state by creation.* Edited by Thankfull Owen and James Barron. In *The Works of Thomas Goodwin, D.D. Sometime President of Magdalen College in Oxford.* London: T. G. [Thomas Goodwin Jr.], 1683. Available at *The Digital Library of Classic Protestant Texts.*

———. *Of the work of the Holy Ghost (the third person of the Trinity) in our salvation.* Edited by Thankfull Owen and James Barron. In *The works of Thomas Goodwin, D.D. Sometime President of Magdalen College in Oxford.* London: T.G. [Thomas Goodwin (Jr.)], 1704. Available at *The Digital Library of Classic Protestant Texts.*

_____. *Thirteen Sermons Preached on Diverse Texts on Scripture, upon Several Occasions.* In In *The Works of Thomas Goodwin, D. D. sometime President of Magdalen College in Oxford.* Edited by Thankfull Owen and James Barron. London: T. G. [Thomas Goodwin (Jr.)], 1681. Available at *The Digital Library of Classic Protestant Texts.*

———. *The Works of Thomas Goodwin, D.D. Sometime President of Magdalene College, Oxford.* Vol. 1, *Containing an Exposition of the First Chapter of the Epistle to the Ephesians.* With general preface by John C. Miller and memoir by Robert Halley. Nichol's Series of Standard Divines: Puritan Period. Edinburgh: James Nichol, 1861.

———. *The Works of Thomas Goodwin, D.D. Sometime President of Magdelene College, Oxford.* Vol. 2, *Containing and Exposition of Various Passages of the Epistle to the Ephesians and Patience and Its Perfect Work, Being an Exposition of James I. 1–5.* With general preface by John C. Miller and memoir by Robert Halley. Nichol's Series of Standard Divines: Puritan Period. Edinburgh: James Nichol, 1862.

———. *The Works of Thomas Goodwin, D.D. Sometime President of Magdelene College, Oxford.* Vol. 4. With general preface by John C. Miller and memoir by Robert Halley. Nichol's Series of Standard Divines: Puritan Period. Edinburgh: James Nichol, 1862.

———. *The Works of Thomas Goodwin. D.D. Sometime President of Magdelene College, Oxford.* Vol. 5, *Of Christ the Mediator.* With general preface by John C. Miller, and memoir by Robert Halley. Nichol's Series of Standard Divines: Puritan Period. Edinburgh: James Nichol, 1863.

———. *The Works of Thomas Goodwin. D.D. Sometime President of Magdelene College, Oxford.* Vol. 6, *The Work of the Holy Ghost in Our Salvation.* With general preface by John C. Miller and memoir by Robert Halley. Nichol's Series of Standard Divines: Puritan Period. Edinburgh: James Nichol, 1863.

———. *The Works of Thomas Goodwin. D.D. Sometime President of Magdelene College, Oxford.* Vol. 7, *Containing: Of the Creatures, and the Condition of Their State by Creation; Of Gospel Holiness in the Heart and Life; Of the Blessed State of Glory which the Saints Possess after Death; Three Several Ages of Christians in Faith and Obedience; Man's Restoration by Grace; On Repentance.* With general preface by John C. Miller and memoir by Robert Halley. Nichol's Series of Standard Divines: Puritan Period. Edinburgh: James Nichol, 1863.

———. *The Works of Thomas Goodwin, D.D. Sometime President of Magdalene College, Oxford.* Vol. 9, *A Discourse on Election, &c. A Discourse of Thankfulness.* With general preface by John C. Miller and memoir by Robert Halley. Nichol's Series of Standard Divines: Puritan Period. Edinburgh: James Nichol, 1864.

Gregory of Nyssa. "On 'Not Three Gods' to Ablabius." Translated by William More and Henry Austin Wilson. In Schaff and Wace, *Nicene and Post-Nicene Fathers,* 5:326–30.

———. "On the Holy Trinity, and of the Godhead of the Holy Spirit to Eustathius." Translated by William More and Henry Austin Wilson. In Schaff and Wace, *Nicene and Post-Nicene Fathers,* 5:331–36.

Gregory Palamas, Saint. *Dialogue between an Orthodox and a Barlaamite.* Translation by Rein Ferwerda. Introduction by Sara J. Denning-Bolle. Binghamton, NY: Global Publications / CEMERS, 1999.

———. *The One Hundred and Fifty Chapters.* Edited and translated by Robert E. Sinkewicz. Studies and Texts 83. Toronto: Pontifical Institute of Mediaeval Studies, 1988.

———. *The Triads.* Edited with an introduction by John Meyendorff. Translated by Nicholas Gendell. With a Preface by Jaroslav Pelikan. Classics of Western Spirituality. Mahwah, NJ: Paulist, 1983.

Grillmeier, Aloys. *Christ in the Christian Tradition.* Vol. 1, *From the Apostolic Age to Chalcedon (451).* 2nd rev. ed. London & Oxford: Mowbrays, 1975.

Grillmeier, Aloys, with Theresia Hainthaler. *Christ in Christian Tradition.* Vol. 2, *From the Council of Chalcedon (451) to Gregory the Great (590–604).* Part 2, *The Church of Constantinople in the Sixth Century.* Translated by Pauline Allen and John Cawte. Louisville, KY: Westminster John Knox, 1995.

Gross, Jules. *The Divinization of the Christian according to the Greek Fathers.* Translated by Paul A. Onica and introduction by Kerry S. Robichaux and Paul A. Onica. Anaheim, CA: A&C, 2002. Originally published as *La divinisation du chrétien d'après le pères grecs: Contribution historique à la doctrine de la grâce.* Paris: J. Gabalda, 1938.

Gunton, Colin E. *Act and Being: Towards a Theology of the Divine Attributes.* London: SCM, 2002.

———. *The Promise of Trinitarian Theology.* 2nd ed. Edinburgh: T&T Clark, 1997.

Gustafson, James M. *Ethics from a Theocentric Perspective: Theology and Ethics.* Chicago: University of Chicago Press, 1981.

Haight, Roger. *The Experience and Language of Grace.* New York: Paulist, 1979.

Hall, Francis J. *Theological Outlines.* Revised by Frank Hudson Hallock. 3rd ed. Eugene, OR: Wipf and Stock, 1933.

Hamilton, Alistair. *The Family of Love.* Cambridge: James Clarke, 1981.

Hanson, R. P. C. *The Search for the Christian Doctrine of God: The Arian Controversy 318–381 ad.* 1st paperback ed. Grand Rapids, MI: Baker Academic, 2005. First published London: T&T Clark, 1988.

Hart, David Bentley. *The Beauty of the Infinite: The Aesthetics of Christian Truth.* Grand Rapids, MI: Eerdmans, 2003.

Hastings, W. Ross. "'Honouring the Spirit': Analysis and Evaluation of Jonathan Edwards' Pneumatological Doctrine of the Incarnation." *International Journal of Systematic Theology* 7, no. 3 (July 2005): 279–99.

Healy, Nicholas J. *The Eschatology of Hans Urs von Balthasar: Being as Communion.* Oxford Theological Monographs. New York: Oxford University Press, 2005.

Hebblethwaite, Brian. *The Incarnation: Collected Essays in Christology.* Cambridge: Cambridge University Press, 1987.

———. *Philosophical Theology and Christian Doctrine.* Exploring the Philosophy of Religion. Edited by Michael L. Peterson. Malden, MA: Blackwell, 2005.

Helm, Paul. "A Forensic Dilemma: John Locke and Jonathan Edwards on Personal Identity." In Helm and Crisp, *Philosophical Theologian*, 45–60.

———. "Maimonides and Calvin on Divine Accommodation." In *Referring to God: Jewish and Christian Philosophical and Theological Perspectives*, ed. Paul Helm, 149–70. New York: St. Martin's, 2000.

Helm, Paul, and Oliver D. Crisp, eds. *Jonathan Edwards: Philosophical Theologian.* Aldershot, UK: Ashgate, 2003.

Henry, Matthew. *Commentary on the Whole Bible.* Vol. 5, *Matthew to John.* Grand Rapids, MI: Christian Classics Ethereal Library, n.d. http://www.ccel.org/ccel/henry/mhc5.html.

Heppe, Heinrich. *Reformed Dogmatics Set Out and Illustrated from the Sources.* Revised and edited by Ernst Bizer. Translated by G. T. Thomson. Foreword by Karl Barth. London: George Allen & Unwin, 1950.

Heron, Alasdair. "*Communicatio Idiomatum* and *Deificatio* of Human Nature: A Reformed Perspective." *Greek Orthodox Theological Review* 43, nos. 1–4 (Spring–Winter 1988): 367–76.

Hill, William J. *The Three-Personed God: The Trinity as a Mystery of Salvation.* Washington, DC: Catholic University of America Press, 1982.

Hodge, Charles. *Systematic Theology.* 3 vols. Grand Rapids, MI: Eerdmans, 1993. Originally published, 1872.

Holmes, Stephen R. "Does Edwards Use a Dispositional Ontology?" in Helm and Crisp, *Jonathan Edwards: Philosophical Theologian*, 99–114.

———. *God of Grace and God of Glory: An Account of the Theology of Jonathan Edwards.* Edinburgh: T&T Clark, 2000.

———. "Reformed Varieties of the *Communicatio Idiomatum*." In *The Person of Christ*. edited by Stephen R. Holmes and Murray A. Rae, 70–86. London: T&T Clark International, 2006.

Hooker, Richard. *A Learned Discourse of Justification, Works, and how the Foundation of Faith is Overthrown.* Grand Rapids, MI: Christian Classics Ethereal Library, n.d. http://www.ccel.org/ccel/hooker/just.ii.html

Hunsinger, George. "Dispositional Soteriology: Jonathan Edwards on Justification by Faith Alone." *Westminster Theological Journal* 66 (2004): 107–20.

Hutcheson, George. *An Exposition of the Gospel of Jesus Christ according to John.* London: Ralph Smith, 1657.

Jenson, Robert W. *America's Theologian: A Recommendation of Jonathan Edwards.* New York: Oxford University Press, 1988.

———. "A 'Protestant Constructive Response' to Christian Unbelief." In *American Apostasy: A Triumph of "Other" Gospels,* edited by Richard John Neuhaus, 56–74. Encounter Series 10. Grand Rapids, MI: Eerdmans, 1989.

———. *Systematic Theology.* Vol. 1, *The Triune God.* New York: Oxford University Press, 1997.

Jewel, John. *A defence of the apology of the Church of England.* In *The works of John Jewel, Bishop of Salisbury.* Edited by John Ayre. Cambridge: University Press, 1848. First published in 1567.

Jinkins, Michael. *A Comparative Study in the Theology of Atonement in Jonathan Edwards and John McLeod Campbell: Atonement and the Character of God.* Lewiston, NY: Edwin Mellen, 1993.

John of Damascus, Saint. *Exposition of the Orthodox Faith.* Translated by S. D. F. Salmond. In Schaff and Wace, *Nicene and Post-Nicene Fathers,* 9.

———. "Fount of Knowledge." In *St John of Damascus: Writings.* Translated by Frederic H. Chase Jr. The Fathers of the Church 37. Washington, DC: Catholic University of America Press, 1958.

———. *Three Treatises on the Divine Images.* Translated and introduction by Andrew Louth. Popular Patristic Series. Edited by John Behr. Crestwood, NY: St Vladimir's Seminary Press, 2003.

Jones, R. Tudur. "Union with Christ: The Existential Nerve of Puritan Piety." *Tyndale Bulletin* 41 (November 1990): 168–208.

Jowers, Dennis W. *The Trinitarian Axiom of Karl Rahner: The Economic Trinity is the Immanent Trinity and Vice Versa.* Lewiston, NY: Edwin Mellen, 2006.

Jüngel, Eberhard. *The Doctrine of the Trinity: God's Being Is in Becoming.* Translated by Horton Harris. Grand Rapids, MI: Eerdmans, 1976.

———. *Justification: The Heart of the Christian Faith.* Translated by Jeffrey F. Cayzer with an introduction by John Webster. London: T&T Clark, 2006.

———. *God as the Mystery of the World: On the Foundation of the Theology of the Crucified One in the Dispute between Theism and Atheism.* Grand Rapids, MI: Eerdmans, 1983.

———. "On the Doctrine of Justification." *International Journal of Systematic Theology* 1, no. 1 (March 1999): 24–52.

Kasper, Walter. *Jesus the Christ.* Mahwah, NJ: Paulist, 1976.

Keating, Daniel A. "Divinization in Cyril: The Appropriation of Divine Life." In Weinandy and Keating, *The Theology of Saint Cyril of Alexandria,* 149–86.

Kelly, J. N. D. *Early Christian Doctrines.* New York: Harper & Brothers, 1958.

Kerr, Fergus. *After Aquinas: Versions of Thomism.* Malden, MA: Blackwell, 2002.

Kirby, W. J. Torrance. *Richard Hooker's Doctrine of Royal Supremacy.* Studies in the History of Christian Thought, vol. 43. Leiden, Netherlands: E. J. Brill, 1990.

Küng, Hans. *The Incarnation of God: An Introduction to Hegel's Theological Thought as Prologemena to a Future Christology.* Translated by J. R. Stephenson. Edinburgh: T&T Clark, 1987.

LaCugna, Catherine M. *God for Us: The Trinity and Christian Life.* New York: HarperCollins, 1991.

Lamont, John. "The Nature of the Hypostatic Union." *Heythrop Journal* 47, no. 1 (2006): 16–25.

Lang, Uwe Michael. "Anhypostatos-Enhypostatos: Church Fathers, Protestant Orthodoxy and Karl Barth." *Journal of Theological Studies* 49, no. 2 (1998): 630–57.

———. *John Philoponus and the Controversies over Chalcedon in the Sixth Century: A Study and Translation of the* Arbiter. Spicilegium Sacrum Lovaniense: Études et Documents 47. Leuven, Belgium: Peeters, 2001.

Lee, Sang Hyun. *The Philosophical Theology of Jonathan Edwards.* Princeton, NJ: Princeton University Press, 1988.

———. *The Philosophical Theology of Jonathan Edwards.* Expanded ed. Princeton, NJ: Princeton University Press, 2000.

———, ed. *The Princeton companion to Jonathan Edwards.* Princeton, NJ: Princeton University Press, 2005.

Leftow, Brian. "Anti Social Trinitarianism." In *The Trinity: An Interdisciplinary Symposium on the Trinity,* edited by Stephen T. Davis, Daniel Kendall, and Gerald O'Collins, 203–50. New York: Oxford University Press, 2002.

———. "A Latin Trinity." *Faith and Philosophy* 21, no. 3 (2004): 304–33.

———. "Modes without Modalism." In *Persons: Human and Divine,* edited by Peter van Inwagen and Dean Zimmerman, 357–76. New York: Oxford University Press, 2007.

———. "A Timeless God Incarnate." In Davis, Kendall and O'Collins, *The Incarnation,* 273–99.

Leget, Carlo. *Living with God: Thomas Aquinas on the Relation between Life on Earth and "Life" after Death.* Publications of the Thomas Instituut te Utrecht, new series, vol. 5. Edited by H. A. G. Braakhuis, K. -W. Merks, H. W. M. Rikhof, and R. A. te Velde. Leuven, Belgium: Peeters, 1997.

Leigh, Edward. *A treatise of divinity consisting of three bookes. The first of which handling the Scripture or word of God. . . . The second handling God, sheweth that there is a God, and what he is. . . . The third handleth the three principall workes of God, decree, creation and providence.* London: William Lee, 1646.

Levering, Matthew. *Scripture and Metaphysics: Aquinas and the Renewal of Trinitarian Theology.* Challenges in Contemporary Theology. Oxford: Blackwell, 2004.

Logan, Samuel T., Jr., "The Doctrine of Justification in the Theology of Jonathan Edwards." *Westminster Theological Journal* 46 (Spring 1984): 26–52.

Lonergan, Bernard J. Collected Works of Bernard Lonergan. Vol. 2, *Verbum: Word and Idea in Aquinas.* Edited by Frederick E. Crowe and Robert M. Doran. Toronto: University of Toronto Press for Lonergan Research Institute of Regis College, 1997.

———. Collected Works of Bernard Lonergan. Vol. 7, *The Ontological and Psychological Constitution of Christ.* Translated by Michael G. Shields from the 4th ed. of *De constitutione Christi ontologica et psychologica.* Toronto: University of Toronto Press for Lonergan Research Institute of Regis College, 2002.

———. Collected Works of Bernard Lonergan. Vol. 12, *The Triune God: Systematics.* Translated by Robert M. Doran and H. Daniel Monsour. Toronto: University of Toronto Press for Lonergan Research Institute of Regis College, 2007.

———. *Grace and Freedom: Operative Grace in the Thought of St. Thomas Aquinas.* Edited by J. Patout Burns, with an introduction by Frederick E. Crowe. London: Darton, Longman & Todd; New York: Herder & Herder, 1971.

Lossky, Vladimir. "Apophasis and Trinitarian Theology." In Clendenin, *Eastern Orthodox Theology*, 149–162.

———. *In the Image and Likeness of God.* Edited by J. H. Erickson and T. E. Bird, with an introduction by John Meyendorff. Crestwood, NY: St. Vladimir's Seminary Press, 1974.

———. *The Mystical Theology of the Eastern Church.* Crestwood, NY: St. Vladimir's Seminary Press, 1997.

Louth, Andrew. *Maximus the Confessor.* The Early Church Fathers. London: Routledge, 1996.

_____. *The Origins of the Christian Mystical Tradition from Plato to Denys.* Oxford: Clarendon, 1981.

———. *St. John Damascene: Tradition and Originality in Byzantine Theology.* Oxford Early Christian Studies. Edited by Gillian Clark and Andrew Louth. Oxford: Oxford University Press, 2002. Reprint, 2004 (page references are to the reprint edition).

Lowance, Mason I., Jr. *Language of Canaan: Metaphor and Symbol in New England from the Puritans to the Transcendentalists.* Cambridge, MA: Harvard University Press, 1980.

Lubheid, Colm, trans. *Pseudo-Dionysius: The Complete Works.* Foreword, notes, and translation collaboration by Paul Rorem. Preface by Rene Roques. Introductions by Jaroslav Pelikan, Jean LeClercq, and Karlfried Froehlich. Classics of Western Spirituality. Mahwah, NJ: Paulist, 1987.

Luitjen, Eric. *Sacramental Forgiveness as a Gift of God: Thomas Aquinas on the Sacrament of Penance.* Thomas Institut Utrecht 8. Nijmegen, Netherlands: Peeters, 2003.

Luther, Martin. "The Last Written Words of Luther: Holy Ponderings of the Reverend Father Martin Luther" (February 16, 1546). Translated by James A. Kellerman. In *Dr. Martin Luthers Werke,* Band 85 (TR 5), 317–18. Weimar: Hermann Boehlaus Nachfolger, 1909. http://www.iclnet.org/pub/resources/text/wittenberg/luther/beggars.txt.

———. *Martin Luther's Basic Theological Writings.* Edited by Timothy F. Lull. Foreword by Jaroslav Pelikan. Minneapolis: Fortress Press, 1989.

———. "Two Kinds of Righteousness." In *Luther's Works.* Vol. 31, *Career of the Reformer I.* Edited by J. J. Pelikan, H. C. Oswald, and H. T. Lehmann. Philadelphia: Fortress Press, 1957.

Macken, John S. *The Autonomy Theme in the* Church Dogmatics: *Karl Barth and His Critics.* Cambridge: Cambridge University Press, 1990.

Macleod, Donald. *The Person of Christ.* Countours of Christian Theology. Downers Grove, IL: InterVarsity, 1998.

Malebranche, Nicolas. *Oeuvres complètes de Malebranche.* Edited by André Robinet. Paris: Vrin, 1958–84.

Maloney, George A. *A Theology of "Uncreated Energies."* The 1978 Pere Marquette Theology Lectures. Milwaukee, WI: Marquette University Press, 1978.

Malysz, Piotr. "Storming Heaven with Karl Barth? Barth's Unwitting Appropriation of the *Genus Maiestaticum* and What Lutherans Can Learn from It." *International Journal of Systematic Theology* 9, no. 1 (January 2007): 73–92.

Mantzarides, George. "Tradition and Renewal in the Theology of Saint Gregory Palamas." *Eastern Churches Review* 9 (1977): 1–18.

Marion, Jean-Luc. *Being Given: Toward a Phenomenology of Givenness.* Translated by Jeffrey L. Kosky. Stanford, CA: Stanford University Press, 2002.

Marshall, Bruce D. "*Ex Occidente Lux?* Aquinas and Eastern Orthodox Theology." *Modern Theology* 20, no. 1 (January 2004): 23–50.

———. *Trinity and Truth.* Cambridge Studies in Christian Doctrine. Cambridge: Cambridge University Press, 2000.

———. "What Does the Spirit Have to Do?" In *Reading John with St Thomas: Theological Exegesis and Speculative Theology*, eEdited by Michael Dauphinais and Matthew Levering, 62–77. Washington, DC: Catholic University of America Press, 2005.

Mascall, E. L. *Christ, the Christian and the Church: A Study of the Incarnation and Its Consequences.* London: Longmans, Green, 1946.

Mastricht, Peter van. *Theoretico-practica theologia, qua, per singula capita theologica, pars exegetica, dogmatica, elenchtica & practica, perpetuâ successione coniugantur.* Traiecti ad Rhenum: Ex officinâ Thomae Appels, 1699.

———. *A Treatise on Regeneration.* Edited by Brandon Withrow. Morgan, PA: Soli Deo Gloria Publications, 2002. First published as part of *Theoretico-Practica Theologia*, 1699, retypeset from 1769 ed.

McCabe, Herbert. "Aquinas on the Trinity." In *Silence and the Word: Negative Theology and Incarnation.* Edited by Oliver Davies and Denys Turner. Cambridge: Cambridge University Press, 2002.

McClymond, Michael J. "Salvation as Divinization: Jonathan Edwards, Gregory Palamas and the Theological Uses of Neoplatonism." In Helm and Crisp, *Jonathan Edwards: Philosophical Theologian*, 139–60.

McClymond, Michael J., and Gerald R. McDermott. *The Theology of Jonathan Edwards.* New York: Oxford University Press, 2012.

McCormack, Bruce L., ed. *Justification in Perspective: Historical Developments and Contemporary Challenges.* Grand Rapids, MI: Baker Academic; Edinburgh: Rutherford House, 2006.

———. "*Justitia aliena*: Karl Barth in Conversation with the Evangelical Doctrine of Imputed Righteousness," in McCormack, *Justification in Perspective*, 167–96.

McDermott, Brian O. *Word Become Flesh: Dimensions in Christology*. New Theology Studies, vol. 9, edited by Peter C. Phan. Collegeville, MN: Liturgical Press, 1993.

McDermott, Gerald R. *Jonathan Edwards Confronts the Gods: Christian Theology, Enlightenment Religion, and Non-Christian Faiths*. New York: Oxford University Press, 2000.

McDonnell, Kilian. *The Baptism of Jesus in the Jordan: The Trinitarian and Cosmic Order of Salvation*. Collegeville, MN: Liturgical Press, 1996.

McGowan, A. T. B. "Justification and the *ordo salutis*." In McCormack, *Justification in Perspective*, 147–66.

McGrath, Alister E. *The Intellectual Origins of the European Reformation*. 2nd ed. Malden, MA: Blackwell, 2004.

———. Iustitia Dei: *A History of the Christian Doctrine of Justification*. 3rd ed. Cambridge: Cambridge University Press, 2005.

———. *A Life of John Calvin: A Study in the Shaping of Western Culture*. Malden, MA: Blackwell, 1990.

———. *Luther's Theology of the Cross: Martin Luther's Theological Breakthrough*. Oxford, UK, and New York: Blackwell, 1990.

McGuckin, John. *Saint Cyril of Alexandria and the Christological Controversy: Its History, Theology and Texts*. Crestwood, NY: St. Vladimir's Theological Seminary Press, 2004.

McIntyre, John. *The Shape of Christology: Studies in the Doctrine of the Person of Christ*. 2nd ed. Edinburgh: T&T Clark, 1998.

Melanchthon, Philip. *Corpus reformatorum*. Vol. 21. Edited by Henricus Ernestus Bindseil. Brunsvigae: C. A. Schwetschke, 1854.

Mersch, Emile. *The Theology of the Mystical Body*. Translated by Cyril Vollert. St. Louis, MO: B. Herder, 1951.

Meyendorff, John. *Christ in Eastern Christian Thought*. Washington, DC: Corpus, 1969.

———. "Humanity: 'Old' and 'New'—Anthropological Considerations." In Meyendorff and Tobias, *Salvation in Christ*, 59–66.

———. *A Study of Gregory Palamas*. Crestwood, NY: St. Vladimir's Seminary Press, 1998.

———. "Theosis in the Eastern Christian Tradition." In *Christian Spirituality: Post-Reformation and Modern*, edited by Louis Dupré, Don E. Saliers, and John Meyendorff, 470–76. World Spirituality: An Encyclopaedic History of the Religious Quest 18. New York: Crossroads, 1989.

Meyendorff, John, and Robert Tobias, eds. *Salvation in Christ: A Lutheran-Orthodox Dialogue.* Minneapolis: Augsburg, 1992.

Meyer, John R. "God's Trinitarian Substance in Athanasian Theology." *Scottish Journal of Theology* 59, no. 1 (2006): 81–97.

Migne, Jacques-Paul. *Patrologiae cursus completus. Series graeca.* 161 vols. Paris, 1857–66.

———. *Patrologiae cursus completus. Series latina.* 221 vols. Paris, 1844–49.

Milbank, John. "Forgiveness and Incarnation." In *Questioning God*, edited by John D. Caputo, Mark Dooley, and Michael J. Scanlon, 92–128. Indiana Series in the Philosophy of Religion. Bloomington: Indiana University Press, 2001.

Miller, Michael R. "Freedom and Grace." In *Gathered for the Journey: Moral Theology in Catholic Perspective*, edited by David M. McCarthy and M. Therese Lysaught, 177–97. Grand Rapids, MI: Eerdmans, 2007.

Miller, Perry. *Images or Shadows of Divine Things.* New Haven: Yale University Press, 1948.

———. *Jonathan Edwards.* Cleveland, OH: World, 1959.

Mœller, Charles, and Gérard Philips. *The Theology of Grace and the Oecumenical Movement.* Translated by R. A. Wilson. London: A. R. Mowbray, 1961.

Moltmann, Jürgen. "The World in God or God in the World." In Bauckham, *God Will Be All in All*, 35–42.

Monsour, H. Daniel. "The Relation between Uncreated and Created Grace in the Halesian *Summa*: A Lonergan Reading." Ph.D. diss., University of St. Michael's College, Toronto, 2000. Online edition available at Theses Canada Portal, Library and Archives Canada, http://www.nlc-bnc.ca/obj/s4/f2/dsk2/ftp02/NQ54051.pdf.

Moran, Dermot. "John Scottus Eriugena." In *Stanford Encyclopedia of Philosophy*, Fall 2008 ed. Edited by Edward N. Zalta. Article published August 28, 2003; substantially revised October 17, 2004. http://plato.stanford.edu/archives/fall2008/entries/scottus-eriugena.

Morimoto, Anri. *Jonathan Edwards and the Catholic Vision of Salvation.* University Park: Pennsylvania State University Press, 1995.

Moss, Jean Dietz. *"Godded with God": Hendrik Niclaes and His Family of Love.* Philadelphia: American Philosophical Society, 1981.

Mosser, Carl. "The Greatest Possible Blessing: Calvin and Deification." *Scottish Journal of Theology* 55 (2002): 36–57.

Muller, Earl. "Real Relations and the Divine: Issues in Thomas's Understanding of God's Relation to the World." *Theological Studies* 56 (1995): 673–95.

Muller, Richard A. *Dictionary of Latin and Greek Theological Terms: Drawn Principally from Protestant Scholastic Theology*. Grand Rapids, MI: Baker Book House, 1985.

———. *Post-Reformation Reformed Dogmatics: The Rise and Development of Reformed Orthodoxy, ca. 1520 to ca. 1725*. Vol. 3, *The Divine Essence and Attributes*. Grand Rapids, MI: Baker Academic, 2003.

———. *Post-Reformation Reformed Dogmatics: The Rise and Development of Reformed Orthodoxy, ca. 1520 to ca. 1725*. Vol. 4, *The Triunity of God*. Grand Rapids, MI: Baker Academic, 2003.

Munk, Linda. "His Dazzling Absence: The Shekinah in Jonathan Edwards." *Early American Literature* 27, no. 1 (1992): 1–30.

Narcisse, Gilbert. *Les Raisons de Dieu: Arguments de Convenance et Esthétique Théologique selon St. Thomas d'Aquin et Hans Urs von Balthasar*. Preface by Jean-Pierre Torrell. Fribourg, Switzerland: Editions Universitaires, 1997.

Negrut, Paul. "Orthodox Soteriology: Theosis." *Churchman* 109, no. 2 (1995): 154–70.

The New Schaff-Herzog Encyclopedia of Religious Knowledge Embracing Biblical, Historical, Doctrinal, and Practical Theology, and Biblical, Theological, and Ecclesiastical Biography from the Earliest Times to the Present Day. 13 vols. Grand Rapids, MI: Baker Book House, 1949–50.

Newman, John Henry. *Lectures on Justification*. London: J. G. & F. Rivington and J. H. Parker, 1838.

Nichols, Stephen J. *An Absolute Sort of Certainty: The Holy Spirit and the Apologetics of Jonathan Edwards*. Phillipsburg, NJ: P&R, 2003.

Niebuhr, Richard R. "Being and Consent." In Lee, *The Princeton Companion to Jonathan Edwards*, 34–43.

Nieden, Marcel. *Organum deitatis: Die Christologie des Thomas de Vio Cajetan*. Studies in Medieval and Reformation Thought 62. Leiden, Netherlands: Brill, 1997.

Nieuwenhove, Rik van, and Joseph Wawrykow, eds. *The Theology of Thomas Aquinas*. Notre Dame, IN: University of Notre Dame Press, 2005.

Norris, John. *Philosophical and Theological Writings*. 8 vols. Edited and introduced by Richard Acworth. Bristol: Thoemmes, 2001.

North, Robert. "Soul-Body Unity and God-Man Unity." *Theological Studies* 30, no. 1 (March 1969): 27–60.

O'Carroll, Michael. *Trinitas: A Theological Encyclopedia of the Holy Trinity*. Wilmington, DE: Michael Glazier, 1987.

O'Collins, Gerald, and Mario Farrugia. *Catholicism: The Story of Catholic Christianity*. Oxford: Oxford University Press, 2003.

Oberman, Heiko Augustinus. *The Harvest of Medieval Theology: Gabriel Biel and Late Medieval Nominalism*. Cambridge, MA: Harvard University Press, 1963.

Oh, Peter S. *Karl Barth's Trinitarian Theology: A Study in Karl Barth's Analogical Use of the Trinitarian Relation*. London: T&T Clark, 2006.

Olevian, Caspar. *In Epistolas D. Pauli Apostoli ad Philippenses & Colossenses, notae, ex Gasparis Oleviani concionibus excerptae, & a Theodoro Beza editae: cum praefatione eiusdem Bezae*. Geneva: Apud Eustathium Vignon, 1580.

Otto, Rudolph. *The Idea of the Holy: An Inquiry into the Non-Rational Factor in the Idea of the Divine and Its Relation to the Rational*. Translated by John W. Harvey. London: Oxford University Press, 1950.

Owen, John. *Christologia: Or, a Declaration of The Glorious Mystery of the Person of Christ, God and Man, to which are Subjoined, Meditations and Discourses on the Glory of Christ*. Vol. 1 of *The Works of John Owen, D.D.* Edited by William H. Goold. New York: Robert Carter & Brothers, 1851.

———. *Containing the Doctrine of Justification by Faith; and Gospel Grounds and Evidences of the Faith of God's Elect*. Vol. 11 of *The Works of John Owen, with Memoirs of His Life and Writings by William Orme*. Edited by Thomas Russell. London: Printed for Richard Baynes, 1826.

———. *Pneumatologia: Or, a discourse concerning the Holy Spirit. Wherein an account is given of his name, nature, personality, dispensation, operations, and effects. His whole work in the old and new creation is explained; the doctrine concerning it vindicated from oppositions and reproaches. The nature also and necessity of gospel-holiness; the difference between grace and morality, or a spiritual life unto God in evangelical obedience and course of moral vertues, are stated and declared*. London: Nathaniel Ponder, 1674.

———. *Theomachia Autexousiastike: A Display of Arminianism*. Vol. 10 of *The Works of John Owen, D.D.* Edited by William H. Goold. New York: Robert Carter & Brothers, 1852.

———. *The Works of John Owen*. Edited by William H. Goold. 16 vols. London: Banner of Truth Trust, 1965–68. Originally published by Johnstone & Hunter, 1850–53.

Paddison, Angus. *Theological Hermeneutics and 1 Thessalonians*. Society for New Testament Studies Monograph Series 133. New York: Cambridge University Press, 2005.

Pannenberg, Wolfhart. *Jesus—God and Man*. Translated by Lewis L. Wilkins and Duane A. Priebe. London: SCM Press, 1968.

———. *Systematic Theology*. 3 vols. Translated by Geoffrey W. Bromiley. Grand Rapids, MI: Eerdmans, 1998.

Patacsi, Gabriel. "Palamism before Palamas." *Eastern Churches Review* 9 (1977): 64–71.

Pauw, Amy Plantinga. "'The Supreme Harmony of All': Jonathan Edwards and the Trinity." Ph.D. diss., Yale University, 1990.

———. *The Supreme Harmony of All: The Trinitarian Theology of Jonathan Edwards*. Grand Rapids, MI: Eerdmans, 2002.

Pelikan, Jaroslav. *The Christian Tradition Christian*. Vol. 5, *Doctrine and Modern Culture*. Chicago: University of Chicago Press, 1989.

Perkins, William. *An exposition of the symbole or creed of the apostles, according to the tenour of the scripture, and the consent of orthodoxe Fathers of the Church*. London: Printed by John Legatt, Printer to the Universitie of Cambridge, 1616.

———. *A golden chaine: Or, the description of theologie, containing the order of the causes of salvation and damnation, according to Gods word. A view whereof is to be seene in the table annexed. Hereunto is adjoyned the order which M. Theodore Beza used in comforting afflicted consciences*. London: Printed by John Legatt, Printer to the Universitie of Cambridge, 1616.

———. *A reformed catholike, or, a declaration shewing how neere we may come to the present church of Rome in sundry points of religion: and wherein we must for ever depart from them*. London: Printed by John Legatt, Printer to the Universitie of Cambridge, 1616.

Perl, Eric D. "Methexis: Creation, Incarnation, Deification in Saint Maximus the Confessor." Ph.D. diss., Yale University, 1991.

Pesarchick, Robert A. *The Trinitarian Foundation of Human Sexuality as Revealed by Christ according to Hans Urs von Balthasar: The Revelatory Significance of the Male Christ and the Male Ministerial Priesthood*. Tesi Gregoriana, Serie Teologia 63. Rome: Gregorian University Press, 2000.

Peter Lombard. *Quator Libri Sententarium*. Edited by Alexis Bugnolo. The Franciscan Archive. http://www.franciscan-archive.org/lombardus/index.html.

Phan, Peter C., ed. *The Gift of the Church: A Textbook on Ecclesiology in Honor of Patrick Granfield, O.S.B.* Collegeville, MN: Liturgical Press, 2000.

Pinnock, Clark H. *Flame of Love: A Theology of the Holy Spirit*. Downers Grove, IL: InterVarsity, 1999.

Placher, William C. *The Domestication of Transcendence: How Modern Thinking about God Went Wrong*. Louisville, KY: Westminster John Knox, 1996.

Pohle, Joseph. *Christology: A Dogmatic Treatise on the Incarnation.* Edited by Arthur Preuss. Whitefish, MT: Kessinger Publishing, 2008.

Polanus von Polansdorf, Amandus. *The substance of Christian religion, soundly set forth in two bookes, . . .* London: R. F. for John Oxenbridge, 1595.

Prestige, G. L. *God in Patristic Thought.* London: SPCK, 1952.

Preston, John. *Life eternall; or, A treatise of the knowledge of the divine essence and attributes. Delivered in XVIII sermons.* London: R. B. [Richard Badger?], 1631.

Pseudo-Dionysius, the Areopagite. *Pseudo-Dionysius: The Complete Works.* Translated by Colm Luibheid. Foreword, notes, and translation collaboration by Paul Rorem. Preface by Réne Roques. Introduced by Jaroslav Pelikan, Jean LeClercq, and Karlfried Froehlich. The Classics of Western Spirituality. Mahwah, NJ: Paulist, 1987.

Pusey, Edward B. *On the Clause "and the Son" in regard to the Eastern Church and the Bonn Conference: A Letter to the Rev. H. P. Liddon, D.D.* Oxford: James Parker ; New York: Potts, Young, 1876.

Rahner, Karl. *Foundations of the Christian Faith: An Introduction to the Idea of Christianity.* Translated by William V. Dych. New York: Crossroad, 1978.

———. "Some Implications of the Scholastic Concept of Uncreated Grace." In *Theological Investigations.* Vol. 1, *God, Christ, Mary and Grace,* 319–46. Translated with an introduction by Cornelius Ernst. 2nd ed. London: Darton, Longman & Todd, 1965.

———. *Theological Investigations.* Vol. 4, *Most Recent Writings.* New York: Crossroad, 1982.

———. *The Trinity.* Translated by Joseph Donceel. London: Herder & Herder, 1970.

Raitt, Jill. *The Colloquy of Montbéliard: Religion and Politics in the Sixteenth Century.* New York: Oxford University Press, 1993.

Rakestraw, Robert V. "Becoming Like God: An Evangelical Doctrine of Theosis." *Journal of Evangelical Theology* 40, no. 2 (June 1997): 257–69.

Ratzinger, Joseph. "The Holy Spirit as Communio: Concerning the Relationship of Pneumatology and Spirituality in Augustine." *Communio: International Catholic Review* 25 (Summer 1998): 324–37.

Reid, Duncan. *Energies of the Spirit: Trinitarian Models in Eastern Orthodox and Western Theology.* American Academy of Religion Academy Series 96. Atlanta, GA: Scholars Press, 1997.

Reynolds, Philip Lyndon. "Efficient Causality and Instrumentality in Thomas Aquinas's Theology of the Sacraments." In *Essays in Medieval Philosophy and*

Theology in Memory of Walter H. Principe: Fortresses and Launching Pads, edited by James R. Ginther and Carl N. Still, 67–84. Aldershot, UK: Ashgate, 2005.

Ridgley, Thomas. *A Body of Divinity: Wherein the Doctrines of the Christian Religion are Explained and Defended Being the Substance of Several Lectures on the Assembly's Larger Catechism.* With notes, original and selected by James P. Wilson. 4 vols. Philadelphia: Printed by and for William W. Woodward, 1815.

Riley, Woodbridge. "Jonathan Edwards." In Scheick, *Critical Essays*, 97–119. Reprinted from *American Philosophy: The Early Schools*, 126–27, 129–30, 142–59, 169–80, 184–87. New York: Dodd, Mead, 1907.

Ritschl, Albrecht. *The Christian Doctrine of Justification and Reconciliation: The Positive Development of the Doctrine.* Translated by H. R. Mackintosh and A. B. Macaulay. Continuum Books, 1966. Reprint, Eugene, OR: Wipf and Stock, 2002.

Romanides, John S. "Notes on the Palamite Controversy and Related Topics." *Greek Orthodox Theological Review* 6, no. 2 (Winter 1960–61): 186–270.

Rorem, Paul. "'Procession and Return' in Thomas Aquinas and His Predecessors." *Princeton Seminary Bulletin*, n.s., 13, no. 2 (1992): 147–63.

Rossum, Joost van. "Gregory of Cyprus and Palamism." In Wiles and Yarnold, *Papers Presented at the Thirteenth International Conference on Patristic Studies*, 626–30.

Rosemann, Philipp W. *Peter Lombard.* Great Medieval Thinkers. New York: Oxford University Press, 2004.

Rupp, George. "The 'Idealism' of Jonathan Edwards." *Harvard Theological Review* 62 (1969): 209–26.

Russell, Norman. *The Doctrine of Deification in the Greek Patristic Tradition.* Oxford Early Christian Studies. Oxford: Oxford University Press, 2004.

———. "'Partakers of the Divine Nature' (2 Peter 1:2) in the Byzantine Tradition." In *Kathegetria: Essays Presented to Joan Hussey on Her 80th Birthday*, edited by J. Chrysostomides. Camberley, UK: Porphyrogenitus, 1988. Available under the same title in the Myrobiblios Library, http://www.myriobiblos.gr/texts/english/Russell_partakers.html.

Russo, Gerry. "Rahner and Palamas: A Unity of Grace." *St. Vladimir's Theological Quarterly* 32, no. 2 (1988): 157–80.

Rutherford, Samuel. *The covenant of life opened; or, a treatise of the covenant of grace.* Edinburgh: Printed by A. A. for Robert Broun, 1655.

Sarot, Marcel. *God, Possibility and Corporeality.* Kampen, Netherlands: Kok Pharos, 1992.

Scanlon, Michael J. "The Ecclesial Dimension of Anthropology." In Phan, *The Gift of the Church*, 193–214.

Schafer, Thomas A. "The Concept of Being in the Thought of Jonathan Edwards." Ph.D. diss., Duke University, 1951.

———. "Jonathan Edwards and Justification by Faith." *Church History* 20 (1951): 55–67.

_____. *Nicene and Post-Nicene Fathers*. Vol. 5, *Gregory of Nyssa: Dogmatic Treatises, etc.* 2nd series. A Select Library of the Christian Church. Peabody, MA: Hendrickson, 1994.

_____. *Nicene and Post-Nicene Fathers*. Vol. 8, *Basil: Letters and Select Works*. 2nd series. A Select Library of the Christian Church. Peabody, MA: Hendrickson, 1994.

_____. *Nicene and Post-Nicene Fathers*. Vol. 9, *Hilary of Poitiers, John of Damascus*. 2nd series. A Select Library of the Christian Church. Peabody, MA: Hendrickson, 1994.

Scheick, William J., ed. *Critical Essays on Jonathan Edwards*. Critical Essays on American Literature. Boston: G. K. Hall, 1980.

Schindler, David C. *Hans Urs von Balthasar and the Dramatic Structure of Truth: A Philosophical Investigation*. Perspectives in Continental Philosophy Series, no. 34. New York: Fordham University Press, 2004.

———. "What's the Difference? On the Metaphysics of Participation in a Christian Context." *Saint Anselm Journal* 3, no. 1 (Fall 2005): 1–27.

Schmid, Heinrich. *The Doctrinal Theology of the Evangelical Lutheran Church*. Translated by Charles A. Hay and Henry E. Jacobs. 3rd rev. ed. Minneapolis: Augsburg, 1899.

———. "The 'Person of Christ,' according to the Older Theologians of the Evangelical Lutheran Church." Translated from the German and Latin by C. P. Krauth. *Mercersburg Review* 1 (1849): 272–306.

Schoot, Henk J. M. *Christ the "Name" of God: Thomas Aquinas on Naming Christ*. Leuven, Belgium: Peeters, 1994.

Schumacher, Matthew. *Knowableness of God: Its Relation to the Theory of Knowledge in St. Thomas*. Notre Dame, IN: University Press, 1905.

Scheick, William J. "Breaking Verbal Icons." In *Design in Puritan American Literature*, 89–119. Lexington, KY: University of Kentucky Press, 1992.

Schweitzer, Don, ed. *Jonathan Edwards as Contemporary: Essays in Honor of Sang Hyun Lee*. New York: Peter Lang, 2010.

———. "Jonathan Edwards' Understanding of Divine Infinity." In Schweitzer, *Jonathan Edwards as Contemporary*, 49–65.

Scrutton, Anastasia. "Emotion in Augustine of Hippo and Thomas Aquinas: A Way Forward for the Im/passibility Debate?" *International Journal of Systematic Theology* 7, no. 2 (April 2005): 169–77.

Sherlock, William. *A vindication of the doctrine of the holy and ever blessed Trinity, and the incarnation of the Son of God. Occasioned by the brief notes on the creed of St. Athanasius, and the brief history of the Unitarians, or Socinians, and containing an answer to both.* London: W. Rogers, 1690.

Shults, F. LeRon. "A Dubious Christological Formula: From Leontius of Byzantium to Karl Barth." *Theological Studies* 57 (September 1996): 431–46.

Singer, Irving. *The Nature of Love.* Vol. 1, *Plato to Luther.* 2nd ed. Chicago: University of Chicago Press, 2009.

Slater, Jonathan. "Salvation as Participation in the Humanity of the Mediator in Calvin's *Institutes of the Christian Religion*: A Reply to Carl Mosser." *Scottish Journal of Theology* 58 (2005): 39–58.

Smith, John. *The Excellency and Nobleness of True Religion.* In Cragg, *The Cambridge Platonists*, 91–140.

Smith, Timothy. "The Context and Character of Thomas' Theory of Appropriations." *Thomist* 63 (1999): 579–612.

South, Robert. "Discourse V: The Scribe Instructed." In *Discourses on Various Subjects and Occasions Selected from the Complete English Edition,* 87–119. Boston: Bowles and Dearborn, 1827.

———. *Tritheism charged upon Dr. Sherlock's new notion of the trinity. And the charge made good, in an answer to the defense of the said notion against the animadversions upon Dr. Sherlock's book, entituled, A vindication of the doctrine of the holy and ever blessed trinity.* London: John Whitlock, 1695.

Stahle, Rachel. "The Trinitarian Spirit of Jonathan Edwards' Theology." Ph.D diss., Boston University, 1999.

Stavropoulos, Christoforos. "Partakers of Divine Nature." In Clendenin, *Eastern Orthodox Theology: A Contemporary Reader,* 183–94.

Stephen, Leslie. "Jonathan Edwards." In Scheick, *Critical Essays*, 73–75.

Stevenson, William B. "The Problem of Trinitarian Processions in Thomas's *Roman Commentary*." *Thomist* 64 (October 2000): 619–29.

Stewart, M. A., ed. *English Philosophy in the Age of Locke.* Vol. 3 of *Oxford Studies in the History of Philosophy.* London: Oxford University Press, 2000.

Strauss, David Friedrich. *The Life of Jesus Critically Examined.* Translated by Marian Evans. New York: Calvin Blanchard, 1860.

Strehle, Stephen. *The Catholic Roots of the Protestant Gospel: Encounter between the Middle Ages and the Reformation*. Studies in the History of Christian Thought. Leiden, Netherlands: E. J. Brill, 1995.

Studebaker, Steven M. "Jonathan Edwards' Social Augustinian Trinitarianism: An Alternative to a Recent Trend." *Scottish Journal of Theology* 56 (2003): 268–85.

———. *Jonathan Edwards' Social Augustinian Trinitarianism in Historical and Contemporary Perspectives*. Piscataway, NJ: Gorgias, 2008.

Stump, Eleonore, *Aquinas*. Arguments of the Philosophers. London: Routledge, 2003.

Strong, Augustus Hopkins. *Systematic Theology: A Compendium and Commonplace Book Designed for the Use of Theological Students*. Vol. 3, *The Doctrine of Salvation*. Philadelphia: Griffith & Rowland, 1909.

Strzelczyk, Grzegorz. *Communicatio Idiomatum: Lo scambio delle proprietà; Storia, status quaestionis e prospettive*. Rome: Pontificia Università Gregoriana, 2004.

Sweeney, Douglas A. "Editor's Introduction." In Edwards, *The Works of Jonathan Edwards*, 23:1–36.

Swinburne, Richard. *The Christian God*. New York: Oxford University Press, 1994.

Tanner, Norman P., ed. *Decrees of the Ecumenical Councils*. Vol. 1, *Nicaea 1 to Lateran V*. Washington, DC: Georgetown University Press, 1990.

Thiel, Udo. "The Trinity and Human Personal Identity." In *English Philosophy in the Age of Locke*, edited by Michael A. Stewart, 217–44. Vol. 3 of *Oxford Studies in the History of Philosophy*. London: Oxford University Press, 2000.

Thomas Aquinas, Saint. *Commentary on the Gospel of John, Chapters 6–12*. Translated by Fabian Larcher and James A. Weisheipl. With introduction and notes by Daniel Keating and Matthew Levering. Washington, DC: Catholic University of America Press, 2010.

———. *Disputed Question: Concerning the Union of the Word Incarnate*. Translated by Jason Lewis Andrew West. Center Valley, PA: Aquinas Translation Project, DeSales University. http://www4.desales.edu/~philtheo/loughlin/ATP/De_Unione/De_Unione1.html.

———. *Disputed Questions on the Virtues*. Edited by E. M. Atkins and Thomas Williams. Cambridge Texts in the History of Philosophy. Cambridge: Cambridge University Press, 2005.

———. *Of God and His Creatures: An Annotated Translation (with Some Abridgement) of the* Summa contra gentiles *of Saint Thomas Aquinas*. Translated by Joseph Rickaby. London: Burns and Oates, 1905.

———. *On the Power of God:* Quæstiones disputatæ de potentia Dei. Translated by the English Dominican fathers. Eugene, OR: Wipf & Stock, 2004.

———. *Quaestio disputata de unione Verbi incarnati.* Translated by Roberto Busa. Taurini, 1953. http://www.corpusthomisticum.org/qdi.html.

_____. *Questiones Disputatae de Veritate, Questions. 1–9.* Translated by Robert W. Mulligan. Chicago: Henry Regnery Company, 1952. http://dhspriory.org/thomas/QDdeVer.htm

———. *St. Thomas Aquinas: Summa Theologica.* 5 vols. Translated by Fathers of the English Dominican Province. New York: Benzinger Bros., 1948. Reprint, Allen, TX: Christian Classics, 1981.

———. *Scriptum super Sententiis.* Translated by Roberto Busa. Parma, 1856. *Corpus Thomisticum.* http://www.corpusthomisticum.org/snp1026.html.

———. *Summa Theologiae*, 3a. 1–6. Vol. 48, *The Incarnate Word: Latin Text, English Translation, Introduction, Notes, Appendices and Glossary.* Edited by J. Hennessey. 2nd edition. The Blackfriars Translation. Cambridge: Cambridge University Press, 2006.

Thunberg, Lars. "'Circumincession' once more: Trinitarian and Christological Implications in an Age of Religious Pluralism." In *Papers presented at the Twelfth International Conference on Patristic Studies held in Oxford, 1995*, edited by Elizabeth A. Livingstone, 364–72. Studia Patristica 29. Leuven, Belgium: Peeters, 1997.

———. *Microcosm and Mediator: The Theological Anthropology of Maximus the Confessor.* 2nd ed. Foreword by A. M. Allchin. Chicago: Open Court, 1995.

_____. *Man and the Cosmos: The Vision of St. Maximus the Confessor.* Foreword by A.M. Allchin. Crestwood, NY: St. Vladimir's Seminary Press, 1985.

Tollefsen, Torstein. "Did Maximus the Confessor have a Concept of Participation?" In Wiles and Yarnold, *Papers Presented at the Thirteenth International Conference on Patristic Studies*, 618–25.

Toon, Peter. *Justification and Sanctification.* Foundations for Faith. Westchester, IL: Crossway Books, 1983.

Törönen, Melchisedec. *Union and Distinction in the Thought of St Maximus the Confessor.* Oxford Early Christian Studies. Oxford: Oxford University Press, 2007.

Torrance, Iain R. *Christology after Chalcedon: Severus of Antioch and Sergius the Monophysite.* Eugene, OR: Wipf and Stock, 1998.

Torrance, Thomas F. *The Christian Doctrine of God: One Being, Three Persons.* Edinburgh: T&T Clark, 1996.

———. *Trinitarian Faith: The Evangelical Theology of the Ancient Catholic Faith.* Edinburgh: T&T Clark, 2006.

———. *Trinitarian Perspectives: Towards Doctrinal Agreement.* Edinburgh: T&T Clark, 1994.

Trelcatius, Lucas. *A briefe institution of the common places of sacred divinitie. Wherein, the truth of every place is proved, and the sophismes of Bellarmine are reprooved.* London: Francis Burton, 1610.

Trueman, Carl R. *John Owen: Reformed Catholic, Renaissance Man.* The Great Theologians. Aldershot, UK: Ashgate, 2007.

Tschipke, Theophil. *Die Menschheit Christi als Heilsorgan der Gottheit: unter besonderer Berücksichtigung der Lehre des heiligen Thomas von Aquin.* Freiburger theologische Studien 55. Freiburg im Breisgau: Herder, 1940. See recent French translation by Philibert Secrétan, *L'humanité du Christ comme instrument de salut de la divinité.* Fribourg: Academic Press, 2003.

Turretin, Francis. *Institutes of Elenctic Theology.* 2 vols. Translated by George Musgrave Giger. Edited by James T. Dennison. Phillipsburg, NJ: P&R, 1992–94.

Turrettini, François. *Institutio theologiae elencticae.* New York: [s.n.], 1847.

Twisse,William, *A discovery of D. Jacksons vanitie. Or a perspective glasse, whereby the admirers of D. Jacksons profound discourses, may see the vanitie and weaknesse of them, in sundry passages, and especially so farre as they tende to the undermining of the doctrine hitherto received.* Amsterdam, 1631.

Tylenda, Joseph N. "Calvin's Understanding of the Communication of Properties." *Westminster Theological Journal* 38 (Fall 1975–Spring 1976): 54–65.

Ussher, James. *A body of divinity: or, the sum and substance of Christian religion. Catechistically propounded and explained, by way of question and answer. Methodically and familiarly handled, for the use of families. To which are adjoined a tract, entitled, Immanuel: or, the mystery of the incarnation of the son of God. To which are added, the life of the author, containing many remarkable passages: his model of Church government, and advices to young ministers. With an alphabetical table. And likewise the principles of Christian religion in short, for the use of younger people.* London: Printed by R. J. for Jonathan Robinson, 1702.

Van Bavel, Tarsicius. "The 'Christus Totus' Idea: A Forgotten Aspect of Augustine's Spirituality." In *Studies in Patristic Christology,* edited by Thomas Finan and Vincent Twomey, 84–94. Dublin, Ireland: Four Courts, 1998.

Venema, Cornelis P. *Accepted and Renewed in Christ: The "Twofold Grace of God" and the Interpretation of Calvin's Theology.* Göttingen, Germany: Vandernhoeck & Ruprecht, 2007.

Waddington, Jeffrey C. "Jonathan Edwards's 'Ambiguous and Somewhat Precarious' Doctrine of Justification?" *Westminster Theological Journal* 66 (2004): 357–72.

Wainwright, William J. "Jonathan Edwards and the Hiddenness of God." In *Divine Hiddenness: New Essays*, edited by Paul K. Moser and Daniel Howard-Snyder, 98–119. Cambridge: Cambridge University Press, 2002.

Walvoord, John F. *The Holy Spirit: A Comprehensive Study of the Person and Work of the Holy Spirit.* Grand Rapids, MI: Zondervan, 1991.

Warfield, B. B. "Calvin's Doctrine of the Trinity." *Princeton Theological Review* 7, no. 4 (1909): 553–652.

Waterworth, J., trans. *The Canons and Decrees of the Sacred and Oecumenical Council of Trent Celebrated under the Sovereign Pontiffs, Paul III, Julius III, and Pius IV, to which are Prefixed Essays on the External and Internal History of the Council.* London: C. Dolman, 1848.

Watson, Thomas. *The beatitudes: Or a discourse upon part of Christs famous sermon on the mount. Whereunto is added Christs various fulnesse. The preciousnesse of the soul. The souls malady and cure. The beauty of grace. The spiritual watch. The heavenly race. The sacred anchor. The trees of righteousnesse. The perfume of love. The good practitioner.* London: Ralph Smith, 1660.

———. *A body of practical divinity, consisting of above one hundred seventy six sermons on the lesser catechism composed by the reverend assembly of divines at Westminster: with a supplement of some sermons on several texts of scripture.* London: Thomas Parkhurst, 1692.

———. *The holy eucharist: Or, the mystery of the Lords supper. Briefly explained.* London: Printed by E. M. for Ralph Smith, 1665.

Watts, Isaac. *The Glory of Christ as God-Man Displayed in Three Discourses.* Boston: Printed by Manning and Loring for David West, 1795.

Wawrykow, Joseph P. "Hypostatic Union." In Van Nieuwenhove and Wawrykow, *Theology of Thomas Aquinas*, 222–51.

———. *The Westminster Handbook to Thomas Aquinas.* Westminster Handbooks to Christian Theology. Louisville, KY: Westminster John Knox, 2005.

Webster, John. *Confessing God: Essays in Dogmatics II.* London: T&T Clark, 2005.

Weinandy, Thomas G. "Aquinas: God *Is* Man: The Marvel of the Incarnation." In Weinandy, Keating, and Yocum, *Aquinas on Doctrine*, 67–89.

———. "Cyril and the Mystery of the Incarnation." In Weinandy and Keating, *The Theology of Saint Cyril of Alexandria*, 23–54.

———. *Does God Suffer?* Edinburgh: T&T Clark, 2000.

———. "Jesus' Filial Vision of the Father." *Pro Ecclesia* 13, no. 2 (Spring 2004): 189–201.

———. *Jesus the Christ*. Huntington, IN: Our Sunday Visitor Publishing Division, 2003.

Weinandy, Thomas G., and Daniel A. Keating, eds. *The Theology of Saint Cyril of Alexandria: A Critical Appreciation*. London: T&T Clark, 2002.

Weinandy, Thomas G., Daniel A. Keating, and John P. Yocum, eds. *Aquinas on Doctrine: A Critical Introduction*. London: T&T Clark, 2004.

Wesche, Kenneth Paul. "The Union of God and Man in Jesus Christ in the Thought of Gregory of Nazianzus." *Saint Vladimir's Theological Quarterly* 28, no. 2 (2006): 83–98.

————, trans. *On the Person of Christ: The Christology of Emperor Justinian.* New York: Saint Vladimir's Seminary Press, 1991.

The Westminster Larger Catechism. Grand Rapids, MI: Christian Classic Ethereal Library. http://www.ccel.org/ccel/anonymous/westminster2.pdf.

White, Thomas Joseph. "The Voluntary Action of the Earthly Christ and the Necessity of the Beatific Vision." *Thomist* 69 (2005): 497–534.

Wiles, M. F., and E. J. Yarnold, eds. *Papers Presented at the Thirteenth International Conference on Patristic Studies held in Oxford 1999*. Studia Patristica 37. Leuven, Belgium: Peeters, 2001.

Willet, Andrew. *Hexapla: That is, a six-fold commentarie upon the most divine epistle of the holy apostle S. Paul to the Romanes: wherein according to the authors former method sixe things are observed in every chapter. 1. The text with the divers readings. 2. Argument and method. 3. The questions discussed. 4. Doctrines noted. 5. Controversies handled. 6. Morall uses observed.* Cambridge, UK: Leonard Greene, 1620.

Williams, A. N. *The Ground of Union: Deification in Aquinas and Palamas*. New York: Oxford University Press, 1999.

Williams, David T. *Vinculum Amoris: A Theology of the Holy Spirit*. Lincoln, NE: iUniverse, 2004.

Willis, E. David. *Calvin's Catholic Christology: The Function of the So-Called Extra Calvinisticum in Calvin's Theology*. Studies in Medieval and Reformation Thought, vol. 2. Leiden, Netherlands: E. J. Brill, 1966.

Wilson, Stephen A. *Virtue Reformed: Rereading Jonathan Edwards's Ethics*. Brill Studies in Intellectual History 132. Leiden, Netherlands: Brill, 2005.

Wilson-Kastner, Patricia. "God's Infinity and His Relationship to Creation in the Theologies of Gregory of Nyssa and Jonathan Edwards." *Foundations* 21 (October 1978): 305–21.

Wippel, John F. *Metaphysical Themes in Thomas Aquinas II.* Studies in Philosophy and the History of Philosophy 47. Washington, DC: Catholic University of America Press, 2007.

Wolfson, Harry Austryn. *The Philosophy of the Church Fathers.* Cambridge, MA: Harvard University Press, 1956.

Yannaras, Christos. "The Distinction between Essence and Energies and Its Importance for Theology." *St. Vladimir's Theological Quarterly* 19, no. 4 (1975): 232–45.

Yarnold, Edward. *The Second Gift: A Study of Grace.* Sarum Lectures. Slough, UK: St. Paul Publications, 1974.

Zakai, Avihu. *Jonathan Edwards's Philosophy of History: The Reenchantment of the World in the Age of Enlightenment.* Princeton, NJ: Princeton University Press, 2003.

Zimany, Roland D. "The Divine Energies in Orthodox Theology." *Diakonia* 11, no. 3 (1976): 281–85.

Zizioulas, John D. *Being as Communion: Studies in Personhood and the Church.* Crestwood, NY: St. Vladimir's Seminary Press, 1997.

———. *Communion and Otherness: Further Studies in Personhood and the Church.* Edited by Paul McPartlan. London: T&T Clark, 2006.

Index

Bombaro, John J., 278n293, 302n6
Bonaventure, 11, 29n45
Braaten, Carl E., 277n272
Bradshaw, David, 36n132, 312n109, 389, 392n5
Brand, David C., 129n102
Bray, Gerald L., 363n8
Brown, John, 264–65n128
Brunner, Emil, 363n5
Budziszewski, J., 267n158
Burke, Patrick, 305n31
Bush, Michael, 181n183
Bush, Randall B., 27n28

Caldwell, Robert W., III, 27n25, 37n142, 183n207, 260n74, 261n81, 261n84
Calvin, John: *autotheos*, 6, 46n228, 357, 358nn2–3; on Christ's suffering, 205; the *exitus-reditus* motif in, 68, 91n187; on the *extra carnem*, 201, 183–84nn212–14; Holy Spirit as bond, 161, 183n208; *in solidum*, 46n228; on the Mediator, 99, 124n26, 194–95, 201, 214n66, 214n69
Cambridge Platonists, 2, 68, 81n75, 294
Cartwright, Thomas A., 357, 358n4
cause: efficient, 69, 79n52, 84n109, 108–10, 116, 126n57, 133n153, 140n237, 154, 172n99, 174n114, 174n120, 176n135, 181n188, 209n11, 247, 262n97, 269n175, 273n224, 290, 291, 292, 305n34, 312n105, 313n119, 313n121, 313–14nn127–28, 314n134, 314nn138–39; final, 55, 64, 67, 69, 86n133, 91n194, 176n135, 262n97, 292, 314n138; formal, 91n194, 262n97, 270n186, 276n268, 290–91, 313n119, 313n127, 314n134, 314n138; material, 32n90, 91n194, 243, 247, 262n97, 269n175,

270n186, 272n211, 314n128; quasi-formal, 290–92, 313–14n128, 314n134, 315n142
Cessario, Romanus, 174n114
Chai, Leon, 83n94, 83n97, 84n109
Chapman, John, 327n265
Chemnitz, Martin, 139–40n224, 172n98, 173n110, 174n115, 177n153, 184n217, 211n37, 227n203, 366, 368, 373n41, 378–79, 380n3, 381n10, 382n18, 384nn35–37, 384n41, 385n50
Cherry, Conrad, 3n3, 87n146, 210n17, 263n107
Cheynell, Francis, 26nn20–21, 357, 358n4, 358n6, 358n10
Christ: beatific vision, 14, 74, 197–98, 204–7, 298, 330, 333, 335; as mediator, 14–15, 24, 98–100, 103–8, 112, 121, 159, 188–89, 194–95, 198, 236, 242–43, 246–48, 253, 291, 387; eternal generation, 10–15, 17–18, 64, 72, 105, 109–12, 117–20, 340, 354, 357; impassibility of the divine nature, 156, 188, 201–2, 206; Logos asarkos, 112, 205; negative and positive righteousness, 246; suffering of, 71, 100, 104, 105, 148, 157, 202–7, 238, 243, 293
circumincessio, circuminsessio. See Trinity: *perichoresis*
Clark, Mary T., 87n144
Clarke, Samuel, 314n135
Clarke, W. Norris, 135n164
Cleenewerck, Laurent A., 27n31, 358n2
Clendenin, Daniel B., 345n23, 352n123
Coakley, Sarah, 385n44
Coffey, David M., 25n9, 27n26, 34n107, 34n112, 36n122, 46n222, 166n32, 176n142, 220n125, 314n134
Colle, Ralph Del, 314n134, 364n14